THIRD EDITION

THE WOMEN'S MOVEMENT

POLITICAL, SOCIOECONOMIC, AND PSYCHOLOGICAL ISSUES

BARBARA SINCLAIR DECKARD

University of California, Riverside

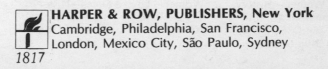

HARPER & ROW, PUBLISHERS, New York
Cambridge, Philadelphia, San Francisco,
London, Mexico City, São Paulo, Sydney

1817

Sponsoring Editor: David Forgione
Project Editor: Nora Helfgott
Designer: Mary Archondes
Senior Production Manager: Kewal K. Sharma
Compositor: ComCom Division of Haddon Craftsmen, Inc.
Printer and Binder: The Murray Printing Company

THE WOMEN'S MOVEMENT: Political, Socioeconomic, and Psychological Issues, Third Edition

Library of Congress Cataloging in Publication Data

Deckard, Barbara Sinclair.
The women's movement, political, socioeconomic, and psychological issues.

   Bibliography: p.
   Includes index.
   1. Women—History.   2. Women—United States—History.
3. Feminism.   I. Title.
HQ1154.D35   1983   305.4'2'09   82-15768
ISBN 0-06-041615-7

To Marga and Thornton Sinclair
with love and gratitude

CONTENTS

PREFACE

In the past decade, increased activity in the feminist movement has resulted in a mass of literature about women. The social, economic, and political status of women in past and present societies and their long struggle for liberation has been explored, yet no attempt has been made to synthesize the old knowledge with the new. This book attempts such a synthesis.

Chapter 1 documents prevalent sexual stereotypes and explains how they function as an ideology. The explanations of the political functions of this ideology set the analytical framework for the book. The rest of Part I (Chapters 2–7) describes and analyzes the present status of women in the United States. Data on psychological theories about women, sex role socialization, the family, working women, and laws affecting women are analyzed, and the theories that have been used to justify this evidence are critiqued. Conservative, liberal, and radical economic theories are examined to see how they explain the patterns of discrimination evident in the data. Part II (Chapters 8–14) begins with a survey of the status of women from primitive societies through the nineteenth century. The present status of women in a variety of capitalist and socialist societies is then discussed. Chapter 10 focuses on the nineteenth-century women's movement in the United States. The growth of the women's movement is examined in light of the social, economic, and political position of women in the nineteenth century. Chapter 11 analyzes why the movement died after 1920 and describes the changes in women's status between 1920 and 1960. Part II concludes with an examination of the contemporary women's movement. Its origin, history, and development are traced, and the issues on which feminists have worked and their accomplishments are described. The final chapter presents and analyzes the three major ideological positions in the movement.

This is not a neutral book. I was a feminist when I began working on it and doing the research has made me more so. The book, while not neutral, is, I think, fair.

Alice Amsden and Nancy Hancock read the manuscript and gave me many helpful suggestions. Sara Sheehan and Marcia Keller contributed a great deal to my understanding of feminist issues and theories. Others who reviewed the first edition and provided suggestions for the second edition include Mary Ellin Colten, Survey Research Center, University of Michigan; Jacqueline J. Snyder, Wichita State University; Mel Steinfield, Department of History, San Diego Mesa College; and Joan Acker, Department of Sociology, University of Oregon. Patricia Ward D'Itri, Michigan State University, Sylvia Brueck, Wichita State University, and Gayle Kimball, California State University, Chico, reviewed the second edition and gave me many helpful suggestions for this third edition. Diana Eddington, Carmen Mathenga, Janet Gropp, and Shirlee Pigeon typed various versions of the manuscript. Howard Sherman helped me understand the intricacies of economic theory, helped with the empirical research, and provided much needed moral support.

I am very much indebted to all of these people. My greatest debt, however, is to the women in the movement—those whom I have met and from whom I have learned, those whose work I have read, and the many thousands whose determination and hard work produced and sustain the feminist movement.

Barbara Sinclair Deckard

part one

AMERICAN
WOMEN
TODAY

INTRODUCTION: SEXUAL STEREOTYPES AS POLITICAL IDEOLOGY

1

What is woman? Writers, past and present, have asked and answered this question over and over again. On the nature of woman everyone seems to consider himself an expert ("himself" because most of the answers come from men).

According to these "experts," woman is emotional rather than logical. In fact, she is not very bright.

> We may thus conclude that it is a general law that there should be naturally ruling elements and elements naturally ruled . . . the rule of the freeman over the slave is one kind of rule; that of the male over the female another. . . . the slave is entirely without the faculty of deliberation; the female indeed possesses it, but in a form which remains inconclusive. . . . [Aristotle]

> Women, then, are only children of larger growth: they have an entertaining tattle, and sometimes wit; but for solid, reasoning good sense, I never knew in my life one that had it, or who reasoned or acted consequentially for four and twenty hours together. [Lord Chesterfield]

> [Woman is] in every respect backward, lacking in reason and true morality . . . a kind of middle step between the child and the man, who is the true human being. [Schopenhauer]

> The chief distinction in the intellectual powers of the two sexes is shown by man attaining to a higher eminence, in whatever he takes up, than woman can attain—whether requiring deep thought, reason, or imagination or merely the use of the senses and hands. [Darwin]

> Feelings, moods and attitudes . . . rule a woman, not facts, reason nor logic. By herself, woman is all mixed up, but superb as an auxiliary. . . . [G. C. Payetter]

3

Everything relating to exploration and cognition, all the forms and kinds of human culture and aspiration that require a strictly objective approach, are with few exceptions, the domain of the masculine intellect, of man's spiritual power, against which women can rarely compete. [Helen Deutsch]

Man is active and independent; woman, passive and dependent. He does, she is.

Women, in general, want to be loved for what they are and men for what they accomplish. The first for their looks and charm, the latter for their actions. [Theodor Reik]

Women are usually more patient in working at unexciting, repetitive tasks. . . . Women on the average have more passivity in the inborn core of their personality. . . . I believe women are designed in their deeper instincts to get more pleasure out of life—not only sexually but socially, occupationally, maternally—when they are not aggressive. To put it another way I think that when women are encouraged to be competitive too many of them become disagreeable. [Benjamin Spock]

Women must give and give and give again because it is their one and only way to obtain happiness for themselves. [well-known American gynecologist]

It is a hard and hateful thing to see proud men, not to speak of enduring them. But it is annoying and impossible to suffer proud women, because in general Nature has given men proud and high spirits, while it has made women humble in character and submissive, more apt for delicate things than for ruling. [Boccaccio]

Women are naturally mothers; their greatest desire and only true fulfillment lies in maternity. In fact, this is one of the few things women are any good at.

. . . As much as women want to be good scientists and engineers, they want, first and foremost, to be womanly companions of men and to be mothers. [Bruno Bettelheim]

Biologically and temperamentally, I believe, women were made to be concerned first and foremost with child care, husband care and home care. [Benjamin Spock]

. . . Woman is nurturance; . . . anatomy decrees the life of a woman. When women grow up without dread of their biological functions and without the subversion of feminist doctrine and therefore enter upon motherhood with a sense of fulfillment and altruistic sentiment, we shall attain the goal of a good life and a secure world in which to live. [Joseph Rheingold]

If woman is naturally stupid, dependent, and passive, then, of course, she is naturally subordinate to the male.

> Wives, submit yourself unto your husbands . . . for the husband is the head of the wife, even as Christ is the head of the church. [Ephesians 5:22–23]

> The whole education of women ought to be relative to men. To please them, to be useful to them, to make themselves loved and honored by them, to educate them when young, to care for them when grown, to counsel them, to console them, and to make life sweet and agreeable to them—these are the duties of women at all times and what should be taught them from their infancy. [Jean-Jacques Rousseau]

> Nature intended women to be our slaves; . . . they are our property, we are not theirs. They belong to us, just as a tree that bears fruit belongs to a gardener. What a mad idea to demand equality for women! . . . Women are nothing but machines for producing children. [Napoleon Bonaparte]

> Man for the field and woman for the hearth:
> Man for the sword and for the needle she:
> Man with the head and woman with the heart:
> Man to command and woman to obey;
> All else confusion. [Alfred, Lord Tennyson]

When woman steps out of her natural role, disaster results:

> A woman who is guided by the head and not the heart is a social pestilence: she has all the defects of the passionate and affectionate woman, with none of her compensations; she is without pity, without love, without virtue, without sex. [Honoré de Balzac]

> Frigidity, as we see it today, is an outgrowth of woman's running away from her biological destiny, which is to be wife, mother, and homemaker. [Dr. Arthur Mandy]

> Women's intellectuality is to a large extent paid for by the loss of valuable feminine qualities; it feeds on the sap of the affective life and results in impoverishment of this life. . . . All observations point to the fact that the intellectual woman is masculinized; in her, warm intuitive knowledge has yielded to cold unproductive thinking. [Helen Deutsch]

> Mom got herself out of the nursery and the kitchen. She then got out of the house. . . . She also got herself the vote, and, although politics never interested her (unless she was exceptionally naive, a hairy foghorn, or a size 40 scorpion) the damage she forthwith did to society was so enormous and so rapid that the best men lost track of things . . . political scurviness, hoodlumism, gangsterism, labor strife, monop-

olistic thuggery, moral degeneration, civil corruption, smuggling, brib-
ery, theft, murder, homosexuality, drunkenness, financial depression,
chaos, and war. [Philip Wylie]

Aside from their often virulent nastiness, the most striking aspect of these quotations is their underlying assumption that all
women are alike. The image of women presented is a stereotype—a
simple-minded, unexamined notion based on prejudice. Similar
statements about blacks (that they all have natural rhythm, for example) are immediately recognized as racist stereotyping. In most cir-
cles, racist slurs are no longer socially acceptable. In contrast, sexism
is the last socially acceptable prejudice. People still tell and laugh
at wife, mother-in-law, and sex jokes that depict women as stupid
and empty-headed, unconcerned with anything but their looks, and
good for only one thing.

The ideology of sexism is so deeply embedded in our society
that, to a considerable extent, most people are unaware they are
prejudiced. The notion that women are inferior to or at least extremely different from men is taken as a self-evident truth:

> Sexism, then, is an "ideology" in the sense that its beliefs and postu-
> lates are well integrated, it functions to direct and guide social and
> political activity, and it rests on assumptions that are not reliably test-
> ed, but that to some degree are accepted on faith.[1]

For example, most tennis pros assumed that Bobby Riggs would beat
Billie Jean King even though she was 20 years younger and one of
the world's best women players. When she beat him, they dismissed
it as an anomaly. When looking at someone, a prejudiced person
will interpret whatever behavior occurs in a way that fits with the
stereotype. A sociologist points out:

> Whatever the facts about sex differences, anti-feminism—like any
> other prejudice—distorts perception and experience. . . . Thus, an
> anti-Semite watching a Jew may see devious or sneaky behavior. But
> in a Christian he would regard such behavior only as quiet, reserved,
> or perhaps even shy.[2]

Since prejudice distorts perception, it is highly resistant to change
even in the face of contrary evidence.

As an example of how prejudiced stereotyping affects behav-

[1] Kirsten Amundsen, The Silenced Majority (Englewood Cliffs, N.J.: Prentice-Hall, 1971), p. 108.

[2] Philip Goldberg, "Are Women Prejudiced Against Women," in Athena Theodore, ed., The Professional Woman (New York: Schenkman, 1971), p. 168.

ior, imagine an employer interviewing a series of people for an executive job. Suppose he believes in the usual stereotypes of women. Suppose the first woman is sophisticated and careful about speaking. He thinks: She is too passive and "feminine" for the job. Suppose the second woman objects to something he says. He thinks: She is an aggressive bitch. Suppose the third person is a man; he gets the job. Prejudiced stereotypes are not harmless; they lead directly to discrimination.

Even in minor ways and unconsciously, most people believe the myths. For example, if a man and woman order tea and coffee in a restaurant, the man will almost always get the coffee and the woman the tea (sometimes even if you ask for it the other way around). Why? Apparently tea is perceived as a light and delicate and therefore feminine drink. In reality, of course, most American women drink coffee. In the same way, if a man and a woman order a soft drink and a cocktail, the waiter or waitress will almost always give the soft drink to the woman without asking. Another myth.

More dangerous is the myth that most women do not work at paid jobs, and that those who do, work only for pin money. Yet in Chapter 5 we shall see that a majority of women of working age now work at two jobs: a paid job in the labor force and their traditional job in the home.

Like most stereotypes, the sexist stereotype is internally inconsistent. Depending upon the purpose, two quite different sets of characteristics are attributed to women. Women cannot be statesmen, captains of industry, or even auto mechanics because they are irrational, flighty, overemotional, sentimental, and unmechanical. On the other hand, women cannot be great poets and painters because they are practical, unadventuresome, unspontaneous, and unimaginative.[3] Unfortunately, inconsistency never destroyed a healthy stereotype, and sexism is still all too robust.

Religion has had a particularly important role in advancing and perpetuating sexist notions. Most of the great religions of the world have been pervaded by sexism. Examples:

> . . . And the rib, which the Lord God had taken from man, made he a woman, and brought her unto the man. . . . And the Lord God said unto the woman, What is this that thou hast done? And the woman said, The serpent beguiled me, and I did eat. . . . Unto the woman he said, I will greatly multiply thy sorrow and thy conception; in sor-

---

[3] Discussion based on Cynthia Ozick, "Women and Creativity," in Vivian Gornick and Barbara Moran, eds., *Woman in Sexist Society* (New York: Signet, 1971), p. 437.

row thou shalt bring forth children; and thy desire shall be to thy husband, and he shall rule over thee. [Genesis 2–3]

The Christian Saint Paul wrote:

Let the woman learn in silence with all subjection. But I suffer not a
woman to teach, nor to usurp authority over the man, but to be in
silence. For Adam was first formed, then Eve. And Adam was not
deceived, but the woman, being deceived, was in the transgression.
Notwithstanding she shall be saved in childbearing, if they continue in faith and charity and holiness with sobriety. [1 Tim. 2:11–
15]

The Christian Bible also declares:

. . . how can he be clean that is born of a woman? [Job 25:4]

And the Pope says:

Woman as a person enjoys a dignity equal with men, but she was
given different tasks by God and by Nature which perfect and complete the work entrusted to men. [Pope John XXIII]

Christianity is equaled, if not surpassed, by other religions. The
male Orthodox Jew recites every morning:

Blessed art Thou, oh Lord our God, King of the Universe, that I was
not born a woman.

The Koran, the Muslim sacred text, says:

Men are superior to women on account of the qualities in which God
has given them pre-eminence.

The Hindu Code of Manu declared:

In childhood a woman must be subject to her father; in youth to her
husband; when her husband is dead, to her sons. A woman must
never be free of subjugation.

Finally, there are the profound sayings of Confucius:

The five worst infirmities that afflict the female are indocility, discontent, slander, jealousy, and silliness. . . . Such is the stupidity of
woman's character, that it is incumbent upon her, in every particular,
to distrust herself and to obey her husband.

The new high priests of Western society—the psychiatrists—
are not much subtler in their sexism, as we shall see in the next chapter. A later examination of the mass media will show that they too
perpetuate sexism.

SEXISM IN LANGUAGE

Sexist thinking is deeply embedded in the English language.[4] Anthropologists have discovered that a society's basic and often unconscious mores are often revealed in its language. We can see many reflections of sexist thinking in our own language.

A linguist writes: "The word *man* originally meant human being, but males appropriated it."[5] This equating of men with the human race causes confusion in important contexts as well as trivial ones. Does *foreman* or *handyman* or *freshman* mean that these positions cannot be filled by women? In fact, the earlier stereotypes implied just that—only men could be supervisory workers, only men were handy, only men should go to college. Or take the sentence "All men are created equal." Many males have argued that this does not apply to women and thus would deny women their democratic rights. In this book we use the language in a sex-neutral way as a reflection of the fact that English is flexible enough to accommodate new ways of thinking without losing fluency or naturalness of expression.

Many words with wicked or evil emotional connotations were sex-neutral in an earlier period. Eventually, however, the wickedness came to be associated with women only. For example, *shrewish* first was applied to males and females, then became associated with a stereotype of women. By contrast, some words gained better emotional connotations when associated with men only. For example, *shrewd* (from the same root as *shrewish*) originally had an evil connotation; but when it became associated with powerful males, its emotional connotation became much more favorable.

The reason for such developments is that language reflects the ideology of the most powerful group in society, and sexism is the ideology of the male, who is dominant in Western society. More precisely, as one linguist writes, "Emotive words acquire their connotations by reflecting the sentiments of the dominant group in a society—in our case white Anglo-Saxon males (WASMs). . . ."[6]

"BUT IT'S NATURAL"

The last resort of those who lack a sound argument is to say: "But it's natural." For example, it is "natural" for a woman to have the whole burden of household and child-rearing chores—even if she

---

[4]See Ethel Strainchamps, "Our Sexist Language," in Gornick and Moran, op. cit., pp. 347–361.
[5]Ibid., p. 350.
[6]Ibid., p. 352.

has an outside job in addition. It is "natural" for women to be passive and submissive; it is "natural" for men to command. It is "natural" for women to be paid less than men. Before 1920, it was said to be "natural" for American men to vote but "unnatural" for women to do so.

What do people mean when they say "It's natural"? Sometimes, *natural* is construed to mean "that which will happen if there is no human intervention."[7] Thus, it is natural for a woman to get pregnant from sex, and unnatural for her to use any means of birth control. But then, isn't it natural for a man to grow a beard, and unnatural for him to shave? What about the use of smallpox and polio vaccines? Are these to be considered unnatural? According to this definition, perpetual pregnancy, beards, and dying of smallpox are all natural. But being natural in this sense does not mean these things are either unchangeable or desirable.

Another argument claims that male dominance is natural because it is based on "innate instincts" or "human nature." If this is true and women are prevented from doing some things by their nature, why must other barriers be erected? For example, if women's nature prevents them from being doctors, why must many medical schools prohibit the admission of all but a small quota from among all the qualified women applicants? If women's nature prevents them from being lawyers, why did many U.S. state laws have to prohibit qualified women law school graduates from practicing in the nineteenth century? The reality, as will be shown in the next chapter, is that there are no such "natural" barriers in the psychology of women.

As John Stuart Mill observed, "Everything which is usual appears natural. The subjection of women to men being a universal custom, any departure from it quite naturally appears unnatural."[8] Usually a person who says something is natural means that it is not just common but desirable. Such statements contain either a giant illogical leap or are simple assertions of preference. Male supremacy— and poverty, disease, and slavery—have been prevalent in many societies. That certainly does not make them desirable. Arguments based on the naturalness of male supremacy and female subordination should be attributed very little value.

[7]The argument here follows the excellent discussion in Christine Pierce, "Natural Law, Language and Women," in Gornick and Moran, op. cit., pp. 242–258.
[8]John Stuart Mill, *The Subjection of Women* (1869).

SEXIST IDEOLOGY AND POWER

The sexist ideology is well integrated and elaborate. Its major premise is that woman is inferior to man. It is sufficiently flexible (inconsistent) that any behavior a woman exhibits can be interpreted to conform with its major premise. The ideology is so pervasive that, until recently, few people were aware of its existence. Its tenets were simply accepted as self-evident truths.

Such an ideology neither develops nor survives without purpose. Its function is to justify and maintain a particular status quo — in this case the dominance of the male over the female. A ruling group always requires an ideology to justify its position of power. All slave societies, for example, develop a set of beliefs stating that slaves are innately inferior to their masters, or even nonhuman. In essence, such beliefs put the onus for the slaves' condition on the slaves themselves. Their status is decreed by their nature or by the gods; it is certainly not the fault of the slave owner.

Ideology is important as a self-justification for the ruling group. It is equally important in its effects on the subordinate group. Members of the subordinate group are inculcated with the ideology from early childhood. To a considerable extent they believe its claims— that they are, in fact, inferior and thus destined to play a subordinate role.

Sexual stereotyping thus is a *political* ideology. Its function is to maintain the power of the dominant group.

This book deals with the ideology of sexism, with the socioeconomic conditions the ideology seeks to justify, and with women's struggles to free themselves and their society from sexism.

THE NATURE OF WOMAN: PSYCHOLOGICAL THEORIES

2

On the subject of what women are really like, everyone is an expert. As we saw in the last chapter, philosophers and novelists, baby doctors and social critics all claim to know exactly what the nature of woman is. Woman, they say, is not very bright; she is emotional and subjective, passive and dependent. Woman is very good at child care and at the sort of repetitive tasks involved in housework. She finds her greatest joy and only true fulfillment in the roles of wife and mother. Woman, clearly, is very, very different from man.

These popular stereotypes should not be accepted without evidence. Perhaps the experts in human psychology have scientifically determined what women are really like. What do the psychologists have to tell us about the nature of women?

PSYCHOLOGICAL SEX DIFFERENCES
Seventy-nine clinically trained psychologists, psychiatrists, and social workers were asked to describe the mature, healthy male and the mature, healthy female.[1] According to these experts, the male is very aggressive, very independent, not at all emotional, very objective, very dominant, not at all easily influenced, and very logical; his feelings are not easily hurt; he can make decisions easily; and he is very self-confident. The normal female is not at all aggressive,

[1] Inge K. Broverman et al., "Sex-Role Stereotypes and Clinical Judgments of Mental Health," in Judith M. Bardwick, ed., *Readings on the Psychology of Women* (New York: Harper & Row, 1972), pp. 320–324.

not at all independent, very emotional, very illogical, very submissive, very sneaky; her feelings are easily hurt; she has difficulty making decisions; and she is not at all self-confident, but very dependent.

The authors of the study remarked about the latter description that "this constellation seems a most unusual way of describing any mature, healthy individual."[2] How had these supposed experts come to such conclusions? Remember, they were not describing the average woman but the healthy, mature woman. In effect, they were saying that this is what women should be like. The experts' ideal is remarkably like the popular stereotype. The stereotype, in turn, reflects what men want women to be.

In a male-dominated world, the woman who at least puts on a good show of conforming to the male ideal seems to get along better than her rebellious sisters. Male control of resources means the "good" woman will be rewarded, while the woman who does not "act like a woman," that is, as a subordinate, will be punished. Those are the facts of life in our society, and psychiatry has traditionally been aimed at getting people to fit into society as it is, not to change it. The clinicians say, "Adjust yourself to the stereotypes; only thus can you be normal and healthy." Meanwhile the costs of conforming to the stereotype—low self-esteem, a tendency toward depression, and economic dependence—are simply not recognized.

Another finding of the Broverman study showed that women are caught in a no-win situation. When the same experts were asked to describe a mature, healthy adult—sex unspecified—their description was very similar to their description of a healthy male and thus very different from their description of a healthy female. Thus if a woman displays the characteristics our society attributes to the healthy adult, she will be considered unfeminine; if she displays the appropriate feminine characteristics, she is not a mature, healthy adult.

Since the clinicians seemed to define adjusting to society's expectations—however destructive they may be—as healthy, their views must be looked upon with considerable suspicion. Nevertheless, there is a modicum of truth in the description when applied to the average woman. Although there is a great deal of overlapping of the sexes on all such traits, studies through the 1960s consistently found that females on the average were more passive-dependent,

[2]Ibid., p. 322.

more fearful and anxious, and less aggressive than males. Differences in self-esteem, in conformity and suggestibility, in need for affiliation, and in achievement need were also frequently found.[3]

What accounts for these differences? The popular view and that held by some psychologists attributes them to biological differences. Other psychologists contend that such differences in behavior are learned, that they are the result of the socialization process.

BIOLOGICAL SEX DIFFERENCES

Men are taller, heavier, and stronger than women. Right? Not exactly. Within any given population group, the average male is taller than the average female, but some women are taller than some men. And the average female in some societies is taller than the average male in other societies. Thus secondary sex characteristics such as the male's greater height, higher muscle-to-fat ratio, more massive skeleton, and more abundant body hair distinguish male and female within a given society but not across societies.[4]

Chromosomal, gonadal, and hormonal sex differences are universal. A normal woman has two X chromosomes; a normal man has an X chromosome and a Y chromosome. The internal and external reproductive and sex organs, of course, differ in normal men and women. The sex hormones secreted and the timing of their secretion differ, with the woman's exhibiting a cyclical pattern.

These differences have provided the basis for a number of theories concerning psychological sex differences. The more sophisticated of these theories argue that since sex hormones, which differ for male and female, enter the brain, different behaviors along sex lines are to be expected. Yet no link between sex hormones and complex behavior patterns has been established. In fact, the relationship between physiological and psychological states seems to depend very much on social context. For example, since adrenalin produces a physiological reaction much like what naturally occurs when a person is very much afraid, one would expect a subject injected with adrenalin to show the psychological symptoms of fear. Yet, when an experimenter put some subjects who were under the influence of adrenalin into a room with someone who was pretending to be euphoric, the subjects became euphoric. When the subjects

[3]Roberta M. Oetzel, "Annotated Bibliography," in Eleanor E. Maccoby, ed., *The Development of Sex Differences* (Stanford, Calif.: Stanford University Press, 1966), pp. 223–321.

[4]Roy G. D'Andrade, "Sex Differences and Cultural Institutions," in Maccoby, op. cit., p. 175.

were put in the presence of someone acting very angry, they became angry.[5] Clearly the subjects' social environment was more important than their physiological state in determining their behavior.

One cannot simply assume that biological differences will result in psychological differences. One *must* provide evidence. This should be kept in mind during the following examination of theories on the origins of psychological sex differences.

ANATOMY IS DESTINY

According to Freud, the normal woman is passive, masochistic, and narcissistic.[6] Woman's inferiority is anatomically based. She is an incomplete—"maimed"—man because she lacks a penis.

Freud saw early childhood development as being similar for both sexes until about age 5. Children then enter the phallic stage, he said, which is characterized by great interest in their own genitals and those of the opposite sex and by considerable masturbatory activity.

At this point the boy's Oedipus complex develops. He desires his mother sexually and would like to kill his father, whom he sees as his rival. He realizes, however, that his father is much more powerful than he is. The boy fears that the father will learn of his desires and, in retaliation, cut off the boy's penis, which gives him so much pleasure. The threat of castration leads the boy to abandon the Oedipus complex.

In the process of destroying these strongly held feelings, the superego develops. The superego includes the conscience and an internal set of standards that are used to evaluate oneself. A man with a strong superego evaluates himself in terms of these internal standards and does not rely heavily on the opinions of others for a feeling of self-worth. In Freud's thought, the development of the superego and the development of civilization are closely bound together.

In the girl, Freud said, the process is different and the outcome less satisfactory. From her observation of little boys, she learns that she lacks a penis and concludes that she has been castrated. Lacking "the only proper genital organ,"[7] the girl develops *penis envy*. In

[5]Naomi Weisstein, "Psychology Constructs the Female, or the Fantasy Life of the Male Psychologist," in Michele Hoffnung Garskof, ed., *Roles Women Play* (Belmont, Calif.: Brooks/Cole, 1971), pp. 76–77.

[6]For a brief summary of Freud's theory of female psychology, see Janet Shibley Hyde and B. G. Rosenberg, *Half the Human Experience: The Psychology of Women* (Lexington, Mass.: D. C. Heath, 1976), pp. 32–38.

[7]Quoted in Judith M. Bardwick, *Psychology of Women* (New York: Harper & Row, 1971), p. 9.

normal development, the girl will eventually transfer her desire for a penis into a desire for a child by her father. "The feminine situation is only established . . . if the wish for a penis is replaced by one for a baby. . . . Her happiness is great if later on this wish for a baby finds fulfillment in reality, and quite especially so if the baby is a little boy who brings the longed-for penis with him."[8]

This process has a number of effects on female psychology, according to Freud. Women do not develop strong superegos. "In the absence of fear of castration the chief motive is lacking which leads boys to surmount the Oedipus complex. Girls remain in it for an indeterminate length of time; they demolish it late and, even so, incompletely. In these circumstances the formation of the super-ego must suffer; it cannot attain the strength and independence which give it its cultural significance . . ."[9]

Because penis envy is never entirely sublimated even in normal women, "envy and jealousy play an even greater part in the mental life of women than of men."[10] "The fact that women must be regarded as having little sense of justice is no doubt related to the predominance of envy in their mental life."[11]

Normal femininity is attained, according to Freud, when the girl represses her own impulses toward activity; that is, when she becomes passive. A woman who is not passive, who wishes to participate in the world outside the home, to pursue an intellectual profession, is neurotic. According to Freud, such desires in a woman are symptoms of penis envy. Not only must the female give up competitive strivings and desires for achievement in the male world; she must also give up clitoral sexuality. Freud refers to the clitoris as a "penis equivalent"[12] and sees clitoral sexuality as masculine. The clitoris is a protruding organ, and it does not require a male penis for enjoyment. Thus it does not fit in with Freud's notion of women as passive. A normal female, according to Freud, transfers her erotic sensitivity from clitoris to vagina. Only vaginal orgasms are normal. A woman who has only clitoral orgasms is considered frigid.

According to Freud, then, women are innately inferior owing to their anatomy. More precisely, in Freudian theory the inferiority

[8]Sigmund Freud, "Anatomy Is Destiny," in Betty and Theodore Roszak, eds., *Masculine/Feminine* (New York: Harper & Row, 1969), p. 24.

[9]Ibid., p. 25.

[10]Ibid., p. 22.

[11]Ibid., p. 29.

[12]Ibid., p. 20.

stems from the female's psychological reaction to her anatomy. Freud leaves little doubt, however, that the female's reaction—her feeling that she has been cheated because she lacks a penis—is realistic and correct. He calls the penis the organ of "power and creativeness"[13] and the female's lack of it, an "anatomical tragedy."[14]

One is tempted to dismiss Freud and his theories as a sick joke. One wonders what happened during his childhood to produce such a penis fixation. Anyone who considers half the human race to be "mutilated creatures"[15] on the basis of the characteristics that make the continuation of the species possible has got to be sick. Unfortunately, we cannot dismiss him so easily; he has had too much effect on our thinking. That his theories could have been—and, in many quarters, still are—taken seriously illustrates the incredible misogyny (hatred of women) prevalent in Western society.

In criticizing Freud, one can point out that his notions were based on observations of affluent Viennese women during the Victorian era. To draw from these observations a generalization for all places and all times is hardly legitimate. His patients were psychologically ill. To generalize from an abnormal to a normal population is also suspect.

One can, however, make an even stronger criticism: Freud never tested his theories. They were based on clinical experience, on insight, not on controlled scientific experiments. Psychologist Naomi Weisstein[16] explains that Freud's "insights" came to him during his psychoanalytic sessions with patients. She notes that this is just as good a way as any other to *formulate* an hypothesis. A scientific hypothesis or theory may be *inspired* by anything, from God to a table of random numbers. A scientific theory, however, is not *confirmed* as valid until it has been tested under controlled conditions. Yet Freud never even attempted to put his theories to such a test. His *Sexual Enlightenment of Children* is usually offered as the scientific proof of the existence of the castration complex. In that work, however, the sole empirical evidence is of a secondhand nature, obtained from the boy's father. Moreover, the father was far from an unbiased observer, since he was also in therapy and enthusiastically believed in Freudian theory. Thus, Freud obtained an insight from one patient, constructed a theory on that basis, and then "con-

---

[13]Quoted in Bardwick, *The Psychology of Women,* op. cit., p. 9.

[14]Quoted in ibid.

[15]Quoted in ibid.

[16]Weisstein, op. cit., pp. 71–72.

firmed" the theory by examining other patients in the light of his pre-conceptions.

Most of Freudian theory has not been scientifically tested. Furthermore, much of it, as now stated, seems to be inherently untestable. Take the notion of penis envy as an example. As we saw earlier, according to Freud, all females experience penis envy, and most never completely get over it. This would seem to be easily tested merely by asking females of various ages if they ever experienced penis envy. Certainly we will find females who deny such an experience, but does this refute the theory? No. According to the Freudians, a female who denies penis envy has simply repressed the experience. In fact, it seems that no evidence that conceivably could exist would refute the theory. If a woman is passive, she has sublimated her penis envy; if she is aggressive, she has also sublimated it, only in another way.

In essence, any conceivable sort of female behavior can be explained by Freudian theory. Because that is so, the theory really explains nothing. It is an ideology, not a scientific theory. A theory, to be scientific, must be testable. It predicts that certain things will happen and others will not. If the theory predicts, for example, that certain types of behavior will not occur and they actually do occur, then the theory is shown to be false. If the predicted behaviors do occur, then our confidence in the validity of the theory increases. If the theory does not forbid any sort of occurrence, it cannot be tested, and so there is no way of determining whether it is true or false. Thus Freudian theory is dogma, not science. People may believe the theory because it makes them feel good, but there is no evidence supporting it.

Some aspects of Freudian theory are testable. One aspect, the notion of the two types of orgasm, has recently been tested and found to be false. Masters and Johnson have conclusively demonstrated that there is only one type of orgasm and that anatomically it is a clitoral orgasm.[17] Female orgasm may be brought on by different types of stimulation—direct clitoral stimulation, intercourse, or even breast manipulation—but the resulting orgasms are physiologically identical. The clitoris is much more sensitive than the vagina and is physiologically similar to the penis. Yet under the influence of Freudian theory, the vaginal orgasm was held to be the only normal form of sexual pleasure. A woman who required clitoral stimulation for orgasm was considered infantile, unfeminine, and frigid.

[17]Susan Lydon, "The Politics of Orgasm," in Garskof, op. cit., p. 64.

WOMAN IS NOT INFERIOR, BUT . . .

A number of psychologists and psychoanalysts agree with Freud that women and men are psychologically very different and that the difference is biologically determined but disagree with the notion of penis envy.

According to Erik Erikson, a well-known exponent of this view, woman's psychology is determined not by the missing penis but by the existence of a "productive inner-bodily space."[18] Woman's "somatic design harbors an 'inner space' destined to bear the offspring of chosen men and, with it, a biological, psychological, and ethical commitment to take care of human infancy."[19] For Erikson, woman's psychology is determined by her procreative potential. In this view, women are not passive; they are active in nonmale ways—bearing and taking care of babies. They are not masochistic; they have "an ability to stand (and to understand) pain as a meaningful aspect of human experience in general and of the feminine role in particular."[20]

Erikson does not deny that women may have interests and abilities that are unrelated to their procreative role. He states, as a general proposition, that women should be given equal rights and that he would not deny them other experiences by "dooming" them to nothing but motherhood. Yet, he claims that everything a woman may do is limited by the fact that she is a woman and can only do things according to her "natural dispositions."[21] What Erikson so magnanimously concedes in general, he nullifies in particular for women. He concedes that a woman's interests may extend beyond children, but then asserts that hers will still be distinctly feminine interests, or that a woman may be capable of competing successfully against men in the masculine sphere, but no "real" woman would want to. Erikson sees the normal woman as an earth mother. She is not inferior to men, but she is very, very different.

On what evidence does he base these conclusions? Erikson conducted an experiment with 150 girls and 150 boys. Within a 2-year period he saw each child 3 times. Each time he put some toys on a table and asked the child to construct some kind of scene with them.[22] He found that boys and girls used space differently. Girls

---

[18]Erik H. Erikson, "Inner and Outer Space: Reflections on Womanhood," in Robert Jay Lifton, ed., *The Woman in America* (Boston: Beacon, 1967), p. 6.

[19]Ibid., p. 5.

[20]Ibid., p. 13.

[21]Ibid., p. 26.

[22]Ibid., p. 7.

tended to build interior scenes in which the people and animals were placed within an enclosure or surrounded by low walls. Boys tended to build either houses with high walls or exterior scenes. In the boys' scenes most of the people and animals were outside the enclosure. "The girls," Erikson concluded, "emphasized inner and the boys outer space."[23]

To draw from such an experiment conclusions concerning the basic psychology of women would seem to be an Olympian leap of logic. Furthermore, since the children involved were from 10 to 12 years old, the possibility that they had already learned what is considered appropriate behavior for boys and for girls is very likely. This was never considered.

Judith Bardwick, in her widely used text *Psychology of Women,* [24] presents another variant on the "woman is different but not necessarily inferior" theme. Like Erikson, she believes that the existence of the female reproductive organs, not the absence of the penis, accounts for the differences. Unlike Erikson, with his rather mystical notion of inner space, Bardwick has a more physiological emphasis. The greater passivity, dependence, and conformity of girls and the greater aggressiveness, independence, and creativity of boys do, according to her, have a biological origin. Chromosomal, hormonal, and anatomical differences result in different potentialities, which are then emphasized or muted by the socialization process.

The evidence Bardwick presents for the genetic origin of these differences is very slim. She admits that "we know astonishingly little about the relationship between particular sex hormones and specific male and female behaviors"[25] but does cite a few findings on sex differences in infancy. For example, some studies report that male infants are somewhat more active and female infants more sensitive to stimuli at birth.[26] Again she admits that "infant research is just beginning, and little of it has been directed towards sex differences."[27] Primate studies are mentioned, but generalizing from monkeys to humans in the area of personality is a questionable practice. A great deal of evidence on sex differences at later ages is available and is cited, but such studies cannot be used to show the genetic origin of sex differences in personalities, since learning could well account for them.

[23]Ibid., p. 9.
[24]Bardwick, *The Psychology of Women,* op. cit., passim.
[25]Ibid., p. 21.
[26]Ibid., p. 93.
[27]Ibid., p. 90.

Although Bardwick does believe in the genetic origin of personality differences, she emphasizes the effect of socialization much more than either Freud or Erikson. Girls are more dependent, less aggressive, and less highly sexed than boys because of genetic and hormonal differences. Because of these inborn traits, the girl's behavior is more acceptable to her parents, so she is less likely to come into conflict with them at an early age. Furthermore, the normal dependent behavior of small children is considered acceptable in girls, so her parents will not penalize and may even reward such behavior. As a result, the girl finds it easy to win the approval of her parents and of other adults and thus is much less likely to develop internal standards of self-worth and independence, at least at an early age. She will depend much more heavily on the opinions and affection of others for her feeling of self-worth, and this dependence on others leads to conformity.

In contrast, Bardwick asserts, the boy's natural aggressiveness and greater sexuality brings him into conflict with his parents early. He is penalized for overaggressive play and for overt sexual activity. If he shows dependent behavior, he is also penalized because this is considered unmasculine. Because he cannot act as he wishes and still obtain parental approval, he turns inward for approval and develops an independent sense of self-worth. Such independence allows for the development of creativity.

Until puberty there are fewer pressures on the girl than on her brother. After puberty, the pressures on her to adopt the feminine role intensify. It is made clear that achievement, at least high achievement, is not feminine, that competition is aggressive and therefore masculine. Because such deviance will threaten her relationships with boys, a girl gives up her attempts at achievement. According to Bardwick, the girl finds it relatively easy to do so because of the personality characteristics she has already developed, particularly her dependence on others for a sense of self-worth. Such dependence also results in the female's placing greater value on interpersonal relationships, especially heterosexual ones, and in her being more empathic, nurturant, and supportive than the male.

Although Bardwick believes these psychological differences have a genetic origin, she feels present socialization practices result in an exaggeration of the differences:

> The sex differences that are present when children enter the school system are most likely to increase until girls and boys are very different. Dependency, affiliation, passivity and conformity versus independence, achievement, activity and aggression are the important vari-

ables. The origin of the differences lies in early constitutional proclivities which the culture enhances by reward and punishment along sex-specific lines.[28]

Psychological differences and society's ideas about appropriate male and female behavior result in a sex role system that assigns tasks on the basis of sex. "While the sexes appear to have characteristic qualities which are more or less functional in different activities, traditional role divisions have been far too restrictive for both sexes."[29]

SOCIETY IS DESTINY

Another group of psychologists holds that the psychological characteristics and behaviors distinguishing male and female are the result not of biology but of socialization. In other words, sex-appropriate responses and behaviors are learned.

There are a number of variants of this view, and the theories are often complex.[30] Social-learning theory is probably the most widely accepted. One psychologist summarizes the theory as follows:

> . . . social-learning theory holds that sex-appropriate responses are rewarded (reinforced) by parents and others, and hence are repeated (increased in frequency). Sex-inappropriate behavior, on the other hand, is likely to be punished and hence to diminish in strength and frequency, i.e., to become extinguished.[31]

According to the social-learning theorists, the society's views concerning sex-appropriate behavior are taught to the child through reward and punishment. A little girl is, for example, encouraged and praised for playing with dolls; a little boy is likely to be penalized for such behavior. Of course, the child does not try out all possible behaviors and then repeat or not repeat them on the basis of others' responses. Children also learn from the observation of live and symbolic models (e.g., television), and they generalize from one type of experience to a class of similar experiences. Children learn from experience what is socially approved behavior for women and what is approved for men. "This learning can affect the child's sex-typed

[28]Ibid., p. 113.

[29]Ibid., p. 217.

[30]For an overview of such theories, see Paul H. Mussen, "Early Sex-Role Development," in Nancy Reeves, ed., *Womankind, Beyond the Stereotypes* (Chicago: Aldine-Atherton, 1971), pp. 393–418.

[31]Ibid., p. 399.

activities by providing information about probable outcomes for responses before they are actually performed."[32]

Walter Mischel, an exponent of this view, points out that aggression and dependence have received special research attention as behaviors differentiating the sexes, and concludes that these differences can be accounted for by social-learning theory.[33] Sex differences in aggression, especially physical aggression, have been documented for 3-year-olds. It has also been found that parents make the greatest distinction between the sexes in this area. Furthermore, in an experiment in which children of both sexes were equally rewarded for aggressive behavior, very little difference between the sexes was found.[34]

Mischel reports that "no strong sex differences in dependency are observed at early ages (e.g., nursery school). . . . At older ages (high school and college) girls are consistently higher on dependency measures."[35] This increase with age in the difference between the sexes suggests that dependence too is learned.

Further evidence that sex-appropriate behavior is learned rather than innate is provided by studies of "persons whose original sex assignment was either incorrect or ambiguous because of the appearance of their external genitalia."[36] The sex to which these people were assigned determined their *gender identity.* That is, a genetic female reared as a male would grow up to think of herself as a male and to act like a male. Furthermore, an attempt to change the sex assignment after very early childhood (18 months to 3 years) is likely to be unsuccessful and to lead to psychological problems. From these studies "the hypothesis has been advanced that gender role is entirely the result of a learning process which is quite independent of chromosomal, gonadal or hormonal sex."[37]

If women are naturally passive and dependent and men naturally aggressive and independent, anthropology should provide evidence of this regularity. If these differences are innate, they should be found in all societies, past and present. In fact, anthropological

[32]Walter Mischel, "A Social-Learning View of Sex Differences in Behavior," in Maccoby, op. cit., p. 60.

[33]Ibid., p. 72.

[34]Ibid., pp. 73–74.

[35]Ibid., p. 74.

[36]David A. Hamburg and Donald T. Lunde, "Sex Hormones in the Development of Sex Differences in Human Behavior," in Maccoby, op. cit., p. 15.

[37]Ibid.

studies show that sex-appropriate characteristics and behavior vary greatly from one society to another.

Margaret Mead studied three New Guinea tribes and found that our assumptions about normal female and male psychology simply do not apply. In two of the tribes, male and female are not expected to, and in fact do not, display different personality traits. All members of Arapesh society are "trained to be co-operative, unaggressive, responsive to the needs and demands of others."[38] Male as well as female are in personality very like our notion of the normal nurturant woman. Among the Mundugumor, in contrast, "both men and women developed as ruthless, aggressive, positively sexed individuals, with the maternal, cherishing aspects of personality at a minimum. Both men and women approximated to a personality type that we in our culture would find only in an undisciplined and very violent male."[39]

In the third tribe, the Tchambuli, sex-linked personality differences are found. "The women [are] the dominant, impersonal, managing partner, the man the less responsible and emotionally dependent person."[40] From our perspective Tchambuli men are feminine; Tchambuli women, masculine.

Mead concludes: "Many, if not all, of the personality traits which we have called masculine or feminine are as lightly linked to sex as are the clothing, the manners, and the form of headdress that a society at a given period assigns to either sex."[41]

FEMINIST REEXAMINATION
OF SEX DIFFERENCE STUDIES

Psychologists with a feminist orientation have attacked theories such as Freud's that purport to explain psychological sex differences on the basis of biological differences. The multitude of empirical studies of sex differences have also been reexamined and frequently found to be wanting.[42] Too often, complex characteristics such as passive dependency or aggression were measured in unitary and simple-

---

[38]Margaret Mead, *Sex and Temperament in Three Primitive Societies* (New York: Dell, 1968), p. 259.

[39]Ibid.

[40]Ibid.

[41]Ibid., p. 260.

[42]See Julia A. Sherman, "Some Psychological 'Facts' About Women: Will the Real Ms. Please Stand Up," in Joan I. Roberts, ed., *Beyond Intellectual Sexism* (New York: David McKay, 1976); and Mary Brown Parlee, "Psychology," *Signs*, vol. 1, no. 1 (autumn 1975).

minded ways. Researchers who found a significant sex difference on one trait and no difference on ten others would report the difference and not the similarities. Illegitimate conclusions were often drawn from the data. Thus the finding that males are consistently better at spatial tasks was interpreted as indicating that men have superior analytic ability.[43]

Psychologist Julia Sherman, who has reviewed the sex-difference literature exhaustively, finds the evidence does not support the notion that women generally are more dependent and passive than men,[44] that they are generally more emotional than men,[45] or that men are superior in abstract and logical thinking.[46] In aggressiveness, the sex difference seems to be restricted to attack aggression; that is, "the male does have a greater tendency to attack or retaliate in certain interpersonal situations."[47] She concludes: "Increased research, improved conceptual models, and cultural change have revealed many sex differences to be more apparent than real."[48]

These reexaminations do not prove there are no psychological differences between the sexes. In fact, given the sex role socialization process, which will be discussed in the next chapter, it would be surprising if there were none. What is clear is that theories such as Freud's assume much greater sex differences than actually seem to exist.

NATURE OR NURTURE?

Are psychological sex differences innate or learned? The evidence indicates that masculinity and femininity are concepts that refer to a society's ideas about what men and women are supposed to be like. A society will socialize its children according to these ideas and thus produce men and women who are very like what society expects them to be. Ideas about what constitutes masculinity and femininity, however, vary from one society to another.

Are there any innate differences between men and women be-

---

[43]Sherman, op. cit., p. 130.

[44]Ibid., p. 119.

[45]Ibid., p. 129.

[46]Ibid., p. 130.

[47]Eleanor Maccoby and Carol Jacklin, "Sex Differences in Intellectual Functioning." Paper presented at the meeting of the Educational Testing Service Invitational Conference on Testing Problems, October 1972, p. 11.

[48]Sherman, op. cit., p. 119.

sides the obvious genital ones? We do not know and probably will never know unless the present socialization process is changed radically. So long as boys and girls are brought up to behave very differently, it will be impossible to disentangle the innate from the learned.

But we do know that human beings are extremely malleable. Psychologists have learned that, by and large, people behave very much the way those around them expect them to behave. A number of studies have shown that the expectations of the experimenter affect the outcome of the experiment. If experimenters are told that their rats are especially good at running mazes, even though in fact they are just average, the rats perform better. If teachers are told that certain students are intellectually promising, even though the students were randomly selected, the students score dramatically higher on IQ tests.[49] Social expectations and social context are crucial: So long as society expects women to be different from men, they are likely to be different.

Intellectual performance is one area in which social expectations seem to have an effect. There are few intellectual differences between the sexes until high school; the few that do exist in the early school years mostly favor girls. In high school, girls begin to fall behind in areas defined as masculine—math in particular.[50] Are innate incapabilities becoming manifest at this period in a girl's life or are girls learning too well what is expected of them? Naomi Weisstein concludes that, given society's expectations about women, "what is surprising is that little girls don't get the message that they are supposed to be stupid until high school; and what is even more remarkable is that some women resist this message even after high school, college, and graduate school."[51]

---

[49]Weisstein, op. cit., p. 75.
[50]Eleanor E. Maccoby, "Sex Differences in Intellectual Functioning" in Maccoby, op. cit., pp. 25–55.
[51]Weisstein, op. cit., p. 81.

THE SELF-FULFILLING PROPHECY: SEX ROLE SOCIALIZATION

3

Before a newborn baby leaves the delivery room, a bracelet with its family name is put around its wrist. If the baby is a girl, the bracelet is pink; if a boy, the bracelet is blue. These different-colored bracelets indicate the importance our society places on sex differences, and this branding is the first act in a sex role socialization process that will result in adult men and women being almost as different as we think they "naturally" are.

SOCIALIZATION AND SOCIETY

Every society has a set of ideas about what people are supposed to believe and how they should act—about what is natural and right in beliefs and behaviors. Children are taught these norms and expectations by parental instruction, in school, and by example.

Although the extent to which this socialization "takes" will vary, most children will grow up to act pretty much as they are expected to. The child internalizes society's standards—he or she comes to believe that certain types of behavior are natural and right. Besides, behavior at odds with society's standards is costly: at best one is considered deviant; at worst, thrown in jail.

All societies have expectations about how people are to behave, but few expect all their members to behave in the same way. What is proper, natural behavior will depend on certain attributes of the person, such as class, age, occupation, or sex. Perhaps because sex is such an obvious differentiating characteristic, almost all societies have sex roles. Women are expected to think and behave differently from men. The societal expectation and belief that women and men are very different tends to be a *self-fulfilling prophecy*. In other words, the socialization process ensures that so long as such beliefs are widely held, girls and boys *will* grow up to be different from each other in just the ways expected. How this process works in the United States is the subject of this chapter.

EARLY CHILDHOOD

The baby is likely to be taken home wrapped in a blanket of the proper color to a nursery decorated in that color—at least if it is the first child of middle-class parents. Although this makes no difference to the baby, it does show the importance the parents attach to its sex. One study of parents' reactions to their newborn infants found that girl babies were described as significantly softer, finer featured, smaller, and less attentive than boy babies, even though there actually was no difference in the size or weight of the two sexes.[1] College students' descriptions of a baby were also found to depend upon the sex they were told the child was. If told the baby was a girl, the students described it as "littler," "weaker," or "cuddlier."[2] These studies indicate that, to a considerable extent, people see what they expect to see. Sex role socialization has led us to expect sex differences even in newborns.

These expectations result in parents treating their male and female children differently. Sex-linked differences in maternal behavior have been observed toward 6-month-old infants.[3] Mothers were found to touch, talk to, and handle their daughters more than their sons. Not surprisingly, at 13 months the girls were more dependent on their mothers. They tended to stay closer to their mothers, to talk to them and touch them more than boys did. Boys tended to show more independence and exploratory behavior, to be more vigorous, to run more and make more noise in their play. The authors of a study of early childhood behavior hypothesized that "in the first year or two, the parents reinforce those behaviors they consider sex-role appropriate and the child learns these sex role behaviors independent of any internal motives."[4]

The overprotection most little girls receive seems to result in

[1]Jeffrey Rubin, Frank Provenzano, and Zella Luria, "The Eye of the Beholder: Parents' View on Sex of Newborns," *American Journal of Orthopsychiatry* 44 (1974), 512–519.

[2]Study by Luria and Rubin reported in *Parade,* February 22, 1976.

[3]Susan Goldberg and Michael Lewis, "Play Behavior in the Year-Old Infant: Early Sex Differences," in Judith M. Bardwick, ed., *Readings on the Psychology of Women* (New York: Harper & Row, 1972), pp. 30–33.

[4]Ibid., p. 33.

one of the few early intellectual differences between boys and girls.[5]
Boys tend to be better at spatial perception, the ability to visualize
objects out of context. This is important because it seems to be related to the sort of analytic thinking required in the sciences. Early
independence training—that is, allowing a child to explore and solve
problems on its own—is conducive to the development of this ability. Girls are much less likely to receive such training. "Overpro-
tected" boys also tend to do less well on spatial perception tests.

Reinforcement of sex role-appropriate behavior takes place in
a variety of subtle and not-so-subtle ways. Boys and girls are given
different toys from a very young age. Boys' toys are more varied,
more likely to encourage activities outside the house, and have a
higher "competency-eliciting value."[6] In nursery school, children
are strongly encouraged to play with the "appropriate" toys.[7] Girls
are more severely reprimanded for noisy and boisterous behavior.[8]
Boys are allowed and often encouraged to be aggressive. One study
found that a father often takes pride in his son's being a "holy terror"
but is worried if his daughter is "bossy."[9] Fathers expect their daughters to be "nice, sweet, pretty, affectionate and well-liked."

These middle-class fathers were much more concerned about
the behavior of their sons than that of their daughters. They worried
about "lack of responsibility and initiative, inadequate performance
in school, insufficiently aggressive or excessively passive behavior,
athletic inadequacies, overconformity, excitability, excessive tearful-
ness . . . and 'childish' behavior."[10] Such behaviors are considered
inappropriate when exhibited by a male child and, presumably, are
penalized. When they appear in girls, they are not a source of worry
and are not discouraged, at least not to the same extent.

Another study of nursery school children found many of the
same patterns.[11] Parents valued malleability, cooperativeness, and

[5]Jo Freeman, "The Social Construction of the Second Sex," in Michele Hoffnung Garskof, ed., *Roles Women Play* (Belmont, Calif.: Brooks/Cole, 1971), pp. 129–130.

[6]Reesa M. Vaughter, "Psychology," *Signs* (autumn 1976): 125–126.

[7]Carol Andreas, *Sex and Caste in America* (Englewood Cliffs, N.J.: Prentice-Hall,
1971), p. 28 passim.

[8]Ibid.

[9]David F. Aberle and Kaspar D. Naegele, "Raising Middle-Class Sons," in Alex In-
keles, ed., *Readings in Modern Sociology* (Englewood Cliffs, N.J.: Prentice-Hall,
1966), p. 104.

[10]Ibid., p. 103.

[11]Kirsten Amundsen, *The Silenced Majority* (Englewood Cliffs, N.J.: Prentice-Hall,
1971), pp. 116–117.

willingness to take direction, but disapproved of assertiveness and quarrelsomeness in girls. In boys, independence, assertiveness, and inquisitiveness were valued; timidity and fearfulness disapproved. The teachers' attitudes were similar to those of the parents. They encouraged boys to be daring and aggressive, but discouraged girls. Their behavior toward a child having trouble climbing to the top of a jungle gym, for example, varied with the sex of the child. A girl would be told, "Take it easy, dear—we'll help you down," while a boy would be told, "That's the boy! You can make it if you want to!"

Thus, from birth male and female children are treated differently and are rewarded for displaying differing types of behavior.

By age 3, children can identify themselves correctly as boy or girl, although they are not clear about the genital differences underlying that distinction. They do know which jobs are performed by men and which by women, and what they report is the traditional, sex-stereotyped division of labor.[12] By age 5 or 6, children are not only clear that there is a distinction between the male and female role but are also aware that the male role is the more highly valued. "Fathers are perceived as more powerful, punitive, aggressive, fearless, instrumentally competent and less nurturant than females. . . . Thus power and prestige appear as one major attribute of children's sex-role stereotypes. . . ."[13] By age 6, children consistently attribute more social power to the father; they consider him smarter than the mother and the boss of the family.[14]

All small children seem to think their own sex is best and to express preferences for others of the same sex. Psychologists explain these findings on the basis of the child's egotism—"what's like me is best." For boys, the same-sex preferences continue throughout childhood. With girls, a decline sets in at the time they learn the greater prestige attributed to the male role. Girls, as they get older, become less and less likely than boys to say their own sex is better.[15] Their opinion of boys and boys' abilities grows better with age, while the boys' opinions of girls grow worse.[16] Girls, then, begin to develop a negative self-image at an early age.

[12]Judith Bardwick, *Psychology of Women* (New York: Harper & Row, 1971), p. 142.

[13]Lawrence Kohlberg, "A Cognitive-Developmental Analysis of Children's Sex-Role Concepts and Attitudes," in Eleanor Maccoby, ed., *The Development of Sex Differences* (Stanford, Calif.: Stanford University Press, 1966), p. 99.

[14]Ibid., p. 102.

[15]Ibid., p. 120.

[16]Freeman, op. cit., p. 125.

In the child's early years the family is the most important socializing agency, but it is not the only one. Children's books and television programs also strongly influence perceptions of what is normal and appropriate. Until very recently, both presented a rigidly sex-stereotyped view. Most books for young children were about boys; when girls or women appeared, they were restricted to traditional feminine pursuits. One mother reports that when she started reading to her daughter at age 2, the little girl would ask questions like "Why aren't the girls fixing their own bikes?" and "Why isn't the little girl riding the horse?" After a few years of such books, the woman found that her daughter was constantly making derogatory remarks about girls—"Girls can't do anything"; "Girls can only do dumb things."[17]

Children's television programs further reinforce the notion that girls are less important and capable than boys. On the highly acclaimed "Sesame Street," females appear less than half as often as males and about one-third as often when the appearance involves any dialogue.[18] The women who do appear are almost always wives and mothers. "Virtually all [the programs] emphasized that there is men's work and then there is women's work—that the men's work is outside the home and the women's work in the home."[19] Of course children are quite aware of which type of work is valued by society.

GRADE SCHOOL

Grammar school continues the sex role socialization process. One study found that more than half of the teachers questioned admitted that they consciously behave differently toward boys and girls. Several studies have found that boys receive more attention from their teachers than girls. While teachers tended to direct more supportive remarks to girls and more critical ones to boys, they were much more likely to reward creative behavior in boys than in girls. "The message to girls is that one does best by being good and being conformist; creativity is reserved for boys."[20]

Having themselves grown up in a sexist society, most teachers, female as well as male, have internalized sexist attitudes. Such attitudes in turn affect their behavior toward their students. Most teach-

---

[17]Quoted in Riverside, California, *Daily Enterprise,* May 31, 1973.

[18]Carolyn Calvery, "Sexism on Sesame Street," available from the author at 11541 Hierra Court, Los Altos, California 94022.

[19]Jo-Ann Gardner, quoted in Judith Hole and Ellen Levine, *Rebirth of Feminism* (New York: Quadrangle, 1971), pp. 250–251.

[20]Bardwick, op. cit., p. 113.

ers probably never *say* girls are inferior to boys; they convey their feelings through their behavior. An occasional teacher is more blatant. A young woman recalls a discussion of a story concerning a male chef when she was in grammar school. One student commented that only a "sissy" would cook because that's a woman's job.

> The teacher's response surprised us all. She informed us calmly that men make the best cooks, just as they make the best dress designers, singers, and laundry workers. "Yes," she said, "anything a woman can do a man can do better."[21]

The attitudes of parents, teachers, and peers affect the child's view of what is natural and right. So, also, do the schoolbooks from which he or she learns to read. These provide one of the child's first views of the wider world outside the neighborhood. What, then, is "reality" as portrayed by elementary schoolbooks?

An excellent study entitled *Dick and Jane as Victims*[22] answers this question. Because the answer is so disturbing, the results will be presented in detail. One hundred and thirty-four elementary school readers currently being used in three suburban New Jersey towns were examined. Fourteen different national publishers were represented, so these would be books used all over the United States.

In the world of elementary readers, there are a lot more boys than girls. There are many more stories about boys. Boys also appear more frequently in illustrations; when girls are shown, they are often just scenery. The ratios speak for themselves.[23]

Boy-centered stories to girl-centered stories	5:2
Adult male main character to adult female main character	3:1
Male biographies to female biographies	6:1
Male animal stories to female animal stories	2:1
Male folk or fantasy stories to female folk or fantasy stories	4:1

In terms of sheer numbers, these books portray a male-dominated world. The numbers by themselves convey to the child

---

[21]Quoted in Florence Howe, "Sexual Stereotypes Start Early," in Marie B. Hecht et al., eds., *The Women, Yes!* (New York: Holt, Rinehart and Winston, 1973), pp. 190–191.

[22]*Dick and Jane as Victims* (Princeton, New Jersey: Women on Words and Images, 1972).

[23]Ibid., p. 6.

the notion that males are more important and more interesting than females. The content of the stories leaves no doubt about it.

Most of the stories are about the development and display of ingenuity, creativity, bravery, perseverance, achievement, adventurousness, curiosity, sportsmanship, autonomy, and self-respect.[24] These traits are generally valued in our society, and their development is presumably an important part of growing up. In the school readers, it is the male who displays such traits by a ratio of 4 to 1.

There are 164 stories emphasizing ingenuity and resourcefulness. The main character in these stories meets a situation with intelligence; he builds things; he uses his wits. In 131, the main character is a boy. The authors of the study comment, "The girl who figures out how to earn bus fare when she finds herself stranded seems like a visitor to these pages."[25]

In stories emphasizing perseverance and initiative, boys outnumber girls 169 to 47. And what sort of obstacles do girls overcome? In one story a girl wins a tennis match despite a dirty tennis dress.

Bravery and heroism are male traits in 143 of the stories and female traits in only 36. Typically boys rescue whole towns and save planes and spaceships; the occasional brave girl rescues younger siblings or small animals.

The acquisition of skills and coming-of-age themes are again found predominantly in stories about boys (151 to 53). In one story a boy kills a grizzly bear while taking care of the family's ranch in his father's absence. (We wonder what his frontier mother did before her son was old enough to protect her.) Any grown-up skills a girl learns tend to be domestic ones.

Stories in which competitiveness and the use of power play a role mostly concern sports. The boys almost always win; when a girl wins, it's often the result of a fluke.

Not only are boys more frequently involved in exploration and adventure stories (216 to 68); their adventures are a lot more exciting. Boys explore in China and meet bears in Yellowstone; girls watch their first snowstorm from inside the house.

When discussing stories on the theme of autonomy and normal assertiveness, the authors comment, "Stories about girls behaving as complete and independent persons are so rare they seem odd."[26]

[24]Ibid., p. 7.
[25]Ibid.
[26]Ibid., p. 13.

The traits considered desirable in our society are depicted in these books as male traits.

When one looks more carefully at how girls are portrayed in these stories, one begins to wish there were no stories about girls at all. The traits of passivity, docility, and dependence are displayed by 119 girls and only 19 boys. Girls cry a lot; they depend on boys to help them with things they should be quite capable of doing themselves; they are shown as spectators of life. In both stories and illustrations, girls spend a large part of their lives watching and admiring boys.

A good part of the rest of their lives is spent doing domestic chores—scrubbing floors, washing dishes, baking cookies—and usually enjoying it. "A girl's inborn aptitude for drudgery is presented in the same spirit as a black person's 'natural rhythm.' "[27] A girl who succeeds at anything nondomestic is seen as exceptional. One biographical story insists, "Amelia Earhart was different from the beginning from other girls."[28]

Girls are not just dependent and domestic; frequently they are just plain stupid. Both boys and girls have mishaps, but the boys' occur because of adventuresomeness, the girls' because of stupidity. If a boy fails at something, he will persevere and finally succeed. Girls give up. Boys are frequently presented as smarter than their mothers, who are, after all, female. The foolish/female, smart/male equation is exemplified "in one amazing story [in which] the author, by some Freudian slip, changes the sex of the stupid *female* kitten in time for 'him' to out-wit the fox!"[29]

If the image of girls is bad, the portrayal of their mothers is even worse. Mother is not really human at all. She is the perfect servant, "a limited, colorless, mindless creature."[30] When a boy is stuck in a tree, he has to wait for his father to come home to rescue him. Mother is evidently incapable of thinking of bringing the ladder. Not only does mother never do anything undomestic; even in this sphere tasks are strictly sex segregated. Father does all the yard work and is the fixer; mother does all the inside work.[31] The notion that tasks might be alternated or even shared appears to be considered heresy. Basically, mother is dull.

[27]Ibid., p. 19.
[28]Quoted in ibid.
[29]Ibid., p. 21.
[30]Ibid., p. 26.
[31]Ibid., p. 27.

Are there any positive role models for girls? Very few. One hundred and forty-seven occupations are shown for men; 26 for women. Mothers, of course, don't work. In the 2760 stories, only three working mothers appear, and they work only out of dire necessity. Fathers, of course, work. Men in these stories are everything from airplane builders to zoo keepers. Women are mostly in the traditional feminine occupations—babysitter, cashier, dressmaker, librarian, school nurse, teacher. The more exotic female "occupations"—fat lady at the circus and witch—are hardly viable role models.

Another study,[32] one of California elementary school texts, found a woman scientist. She was the only working woman in a series of descriptions of present-day professionals, and the text says twice that she is working on an idea not her own. The men scientists are shown as doing work that requires originality.

The biographical stories do offer some worthy female role models, but not many. There were 119 stories about 88 different men, but only 27 stories about 17 women. Boys are offered the full range of role models, from Albert Einstein to Mickey Mantle. There is a biography of Alexander the Great, but none of Queen Elizabeth I. Susan B. Anthony and other women's leaders are, of course, not included. The California study found a story about Marie Curie in which she is made to appear as little more than an assistant to her husband.[33]

According to these books, then, the normal girl is dependent, fearful, and incompetent. Girls are not even shown as excelling in schoolwork, as they actually do in grade school. In some cases the point that a girl should not be assertive is made in a really gross fashion. In one story an Indian girl who wanted to be tall, brave, and strong like the men is turned into a shadow for her presumption. And what happens when the girls in these stories grow up? Not much. They become textbook mothers—household drudges incompetent at anything outside their narrow province. The California study did not find one story in which the mother so much as suggests a solution in a family crisis. Textbook mothers don't even drive cars (which, given their IQ, is probably a good thing).

No wonder, then, that textbook boys have such a low opinion of females. The New Jersey study found 67 stories in which one sex demeans the other; girls are victims in 65 cases, boys in 2. Boys at-

[32]Marjorie B. U'Ren, "The Image of Women in Textbooks," in Vivian Gornick and Barbara K. Moran, eds., *Woman in Sexist Society* (New York: Signet, 1971), p. 324.
[33]Ibid., p. 323.

tack and ridicule girls as being "foolish, vain, silly, dumb, boring, no good at games and sports, etc., ad nauseam."[34] In one story, "Smart Annabelle," the title character asks a group of boys about the contraption they are building. She is put into her place with the comment, "We are willing to share our great thoughts with mankind. However, you happen to be a girl."[35] Such behavior by boys is never condemned or even commented on. Even worse, in these stories girls agree with boys' low opinions of their sex and frequently put themselves down with remarks like: "I'm just a girl but I know enough not to do that," and "Even I can do it and you know how stupid I am."[36]

The image of females conveyed by these readers is almost wholly negative. Little girls are generally nicer than little boys, but, as is made clear, nice is dull. Girls are also self-sacrificing, an admirable trait when displayed in moderation. But the readers portray self-abnegation as a natural component of the female personality, thus clearly implying that if a girl ever puts herself first she is some sort of monster. "The readers present a twisted view that happiness for girls lies chiefly in giving happiness to boys and men. Success, excitement, confidence, and status must be derived from association with the 'powerful' sex."[37]

The image of males, while much more positive, does contain some disturbing elements. Ingenuity, independence, creativity, and bravery are presented as admirable male traits, but excessive aggression and even dishonesty are not clearly condemned. Even when the fantasy and animal stories were excluded, almost 100 stories condoning meanness and cruelty in the story line were found. The study concludes that "boys are being given permission to vent a twisted type of aggression and sadism."[38] As far as dishonesty goes, the authors comment: "There is a blurry line drawn between praiseworthy enterprise and rather shady accomplishment in which a bright lad with a head on his shoulders bends the rules to his needs."[39]

Boys are being taught that overt aggressiveness is at least normal—if not praiseworthy—male behavior, and that winning is more important than playing by the rules. They are also taught that display-

---

[34]*Dick and Jane as Victims,* op. cit., p. 21.
[35]Quoted in ibid., p. 2.
[36]Quoted in ibid., p. 21.
[37]Ibid., p. 30.
[38]Ibid., p. 22.
[39]Ibid., p. 15.

ing emotion is unmasculine. Showing emotions is a feminine trait and one that attests to the female's weakness and foolishness. Under the most extreme circumstances boys must keep calm; in contrast, girls become terrified and cry on the slightest provocation. "Only on the pages of a reader does a girl weep non-stop from morning to night over a broken doll. Only on the pages of a reader does a boy remain impassive while his canoe proceeds out of control through the rapids."[40]

The images the texts present for children to model themselves upon are almost completely negative in the case of girls and contain destructive elements in the case of boys. But do these books really have an effect? They might not have much of one if these were the only forces pushing children into sex-stereotyped attitudes and behaviors. But in fact the texts present and reinforce society's attitudes toward men and women.

Television carries much the same message as the children's readers. A study of the most-watched prime-time shows during the 1973 viewing season found that 61 percent of the major characters were male.[41] On the adventure shows, 85 percent were male. Thus tv, which takes up so many hours of most children's time, portrays a predominantly male world. The women who do appear tend to be stereotyped by occupation—they are housewives, teachers, secretaries, and waitresses.[42] Only rarely does a professional woman appear. On the adventure shows particularly, women are depicted as incompetent. Forty-six percent of male behaviors but only 14 percent of female behaviors were classified as displaying competence; in contrast, 3 percent of male but 31 percent of female behaviors displayed incompetence.[43]

Sex role stereotyping thus begins at birth and is conveyed by most of the institutions in our society. Family, school, and the media in concert teach children to think and act in sex-appropriate ways.

In many ways, until adolescence, the pressures are greater on the boy. Girls are allowed and encouraged to be dependent, but this is normal behavior for a small child. Boys, from a very young age, are told not to cry, not to run to mother but to fight back, to "be a man," not to "act like a girl."

While independence is important for a child's intellectual de-

[40]Ibid., p. 22.
[41]*Channeling Children* (Princeton, N.J.: Women on Words and Images, 1975), p. 19.
[42]Ibid., pp. 19–21.
[43]Ibid., pp. 22–25.

velopment, pressuring a little boy to be physically aggressive and emotionally impassive is likely to leave scars. The child knows he is not really the person his parents expect him to be, even if he outwardly displays the expected behavior. Not surprisingly, many boys grow up with doubts about their masculinity, and many compensate for their doubts through overly "masculine" behavior. A man who values physical strength and aggressiveness above all else, who is convinced that any display of emotion or sensitivity to others' feelings is a feminine characteristic, is likely to find life very difficult. In a complex, industrial society there are very few comfortable niches for the John Waynes of the world.

For little boys the male role is frequently defined as the opposite of the female role. Fathers and mothers often tell a boy, when he is doing something of which they disapprove, that he is acting like a girl. This clearly contributes to the virulent antigirl feelings expressed by many little boys. One woman wrote to ask why girls could not be included in the Tonka Toys slogan, which says, "You can't raise boys without Tonka Toys." The company replied that if little boys know that girls also play with a toy, they will not want it.[44]

Dislike and disparagement of girls is fostered by child-rearing practices and by school texts. The texts seldom show cross-sex friendships, and most organized recreational activities for grade school children are sex segregated. Cub Scouts is for boys only; Brownies and Bluebirds are for girls. Such segregation again reinforces the notion that boys and girls are very different.

The idea that males are naturally brave, independent, and resourceful while females are timid and dependent tends to be a self-fulfilling prophecy. Parents base their child-rearing practices on this idea. Thus boys are given more independence at an earlier age than girls. They are allowed to play away from home, to walk to school alone, to pick their own activities, movies, and books earlier than their sisters. Boys are also given more personal privacy—to pick friends and girlfriends and to come and go as they please without parental consent. Psychologist Mirra Komarovsky concludes, "Parents tend to speed up, most often unwittingly, but also deliberately, the emancipation of the boy from the family, while they retard it in the case of his sister."[45]

That males are physically strong and females weak is another

[44]Hole and Levine, op. cit., p. 337.

[45]Mirra Komarovsky, "Functional Analysis of Sex Roles," in Marvin B. Sussman, ed., *Sourcebook in Marriage and the Family* (Boston: Houghton Mifflin, 1968), p. 261.

self-fulfilling prophecy. Boys are strongly encouraged and sometimes forced to participate in athletics from a very early age. Being good at sports is an important element of "masculinity" in our society. A boy who doesn't love baseball and football is considered a sissy, if not an incipient homosexual. A boy learns early that athletic prowess brings prestige with his peers and approval from his parents.

Delicacy and even physical weakness are still components of our notion of femininity. Girls are not encouraged to participate in athletics. Sometimes they are actively discouraged. "Several years ago in California there was a movement trying to say that it's too strenuous for girls to compete in sports," an Indio, California, school principal reports.[46]

Girls who wish to participate often find little opportunity. The Little League, until very recently, admitted only boys, and there was no comparable organization for girls. Although in high school some organized sports are available to girls, the bulk of the money and effort goes into boys' sports. Lucy Komisar reports that "the Syracuse school system spent about $90,000 for boys' extracurricular athletics compared to $200 for girls."[47] Until recently women coaches generally got no coaching pay. Girls' teams did not get special equipment; they had to make do with equipment used in gym classes, which was often in poor shape. If the girls wanted new equipment, uniforms, or travel money, they had to raise it themselves through bake sales and the like.[48]

The low value put on women's athletics will discourage many girls. They will grow up just about as they are expected to—not delicate or weak, but much less strong and physically fit than they could be.

ADOLESCENCE

When children enter adolescence, they are aware of and have to a large extent internalized society's views of sex-appropriate attitudes and behavior. Good girls are sweet, obedient, and docile; they grow up to be mommies. Good boys are "little men"—daring and aggressive; they grow up to be presidents or at least fire fighters. Until this point, overt socialization pressures have been directed more at boys than at girls. After all, turning a child into John Wayne is no easy task. Girls have been allowed and encouraged to remain child-

[46]Quoted in Riverside, California, *Press Enterprise,* May 27, 1973.
[47]Lucy Komisar, *The New Feminism* (New York: Warner Paperback Library, 1972), p. 32.
[48]Riverside, California, *Press Enterprise,* May 27, 1973.

ish—that is, dependent. They have also been encouraged to be little ladies, although most parents will condone a certain amount of tomboyishness in a preadolescent girl.

During adolescence the situation changes. The pressure on the boy to achieve academically and athletically continues. The pressure on the girl to be feminine increases enormously. Mothers particularly are terribly concerned that their daughters be feminine and popular and may push them into absurdly early dating. Padded bras for 10-year-olds are sold, and it's not the little girls who pay for them. Peer pressures become tremendously important in adolescence. Being popular becomes crucial, and for a girl that means being popular with boys as a female. In grade school, the tomboy or girl clown may be popular, and this sort of popularity may continue. But everyone knows that it's not the right sort of popularity. It doesn't get her dates.

Being popular in high school means living up to boys' expectations of what a girl is supposed to be like. She should be pretty; she should not be too smart or talk in class much; she should be supportive and admiring of the boys she is with. In one study, 40 percent of the girls interviewed admitted to "playing dumb" on dates, at least occasionally.[49] And of course, not all girls need to *play* dumb. The really popular, successful high school girl is not a "brain" or even an athlete; she is the cheerleader. She embodies the supportive and admiring role assigned to girls. She is defined in terms of her relationship to boys.

Because of their early upbringing, girls are less likely to have developed an independent sense of self-worth, are more likely to depend on the opinions of others for a feeling of worth and thus to define themselves in terms of their relationships with others. Unlike the boy, the girl is not encouraged to be independent, to explore and solve problems for herself. The girl remains more dependent and relies on the family for her feelings of self-worth. Now, in adolescence, she is encouraged to define herself in relation to boys. She is successful not if she accomplishes something intellectually, artistically, or athletically, but only if boys like her.

Dating, which can be honestly labeled one of the barbaric rituals of our society, intensifies this process. Awakening sexual drives and the societal prohibition against their expression would make adolescence a difficult time in any case. The dating ritual makes it acutely painful for the great majority. Because boys and girls have

[49]Mirra Komarovsky, "Cultural Contradictions and Sex Roles," in Bardwick, *Readings on the Psychology of Women,* op. cit., p. 60.

been segregated in play activities, they find it very difficult to talk together, much less be real friends. The accepted dating procedure reinforces the female/passive, male/aggressive stereotype. The boy must call the girl; she must passively sit and wait. The boy who has managed to get by and hide the fact that he's not really John Wayne is now expected to be James Bond. If not enough boys call, the girl is a failure as a woman. The fact that the boy is expected to pay for both himself and his date not only places a financial burden on him but encourages in both parties the notion of woman as passive object. "I always feel like I'm being rented for the evening," one girl commented. "I have to be nice and charming and do what he wants to do because he's paying."[50]

The dating ritual reinforces the tendency already instilled in the girl to see herself as passive and to define herself in terms of her relationships with men. It engenders conflicts among girls because they are in competition for the attentions of the same set of boys. The canard that women cannot be true friends contains a grain of truth. Many women do go through life regarding other women as competitors. This is not a healthy sort of competition in which winning depends on the development and expression of skills and abilities. It is, rather, an expression of the slave mentality. Winning depends not on what you can do but on the capricious choice of the master.

The dating ritual also places a tremendous premium on good looks. No girl growing up in America can escape the conclusion that being feminine depends not only on appropriate behavior but also on being pretty. From television, movies, and women's magazines she may well conclude that without beauty happiness is impossible, and her experiences with peers are likely to confirm that conclusion. Boys, too, have been socialized to regard appearance as a girl's most important characteristic. Dating a plain girl, however interesting she may be, means loss of social prestige.

Who determines the standard of beauty? The media, including Hollywood, decree the ideal. The ideal allows for little variety and individuality and, of course, excludes the vast majority of women.

All girls, not just the really plain ones, suffer from this inordinate emphasis on looks. Is there a girl who, during her teen years, was not convinced that some aspect of her looks was just awful? She is too short or too tall, too fat or too thin; her breasts are too small or too big; she has a mole on her face; her nose is too big or crooked; her ears stick out. When beauty becomes the one and only

[50]Quoted in Komisar, op. cit., p. 39.

passport to happiness, a morbid sort of self-consciousness results. A girl becomes sure that a flaw so minor no one notices it completely ruins her looks and thus her life. A pimple becomes a cosmic disaster.

Such a preoccupation with looks, while destructive for the girl, is good for the economy. She is willing to believe the wildest advertising claims and will spend any money she has on clothes and cosmetics. Perhaps this product will finally make her look like Raquel Welch or whoever is the latest sex symbol. The girl begins to regard herself as a product that must be adorned and properly displayed so as to command the highest possible price.

The media, of course, encourage such a view. Advertising, with its insistence that you aren't a real woman and will never catch a man unless you use a certain eye shadow or vaginal spray or whatever, is a major offender. The features in women's magazines are just as bad. *Seventeen,* which is aimed at high school girls, devotes most of its space to fashions, makeup, and hair styling. The message is clear: Success for a girl means attracting boys, and that requires making the best of your physical resources. (Behavioral tips are also given: Be sweet and charming, a little helpless, and not too smart. And don't be domineering—that is, don't show that you have a mind of your own.)

Given these preoccupations, it's remarkable that girls do as well as they do academically. Throughout grade school, girls are ahead of boys academically. In high school, their grades are on the average as good as boys, and more girls graduate than boys. But girls do begin to slip in some areas—those that are defined as masculine. Thus on college entrance exams the sexes do equally well on the verbal aptitude section, but the boys score significantly higher on math. If the problems are reworded so that they deal with "typically" feminine pursuits (cooking, for example), the girls' performances improve.[51] "It's around the eighth or ninth grade that this kind of thing begins to occur," one teacher said. "Girls don't like to answer in class; they don't volunteer very often. If you call on a girl, she'll much more likely give you a blank stare while boys will try to think of an answer or make one up. Often, even if girls know the answer, they giggle and act stupid. They're always putting themselves down. . . . Even if girls don't have trouble with math, they say they do. They think math is somehow for boys."[52] If an occasional girl does not

[51] Sandra L. and Daryl J. Bem, "Training the Woman to Know Her Place: The Power of a Nonconscious Ideology," in Garskof, op. cit., pp. 87–88.
[52] Quoted in Komisar, op. cit., p. 34.

catch on, the teacher may well set her straight. A New York high school student explained:

> Well, within my physics class last year, our teacher asked if there was anyone interested in being a lab assistant, in the physics lab, and when I raised my hand, he told all the girls to put their hands down because he was only interested in working with boys.[53]

The expectations of a girl with respect to academic performance are contradictory. She is aware that achievement is a societal value. Particularly if they are middle class, her parents will expect her to do well at school. At the same time her mother, especially, is likely to warn her not to do too well. "Let him think he's smarter," she'll be told. Not surprisingly, many girls feel resentment. One high school girl complained that her family told her to work hard at school in order to get into a top university. Simultaneously, however, they compared her to her friend next door who was "pretty and sweet" and very popular. So they also hounded her to work on her appearance and have a "successful" social life. "They were overlooking the fact that this carefree friend of mine had little time left for school work and had failed several subjects. It seemed that my family had expected me to become Eve Curie and Hedy Lamarr wrapped up in one."[54]

Expectations about careers for girls are considerably less ambiguous. Boys are encouraged to think about growing up to be something from a very early age; in high school the pressure seriously to consider career plans intensifies. If the boy is middle class and not mentally deficient, it is assumed that he will go into a profession or into business. Girls may be encouraged to prepare for a job but seldom for a career. They have been taught from earliest childhood that their most important adult role will be that of wife and mother. This is never presented to girls as a matter of choice: You're either normal or not. A girl who didn't want to grow up and have babies would be considered some kind of freak, if not a downright monster.

Typically it is the mother who impresses the importance of marriage on her daughters. But fathers are in complete agreement. A study of middle-class fathers found that the men interviewed expected their daughters to get married and preferred marriage over

[53]Quoted in Howe, op. cit., p. 194.
[54]Komarovsky, "Cultural Contradictions and Sex Roles," op. cit., p. 59.

a career for them.[55] Half were willing to accept the possibility of a career for their daughters; the rest completely rejected the idea. Only two wanted their daughters to know how to earn a living.

Schools do little to make up this deficit. The career education materials used at the primary and secondary school level tend to perpetuate sex stereotypes. One careful study found that through the text or the illustrations, most occupations were presented as being either male or female; few were clearly shown as appropriate for both sexes.[56] In both grade school and high school, many more male occupations were presented, and the female occupations were, by and large, traditional.[57]

Girls but not boys are told that good grooming is important to job success. "Good posture, attractive glasses, manicured hands, smooth arms and legs, proper girdles to firm buttocks—all enhance the physical qualities we have inherited. The secretary who does not make the most of her physical attributes is not doing herself justice."[58] Combining family responsibilities with those of the job are seen as a female problem. Women are frequently portrayed as quitting jobs to get married.[59] Even those materials prepared under the impetus of the women's movement to combat sex stereotyping sometimes assume that the family is the woman's responsibility and that she should make her career choice with this in mind. Thus girls are advised that "a dental practice can often be adapted to the schedule of a woman who wants to have a family. An office can be established in her home, and a part-time practice can be maintained."[60] The girl who would like to be a successful doctor as well as a wife and mother is told that, among other things, she'd better have "the constitution of an ox."[61]

Boys are not only encouraged to begin career planning early, they are also provided with a wealth of role models. In textbooks, television, and films and in their everyday life, they see men in a variety of careers. In contrast, the role models to which girls are exposed are very limited. Betty Friedan remarks that, aside from women who were full-time wives and mothers, "the only other kind of women

---

[55] Aberle and Naegele, op. cit., p. 102.
[56] *Help Wanted: Sexism in Career Education Materials* (Princeton, N.J.: Women on Words and Images, 1975), p. 7.
[57] Ibid., p. 7, p. 9 passim.
[58] Ibid., p. 17.
[59] Ibid., pp. 16–17.
[60] Ibid., p. 23.
[61] Ibid., p. 23.

I knew growing up were the old maid high-school teachers; the librarian; and the one woman doctor in our town, who cut her hair like a man."[62] A younger woman recalls that at an early age she was already sure she did not want to be like her mother. But the only women she knew who were not full-time mothers were teachers, librarians, secretaries, and waitresses, all of whom she considered dull.[63]

Schoolbooks, as we saw earlier, present an even more restricted set of female role models. In one American history text, for example, only 26 of the 643 people mentioned are women. "If we are to accept the view of our society presented by our history text," several girls using the book wrote, "ours is a society without women."[64] In six richly illustrated high school science texts, Florence Howe reports that the only women she found in illustrations were one doctor, one scientist, one lab assistant, and Rachel Carson.[65] A high school text entitled *Representative Men: Heroes of Our Time* featured two women—Elizabeth Taylor and Jacqueline Onassis.[66]

The image of women in the media is largely a restricted, stereotyped one and frequently just plain insulting. Television commercials are a major offender with their presentation of women as either housewife-mothers or sex kittens. The former are always shallow—their major concern is having the whitest laundry in the neighborhood—and often stupid. The latter are always dumb and sometimes masochistic. For both, pleasing a man is the primary purpose in life.

On television programs one does find an occasional career girl. But what do these "girls" actually do? Taking the highly acclaimed "Mary Tyler Moore Show" as an example, one reviewer asked, "Why can't the writers find something for Mary to do other than waiting on the men in her office, or worrying about the flowers on her desk, or solving the mini-crises of her friends?"[67] Surveying evening television programs, the reviewer found only one truly liberated woman—Miss Kitty, the nineteenth-century saloonkeeper on "Gunsmoke." "She is the only woman character on nighttime television who is her own woman, who is successful in her own right and who

[62]Quoted in Cynthia Epstein, *Woman's Place* (Berkeley: University of California Press, 1971), p. 55.
[63]Roberta Salper, *Female Liberation* (New York: Knopf, 1972), p. 14.
[64]Quoted in Hole and Levine, op. cit., p. 333.
[65]Howe, op. cit., p. 194.
[66]Ibid., p. 197.
[67]Judy Klemesrud, in Riverside, California, *Press Enterprise,* May 31, 1973.

doesn't bask in the reflection of some man." The reviewer concludes that the vast majority of women on prime-time television are "unliberated ding-a-lings, sex kittens, kooky housewives, lovable widows, crimefighters' secretaries and nosy nurses."

Many young girls never see, much less get to know, even one intelligent, dedicated professional woman who could serve as a role model. And role models are important. Daughters of working mothers are more likely to expect to hold a job themselves. They consider working normal rather than extraordinary for a woman.[68] One study found that 66 percent of career-oriented college women were daughters of working women.[69] In contrast, only 22 percent of women not oriented toward a career had working mothers.

The educational system itself encourages girls to live up to sex stereotypes in their career planning or lack of it. Girls are encouraged to take home economics, boys to take shop. Until it became illegal, in many schools more than encouragement was involved; girls were not allowed to take shop courses. A few high schools required girls to take home economics in order to graduate. Of course by the time high school age is reached, such rules usually are not necessary. A social studies teacher reports: "I've heard girls say they want to take auto mechanics, and the guidance counselors and the mothers threw fits and absolutely shamed those girls out of wanting to take those courses."[70] Career day is a common event in many high schools. Doctors, lawyers, and engineers are brought in to talk to the boys; nurses and airline stewardesses, to talk to the girls.

In some areas sex-segregated public high schools remain. Until recently all but one of New York City's special scientific high schools for especially capable students restricted admission to boys.

But what if, after all this, a girl is still interested in a career? What sort of advice is she likely to receive from the guidance counselors? "They ask girls whether the careers they have in mind would 'fit in' with marriage and a family."[71] Again, it is simply assumed that every girl's primary adult role is that of wife and mother and that she will, of course, subordinate all else to that role. Sometimes the message is conveyed in a blunter fashion. A bright female college student who

---

[68]Ruth E. Hartley, "American Core Culture: Changes and Continuities," in Georgene Seward and Robert Williamson, eds., *Sex Roles in Changing Society* (New York: Random House, 1970), p. 129.

[69]Elizabeth Almquist and Shirley Angrist, "Role Model Influences on College Women's Career Aspirations," in Athena Theodore, ed., *The Professional Woman* (Cambridge, Mass.: Schenkman, 1971), p. 301.

[70]Quoted in Komisar, op. cit., p. 33.

[71]Ibid., p. 36.

wanted to be a doctor was told by her adviser that the only reason women go to medical school is to catch a husband. "Why don't you do something more appropriate, dear?" the adviser asked.[72]

When a girl receives her high school diploma, what has she learned? Probably some English, math, and history; her proper place in the scheme of things almost certainly. She has learned that men and women are very different. Males are physically strong and emotionally impassive; they are good at math and science and in mechanical matters; they are natural leaders. Women, in contrast, are designed by nature to play the supportive role whether in a job as nurse or secretary or in the family. Women are not good at math or science or mechanical matters; they are emotional rather than logical. A woman can find personal fulfillment only by marrying the right man and bearing his children. And this is enough for any normal woman. She does not need a career for personal fulfillment. Interest in a demanding career is, in fact, a sign of selfishness in a woman. Furthermore, given her intellectual and emotional traits, she is not likely to succeed at one if she tries. Again, the girl learns not only that men and women are different but that men are better. The traits attributed to men are those generally valued by our society.

More boys than girls go to college. For young people of both sexes, the chance of going beyond high school is related to the income of their parents. But at all income levels girls are less likely than their brothers to continue with their education. In working-class families, if there is enough money to send only one of the children to college, it will be the boy. His sister may even be expected to help send him through. Mrs. Danielli, a working-class housewife, said that she was considered something of a "women's libber" for insisting that her daughters also go to college.

> Everyone in the family thought our three girls would go to work to help put my son Johnny through. . . . I told my husband, "Joe, if one of our kids is going to college, all of them are. Your girls aren't gonna have 10 children like your mama—they've gotta do something with their lives just like our boy." Both of our families were shocked when our oldest girl went off to college—Joe's papa kept asking if we didn't need the extra money she could bring in working as a typist. We needed the money, all right, but I never gave in. . . .[73]

[72]Quoted in Joan Flannigan, "Women in the Professions," in New York City Commission on Human Rights, *Women's Role in Contemporary Society* (New York: Avon, 1972), p. 358.

[73]Quoted in Susan Jacoby in Riverside, California, *Press Enterprise,* June 17, 1973.

In middle-class families where money is less of a problem, girls are more likely to go to college, but still not as likely as their brothers. Of the top 40 percent of high school graduates, about half go to college; two-thirds of those who do not are female.[74]

What happens to the young woman whose education ends with high school? She may marry immediately, get a job, or both. In any case, her chance of ever breaking out of the rigidly stereotyped female role is slim. Any job she can get will almost certainly be a typical female job—low-paid, dull, and dead-end. After a few years at such a job, marriage, motherhood, and full-time housewifery may seem a welcome change. But when the children are small, she will have little time for self-development; when they enter school, she will probably have to go back to work to help make ends meet.

All the bright promises about the fulfillment inherent in being a "real" woman, a wife and mother, do not materialize. With a dull job, in or out of the home, and few inner resources, a woman is likely to take out her frustrations on her husband and children. She feels that they must succeed in order to make up for her empty life. Never aware of why she is not content and feeling guilty about it, she will raise her son to be the aggressive, successful, supermasculine man that her husband probably isn't, her daughter to be the "real" woman who finds the fulfillment she herself has never found in the traditional role.

COLLEGE

The young woman who goes to college has another chance to break out of the stereotyped role society has decreed for her. The college years may be a period of intensified social pressures to adopt appropriate feminine role behavior, or they may be a period of widening horizons and newly perceived possibilities.

It is often assumed that the only reason the young woman goes to college is to catch a husband. Sometimes it's true. After all, that's what she has been taught is her main purpose in life. One study found that the relation between college freshmen's desire to please their parents and their desire to attend graduate or professional school was +.47 for men and −.37 for women.[75] That is, men who wanted to please their parents were interested in further career-oriented education but women concerned about pleasing their parents were not.

The young woman's college experience may either reinforce

[74]Epstein, op. cit., p. 59.
[75]Walter L. Wallace, "The Perspective of College Women," in Theodore, op. cit., p. 385.

or begin to erode previous socialization. A sorority type of college, with its emphasis on football and beauty queens, will act as reinforcement. But for many girls, going away to college offers a first taste of independence. As we have seen, girls are brought up to be more dependent on the family than their brothers. Leaving home to go to college allows and even forces the young woman to make her own decisions, to develop a certain amount of self-reliance. But sororities act as family surrogates. The social pressures operating within a sorority encourage conformity and discourage independence. Generally they also institutionalize husband-catching.

This sort of college life seems to be on its way out or at least is becoming much less prevalent. The new style in college life emphasizes informality and "doing your own thing." Young women now have greater freedom from conventional social pressures, but neither they nor their fellow students who are male can completely escape previous socialization. Girls may wear tee shirts and blue jeans rather than pleated skirts and bobby socks. Beauty parlor curls may have given way to long, straight hair. Young men and women may sleep together pretty much whenever they want to, and they may set up housekeeping together.

Under the surface, however, the traditional assumptions about the male and female persist. Men are expected to be the leaders in academic and social life. In class, men are much more likely to speak up than women. Men tend to dominate college politics. The division of labor when male and female students live together again tends to be highly traditional: She does the cooking and cleaning and shopping; he does the yard work if there's any to be done. And what about the image of women as sex objects? Under pressure from the growing women's movement, the present generation of college men may be more likely than their fathers to regard women as people first and as bodies second. But the circulation of *Playboy* doesn't seem to be decreasing, and its readership is heavily young, male, and college educated.

During the college years, the results of early sex role socialization become starkly obvious. Most young women have developed very clearly negative self-images. A 1968 study asked college students to rate the typical adult male, the typical adult female, and themselves on 122 bipolar items describing personal characteristics.[76] Male and female students agreed closely on their descriptions of the typical adult male and female—and both judged the typically male traits as more socially desirable. Furthermore, the women stu-

[76]Hartley, op. cit., p. 138.

dents attributed to themselves the typically female but socially less desirable traits. These women saw themselves as not at all resourceful or intellectual or competent or intelligent or realistic, as very immature, very subjective, very submissive, and very easily influenced.

Given these negative self-images, it's not surprising that women lack self-confidence. Numerous studies have found that, on a wide variety of tasks, women's expectations about their performance are lower than men's expectations.[77] Generally in these experiments, a task is described and the subject asked to predict his or her performance in completing it. On tasks as widely divergent as solving anagrams, taking tests of verbal intelligence and arithmetic abilities, and a marble-dropping game, males consistently expect to do better than females do. Explicitly labeling the task to be performed as feminine raises women's expectations to about the level of the men's.

Women, then, generally do not expect to succeed. When they do, does it raise their self-confidence and lead to higher expectations in the future? In fact, on most of the tasks used in these experiments, men and women performed about the same. Yet men and women explained their performance differently. Women attributed their success to luck while men attributed their success to ability. Women were more likely to explain their failure as a lack of ability while men seldom did.[78] If success is seen as the result of luck not of competence, it is unlikely to build self-confidence.

If men and women are asked to explain other people's success, the same attribution pattern is found. Both men and women explain a woman's success as being due to luck; a man's, as due to skill.[79] What if the success is one that can't possibly be due to luck? In an experiment, subjects were asked to explain the success of a surgeon identified as either Dr. Marcia Greer or Dr. Mark Greer.[80] The male subjects attributed greater ability to Mark; Marcia was seen as having worked harder and having had an easier task. The women subjects also thought Marcia had worked harder, but they did not see her task as easier. A similar study found that high school girls attributed female failure to lack of ability and female success to luck, easy courses, and even cheating on exams.[81]

A study by Philip Goldberg further demonstrates the extent to

[77]Kay Deaux, *The Behavior of Women and Men* (Belmont, Calif.: Brooks/Cole, 1976), pp. 38–39.
[78]Ibid., p. 41.
[79]Ibid., p. 30.
[80]Ibid., pp. 31–32.
[81]Ibid., p. 32.

which women have a negative image of women in general.[82] Female college students were asked to evaluate short articles on art history, dietetics, education, city planning, linguistics, and law. Two sets of booklets containing the articles had been prepared, the only difference being the authors' names. In one set, a given article was attributed to a male author, for example, John T. McKay; in the other set, the same article was attributed to a female author, Joan T. McKay. Each booklet contained articles by three "male" and three "female" authors.

The women students consistently rated "male" authors higher than "female" authors, even in traditionally feminine fields such as elementary school teaching and dietetics. The author of the study concluded that the belief in women's inferiority, particularly in the intellectual and professional sphere, distorted these students' perceptions.[83] Facts were interpreted in such a way as to support the belief. The same experiment was run using male students as subjects, and the results were similar. The male students also consistently rated the "male" authors higher.[84]

Since many young women have internalized the assumption that women are intellectually inferior to men, it is hardly surprising that few strive for professional achievement. Still, many college women are academically successful, and career opportunities for women are expanding. Given the high premium our society places on achievement, why is the number of women in the professions not increasing more quickly?

Psychologist Matina Horner has suggested the presence of "the motive to avoid success" as a psychological barrier to success in women. She says that the motive to avoid success "exists and receives its impetus from the expectancy held by most women that success, especially in competitive achievement situations, will be followed by negative consequences for them. Among these are social rejection and feelings of being unfeminine or inadequate as women."[85]

Horner asked students to write a short story, beginning with the sentence, "At the end of first term finals Anne/John finds herself/himself at the top of her/his medical school class." From the content

[82]Philip Goldberg, "Are Women Prejudiced Against Women?" in Theodore, op. cit., pp. 167–172.

[83]Ibid., p. 168.

[84]Bem, op. cit., p. 85.

[85]Matina Horner, "The Motive to Avoid Success and Changing Aspirations of College Women," in Bardwick, ed., *Readings on the Psychology of Women,* op. cit., p. 62.

of the stories it was determined whether fear of success imagery was present. Although only 10 percent of the male stories showed fear of success, 65 percent of the female did.

Many of the female stories showed fear of social rejection as a result of academic success. In a number, Anne is faced with losing her boyfriend; in others she doesn't have one because she's too smart. In another group of stories, Anne's success makes her worry about her normality or femininity. One story says explicitly that Anne is no longer certain about a medical career because she wonders if it's "normal" for a woman to be a doctor. Another account, which says that Anne starts to feel guilty, supplies a classic conclusion: "She will finally have a nervous breakdown and quit med school and marry a successful young doctor."[86] In their stories, some of the women students simply denied the situation in the lead line. One such story claims that Anne doesn't really exist but that a group of medical students created her as a code name to play a joke on their professors. In another, medical school is taken to mean nursing school. A few stories were truly bizarre. In one, Anne's classmates "jump on her in a body and beat her. She is maimed for life."[87]

In a variant on the basic experiment, students at an outstanding eastern women's college were asked to describe Anne. More than 70 percent said she was unattractive in face, figure, or manners: "Wears long skirts. Not feminine; masculine looking. Has short hair."

Horner's study has been criticized on a number of grounds.[88] Because she did not provide a detailed manual for scoring fear of success imagery, a good deal of subjectivity may have crept into the scoring. This may explain the contradictory results found by other researchers using the same technique. She has not adequately shown, some claim, that fear of success is actually a motive and that it does predict behavior.

The results of further studies using Horner's technique suggest that some of the subjects may not be displaying their internalized motives in the stories they write. Rather, as psychologist Kay Deaux points out, they may be "responding to a stereotype and writing what they think an average male or an average female might do in that particular situation."[89] In one experiment men and women were

[86]Matina Horner, "Femininity and Successful Achievement: A Basic Inconsistency," in Garskof, op. cit., pp. 111–113.

[87]Ibid., p. 114.

[88]David Tresemer, "Fear of Success: Popular But Unproven," *Psychology Today,* 7 (March 1974).

[89]Deaux, op. cit., p. 51.

asked to write about both Anne and John. Regardless of the sex of the writer, the stories about Anne showed more fear of success imagery than those about John.[90] In another experiment, nursing school was substituted for medical school for some of the subjects. Both men and women displayed more fear of success imagery for Anne in medical school and John in nursing school than for the situations in which sex and occupation were linked in the stereotyped manner.[91]

Taken together, these experiments show that both men and women expect negative consequences when a member of either sex succeeds in a situation considered non–sex-appropriate. Since the occupations sex-typed as male are more highly valued in our society, women are placed in a no-win situation.

THE COSTS OF SEX ROLE STEREOTYPING

In this chapter, we have seen how society molds the child along sex-specific lines. That this process is costly for women hardly needs to be argued. The costs of sex role socialization to men are perhaps less obvious but nevertheless very real.[92] The stereotypical masculine male is aggressive, emotionally impassive, self-sufficient, athletic, brave in the face of danger, a natural leader, and competent at any task defined as masculine. Living up to this image is expecting a lot of any human being, and feeling that one should is likely to produce anxiety and insecurity. Furthermore, in the complex world in which we live, some of these traits are counterproductive. Physical aggressiveness is more likely to lead to jail than to success; a definition of bravery that extends to foolhardiness may get you killed. The male who learns to be emotionally impassive, to hide his feelings from others and often from himself, denies himself a valuable outlet and cuts himself off from an important aspect of human experience.

Sex role stereotyping also limits the options open to men. The male child is frequently expected to be good at athletics whether or not he has the slightest interest or aptitude for them. In many families, an interest in music, art, or dance is discouraged in boys. A male who desires to enter a "female" field—nursing or kindergarten teaching, for example—is considered even more deviant than a woman in a "male" field.

Not only is the male expected to enter an appropriate field, he is expected to be a success. Whatever other attributes he may

90Ibid., p. 52.
91Ibid., pp. 52–53.
92Warren Farrell, *The Liberated Man* (New York: Random House, 1974).

have, he will be largely judged by his career success. While to many men, women are sex objects, men are frequently success objects to women. Because career success is defined as central to masculinity in our society, men often sacrifice all other values in pursuing it.

If masculinity and femininity as defined by our society are destructive of human individuality, what is the alternative? A reassessment of the value of "feminine" and "masculine" traits and an attempt to inculcate those traits that are considered valuable in both boys and girls would seem to be the answer. Studies have found that high-achieving and highly creative children are much less sex-stereotyped in behavior than their less outstanding peers.[93] Androgynous people—those who display both masculine and feminine characteristics—have higher self-esteem, achieve more in school, and seem to be more adaptable.[94] There *are* better alternatives than assigning traits and behaviors on the basis of sex. Society has constructed the feminine female and the masculine male; our task is to see that, in the future, society constructs the full human being.

HOW MUCH CHANGE?

Most of the studies upon which the preceding discussion of socialization is based are from the 1960s and early 1970s. Has the last decade seen significant change? Because socialization is a complex and multifaceted process, a great many studies are required before that question can be answered unequivocally. Such a body of research does not yet exist, so our assessment will have to be tentative.

Some studies indicate a change in attitudes among parents. The authors of a 1976 study of fathers mostly from the middle class concluded, "Unlike the fathers of the fifties, worried about their sons' careers and wishing some vague sort of marital bliss for their daughters, the fathers in our study were concerned with their daughters' full human potential."[95] A number of the fathers were specifically concerned that their daughters not be limited by sex role stereotypes. The same study found, in contrast to the findings of research during the 1960s, that parents did not show a difference in the ages at which they would grant independence to girls and boys.[96] A nationwide survey sample found that women in 1980 were less likely to sex-type

[93]Ibid., pp. 34–35.
[94]Deaux, op. cit., pp. 139–140.
[95]Caryl Rivers, Rosalind Barnett, and Grace Baruch, *Beyond Sugar and Spice* (New York: Putnam, 1979), p. 59–60.
[96]Ibid., p. 135.

household chores than they had been in 1974.[97] Women were asked whether children of both sexes might be expected to perform certain chores or if only boys or only girls should be. In 1974, 54 percent said that both boys and girls could be expected to mow the lawn; by 1980, 70 percent said so. In 1974, only 39 percent said both sexes should be asked to mend their clothes; by 1980, this had increased to 56 percent. In fact, by 1980 a majority of the women saw all of the chores as appropriate to both sexes, and a very large majority of the women felt that most of them were.

Unfortunately, attitude changes do not always translate into changes in behavior. Psychologist Beverly Fagot recently completed a study in which she compared parents' attitudes and their behavior towards their 2-year-old children. The parents' attitudes about bringing up their children were nonstereotyped. Fagot says, "These parents would not restrict playmates to one sex, nor would they avoid buying an opposite-sex toy if the child wanted it. They planned to encourage their child to follow up interests, regardless of the sex-appropriateness of the interest, as the child grew older. Eighty percent planned to actively encourage a viewpoint of sex equity. . . ."[98] When Fagot observed the parents' behavior toward their children, however, she found that it often contradicted the attitudes they had expressed. Parents were, for example, likely to react positively when their daughters asked for help and negatively when their sons did. When the girls "manipulated objects," they were given more negative feedback than boys. Thus girls but not boys were discouraged from exploring objects and thereby learning about the physical world. Fagot concluded that although there were not a great number of areas in which parents treated girls and boys differently, "the few areas where we do find significant differences have great consequences for the developmental process."[99] Clearly, notions about sex roles are very deeply ingrained; even when people change their attitudes on the conscious or intellectual level, they may unconsciously express older notions in their behavior.

What sort of messages are children receiving from other important forms of socialization? In response to pressure from feminists, schoolbook publishers promised to make changes. The first crop of books that resulted was a disappointment by and large; in it, token-

---

[97]The Roper Organization, *The 1980 Virginia Slims American Women's Opinion Poll,* p. 68.
[98]Quoted in Rivers, op. cit., p. 101.
[99]Quoted in ibid., p. 101.

ism was the norm.[100] There are reports that some progress has been made in the last few years, but no systematic studies exist. A considerable number of very good nontext children's books are now available. But since parents must seek these out from among a mass of traditional works, only the children of middle-class parents with a feminist bent are likely to get much exposure to them.

Systematic studies do not show much change in television.[101] In its portrayal of women, "Sesame Street" has improved immensely. Commercial television seems to show women in nontraditional roles a little more frequently and in really degrading positions a little less frequently. Nevertheless, television still presents a stereotyped picture of the sexes. Studies have found that children who watch a lot of tv have more stereotyped perceptions than children who are light viewers. The authors of one recent study said that their data "suggest that heavy television viewing may contribute significantly to children's acquisition of stereotypic perceptions of behavior and psychological characteristics associated with males and females."[102]

On the whole, the messages children receive from the media still portray sex roles in a fairly traditional way. Consequently, as a recent study found, "Preschool children possess pronounced stereotypes about sex differences in emotionality."[103] The children in the study associated anger with maleness, and happiness, sadness, and fear with femaleness. Children also still tend to sex-type occupations. A recent study of children aged 2½ through 8 found that even the youngest classified doctor a male occupation and secretary a female occupation.[104] Sex-typing of these and other jobs increased with age. Another study of third through twelfth graders offers somewhat more encouraging findings. The researchers reported that the third graders endorsed a highly sex-typed occupational world, but that the degree of stereotyping decreased with age—more dramatically among girls than among boys. Even so, 44 percent of the twelfth graders said that 7 or more of the 13 occupations asked about should only be performed by either men or women; 55 percent of the

[100]"Any Change in Sexist Texts?" *Women's Studies Newsletter* 2, no. 3 (1974), p. 3.

[101]U. S. Commission on Civil Rights, *Window Dressing on the Set: An Update,* January 1979.

[102]Paul E. McGhee and Terry Frueh, "Television Viewing and the Learning of Sex-Role Stereotypes," *Sex Roles* 6 (April 1980), 185.

[103]Dana W. Birnbaum, T. A. Nosanchuk, and W. L. Croll, "Children's Stereotypes about Sex Differences in Emotionality," *Sex Roles* 6 (June 1980), 435.

[104]Linda Gettys and Arnie Cann, "Children's Perceptions of Occupational Sex Stereotypes," *Sex Roles* 7 (March 1981), 301–308.

twelfth grade boys and 36 percent of the twelfth grade girls gave such responses.[105]

Earlier studies as well as much anecdotal evidence indicate that girls lower their achievement levels at puberty so as to avoid competition with boys. In a 1978 study, fifth, seventh, and ninth graders were given a test described as an intelligence test.[106] Boys and girls were seated opposite each other. After the first part of the test had been completed, each child was taken aside and told he or she had done better than the opposite sex child across the table. The children were then sent back to do the second part of the test. Both the male and female fifth graders tended to increase their performance on the second test. Among seventh graders, however, the pattern was radically different. The boys tended to increase their scores but 80 percent of the girls decreased theirs. About half of the ninth grade girls decreased their performance. Asked about competing intellectually with the opposite sex, almost all of the seventh grade girls said they did not like to beat a boy. Several explicitly said, "I'd rather be popular than have good grades or win a game against a boy." Most of the ninth grade girls responded similarly, but the few who did not kept their scores up on the second test.

Nationwide surveys of high school seniors in 1976 and 1977, nevertheless, found that most of the girls expected to work outside the home for most of their adult lives and many expected to work in high-level occupations.[107] Asked "What do you think you will be doing 30 years from now?" only 11 percent said they thought they would be full-time homemakers; 44 percent expected to hold professional jobs. Almost as many girls as boys expected work to be central to their lives: 72 percent of the girls and 76 percent of the boys. More than half the girls—56 percent—said it was important that their job be of high prestige.

Recent studies of young adults—mostly college students—also suggest some change. In an experiment similar to the Broverman study referred to in Chapter 2, undergraduates were asked to describe a socially competent, healthy adult man, a healthy adult woman, or a healthy adult, sex unspecified.[108] The male students

[105]Scott Cummings and Delbert Taebel, "Sexual Inequality and the Reproduction of Consciousness: An Analysis of Sex-Role Stereotyping Among Children," *Sex Roles* 6 (August 1980), 631–644.

[106]Reported in Rivers, op. cit., pp. 157–158.

[107]Ibid., p. 171.

[108]Jeanne Brooks-Gunn and Melanie Fisch, "Psychological Androgyny and College Students' Judgements of Mental Health," *Sex Roles* 6 (August 1980), 575–580.

described the healthy man as similar to the adult standard and the healthy woman as different. The female students, however, did not perceive the healthy woman as different from the adult standard. This study suggests that current female college students are less likely than their predecessors to attribute negative characteristics to normal women. A recent replication of the Goldberg study of reactions to articles authored by "males" and "females" indicates that female college students are less likely now than they were in the past to derogate work attributed to a woman.[109] Males, both student and nonstudent, as well as older nonstudent females tended to respond in fairly prejudiced and stereotyped ways. Still another study of college students found that neither males nor females subscribed to the traditional belief that success-oriented women were unattractive or unromantic.[110]

An examination of recent studies produces a rather ambiguous picture. Certainly the socialization process has not been revolutionized; sexist messages in the typical child's environment still outnumber nonsexist messages. But the lack of a total transformation should neither surprise nor discourage us. Because the sex role socialization process involves all facets of our society, changing it will also. That more options are presented to children and young adults now is encouraging; messages about sex roles are no longer homogeneously traditional. Some children, such as girls from upper–middle-class families, are probably more likely to receive exposure to untraditional messages than others. Consequently the impact of changes in sex roles is likely to be spread unevenly across the population for some time to come. Society does not yet construct the full human being, but a significant beginning has been made.

---

[109]Madeleine M. Gross and Robert A. Geffner, "Are the Times Changing? An Analysis of Sex Role Prejudice," *Sex Roles* 6 (October 1980), 713–722.

[110]Ronald L. Micheline, Donald Eisen, and Stephan R. Snodgrass, "Success Orientation and the Attractiveness of Competent Males and Females," *Sex Roles* 7 (April 1981), 391–401.

THE FAMILY:
REFUGE OR PRISON?

4

They stare at you from the television screen, the pages of magazines, the billboards—the pretty, smiling woman; the tall, competent-looking man; the cute, clean children. No label is necessary for us to recognize them as the typical American family. Ask any man or woman on the street and they will tell you that the family, consisting of husband, wife, and children, is not just typical but natural and universal—decreed by God or determined by biology. An occasional fun-loving bachelor may have escaped marriage; a few women are simply too ugly to catch any man; some couples are unable to have children, poor things. These cases are exceptions and are abnormal. Our society enforces a belief that the proper, accepted, normal state for an adult is marriage and parenthood. Furthermore, the closer one comes to the typical family of advertising fame, the happier and certainly the more normal one will be. The pretty wife stays home taking care of her house, her gadgets, and cute children; the husband goes out to work to make it possible to buy the gadgets and a college education for the children. This division of labor is not just typical; it is natural, universal, and good.

Popular stereotypes can hardly be considered scientific knowledge. What do social scientists have to tell us about the family? Sociologists of the structural-functional school agree to a remarkable extent with the popular stereotypes, although of course their language is much more impressive. These sociologists say that the nuclear family, consisting of a man, a woman, and their children, is universal. It is universal because it performs certain functions that are necessary if the society is to survive. Some functions that used to be performed within the family (economic production, for example) are now performed elsewhere. The family still acts as the "primary agent of socialization of the child" and is the "primary basis of security for the normal adult."[1] For the family to function effectively, a division of labor is required: the husband's function is instrumental (i.e., task oriented); the wife's, expressive (i.e., she provides emotional support). In concrete terms, the husband works outside the home to support the family financially; the wife is housekeeper, mother, and binder of psychic wounds for both husband and children.

The structural-functional theorists essentially agree with the popular view that the nuclear family and the present division of labor within it is both natural and good. They do not provide evidence that the functions the family performs cannot be performed by other institutions. They do not explain why the woman should invariably perform the expressive function and the man the instrumental. More basically, they do not ask whether the maintenance of society as it now is should be the overriding goal. Certainly the abolition of the nuclear family would result in major societal changes, but would these changes be for the better or for the worse? The answer depends to a large extent on how one evaluates the present situation. Instead of asking whether the nuclear family is functional for society, we should ask if it is functional for its component units—for the woman, the man, and the children.

Surprisingly, the popular view recognizes more ambiguity concerning the benefits of marriage and family life than the structural functionalists do. According to the stereotype, women want to get married and men do not. This is natural because women get the greatest benefits out of marriage—someone to support them and children to fulfill their natural maternal instincts. Men, in contrast, must work in order to support their often spendthrift wives and, since men are not naturally monogamous, must restrain their natural sexuality. Why men get married at all in this age of easily available sex, and how this view fits with the simultaneously held view that family life is natural, is never explained. Inconsistencies, however, have never destroyed a stereotype. In the popular view it is clearly the woman who benefits most from marriage.

The sociologists don't seem to be interested in who benefits and how much. They seem to think that if everyone performs his or her proper function, everyone benefits.

---

[1] Talcott Parsons, "The Normal American Family," in Arlene and Jerome Skolnick, eds., *Family in Transition* (Boston: Little, Brown, 1971), p. 402.

In examining the empirical evidence on the modern American family, we will ask who benefits, or (in the jargon) for whom the institution is functional.

THE MYTH

What does a young woman expect of marriage, and what does she actually get? She has been taught that the choice of a marriage partner is the most important decision she will ever make. In marriage she expects to fulfill her true nature as loving wife and mother. This, she has been taught, is the most creative career possible for a woman. She is, in effect, promised instant and complete happiness.

Especially if she is quite young, the bride's image of marriage is likely to come straight from the pages of popular magazines and the tv screen. She sees herself as the glamorous, creative homemaker decorating her house à la *House Beautiful* and cooking gourmet meals. Beautifully dressed, she greets her smiling husband when he comes home from work. They spend a peaceful, intimate hour discussing the events of the day. She, of course, is an interested and sympathetic listener; he, of course, wants to share all aspects of his life with her and values her advice. Some evenings they entertain couples as beautiful and smiling as themselves; other evenings they go out.

Did the young woman have dreams or plans for doing something more with her life? She will, she is sure, manage to keep up in some way. If she has artistic talent, she can write or paint at home. Otherwise, she can at least read good books. This will provide intellectual stimulation for her and keep her interesting to her husband.

Not long after marriage she will become pregnant. Having a baby—an act that she has been told is more creative than painting the *Last Supper*— will complete her happiness. She sees a cute, smiling baby that she can play with, take for walks, and show off to her friends. She may look a few years further into the future and see herself, still vivacious and pretty, as the mother of several clean, attractive grammar school children. Throughout, she is happy and fulfilled as wife, mother, and homemaker. She has lived the American dream.

REALITY: THE MIDDLE-CLASS VERSION

Today it is more likely that the middle-class, like the working-class, woman will work until she is pregnant with her first child. During the time she is working outside the home, she will find she has two jobs. She is expected to do most of the housework. It is, after all, woman's work. Her husband may help out, but it is clearly under-stood that the inside housework is her responsibility.

Whether she is working or not, the first part of the myth crum-bles quickly. Housework is neither interesting nor creative; in the graphic phrase of the women's movement, it is "shit work." For those with the talent and interest, decorating and gourmet cooking are creative and fun. But most housework consists of mopping floors, washing dishes, and cleaning toilet bowls. Not only is it boring, it is repetitive and never-ending. Housework does not stay done; a chore done today must be done again tomorrow or, at best, next week. Thus it provides no real feeling of accomplishment. Studies have found that doing housework is a perfect job for the feeble-minded.[2]

When the first baby is born, the young woman is likely to be-come a full-time housewife and mother. The media tend to present a baby as a wonderful toy—gurgling, smiling, and doing cute things. While babies are wonderful and lovable, they are also a great deal of trouble. They cry as well as smile. Changing a dirty diaper is not a fulfilling experience.

A baby increases the amount of housework that must be done. More serious, with the arrival of the child the young woman loses control over her own schedule. As one young mother explained, "Suddenly I had to devote myself to the child totally. I was under the illusion that the baby was going to fit into my life, and I found I had to switch my life and my schedule to fit *him.*"[3] A baby is not a toy that can be put away when one is tired of it. The young mother is always on duty. She cannot take time off to read or rest. When the child becomes mobile, the problem becomes especially acute. A toddler must be watched. The housework must still be done. Nei-ther of these tasks require the woman's full attention, but they require enough of it so that she cannot do anything else. "In industry the most fatiguing jobs are those which only partially occupy the work-er's attention, but at the same time prevent him from concentrating on anything else. Many young wives say that this mental gray-out is what bothers them most in caring for home and children. 'After a while, your mind becomes a blank,' they say. 'You can't concen-trate on anything. It's like sleep-walking.' "[4]

The child also severely restricts the woman's mobility. Isolated

[2]Betty Friedan, *The Feminine Mystique* (New York: Dell, 1964), p. 244.
[3]Quoted in Betty Rollin, "Motherhood: Who Needs It?" in Skolnick, op. cit., p. 351.
[4]Quoted in Friedan, op. cit., p. 240.

in her own home in suburbia, she spends most of her time with people under 6 years old. She is progressively cut off from participation in the world outside the home. There is, of course, the television set, but as Myrdal and Klein point out:

> The isolated woman at home may well be kept "in touch" with events, but she feels that the events are not in touch with her, that they happen without her participation. The wealth of information which is brought to her without any effort on her part does not lose its vicariousness. It increases rather than allays her sense of isolation and of being left out.[5]

The lack of adult conversation is a universal complaint among young American housewives. In the past, housework was much more physically taxing, but at least the woman had other adults around for help and companionship. "The idea of imprisoning each woman alone in a small, self-contained, and architecturally isolated dwelling is a modern invention dependent upon an advanced technology," Philip Slater says. "In Muslim societies, for example, the wife may be a prisoner, but she is at least not in solitary confinement. In our society the housewife may move about freely, but since she has nowhere in particular to go and is not a part of anything, her prison needs no walls. . . . Most of her social and emotional needs must be satisfied by her children, who are hardly adequate to the task."[6]

The young woman's good intentions about staying intellectually or artistically active dissipate. One cannot read a serious book, much less write a novel, in 10-minute snatches. Connected, uninterrupted time is needed, and this the young mother does not have.

Progressively she becomes more and more dependent on her husband as her only link with the outside world. Yet the couple find they have less and less to talk about. Their experiences are too divergent. She becomes boring because her experiences are boring. Small household catastrophes and a few cute stories about the children do not make for stimulating conversation. One of the results is the sort of sex segregation one used to see at suburban parties—the men in one part of the room discussing business and politics, the women in the other talking about children and home.

---

[5]A. Myrdal and V. Klein, *Women's Two Roles* (London: Routledge and Kegan Paul, 1968), p. 148.
[6]Quoted in Jessie Bernard, *The Future of Marriage* (New York: Bantam, 1973), p. 50.

Eventually, of course, all the kids are in school. For the average American woman this occurs when she is 34 years old.[7] There is still housework to do, and school-age children do require care, but finally the woman has some uninterrupted time. What can she do with it?

At this point she could return to work. Some women are prevented from going back to work by the strong disapproval of their husbands. Such men have so strongly internalized the notion that the provider role defines masculinity that their whole sex identity is threatened by a working wife. Even if the husband is supportive, the wife's return to work is not easy. The middle-class woman may well have completed college, but usually she has not been trained for a career. Too often the only jobs she can get are not commensurate with her education. A clerical job is frequently the best she can do. Many women find that even such jobs are better than staying home. Working at all may provide a feeling of independence as well as social stimulation. The financial costs of holding a job—transportation, new clothes, and especially babysitters—may, however, be greater than what she earns. If the husband prefers that she not work, he can use this as an argument.

For the professionally trained woman, the return to work may be even more difficult. Her training is likely to be out of date, and she has probably found it impossible to keep up with the professional literature. In order to become competitive with recent graduates she will have to retool, and she may very much fear that she is no longer capable of the analytic thinking and sustained concentration required. Assuming that she survives the retooling process, she will still have difficulty finding a good position. In addition to the prejudice against women, she will face prejudice on the basis of her age. As the prestige professions require extremely long hours, she may want a part-time job, but such jobs are often difficult to find and are marginal in pay and prestige. Even with a Harvard Ph.D., she may well end up teaching at Podunk Community College.

There are alternative ways of filling one's day. Volunteer work has long been considered an appropriate outlet for middle-class female energies. More and more, however, such work is becoming professionalized. The tasks for which unpaid volunteers are used are busywork jobs that are neither stimulating nor creative. Especially

[7]Mirra Komarovsky, in New York City Commission on Human Rights, *Women's Role in Contemporary Society* (New York: Avon, 1972), p. 64.

in the suburbs, the volunteer is likely to end up stuffing envelopes and answering phones.

Artistic endeavors would seem to be easier than any sort of outside work for the woman to fit in with her still considerable responsibilities in the home. Most women, however, like most men, do not have a real talent for writing or painting. Furthermore, developing a serious talent requires a strong commitment in time and energy. The housewife's artistic endeavors tend to degenerate into dilettantism. For a month she will attempt to write a novel; then she will take up painting, followed perhaps by potting and then weaving.

Some women do manage to develop a full and interesting life of their own without taking a paid job. A few seriously develop an artistic talent; others become deeply involved in community affairs or in politics. Such involvement requires considerable chunks of time at regular intervals. Finding this time takes *more* organization and determination for the woman who is "only" a housewife than for the woman holding a paid job. A working woman's family understands that she must go to work regularly. Even so, in two-job families, the woman and not the man is expected to stay home with a sick child. Nevertheless, the family recognizes that the woman will be away from the home during her working hours and should not be disturbed unless a real emergency arises. The woman who does not hold a paid job constantly has to justify and protect her time from encroachments. As she is not getting paid for her efforts, her family is unlikely to take them seriously and thus will expect her to change her schedule to suit them. She will need a great deal of determination and sense of her own rights as an individual if she is seriously to pursue her non–family-related interests.

Whether she works at a paid job or pursues another interest, the woman is expected to keep it from interfering with her principal functions in the family. Working just because she enjoys doing so is suspect. Women are expected to be service oriented, not achievement oriented. A woman who feels that achievement is necessary for her self-realization is considered selfish. A working woman married to a man making quite a large salary often claims she works because the family needs the money. Working in order to help her family is considered legitimate; working because she enjoys it is not.

For the married woman, her husband and children must always come first; her own needs and desires, last. When the children reach school age, they no longer require constant attention, but the emotional-expressive function assigned to the woman is still required of her. Called the "stroking function" by sociologist Jessie Bernard, it consists of showing solidarity, raising the status of others, giving help, rewarding, agreeing, concurring, complying, understanding, and passively accepting.[8] The woman is expected to give emotional support and comfort to other family members, to make them feel they are good and worthwhile human beings.

The stroking function is a vitally important one; everyone needs stroking at least occasionally. Here precisely is the problem of specializing the function in the wife. Who raises *her* status? Who agrees with and passively accepts *her?* Despite its glamorization in the media, housework is not highly valued in our society. Nor does it provide intrinsic satisfaction. For many women child rearing does provide such satisfaction, but intermittently and interspersed with a great deal of frustration. Thus the woman needs emotional support and assurance that she is a worthwhile human being at least as much as the man. But the stroking function is seen as her responsibility, so she is not likely to receive much of it. Boys are brought up to believe that the characteristics associated with emotional support—empathy, sympathy, and showing tender emotions—are female traits. Men feel uncomfortable and unmasculine displaying such traits and thus are not very good at doing so. Yet they expect women—not only, but especially, their wives—always to provide such support with little or no reciprocation.

A man generally expects his wife to center her life around him. She should not need anything but a husband who is a good provider and healthy children to make her happy, he thinks. After all, both he and she have been taught that a normal woman finds total fulfillment in this way. He is surprised and upset if the pretty, admiring girl he married turns into a nagging shrew. Being barred from achieving on her own, the wife may put all her excess energy into her husband's career. He may be satisfied with his present position; she demands greater and greater success. Aware of his weak spots, she may question his masculinity if he does not live up to her expectations. He will be hurt and angry; he may seek out other female companionship to provide the stroking his wife withholds. He probably considers his wife overly money-hungry and status conscious. He is unlikely to realize that she is trying to live his life because she does not have one of her own.

The traditional American family structure does not seem to be good for the wife and can also be pretty hard on the husband. What about the children? Surely the children must benefit from having a loving mother always around. Child psychologists have found that

[8]Jessie Bernard, *Women and the Public Interest* (Chicago: Aldine, 1971), p. 88.

this is not always so. Children can be overmothered. Such children are overly dependent on their mothers; they tend to be passive and remain infantile. Overmothering stunts a child's emotional and intellectual development. Small children who are not given independence to explore and solve problems on their own are unlikely to develop the ability to think analytically.[9] Such children often do not develop an independent sense of self-worth.

A woman may overmother her children because she believes this is the proper mother's role. Child-care books and popular Freudian psychology convey the impression that, by sins of omission or commission, she can easily scar her child for life. Her full-time loving presence is said to be essential for the child's healthy development. She is never told that she can scar her children as well as herself by paying too much attention to them.

Excessive mothering is often a result of the woman's lack of a life of her own. She may attempt to live vicariously through her children to experience through them all the things she has missed. Her daughter must be the prettiest and most popular girl in her class; her son, the smartest and most athletically proficient. She may push her daughter into dating at an absurdly early age so that she can relive the most exciting part of her life. She will give up anything and everything for her children. Nothing is too good for them. They need not help around the house or get part-time jobs. The only thing she will not give them is their independence.

When their children leave home, such supermothers find adjustment especially difficult. Depression severe enough to require hospitalization is a not-infrequent problem.[10] For most full-time housewives, the children's leaving home means a loss of function and, often, of identity. The woman frequently feels that no one needs her any more, and because she has based her life on satisfying others' needs, she now sees herself as superfluous. She has nothing to live for, nothing to do. All the free time is seen as a curse, not a benefit. Because over the years her interests have been so narrowly centered on her family, her wider interests have atrophied. Now she has no idea what to do with the 20 or 30 years of life left to her.

Even if her husband understands her problem, there is often

[9]Eleanor E. Maccoby, "Sex Differences in Intellectual Functioning," in Eleanor E. Maccoby, ed., *The Development of Sex Differences* (Stanford, Calif.: Stanford University Press, 1966), pp. 25–55.

[10]Pauline Bart, "Depression in Middle-Aged Women," in Judith Bardwick, ed., *Readings on the Psychology of Women* (New York: Harper & Row, 1972), pp. 134 –142.

little he can do to help. If he is successful, his career may well require increasing amounts of time. Even if he does have time to spend with his wife, they may find they have so little in common that neither finds much satisfaction in being together.

The middle-class American ideal is the companionate marriage in which husband and wife are friends. But the typical division of labor in the family along sex lines makes the ideal almost impossible to achieve. Friendship requires common interests. The very different lives that husband and wife lead tend to erode any common interests they may have had and does not encourage the development of new ones. Friendship also requires equality. Even if the couple consciously tries to attain an egalitarian marriage, so long as the traditional division of labor is maintained, the husband will be "more equal." He is the provider, not only of money but of status. Especially if he is successful, society values what he does; she is just a housewife. Their friends are likely to be his friends and co-workers; in their company, she is just his wife. Because his provider function is essential for the family's survival, major family decisions are made in terms of how they affect his career. He need not and usually does not act like the authoritarian *paterfamilias* of the Victorian age. His power and status are derived from his function in the family and are secure so long as the traditional division of labor is maintained.

REALITY: THE WORKING-CLASS VERSION

While the middle class pays lip service to the ideal of egalitarian marriage, in the working class older, more traditional values prevail. In her study of blue-collar families, Lillian Rubin found that both men and women believe that the man should be the ultimate authority in the family.[11] Thus, in discussing something she wanted to do—such as going back to school—the blue-collar wife will frequently conclude, "He won't let me."[12] In contrast, middle-class wives do not speak in terms of getting *permission* from their husbands.

The difference may be one of style and language rather than of substance. The working-class man simply tells his wife she cannot do certain things; the middle-class husband, with his greater verbal skills, uses a subtler form of coercion. Thus one middle-class husband told his wife that whether or not to get an abortion was her decision.

[11] Lillian Breslow Rubin, *Worlds of Pain: Life in the Working Class Family* (New York: Basic Books, 1976), p. 96.
[12] Ibid.

However, if she did, he would never consent to having another child.[13]

The differing economic circumstances of middle- and working-class families also have an effect. The blue-collar families Lillian Rubin interviewed were not poor according to U.S. government standards at that time; their median income was $12,300.[14] Nevertheless, they were economically insecure; for almost all, paying the bills was a continuous struggle. In most families, regardless of class, men have the ultimate power in important spending decisions.[15] In blue-collar families where money is tighter, the husband's power may have a greater effect on the wife's life because harder choices have to be made. When money is scarce, conflicts about spending priorities can seldom be resolved by saying, "Let's buy both."

On housework, Rubin found that a highly traditional division of labor prevailed in these blue-collar families. All agreed that housework is the woman's job; her husband may help her, but it is her responsibility. As one man said:

> That's just the way life is. It's her job to keep the house and children and my job to earn the money. My wife couldn't do my job and I couldn't be as good a cook and housekeeper as she is. So we just ought to do what we do best.[16]

If the wife works outside the home, as more than half the women interviewed do, the burden is especially great. These families lack the money to hire any outside help as middle-class families often can. Asked "Whose life is easier, a man's or a woman's?" the wives often expressed their frustration:

> I get mad sometimes and wish I could change places with him. It would be a relief to worry only about one thing. It feels like I drag around such a heavy load.[17]

Despite the double burden these working wives carry, most enjoy holding a job.[18] The jobs these women have—salesclerk, waitress, factory worker—are by no means glamorous, yet they do provide satisfactions not available at home. As a factory worker said:

[13]Ibid., p. 97.
[14]Ibid., p. 106.
[15]Ibid., p. 108.
[16]Ibid., p. 100.
[17]Ibid., p. 106.
[18]Ibid., pp. 168–169.

> I really love going to work. I guess it's because it gets me away from the home. It's not that I don't love my home; I do, but you get awfully tired of just keeping house and doing those housewifely things.[19]

Another working woman said about her job, "I'm good at it, and I like that feeling. It's good to feel like you're competent."[20]

Thus, although most of these women work out of economic necessity, they do find other satisfactions in holding a job. Getting out of the house, a sense of competence, some feeling of independence are the less tangible rewards. There are, however, costs involved beyond those of the double burden. In a society in which men so heavily define their masculinity in terms of the provider role, the wife's working may be seen as a threat. As one woman said, "I guess it's a matter of pride with him. It makes him feel bad, like he's not supporting us good enough."[21] A number of the husbands of working women feel that their wives have become too independent, that their authority is threatened:

> I'd like to feel like I wear the pants in the family. Once my decision is made, it should be made, and that's it. She should just carry it out. But it doesn't work that way around here. Because she's working and making money, she thinks she can argue back whenever she feels like it.[22]

In her study of blue-collar marriage in the late 1950s, sociologist Mirra Komarovsky found that many of the husbands and wives she interviewed did not expect to be friends as well.[23] Men and women were seen as having sufficiently different interests that cross-sex friendship was not really possible. Thus husband and wife had few mutual friends. The wife had female friends whom she saw during the day; the husband, male friends whom he saw on his night or nights out.

Lillian Rubin's study indicates that expectations are changing. The wife in a blue-collar family especially does expect marriage to be more than an economic and sexual arrangement. Though she often cannot express her desires clearly, she wants communication and companionship.

[19]Ibid., p. 170.
[20]Ibid., p. 172.
[21]Ibid., p. 173.
[22]Ibid., p. 177.
[23]Mirra Komarovsky, *Blue-Collar Marriage* (New York: Vintage Books, 1967), p. 112 passim.

I keep talking to him about communication, and he says, "Okay so we're talking, now what do you want?" And I don't know what to say then, but I know it's not what I mean.[24]

The men, not knowing what is expected of them, feel confused and threatened. The socialization process, which is more sex-stereotyped in working-class than in middle-class families,[25] has produced in the man a "trained incapacity to share."[26] "The ideal of masculinity into which they were socialized inhibits expressiveness both directly, with its emphasis on reserve, and indirectly by identifying personal exchange with the feminine role."[27] She wants to talk about their inner feelings, to establish a truly intimate relationship. He may try but he literally does not know how. As one man said:

I sometimes think I'm selfish. She's the support—the moral support—in the family. But when she needs support, I just don't give it to her. Maybe it's not just selfishness, it's that I don't know what she wants and I don't know how.[28]

Many of the wives, while dissatisfied and yearning for a deeper relationship, for something more out of life, also feel guilty about the new demands they are making on their husbands.

What do I have to complain about? Jim's a steady worker; he doesn't drink; he doesn't hit me.[29]

Some even question whether they are normal.

. . . I worry sometimes that maybe there's something the matter with me that I'm not satisfied with what I've got.[30]

Lillian Rubin concludes that for most of the couples interviewed, "despite the yearning for more, relations between husband and wife are benumbed, filled with silence; life seems empty and meaningless."[31]

[24]Rubin, op. cit., p. 120.
[25]Ibid., pp. 125–127.
[26]Komarovsky, op. cit., p. 156.
[27]Ibid.
[28]Rubin, op. cit., p. 129.
[29]Ibid., p. 19.
[30]Ibid., p. 132.
[31]Ibid., p. 123.

MARRIAGE AND THE FAMILY—
IS IT GOOD FOR HUMAN BEINGS?

If the description of the family presented here is correct, the traditional family structure is not good for human beings. The woman in particular is trapped in a situation that provides little opportunity for intellectual growth or the satisfactions of achievement. The man at least gets a maid.

Certainly there must be women who are content with the traditional female role of housewife and mother, but available evidence indicates that the happy housewife may indeed be relatively rare.[32] A number of studies have found that women of all social classes express more dissatisfaction with marriage than do men.[33] "More wives than husbands report marital frustration and dissatisfaction; more report negative feelings; more wives than husbands report marital problems; more wives than husbands consider their marriages unhappy, have considered separation or divorce, have regretted their marriages; and fewer report positive companionship."[34]

Many widows do not want to remarry. A study by the Department of Health, Education, and Welfare of 390 Chicago widows found that only one-fifth said they would like to marry again. The other 80 percent said no and gave as their reason, "I'm free and independent now."[35] A study of people over 65 found that the wives envied the widows for their freedom, independence, and fun in life. The wives felt "they were unfortunate, in contrast with the widows, in being stuck in the house at the beck and call of a usually temperamental and demanding retired husband."[36]

More disturbing are the figures on mental health. According to Jessie Bernard, "being a housewife makes women sick."[37] When married men and married women are compared, the men show up much better on various indexes of mental health. "More married women than married men show phobic reactions, depression and passivity; greater than expected frequency of symptoms of psychological distress; and mental-health impairment."[38]

Are women simply less stable psychologically than men? No; the poorer mental health of married women is not due to a general

---

[32]Friedan, op. cit., p. 227.
[33]Komarovsky, op. cit., p. 199.
[34]Bernard, *The Future of Marriage,* op. cit., p. 28.
[35]Riverside, California, *Press Enterprise,* October 11, 1973.
[36]Barbara Seaman, *Free and Female* (Greenwich, Conn.: Fawcett, 1973), p. 224n.
[37]Bernard, *The Future of Marriage,* op. cit., p. 53.
[38]Ibid., p. 30.

sex difference. On the same measures, unmarried women show up as mentally healthier than both married women and unmarried men. "Many symptoms of psychological distress show up more frequently than expected among married women: nervous breakdowns, nervousness, inertia, insomnia, trembling hands, nightmares, perspiring hands, fainting, headaches, dizziness and heart palpitations. They show up less frequently than expected among unmarried women."[39] Unmarried women's mental health also compares very favorably with that of unmarried men. "Single women show far less than the expected frequency of symptoms of psychological distress as compared with single men. . . . Single women suffer far less than single men from neurotic and antisocial tendencies. More single men than single women are depressed and passive."[40] When unmarried women and married men are compared, little overall mental health difference is found, although the women show a markedly smaller incidence of psychological distress symptoms such as nervousness and insomnia.[41]

The data would seem to show that marriage is good for men and bad for women. Perhaps, however, some of these differences are due to selective factors. That is, maybe mentally healthy men and mentally sick women tend to marry more frequently than mentally sick men and mentally healthy women. Bernard believes that such selection may account for some but far from all the difference. "In our society, the husband is assigned superior status. It helps if he actually *is* somewhat superior in ways—in height, for example, or age or education or occupation—for such superiority, however slight, makes it easier for both partners to conform to the structural imperatives."[42]

Men may tend to marry women to whom they can feel superior, women to marry men they can look up to. If women tend to marry up and men to marry down, then "bottom-of-the-barrel" men and "cream-of-the-crop" women are least likely to marry.

The selective process cannot, however, completely explain the poor mental health of wives because almost everyone does eventually get married. Something about the woman's marriage must account for the problem. A comparison between working women, many of whom are married, and housewives is illuminating. Working women, whatever their marital status, are on the average far health-

[39]Ibid., p. 32.
[40]Ibid., p. 33.
[41]Ibid., p. 35; also see Table 23, p. 343.
[42]Ibid., p. 35.

ier mentally than housewives. "Far fewer than expected of the working women and more than expected of the housewives, for example, had actually had a nervous breakdown. Fewer than expected of the working women and more than expected of the housewives suffered from nervousness, inertia, insomnia, trembling hands, nightmares, perspiring hands, fainting, headaches, dizziness, and heart palpitations."[43] Clearly, being only a housewife is the problem: It literally makes many women sick.

The nuclear family structure, with its strict division of labor along sex lines and the resulting isolation of wives in the home, is not functional for women. For men, the balance between costs and benefits is less clear. In mental health and reported happiness, married men far surpass single men. On the other hand, if there is strict adherence to the traditional division of labor, the husband is solely responsible for the support of his wife and children. This may mean very long working hours, considerable anxiety, and little freedom to change the type of work he does if he should desire to do so. Furthermore, as his wife becomes more and more unhappy with her lot she also becomes more likely to take it out on him.

The family as we know it today presents some serious problems for children, too. Living their first 6 years of life almost exclusively in the company of a woman who is harried, often depressed and unhappy and, not infrequently, on the brink of serious mental illness, must have a deleterious effect on children. As one young mother said,

> I feel it should be more widely recognized that it is in the very nature of a mother's position in our society, to avenge her own frustrations on a small, helpless child; whether this takes the form of tyranny, or of a smothering affection that asks the child to be a substitute for all she has missed.[44]

THE AMERICAN FAMILY AND MYTH
AS SOCIAL SCIENCE

A critique of the nuclear family is useful only if better alternatives can be found. Many people, social scientists as well as ordinary people, contend this is not possible. The nuclear family, they say, is uni-

---

[43]Ibid., p. 52.

[44]Quoted in Rochelle Wortis, "Acceptance of the Concept of the Maternal Role by Behavioral Scientists," in Helen Wortis and Clara Rabinowitz, eds., *The Women's Movement* (New York: Wiley, 1972), pp. 41–42.

versal and is based on our biological nature. Women must have babies for their own good, not just for the continuation of the species. Motherhood is a biological imperative; no woman can find true fulfillment without having children. The division of labor within the family is decreed by nature; since women have the babies, they must stay home and take care of them. Any absence of the mother will have disastrous psychological and intellectual effects on the child. The father performs the instrumental function; he is the provider, a role for which (the biological determinists contend) he is well fitted by virtue of his natural aggressiveness, innovativeness, and independence. According to the sociologists, however, the male cannot effectively perform his function unless the female performs her expressive function. That is, the husband is dependent on his wife for emotional support or, in Bernard's term, stroking. If a woman has a career in the cruel, competitive world outside the home, she is unlikely to be effective at stroking, since her husband will see her as a competitor and not as a quiet port in a stormy world. According to Talcott Parsons, if both husband and wife have careers, the resulting competition between them is likely to have a disruptive effect on the solidarity of the marriage.[45]

If we are to determine whether alternatives to the nuclear family are possible and desirable, we must examine each of these tenets.

George Murdock, a well-known anthropologist, contends that the nuclear family is universal.[46] But when one examines his much-reprinted article on the topic, one finds that his definition of the term *nuclear family* is very broad. So long as a man, a woman, and their children live together, no matter who else lives with them, there is, according to Murdock, a nuclear family. Under this definition Murdock includes both polygamous and extended families, since in these forms of the family a man, a woman, and their children also live together. In common usage the term *nuclear family* refers to the isolated family, composed solely of a man, a woman, and their children. Of the 192 societies on which Murdock had data, 42 had isolated nuclear families, 53 had polygamous families, and 92 had some form of extended family.[47] Obviously the isolated nuclear family is atypi-

[45]Talcott Parsons, "The Kinship System of the Contemporary United States," in Talcott Parsons, ed., *Essays in Sociological Theory,* rev. ed. (New York: Free Press, 1954), p. 192.

[46]George Peter Murdock, "The Universality of the Nuclear Family," in Norman Bell and Ezra Vogel, eds., *A Modern Introduction to the Family* (New York: Free Press, 1960), pp. 37–44.

[47]Ibid., p. 38.

cal. Furthermore, a few cases of "visit" marriages, in which a man does not live with his wife and children, have since been discovered.[48] An extended discussion of different forms of the family will be undertaken in a later chapter. Data so far presented show clearly that the nuclear family consisting solely of a man, a woman, and their children is far from universal, and thus it cannot be biologically determined.

Is motherhood natural? This question really consists of two parts. Do women *need* to be mothers in order to find fulfillment? Does mothering—that is, taking care of children—come naturally to women?

There is no evidence that women have a biological need for children. "Women don't need to be mothers any more than they need spaghetti," says Dr. Richard Rabkin, a New York psychiatrist. "But if you're in a world where everyone is eating spaghetti, thinking they need it and want it, you will think so too."[49]

If there were such a biological need, the motherhood-is-bliss myth and all the social pressures on women to become mothers would be unnecessary. As sociologist William Goode says, "There is no innate drive for children. Otherwise, the enormous cultural pressures that there are to reproduce wouldn't exist. There are no cultural pressures to sell you on getting your hand out of the fire."[50]

A woman's desire to have children is due to her psychological, not her biological, state. Do women, then, have a psychological need for children? To the extent that they do, the need is a socially developed one. Nevertheless, despite the motherhood-is-bliss myth, many women find it more frustrating than blissful. As one young mother said, "In the abstract sense, I'd have several [children]. . . . In the non-abstract, I would not have any. . . ."[51] A number of studies have found that childless marriages are happier.[52]

A look through the newspaper should convince anyone that women are not naturally good mothers. Cases of child neglect and physical abuse are far from rare. The complex behavioral pattern we call mothering is learned, not innate. Even among the apes, mothering does not come naturally. A female primate reared in isolation where she has no opportunity to learn from others of her species

[48]Clyde Kluckhohn, "Variations in the Human Family," in ibid., p. 45.
[49]Quoted in Rollin, op. cit., p. 346.
[50]Quoted in ibid.
[51]Quoted in ibid., p. 351.
[52]Ibid., p. 352.

will often reject her baby. She will not care for it properly and may kill it or let it die from neglect.[53]

If women have no biological need nor special aptitude for motherhood, why should society expect all women to become mothers? As long as population growth was considered desirable and pregnancy could not be prevented, such expectations made some sense. But in an already overpopulated world pushing women into motherhood no matter how unprepared and unfit they are is not only foolish but dangerous.

> One of the most absurd aspects of the Myth is the underlying assumption that, since most women are biologically equipped to bear children, they are psychologically, mentally, emotionally, and technically equipped (or interested) to rear them. . . ."[54]

If a woman does have children, should she necessarily be expected to assume sole responsibility for their care? Many women would like to escape the isolation and monotony of suburbia by working at least part-time when their children are small. Some have been deterred by the experts, who warn them about the effects on the child of "maternal deprivation."[55] Women have been told that any separation of mother and child during the child's first few years will have serious deleterious effects on the child.

The evidence supporting the notion of maternal deprivation is far from convincing. Studies of children in hospitals and orphanages show that such institutionalization frequently does have negative effects. But such a traumatic separation of the child from its home and family cannot be equated with the routinized and shorter separation that occurs if the mother works. Studies of children of working mothers find no deleterious effects.[56]

Anthropological evidence shows that the American child rearing pattern is atypical:

> There is no known primitive society where mothers spend as much time with their children as they do in America today. . . . in the primitive cultures child care is much less the exclusive responsibility of the mother. In less complex societies the job is shared by father, mother, grandmother, aunt, big sister and women "too old for heavy work" who perform as general babysitters.[57]

[53]Sally Linton, "Primate Studies and Sex Differences," in Skolnick, op. cit., p. 194.
[54]Rollin, op. cit., p. 352.
[55]Wortis, op. cit., pp. 35–36.
[56]Seaman, op. cit., pp. 290–291.
[57]Ibid., p. 222.

Placing upon the mother the sole responsibility of child care is bad for her and bad for the child. According to Margaret Mead,

> At present the specific biological situation of the continuing relationship of the child to its biological mother and its need for care by human beings are being hopelessly confused in the growing insistence that child and biological mother, or mother surrogate, must never be separated, that all separation, even for a few days is inevitably damaging, and that if long enough it does irreversible damage. This . . . is a new and subtle form of antifeminism in which men—under the guise of exalting the importance of maternity—are tying women more tightly to their children than has been thought necessary since the invention of bottle feeding and baby carriages. Actually, anthropological evidence gives no support at present to the value of such an accentuation of the tie between mother and child. . . . On the contrary, cross-cultural studies suggest that adjustment is most facilitated if the child is cared for by many warm friendly people.[58]

Children do not need and are better off without a mother who spends every waking moment with them. What they do need is "consistent care; sensitivity of the care-taking adult(s) in responding to the infant's needs; a stable environment the characteristics of which the growing infant can learn to identify; continuity of experience within the infant's environment; and physical and intellectual stimulation, love, and affection."[59] The caretaking adult need not be the child's mother and, in fact, need not be female. A recent study found that children can become just as attached to a male as to a female if the man spends sufficient time with them.[60]

Margaret Mead's contention that children are best off if cared for by many warm, friendly people is gaining increasing recognition. Urie Bronfenbrenner says, "The young child does not require care by the same person all the time, and indeed profits from the intercession of others, notably his father."[61] Some social scientists go a good deal further. "A number of recent theories of schizophrenia have argued that the isolated nuclear family provides a fertile setting for driving children crazy. In the isolation of the nuclear family, the parent can easily deny some aspect of reality, usually the parents' behavior

---

[58]Margaret Mead, "A Cultural Anthropologist's Approach to Maternal Deprivation," in *Deprivation of Maternal Care: A Reassessment of Its Effects,* Public Health Papers, No. 14 (Geneva: World Health Organization, 1962).

[59]Wortis, op. cit., p. 40.

[60]Seaman, op. cit., p. 295.

[61]Quoted in ibid., p. 282.

or motives, thus causing the child to doubt his own perceptions. For example, the parent may act very angry or sexy, yet deny he or she is doing so."[62]

If the child does not need the constant presence of its mother, then one of the major arguments for the present division of labor in the family is destroyed. According to the second argument, a strict division of labor along sex lines is necessary to prevent competition between husband and wife that would threaten the solidarity of the family.

Lynda Holmstrom's study of two-career families shows that feelings of competitiveness are far from inevitable in such families. Sixty-five percent of the couples she studied reported no such feelings and gave no indication during their interviews that they actually felt competitive.[63] Whether two people feel that they are in competition is not simply a function of the situation; it depends on their perception of the situation. As one wife said, "We identify very much with each other. . . . We will be in competition *together* against some other person, not in competition with each other."[64] Feelings of competitiveness were not related to whether the couple were in the same field. Such feelings, "especially among the men, were associated with other feelings such as lack of self-assurance, feeling threatened, not feeling competent in a given area, feeling inadequate, or 'pride of the male ego.' "[65]

According to Parsons, "So long as lines of achievement are segregated and not directly comparable, there is less opportunity for jealousy, a sense of inferiority, etc., to develop."[66] But Holmstrom found that the sex-linked division of labor is not sufficient to prevent jealousy and a sense of inferiority. Several wives who had given up their careers to play the traditional female role were clearly resentful.

> I think that I do occasionally feel just a little resentment as to my role as opposed to my husband's role. After all, I made things as easy for him so that he has all the time he can available for his work. . . . I sometimes wonder a bit now (laughter) . . . is this fair (laughter) that I should be doing all the work?

[62]Skolnick and Skolnick, *Family in Transition,* op. cit., p. 306.

[63]Lynda Lytle Holmstrom, *The Two-Career Family* (Cambridge, Mass.: Schenkman, 1972), p. 105.

[64]Ibid., p. 103.

[65]Ibid., p. 109.

[66]Parsons, "The Kinship System of the Contemporary United States," op. cit., p. 192.

> I am intensely envious of the prerogative of a man to devote himself to a career without giving up the family. It is grossly unfair that he should have both. I feel that I can't. I have moments of bitterness about this.[67]

The traditional division of labor relegates women to an inferior status and thus frequently breeds jealousy and resentment.

A final argument for maintaining the traditional division of labor is based on the fragility of the male ego. Having to compete against women and possibly even coming out second best will undermine the man's sense of masculinity. Mental illness and even impotence may result. So long as males are taught that they are superior to all females, a competent woman will be seen as a threat. But to argue that women should stay in their place to avoid damaging the ego of the superordinant male is similar to arguing that Southern blacks should have stayed in their place to avoid damaging the fragile egos of Southern whites.

None of the arguments for maintaining the status quo is persuasive. But in them, as so often happens, social scientists have attempted "to justify a particular, local and almost certainly, temporary, economic and cultural pattern as an eternal biological law."[68]

RECENT TRENDS

While conservative social scientists continue to defend such theories against feminist attacks, the American family is changing. In 1976, 64.9 percent of all households included a husband and wife; 11 percent included a woman and dependents (but no husband); 3.4 percent included a man and dependents (but no wife); and 20.6 percent consisted of single individuals.[69] Thus married-couple households were still the norm, but other forms were far from rare. The supposedly typical family consisting of a breadwinning husband, a wife who did not work, and one or more children under the age of 18 had become distinctly atypical, accounting for only 19.1 percent of all households. Today, because increasing numbers of women have entered the labor force, fewer than 15 percent of all households conform to the erstwhile norm.

---

[67]Holmstrom, op. cit., p. 116.

[68]Quoted in Wortis, op. cit., p. 38.

[69]Data in the paragraph are from Nancy Smith Barrett, "Data Needs for Evaluating the Labor Market Status of Women." Paper prepared for the Census Bureau Conference on Issues in Federal Statistical Needs Relating to Women, April 27–28, 1978, Table 2.

What has been the effect of this transformation on family life? Careful and up-to-date studies are rare, but we do know from older research that a working wife has more influence in the family. Certainly, attitudes have changed. When, in 1962, a sample of women was asked to respond to the statement "Most of the important decisions in the life of the family should be made by the man of the house," fewer than one-third disagreed.[70] In 1977, slightly more than two-thirds disagreed. We also know that, by and large, working wives tend to be healthier mentally than housewives. Recent studies do continue to show that when a wife takes a job, she assumes a double burden and that her husband does not increase significantly his share of the housework. Studies done in 1975 through 1977 found that women did 80 to 90 percent of the housework: The full-time homemaker spent 8 hours a day, 7 days a week, on housework; the wife employed full time spent 5 hours a day, 7 days a week on housework.[71] Not only was the husband's contribution to household labor minimal even if his wife was employed, he seldom assumed responsibility for the tasks he did perform. That is, although a husband might help out his wife by taking out the garbage or occasionally buying groceries, reminding him or making the shopping list remained her responsibility. The researcher found that the division of household labor did not vary across classes; it was no more equal in middle-class families than working-class families.

Certainly the husband and wife in some families have made a real effort to change the traditional division of labor. Such families are, however, still relatively rare. A nationwide survey found that only 5 percent of the families questioned had made a conscious effort to change.[72] But even for those who do, changing the division of labor is not easy. Because of their upbringing, women are more likely to know how to cook and men how to make repairs; unfortunately for women, cooking has to be done every day while repairs are needed much less frequently. Sexist attitudes are deeply ingrained; even couples who think they are liberated are seldom totally free from traditional notions or habits picked up in childhood. Several studies have found that men and women exaggerate the husband's actual contribution to housework, with men exaggerating more.[73] Such exaggeration is, in part, due to the deep-seated notion that housework is basically women's work. A divorced father who

[70]*Institute for Social Research Newsletter* (winter 1980):3.

[71]*Los Angeles Times,* July 25, 1980.

[72]Ibid.

[73]Ibid.

has custody of his three children said, "When I was married I thought I was doing 50 percent of the work. Now that I have to do it all, I realize I was doing only about 30 percent."[74]

In women, the combination of traditional and feminist attitudes sometimes leads to the "superwoman" syndrome. Determined to succeed at a demanding job, a woman may feel guilty if she does not also do all the things a housewife does. She may not feel she is a good mother unless she bakes cookies instead of buying them. When entertaining her husband's colleagues, she may feel she must cook a lavish gourmet feast rather than prepare a simple dinner or take them out to a restaurant. This syndrome is clearly a prescription for disaster.

It *is* possible to combine a demanding and satisfying career with marriage and motherhood. Psychologist Abigail Stewart found that high role-combination—that is, being wife, mother, and worker—was not a source of psychological distress; on the contrary, it was associated with personal fulfillment.[75] Judith Birnbaum found married professional women to be happy, to have high self-esteem, and to feel personally competent and worthwhile.[76] Although these women sometimes worried about whether they spent enough time with their children, they believed themselves to be good mothers.

What will the families of tomorrow be like? Is the truly egalitarian marriage just around the corner? An examination of the attitudes of young people may provide some answers. Surveys of high school seniors indicate marriage is likely to remain the norm; 80 percent said they would eventually marry.[77] The seniors were asked to rate a variety of family/work arrangements as either "desirable," "acceptable," "somewhat acceptable," or "not at all acceptable."[78] When no preschool children are involved, most of the seniors believed the wife should work. Only 25 percent of the males and 14 percent of the females felt it would be unacceptable for both partners to work full time in this situation, while to 38 percent of the females and 13 percent of the males the traditional arrangement was unacceptable. When preschool children are present, however, the seniors endorsed more traditional patterns: 41 percent said the most desir-

---

[74]Caryl Rivers, Rosalind Barnett, and Grace Baruch, *Beyond Sugar and Spice* (New York: Putnam, 1979), p. 304.

[75]Ibid., p. 281.

[76]Ibid., p. 280.

[77]*Institute for Social Research Newsletter* (winter 1981):8.

[78]The following is based upon a discussion in the *Institute for Social Research Newsletter* (spring 1979):3–5.

able arrangement would be for the husband to work and the wife to stay home. A great many—especially of the females—did say it would be acceptable for the wife to work half time. If both parents work, the seniors believed child care should be divided equally; but even when the woman does *not* work, the seniors endorsed a major child-care role for the husband. Although the high school seniors also thought a working couple should share housework, they did not feel as strongly about this as about shared child care. Females favored equal division of housework more strongly than males.

This study shows that today's young people hold an amalgam of old and new beliefs about marriage. In some cases, real life will force them to make hard choices. The survey found that many of the girls expected to hold professional jobs with high prestige. These women are likely to find that such jobs do not allow for part-time work or an in-and-out employment pattern. Whether the boys will follow through on their good intentions about sharing child care and housework is another big question. The truly egalitarian marriage is not likely to be the norm in the immediate future. Nevertheless, the current generation of high school students enters adulthood with very different attitudes about marriage than their parents held at the same age. Certainly they have a better chance for devising family arrangements that will be good for men, women, and children.

THE EXPLOITATION
OF WORKING WOMEN

5

"Everyone knows that women don't work for the same reasons as men. They work for other reasons, for self-gratification, so they really can't be counted the same."[1] This statement, attributed to a high official in Gerald Ford's administration, reflects one of the many myths about working women. In this chapter, myth and reality will be explored.

MYTHS ABOUT WORKING WOMEN

Many people still believe that working women are atypical. Yet, according to 1981 census data, women account for 42 percent of the labor force.[2] In fact, 63 percent of women between the ages of 20 and 64 are in the labor force. Well over 40 million women hold paid jobs. Of all American males age 16 and over, 78 percent are in the labor force. Of all American females age 16 and over, 52 percent are in the labor force. Rather than the exception, the working woman has become the norm. More than 90 percent of all women now do paid work at some point in their lives; and, of course, almost all women also do unpaid work in the home.

The myth implies that only young, single women work outside the home, and then only for a short time before they get married. This was partially true a quarter of a century ago. Now, however, the typical working woman is married. In 1980, 50.2 percent of all

---

[1]Statement of William Seidman, quoted by Walter Mondale in *Los Angeles Times,* October 23, 1976.

[2]Data in this paragraph from U.S. Department of Labor, *Employment and Earnings* (November .1981).

married women living with their husbands and 60.3 percent of those between the ages of 16 and 44 were in the labor force.[3] According to the myth, these women are childless, but the census reveals that, on the contrary, 61.8 percent of mothers who have children between ages 6 and 17 and who are living with their husbands have jobs outside the home. Even among mothers with children under 6, 44.9 percent work.

Figure 5.1 shows how the pattern of labor force participation by women of different ages has changed over the years. In 1890 most working women were young; after their early twenties, most dropped out of the labor force. By 1940, there were many more women working, but the pattern had not really changed; women still tended to quit working during the child-rearing years and not return. The 1960 pattern is dramatically different; women still left the labor force during their late twenties, but when their children reached school age, many returned. The 1975 curve again shows a major change; the tendency for women to drop out of the labor force during their late twenties and early thirties is much less pronounced. Nowadays, fewer women leave the labor force during their child-rearing years, and of those who do, most return. Figures from 1980 show a culmination of this trend. Of women between 20 and 24,

[3]Data in this paragraph from U.S. Department of Commerce, *Population Profile of the United States: 1980,* Series P-20, No. 363, p. 35.

FIGURE 5.1

Patterns of Labor Force Participation by Women of Different Ages, 1890–1975

Source: U.S. Department of Labor, *Employment and Training Report of the President,* 1976, p. 143.

TABLE 5.1
Education and Labor Force Participation, 1979

Education	Percent of women working
Less than high school graduate	33.9%
High school graduate	57.1
1 to 3 years of college	59.8
4 or more years of college	67.1

Source: U.S. Department of Labor, *Perspectives on Working Women: A Databook* (October 1980), p. 44.

67.7 percent are in the labor force.[4] Of those in the 25 to 34 and the 35 to 44 age categories, slightly more than 65 percent are in the labor force. Thus the tendency to drop out has almost completely disappeared.

It is a waste to educate women, it has frequently been claimed; they will only get married and waste their training. The evidence presented so far casts doubt on that statement, and Table 5.1 shows it just is not so. The more education a woman has, the more likely she is to hold a job. More than 90 percent of women with Ph.D.s work outside the home. Women with very little education don't work because they cannot find jobs.

Sexist mythology would lead us to believe that women at least work at jobs that are physically undemanding. Yet more than 5 million women work in factories. According to a woman who works in one, the only kind of job women are allowed to do in the factories is "the fast, picky shitwork."[5] She also testified that promotion was almost unheard of for factory women. Moreover, these women all had a second job at home. This meant that before and after their 8-hour workday, they had to care for children, cook, and clean the house. Many of them also had to spend a large portion of their paychecks for babysitters. But jobs in factories are not the only physically demanding work women do. One million women work as domestic servants, 329,000 as farm laborers, and 516,000 as nonfarm laborers.[6]

And almost all women, whether they "work" or not, do house-

[4]U.S. Department of Labor, *Perspectives on Working Women: A Databook,* October 1980, p. 4.

[5]Jean Tepperman, "Two Jobs: Women Who Work in Factories," in Robin Morgan, ed., *Sisterhood is Powerful* (New York: Vintage Books, 1970), p. 118.

[6]*Population Profile,* op. cit., p. 36.

work. It has been estimated—in 1918, 1928, and again in 1968—that the housework labor done by women equals *one-fourth of the U.S. gross national product.* [7] Why is it not included in the calculation of the GNP? One reason is the sexist attitude that housework is easy, that women sit in pampered leisure. The other reason is the more general attitude of capitalist society that a product or service is only really "worth" something if it is bought and sold for money on the market.

In addition to unpaid home labor, about 13 million women do volunteer work. It has been estimated that the monetary worth of volunteer work in 1965 was $14.2 *billion.* [8] Women are hooked on this unpaid volunteer work largely on the basis of sexist ideology and discrimination. Husbands, friends, and women's own social conditioning are all elements that discourage careers. Volunteer work is seen not as a permanent career, but as proper, temporary charity work. Moreover, our capitalist system does not guarantee full employment, and older women have a hard time getting any job. Most volunteers are women over 40 with grown children for whom no other interesting work (or no work at all) is available. [9]

Why do women work?
According to the popular stereotype, women work for fun or for "pin money"—and can therefore be paid less, hired last, and fired first. In 1950, acting on this stereotype, a Detroit labor union voted that all women should be fired so that unemployed men could be hired. When Congresswoman Martha Griffiths mentioned this injustice to the Detroit head of the National Labor Relations Board, he said: "Well, I think it is wrong to permit a woman with top seniority to remain on a job and lay off a man supporting a wife and five kids when all the woman is doing with her money is buying good clothes, Cadillacs, and going to Florida." [10]

Here is a man—who should know better—accepting the extreme stereotype. What woman (or man) working in a factory buys Cadillacs or Florida vacations? In fact, 44.5 percent of working

[7]Juanita Kreps, *Sex in the Marketplace* (Baltimore: Johns Hopkins Press, 1971), p. 67.

[8]Doris Gold, "Women and Voluntarism," in Vivian Gornick and Barbara Moran, eds., *Women in Sexist Society* (New York: Signet, 1972), p. 534.

[9]Ibid.

[10]Quoted by Martha Griffiths in Mary Thompson, ed., *Voices of the New Feminism* (Boston: Beacon, 1970), p. 107.

women are single, divorced, separated, or widowed; many of them have children.[11] About one-fifth of working women are married to men who make less than $10,000 a year. Together, these two groups of women who absolutely must work to support their families comprise almost two-thirds of all working women.

Many middle-class families are middle-class only because the wife brings in a second income. In 1978, working wives contributed an average of 26.1 percent to their family's incomes; wives who worked full time contributed 37.6 percent.[12] Two-paycheck families accounted for 60 percent of all families who had incomes over $20,000.[13] Families in which both the husband and the wife worked were also less likely to be poor than more traditional families in which the husband was the only earner. Only 5 percent of two-paycheck families fall into the bottom fifth of the family income distribution pyramid while 15 percent of traditional families do.

Do women get equal pay?

There is a myth that, in this country, people get paid what they are worth. Unfortunately, it is only a myth. One proof of this is the fact that under the Equal Pay Act of 1963, the courts have found extensive wage discrimination against women and have forced companies to give back-pay of $18.7 million to 54,000 women.[14] This legally determined discrimination is only the tip of the iceberg. In 1977, women who worked fulltime, year-round were paid on the average only 59 percent of what men were paid. The average male worker made $116 more a *week* than the average female worker.[15] The gap between men's and women's wages has been increasing. In 1960, for example, women made 61 percent as much as men. By race and sex, the pecking order is very clear (see Table 5.2).

Even the median wage for white males is under what the Bureau of Labor Statistics considers "moderate, but adequate." This is why so many wives must work. But the black man's wage is much lower, which is why even more black wives must work. Still lower is the white woman's wage, showing even greater economic discrimination. And lowest of all, reflecting the double burden of

[11]*AFL-CIO American Federationist,* April 1980, p. 15.

[12]*Perspectives,* op. cit., p. 57.

[13]Howard Hayghe, "Husbands and Wives as Earners: An Analysis of Family Data," *Monthly Labor Review* 104 (February 1981), 50.

[14]Kreps, op. cit., p. 92.

[15]U.S. Department of Labor, Women's Bureau, *The Earnings Gap Between Women and Men* (1979), p. 1.

TABLE 5.2
Median Wage or Salary Income of Full-Time,
Year-Round Workers, 1977

Group	Wage	Wage as percent of white male's wage
White men	$15,230	100%
Black men	10,618	70
White women	8,787	58
Black women	8,217	54

Source: U.S. Department of Labor, Women's Bureau, *The Earnings Gap Between Women and Men* (1979), p. 20.

racist and sexist discrimination, is the wage of the black woman. And remember, these are all wages for full-time, year-round workers.

The same dreary picture shows up in the figures on poverty. In 1980, almost half of all families below the poverty level were headed by women—that is, there was no husband present. Half of all families headed by black women fell below the poverty level, and a quarter of those headed by white women did.[16] In 1979, 30.9 percent of women full-time workers made less than $149 per week, and 56.9 percent made less than $200 per week; among men, only 9.4 and 21.3 percent respectively earned such low salaries.[17] On the other end of the scale, 25.7 percent of men but only 4.4 percent of women full-time workers made $400 or more per week.

Are women paid according to their education?

Perhaps women have lower wages because of less training and education. No; in spite of discrimination in higher education, the woman worker has exactly the same educational level as the male worker. The median level for both in 1979 was 12.6 years—yet as we have seen, the woman's wages are only 59 percent of the man's. When we compare income by sex at different levels of schooling, we find that a woman with a high school education gets lower wages than a man with fewer than 8 years of elementary school education (see Table 5.3). A woman with some college education is paid far less than a man with only some high school education, and a woman with a college diploma is paid less than a man with a high school diploma.

[16]Labor Research Association, *Economic Notes* (September 1981): 8.

[17]*Perspectives,* op. cit., p. 50.

TABLE 5.3

Median Income by Sex and Education, 1977 (Full-Time, Year-Round Workers, 25 Years and Over)

Education	Women's median income	Men's median income	Difference
Elementary school			
Less than 8 years	$ 6,074	$ 9,419	$3,345
8 years	6,564	12,083	5,519
High school			
1 to 3 years	7,387	13,120	5,733
4 years	8,894	15,434	6,540
College			
1 to 3 years	10,157	16,235	6,078
4 years	11,609	19,603	7,998
5 years or more	14,338	21,941	7,603

Source: U.S. Department of Labor, Women's Bureau, *The Earnings Gap Between Women and Men* (1979), p. 15.

TABLE 5.4

Women's Median Earnings as a Percentage of Men's by Education and Occupation, 1973 (Full-Time, Year-Round Workers, 18 Years and Over)

Occupation	Total	Elementary, 8 years or less	High school 1 to 3 years	High school 4 years	College 1 to 3 years	College 4 years or more
Total	58.5%	56.8%	56.3%	57.3%	59.0%	60.9%
White-collar workers	54.9	58.0	56.8	56.6	55.8	59.8
Professional and technical workers	66.1	62.5	58.1	65.4	68.9	63.9
Managers and administrators (except farm)	54.3	62.4	56.0	55.1	59.2	59.9
Clerical and sales workers	57.7	59.8	58.5	59.8	58.2	53.9
Blue-collar workers	54.0	55.4	56.3	54.0	54.4	54.2
Service workers	55.2	60.2	58.1	52.1	56.9	58.4

Source: U.S. Department of Labor, Women's Bureau, *1975 Handbook on Women Workers,* p. 195.

When we compare men and women with the same education working at similar jobs, we get the same depressing results (see Table 5.4). Women white-collar workers with 4 years of high school make only 56.6 percent as much as male white-collar workers with the same education; women managers and administrators with at least a college degree make 59.9 percent of what a man with a comparable job makes. The smallest percentage difference is for professional and technical workers with 1 to 3 years of college, and even in that category, women make less than 70 percent of what men do.

A Bureau of Labor Statistics study found that "in each of eight occupations studied for men and women in the same jobs, men always were paid more than women."[18] Thus female class A accounting clerks received on the average 82 percent as much as males doing the same work. Women payroll clerks were paid 77 percent of what male payroll clerks received.

Education is, of course, not the only factor influencing income. Many economists have long believed that better data on job qualifications would explain the earnings gap. But, in a recent study by the Institute for Social Research, more precise measures of qualifications were obtained. The study clearly showed that "differences in job qualifications such as education, on-the-job training, and general work experience fail to explain much of the very large wage gap between white men and other workers. Average differences in these kinds of qualifications account for less than one-third of the wage gap between white men and black women, less than half of the gap between white men and white women, and less than two-thirds of the gap between white men and black men."[19] The researchers also found that time spent in on-the-job training is more valuable than time spent acquiring general work experience and that white men have considerably greater access to jobs offering such training than do women or black males.

Are women promoted equally with men?
In each area of the economy there is evidence that women receive lower-level jobs to start with and are less likely to be promoted than men of equal training and experience. Look at almost any company or educational institution, or at government employment, and you will find large numbers of poorly paid women (and minority males) in the bottom ranks and a few highly paid white males at the top.

[18]U.S. Department of Labor, Women's Bureau, *1975 Handbook on Women Workers,* pp. 145–147.
[19]*Institute for Social Research Newsletter* (spring 1978): 7.

Thus American Telephone and Telegraph, which is the single largest employer of women in the United States, systematically excluded women from both higher-level management jobs and from better-paying craft jobs. Table 5.5 shows the situation at New York Bell. In 1970, only 1.1 percent of all craft jobs in the entire Bell System were held by women. Telephone operators were 99.9 percent female.[20] AT&T was sued for sex and race discrimination and in 1973 was ordered to rectify its hiring practices. Although there seems to be some improvement, it has been slow. At Pacific Telephone, one of the AT&T operating companies, only 2.5 percent of the top supervisors were women in 1977.[21]

Banks have also been major offenders. A recent survey of 24 major banks found that women were 63 percent of all workers but only 13 percent of bank officers. Even this small percentage is an increase over 1971, when only 6.4 percent of the officers were women.[22] The same pyramid of pay and prestige is found in education. About 88 percent of elementary school teachers are women, yet elementary school principals and administrators are 78 percent male. Approximately half of high school teachers are women, but 96.5 percent of high school principals are men.[23]

[20]Barbara Allan Babcock, Ann E. Freedman, Eleanor Holmes Norton, Susan C. Ross, *Sex Discrimination and the Law* (Boston: Little Brown, 1975), p. 292.

[21]*Los Angeles Times,* February 6, 1977.

[22]Ibid.

[23]Carol A. Whitehurst, *Women in America: The Oppressed Majority* (Santa Monica, Calif.: Goodyear, 1977), p. 61.

TABLE   5.5
Women at New York Bell Telephone, 1970

Job	Percentage of women to total
Top-level managers (18 men)	0%
4th-level managers (80 men)	0
3d-level managers	0
2d-level managers	23
1st-level managers	95
Supervisors (2,000 women)	100
Operators (21,000 women)	100

Source: James Horris, Assistant Vice-President, Bell Telephone, in New York Commission on Human Rights, Hearings on *Women's Role in Contemporary Society* (New York: Discus Books, 1972), pp. 232–255.

One way many companies pay women less—without appearing to discriminate—is to create a new job title for women to do a job previously done by men under another name and for higher pay. "Men and women often do exactly the same thing in all but name and pay. . . . Management consultants frequently turn up men and women doing the same job under differing titles when they analyze what each employee really does."[24]

In fact, until recently, when the law made it illegal, most private employers openly admitted to sexist discrimination. As late as 1961 a questionnaire on sex discrimination was answered by the 1900 employers in the National Office Managers Association. A third of them admitted quite honestly that they always paid women less than men.[25]

Surely, however, women are treated equally in public employment. False! Look at the example set by the federal government (see Table 5.6). The U.S. Civil Service is another pyramid with thousands of women in low-paying jobs at the bottom and a small number of well-paid men on the top. Although women made up 43.1 percent of federal white-collar employees, very few reached the top policy-making positions. In late 1977, there were only 16 women in government service jobs graded 18 and only 55 in jobs graded 17. Yet even these sad figures are an improvement

[24]Caroline Bird, *Born Female* (New York: Pocket Books, 1969), p. 63.
[25]Ibid., p. 62.

TABLE 5.6
**Women in the Federal Civil Service System
    (Full-Time, White-Collar Employees,
    November 30, 1977)**

Grade groups	Percentage of women to total grade group	Mean* salary
17–18	3.3%	47,500
13–16	5.8	35,703
9–12	25.9	18,951
5–8	61.5	12,412
1–4	77.2	7,935

*Average over grades in group of basic pay for employees in step 1 of the grade as of October 1978.
Source: Statement of Nancy S. Barrett, Hearings on *The Coming Decade: American Women and Human Resources Policies and Programs,* U.S. Senate Committee on Human Resources, February 9, 1979, Table 1.

over the situation in 1973, when women made up only 1.8 percent of GS grade 17 and above and only 4.6 percent of the grades 13 through 16.[26]

A look at men's and women's earnings over the life cycle gives another perspective on the same problem. Men's earnings rise sharply in the mid-twenties and thirties. Males 35 to 44 are earning twice the median income of those who are 18 to 24. But women's earnings do not make a comparable jump. The median income of full-time, year-round women workers between the ages of 35 and 44 is not even $2000 more than the median for 18- to 24-year-old women. The difference for men is about $8000.[27] A woman simply is not allowed to move upward in the career ladder the way the average man does.

Are women more often absent?
Do they quit more often?

The first sexist apologia for lower-pay, low-level jobs, and few promotions for women is that women are inherently inferior. This can no longer be said in public, however, so the second sexist apologia is that men "need more money to support their families." We have already seen that this is utterly false for most working women; women are the sole or a main support of most of the neediest families. The third and fourth sexist apologias are that women are absent from work more often because they have to care for their families, and that women quit their jobs more often because they get pregnant.

Now it is true that women are forced, often involuntarily, to drop out to have families, and it is true that they bear the burden of a second job at home. It is also true that women are given precious little help with these burdens by employers, husbands, or government; maternity leaves and child-care facilities are almost nonexistent. Astoundingly, however, in spite of these extra burdens, women in general are *not* absent more often, and women do *not* quit their jobs more often.

A very extensive Labor Department study concludes from all the earlier studies and from its own statistics: "Women workers have favorable records of attendance and labor turnover when compared

[26] *1975 Handbook,* op. cit., p. 117.

[27] U.S. Congress, Senate, Committee on Human Resources, Hearings on *The Coming Decade: American Women and Human Resources Policies and Programs,* Statement of Nancy S. Barnett, February 9, 1979, p. 4.

with men employed at similar job levels and under similar circumstances." One can predict absenteeism and turnover much better from (1) the skill level of the job, (2) the age of the worker, and (3) the length of service with the employer than from "the mere fact that the worker is a man or a woman."[28]

True, some studies find very slightly higher *aggregate* rates of absence or turnover for women. A 1967 study found the average woman worker lost 5.6 days a year from illness or injury, while the average male worker lost 5.3 days. But this study overlooked the fact that discrimination forces most women into miserable jobs in which *all* workers are ill or injured more often—and men in these jobs are absent more often than women. Similarly, a 1968 study found that 2.6 women per 100 quit their jobs voluntarily that year while 2.2 men quit voluntarily. Again, this overlooks the fact that most women are pushed into jobs everyone tries to quit at the first opportunity—and that men quit more often.[29] In fact, as another study shows, from January 1965 to January 1966 only 7 percent of women but 10 percent of men workers changed occupations. Moreover, from 1957 to 1960 an average of only 6 percent of women workers but 8 percent of men changed the region of their main job.[30] The truth may be that women workers are less likely to change jobs than men because, as a result of discrimination, they have fewer options.

Particularly at higher job levels, there are no differences between labor turnover for men and women workers. Thus turnover was reported "about the same" for men and women at the same grades in a study of 65 large chemical and pharmaceutical laboratories.[31] The notion that a woman worker on any particular job is more likely to be absent or quit than a man is quite wrong; the opposite is more often true in lower-level jobs. Such notions are pure sexist myths—and are used, consciously or unconsciously, to pay women lower wages, to refuse to promote them, or not to hire them at all.

DISCRIMINATION BY SEGREGATION

Although many women are paid less for doing the same jobs as men, the major cause of the wage gap between men and women is employment segregation. Employer prejudice and women's own inter-

---

[28]U.S. Department of Labor, Women's Bureau, *Facts About Women's Absenteeism and Labor Turnover* (Washington, D.C.: Government Printing Office, 1969), p. 1.

[29]Ibid., p. 2.

[30]Ibid., pp. 3, 5.

[31]Ibid., p. 7.

nalized sex role socialization keep most women out of better-paying "men's" jobs and herd them into low-paying, dead-end "women's" jobs.

Even in the most general classifications used by the Census Bureau, the pattern of segregation is apparent (see Table 5.7). Men dominate in the better-paying occupations: managers, administrators, and craft workers. Of course not all male jobs are well paid; nonfarm laborers are mostly men. Clerical work, domestic service, and other service occupations, which are less prestigious and do not pay as well, are predominantly female. Of all women at work, 35 percent are clerical workers.[32]

More detailed occupational classifications show that few occupations are truly mixed and that women are much more concentrated in a few occupations than men are. In 1975, women made up 90 percent or more of the workers in 41 of the 419 occupations identified in government data.[33] Forty percent of all female workers

[32]U.S. Department of Labor, Bureau of Labor Statistics, *Employment and Unemployment: A Report on 1980* (Washington, D.C.: Government Printing Office), pp. 22–23.

[33]Nancy Rytina, "Occupational Segregation and Earnings Differences by Sex," *Monthly Labor Review* 104 (January 1981), 50.

TABLE 5.7
Occupation, by Sex, 1980

Occupation	Women as percent of total in occupation
Mainly male occupations	
Craft and kindred workers	6.0%
Nonfarm laborers	11.6
Managers and administrators, except farm	20.7
Mixed occupations	
Factory operatives, except transport	40.1
Professional and technical workers	44.3
Salespeople	45.3
Mainly female occupations	
Service (other than domestic)	58.9
Clerical workers	80.1
Private household workers	97.5

Source: U.S. Department of Commerce, *Population Profile of the United States: 1980,* Series P–20, No. 363, July 1981, p. 36.

were to be found in these occupations—10 percent of the total. There were many more predominantly male occupations—179 in which 90 percent of the workers were men and in which almost 50 percent of all men were employed. Data from 1980 show that 55 percent of working women are clerical workers, retail sales workers, sewers and stitchers, waitresses, private household workers, nurses, or non–college-teachers.[34] These are all predominately female occupations. Women make up a little more than 70 percent of retail sales persons and of non–college-teachers. The other occupations are over 80 percent female.

This crowding of women into a few types of jobs depresses their wages and increases unemployment. Between 1965 and 1975, for example, 44 percent of the growth in female employment was in clerical jobs. According to economist Nancy Barrett, "At the same time, clerical unemployment rose from 11.1 percent in 1965 to 14.6 percent in 1976 and the average clerical wage dropped sharply relative to the average wage for the work force as a whole."[35]

Under pressure from the women's movement, some previously all-male preserves are being breached. Progress in the professions, which will be discussed in the next chapter, has gotten most of the media attention, but just as important are the inroads women have made into the skilled trades. Between 1960 and 1970, the number of women carpenters rose from 3,300 to 11,000; electricians from 2,500 to 8,700; plumbers from 1,000 to 4,000; auto mechanics from 2,300 to 11,000; and tool and die makers from 1,100 to 4,200.[36] In some of these trades, women made further gains between 1970 and 1980. Thus, by 1980, there were 17,775 women carpenters.[37] During the 1970s, apprenticeship programs in the skilled trades were being opened to women and, by the end of the decade, women made up about 2 percent of the workers in skilled trades.[38] Such jobs pay a great deal more than "women's" jobs that require comparable education. For the woman who does not have the opportunity to train for a profession, the skilled trades offer a chance to escape from near poverty-level wages. But although the figures offer hope for the

---

[34]*Employment and Unemployment,* op. cit., pp. 22–23.

[35]Nancy Barrett, "Data Needs for Evaluating the Labor Market Status of Women." Paper prepared for the Census Bureau Conference on Issues in Federal Statistical Needs Relating to Women, April 27–28, 1978, p. 5.

[36]Mary Dublin Keyserling, "The Economic Status of Women in the United States," *American Economic Review* 66 (May 1975), p. 210.

[37]*Employment and Unemployment,* op. cit., pp. 22–23.

[38]*Federationist,* op. cit., p. 2.

future, they do not mean that sex segregation is ended. Women still constitute only a tiny proportion of skilled trade workers.

Rationalizations for segregation

Segregation in employment is frequently defended as natural; because of supposed biological and psychological differences some jobs are considered to be "obviously" women's jobs and others just as "obviously" men's jobs. Our earlier discussion of psychological sex differences showed that there simply is no evidence to support such views. Biological differences may disqualify most women for a very few jobs. Few women are large enough and strong enough to be professional football players—but the same is true of men. About the only jobs for which the sex of the worker is crucial are semen donor and wet nurse.

If the present division of labor were "natural," it should be worldwide. But a study of 324 primitive societies by anthropologist G. P. Murdock found that every occupation done by men in one was done by women in another, and vice versa. Even child care was not invariably women's work. The only exception was metal working, which was always done by men. Yet during World War II, when a labor shortage forced U.S. employers to hire women, they suddenly discovered that women were good at metal working. Rosie the Riveter, who appeared on recruiting posters, became a national heroine. Today, almost all jobs done mainly by men or by women in one country are done by the other sex elsewhere. For example, in the United States being a doctor is considered too unpleasant or difficult for women, but it is considered a "nurturing" or "woman's job" in the Soviet Union. In the United States, women are told to go into nursing because it is a "nurturing, woman's job." But why not become a doctor? There's less heavy lifting and the pay is a lot better.

The sexist defense of segregation, including "explanations" by some sociologists, often rests on the notion that women's jobs are natural extensions of women's family role. But the largest number of employed women are typists whose role at home calls for no typing at all. What women do at home does include cooking and child care, yet men have the top posts in restaurant cooking and in academic child-study programs. Moreover, the housewife may gain expertise in dressmaking and in the use of cosmetics, but men hold the top positions in both the cosmetics industry and the dress designing and manufacturing industries.

In terms of tasks performed, the argument is nonsense. It is true, however, that in the world of work, as in the home, women are cast in the role of auxiliaries, as the support troops, while men are cast as the decision makers. Thus a good secretary is expected to do more than type and take dictation. She is expected to take care of all the picky details—getting coffee, reminding her boss of his appointments, shielding him from people he does not want to see, sometimes even buying birthday presents for members of his family. She is expected to do all this so that he can concentrate on really important tasks. In general, women's jobs are those considered too boring and too unimportant to occupy men. It is the notion that women are naturally subordinate to men that is carried over from the home to the employment world. Only when we realize this can we understand the seeming inconsistency in the sex stereotyping of particular jobs.

Women supposedly are physically weaker than men, but nurses and waitresses carry heavy loads, while doctors and chefs do the "women's jobs" of nurturing and cooking. And this is not a matter of choice! There are many obstacles standing in the way of a woman who wants to be a doctor. And becoming a chef is just as hard. In New York City a woman went through a 40-week union training program in culinary art to be a chef or cook only to be turned down for hundreds of such jobs. The union said not to worry: "It is very easy, we will just switch you to a waitress local."[39] Their assumption was that a woman can cook at home but not in an expensive restaurant. There was a case in which a man was denied a job as an electronic circuit assembler since women have more "finger dexterity."[40] Yet some medical schools have said that women can't be brain surgeons because it "takes a steady hand." Similarly, well-paid accountants are mostly men "because women have no head for figures," but most poorly paid bookkeepers—who do much more arithmetic—are women. Finally, we note that employers give many reasons for preferring men to women but usually can't say or write anything coherent when pushed to justify them. "In 1962 a Presidential order requesting all Federal appointing officers to give reasons for requesting a man or a woman for a job opening cut down requests for candidates of a certain sex to one percent of their former volume."[41]

It must be emphasized that one result of sex segregation is low wages and little prestige in all "women's occupations." Waitresses are paid and respected less than chefs, bookkeepers less than ac-

---

[39]Carol Jacobson, in New York Commission on Human Rights, *Women's Role in Contemporary Society* (New York: Discus Books, 1972), p. 447.

[40]See Kreps, op. cit., p. 95; and Bird, op. cit., p. 69.

[41]Bird, op. cit., p. 68.

countants, nurses less than doctors, and electronic assemblers less than brain surgeons. Most economists now agree that one reason for the low wages is that the overcrowding of women in these occupations raises the supply above the demand. Since the 1950s, the number of women in the labor market has increased rapidly. But most of the increase was in these "women's" occupations, the so-called "pink-collar ghettos," so the oversupply forced women's wages down further. Another reason for low wages is weak unionization, which we will investigate later. Needless to say, employers welcome the endless supply of cheap labor that women provide.

The obstacle course

Juanita Kreps, a liberal-establishment economist and Secretary of Commerce in the Carter Administration, examined "women's jobs" and commented: "It is not difficult to explain, in simple demand and supply terms, why the wages in these over-supplied fields remain low; but why is a service offered when the wage is so low?"[42] It is indeed a mystery to the neoclassical economist who pictures an idealized worker with no constraints on him or her, making a perfectly rational choice on the basis of perfect knowledge of all the possibilities. The mystery is deepened because the question is misstated. The woman does not voluntarily "offer" her services (nor "prefer" nor "have a taste for"), but is pushed into these fields by extreme social pressure—some of which is internalized.

For women, getting into women's jobs is like sliding down a greased incline, while getting into men's jobs is like running an obstacle course. The first obstacle is the socialization of men and women from birth; Johnny gets a toy stethoscope while Jeanie gets a nurse's cap. Throughout her development, the "proper role" is instilled into a woman by family, school, church, and the media. This means that women (and men) internalize a conception of male and female jobs. So most women never even think of trying for the higher-status, higher-paying "male jobs."

Suppose a brilliant and independent young woman does overcome the brainwashing that has taught her to think of jobs as sex-typed and decides to become a lawyer rather than a secretary. The second obstacle on the course is marriage under the present sexist social conditions. If she marries a typical middle-class man, it is assumed that when they have children she (but not he) will drop out of school to take care of the children and the house (and sometimes get a secretarial job to help him finish). If she somehow manages

[42]Kreps, op. cit., p. ix.

to finish college and then law school, circumstances still hinder her from getting a job. Because the husband's career comes first, she can look for a job only in the same geographic area as he does. Because children and housework are her responsibility, she can only work limited hours. Because of brainwashing, no one considers the possibility that husband and society should share these burdens.

Suppose the woman is not only brilliant but ingenious enough to manage all this. The third and cruelest obstacle is discrimination. She may face discrimination in getting admitted to law school. If she gets in, she may be awarded fewer fellowships and lower grades than she deserves because many law professors are prejudiced against women. And if she graduates, many law firms won't hire her. The same discrimination exists in many nonprofessional jobs: Discrimination prevents a woman from being an airline pilot rather than a stewardess, or a chef rather than a waitress. Also, as was noted earlier, most women who work do so out of necessity. Therefore if a woman can't get a job as a pilot but is offered one as a stewardess, she must take it. The combination of socialization, marital constraints, and discrimination in other areas amply explains the "mystery" of why millions of women "prefer" boring, dead-end jobs with low wages.

The question may be asked, *why* do some jobs become "women's" and others "men's"? U.S. history shows that the key to sex-typed jobs for women is low wages and low status. Before 1880, almost all clerical and sales workers were men, who had decent pay and prestige. Then there was a demand for many more cheap but competent clerks and sales workers, so women were substituted at low wages. Similarly, the earliest public school teachers were men; after the Civil War, women were recruited for about one-fourth the pay, and naturally, the status of teaching dropped. Similarly, women became nurses when the work was mostly unpaid volunteer work done under miserable conditions.

Being a bank teller was considered a good, well-paid, man's job until World War II, when—of necessity—banks substituted women. Then the job lost status, partially because of routinization and the new "supermarket" atmosphere, but also because women were doing it. As a result, women were kept on at low wages; now every sexist knows that bank teller is a "woman's job" by "nature."

By contrast, in 1940, when 90 percent of them were female, librarians received low pay and low status. After World War II, however, many men on the GI bill found that they could become librarians in just 1 year of graduate work; jobs were plentiful, and veterans were not worried about being called "sissies." At the same time, libraries became more important. The war showed the importance of knowledge, and computers were soon introduced. Now men hold most of the top library jobs, and sexists among them say the job of head librarian is too important to be trusted to a woman. Most of the lowest-paying library jobs, however, still belong to women.

One important mechanism for maintaining the segregated status quo are the procedures used by employment agencies. The law says they can no longer keep separate male and female files, but they get around the law by using pink and blue cards, separate interviewers, and other devices. For example, Susan Sands, who has a B.A. in applied science and 9 years of experience in technical publishing, asked several employment agencies in New York State to help her get work. One agency tried to get her to take a secretary's job in a "lovely office" where she could "get the knack" of technical publishing. Another sent her to a typing/bookkeeping/phone-answering job. Sands said the employment agencies "should call themselves what they are—slave peddlers."[43]

In a similar case, Gloria Greenberg went to the employment agencies with 8 years experience in the New York State Department of Labor, including 1½ years at the executive level. They asked her: "What about typing and stenographic skills?" "Would your husband approve of your doing such and such a job?" "Why is an attractive girl like you not satisfied to raise a family?"[44]

Recruiters and colleagues still ask women, even executive and professional women: "Can you type?" A woman engineer in a West Coast space-research company was pushed into acting as secretary for a conference of engineers. She said, "They tried it only once. They asked me to take notes at a conference—and I did." But she didn't take down the very long-winded discussion, she just summarized it and added her own sarcastic comments: "Target Date: None" and "Action Required: Policy Definition." They never used her secretarial skills again.[45]

Men often say they would hire women who were "qualified," usually meaning superwomen. One management expert said any woman could get a job if she had a Master's in Business Administration from Harvard. This idea was tested by a study of the recruiting experiences of a group of women who did have M.B.A.s from Harvard. It was found that they received fewer job offers than the men in their classes. The women were offered jobs in research or testing,

[43]Susan Sands, in New York Commission on Human Rights, op. cit., p. 405.
[44]Gloria Greenberg in ibid., p. 414.
[45]Bird, op. cit., p. 46.

not jobs handling accounts. One recruiter said bluntly: "We don't feel our clients will accept a woman account executive."[46] Strange that a woman's face is necessary as a low-paid receptionist for men but impossible as a high-paid account executive for men.

DISCRIMINATION BY UNEMPLOYMENT

There is a myth that all women without paid jobs stay at home voluntarily. Not true. Women are more likely to be unemployed than men. Because of sexism, they are the last hired and first fired (see Table 5.8). Racial discrimination is also shown in the greater unemployment of black men. Double discrimination, because of racism and sexism, is revealed in the even higher unemployment of black women.

Many employers have admitted to sex discrimination in their hiring and firing practices, excusing it on the basis of the myth that men need money to support families, whereas women work just for pin money. We have seen that the reality is quite different; most women also work from necessity.

In addition to direct discrimination in employment, the higher unemployment of women is due to the segregation of jobs, which very much narrows the range of their job opportunities. Furthermore, and not by coincidence, the jobs considered women's jobs are mostly in areas with extreme fluctuation of demand, such as clerical work. Thus women form a convenient reserve army of workers for business, available for low wages during wartime expansions and other temporary booms, but easily (employers hope) sent back to the home during recessions.

In addition to those who are actually unemployed, many women can find only part-time employment; they form a cheap, marginal work force. In 1978, almost 70 percent of women workers had full-time jobs sometime during the year, but only a little over

[46]Ibid.

TABLE 5.8
Unemployment Rates, 1979

	Men	Women
White	4.4	5.9
Black and other	10.3	12.3

Source: U.S. Department of Labor, Perspectives on Working Women: A Databook (October 1980), pp. 62–63.

40 percent of working women were employed full-time during the entire year.[47] This temporary or part-time work results in another very important type of discrimination against women who are forced to accept it. The U.S. government reports that 24 percent of all wages (somewhat less in factory work) come in the form of fringe benefits.[48] But these fringe benefits are given only to full-time workers and/or to those who have worked a certain length of time. Women who work part-time or only part of the year are often not eligible.

It must also be emphasized that "unemployment" is officially defined in such a way that the official figures seriously understate it, particularly among women. In the first place, part-time workers, even those working only 1 hour a week, are considered "employed." Second, if a woman can't get a job for a long time and finally gives up, she is not considered unemployed. Even the Women's Bureau of the U.S. Department of Labor admits, with regard to unemployment data on women, that available figures may be deceptively low, because they do not include the many women who have stopped looking for employment because the current job market seems so hopeless. "Since no account is taken of the many who have given up job-hunting because it seemed hopeless, these figures may be deceptively low."

Table 5.9 shows the official unemployment rate and a corrected rate that takes into account discouraged and part-time workers who would like to work full time. Clearly, for all workers actual unemployment is much higher than official unemployment. Furthermore, when the figures are corrected, the gap between men and women increases.

[47]*Perspectives,* op. cit., p. 16.
[48]Bird, op. cit., p. 66.

TABLE 5.9
Corrected and Official Unemployment Rates by Race and Sex (June 1975)

Category	Official unemployment	Minimum corrected unemployment*
White men	7.6	9.9
White women	9.4	13.3
Black men	15.4	20.1
Black women	15.5	22.9

*The more conservative of two ways of correcting is given.
Source: Howard J. Sherman, *Stagflation* (New York: Harper & Row, 1976), p. 16.

To add insult to injury, recent Republican administrations have not seen women's unemployment as a serious problem. Spokesmen for the Nixon and Ford administration, as well as President Reagan himself, have claimed that the unemployment situation is not as bad as the official figures make it look because there are now so many women and young people in the labor force. The implication is that women and young people do not really *need* to work and thus their unemployment does not really count.

IS DISCRIMINATION AN IRRATIONAL PREFERENCE?

There is a myth that only irrational males want sexual discrimination and that it's just a matter of their inexplicable tastes or preferences. The economist Gary Becker, whose work is considered definitive by conservatives, says: "Discrimination and prejudice are not usually said to occur when someone prefers looking at a glamorous Hollywood actress rather than at some other woman; yet they are said to occur when he prefers living next to whites rather than next to Negroes. At best, calling just one of these actions 'discrimination' requires making subtle and rather secondary distinctions."[49] Note that he thinks discrimination against blacks is as trivial as preferring apples to oranges, and that he uses a sexist example to make his point.

Ray Franklin and Solomon Resnick point out that Becker is wrong to consider discrimination as trivial, as "just" a preference: "Becker errs because his analysis ignores the distribution of power and the use of the double standard."[50] First, employers, union leaders, and military and government leaders are white males who have power to discriminate. Second, employers choose by a double standard—they assume that white males are good, qualified workers, while blacks and women are not, and the burden of proof is on blacks and women to show themselves qualified. Even where there are laws against discrimination, control of the power structure means the laws are frequently not enforced. Prejudiced propaganda is perpetuated through the media, church, and schools, and blacks and women continue to get inferior training.

Conservatives such as Milton Friedman claim that discrimination by business is irrational because business loses profits by it. The theory is this: Suppose there are equally qualified male and female

[49]Gary Becker, *The Economics of Discrimination* (Chicago: University of Chicago Press, 1957), p. 5.
[50]Ray Franklin and Solomon Resnick, *The Political Economy of Racism* (New York: Holt, Rinehart & Winston, 1973), p. 16.

workers. Suppose only males are hired because of prejudice. Female workers, because of discrimination against them elsewhere, could be hired more cheaply. Therefore the capitalist who hires only males must be paying higher wages. Under competition there is no way to pass on this higher cost, so business must pay the price of the irrational exclusion of women. In Friedman's opinion, there is a high degree of competition in most of the U.S. economy; thus capitalists who discriminate pay for it in much higher costs.[51] He argues that, since capitalists who discriminate lose money, the prejudiced capitalists who are so irrational as not to hire qualified women will be bankrupted by the competition of those who do hire women at lower wages. Therefore, Friedman claims there is very little discrimination now and the little that does remain will disappear in long-run equilibrium under capitalism.

Some extreme conservatives use this argument to prove the inferiority of women. Since women still receive lower pay and poorer jobs, and since this is not due to discrimination by employers (assuming the economy is in competitive equilibrium), the woman worker must be inferior, they argue. Some conservatives say the inferiority is due to past discrimination, but true sexists claim that the inferiority is inherent. One economist, Angus Black, said bluntly: "If a woman were more like a man, she'd be treated as such."[52]

Liberals like Martin Bronfenbrenner[53] agree with Friedman on the high cost of discrimination under competition but emphasize the influence of monopoly and monopoly power. Given pervasive monopoly power, business *can* discriminate in long-run equilibrium with less loss. All traditional economists, both conservative and liberal, thus agree on the main points and differ only in emphasis: (1) Discrimination by employers reflects an inexplicable "preference" (like apples instead of oranges); (2) capitalists must pay a cost, heavy or light, for it; (3) so more competition will tend to eliminate those capitalists and automatically end discrimination.

The only major difference between liberals and conservatives is that the liberals realize there is a great amount of discrimination, while the conservatives deny there is any. Thus the liberal economists advocate reforms, while the conservatives believe reforms are

[51]Milton Friedman, *Capitalism and Freedom* (Chicago: University of Chicago Press, 1957), pp. 108 ff.

[52]Angus Black, *A Radical's Guide to Economic Reality* (New York: Holt, Rinehart & Winston, 1970), p. 37.

[53]Martin Bronfenbrenner, "Potential Monopsony in Labor Markets," *Industrial and Labor Relations Review* 9 (April 1956), 577–588.

unnecessary. Both agree that the radicals are totally incorrect in saying that capitalists benefit from sex discrimination. For example, liberal economist Barbara Bergmann ridicules the idea that capitalists conspire together in a Watergate-like plot to discriminate against women in order to make more profits. She says that the status quo of large-scale discrimination against women only helps male workers, not male capitalists. She admits that the capitalist employers are the ones who do the actual discriminating, but denies that they profit from it: "The employers actually tend to lose financially, since profits are lowered when cheap female help is spurned in favor of high-priced male help."[54] Thus she accepts Milton Friedman's basic argument.

If capitalists are in business to make profit, why do they systematically choose to lose money? This is not a problem for Friedman, because he simply denies that there is much discrimination. It is a problem for Bergmann, however, because she shows the vast extent of discrimination against women, while continuing to argue that capitalists lose money from it. Her answer to the riddle is that capitalists lose financially, but they gain psychologically: "It feels so good to have women in their 'place.' "[55] She does not seem to find it astounding that such irrational behavior has persisted for many decades under capitalism.

This split over whether sex discrimination is due to an irrational response by all men or to a desire for profit by the capitalist class is not limited to professional economists; it is also a very controversial issue within the women's movement. Some feminists claim that all men benefit from sexist discrimination. Like the traditional economists, they do not claim that the benefits are material in most cases, but that all men benefit psychologically from the oppression of women. It follows from this, as June Safer of the New York Feminists asserts, that all "men are enemies," not just capitalist men.[56] On the contrary, Frances Beale of the Third World Women's Alliance argues that "male chauvinism and racism is economically profitable" to the capitalist system.[57] She says explicitly that men do not merely get a vicarious pleasure out of sex discrimination, but exploit women workers in order to make more profits.

[54]Barbara Bergmann, "Economics of Women's Liberation," *Challenge* 16 (May–June 1973), 14.

[55]Ibid.

[56]June Safer, in New York Commission on Human Rights, op. cit., p. 135.

[57]Frances Beale, in ibid., p. 134. See also Marilyn Goldberg, "Economic Exploitation of Women," *Review of Radical Political Economics* 2 (spring 1970), 3.

It is important to distinguish between the whole system of labor-capital relations and the attitudes of individual capitalists and workers. Radicals claim only that the whole system profits from sex discrimination, so that it is "rational" from the viewpoint of the system as a whole. Certainly, many men hold irrational sexist prejudices—including workers, who lose from discrimination in the aggregate—and these prejudices are the immediate causes of discrimination. Because of their own sexist prejudices, many employers *perceive* all male workers as better than all female workers, so often they do not even seriously consider a woman who is equally or better qualified than a man for a good job. This is the case in many businesses, in government, and in most universities. A large number of studies have shown that employers, having very imperfect knowledge about workers, just take the easy way out by classifying all black and/or female workers as inferior to white male applicants.[58]

Not only do employers exhibit this prejudice (some even in the face of evidence to the contrary), but foremen add their own racist and/or sexist prejudices to increase the discrimination. Over 20 percent of all white males with jobs in the economy are foremen (or kindred workers); less than 14 percent of black males are foremen; only 1 percent of white women and much less than 1 percent of black women are "foremen."[59]

It is also true that many male workers perceive women as inferior and/or as rivals. Male workers have this perception because of their own sexist upbringing in this society. Certainly employers do sometimes respond to the prejudices of male workers, but they also use some alleged (and nonexistent) workers' prejudices as convenient excuses for their own actions. Finally, it is true that many male clients, industrial purchasers, and advertisers perceive women as inferior. Certainly capitalists do pander to the prejudices of these buyers, but again they also use buyers' prejudices as convenient justifications for their own behavior.

Can we believe, however, that such prejudices would have been allowed to influence corporate behavior for so many decades if it were not profitable? Can we conceivably believe, as some economists contend, that these prejudices continue unabated even though they cause large losses to the capitalist system? In fact, it is possible to present an impressive list of the ways in which sexism is very profitable to U.S. capitalists.

[58]Michael Spence, *Market Signalling, Discussion Paper, Public Policy Program,* no. 4. (Cambridge, Mass.: Harvard University, Kennedy School of Government, 1972).
[59]Franklin and Resnick, op. cit., p. 46.

IS SEXIST PREJUDICE PROFITABLE?

It will be shown here that sex discrimination and prejudices are profitable in dollars and cents, after which the question of noneconomic benefits to the ruling elite will also be investigated.

Segregation and lower wages

First, it is important to review one crucial point concerning the reality of women at work. Women and men are mostly segregated at work, so that half of all women workers are in occupations that are over 70 percent female. On the other side of the segregated job world, most males are in occupations that are well over 70 percent male. There are some mixed occupations, but they are so few that they may be ignored here in order to simplify the analysis.

What is the situation in the mostly female occupations? The evidence shows that in areas where most of the labor force is female, the pay for *both* men and women is lower, even though workers in many of those areas have higher qualifications (shown in more education) than the average worker. This may be shown for all the clerical occupations in which women predominate (see Table 5.10). The table reveals that, in every clerical occupation where women are in the majority, women's wages are much lower than the average American male's wage, although the women's education is above the average American male's education. The women's wages are also very considerably below those of men who are in the same occupation, yet their education is almost the same as the men's. But these four facts only tell us what we knew already, that women suffer from job segregation and discrimination. More interesting is the fact that men in these occupations had much lower wages than the average American male worker, even though these men had more education than the average American male worker. Therefore, *sexist discrimination not only hurts women workers, it also hurts men workers*—and the lower wages produce higher profits.

To understand the much lower wages of all workers in the mostly female sectors, it is necessary to understand that these sectors differ systematically in several other characteristics from the mostly male sectors. Most important, one careful study shows that the industries into which women are largely segregated, such as the service areas and the garment industry, are small and relatively competitive, whereas the male-dominated industries are large and highly specialized.[60] Because of the competitive nature of the mostly fe-

[60]See the discussion and data in Mary Stevenson, "Women's Wages and Job Segregation," *Politics and Society* 4 (fall 1973), 92–93.

TABLE 5.10
Education and Income of Clerical Workers, 1970*

Occupation	Percentage by which median education is above or below median of all U.S. male workers		Percentage by which median earnings are above or below median of all U.S. male workers	
	Men	Women	Men	Women
Bank teller	+4%	+2%	−25%	−45%
Bookkeeper	+4	+2	−3	−41
Cashier	0	−2	−59	−68
File clerk	+2	+1	−35	−55
Library attendant and assistant	+13	+7	−80	−73
Key punch operator	+2	+2	−2	−40
Payroll & time-keeping clerk	+2	+2	+3	−32
Receptionist	+5	+2	−44	−56
Secretary	+5	+3	−1	−37
Telephone operator	+2	+1	−15	−44
Typist	+2	+2	−21	−47

*In all occupations listed, women are a majority of the total.
Source: Department of Commerce, *1970 Census of Population,* Subject Report PC(2)–7A, Occupational Characteristics, Table 1.

male industries, they have low rates of profit. On the other hand, the more specialized male industries use their monopoly power to achieve a higher rate of profit.[61]

The mostly female, more competitive sector also pays much lower wages for all employees than does the mostly male sector.[62] Finally, the unions in the female industries and occupations are by and large much weaker than those in the male industries. Of course, these are generalizations and do not hold true in every case. Nevertheless, the attributes of a high percentage of female employees, competition, low profits, low wages, and weak unions do tend to be found together.

Now, several questions may be asked and answered. The first is why the average wage of women is much lower than that of

[61]See Howard Sherman, *Profits in the United States* (Ithaca: Cornell University Press, 1972), p. 89 ff.

[62]See Barry Bluestone, "Economic Crisis and the Law of Uneven Development," *Politics and Society* 3 (fall 1973), 65–82.

men. A large part of the answer is that women are mainly in the low-wage areas. Why are they in the low-wage areas? Partly this is because they are discriminated against in the other areas and partly because their own sexist conditioning tells them these low-wage areas are the proper places for them to be. Thus women congregate in certain occupations because it is much, much harder for them to move into the better paying areas. Discrimination, sexist conditioning, and family circumstances all work to keep women in traditional female jobs.

A related question is: Why do employers segregate women into these particular areas? The key to answering this is to recognize that, in the competitive sectors, employers are forced to economize in every way. Even though they may be as prejudiced as employers in the monopoly sector, their small profits force them to hire women if they can pay them lower wages. In fact, when they discover out of necessity that women can do the jobs as well as men but will work for lower wages, they scramble to hire women.

If higher profits are to be made by hiring women at lower wages, why don't employers in the monopoly sector do this as well? One could refer to their biased perceptions about women, but it was shown that these could be overcome. One could refer to the biases of strong male unions, but these have also been overcome when it was important for employers' profits. The key point is that there is less reason to resist high wages in this sector. The monopoly power of these capitalists can be used to pass on to the consumer all of the higher wages. In fact, a small increase in wages is often used by the monopolists as the excuse for a major price increase. Also, the high salaries these businesses pay are used to defray their profit margins, and thus to reduce their taxes.

Finally, it may be asked why wages are kept much lower for *all* workers in the mostly female industries. As was shown earlier, both discrimination and socialization push women into these areas, so there is great overcrowding of labor in this sector. The excess supply is one reason for lower wages. Furthermore, the fact that competitive employers cannot simply pass on wage increases to consumers means that they are more likely to run sweat shops. And, because of weak unions, workers in this area are greatly handicapped in fighting for higher wages.

Why are the unions much weaker in the mostly female, more competitive sector? One reason is that the oversupply of labor decreases bargaining power, while the competitive employers are forced to protect their own limited profits by tough bargaining. Moreover, many of these industries and occupations are quite spread out geographically. It is much easier to organize one enormous factory in the monopoly sector than it is to organize a thousand smaller ones in the competitive sector. Many women and much competition are found particularly in the service industries, which are also spread out and harder to organize. Yet another important factor is that some of these areas have significant numbers of men as well as women, so the situation is ideal for sexist prejudice to divide the workers, weaken their unions, and make them easy to rule.

Divide and rule

For the entire country, one out of every four male workers but only one out of every seven female workers is unionized.[63] One reason for the lower proportion of women in unions is that the areas in which most of them work are harder to organize. The other reason is the hostility or indifference of union men and union leaders toward women, an attitude fostered by their own prejudices. The degree of sexism in unions may be observed by the fact that most union executive boards are exclusively male, even though women do average about 20 percent of all union members. Even in unions such as the International Ladies Garment Workers, where women constitute over three-fourths of the members, only a few token women are on the executive board.

Jean Tepperman reports that women in the factories where she worked were very angry and would have liked a militant union to act on their grievances, but never even dreamed of having such a union. The women thought of unions as run by men who were selling them something like car insurance. The women joined the union because they were forced to and because they thought that, without it, their situation might be even worse. Tepperman says: "The way most people chose between the unions was to compare prices (union dues) against the product (the list of union promises), adjusted by how much you felt they were lying."[64] The unions did very little, if anything, for the women's specific grievances.

Union men often pay for their prejudices in broken unions and lower wages. In a strike by Standard Oil workers in San Francisco, the union was beaten because of its own prejudices against women. "Women at Standard Oil have the least chance for advancement and decent pay, and the union has done little to fight this. Not surprising-

[63]Kirsten Amundsen, *The Silenced Majority* (Englewood Cliffs, N.J.: Prentice-Hall, 1971), p. 96.
[64]Tepperman, op. cit., p. 120.

ly, women formed the core of the back-to-work move that eventually broke the strike."[65]

The liberal economist Morris Silver finds that prejudice between black and white workers makes unions more difficult and thus may lower the total wage bill. Therefore, "far from being indifferent to the existence of discriminatory attitudes on the part of workers, the capitalist gains from them and may find it profitable to invest in their creation."[66] The same conclusion obviously holds for sexist attitudes toward women.

Other functions of sex discrimination

In addition to lower wages and weaker unions, discrimination helps provide a handy but disposable labor force. The process has been well described by Franklin and Resnick in the case of racism. If an employer has 10 black and 10 white workers, and must fire half for a couple of months, which will he fire? "If he is rational and seeks to minimize his labor turnover costs, he will lay off his ten black workers on the assumption that they will be unlikely to get permanent or better jobs elsewhere because of the discriminatory practices of other employers."[67] Obviously women workers are treated the same way by "rational" employers.

Another reason sexism is profitable to capitalists is the closely related factor of savings on fringe benefits. It is now common for employers to keep a permanent crew of skilled white males plus a large number of temporary women (and black) workers. The temporary workers are usually fired in fewer than 90 days. Under most laws this is soon enough to disqualify them for fringe benefits such as vacation pay, sick leave, extra medical benefits, employer contributions to pension plans, and unemployment insurance.

Sexism is also profitable because it instills the desire to consume in women. The sexist image of the good woman shows her in her kitchen surrounded by the very latest gadgets, made up with miracle cosmetics, and using the latest laundry detergent, dishwasher soap, and wall cleaner. This image helps business sell billions of dollars of unnecessary (or even harmful) goods.

Still another reason sexism is profitable is that women's unpaid work in the home is crucial to the paid labor force. In other words, women raise children to be workers, and they cook and clean and

---

[65]Kathy McAfee and Myrna Wood, "Bread and Roses," in Roberta Salper, ed., *Female Liberation* (New York: Knopf, 1972), p. 155.

[66]Quoted in Franklin and Resnick, op. cit., p. 23.

[67]Franklin and Resnick, op. cit., p. 20.

take care of adult male workers. These valuable services are unpaid. Such housework is valued at about one-fourth of the GNP, though it is not counted in the official GNP. If business had to pay women *in full* to raise and clean and cook for the labor force, profits would be much, much lower.

Women in the family are not only profitable to capitalism because of their unpaid material labor, but perhaps even more for the psychological jobs they perform in the family. The woman in the sexist family must play a certain role as wife and mother. That role includes keeping the family safe and stable, which sometimes means "adjusting" it to harsh realities. As a mother, she is expected to tell her children to behave docilely in school. Later, she is the one who must train her children to be "good" workers, that is, to be quiet and disciplined, and yet at the same time enterprising and competitive with other workers.[68]

As a wife, she is often the one to caution her husband not to involve himself in a strike lest he lose his job. Both his wife's influence and his family responsibilities then join to reduce the husband's mobility, his resistance to low wages, and his ability to strike.[69] At the same time, wives act as lightning rods for the reactions of men to the system. If he is angered by the boss on the job, a husband can come home and act as a petty dictator to his wife and children. He can let out his frustrations within the family, rather than against the system. As head of the household, he also enforces the child's acceptance of authority and belief in a hierarchical view of all social relations, a view which is very helpful to factory management.[70]

As a result of their dependent role in the sexist family, women are socialized to be passive, submissive, and docile as workers. Employers can also more easily exploit wives as cheap labor because women are socialized to believe the myth that they work for pin money or just "supplementary" income, that their work is only temporary, and that they must only work close to their homes for limited hours. Yet this "supplementary" income is now massive enough so that many husbands may be more willing to settle for lower wages. The mother also trains her daughter to be a good mother, and the process begins again.

The last, but not the least important, way in which capitalism

---

[68]See Peggy Morton, "A Woman's Work Is Never Done," in Edith Altback, ed., *From Feminism to Liberation* (Cambridge, Mass.: Schenkman, 1971), pp. 211–228.

[69]See Margaret Benson, "Political Economy of Women's Liberation," in ibid., p. 199–210.

[70]See McAfee and Wood, op. cit., p. 156.

profits from sexism comes in increased support for political stability. On the one hand, women's psychological role in the sexist family has the same effects politically as it does economically. It tends to make a woman more fearful and conservative; she tends to influence her husband in this direction and to pass it on to her son and especially to her daughter. Sexism is used for political "divide and rule" in many of the same ways as racism. Some white politicians blame all urban problems on blacks. Hitler blamed unemployment on Jewish capitalists and agitation on Jewish communists. President Reagan blamed unemployment (and accompanying pressure for low wages) on the competition of women workers. Thus women provide a scapegoat for men's problems rather than becoming an ally against a dehumanizing system.

The effects of dividing and ruling by sexism are also evident in radical movements. Many examples can be found in U.S. history. In the late 1960s, the Students for a Democratic Society and other organizations of the New Left wasted women's talents and were weakened by resulting male-female struggles. It should also be noted that the establishment sociologist and current U.S. Senator Daniel Moynihan helped divide and weaken the black movement with his "theory" that black women are domineering matriarchs who psychologically castrate their men. Finally, it is saddest to note how universities and corporations can sometimes play women against blacks and other minority males in awarding scarce jobs.

In conclusion, sexism yields profits for capitalists by splitting unions and radical organizations, getting cheaper labor from women *and* men, obtaining a flexible reserve army of unemployed workers, saving on fringe benefits, giving an outlet to men's frustrations, providing unpaid maintenance for the labor force, and socializing women to economic and political conservatism. On the other hand, sexism is costly to society, which loses many of the potential talents of women. It is detrimental to women themselves, resulting in low wages and unemployment, the stifling of their creativity and personality, and their subordinate and often unhappy home lives. It is also detrimental to male workers, as it results in lower wages, weaker unions, less political strength, and unhappy home lives.

PROFESSIONAL WOMEN: THE OBSTACLE COURSE

6

"The nature and proper timidity and delicacy which belongs to the female sex evidently unfits it for many of the occupations of civil life." So wrote the justices of the Supreme Court when, in 1872, they denied Myra Bradwell the right to practice law. Although the legal barriers have now been abolished, most women are still effectively excluded from the prestige professions.

Current data reveal a systematic pattern in which women are heavily represented in some professions but hardly visible in others. Despite some recent gains, there are still few women in the prestige professions such as law, medicine, and engineering; but some low-paying and low-prestige "professions" such as nursing and elementary school teaching are almost wholly female. Women are segregated in the professions quite as much as they are in the work force as a whole.

PATTERNS OF SEGREGATION IN THE PROFESSIONS

In 1980, women accounted for 44.3 percent of what the census calls "professional and technical workers."[1] This figure is, however, misleading because the category includes a large number of quite disparate occupations. Half of all the women in this category are nurses or elementary or secondary school teachers, jobs that are low in pay and in prestige.

[1]1980 data in this section are from U.S. Department of Labor, Bureau of Labor Statistics, *Employment and Unemployment* (Washington, D.C.: Government Printing Office, 1981), pp. 22–23.

In the high-paying and high-prestige professions, the situation is very different. In 1980, women made up only 4 percent of engineers, 13 percent of lawyers, 13.4 percent of doctors, 4.3 percent of dentists, and 6.7 percent of architects. Yet these low figures are an improvement over 1960, when only 3.5 percent of lawyers and 6.8 percent of doctors were women. In the academic world the picture is a little better, but not much. Women make up 33.9 percent of university and college teachers but, as we will see later, they are found mostly in the less prestigious schools and in the lower ranking positions. The university is still predominately a male preserve.

The picture is quite different in the lower-paying professions into which women are segregated. According to 1980 data, women account for 96.5 percent of all nurses, 65 percent of all social workers, 85 percent of all librarians, and 83.7 percent of all elementary school teachers. An interesting area in transition is high school teaching; formerly almost all female, it is now only 46 percent female. Because its pay and prestige have risen somewhat, men have invaded the area, taking most of the higher-paying positions.

WAGES IN THE "FEMALE" PROFESSIONS

In those professions where women predominate, *both* men and women receive lower wages even though they have higher educational qualifications than the average worker (see Table 6.1 and compare it with Table 5.10). In every single professional area with a majority of women, the male professionals' wages are far below what their education would ordinarily merit and the female professionals' wages are much farther below what their education should merit. In a few areas the men's wages are slightly above the average (though their education merits more); in no area do the women's wages even approach the average. These low wages are due to overcrowding as a result of segregation of women professionals. Weakened bargaining power, disunity, and lack of unions due to men's sexist attitudes, women's socialization, and successful "divide and rule" tactics by employers are further contributing factors.

Why then have women not invaded the men's professions in greater numbers? For a woman to achieve success in a prestige profession means overcoming an enormous number of barriers. These obstacles to success may be divided, somewhat arbitrarily, into three major categories: the sexist socialization of women, discrimination against women by men who are sexist because of their socialization, and the traditional structure of the professions and the family.

TABLE 6.1
Education and Income in Selected "Female" Professions, 1970*

Profession	Percentage by which median education is above median of all U.S. male workers		Percentage by which median earnings are above or below median of all U.S. male workers	
	Male	Female	Male	Female
Librarian	+38%	+35%	+1%	−19%
Dietician	+3	+5	−21	−41
Registered nurse	+10	+8	−8	−26
Therapist	+30	+33	+3	−29
Clinical lab technician	+20	+19	−5	−27
Therapy assistant	+5	+2	−9	−50
Religious worker	+34	+20	−21	−68
Social and recreational worker	+34	+33	+4	−19
Elementary teacher	+37	+35	+7	−14
Kindergarten teacher	+31	+29	−31	−60

*In all professions listed, women are a majority of the total.
Source: Department of Commerce, *1970 Census of Population*, Subject Report PC(2)–7A, Occupational Characteristics, Table 1.

THE SOCIALIZATION OF WOMEN

Women are socialized from infancy to accept certain roles and to reject others as "unfeminine." These roles are taught to them in the family, churches, schools, and media. Thus for Christmas a girl gets either a dollhouse so she can learn to be a "mommy" or a nurse's outfit; a boy gets a doctor's kit or an astronaut's helmet. Even when parents attempt to rear their children in a nonsexist fashion, peer pressure often undermines their efforts in everything from choice of toys to choice of high school courses. Math and science are still considered masculine disciplines. Consequently, high school girls are still much less likely to take these courses. This results in a narrowing of the majors girls can pursue in college and, thus, a narrowing of career options. Most high schools do little to make girls aware of this. More generally, the creativeness and independence necessary for professional work are still suspect qualities in women.

The lack of role models is another problem. Although girls growing up now are quite likely to have working mothers, these mothers will probably hold women's jobs. Because women are still relatively rare in the prestige professions, girls are not likely to know professional women personally. The media are more likely today than they were a few years ago to show professional women, but the vast majority of role models and major characters are still male. At college, most of the professors, especially in disciplines outside the humanities, will be men.

This socialization makes the average woman less apt to try to enter a profession and less apt to be successful in the attempt than a man, but this internal barrier is not the most important obstacle a woman faces. It is strongly reinforced by sex discrimination at all levels and by external structural barriers.

DISCRIMINATION IN THE PRESTIGE PROFESSIONS

The immediate cause of sex discrimination is the sexist attitude of male professionals, attributable both to their own sexist socialization and to their selfish interests (the latter being usually much less important and often unconscious). For example, a New York professor of art says "art is male, . . . aesthetic values are in masculine terms."[2] How can he act equally toward male and female students?

Following are other sexist comments made by male faculty members to women graduate students and even to women faculty.[3]

> "A pretty girl like you will certainly get married; why don't you stop with an M.A.?"

> "You're so cute. I can't see you as a professor of anything."

> "Women are intrinsically inferior."

> "Any woman who has got this far has got to be a kook."

Another man said to a prospective female faculty member that the department already had "too many" women. Still another told a candidate that he could not take women seriously in his profession. Another looked at a woman who was being interviewed for a job and asked her age; then, he said she probably couldn't handle the job because she didn't look like the "academic" type. A dean told a woman who was trying to enter graduate school that they would take any man, but that a woman should have at least an A— average from Bryn Mawr. Another dean told a young widow (with a 5-year-old child) that she didn't need to go to gradu-

---

[2]Quoted in Judith Hole and Ellen Levine, *Rebirth of Feminism* (New York: Quadrangle, 1971), p. 366.

[3]Quoted by Ann Harris in New York Commission on Human Rights, *Women's Role in Contemporary Society* (New York: Avon, 1972), pp. 587–588.

ate school because she was quite attractive and could easily find a man to marry her. And, he added, he wouldn't give her a fellowship because men needed aid more than she did. Finally, over 50 percent of 3000 academic men replied to a questionnaire that the prime responsibility of a woman is to be a mother and wife, that women don't have as much need to achieve as men, and that women do have an equal opportunity to achieve their full potential (presumably while staying at home).[4] A majority also believed the myth that women have higher job turnover and sick-leave rates, and most believed that women cannot deal with men who are their subordinates.

Such sexist attitudes on the part of academic men are not merely curiosities, they distort their judgments of women as students and as colleagues. As one careful study in educational psychology puts it, "The expectations and prejudices of those who judge the performance of anything from white rats to human beings are reflected in the judgments they make."[5] Thus sexist prejudices affect judgments on admissions, grading, hiring, and promotion of women. There is even evidence that they negatively affect the performance of women students.

The beliefs of prejudiced people bias the way in which they perceive women, furnishing distorted "facts" to confirm their prejudices. The John McKay/Joan McKay experiment described in Chapter 3 shows that both male and female students tend to be sexist in just this way.[6] Their biases do distort their perceptions of women. Does this mean that students and colleagues and reviewers evaluate books and articles by women differently from those by men? Does it mean that student evaluations of teaching are biased against women? It probably does.

Admissions

In this era of equality it is still true that "girls need higher grades for admission to many institutions."[7] For example, in 1970 the University of North Carolina at Chapel Hill still said openly: "Admission of women on the freshman level will be restricted to those who are

[4]Ibid., p. 584.

[5]R. Rosenthal and L. Jacobson, *Pygmalion in the Classroom: Teacher Expectation and Pupils' Intellectual Development* (New York: Holt, Rinehart and Winston, 1968).

[6]Philip Goldberg, "Are Women Prejudiced Against Women?" in Athena Theodore, ed., *The Professional Woman* (Cambridge, Mass.: Schenkman, 1971), p. 168.

[7]Bernice Sandler, in U.S. Congress, House, Committee on the Judiciary, Hearings on *Equal Rights for Men and Women* (Washington, D.C.: Government Printing Office, 1971), p. 267.

especially well-qualified." Maximum quotas for women graduate students have been exposed in departments of art, genetics, and journalism, as well as in law and medical schools.

In a 1969 survey, deans of medical schools were asked about their policies for admitting women.[8] The following are some selected answers: Dean A, "We have refused to admit women with children." Dean B, "We would not admit a married student unless she was quite outstanding." Dean C, "I have enough trouble understanding my wife and daughters without attempting to explain the questions in this paragraph." Dean D (orally to a woman applicant, a Phi Beta Kappa in chemistry), "I cannot accept you this year because I have my quota of women. . . . My God, I don't know what I am going to do with all these female over-achievers who keep applying." In medical school some male doctors and students perpetuate these sexist attitudes. A male medical student said to a female, "You don't belong here, sweetie, you took the place of some guy who could make a more significant contribution than you will."

In 1968, the chairman of a political science department said: "We don't discriminate against women. We just put all the applications from women at the bottom of the stack; when we run out of qualified men, we consider women."[9] And in the debate on the Civil Rights Act of 1964, a congressman pointed out that in Virginia "21,000 women were turned down for college entrance during a period when not one male applicant was rejected."[10] As a result of such discrimination, women college freshmen have higher high school grades than men. Entering women graduate students also have higher college grades than men.

Partly as a result of socialization and partly as a result of biased admissions policies, the ratio of women to all students declines at higher levels. In 1970, women received 51 percent of the high school diplomas but only 42 percent of the B.A.s, 40 percent of M.A.s, and 13 percent of Ph.D. degrees.[11] In the last few years, the situation has improved somewhat. By 1978, the number of women and men in colleges had essentially reached equality.[12] Women re-

[8]Reported by Joan Flannigan, in New York Commission on Human Rights, op. cit., p. 359.

[9]Reported in Lucy Komisar, *The New Feminism* (New York: Warner Books, 1972), p. 137.

[10]Doris Pullen, "The Educational Establishment," in Mary Thompson, ed., *Voices of the New Feminism* (Boston: Beacon, 1970), p. 133.

[11]Rudolph Blitz, "Women in the Professions," *Monthly Labor Review* 97 (May 1974): 38.

[12]National Center for Education Statistics, *Digest of Education Statistics 1980*, p. 93.

ceived 47.1 percent of the B.A.'s, 48.3 percent of the M.A.'s, and 26.4 percent of the Ph.D.'s in 1977–1978.[13] Women still tended to get their degrees in traditionally female fields, however. Thus, more than half the masters degrees and 34.9 percent of the Ph.D.'s earned by women in 1977–1978 were in education.[14]

Financial aid

Many of the best scholarships were limited to men until recently. This was the case, for instance, at New York University Law School before a major protest by women forced a change in policy. Even without formal limitations, most male-dominated faculty committees award more financial aid to male than female graduate students on the stereotyped grounds that "the men need the money more" and "the men are the more devoted students."

One woman graduate student reported that both she and her husband had applied for fellowships.[15] Even though she had the higher grades, he received a fellowship and she did not. Why? He was married and had a child; thus he needed the money and was considered a good risk because he had settled down. She was told that because she was married and had a child, she was a poor risk. Not only do institutions give less aid to women, parents also reveal the usual sexist attitude by giving more financial aid to their sons than to their daughters who are in school.

A comprehensive study of all college faculty in Minnesota found that women more often than men financed their graduate training out of their own personal savings: ". . . men far exceeded women in the use of scholarships and fellowships, staff appointments as teaching research assistants, GI aids and 'earnings of a spouse'."[16] Yet remember that the average graduate woman has better college grades than the average graduate man.

In a careful study of all departments of political science, it was found that all four groups questioned—female and male graduate students, female and male faculty—put bias in financial assistance and scholarships near the top of their lists of types of discrimination against women graduate students.[17] In fact, in 1970, female graduate students in political science, *who had top honors in col-*

[13]Ibid., p. 120.

[14]Ibid., pp. 119–120.

[15]Riverside, California, *Daily Enterprise,* May 15, 1974.

[16]Ruth Eckert and John Stecklein, "Academic Women," in Theodore, op. cit., p. 349.

[17]Jean and Philip Converse, "Status of Women as Students and Professionals in Political Science," *P.S.* 4 (summer 1971), 342.

lege, were supported 50 percent by fellowships but only 17 percent by assistantships, and 33 percent were forced to support themselves with their own resources. Among male graduate students with similar top honors, 50 percent were supported by fellowships but 47 percent received assistantships and only 3 percent were forced to use their own resources.[18] There is more discretion (and hence more room for prejudice) in awarding teaching assistantships than in awarding fellowships, since the latter are awarded almost exclusively on the basis of grades. Whatever the reason, almost all men with top honors got support, while one-third of the women did not.

Training
Most of the discrimination in training that has been objectively proved is the discrimination in financial aid just mentioned. In addition, however, the sexist attitudes of faculty obviously prejudice their handling and evaluation of women students. This is most evident in the areas of medicine and law. A recent graduate of Harvard Law School reports that as late as 1970, several professors still had "ladies days," when they asked female law students cute questions about supposedly female areas of the law. On all other days women students were ignored.[19] No women were admitted to Harvard Law School until 1950, and only about 3 percent of its students have been female since then. Until 1970, the only eating place in the law school, Lincoln's Inn, did not admit women. Women couldn't play on the squash courts at Harvard until 1971. The absence of women faculty members at Harvard Law School was not only an instance of discrimination but also deprived female students of successful role models.

Women law school graduates in Indiana were subjected to blatant sexism on the 1973 bar examination. One of the major questions ridiculed women involved in the women's movement. The hypothetical case the students were to analyze concerned an article written by a mythical movement activist named Ms. Clytemnestra Toris, the editor-publisher of *The Daily Dildo.* The article was described as "infantile, sophomoric and freshmanic . . . poorly reasoned, unresearched and written with her usual strident and shrill hysteria."[20]The

---

[18]Ibid.,p.339.
[19]See Brenda Easteau, "Law and Women," in Jonathan Black, *Radical Lawyers* (New York: Avon, 1971), p. 240.
[20]*Women's Rights Law Reporter* (April 1974): 38. The entire question is reproduced on pp. 37–39.

question was not just offensive and tasteless, it very likely had a negative impact on women's performance on the exam. The response it deserved would not have received a passing grade.

Entry and hiring

Women were simply prohibited from entering medicine and law for much of the nineteenth century. As late as 1872, the United States Supreme Court agreed that the state of Illinois could refuse to admit a woman (Myra Bradwell) to practice law.

Until recently, blatant hiring discrimination was typical in the prestige professions. As late as March 1970, the psychology department of Lehman College (of City University of New York) advertised for a faculty vacancy: "prefer male, but will consider either."[21] Theodore Lowi, a well-known political scientist, reported that "A very high proportion of my graduate students were women, and collectively they were in every respect the equal of the male candidates. Yet, I had tremendous difficulty getting interviews for them."[22] Women lawyers often met similar problems. Many were told by employment agencies: "Well, we don't have anything for a woman lawyer, but we have some openings for legal secretaries."[23] A female law student at Harvard reported that when she graduated in 1970, she was refused four separate law jobs on the simple ground that she was a woman. In the 1970 Harvard class 99 percent of the men, but only 44 percent of the women, received two or more job offers. Moreover, 72 percent of the men, but only 52 percent of the women, got jobs with law firms.[24] In 1967, in a study of 1300 women law graduates, the women reported 1963 separate cases in which they were told "we do not hire women" by law firms, banks, unions, corporations, and government agencies.[25] The same survey asked the women lawyers if they had suffered sex discrimination in hiring or other ways: 50 percent said yes with "certainty"; another 18 percent said "probably."

One need not rely upon such reports for proof; a number of careful studies provide more evidence. In one, the subjects were 30 male undergraduate industrial management students and 30 male

[21]Bernice Sandler, "Patterns of Discrimination and Discouragement in Higher Education," in New York Commission on Human Rights, op. cit., p. 575.

[22]Women's Caucus for Political Science, *Newsletter* (fall 1973).

[23]Sue Caplan, in New York Commission on Human Rights, op. cit., p. 408.

[24]Easteau, op. cit., p. 245.

[25]See James White, "Women in the Law," *Michigan Law Review* 65 (April 1967), 1053.

professional interviewers representing a wide range of companies. Each was given 12 resumes and asked to rate and rank the applicants as to suitability for a management position. Both groups rated male applicants higher than female applicants, and 72 percent chose a male for the first-rank position. Since the resumes were identical except for the sex of the applicant, this study provides clear evidence of discrimination on the basis of sex.[26]

In another study, chairmen of psychology departments were sent descriptions of ten hypothetical young psychology Ph.D.'s.[27] They were asked to rank the candidates and to indicate at what level the candidate should be offered a position. The sex of the hypothetical candidates was systematically varied. Male candidates were consistently deemed worthy of higher level positions than identical female candidates and were generally ranked higher in terms of desirability. When a description indicated the candidate was female, the modal position considered appropriate was that of assistant professor; for males, associate professor was the appropriate modal position. None of the respondents considered any of the women candidates ready for a full professorship, although some did consider identical men candidates for that position. These studies show that women per se tend to be perceived as less qualified even when there is no supporting evidence.

The last decade has seen considerable improvement. In law, for example, the large prestigious firms have begun to hire women in significant numbers: In 1980, 21.5 percent of the lawyers working for the 50 largest firms were women.[28]

Still, discrimination has by no means disappeared. In law, women are still overrepresented in the less professionally prestigious and monetarily rewarding specialities.[29] In academia, women are found disproportionately in the smaller teaching colleges, as opposed to the more prestigious research-oriented universities.[30] This, of course, has a negative impact upon academic women's further career success. The fact that a higher percentage of women must take

[26]Robert Dipboye, Howard Franklin, Kent Wilback, "Relative Importance of Applicant Sex, Attractiveness, and Scholastic Standing in Evaluation of Job Applicant Resumes," *Journal of Applied Psychology* 60 (February 1975), 39–43.

[27]L. S. Fidell, "Empirical Verification of Sex Discrimination in Hiring Practices in Psychology," *American Psychologist* 25 (December 1970), 1094–1098.

[28]Cynthia Fuchs Epstein, *Women in Law* (New York: Basic Books, 1981), p. 75.

[29]Ibid., p. 381.

[30]Cynthia Epstein, *Woman's Place* (Berkeley: University of California Press, 1971), p. 180. See also Jessie Bernard, *Academic Women* (University Park: Pennsylvania State University Press, 1946), p. 93.

jobs in the smallest colleges (and at the lowest levels) not only lowers their average pay but handicaps them in other ways: "Being burdened with the heavier teaching and service loads characteristic of junior-level positions, they . . . had little opportunity to do research and scholarly writing."[31]

Since most women are in small colleges with big teaching loads, Kreps talks about "apparent preference for teaching."[32] She quotes Jessie Bernard in saying that women follow this teaching pattern where men follow the research pattern: "Women tend to serve in institutions which emphasize different functions, and they themselves are attracted to different kinds of functions." Nonsense! This is not primarily a preference; it is due mainly to discrimination. Kreps and Bernard admit that there is some discrimination, but do not see that this pattern must be due *mostly* to discrimination. Certainly undergraduate socialization might lead some women to emphasize teaching, since they are told that teaching is "more feminine" than research. Kreps admits that most women receive Ph.D.'s from the same universities as men—where graduate socialization is fiercely in favor of research. Therefore, she should also admit that the difference in job patterns must be due primarily to discrimination.

There is also segregation of academic women by area: Most women are in history, English, sociology, and Romance languages. Because of the oversupply of women, these areas have lower-than-average salaries. They are also considered "women's areas" *because* of the low wages. Kreps again makes the mistake of thinking women simply prefer or are solely interested in these areas: "What we do not know is the extent of women's interests in the future in areas other than the humanities."[33] Academic women are not born with interests in these specialties, they are herded into them by sexist socialization in their upbringing and training and by present discrimination, which keeps them out of other areas.

Another problem of discrimination in hiring is the existence of antinepotism rules at many U.S. colleges and universities. The antinepotism rules merely specify that two related individuals cannot be hired in the same academic unit. The rules have the worthy purpose of preventing favoritism due to family ties in hiring and promotion, and they sound fair. The problem arises because a large percentage of academic women marry men in the same field. In 1967,

---

[31]Eckert and Stecklein, op. cit., p. 352.

[32]Juanita Kreps, *Sex in the Marketplace* (Baltimore: Johns Hopkins Press, 1971), p. 59.

[33]Ibid., p. 60.

55 percent of married women with professional and engineering degrees were married to men with the same degrees.[34] In practice, therefore, the rules discriminate against many academic women because no one ever suggests hiring the wife and letting the husband stay home.

The dimensions of the problem are apparent in a study of 18 of the most creative U.S. women mathematicians, each selected as being far above the average by mathematicians—most of them male—in their specialized fields.[35] The main point of the study is that the personalities of the women mathematicians are very similar to those of all other women (surely this is not surprising), but that they have more of the qualities found in most creative people, such as independence, flexibility, and pleasure in research. The study then mentions, almost casually, that the most creative *male* mathematicians "held important positions" at prestigious universities. In contrast, only two or three of the creative women taught graduate students, and one-third, including some of the highest rated, had no regular position at all. Several had young children. Most of the married ones were married to mathematicians, so that nepotism was a constant problem.[36]

In the last few years, many institutions have abolished their antinepotism rules. Most, however, are still leery of hiring a married couple. Since sexism results in men being perceived as more qualified than women with identical records, this leeriness works to the detriment of women. Too often a superbly qualified woman will be used for academic slave labor by a university where her husband holds a full-time position. She will be hired on a part-time basis at low pay to teach courses when the department needs her and let go when not needed.

Working conditions
Women do not have as much access to colleagues for serious discussions and information. Yet this access is crucial in the professions, because so much important information is still unpublished and because one needs the stimulation. Some men simply won't hold a serious discussion with any woman. Some important meetings are routinely held in explicitly men-only clubs or men's associations or implicitly men-only golf courses or luncheons. An amusing illustra-

[34]Jessie Bernard, *Women and the Public Interest* (Chicago: Aldine, 1971), p. 190.
[35]See Ravena Helson, "Women Mathematicians," in Judith Bardwick, ed., *Readings on the Psychology of Women* (New York: Harper & Row, 1972), pp. 93–100.
[36]Ibid., p. 97.

tion of this problem appeared in the late 1960s in the political profession. At a Washington party given by Perle Mesta, one of the guests was a woman senator. After dinner the men retired to another room to discuss politics, while the women were supposed to engage in "women's talk." After consideration, the woman senator joined the men. Although this tale had a happy ending for the senator, it prompts the question: How many times are women professionals (and all women) hopelessly segregated at parties?

In most professions it is important for a student to be the protégé of some prominent member, but men will seldom accept women as protégés and won't push to get them employed even when they do. The famous anthropologist Ruth Benedict was the protégé of Franz Boas, but he thought she didn't need much money because her husband supported her, and that she would never work hard. He helped get her an assistant professorship only after she separated from her husband.[37] Another particularly unpleasant but well documented problem of professional women is that secretaries (and other staff) are far more willing to carry out important tasks for males than for females. This results, of course, from the sexist socialization of the secretaries, even though most are women.

Journalism, as a male-dominated field, has all the problems mentioned earlier. But there are also some additional ones with the "personalities" women must interview. While at a public bill-signing ceremony in the White House in 1973, President Nixon had some sexist "fun" with reporter Helen Thomas. He said, "Helen, are you still wearing slacks? Do you prefer them actually? . . . Slacks can do something for some people and some it can't. I think you do very well—turn around. . . . Do they cost less than a gown?" "No," she replied. " 'Then change,' the President suggested, and everyone in the room laughed."[38]

Women in male-dominated professions often find themselves isolated. Being a member of the "old-boy network" may be necessary for career advancement and simply for having a real say in decisions. According to a women medical school professor, "In Tucson, students and professors go quail hunting together; in Los Angeles, it might be sailing. Whatever the form of camaraderie, women lose out because they're not invited."[39] Women also find themselves evaluated by different standards than are applied to their male peers. Thus a woman professor was criticized for wearing slacks, for refus-

[37]Epstein, op. cit., p. 170.
[38]Washington *Post,* August 7, 1973.
[39]*Los Angeles Times,* November 11, 1981.

ing to use sexist language, and for employing an informal teaching style. A colleague even said to her, "I'm suspicious of the quality of your articles, given their quantity."[40] A woman engineer, the first in her department, was first seated near the secretaries and the men expected her to answer the telephones. "I told them I was not going to do that. They don't. I am there to be an engineer."[41]

A woman who is very successful early in her career may find herself a subject of malicious rumors. Many people are unwilling to attribute such success to ability and hard work; rather, they assume a woman's rapid rise is the result of having slept with the boss. Mary Cunningham, a 29-year-old MBA from Harvard, was promoted to vice-president of strategic planning at Bendix Corp. Rumors that her rapid advancement was the result of a personal relationship with Bendix's chairman got so bad that she was forced to resign. This is not an atypical case. An experienced business woman said she has heard similar rumors about other top business women "more times than I care to recount."[42] A young man who was rapidly promoted said, "I'd be willing to bet that if a woman my age was promoted to executive vice-president, people would say she could only do so by hanky-panky with the president."[43]

This problem is not just an annoyance; it is a serious barrier to women's advancement. "It's a truism of American business that young people who rise rapidly have a mentor, someone who knows their abilities and will push for them despite their age,"[44] a senior executive explained. Men are not often willing to take women on as their protégés. If the price for doing so includes being accused of sleeping with her, even fewer will be willing to do so.

Promotion
The preceding sections show the poorer working conditions of women professionals, biases in evaluations by colleagues and outside reviewers, and poorer initial jobs. It follows that promotion is more difficult and less frequent for women. Obviously, if a woman is perfect, a superwoman, she can get promoted. Obviously too, the average woman is promoted less than the average man. In 1960 the National Academy of Sciences studied a group of men and women,

[40]Linda L. Nielsen, "Sexism and Self-Healing in the University," *Harvard Education Review* 49, no. 4 (1979), 469.
[41]*Los Angeles Times,* June 29, 1981.
[42]*Los Angeles Times,* October 5, 1980.
[43]Ibid.
[44]Ibid.

all of whom received Ph.D.'s in 1935. The study found that women took 2 to 5 years longer to become full professors in the natural sciences and 5 to 10 years longer in the social sciences. In fact, it was found that only 50 percent of women with Ph.D.'s and 20 years' teaching experience were full professors, but 90 percent of men Ph.D.'s with the same teaching experience were full professors.[45]

A more recent study examined men and women who received their Ph.D.'s between 1970 and 1974. Table 6.2 shows the 1979 rank of those who held academic positions. Men were more than twice as likely as women to have been promoted to full professor; more than half the women were still assistant professors or instructors.

A recent study of Harvard Law School graduates found that, 7 years after graduation, 25 percent of the men but only 1 percent of the women were partners in law firms. An American Chemical Society survey reported that although men and women chemists start with nearly equal salaries, after a few years, women are found to have clustered in middle management and men to have moved into upper management.[46]

The pyramid effect
Discrimination in hiring and promotion boxes women into the lower levels of their professions. Most elementary school teachers are women, but the majority of principals are men. About half of all high

---

[45]Kreps, op. cit., p. 53, and Sandler, in New York Commission on Human Rights, op. cit., p. 569.
[46]Los Angeles Times, February 14, 1982.

TABLE   6.2
1979 Rank of Academically Employed Men and Women Who Received Their Ph.D.'s Between 1970 and 1974

Rank	Men	Women
Professor	13.3%	6.3
Associate Professor	48.7	39.2
Assistant Professor	36.8	50.2
Instructor	1.2	4.3

Source: National Research Council—Commission on Human Resources, 1979 Survey of Doctorate Recipients.

TABLE 6.3

Women Faculty at U.S. Colleges and Universities—1978–1979

Rank	Percentage of women
Professor	9.6%
Associate Professor	18.9
Assistant Professor	32.9
Instructor	51.4

Source: National Center for Education Statistics, *Digest of Educational Statistics 1980,* p. 107.

school teachers are women, but most of the principals are men. In the huge Los Angeles school district, for example, women make up 70 percent of the teaching staff but hold only 12 percent of the high school principalships, 16 percent of the junior high and 35 percent of the elementary school principalships.[47] Similarly, most librarians are women, but most chief librarians and library administrators are men. In social work, most caseworkers are women, but most supervisors are men. Most nurses are women, but most doctors are men. Most legal secretaries are women, but most lawyers are men. In advertising and journalism, most researchers are women, but the more prestigious job of writing is mainly reserved for men.

In the academic world, there is a very definite prestige and pay pyramid extending from the many lowly instructorships to the few full professorships. Fewer women hold positions on the higher rungs of the ladder (see Table 6.3). Half the instructors, who are poorly paid and frequently not on the promotion ladder, are women. The well-paid and prestigious full professorships are held predominantly by men.

Women teach at the less prestigious schools. A mid-1970s study found that women constituted 32.3 percent of the faculty at two-year schools, 23.2 percent at four-year schools, and 17.1 percent at universities.[48] The California higher education system shows the same pattern. At the two-year community colleges, which are the lowest in prestige, women were 31.4 percent of tenured faculty in 1979. Women made up 17.6 percent of the tenured faculty of the state colleges. At the prestigious University of California, only

[47]*Los Angeles Times,* February 11, 1981.

[48]Reported in Leigh Beinen, Alicia Ostriker, and J. P. Ostriker, "Sex Discrimination in the Universities: Faculty Problems and No Solutions," *Women's Rights Law Reporter* 2 (March 1975), 5.

TABLE 6.4
**Women as Full-Time Tenure-Track Faculty
in Ph.D.-Granting Departments
of Political Science, 1980**

Rank	Percent of women to total
Professor	3.4
Associate Professor	8.3
Assistant Professor	20.4

Source: Report by Committee on the Status of Women in the Profession, *P.S.* 13 (spring 1980), 221–223.

7.5 percent of the tenured faculty and 11 percent of the total faculty were women.[49] The most prestigious schools are the least likely to hire and promote women. In the academic year 1969–1970, there were no women among the 350 associate and full professors in the Faculty of Arts and Sciences at Harvard.[50] Five years later, after a great deal of pressure on academic institutions by the women's movement, there were 13. During the 1974–1975 academic year, 55 women held associate or full professorships at Princeton, Yale, Harvard, and Columbia. These women constituted 2.7 percent of the total faculty in those ranks—a very modest increase over the 1.0 percent that women held in 1969–1970.

The pattern of relegating women to the lower ranks and the less prestigious schools is found with monotonous regularity in every discipline one examines. Taking political science as an example, we see that in 1980 only 3.4 percent of the professors in departments that granted Ph.D.'s were women (see Table 6.4). Granting the Ph.D. is a minimum definition of a prestigious department or a department to which aspiring women scholars will want to go for training. Yet there are only 34 women full professors and 44 women associate professors at all these schools combined.[51] The role model problem for women graduate students is obvious. In departments that grant master's degrees but not Ph.D.'s, the situation is better—but only in comparison. There, 5.3 percent of full professors and 16.8 percent of associate professors are women. The most prestigious depart-

[49]*Los Angeles Times,* October 18, 1981.
[50]Beinen, op. cit., pp. 5–6.
[51]All data on political science from a report by the Committee on the Status of Women in the Profession, *P.S.* 13 (spring 1980), 221–223.

ments are again the worst offenders. Yale has no woman at either the associate or full professor level; Michigan has one; Harvard and Berkeley have two each.

Academic men have an interesting use of the word *qualified.* Department chairmen often say: "I would be glad to hire a *qualified* woman if I could find one." But they define qualified very differently for women than for men. When it is applied to women, *qualified* really means "best in their field." A University of Chicago history professor said his department "would be happy to hire more women, but there were only three good women historians in the country, and none of them were available."[52]

Other professions are just as guilty of relegating women to lower-paying and less prestigious positions. Although the number of women in law is increasing rapidly, women account for only 2 percent of the partners in the nation's 50 largest law firms, 5 percent of the professors in law schools and 4 percent of all judges.[53] The American Bar Association has never elected a woman to its board of governors nor as chair of its House of Delegates, in which only 14 out of 380 delegates are women. Men dominate the Association's committees and, so far, women have had little success in breaking into the higher ranks. The Association's discriminatory treatment of women candidates for federal judgeships is one negative result of this male domination. A study of judicial nominations for 1976–1979 shows that the ABA rated 70 percent of the men nominated for judgeships in the federal circuit courts of appeals qualified nominees but only 40 percent of the women; 54 percent of the men but only 8 percent of the women nominated to the federal district courts were rated as qualified.

In positions of prestige and power in medicine, too, women are underrepresented. Only 3.6 percent of professorships and 2 percent of department heads in U.S. medical schools are women. No woman is a full dean.[54] In medical school, women are overtly and covertly pressured to enter the traditional female specialties, which are lower in pay and prestige. "Before [being admitted to] medical school, race was the biggest issue," a black woman obstetrician explained. "After I was in medical school, sex was the biggest thing. We [the female students] were expected to do pediatrics, psychiatry,

---

[52]Sandler, in New York Commission on Human Rights, op. cit., p. 570.

[53]The data on law in this paragraph are from Riverside, California, *Press Enterprise,* February 15, 1981.

[54]*Los Angeles Times,* November 11, 1981.

radiology, anesthesia or pathology. Certainly not anything in general medicine and definitely not surgery."[55] If a woman persists in persuing a "male" speciality, she must do so in the face of stiff resistance from peers and professors. "If the whole time you are doing surgery, everyone is hostile and negative, that is bound to affect you," another woman doctor explained.[56] Physicians, after they have finished their speciality training, must rely on other doctors for referrals. "They never even consider referring to you unless the patient specifically asks for a woman physician," a woman doctor reported.[57] In the last few years, patient prejudice seems to have almost disappeared, women physicians say. They are no longer asked constantly if they are the nurse. According to Dr. Marlys Witte, a professor of surgery at the University of Arizona College of Medicine, "The problem now is among peers."[58]

Earnings

In all the professions, women on the average are paid less than men. Table 6.5 presents data on selected professions taken from the 1970 census. In each profession, women are paid substantially less. An apologist might argue that women's lower earnings merely reflect less training or experience. Such differences do not account for anywhere near all the differences in earnings. In academia, for example,

[55]*Los Angeles Times,* July 12, 1981.
[56]Ibid.
[57]*Los Angeles Times,* November 11, 1981.
[58]Ibid.

TABLE   6.5
Median Earnings in Selected Professions, 1970

Profession	Men	Women	Women's earnings as a percentage of men's
Physician	$25,000+	$9788	less than 39%
Lawyer	18,749	8980	48
Engineer	13,151	9648	73
Life and physical scientist	12,025	7518	63
Social scientist	13,280	7687	58
College and university teacher	11,248	6220	55

Source: Department of Commerce, *1970 Census of Population,* Subject Reports, Occupational Characteristics, PC(2)-7A, Table 1.

women at each rank earn less than men, the difference for all ranks combined averaging 18 percent.[59] Women engineers with 11 years of experience earned $2500 a year less than men with the same amount of experience.[60] When both education and type of employer were held constant, women chemists were found consistently to make less than comparable males (see Table 6.6). Furthermore, women with a master's degree make less than men with only a bachelor's, and women Ph.D.'s make only slightly more than men with only the master's.

Perhaps the most careful research survey of all was done by James White on salaries of women lawyers.[61] Using a sample of 1300 female and 1300 male law graduates, he found that the median salary of the women was $1500 less than the men's in the first year after graduation. Ten years later, the median salary of the men was $8300 higher than that of the women. Of course it could always be said that these enormous differences were due to factors other than discrimination, but in White's survey every conceivable factor was taken into consideration.

First, the men may have graduated from better or more prestigious law schools. White used all the women graduates from a list of schools and asked the schools to select at random an equal number of men graduates, so there were the same percentages by sex from low- and high-prestige schools. Second, perhaps the men had

[59]Mary Keyserling, "The Economic Status of Women in the United States," *American Economic Review* 66 (May 1976), 206.

[60]U.S. Department of Labor, Woman's Bureau, *1975 Handbook on Women Workers*, p. 158.

[61]White, op. cit.

TABLE   6.6
Average Salaries (in Thousands of Dollars) of Chemists Who Were Members of the American Chemical Society, March 1974

Type of employer	B.A.		M.A.		Ph.D.	
	Women	Men	Women	Men	Women	Men
Industry	$13.3	$18.0	$14.0	$20.0	$21.0	$23.4
Educational institution	9.0	11.5	11.0	14.0	15.0	17.5
Government	15.2	18.7	15.0	19.5	20.9	24.0

Source: U.S. Department of Labor, Women's Bureau, *1975 Handbook on Women Workers*, p. 158.

more experience. White's sample took men and women from the same graduating classes. Third, perhaps more men worked full time than the women. White used only women who worked full time at law. Fourth, perhaps the men happened to be brighter than the women. There was no significant difference in law-class standing nor in law review participation. Fifth, perhaps relatively more women than men worked for low-paying employers. Yes, women were more likely to work for the government, where pay is relatively low, rather than for private firms. But they were paid less (in similar proportions) in *both* areas, so employer segregation was an additional cause but not the only cause of lower wages. Sixth, perhaps relatively more women worked in low-paying specialties. Yes, White found, women were forced to work relatively more in the low-paying areas—trusts and estates and domestic relations. But they were paid less (in similar proportions) in all fields, so the segregation by field also explained some but not all of the lower wages. Eliminating all these excuses, White concluded that sex discrimination as well as segregation accounts for the lower wages.

Another study of matched graduates from the classes of 1953–1959 of Harvard Law School found that in 1970, some 70 percent of the full-time women lawyers were making less than $20,000, whereas only 16 percent of the men lawyers were making less than $20,000.[62]

In political science, a survey by the American Political Science Association found that in 1970 men faculty averaged $17,000 a year, but women faculty only $10,500.[63] Careful corrections for possession of Ph.D. training, quality of graduate school, and amount of professional work experience still found women with the same training and experience making $3750 a year less than comparable males.[64] The survey then corrected for every other conceivable factor, including productivity, and still found that "as far as we can carry inquiry there remains significant differentials by sex in annual incomes after a wide variety of extenuating circumstances are dutifully taken into account."[65]

Fringe benefits
The biggest problem in the area of fringe benefits comes with preg-

[62]See Easteau, op. cit., p. 246.
[63]Converse, op. cit., p. 342.
[64]Ibid., p. 343.
[65]Ibid., p. 345.

nancy, which is often not included under possible sicknesses, either for sick leave or for free medical care. Yet even counting pregnancy, men have longer absences from work than women. At a California college, a woman faculty member was refused a 2-week sick leave to have a baby. Yet the same college allows "sick leave" for a male faculty member to help at home when his wife has a baby! Furthermore, until recently, at many colleges and most elementary and high schools, a woman could not get a short, paid sick leave for pregnancy, but she was *required* to take an *unpaid* leave of up to a year's length.

OBSTACLES OF TRADITIONAL FAMILY STRUCTURE

A woman is expected to do the housework regardless of her job, so the average American woman Ph.D. spends 28 hours a week on household tasks.[66] A number of studies have shown that when the wife goes to work, the husband does not increase the amount of housework he does. It is also expected by traditional sexists that a woman will follow her husband wherever he decides to go. This traditional family folkway restricts the geographic mobility of professional women, so their choice of jobs is much more limited than other professionals'.

Because of child care and housework duties in traditional families, about half of all professional women interrupt their careers for family purposes. These interruptions have drastic negative effects. A study of 300 professional women shows that "the achievement level of women with interrupted work histories was far below that of women with uninterrupted work histories, fewer than a third as many showing a high achievement level [7 percent to 23 percent] and five times as many showing a low achievement level [36 percent to only 7 percent]."[67] Dropping out and then going back to a career also presents more difficult problems of adjustment for her and her family.

Women in our society are forced to interrupt careers for children because society does not provide decent child care, nor does it provide maternity leaves. If women were given one- or two-month maternity leaves with pay, as in some countries, plus more unpaid leave if necessary, plus publicly run high-quality child care, they would not have to interrupt their careers—assuming that the husband is also willing to do his share of housework and child care.

[66]See Patricia Grahame, "Women in Academe," in Theodore, *op. cit.,* p. 729.
[67]*1975 Handbook,* op. cit., p. 174.

This alternative is actually cheaper for society because more professional women would continue to work full time and would achieve more.

In our society women have long faced a cruel dilemma: career *or* marriage. As a result, professional women were more likely to remain unmarried than other women. As late as 1950, only 59 percent of women with Ph.D.'s were married.[68] There has been some change. A 1966 study found that 72 percent of women Ph.D.'s were married, and some lived with men without being married. It is important to note that these lower percentages of married professional women do not represent inherent psychological preferences for a life without love or sex. Some were driven to "choose" a career instead of marriage because of the rigid and sexist structure of the professions and of the traditional family, which made it impossible to have both. Furthermore, there was and is discrimination against married women. In elementary teaching in the nineteenth century and in some colleges as late as the 1930s, there were rules firing women who got married! Discrimination, combined with lack of child-care facilities and unsympathetic husbands, forced women into a cruel choice, and the situation is changing only slowly.

EXCUSES FOR DISCRIMINATION

The first excuse is that education (and jobs) are wasted on women because they drop out. A study based on a large sample of women Ph.D.'s in 1966 found that 96 percent of the unmarried ones worked full time![69] Where the obstacle of marriage was added, 91 percent of the married women Ph.D.'s without children worked (87 percent full time and 4 percent part time). Even when the obstacle of children was added, most highly educated women still did professional work. The percentage of all married women Ph.D.'s with children working professionally is astonishing—85 percent, including 60 percent full time and 25 percent part time.[70]

Thus the notion that women Ph.D.'s drop out is pure myth. It is true that earlier studies showed about 40 percent of all professional women interrupting their careers at some time, mostly to raise small children. Giving birth is not what causes the problem (unless women are not given a brief sick leave). What causes the interruption is the socially determined fact that women alone are responsible for child

[68]Ibid., p. 187.
[69]See Rita Simon et al., "The Woman Ph.D.," in Bardwick, op. cit., p. 83.
[70]Data from ibid., p. 84. Also see Helen Astin, "Participation of Women Doctorates in the Labor Force," in Theodore, op. cit., p. 445.

care. If there were decent child-care facilities and the husband did his half, there need be no interruption. Furthermore, an almost identical number of men, about 50 percent, also interrupt their careers, mostly for military service. It is surely a "curious paradox of human values" that "men have been only slightly criticized for career interruptions in which their task was to kill off other members of the human race; but women have been severely criticized for taking time away from their profession in order to raise the next generation."[71]

Despite the burden of child care, more recent women Ph.D.'s seem less likely to interrupt their careers than older professional women were. A study of women who received the Ph.D. in 1957–1958 found that 91 percent were working, 81 percent full time; 79 percent had not interrupted their careers in the ten years after receiving their doctorate.[72] It need only be added that professional women, in spite of emergency family problems, show no more tardiness or absenteeism than professional men—which is very little in both cases.

The second major excuse for discrimination is that women are less productive; in academia it is claimed that they publish less. Some early studies did find that women faculty were less productive than men in producing books and articles, and in the number of grants they obtained. These studies, however, were unscientific in that they ignored the variables of location and rank. We have seen that women are located disproportionately in the smaller departments of poorer colleges at the lower academic ranks, all of which means heavier teaching loads and less time to do research. In spite of poorer working conditions and in spite of the sexist structure of most families, *women faculty produce identically with men in the same locations and ranks.*[73] The most recent study found that the average woman Ph.D. produced as many books and articles as the average man (without consideration of rank or location!), with slightly less for unmarried women, equal for married women with children, and slightly more for married women without children.[74] The differences are so slight that they could easily be due to sampling biases.

The silliest excuse for wage or financial aid discrimination is that women don't need the money as much as men do. If they are married, their husbands can support them. If they are unmarried,

[71]Lynda Holmstrom, "Career Patterns," in Theodore, op. cit., p. 525.
[72]Bienen et al., op. cit., p. 9.
[73]See Bernard, *Academic Women,* op. cit., pp. 160–170.
[74]Simon, op. cit., p. 90.

they don't need much money because they have no family. Of course many professional women are unmarried heads of households, and many more are equal contributors to a household. At any rate, the excuse is feeble; a capitalist society does not pay people on the basis of their needs.

PROGRESS IN THE PRESTIGE PROFESSIONS

The women's movement has changed attitudes among women. Women are much more likely now than ever before to aspire to a career in one of the prestige professions. Discrimination in admissions and in hiring is now illegal. Although many barriers remain, some real progress has been made. Table 6.7 shows the increase in the proportion of women receiving professional degrees between the early and the late 1970s. During the 1980–1981 school year, 26 percent of all medical students and 34 percent of law school students were women.[75] Even in engineering, women are beginning to be represented. In 1971–1972, women received only 1 percent of engineering B.A.'s; this increased to 4.5 percent in 1976–1977.[76] In 1980–1981, 15 to 20 percent of engineering students were reported to be women.[77]

[75] *Los Angeles Times,* July 12, 1981, and University of California *Bulletin,* October 19, 1981.

[76] National Center for Education Statistics, *Degree Awards to Women: An Update* (1979), pp. 26–27.

[77] *Los Angeles Times,* June 29, 1981.

TABLE 6.7
Women in the Prestige Professions
  (Percent of First Professional Degree
  Recipients Who Are Women)

Field	1971–1972	1977–1978
Medicine	9.0%	21.5
Law	7.2	26.0
Dentistry	1.2	10.9
Optometry	2.2	13.1
Veterinary	9.4	24.5

Sources: National Center for Education Statistics, *Degree Awards to Women: An Update* (1979), p. 30 and *Digest of Education Statistics 1980,* p. 128.

AFFIRMATIVE ACTION AND "REVERSE DISCRIMINATION"

The progress that has been made, modest as it is, has resulted in cries of "reverse discrimination." Charges that the government is forcing universities and corporations to hire unqualified women and minority males are often heard. Because of the tight job market, attacks on affirmative action have been especially virulent in the university. Young white males find it easy to blame women and minority men for their difficulty in getting jobs and they are often encouraged to do so by older white men. Yet there seems to be no single well-documented case of reverse discrimination.

In fact, despite the evidence of continued discrimination against women and blacks, the federal government has done relatively little to ensure that universities make truly nondiscriminatory hiring and promotion decisions. "The government has never really taken this issue on, contrary to myth," said Bernice Sandler, director of the project on the Status and Education of Women, sponsored by the Association of American Colleges. "There have been very few investigations, even fewer critical findings and no funds have ever been cut off, despite the threats."[78]

Academic institutions have developed a variety of techniques to avoid complying in good faith with affirmative action guidelines.[79] Government pressure, which was spotty in the 1970s, has been virtually nonexistent during the Reagan administration. In the 1980s, women will have to produce the pressure for change if any progress is to be made.

[78]*Los Angeles Times,* October 18, 1981.
[79]See Deborah S. Rosenfelt with Gloria DeSole, "Affirmative Action: The Verdict Is Still Out," *Radical Teacher* (March 1979): 4.

WOMEN AND
THE LAW

7

A society's standards as to what is natural and right are reflected in its laws. An examination of the differential treatment of men and women in U.S. federal and state law reveals more than inequalities. It provides another perspective on society's image of women. Under the impetus of the women's movement, that image is beginning to change, and this too is reflected in recent developments in the law.

THE DOUBLE STANDARD INSTITUTIONALIZED:
WOMEN, SEX, AND THE LAW

When it comes to sexual matters, the American woman, according to the law, is a delicate and pure creature who must be protected. To effect such protection, even free speech is not too much to give up. Many states have laws prohibiting obscene or vulgar language in the presence of women. An Arizona statute provides that a person who "in the presence of or hearing of any woman or child, or in a public place, uses vulgar, abusive or obscene language, is guilty of a misdemeanor. . . ."[1] In at least 12 states, inpugning the chastity of a woman is a criminal offense.[2] Many states used to require only the male to get a venereal disease test before issuing him a marriage

[1] Quoted in Leo Kanowitz, *Women and the Law* (Albuquerque: University of New Mexico Press, 1969), p. 175.

[2] Lois J. Frankel, "Sex Discrimination in the Criminal Law: The Effect of the Equal Rights Amendment," *American Criminal Law Review* 2 (winter 1973), 485.

license. In Washington state as late as 1969 the requirement still applied only to men.[3] Obviously the pure, delicate female would not need such a test.

In most states, if an adult male has sexual intercourse with a female who is below a certain age, he is committing the crime of statutory rape. These laws are based on the incapacity of the underage female to give meaningful consent, a principle on which many laws that treat minors differently from adults are based. But why is it assumed that, in the sexual realm, underage males can give meaningful consent? In very few states can an adult female be guilty of statutory rape, and in states where the crime is defined without regard to the sex of the adult, women are not prosecuted. Professor Kanowitz was told in an interview with a California prosecuting attorney that "a district attorney would 'feel silly' if he were to prosecute a 22 year old girl . . . for having sexual relations with a 17 year old boy. No such compunction would arise, however, in prosecuting a 22 year old male for statutory rape because he had engaged in sexual intercourse with a 17 year old girl."[4] The law and the way it is enforced obviously reflect the double standard. Tennessee carries the protection of the female "child" to an absurd point; there the age of meaningful consent is 21.[5] In most states, a female can get married without her parents' consent before that.

Although the laws against forcible rape are intended to protect women, the manner of their enforcement reveals the other side of the double standard. In many states, the maximum penalty for rape is as severe as that for murder—indicating, perhaps, that a violated woman might as well be dead. If a rape victim attempts to bring charges under these laws, however, she frequently suffers more than the rapist. Her character will be attacked, her past sex life scrutinized. Until recently, any and all questions about her sex life were permissible. A common defense tactic has been to discredit the woman by questioning her about her sex life in excruciating and insulting detail. If the jury can be convinced she is promiscuous, they are likely to decide that she consented or, if not, that she deserved being raped.

The notion that a sexually active woman cannot really be raped is very strong; in some places, it is enshrined in the law. Thus, in Cali-

[3]Kanowitz, op. cit., p. 13.
[4]Quoted in ibid., p. 246.
[5]Ibid., p. 21.

fornia, the judge was required to read this "unchastity instruction" to the jury:

> Evidence was received for the purpose of showing that the female person named in the information was a woman of unchaste character. A woman of unchaste character can be the victim of forcible rape but it may be inferred that a woman who has previously consented to sexual intercourse would be more likely to consent again. Such evidence may be considered by you only for such bearing as it may have on the question of whether or not she gave her consent to the alleged sexual act and in judging her credibility.[6]

The attitude expressed in this instruction lends credence to the claims of some lawyers that rape laws are really property laws. Rather than to protect the women, their purpose is to protect a man's private property—his wife or daughters. As an "unchaste" woman who does not "belong" to any particular man is neither valuable nor private property, she is not worth protecting.

The rape laws are further predicated on the assumption that women are liars, for much stricter standards of proof are required than in crimes of comparable seriousness. The woman's word must be corroborated by other testimony.[7] In other crimes, the victim's testimony is sufficient. In California, the judge was required to read the following cautionary instruction to the jury:

> A charge such as that made against the defendant in this case is one which is easily made and, once made, difficult to defend against, even if the person accused is innocent. Therefore the law requires that you examine the testimony of the female person named in the information with caution.[8]

Too many judges and lawyers seem to subscribe to the notion that women frequently make false charges of rape. The author of a 1970 law review article states, "Women often falsely accuse men of sexual attacks to extort money, to force marriage, to satisfy a childish desire for notoriety, to attain personal revenge."[9] Although there is no evidence to support these charges, it has been suggested that all women

---

[6]CALJIC 10.06 (1970 Rev.).

[7]Susan C. Ross, *The Rights of Women* (New York: Avon, 1973) p. 181.

[8]Quoted in American Civil Liberties Union of Southern California news release, May 2, 1974.

[9]Quoted in Barbara Allen Babcock, Ann E. Freedman, Eleanor Holmes Norton, and Susan C. Ross, *Sex Discrimination and the Law: Causes and Remedies* (Boston: Little, Brown, 1975) p. 855.

who bring rape accusations be forced to submit to psychiatric examination.[10]

In some states, a woman must physically resist the rapist; otherwise she is considered to have consented.[11] A typical judge's instruction on nonconsent reads: "Mere verbal protestations and a pretense of resistance are not sufficient to show want of consent. If the female fails to take such measures to frustrate the execution of the male's design as she is able to make and are called for under the circumstances, the inference may be drawn that she did in fact consent."[12] Lack of resistance to a robbery, a mugging, or any other violent crime is not taken as implying consent. Rather, it is often seen as the victim's surest way of surviving the incident. Whatever the law, if the woman cannot show considerable visible injury, the jury will frequently assume that she actually consented.

Given the severity of the penalties for rape, strict standards of proof must be maintained. But justice for the accused rapist does not require the sort of brutal treatment to which the victim is often subjected. The abuse heaped upon the victim reflects society's view that there are two types of women—the pure and the evil. For women, evil is associated with sexuality. It seems to be assumed that good women don't let such things happen to them, that any woman who really wants to resist can do so successfully. The fact that this contradicts a major tenet of the male mystique—the vastly superior strength of the male—and ignores the existence of guns and knives is simply overlooked.

Under pressure from the women's movement, some states have changed their rape laws. In 1974, California, Florida, Iowa, and Michigan passed laws prohibiting introduction of evidence about the victim's previous sexual conduct unless the defendent first demonstrates to the judge that the evidence is relevant to a fact at issue in the case.[13] Some states have repealed laws requiring the more offensive cautionary instructions. On the matter of resistance, progress is also evident. A number of courts have rejected the contention that anything less than resistance to the point of serious physical injury implies consent.[14]

By 1980 every state had considered and most had passed some form of rape reform legislation. Much of the activity occurred be-

[10]Ibid., p. 860.
[11]Ross, op. cit., p. 183.
[12]Babcock, op. cit., pp. 826–827.
[13]*Women's Rights Law Reporter,* March 1975, p. 38.
[14]Ibid., p. 38.

tween 1976 and 1979, when 32 states amended their rape or sex offense laws.[15] One thrust has been toward replacing the single crime of rape with a series of graded offenses and toward reducing the penalties for rape. The rationale for this is that juries will be more likely to convict if the penalties are less severe. A second thrust has been toward limiting the admissibility of evidence of a victim's prior sexual conduct with persons other than the defendant. By 1979, 41 states had passed some legislation of this sort.[16] Typically, a pretrial hearing to determine the relevance of this sort of information is required.

Unfortunately, this impressive progress may be illusionary, at least in part. Leigh Bienen, an expert on rape laws, discusses a number of reasons why such reforms may not accomplish their stated objectives.[17] Many of the statutes exclude evidence of only one particular type or evidence introduced for one particular purpose and thus may have limited practical effects. For example, although evidence of prior sexual activity may not be used to prove consent, it sometimes may be brought out by the prosecution to attack the victims' credibility. Some of the new laws may be drafted too broadly and thus be subject to constitutional challenge. If judges and lawyers are unaware of the new laws, the laws will have little effect. A study of how a reform law in Florida worked in practice found this to be a problem. Since the vast majority of rape cases are handled through plea bargaining, the limitations on admissible evidence may have little effect, while the reduction in penalties may result in shorter sentences. Despite this sobering appraisal, Bienen says, "The educational side effects of getting rape reform legislation passed, rather than the direct substantive impact upon the processes of the criminal justice system, may be most important."[18]

Another area in which some modest changes have occurred is in what is called the *spousal exception.* Under English common law, a man could not be found guilty of raping his wife.[19] This spousal exemption was carried over into American law. Three states have recently eliminated it, and more than 20 have modified it, typically by stipulating that the spousal exemption does not apply when the

[15]Leigh Bienen, "Rape III—National Developments in Rape Reform Legislation," *Women's Rights Law Reporter* 6 (spring 1980), 170–213.
[16]Ibid., p. 197.
[17]Ibid., p. 206.
[18]Ibid., p. 212.
[19]Ibid., p. 184.

parties are legally separated or living apart.[20] It is much too early to determine whether these legal changes will have much practical effect.

The double standard in sexuality is also reflected in elements of divorce law. A number of states provided that a wife's having had intercourse with another man before marriage was grounds for divorce. A husband's similar behavior was not.[21] In some states, a single act of adultery was grounds against the wife but not against the husband. This is still the case in Kentucky.[22] The "unwritten law" defense is actually in the legal code in several states, including New Mexico, Texas, and Utah.[23] It provides that a husband may kill his wife's lover without penalty if he catches them in the act of adultery. If the wife should kill her husband's lover, it would be considered murder.

That it is much worse for women than men to have intercourse outside the bonds of marriage and that if a woman does so she must be made to pay for it are pervasive notions in our society that are only beginning to be cast aside. The "man in the house" rule, applied by many states to female welfare recipients until it was struck down by the Supreme Court in 1968, is a particularly vicious example of these notions.[24] The rule specified that if a man spent the night in her house, a woman could lose her welfare benefits. The public justification for the rule was that if a man lived with her, he could support her and her children. The actual purpose was punitive.

Pregnant girls are routinely expelled from high school, frequently even if they are married. A federal district court has declared the practice of excluding unwed mothers from the public schools unconstitutional. "The fact that a girl has one child out of wedlock does not forever brand her as a scarlet woman undeserving of any chance for rehabilitation or the opportunity for further education," the court said.[25] Thus the court clearly recognized the punitive intention of such rules and their basis in the notion that good girls are sexually pure and bad girls must be made to pay for their behavior.

[20]Ibid., p. 179.
[21]Kanowitz, op. cit., p. 14.
[22]Ibid., p. 96.
[23]Ibid., p. 92.
[24]See Babcock, op. cit., pp. 761–770.
[25]Quoted by Martha Griffiths, in U. S. Congress, House, Committee on the Judiciary, Hearings on *Equal Rights for Men and Women* (Washington, D.C.: Government Printing Office, 1971), p. 38.

The same notion seems to account for a good deal of the opposition to legal abortion. An all-too-common sentiment is: If a woman gets herself into a position in which she may get pregnant, well she's just got to take the consequences. Actually, the right to abortion on request before quickening (about 4 months) had been recognized in common law—before laws prohibiting abortion except to save the life of the mother were adopted by the states during the second half of the nineteenth century—a time of general sexual repression.

A number of states did pass reform laws during the period from 1967 to 1970, but even these laws were still highly restrictive. Abortions could now be obtained if pregnancy would gravely impair the woman's physical or mental health, if the baby was likely to be deformed, or if pregnancy was the result of rape or incest. In 1970, three states—Hawaii, Alaska, and New York—passed much more liberal laws. These came close to abortion on request, although some restrictions on how late in the pregnancy an abortion could be performed were maintained. By 1972, a large number of cases had been brought, and some state abortion laws had been declared unconstitutional by lower courts. In early 1973, the Supreme Court, in the landmark decisions of *Roe* v. *Wade* and *Doe* v. *Bolton,* upheld a woman's constitutional right to abortion.[26] The Court declared that during the first 3 months of pregnancy, the decision on abortion should be left to the woman and her doctor. During the second 3 months, a state may regulate abortion if the regulations are reasonably necessary to protect the woman's health. During the last 3 months, the state may, but need not, ban abortion except to save the mother's life. In *Doe* v. *Bolton,* the Court struck down the requirement of approval by a three-doctor committee and a requirement for special accreditation for hospitals performing abortions.

Attempts to circumvent the decision began immediately. Laws passed in Rhode Island and Utah that, in effect, ignored the decision were also struck down immediately.[27] Laws requiring the consent of the woman's husband were declared unconstitutional by the Supreme Court.[28] The Court further ruled that the states may not impose "blanket" restrictions requiring all minor females to get the consent of a parent.[29]

The U.S. Congress has passed a provision allowing hospitals, even if they receive federal money, to refuse to perform abortions

[26]*Congressional Quarterly Weekly Report* 31 (January 27, 1973), 142.
[27]Babcock, op. cit., p. 380.
[28]Riverside, California, *Daily Enterprise,* July 2, 1976.
[29]Ibid.

on the basis of "religious beliefs and moral convictions."[30] Several federal district courts, on the other hand, have ruled that public hospitals may not refuse to perform abortions.[31] This is an area in which law and practice are still in a state of flux.

Ensuring that poor women have access to abortion has been another problem area. For a while, a number of states refused Medicaid payments for elective abortions, but the courts generally struck down such provisions.[32] In 1976, the U.S. Congress passed the Hyde Amendment, a similar provision denying medicaid reimbursements for elective abortions. A federal district court declared it unconstitutional and ordered the Department of Health, Education, and Welfare to continue medicaid funding.

In June 1977, the Supreme Court ruled that neither the Constitution nor federal Medicaid law requires state governments to pay for elective abortions. While the Hyde Amendment prohibiting the federal government from paying for elective abortions was not at issue, the Court's decision made it unlikely that such provisions would be struck down, and the injunction against its enforcement was lifted.

Each year from 1976 on, Congress approved some version of the Hyde Amendment. By 1980, the conditions under which the federal government would pay for an abortion had become extremely restrictive. Only if the woman's life would be endangered or if the pregnancy were the result of rape or incest promptly reported to the authorities would a poor woman be eligible for a Medicaid abortion. On June 30, 1980, the Supreme Court, in the case of *Harris* v. *McRae,* upheld the constitutionality of the Hyde Amendment. At the same time, in the case of *Williams* v. *Zbaraz,* it upheld an even more restrictive state law barring state medical assistance for all abortions except those "necessary for the preservation of the life of the woman."[33]

Justice Stewart, for the five-man majority, argued, "[Al]though government may not place obstacles in the path of a woman's exercise of her freedom of choice, it need not remove those not of its own creation. Indigency falls in that latter category."[34] In dissent, Justice Brennan wrote:

[30]Babcock, op. cit., p. 983.

[31]U.S. Department of Labor, Women's Bureau, *1975 Handbook on Women Workers* (Washington, D.C.: Government Printing Office), p. 381.

[32]Ibid., pp. 380–381.

[33]*Congressional Quarterly Weekly Report* 38 (July 5, 1980), 1860.

[34]Ibid., p. 1861.

[T]he Hyde Amendment is a transparent attempt by the Legislative Branch to impose the political majority's judgment of the morally acceptable and socially desirable preference on a sensitive and intimate decision that the Constitution entrusts to the individual.

Worse yet, the Hyde Amendment does not foist that majoritarian viewpoint with equal measure upon everyone in our Nation, rich and poor alike; rather, it imposes that viewpoint only upon that segment of our society which, because of its position of political powerlessness, is least able to defend its privacy rights from the encroachments of state-mandated morality.

By thus injecting coercive financial incentives favoring childbirth into a decision that is constitutionally guaranteed to be free from governmental intrusion, the Hyde Amendment deprives the indigent woman of her freedom to choose abortion over maternity, thereby impinging on the due process liberty right recognized in *Roe* v. *Wade*. By funding all of the expenses associated with childbirth and none of the expenses incurred in terminating pregnancy, the government literally makes an offer that the indigent woman cannot afford to refuse.[35]

States may still pay for abortions not covered by the Hyde Amendment, but since they have to finance the full cost, pressure to cease such funding has increased. Even before these decisions, only nine states and the District of Columbia were voluntarily paying for abortions with their own money.[36] Many poor women again face the choice of illegal, unsafe abortions performed by back-alley butchers or forced motherhood.

Laws concerning contraceptives are another institutionalized expression of American puritanism. As late as 1968, 60 percent of the states had laws restricting the dispersal and use of contraceptives.[37] Frequently the restrictions have taken the form of denying contraceptives to the young or unmarried. Legally, these prohibitions apply to both sexes equally, but since it is the female who gets pregnant, she is the one who suffers. A proposed Reagan administration regulation would require notification of the parents when a minor female seeks contraceptives from a federally financed clinic.

In 1965, in the Griswold decision, the Supreme Court threw out a Connecticut law against *using* contraceptives. The decision was based on the law's hampering doctors in the practice of medi-

[35]Ibid., pp. 1861–1862.
[36]Ibid., p. 1860.
[37]Lucinda Cisier, "Unfinished Business: Birth Control and Women's Liberation," in Robin Morgan, ed., *Sisterhood is Powerful* (New York: Vintage Books, 1970), p. 249.

cine and on the violation of marital privacy.[38] A Massachusetts law banning contraceptives for unmarried people was struck down by the Supreme Court in 1971.[39]

When women do not live up to society's image of them as good and pure, the law punishes them. The prostitute is the antithesis of society's ideal woman and is treated as such. She and her customer are treated very differently. He is seldom prosecuted, even if there is a law against patronizing a prostitute.[40] In New York State, the prostitute faces a maximum sentence of three months; the maximum for the customer is 15 days.[41] She can be convicted on the uncorroborated testimony of a policeman posing as a customer. The pimp cannot be convicted on her uncorroborated testimony.[42]

WHEN SHE IS BAD SHE IS HORRID: CRIMINAL PENALTIES FOR WOMEN

The proposition that women are by nature good and pure has a corollary: Bad women, perhaps because they are unnatural, are a lot worse than bad men.

Law and practice with respect to juveniles presents a good example of this principle. The New York State Family Court Act relating to "persons in need of supervision" provides that youths who are "habitually truant, incorrigible, ungovernable or habitually disobedient and beyond lawful control of a parent or guardian" may be imprisoned.[43] The law applies to boys up to age 16: If a boy is imprisoned before he is 16, he may be kept until he is 18. For a girl, however, the age of applicability is 18, and she may be kept until she is 20. This law applies only to noncriminal conduct and, for girls, is used primarily for sexual misconduct.

Sally Gold, a member of the legal staff of the New York City Department of Consumer Affairs, made a study[44] of juvenile delinquents in jails and "homes" across the country. She found that more than half of the girls incarcerated were in for noncriminal conduct such as sexual activity, while only one-fifth of the boys were in for

[38]Ibid., p. 250.

[39]*Eisenstadt* v. *Baird* in *Women's Rights Law Reporter* 1 (spring 1972), 39.

[40]Kanowitz, op. cit., p. 16.

[41]New York City Commission on Human Rights, *Women's Role in Contemporary Society* (New York: Avon, 1972), p. 43.

[42]Norman Dorsen, in ibid., p. 507.

[43]Quoted by Sally Gold, in ibid., pp. 512–513.

[44]Ibid., p. 515.

noncriminal matters. The crimes that girls did commit tended to be minor—shoplifting rather than car theft or burglary—yet girls served significantly longer terms than boys. Even though their crimes or conduct were usually less serious than those of boys, girls were no more frequently let off with a warning. They were sent to reform schools as frequently as boys.

State statutes requiring that women be more severely sentenced than men for committing the same crime have recently come under attack. A lower court upheld, but the Pennsylvania Supreme Court struck down, the Muncy Act, which provided that "women sentenced for offenses punishable by imprisonment for more than one year *must* be sentenced to the maximum permissible term. Men, on the other hand, *may* be sentenced to lesser terms."[45] In 1968, a federal district court struck down a similar Connecticut law.[46] Several other states have such laws, but after these decisions they seemed vulnerable to attack. On October 27, 1971, however, the New Jersey Supreme Court upheld a sentencing law similar to the Muncy Act.[47]

CITIZENSHIP SECOND CLASS: WOMEN'S POLITICAL RIGHTS

In 1851, Ernestine Rose, an early feminist, summed up the political position of women in the United States thus: "In the laws of the land she has no rights; in the government she has no voice."[48] The voice was a long time in coming. Despite the work of women's groups, women were not included in the Fourteenth and Fifteenth Amendments to the Constitution, which granted blacks the rights of citizenship, including the right to vote.

Some hoped that the Supreme Court might interpret the Fourteenth Amendment so as to give women the vote. But in 1875, in the case of *Minor* v. *Happersett,* the court ruled that while women were citizens, suffrage was not one of the privileges and immunities of citizenship protected by the Fourteenth Amendment. The battle

[45]Kanowitz, op. cit., p. 168.

[46]Ibid., p. 197.

[47]*State* v. *Costello.* For a discussion of this and similar statutes and cases, see Carolyn Engel Temin, "Discriminatory Sentencing of Women Offenders: The Argument for the ERA in a Nutshell," *American Criminal Law Review* 2, no. 2 (winter 1973), 357–361.

[48]Ernestine Rose, "On Legal Discrimination," in Aileen S. Kraditor, ed., *Up from the Pedestal* (New York: Quadrangle, 1968), p. 224.

would have to be won in the political arena where women, lacking the vote, had very little power. Starting in 1890 with Wyoming, women did gain the vote in a number of states, but only after the ratification of the Twentieth Amendment in August 1920 were all American women enfranchised. The winning of the vote did not bring about equality. Until 1933 an American woman lost her citizenship if she married an alien. An American man did not.

Equal rights and responsibilities in jury service still have not been established. In 1880, the Supreme Court held that a West Virginia law barring blacks from jury service was unconstitutional but that it was not unconstitutional to bar women.[49] Not until 1966 did a federal district court rule that the exclusion of women from juries was a violation of the Fourteenth Amendment's equal protection clause. In *White* v. *Crook,* the courts struck down an Alabama law, and the ruling also applies to similar laws in Mississippi and South Carolina, the other two states that completely excluded women from juries.[50] Despite this ruling, during the late 1960s women served on juries on the same basis as men in only 32 states. In others, women were granted special exemptions not available to men; in 15, sex alone was a valid exemption. Three states required a woman to register with a clerk of the court if she wished to be considered for jury service.

These special "privileges" were based on the stereotyped notion that women's place is in the home. The Supreme Court, upholding Florida's registration law in 1960, said:

> Woman is still regarded as the center of home and family life. We cannot say that it is constitutionally impermissible for a State, acting in pursuit of the general welfare, to conclude that a woman should be relieved from the civic duty of jury service unless she herself determines that such service is consistent with her own special responsibilities.[51]

Leo Kanowitz, a professor of law, concludes that such special exemptions "freeze the position of women as second-class citizens in the field of political rights. . . . They also express present day vestiges of male supremacy doctrines."[52] Furthermore, if a woman wishes to perform her civic duty, such laws can result in a real hard-

---

[49]*Strauder* v. *West Virginia,* 100 U.S. 303.
[50]Kanowitz, op. cit., pp. 28–29.
[51]*Hoyt* v. *Florida,* quoted in ibid., p. 30.
[52]Ibid., p. 31.

ship. New York State allowed women to refuse jury service on the basis of sex alone. As a result, New York City would not pay the salary of a female employee if she chose to serve. Male employees' salaries were paid during jury service. In 1968, this practice was tested in the courts and upheld.[53]

Finally, in 1975 the Supreme Court declared unconstitutional a Louisiana law that automatically exempted women from jury service unless they volunteered to serve.[54] By that time, only seven states still provided an unqualified exemption for women and only Louisiana required women to volunteer before they would be eligible.[55] Under *Taylor* v. *Louisiana,* states may still grant exemptions to men and women on different grounds so long as the result is a "reasonably representative" jury.[56] In *Duren* v. *Missouri,* decided in 1979, the Supreme Court invalidated a Missouri law giving women the option of being exempted from jury service because of their sex.[57] The Court held that the procedure was a violation of the defendant's right to a jury of a fair cross-section of the community. The Court still did not apply the equal protection clause recognizing harm to the excluded class as well as to the litigant. Thus equality in jury services has still not been established.

A Supreme Court decision handed down in mid-1981 represents a serious blow to equal rights and responsibilities for women and men. In *Rosteker* v. *Goldberg,* the Court ruled that the government may exclude women from the military draft and registration for it. The Court emphasized its traditional deference to Congress in the exercise of its constitutional responsibility to raise and regulate the armed forces, thus presumably signaling that it did not intend the decision to be read as backtracking on women's rights generally. Even so, women are likely to pay heavily for the "privilege" of being exempted from the draft. Justice Marshall in dissent expressed this well. An all-male draft registration, Marshall said, "categorically excludes women from a fundamental civic obligation." With its decision, he said, "the Court today places its imprimatur on one of the most potent remaining public expressions of ancient canards about the proper role of women."[58]

[53]Rose Aronoff, in New York City Commission on Human Rights, *Women's Role in Contemporary Society* (New York: Avon, 1972), p. 562.
[54]*Women's Rights Law Reporter* (March 1975): 33.
[55]Ibid., p. 34.
[56]Ibid., p. 36.
[57]*Women's Rights Law Reporter* (winter-spring 1979): 81–82.
[58]*Congressional Quarterly Weekly Report* 39 (July 27, 1981), 1149.

A SLOW RESURRECTION FROM CIVIL DEATH: MARRIED WOMEN'S RIGHTS

"By marriage, the husband and wife are one person in law; that is, the very being or legal existence of the woman is suspended during the marriage, or at least is incorporated and consolidated."[59] This is the doctrine of coverture as described by Judge Blackstone. A basic principle of English common law, its result was that, upon marriage, a woman lost even the rights she possessed when single. Much of her property became her husband's, and all fell under his complete control. He did not even have to account to her. She could not transfer her property, enter into contracts, or sue or be sued. Marriage meant, in effect, civil death.[60]

Coverture in America

English common law was somewhat less stringently applied in America. Colonial courts had recognized some rights of the wife—to live with her husband in house and bed, to receive support from him even if he abandoned her, to be protected from violence at his hands—although none of these really minimal rights had been recognized in England. The wife was also entitled to inherit the life use of one-third of her husband's estate.[61]

The rich protected their daughters' property through marriage contracts and trusts. Without such an arrangement, if the marriage ended in separation or divorce the husband was entitled to everything—even the wife's clothes.

Starting in 1839, a series of Married Women's Property Acts were passed in a number of states. The earlier laws gave women a right to the property they brought to marriage; later ones gave them a right to the wages they earned. The New York Married Women's Property Act of 1848 provided that the real and personal property that a woman brings with her to marriage "shall not be subject to the disposal of her husband nor be liable for his debts and shall continue her sole and separate property as if she were a single female."[62] This law was passed after a 12-year campaign by feminists. Success was, however, probably due largely to the interest of the wealthy in protecting their daughters' property rights. Ernestine Rose, a femi-

[59]Quoted in Kanowitz, op. cit., p. 35.
[60]Ibid., p. 36.
[61]Andrew Sinclair, The Emancipation of the American Woman (New York: Harper & Row, 1965), p. 84.
[62]Married Women's Property Act, New York, 1848, in Miriam Schneir, ed., Feminism: The Essential Historical Writings (New York: Vintage Books, 1972), p. 73.

nist leader in the campaign, said the act was "not much . . . only for the favored few and not for the suffering many. But it was a beginning and an important step."[63]

The New York Married Women's Property Act of 1860 was of more importance to the average woman. It gave her the right to her earnings and declared her "to be the joint guardian of her children, with her husband, with equal powers, rights and duties. . . . "[64]

Property rights

At present, a married woman's property rights depend on the state in which she lives. In the 42 common law states, the property each spouse brings to marriage and that which each earns is his or her separate property. A wife thus has no present interest in or control over any of her husband's earnings, although upon his death she is entitled to receive a specific share of his property—usually one-third or one-half. A wife who does not work is dependent on her husband's generosity for anything beyond basic support. One New York husband refused to give his wife money for tuition when she wished to complete her education.[65] Under the law, this was his right.

In the eight community property states, marriage is seen as a type of partnership, and the couple's earnings are considered community property. However, until recently the husband had the exclusive right to manage and control that property. In California, for example, the husband was declared by law to be the "head of the family." Until it was changed in the mid-1970s, his control of community property, while no longer absolute, was extensive. He had to obtain his wife's signature to give away, sell, or mortgage real community property; and a 1951 law gave the wife the right to manage and control community property earned by her.[66] But the husband could still dispose of community property such as cars and furniture without his wife's consent, although she could not do likewise. Furthermore, as lawyer Roberta Ralph pointed out, "since a woman doesn't have management and control, she has no say in investments her husband makes. He can go and buy a diamond mine in Alaska.

[63]Rose, quoted in ibid.

[64]Married Women's Property Act of 1860, in ibid., p. 123.

[65]A housewife, in New York City Commission on Human Rights, op. cit., pp. 792–793.

[66]Kanowitz, op. cit., p. 65.

She can say, 'No dear, I don't think so.' And he can say, 'Shut up, dear, I make the decisions.' "[67]

Even after the death of one spouse, the inequality continued. If the wife died first and if she had left her share of the community property to her husband, he did not have to go through probate court. If the husband died first, however, the wife had to probate everything, including her own share. Probate is expensive and inconvenient. The estate could be tied up for months or even years, during which time the woman had no money. She could get support money to tide her over by court action, but again, this costs money and is inconvenient.

Under pressure from feminists, bills to equalize the positions of men and women were passed by the California state legislature. A bill giving wives control equal with their husbands' over community property was signed into law on October 2, 1973, and became effective on January 1, 1975.[68] A bill equalizing procedures for inheriting community property was approved in early 1974 and became effective at the beginning of 1975.

Despite the nineteenth-century Married Women's Property Acts, a number of states still restrict a woman's right to make contracts and her right to engage in business on her own.[69] In Kentucky a woman cannot by herself be sure of (i.e., guarantee) anyone's debt except her husband's. In Georgia, on the other hand, she may not use her separate estate to pay her husband's debts. Some states will not let a woman mortgage or lease her real property unless her husband is involved in the transaction. Maryland places limits on a woman's right to sue and be sued in her own name. Utah places limitations on her right to serve in a position of trust. An Idaho statute providing that "the court is to prefer male over female when persons otherwise entitled to a selection apply to be named an administrator of a descendant's estate" was recently ruled unconstitutional by the Supreme Court.[70]

In five states, a wife must get court approval to engage in an independent business. In Florida, for example, she must present a petition setting forth her name, age, "and her character, habits, edu-

[67]Quoted by Barbara Fryer in Riverside, California, *Daily Enterprise,* June 25, 1973.
[68]Press Release of California State Senator Mervyn M. Dymally, October 5, 1973.
[69]Kanowitz, op. cit., p. 56.
[70]Association of the Bar of the City of New York, Committee on Federal Legislation, "Amending the Constitution to Prohibit State Discrimination Based on Sex," in House Hearings on *Equal Rights for Men and Women,* op. cit., p. 633.

cation and mental capacity for business, and briefly set out the reasons why such disabilities [to engage in her own business] should be removed."[71] In New York State, a woman applying for a liquor license must submit a personal history from her husband or nearest male relative.[72]

Domicile

A married woman's domicile (roughly, her legal residence) follows her husband's. Some states make certain exceptions, but this is the general rule. Domicile is important because it determines such matters as where one can obtain a divorce, where probate will take place, where one has the right to vote and hold public office or receive welfare benefits, and where one qualifies for residence tuition at state schools.

A husband can choose any reasonable domicile, and his wife is legally bound to abide by his choice. Of course at present a real and serious conflict on where to live would most likely result in divorce. The law cannot be used to force a woman to live in a place she considers totally unacceptable. But the existence of the law does mean that if a husband and wife, for financial or other reasons, want to maintain separate domiciles, they may not. It is another enshrinement in the law of the second-class citizenship of women.

In several domicile cases decided in 1971, the courts ruled in favor of the women plaintiffs.[73] The University of Arizona defined resident women married to nonresident men as nonresidents and thus required them to pay the higher out-of-state tuition. The judge did not rule on the broader issue of domicile but simply held the rule to be unreasonable. In a similar Colorado case, the judge ruled that the law that read "the domicile of a married woman is normally that of her husband" did not apply for the purpose of tuition at state schools.[74] In a Florida case, a woman married to a foreigner who had never provided a home was allowed to retain her own domicile. *"Normally* and perhaps *presumptively,* but not *inevitably,* a wife acquires the husband's domicile upon marriage,"* the court said.[75]

These cases show the problems that domicile laws create for married women. Although the women plaintiffs won these cases, all

[71]Quoted in Kanowitz, op. cit., p. 57.
[72]*Ms.* 5 (May 1977), 20.
[73]*Women's Rights Law Reporter* 1 (spring 1972), 25 passim.
[74]Quoted in ibid., p. 25.
[75]Quoted in ibid.

were decided on very narrow grounds and did not change the basic law on domicile.

A married woman's name

By custom, women have taken the name of their husband upon marriage. The common law would indicate that this is an option and not a requirement, some lawyers contend.[76] Under the common law any person may adopt any name he or she likes so long as fraud is not intended. Only one state, Hawaii, specifically required by law that a woman take her husband's name.

Many lawyers say that by common law rule a wife must assume her husband's surname. A great many state laws are based on this presumption. Statutes relating to the issuance of drivers' licenses often require a woman to notify a state agency of a change in name upon marriage. Voter registration laws frequently require that a woman reregister in her married name. Administrative rules at the state and local levels also frequently require a married woman to use her husband's name. When such laws and rules have been tested in court, the results have been varied.[77] In the 1971 case of *Forbuse* v. *Wallace,* an Alabama requirement that women use their married names in applying for drivers' licenses was upheld by the Supreme Court. Maryland's requirement that a woman use her husband's name in registering to vote was struck down by the state court of appeals in 1972.

Women contend that having to take their husband's name is a submergence of their personality and another example of the demeaning doctrine of coverture. The requirement also has practical consequences. *Newsweek* reports that "in Lowell, Massachusetts, counselor Gail Dunfey was marked absent from city-council meetings because she insisted upon using her own name—under which she had been elected—and not her husband's."[78]

Many states do have formal procedures for changing one's name, but married women are frequently excluded from these provisions. In Iowa, for example, a married woman cannot change her name, but if her husband changes his, the new name automatically becomes her legal surname.[79] Even if state law allows her to change her name, she is frequently harassed if she attempts to do

---

[76]See Priscilla Ruth MacDougall, "Married Women's Common Law Right to Their Own Surnames," *Women's Rights Law Reporter* 1 (fall-winter 1972–1973).

[77]Ibid., pp. 2–3.

[78]*Newsweek,* August 20, 1973.

[79]Kanowitz, op. cit., p. 43.

so. "In Indiana, where a woman sought to restore her maiden name, State Attorney General Theodore Sendak suggested that her 'need was not for a change of name but for a competent psychiatrist.' "[80]

Several state court decisions and rulings by state attorneys general have held that women need not assume their husbands' names upon marriage. The Hawaii statute requiring a woman to take her husband's name has been struck down as contrary to the state constitution.[81] By 1981, Priscilla Ruth MacDougall, the foremost expert in the area, could state, "Women's right to retain or change their names irrespective of their marital status on the same basis as men in the United States is all but a universally recognized legal right."[82]

The law of support

If a woman loses many rights upon marriage, she does, it is claimed, gain security. The husband is responsible for supporting his wife and children. In some states, a wife is legally responsible for supporting her husband under certain circumstances—if he is disabled, for example. Nevertheless, the main burden of support falls upon the husband.

These laws are based, some legal scholars contend, on the notion that a wife is her husband's property.[83] He owns her and therefore must take care of her. Certainly the laws are an expression of rigid sex-role stereotyping. The husband's obligation applies whether or not his wife can support herself. The law is not based on functional relationships within the family—on whether, in fact, the wife stays home and takes care of the children while the husband is the major breadwinner. It is based simply on sex.

While women are more likely to stay home and take care of children and thus require support from their husbands than vice versa, support laws need not be based on sexist premises. The National Commission on Uniform State Laws has drafted a Uniform Marriage and Divorce Act that completely avoids mention of sex. "It provides for alimony for either spouse (called 'maintenance'), child support obligations for both spouses in accordance with their means, and custody of children based upon the welfare of the

---

[80]*Newsweek,* August 20, 1973.

[81]*1975 Handbook,* op. cit., pp. 386–388.

[82]*Spokeswoman* (August 1981): 7.

[83]Kanowitz, op. cit., p. 71.

child."[84] The act bases support obligations on the circumstances of a given case and not on sex per se. It avoids the offensive assumption that all women are incapable of taking care of themselves and makes the law a great deal fairer for both husband and wife.

By 1978, 38 states had adopted sex-neutral laws with similar provisions concerning alimony. But many women are still feeling the effects of traditional support laws, which do not offer them much protection. While a woman is living with her husband, there is very little she can do to ensure enforcement.[85] If he is a gambler, an alcoholic, or just doesn't want to work, it is too bad for her. Contrary to public opinion, the divorced wife usually ends up with the short end of the stick. An American Bar Association study found that temporary alimony was awarded in less than 10 percent of the cases; permanent alimony, in about 2 percent.[86] In general, the ex-husband's child support payments covered less than half of the cost of actually supporting the children. Furthermore, alimony and child support are difficult to collect. A study found that 10 years after divorce, 87 percent of the husbands were no longer meeting such court-ordered payments.[87]

The assumption that the man is the primary breadwinner has been used to deny women employee benefits that are routinely extended to men. Army rules formerly stipulated that male members of the armed forces could claim their wives as dependents, whether or not the wife was in fact dependent. The dependency status entitled them to a supplementary housing allowance and various medical and dental benefits. A female member of the armed forces could claim her husband as a dependent only if she could show that she provided more than half of his support. First Lieutenant Frontiero brought suit against the army. In January 1973, the Supreme Court ruled in her favor and threw out the discriminatory statutes as violating the Fourteenth Amendment's equal protection clause.[88]

In private employment, similar discrimination in fringe benefits frequently takes place. A number of such cases have been taken to the Equal Employment Opportunity Commission, which has, in turn, ruled that "the assumption that any working female is dependent

[84]Citizen's Advisory Council on the Status of Women, "The Equal Rights Amendment—What It Will and Won't Do," in House Hearings on *Equal Rights for Men and Women,* op. cit., p. 564.

[85]Lisa Cronin Wohl, "The Sweetheart of the Silent Majority," *Ms.* 2 (March 1974), 56.

[86]Cited in ibid.

[87]Cited in ibid., p. 57.

[88]*Women's Rights Law Reporter* (spring-summer 1973):82–83.

upon her husband for her support, regardless of the extent to which she contributes to the actual support and maintenance of her family, is plainly indefensible."[89] In one such case, the employer financed health insurance for the dependents of married men but not for those of married women on the basis that men were heads of household or primary breadwinners, but women were not.

Many provisions of the social security law are also based on the assumption that the family is dependent on the male breadwinner. In a series of recent decisions, the Supreme Court has struck down a number of discriminatory aspects. Until it was declared unconstitutional in 1975, an unemployed widow with children received benefits based on her deceased husband's earnings, but a comparably placed widower did not.[90] Under social security law, a husband, to be eligible for dependency benefits when his wife dies, retires, or becomes disabled, had to prove that he was dependent on his wife for at least half of his support. There was no such requirement for wives.[91] In two decisions handed down in March 1977, the Supreme Court declared these provisions unconstitutional.[92] Interestingly, the justices could not agree on whether the law discriminated against men or women. One can argue either way, but the result of the provisions was that a woman paid as much social security tax as a comparably placed man, yet she and her husband received smaller payments when she retired.

Credit
Prior to passage of the Equal Credit Opportunity Act, home mortgage financing practices were dominated by the same stereotyped assumptions. Although the amount one can borrow for buying a home depends on one's income, most lending institutions would not give full credit for the wife's income. They assumed that the husband was the main breadwinner and the wife a temporary worker. One survey of lending practices found that in general, if the wife was not a professional, no allowance was made for her income if she was under 35, half was counted if she was between 35 and 42, and only thereafter was her full income counted.[93]

Such practices were not restricted to private lending institu-

---

[89]Quoted in ibid., p. 89.
[90]*Women's Rights Law Reporter* (September 1975): 13.
[91]Ibid.
[92]*Los Angeles Times,* March 22, 1977.
[93]Dennis Kendig, "Discrimination Against Women in Home Mortgage Financing," *Yale Review of Law and Social Action* 3 (winter 1973), 164.

tions; the Veterans Administration had the same type of policy.[94] For example, a 29-year-old woman and her husband wished to buy a home for which they would be eligible only if her income were counted. This woman had worked full time since graduating from high school. The longest she had ever taken off from work was 2 months, when she had her only child, 8 years before. She had also completed 2 years of college in night school and was working for her degree, which would increase her earning potential. She had, in fact, owned a house in another state, and her payment record was good. When they applied for the loan, she and her husband were renting an apartment that cost $50 per month more than what their mortgage payments would be, and they had never had difficulty paying their rent.

What was the VA's response to their request? The woman is of childbearing age, the VA said, so her income cannot be counted. However, her income could be counted if her doctor would specify that she was incapable of having more children or if she would sign an affidavit saying she was using birth control and intended to continue and not have more children. The woman considered this an invasion of her rights and refused to sign.

The 1974 Equal Credit Opportunity Act outlaws discrimination on the basis of sex or marital status in any aspect of a credit transaction.[95] Creditors may not discount income from part-time work, they may not ask about a woman's childbearing intentions, and they must, if requested, give reasons for denying credit.

The act is a big step forward but it is far from perfect. Feminists had hoped that creditors would have to give an explanation for all denials of credit, but opposition from businesses weakened that provision. Creditors are required to record family accounts in the names of both spouses only if requested—a provision that enables a woman to establish her own credit identity. Many women may not be aware that this is important and may not take advantage of the provision. If they do not, they will find that, as in the past, upon divorce or widowhood, in the eyes of potential lenders they are nonpersons. Penalties for discrimination under the act are rather mild, and enforcement authority is dispersed among a number of federal agencies. The act, then, is no panacea; it is a useful weapon in the fight for equal rights. But women themselves will have to take on the major burden of seeing that it is enforced.

[94]Ibid., pp. 168–169.
[95]The following discussion is based on Lisa Cronin Wohl, "Equal Credit Opportunity Act: Some Good News, Some Not So Good," *MS.* (March 1977).

SINGLE WOMEN: THERE OUGHT TO BE A LAW

In the past, problems specific to the single woman stemmed from the lack of antidiscrimination laws rather than from the existence of discriminatory law. Under the common law, even at a time when married women had almost no rights, single women's property and contract rights were the same as those of men. But even at present, the single woman who is not rich finds that in practice her rights in financial transactions are limited.

Getting credit of any sort is frequently difficult, if not impossible, for the single woman. She is often refused credit cards. If she wishes to buy a home, she will have great difficulty getting financing, even if her financial status is clearly adequate.[96] A 28-year-old woman attempted to get mortgage financing for a $34,500 townhouse she wished to buy. This woman had a master's degree, an annual salary of $12,000, $9,000 in cash, and no debts. Yet no bank was willing to give her a loan. She had not even been able to get a credit card. Until passage of the Equal Credit Opportunities Act, such discrimination was not illegal.

Until recently, most areas had no laws prohibiting discrimination against women in housing or in public accommodations. In New York City, for example, a number of landlords would not rent to single women, claiming that the financial risk was too high.[97] Such policies were prevalent in the most desirable areas. Thus it was estimated that in 1970 there were about 1000 buildings in New York City's Upper East Side that refused to rent to single women. Even public housing authorities discriminated. Carter Burden, a member of the New York City Council, reported that a single woman who had applied to nearly every middle-income housing development during the past 15 years had been turned down consistently because she was single.[98]

Nightclubs, cocktail lounges, and even some restaurants will not admit unescorted women. The policy has frequently been justified as necessary to discourage prostitutes.[99] That in itself says a great deal about how women are viewed.

From 1970 on, a number of states passed laws prohibiting discrimination on the basis of sex in places of public accommodation.[100] Such discrimination is still not prohibited by federal law, al-

[96]Ibid., p. 171.
[97]Carol Greitzer, in New York City Commission on Human Rights, op. cit., p. 146.
[98]Carter Burden, in ibid., p. 151.
[99]Babcock, op. cit., p. 1059.
[100]Ibid., p. 1057.

though discrimination against minority males is illegal under Title II of the 1964 Civil Rights Act.

WOMEN AS WORKERS: LAWS ON EMPLOYMENT

Laws affecting women as workers again reflect society's sexist image of women. Women have been relegated to low-paid, low-prestige, dead-end jobs, and employment laws often seemed designed to keep women from bettering their position. Recently, however, legislation to end sex discrimination in employment has been passed, and women have been going to court to force compliance with these laws. The picture, then, is a mixed one: continuing discrimination and considerable progress.

Women need not apply

In 1872, the Supreme Court upheld an Illinois law prohibiting women from practicing law. Myra Bradwell, the plaintiff, claimed that the law was an abridgment of the privileges and immunities of citizenship guaranteed by the Fourteenth Amendment and thus was unconstitutional. The court disagreed, basing its decision on the "nature" of women.

> . . . the civil law, as well as nature herself, has always recognized a wide difference in the respective spheres and destinies of man and woman. Man is, or should be, woman's protector and defender. The natural and proper timidity and delicacy which belongs to the female sex evidently unfits it for many of the occupations of civil life. The constitution of the family organization, which is founded in the divine ordinance, as well as in the nature of things, indicates the domestic sphere as that which properly belongs to the domain and functions of womanhood. The harmony, not to say identity, of interests and views which belong, or should belong to the family institution is repugnant to the idea of a woman adopting a distinct and independent career from that of her husband. So firmly fixed was this sentiment in the founders of the common law that it became a maxim of that system of jurisprudence that a woman had no legal existence separate from her husband, who was regarded as her head and representative in the social state; and notwithstanding some recent modifications of this civil status, many of the special rules of law flowing from and dependent upon this cardinal principle still exist in full force in most states. One of these is, that a married woman is incapable, without her husband's consent, of making contracts which shall be binding on her or him. This very incapacity was one circumstance which the Supreme Court of Illinois deemed important in rendering a married woman incompetent fully to perform the duties and trusts that belong to the office of an attorney and counselor.

It is true that many women are unmarried and not affected by any of the duties, complications, and incapacities arising out of the married state, but these are exceptions to the general rule. *The paramount destiny and mission of woman are to fulfill the noble and benign offices of wife and mother.* This is the law of the Creator. And the rule of civil society must be adapted to the general constitution of things, and cannot be based upon exceptional cases.

. . . in my opinion, in view of the peculiar characteristics, destiny, and mission of woman, it is within the province of the legislature to ordain what offices, positions, and callings shall be filled and discharged by men, and shall receive the benefit of those energies and responsibilities, and that decision and firmness which are presumed to predominate in the sterner sex.

For these reasons I think that the laws of Illinois now complained of are not obnoxious to the charge of abridging any of the privileges and immunities of citizens of the United States.[101]

More than 20 years later, the Court upheld a similar law in Virginia. Not until 1921 did women gain the right to practice law in all states. The right was won not through court action but by changes in state legislation.

Many states barred women from such occupations as mining, wrestling, and bartending. In 1948, in *Goesart* v. *Cleary,* the Supreme Court upheld a Michigan bartending prohibition saying "Bartending by women may, in the allowable legislative judgment, give rise to moral and social problems. . . ."[102]

These laws as well as the judicial decisions upholding them are based on sexist premises. But more than the notion that women are weak, incompetent creatures who need protection is involved. The Michigan law exempted the wives and daughters of bar owners from the bartending prohibition. Michigan law did not prohibit women from working as waitresses in a bar. In the Goesart decision, Justice Frankfurter wrote, "Since the line [the legislators] have drawn is not without a basis in reason, we cannot give ear to the suggestion that the real impulse behind this legislation was an unchivalrous desire of male bartenders to monopolize the calling."[103] Given the difference in pay between the jobs of bartender and waitress, that in fact seems a reasonable conclusion.

The Court, however, in this and other cases, decided that the

---

[101]*Bradwell* v. *Illinois,* quoted by Diane B. Schulder, "Does the Law Oppress Women?" in Morgan, op. cit., pp. 147–148.
[102]Quoted in Kanowitz, op. cit., p. 33.
[103]Quoted in ibid., p. 180.

grossest stereotypes about women provide a reasonable reason for discrimination.

Protective laws

Most states have protective labor laws that apply to women only. Laws establishing maximum hours, minimum wages, weight-lifting ceilings, mandatory rest periods, or lunch breaks and prohibiting certain types of night work are considered protective laws. The states vary greatly both in terms of which types of protections are included and in the specific standards set.

In the late nineteenth and early twentieth centuries, many states passed non—sex-based protective laws. Working conditions in industry were abominable; many people were forced to work 12 to 14 hours a day, often 7 days a week, for starvation wages. In 1905 the Supreme Court declared a maximum hours law for bakers unconstitutional (*Lochner* v. *New York*).[104] The states realized that other such laws would not survive a judicial challenge. Then, in 1908, the Court upheld an Oregon maximum hours law for women only.[105] Many of the early protective laws, then, were restricted to women because only thus would they survive the Court. Half a loaf was considered better than none.

The Court based its decision in *Muller* v. *Oregon* on the biological differences between the sexes: "The two sexes differ in structure of body, in the functions to be performed by each, in the amount of physical strength. . . ."[106] Woman's inferior physical strength, the Court asserted, meant she was incapable of taking care of herself and must look to men for protection:

> History discloses the fact that woman has always been dependent upon man. . . . As minors, though not to the same extent, she has been looked upon in the courts as needing especial care that her rights may be preserved. . . . Differentiated by these matters from the other sex, she is properly placed in a class by herself and the legislation designed for her protection may be sustained, even when like legislation is not necessary for men, and could not be sustained. It is impossible to close one's eyes to the fact that she still looks to her brother and depends upon him.[107]

According to Kanowitz, this language provided the basis for the principle that

[104]*Lochner* v. *New York,* 198 U.S. 45 (1905).
[105]*Muller* v. *Oregon,* 208 U.S. 412 (1908).
[106]Quoted in Kanowitz, op. cit., p. 153.
[107]Quoted in ibid., pp. 153–154.

. . . sex is a valid basis for classification . . . a principle that is often repeated mechanically without regard to the purposes of the statute in question or the reasonableness of the relationship between that purpose and the sex-based classification. The subsequent reliance in judicial decisions upon the Muller language is a classic example of the misuse of precedent. . . .[108]

While the early sex-specific protective laws were a way of circumventing a conservative Court, later ones sprang from less noble motives. In the early 1930s, there was a movement to bar women from night work in a number of industries, including wool manufacturing and textiles. Its purpose was "to solve the unemployment situation by throwing women out of work."[109] Until they were revised in 1969, the New York State labor laws specified maximum hours for women but made exceptions for women working in restaurants in rural places of 1500 or less or in factory jobs in the canning of fruit or sauerkraut.[110] The law further specified that no woman could work after midnight in a factory or in a dining room or kitchen unless she obtained a special permit. Hat check girls, cigarette girls, and ladies room attendants did not require a permit. Generally, the maximum hours and no night work laws did not cover domestics and cleaning women. *Thus jobs have been covered or exempted depending on the convenience of employers and of competing males.*

"Most of the so-called protective legislation has really been to protect men's rights in better paying jobs," Congresswoman Martha Griffiths stated.[111] Both maximum hours and weight-lifting laws have been used to deny women promotion. To give just one example, Southern Bell refused to promote a woman to switchman because of Georgia weight-lifting laws. Her salary was $78 per week; as a switchman she would have made $135 per week.[112]

The 1963 Equal Pay Act
and Title VII of the 1964 Civil Rights Act
In 1963 and 1964, the first federal laws prohibiting sex discrimination in employment were passed. The 1963 act specified that men

---

[108]Ibid., p. 152.

[109]Burnita Sheldon Matthews, statement during Senate Hearings on the Equal Rights Amendment, in Kraditor, op. cit., p. 295.

[110]Mary Ann Krupsak, Assemblywoman, New York State Assembly, in New York City Commission on Human Rights, op. cit., pp. 330–331.

[111]House Hearings on *Equal Rights for Men and Women,* op. cit., p. 176.

[112]Faith A. Seidenberg, "The Submissive Majority: Modern Trends in the Law Concerning Women's Rights," in Jonathan Black, ed., *Radical Lawyers* (New York: Avon, 1971), p. 236.

and women must receive equal pay "on jobs the performance of which requires equal skill, effort and responsibility and which are performed under similar working conditions. . . ."[113] The act was passed as an amendment to the Fair Labor Standards Act and thus covers the same employees. Executive, professional, and administrative jobs were not included until June 1972, when the Equal Pay Act was extended to cover such jobs.[114]

In *Shultz* v. *Wheaton Glass Company* (1970), the first circuit court decision on the Equal Pay Act, the court ruled that jobs meriting equal pay need not be identical but only substantially equal.[115] Following this decision, most courts have ruled that different pay rates are justified only if there is a substantial difference in the effort, skill, or responsibility required. In *Shultz* v. *Hayes Industries, Inc.,* for example, the company argued that only men helped in changing the die in the machines and that this justified the pay differential. The court disagreed, saying the infrequency of the extra task did not justify the men's receiving 40 cents per hour more.[116]

Title VII of the Civil Rights Act states that it "shall be an unlawful employment practice" for a covered employer, because of race, color, religion, sex, or national origin

(1) to fail or refuse to hire or to discharge any individual or otherwise to discriminate against any individual with respect to his compensation, terms, conditions, or privileges of employment . . . or

(2) to limit, segregate or classify his employees in any way which would deprive or tend to deprive any individual of employment opportunities or adversely affect his status as an employee. . . .[117]

The act covers employers and labor unions having 25 or more employees or members and employment agencies that deal with such employers. Educational institutions and government agencies were exempted.

The Equal Employment Opportunity Commission (EEOC) established by the act may investigate complaints and attempt to conciliate the matter. If conciliation fails, the person injured may bring suit in federal court. The U.S. Attorney General may intervene in cases of "general public importance." Upon finding an intentional

---

[113]Quoted in Kanowitz, op. cit., p. 138.

[114]Judith Hole and Ellen Levine, *Rebirth of Feminism* (New York: Quadrangle, 1971), p. 428.

[115]Babcock, op. cit., p. 445.

[116]*Women's Rights Law Reporter* 2 (spring-summer 1973), 72.

[117]Quoted in Kanowitz, op. cit., p. 108.

unlawful employment practice, the federal courts may enjoin the defendant from engaging in it and order reinstatement or hiring of employees with or without back pay. If there is a pattern of intentional violations, the attorney general may also bring a civil action in a federal district court. Under the original act, the EEOC could initiate a court proceeding on its own only to compel compliance with a previously issued order under the provisions just stated.

In 1972, the commission's powers were extended. It was given the power directly to sue an employer in federal court for violation of the civil rights laws. It was not, however, given the power to issue cease and desist orders. The EEOC's authority was also extended to educational institutions and to government employment.[118]

Title VII states that it is legal to discriminate on the basis of sex, religion, or national origin, but not race, where these characteristics are a "bona fide occupational qualification reasonably necessary to the normal operation of that particular business or enterprise."[119] This provision is potentially a major loophole, and much of the litigation under the act has centered on what are bona fide occupational qualifications (bfoq's).

EEOC guidelines specified that the bfoq provision was to be interpreted narrowly. According to Commissioner Jerolyn Lyle, "sex is a bona fide occupational qualification only when necessary for authenticity or genuineness of job performance such as acting or modeling."[120] The following are violations of Title VII:

(1) Refusing to hire women on the basis of assumed comparative employment characteristics of women in general.

(2) Refusing to hire women on the basis of stereotyped characteristics of the sexes.

(3) Refusing to hire women because of real or assumed negative preferences of persons who would become their co-workers.

(4) Refusing to hire women because separate facilities woud have to be provided, unless clearly unreasonably high expenses would be incurred thereby.[121]

In *Diaz* v. *Pan American Airways, Inc.,* the airline contended that sex is a bfoq for the position of cabin attendant.[122] Passengers prefer female stewardesses because they are more comforting, the

[118]*Congressional Quarterly Weekly Report* 30, no. 9 (February 26, 1972), 456.
[119]Quoted in Kanowitz, op. cit., p. 109.
[120]Jerolyn Lyle, in New York City Commission on Human Rights, op. cit., p. 293.
[121]Quoted in ibid.
[122]*Women's Rights Law Reporter* 1 (fall-winter 1972–1973), 52–53.

company claimed. The Fifth Circuit Court found for the male plaintiff, saying that customer prejudice does not justify discrimination.

Denying a woman promotion on the assumption that women resent taking orders from other women is a violation of Title VII, the EEOC has decided. The case was brought by a bank employee who had been refused promotion to trust officer. A memo from a vice-president to the woman's supervisor said, "My observation is that [charging party] is a most capable employee, but long experience in personnel work makes me question the advisability of having a woman supervise all female employees. . . ."[123]

The relationship between the bfoq provision and state protective laws has presented especially troublesome questions. If state protective laws were interpreted as making sex a bfoq for jobs covered by such laws, the sex provision of Title VII would, to a large extent, be nullified.

The EEOC's position on this question has vacillated. In December 1965, the EEOC's first guidelines did allow state protective laws to be interpreted as a bfoq exception to Title VII so long as the laws actually protected rather than discriminated against women. It did not, however, specify how this distinction was to be determined. In its next set of guidelines, issued in August 1966, the EEOC claimed it did not have the authority to determine the relationship between the protective laws and Title VII. This was up to the courts to decide. Reversing its own decision in February 1968, the EEOC said it would decide on a case-by-case basis whether state laws were discriminatory and thus should be superseded by Title VII. Finally, in August 1969, the EEOC declared that state laws were in general no longer protective and were superseded by Title VII.

There have been a number of court cases in which the relationship between Title VII and state protective laws was at issue. The courts have held that state protective laws may not be used to deny women jobs and promotions. Title VII as federal law supersedes the state protective laws.

In 1968, in *Rosenfeld* v. *Southern Pacific Co.,* the court held that California's maximum hours and weight-lifting laws were invalid.[124] Ms. Rosenfeld had been rejected for the job of agent-telegrapher without any evaluation of her ability to do the job, even though she was the senior employee applying. The court ordered that she be considered for any future job without regard to sex.

Ms. Weeks was refused a job as a switchman because of a state

[123]Quoted in ibid., p. 56.
[124]Ibid., p. 36.

30-pound weight-lifting limit. The court of appeals in 1969 decided in favor of Weeks and said, "An employer has the burden of proving that he had reasonable cause to believe, that is, a factual basis for believing, that all or substantially all women would be unable to perform safely and efficiently the duties of the job involved."[125]

In *Bowe* v. *Colgate-Palmolive Co.*, the court of appeals struck down a company weight-lifting limit, saying Title VII prohibits "stereotyped characterization of the sexes [which precludes] consideration of individual capacities as to physical strength and particular job requirements."[126]

These three cases, all decided in 1968 and 1969, are considered particularly important as trend setters. The principles established—that state protective laws cannot be used to deny women jobs or promotion, that the burden of proof regarding bfoq falls upon the employer, that stereotyped notions about women may not be used to establish bfoq—have been used in a large number of subsequent decisions.

Cases challenging somewhat subtler forms of discrimination have also been brought. In *Griggs* v. *Duke Power Co.* (1971), the Supreme Court ruled that aptitude tests must be job related, saying that the employer has "the burden of showing that any given requirement has a manifest relationship to the employment in question."[127] In that case, the plaintiff charged that the non–job-related aptitude test that was used discriminated against him on the basis of race, but the ruling is also applicable to sex.

The New York State Division of Human Rights found the New York City Department of Parks and Recreation's height and weight requirements (5 feet 7 inches and 135 pounds) for lifeguards discriminatory, since the department had not shown that meeting the requirements was essential to the job.[128] In a similar case, the EEOC struck down a minimum height requirement of 5 feet 7 inches for bus drivers, saying that it had a "substantially disproportionate effect" on women as a class and that "business convenience may not be equated with business necessity."[129] In a very important 1976 decision, a three-judge federal court invalidated Alabama's height and weight requirements for police personnel.[130] The court found

---

[125]*Weeks* v. *Southern Bell Telephone and Telegraph Co.,* quoted in ibid., p. 37.
[126]Quoted in ibid.
[127]Quoted in ibid., p. 45.
[128]Ibid., p. 58.
[129]Quoted in ibid., p. 39.
[130]*Poverty Law Report* 4 (September–October 1976), 3.

that the requirements had a disproportionate effect on women applicants: For state troopers, the minimums were 5 feet 8 inches and 160 pounds. It concluded that the requirements had not been shown to be sufficiently job related so as to further the legitimate interests of the state. The judges said: "One lesson the women's rights movement has taught us is that many long-hailed conceptions concerning the sexes have been found to be erroneous when exposed to the light of empirical data and objectivity."[131] Since 97 percent of the nation's police jobs have some minimum height and weight requirements, this decision is likely to set an important precedent.

In a number of cases, employers have claimed that their decision was based not on the sex of the employee or potential employee but on some other characteristic such as marital state or parenthood. The complainants have charged sex discrimination because males with the given characteristic were treated differently from females. The argument in these cases centers on whether sex plus some other characteristic is a legal ground for discrimination. If such an argument were allowed to stand, Title VII would lose much of its usefulness.

Ida Phillips, who was making $45 a week as a waitress, applied for the position of assembly line trainee at $2.25 an hour. Martin Marietta Corporation turned her down, saying that the company did not hire women with preschool children. She brought suit, and the case was decided by the Supreme Court in 1971. The Court held that the company could not automatically preclude mothers of preschool children from consideration when it did not do the same with fathers. But it added that "the existence of such conflicting family obligations, if demonstrably more relevant to job performance for a woman than for a man, could arguably be a basis for distinction under [the bfoq provision]."[132] The Court thus left the door open to a sex-plus argument.

In a concurring opinion, Justice Marshall wrote, "I fear that in this case . . . the Court has fallen into the trap of assuming that the Act permits ancient canards about the proper role of women to be a basis for discrimination. Congress, however, sought just the opposite result."[133] Martin Marietta did not attempt to show that the bfoq provision applied in its case. Following the *Phillips* decision, a number of lower courts have ruled on the airline's rules that female but not male cabin attendants must not be married or over 32. The airlines

[131]Quoted in ibid., p. 3.
[132]Quoted in ibid., p. 59.
[133]Quoted in ibid.

lost all these cases, and the sex-plus defense has fallen into disuse.[134]

Many employers force women to take an unpaid maternity leave of several months or more, and some fire a pregnant woman outright. EEOC guidelines declare that firing or refusing to hire a pregnant woman is a violation of Title VII. According to 1972 EEOC guidelines, pregnancy must be treated like any other temporary disability.[135]

A number of cases challenging enforced maternity leave have been brought.[136] The Supreme Court agreed to hear two such cases during its 1973 term. One involved two junior high school teachers. The school board's policy required that they quit work after the fourth month of pregnancy and not return until the school term on the first day of which the child is at least 3 months old. For the two women bringing the suit, the rule would have resulted in almost a year of unemployment. The attorneys for the employers in the two cases, the Cleveland Board of Education and the Chesterfield County School Board, based their arguments on pregnant women's inability to do the job efficiently. In oral arguments before the Court, they claimed that "pregnant women are subject to 'certain medical conditions,' urinate more frequently, lose their sense of balance and become prone to falling down. . . . Moreover, they are forced to miss class in order to see their obstetricians as many as 13 times in the last three months of pregnancy."[137] On January 21, 1974, the Supreme Court struck down mandatory maternity leave policies, declaring such rules to be a violation of the teachers' constitutional right to due process.

In two subsequent pregnancy-related decisions, the Supreme Court decided against the women plaintiffs. The Court upheld the California temporary disability insurance program which denies benefits for pregnancy-related disabilities *(Geduldig* v. *Aiello).*[138] Dissenting, Justice Brennan wrote:

> . . . the economic effects caused by pregnancy related disabilities are functionally indistinguishable from the effects caused by any other disability: wages are lost due to a physical inability to work, and medical expenses are incurred for the delivery of the child and for postpartum care. In my view, by singling out for less favorable treatment a gender-linked disability peculiar to women, the State has created a double standard for disability compensation: a limitation is imposed upon the disabilities for which women workers may recover, while men receive

[134]*Signs* (September 1976):70, and Babcock, op. cit., p. 246.
[135]*Women's Rights Law Reporter* 2 (spring–summer 1972), 90.
[136]Ibid., p. 65.
[137]Riverside, California, *Daily Enterprise,* October 17, 1973.
[138]Babcock, op. cit., p. 318.

full compensation for all disabilities suffered, including those that affect only or primarily their sex, such as prostatectomies, circumcision, hemophilia and gout. In effect, one set of rules is applied to females and another to males. Such dissimilar treatment of men and women, on the basis of physical characteristics inextricably linked to one sex, inevitably constitutes sex discrimination.[139]

An even more serious setback for women occurred on December 7, 1976, when the Supreme Court handed down its decision on *General Electric Co.* v. *Gilbert.*[140] GE's disability insurance covers almost every possible disability—including recovery from hair transplants and plastic surgery—but excludes pregnancy. Ms. Gilbert sued under Title VII. Despite the plan's covering disabilities unique to men (prostatectomies, vasectomies, and circumcisions, for example), a majority of the justices ruled that the exclusion of pregnancy is not sex discrimination. Writing for the majority, Justice Rehnquist stated: "Gender based discrimination does not result simply because an employer's disability benefits program is less than all inclusive."[141] Justice Brennan, in dissent, called the majority's assumption that the GE plan was sex-neutral "purely fanciful."[142] According to Ruth Bader Ginsburg, a judge for the District of Columbia Circuit Court, the decision takes "pregnancy out of Title VII. It means that an employer can say when you're pregnant, 'Go, I don't want you any more.' It gives an employer carte blanche to treat a woman as if she were a temporary member of the labor force."[143]

Congress responded to feminists' outrage at that decision and, in 1978, amended Title VII to make explicit that discrimination on the basis of pregnancy is sex discrimination under that title. Essentially, Congress enacted into law the strong EEOC guidelines the court had rejected in *Gilbert.*[144] Thus employers may not fire or refuse to hire a woman just because she is pregnant, or deprive a woman of seniority rights because she takes a maternity leave. Also, health and disability plans may not exclude pregnancy.[145]

In 1979, the Supreme Court handed down another damaging decision—one that neither the U.S. Congress nor the state legisla-

---

[139]Quoted in ibid., p. 130.

[140]*Los Angeles Times,* December 8, 1976.

[141]Quoted in ibid.

[142]Quoted in ibid.

[143]Quoted in *Newsweek,* December 26, 1976.

[144]Nancy Erickson, "Pregnancy Discrimination: An Analytical Approach," *Women's Rights Law Reporter* 5 (winter-spring 1979), 102–103.

[145]*Washington Post,* November 27, 1978.

tures are likely to reverse. The court ruled that giving veterans preference in government employment does not constitute illegal sex discrimination despite the fact that, until recently, women's participation in the military was severely restricted by law.[146] At issue was a Massachusetts statute that automatically places any veteran passing a competitive test at the top of the civil service hiring list. Helen Feeney sued after being bumped three times from the top of job lists by veterans.

Sexual harassment

Although large numbers of women have been subject to sexual harassment on the job, few were willing to talk about it publicly until recently. Women too often felt that somehow it was their own fault and most felt powerless to do anything about it. In the 1970s, largely because of the women's movement, more and more women began to talk openly about the problem, and some filed suit. Since 1975, a marked increase in sexual harassment suits has occurred.[147] In 1978, a district court judge found Johns-Manville Corporation guilty of sex discrimination under Title VII in a sexual harassment case. "An employer is liable under Title VII when refusal of a supervisor's unsolicited sexual advances is the basis of the employee's termination," the judge wrote.[148]

In 1980, the EEOC issued strong guidelines. In them, sexual harassment was broadly defined and termed a violation of Section 703 of Title VII. According to the guidelines, unwelcome sexual advances, requests for sexual favors, and other verbal or physical conduct of a sexual nature constitute sexual harassment when (1) submission to such conduct is made either explicitly or implicitly a term or condition of an individual's employment, (2) submission to or rejection of such conduct by an individual is used as the basis for employment decisions affecting such individual, or (3) such conduct has the purpose or effect of substantially interfering with an individual's work performance or creating an intimidating, hostile, or offensive working environment.[149] The third point is especially important because it recognizes that sexual harassment is not limited to "sleep

---

[146]*Newsweek,* June 18, 1979, p. 52.

[147]Mary C. Meyer, Inge M. Berchhold, Jeannenne L. Oestreich, and Frederick J. Collins, *Sexual Harassment* (New York: Petrocelli Books, Inc., 1981), p. 11.

[148]Quoted in Ibid., p. 11.

[149]Joan Vermuelen, "Comments on the Equal Employment Opportunity Commission's Proposed Amendment Adding Section 1604.11, Sexual Harassment, to Its Guidelines on Sexual Discrimination," *Women's Rights Law Reporter* 6 (summer 1980), 288.

with me or I'll fire you" situations. Certain forms of behavior—leering, touching, obscene suggestions—can make a woman's job environment unbearable without such threats.

The guidelines make an employer liable for the acts of its agents and supervisory employees as well as for the acts of coworkers and customers if nothing is done after a complaint.[150] Additionally, the guidelines put responsibility on employers to forestall sexual harassment and urge them to take all steps necessary to prevent sexual harassment, such as affirmatively raising the subject, expressing strong disapproval of harassment, developing appropriate sanctions, informing employees of their right to raise—and of ways of raising—the issue of harassment under Title VII, and developing methods to sensitize all concerned.[151]

Sexual harassment is not likely to disappear. Still, the guidelines may raise some consciousnesses. Certainly they provide a strong basis for those women who decide to bring suit.

Title IX
Equal opportunity in education is a prerequisite to equal job opportunities. In 1972, Congress passed the Education Amendments, Title IX of which states, "No person in the United States shall, on the basis of sex, be excluded from participation in, be denied the benefits of or be subjected to discrimination under any education program or activity receiving Federal financial assistance."[152] With certain exemptions, the law bars sex discrimination in admissions and in the treatment of students once they are admitted. Schools may not require women to have a higher grade point average than men in order to be admitted nor may they use quotas to balance the number of men and women. Schools may not restrict courses to members of one sex nor may they discriminate in financial aid or in student health and insurance benefits. All facilities must be available, without discrimination, to members of both sexes. Separate housing and separate locker rooms are permissible but the facilities must be comparable.

The most publicized controversy over Title IX has occurred in the area of athletics. The most recent guidelines, announced in December 1979, require that athletic scholarship money must be divided proportionately among men and women.[153] If, for example, women make up one-third of the athletes, they should receive a third

[150]Ibid., pp. 290–292.
[151]Ibid., p. 293.
[152]Peer, "Summary of the Regulation for Title IX, Education Amendments of 1972."
[153]Peer Perspective 6 (March 1980), 1.

of the scholarship money. Other athletic benefits, opportunities, and treatment must be "equivalent" in availability, quality, and kind for both sexes. This does not necessarily mean that the amount of money spent must be proportionate.

Title IX, though a useful tool in the fight for equal education rights, does have some serious weaknesses. Most notably, the admissions policies of primary and secondary schools are exempted, as are admissions to private undergraduate institutions. This exclusion allowed the`Supreme Court to affirm a lower court decision in *Vorcheimer* v. *School District of Philadelphia* concerning single sex high schools.[154] Philadelphia maintains two high schools for academically superior students—one for boys and one for girls. The boys' school is superior, especially in its science facilities, and Susan Vorcheimer was especially interested in science when she applied for admission there. Because of the Title IX loophole, the court ruled that barring her from admission was not a violation of her legal rights.

Two current legal issues concerning Title IX will seriously affect the impact of the law on educational opportunity. From the beginning the federal government has taken the position that Title IX barred discrimination against employees of educational institutions as well as against students. This interpretation, which was written into the regulations, was challenged. Decisions at the circuit-court level were mixed, though most subscribed to the narrow interpretation.[155] The Supreme Court in mid-1982 upheld the broad interpretation.

Another and perhaps even more serious issue concerns whether Title IX applies only to programs that directly receive federal aid or whether it applies generally to institutions that receive federal funds. The program-specific interpretation would severely limit the impact of Title IX. The federal government has subscribed to the broad interpretation and has been challenged in court. The cases brought have dealt with athletics which seldom receive federal assistance directly. During 1981, three federal district judges ruled on the issue and they split two-to-one in favor of the program-specific interpretation.[156] The Supreme Court will have to decide on this issue, too.

---

[154]Andrea Novick and David Griffiths, "Sex-Segregated Public Schools: *Vorcheimer* v. *School District of Philadelphia* and the Judicial Definition of an Equal Education for Women," *Women's Rights Law Reporter* 4 (winter 1978), 79–96.

[155]*Peer Perspective* 6 (September 1980), 1.

[156]*Peer Perspective* 7 (November 1981), 7.

THE EQUAL RIGHTS AMENDMENT

The federal Equal Rights Amendment reads: "Equality of rights under the law shall not be denied or abridged by the United States or by any State on account of sex." Approved by the United States Congress on March 22, 1972, it was defeated on June 30, 1982—3 states short of the 38 needed for ratification. The defeat represents a major blow to women's rights, and, many feel, a conservative backlash to advances made by the women's movement during the past decade.

Opposing arguments took two forms: first, that the amendment was unnecessary to secure equality and, second, that it would have harmful effects. A number of lawyers, including some feminists, argued that existing constitutional amendments already provided the basis for sexual equality under the law. They contended that the Fifth and Fourteenth Amendments, which guarantee due process and equal protection under the law, can and should be interpreted by the Supreme Court to outlaw sex discrimination. ERA supporters answered that although the Court can and should have so interpreted the Constitution, it has not. The Senate Judiciary Committee report on the ERA stated: "If the Supreme Court were to hold that discrimination based on sex, like discrimination based on race, is inherently 'suspect' and cannot be justified in the absence of a 'compelling and overriding state interest,' then part of the reason for the Amendment would disappear. But the Court has persistently refused so to hold."[157]

Until 1971, the Supreme Court had never ruled favorably in a sex discrimination case. Its recent decisions striking down state laws as discriminatory have been based on narrow grounds. In *Reed* v. *Reed,* the Court used the standard of "reasonableness," which puts the burden of proof that a discriminatory law is unreasonable on the woman plaintiff.[158] Under this standard, a law distinguishing between men and women will be upheld so long as it bears a "reasonable relationship" to a permissible legislative objective. In *Frontiero* v. *Richardson,* the Court used a somewhat stricter standard, and a plurality but not a majority declared that "classifications based upon sex, like classifications based on race, alienage or national origin . . . are inherently suspect" and therefore subject to "close judicial scrutiny."[159] Three other justices, however, specifically said that

[157]U.S. Congress, Senate, Committee on the Judiciary, *Equal Rights for Men and Women,* March 14, 1972, p. 10.
[158]Ibid.
[159]Quoted in *Women's Rights Law Reporter* (summer 1973): 3.

it was "unnecessary for the Court in this case to characterize sex as a suspect classification, with all of the far-reaching implications of such a holding."[160] This and cases decided subsequently suggest that, until there is an Equal Rights Amendment to the Constitution, a majority is unlikely to declare sex a suspect classification—a ruling that would shift the burden of proof from the woman plaintiff to the state.[161]

Another group of opponents based their opposition on the potentially "terrifying consequences" of the ERA. According to Dr. Pincus, who was quoted with approval by Senator Sam Ervin, "the Equal Rights Amendment and many of the other goals of its proponents will bring social disruption, unhappiness and increasing rates of divorce and desertion. Weakening of family ties may also lead to increased rates of alcoholism, suicide, and possible sexual deviation."[162]

Opponents of the ERA contended that under it, laws that protect married women would be struck down. A husband would no longer be required to support his wife and children. If the marriage ends in divorce, the woman would have no right to alimony and child support nor any special right to child custody. A marriage law basing rights and obligations not on sex but on circumstances has already been written and recommended to the states. As pointed out earlier, such a law is a great deal fairer to both husband and wife and would not be unconstitutional. Actually, the ERA may well have given the unemployed wife greater protection than she now has. According to Common Cause, the ERA would "require state law to recognize the contribution of the homemaker who takes care of home and family . . . [it] would entitle the homemaker to financial support in compensation for her services as homemaker."[163]

A recent study of the effects of state ERAs support this position. "Fairer decisions on divorce to homemakers, to children and the husbands are resulting,"[164] the report found. The director of the Pennsylvania state commission for women said that the state's ERA had substantially improved the status of homemakers and mothers: "In child support cases the court said a homemaker's care of the children must be considered an economic contribution in assessing sup-

[160]Ibid., p. 4.
[161]Babcock, op. cit., pp. 122–125.
[162]Minority Views of Mr. Ervin, in ibid., p. 48.
[163]Quoted in Wohl, op. cit., p. 57.
[164]Quoted in Riverside, California, *Daily Enterprise,* July 9, 1976.

port obligations. For the first time, a woman's work in the home is legally recognized."[165]

A number of unions based their opposition to the ERA on the conflict between the amendment and state protective laws. The ERA would have made sex-specific protective laws unconstitutional. Since the courts have been striking down protective laws as in conflict with Title VII, this argument is of little relevance. Many such laws did not, in fact, protect women. Protective laws that really do protect can be extended to men and thus escape constitutional challenge. Some lawyers contend that, when such laws are challenged, the courts have the power to extend the truly protective provisions to cover men, and in some cases this had been done.[166]

Women would be drafted into the armed services, ERA opponents said with horror. There is no draft in effect now, but if it were reinstated, women would be eligible on the same basis as men. Although many people, men as well as women, would consider army service an unwelcome interruption in their lives, it is difficult to understand opponents' horror. Women serve as volunteers in the armed services now. During peacetime, the tasks performed by most recruits are of the office work variety. Whether, in time of war, women would be required to serve in combat depends on whether they are judged physically capable of such duty. If having women killing and being killed in the front lines seems so much worse than placing men in the same position, perhaps we had better work harder at avoiding wars.

Military service is usually regarded as a burden by those debating the ERA. Some supporters have, however, pointed out that such service offers advantages as well. For the poor, the armed services have offered upward mobility. Job training is often available, and the GI Bill makes further education possible after leaving the military. Veteran status also carries with it numerous benefits, such as eligibility for VA loans. Until recently women were limited by law to 2 percent of the total military forces, and there are still informal limits in effect.[167] Women must also meet higher requirements in order to enlist. To become officers, women compete only against one another for a very limited number of openings. The ERA would have made such unequal treatment unconstitutional.

The clinching argument against the amendment, according to opponents, was that it would force desegregation of restrooms, pris-

[165]Quoted in ibid.
[166]*Hayes* v. *Potlatch Forests, Inc.* See Babcock, op. cit., pp. 283–285.
[167]Ross, op. cit., pp. 132–133.

ons, and the like. Representative Abner Mikva has called this the "toilet training trauma,"[168] and most supporters recognize that such arguments stem from hysterical, not realistic, interpretation of the amendment. In any case, the Supreme Court has recognized a right to privacy, which ERA supporters say would be applied in such cases.

The arguments against the amendment were unconvincing. Wives and children would not be left without financial support; men and women would not be forced to use restrooms together.

What the amendment would have done is render all state and federal laws and practices that treat men and women unequally unconstitutional. The vestiges of the doctrine of coverture that remain in some state property laws would have been swept away. For example, laws that require the husband's signature when the wife sells some of her property but do not require her signature when he is the seller would have been invalidated. A number of states would have been required to change their laws on jury service. Men and women would have been eligible for such service on the same basis; grounds for exemption could not differ for the sexes.

The ERA would have had important consequences in the area of public education by backing up Title IX which, as we have seen, has some major defects and may be further weakened by new court rulings.

The ERA would have prohibited all levels of government from discriminating against women in public employment and in job-training programs. Since teachers and professors in public schools and universities are public employees, this would have involved a large number of people. The armed services would have been required to enlist women on the same basis as men.

The ERA would not have been a panacea. Purely private discriminatory practices could never be covered by law. Suits would have had to be brought to enforce the amendment. Still, ratification would have declared equality of the sexes a national policy and would have provided a sound constitutional basis for challenging sexual discrimination.

---

[168]Abner Mikva, in House Hearings on *Equal Rights for Men and Women,* op. cit., p. 86.

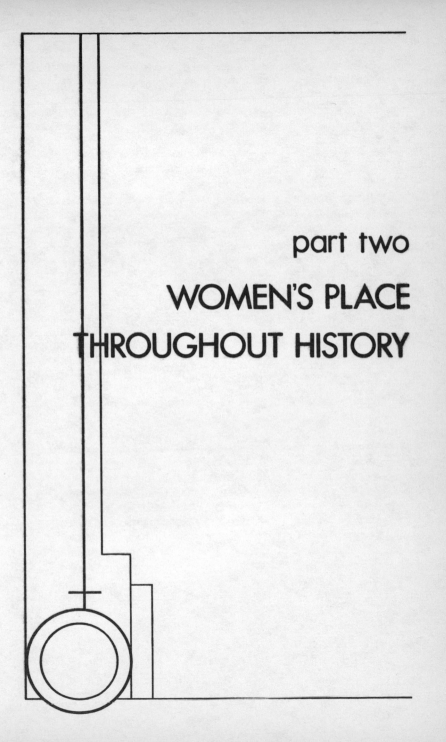

part two

WOMEN'S PLACE
THROUGHOUT HISTORY

WOMEN'S PLACE: FROM HUNTING AND GATHERING SOCIETIES TO CAPITALISM

8

Among anthropologists and historians there are two conflicting approaches to the position of women in earlier societies. A few still cling to the old approach, which claims that nothing ever has or ever will change because the status and role of women and men are determined by biology. In contrast, most anthropologists agree that a tremendous variety of social and sexual relationships, attitudes, and behavior is found in various societies. With regard to the forms of the family, the typical personality characteristics of male and female, and the status and occupations of women and men, almost anything found in one society can be found to be exactly opposite in some other society.

WOMEN IN PRIMITIVE SOCIETIES

Margaret Mead's[1] classic anthropological study of the relationship between sex and personality, or temperament, was discussed in Chapter 2. Of the three New Guinea tribes she investigated, among the Arapesh the personalities of both sexes are, according to our notions, "feminine"; among the Mundugumor, in contrast, both sexes have personalities stereotyped in our society as "masculine." In neither society do the people believe that personality should vary with sex and, in fact, it does not. The Tchambuli do show a relationship between sex and personality, but in this tribe, the normal male shows "feminine" personality traits and the normal female, "masculine" traits. Mead concludes that social conditioning, not biology, ac-

---

[1]Margaret Mead, *Sex and Temperament in Three Primitive Societies* (New York: Dell, 1935, 1971).

counts for these differences. The average Arapesh is gentle and co-operative because he or she has been brought up in a society where that is the expected behavior. The average Mundugumor is violent and aggressive—not by nature, but because of the society's socialization process. A child born into one of these tribes and reared in the other would grow up to display the personality and behavior characteristic of the tribe in which it was socialized.

Not merely the attitudes but the actual relations and status of men and women differ in various societies. In hunting and gathering societies, which were the predominant form during 99 percent of human history, men and women were roughly equal.[2] Slave societies, in contrast, were characterized by female subordination. Moreover, family organization and forms of marriage differ drastically in various periods and societies. The nuclear family, with husband and wife and their children living in an isolated household, is not eternal, omnipresent, or "natural." In fact, in most primitive societies the band or clan had much more social importance than the family.

Most clan societies are *patrilineal,* meaning that descent and inheritance are calculated through the father. After she is married a woman usually goes to live with her husband's family, and in some cases, if a man dies his brother must support and may marry his widow. All the kin terms relate the husband, wife, and children to the man's clan relatives. Many, but not all, patrilineal societies are also *patriarchal;* that is, male dominated. Yet there are also many clan societies that are *matrilineal,* with descent and inheritance passed down through the mother, kinship calculated to the mother's clan, and the husband moving to live with the wife's clan. In some cases, if a man is widowed he may marry his wife's sister. Matrilineal societies still exist among American and Canadian Indians, in some areas of Africa, and among the Dravidians of India.[3] In most matrilineal societies the status of women is high. There is, however, very little evidence of *matriarchy* or clear female dominance.

Marriages of one man and many women are also not uncommon. Polygyny is allowed in most Muslim societies and was practiced among the Mormons in nineteenth-century Utah. In practice, however, only the very wealthy man can afford many wives, so it has never been common among the working classes. On the other

---

[2]Ruby Rohrlicht-Lequitl, "Gatherer-Hunters," in Barbara Bellow Watson, ed., *Women's Studies: The Social Realities* (New York: Harper's College Press, 1976), pp. 181–201.

[3]Jacquetta Hawkes and Sir Leonard Woolley, *Prehistory and the Beginning of Civilization* (New York: Harper & Row, 1963), p. 122.

hand, there are a few societies in which one woman marries several men. Among the Todas of India, a woman marries a man and all his brothers, and no one cares who the biological father of her children is.

There are no undisputed cases of group marriage in primitive societies, but societies differ greatly in their views on sex. Among many Eskimo tribes, the wife would normally offer sexual hospitality to each visitor from afar. Among the 50 people of the Emerillon tribe of French Guiana, "marriages" are so short-lived that almost everybody marries everyone else of the opposite sex at some time.[4] In the Muria tribe of India, all adolescent boys and girls live together in communal huts with a high degree of sexual freedom, although adolescent lovers are not later permitted to marry.[5]

THE SEXUAL DIVISION OF LABOR

So far, it can be observed that the attitudes and status of women and men, as well as the forms of marriage and family, differ drastically in various societies. How and why?

Some argue that the biology of sex itself determines that women are limited to home and children and must play an inferior role in the economy, in public affairs, and even in the home. According to this view, all social forms everywhere can be explained by biological determinism. Strangely, some radical feminists, like Shulamith Firestone, also take this approach. Firestone argues that male domination is, at origin, due to women's reproductive role.[6] She therefore advocates test-tube babies as the only solution; she seems to forget that childbearing by itself is not very time consuming, and there is no biological reason, given baby bottles, to leave child rearing exclusively to women.

The problem with this approach is that the biology of sex is a constant throughout history and a constant cannot be used to explain changes in societies. For example, French geography cannot be used to explain the French revolution because it was the same before and after. Similarly, sex cannot be used to explain changes in marriage forms or the status of women because sex has remained constant. Neither can the biology of sex be used to explain differences between societies because it is the same in each society: the

---

[4]Claude Levi-Strauss, "The Family," in Arlene and Jerome Skolnick, *Family in Transition* (Boston: Little, Brown, 1971), p. 60.

[5]Ibid., p. 62.

[6]See, e.g., Shulamith Firestone, *The Dialectic of Sex* (New York: Bantam, 1970), passim.

biology of American men and women is no different from that of the Tchambuli of New Guinea.

What we find is that the status of women and the form of marriage are closely related to the division of labor between the sexes and the occupational roles of women and men. An anthropologist writes: "The most important clue to woman's status anywhere is her degree of participation in economic life and her control over property and the products she produces. . . ."[7]

Because it is more efficient and aids survival, every known society divides and specializes labor tasks to some degree. In every known society, women and men do somewhat different tasks (though some still unknown, very primitive societies may have no such division of labor). But the division of labor by sex is totally different in different societies. Whatever one sex does in one society, the other sex does in some other one.

Only 6 percent of all U.S. doctors are women, but Soviet doctors are about 75 percent female. American men seldom take responsibility for child care, but in the Nambikwara tribe fathers take care of babies and clean them when they soil themselves, while many young Nambikwara women disdain domestic activities and prefer hunting and even war expeditions.[8] Most Americans think it is "natural" for men to do the heavy work in society, but women carry all the heavy burdens in about four times as many societies as men do.[9] Likewise, although some would argue that it is "natural" for men to be the providers, there are many societies—such as the Alorese of Eastern Indonesia or the Otomi Indians of Mexico—where women do all the heavy labor while their husbands lie in the shade and gossip.

In most primitive societies the group doing the labor and providing the food has a high status, while the opposite is often true in more advanced societies. We saw that among the Tchambuli of New Guinea, women tend to be aggressive and dominant, men passive and responsive. This is closely related to the fact that Tchambuli women fish and sell their catch in the market while Tchambuli men do the shopping, wear jewelry, love to dance and paint. Thus male and female personalities and status are intimately connected in each society to their economic role. Moreover, just as Mead shows how

[7]Ruby Leavitt, in Vivian Gornick and Barbara Moran, eds., *Women in Sexist Society* (New York: Signet Books, 1971), p. 396.

[8]Levi-Strauss, op. cit., p. 62.

[9]Lucy Komisar, *The New Feminism* (New York: Warner Paperback Library, 1972), p. 159.

society conditions each sex to a particular personality and status, she shows how they are conditioned to accept a certain economic role, a certain part in the division of labor.

Why is the ideology and the whole conditioning process what it is in each society? The basic answer is that in the long run an ideology develops that conditions people to accept what is necessary for the operation and survival of the society under existing power relationships. Different economic conditions require different divisions of labor, and the society will socialize people to think that the division is natural. One archeologist writes, ". . . in the long run an ideology can survive only if it facilitates the smooth and efficient functioning of the economy. If it hampers that, the society—and with it the ideology—must perish in the end."[10] Of course one should emphasize "in the long run." Evolution, even social evolution, takes a long time to eliminate the losers and declare the fittest to be winners. Thus in the short run—which may be a very long time—an ideology may hamper the most efficient working of the society. The ideology may come into being when it is useful and necessary for survival. But each division of labor implies the equality or, often, the dominance of some group. Once a group has power, whether it is slave owners in Rome or white males in America, that group makes every effort to defend and propagate the existing ideology to maintain its position.

We shall see in following sections that the sexist ideology of male supremacy grew out of a division of labor by sex, which was very useful to efficient social development *when it first arose.* Now it hampers further development, but it is promoted, consciously or unconsciously, by males with great power in our society—and by all of us unconsciously, since that is the way we have been conditioned.

HUNTING AND GATHERING SOCIETIES
(OLD STONE AGE)

For 1 to 2 million years, human societies were based on hunting animals and gathering wild food. The available evidence indicates that the men did most of the hunting, while the women gathered fruits, vegetables, and grains. So this first division of labor was along sexual lines. In this very limited sense, Firestone and the male sexists are correct: It appears that the biological facts of childbirth and nursing

---

[10]Gordon Childe, *What Happened in History* (Baltimore: Penguin, 1954, 1971), p. 24.

did limit women's mobility, so it made more sense for men to do the wide-ranging hunting.

This does not mean that women played an inferior role. On the contrary, everything indicates that they worked just as long and hard as the men, their economic contribution was at least as important and more stable, and their status roughly equal. One should not think of "status" in its complex modern forms when speaking of early societies. These were small groups, all relatives, of 20 to 200 people. There was little private property except one's immediate tools or weapons, and very little wealth or property of any kind. There was no government. People worked as a collective unit and shared collectively by tradition and out of the necessity for survival. "The large collective household *was* the community, and within it both sexes worked to produce the goods necessary for livelihood. . . . Women usually furnished a large share—often the major share—of the food."[11] Many hunter-gatherers, such as the Bushmen of the Kalahari Desert, depended primarily on fruits and vegetables gathered by women; the meat provided by men was a luxury.

When Europeans from capitalist societies first came into contact with some of these primitive hunting-gathering societies, they were both shocked and confused by the high status of women and the role of the extended family or collective community. For example, in the seventeenth century, Jesuit missionaries encountered the Naskapi tribe of Canada. The Jesuits were shocked at the great power women possessed to decide where to live and what projects to undertake; they scolded the men for not being masters in their own homes "as in France." They were particularly worried about the degree of sexual freedom women enjoyed—men often didn't know who their biological children were. The Naskapi, however, thought that this objection was nonsensical and that the French were immoral to love only their own children. The Naskapi said: "You French people love only your own children; but we love all the children of our tribe."[12]

AGRICULTURAL VERSUS HERDING SOCIETIES (NEW STONE AGE)

For hundreds of thousands of years, women and men slowly improved their tools and weapons without major changes in social

---

[11]Eleanor Leacock, anthropologist, in Introduction to Frederick Engels, *The Origin of the Family, Private Property, and the State* (New York: New World Paperbacks, 1972), pp. 33–34.

[12]Quoted in ibid., p. 38.

structure. Eventually enough progress was made in improving implements and methods of work to affect social conditions. This change from the Old to the New Stone Age is called the Neolithic Revolution. It occurred 10,000 to 12,000 years ago in the Middle East, somewhat later in other areas, and not at all among a few still-existing primitive tribes.

Two different "discoveries" occurred in the Neolithic Revolution. One was agriculture, the domestication of plants. The other was herding, the domestication of animals. Most societies discovered or emphasized one or the other long before they could do both. In a majority of cases agriculture probably came first.

What does this have to do with the relations of men and women? Everything. There was no change in human biology, but a major social change depending on which sex discovered what. Since men had been hunting, men were the inventors of systematic herding. Since women had been gathering plants, women were the inventors of systematic agriculture.

> It is generally accepted that owing to her ancient role as the gatherer of vegetable foods, woman was responsible for the invention and development of agriculture. Modern analogies indicate that so long as the ground was prepared by hoeing and not by ploughing woman remained the cultivator.[13]

The business of learning agriculture, selection, planting, weeding, and so forth was an extended process that took place over many hundreds of thousands of years. To accomplish it, women had to invent many other things besides methods of cultivation and better hoes. They learned enough chemistry to make pottery that would hold water and could be cooked in. "It has never been doubted that . . . pottery was both shaped and decorated by women."[14] Women learned enough mechanics to construct looms for spinning textiles, as well as better ways of home building (which is a purely feminine occupation in some neolithic tribes). They also learned—and shaped tools for—grinding wheat, constructing ovens, and taking advantage of the biochemistry of yeast to make bread.

In mainly agricultural societies of the primitive hoe type, women were the most important food providers. The meat provided by male hunters was much less significant in quantity and more unstable in supply. As a result, women had a very high status: "The earliest Neolithic societies throughout their range in time and space

---

[13]Hawkes and Woolley, op. cit., p. 265.
[14]Ibid., p. 331.

gave woman the highest status she had ever known."[15] Of course, in class-divided societies the fact that a group does a lot of work does not mean it has high status—quite the contrary. But these societies were still communal, doing work collectively without rulers or bosses. The group that performed a task made all the decisions concerning it. Therefore, the fact that women were often the main food-providing group meant that they made many of the most important social decisions.[16]

Just as the high status of women is strongly correlated with primitive agriculture, so too is the existence of matrilineal clans. When the number of people in a tribe grew to 300 or 400, the old anarchical family structure was no longer possible. The denser population that resulted from agricultural productivity required a new form of organization. The anarchical family was replaced, at a very early date in many places, by the clan system. The evidence from contemporary primitive tribes indicates that they are composed of groups of clans, with the family being of little social importance. Everyone in the clan is supposed to be descended from some mythical ancestor. This ancestor is their symbol of *Totem,* which may be a plant or animal important in the economic life of the tribe.[17] The clan system lasted through the Neolithic Revolution. The clan, not the family, normally held the land in common. An individual "family" might be allocated a plot, but only for immediate use and usually for 1 year only. Pastures were always held in common by the whole clan, as is still the case in many primitive agricultural societies.

Where a society is almost totally dependent on agriculture and women do most of this work, descent and kinship are usually calculated from the female—that is, the clan is matrilineal. Where a society is primarily based on animal herding and men do most of this work, descent and kinship are usually calculated from the male—that is, the clan is patrilineal.[18] Matriliny, early agriculture, and female influence are highly but not perfectly correlated, as are patriliny, herding, and male influence.

Many good examples of matrilineal societies in which women have a high status are found among American Indian cultures. The Hopi technology is similar to the technologies of the New Stone Age, as are their social relations. The Hopi have a matrilineal clan, the

[15]Ibid., p. 264.
[16]Leacock, op. cit., p. 34.
[17]Childe, op. cit., p. 53.
[18]Ibid., p. 73.

leadership of which is mainly in the hands of the older active women.[19] The family group includes a woman's brothers, but not the women who marry them. The whole clan owns the land together and there is no privileged class. The group of men collectively owns the livestock, but the group of women owns the houses, the furnishings, and all the vegetable food. Since vegetables provide most of the food supply, the women are socially and economically secure regardless of whether they are married or not.[20] A woman is always elected clan leader, though her brother leads all ceremonies.

Predominantly livestock-raising tribes were most likely to develop patrilineal clans, since male hunters first tamed animals. Men also invented new weapons and other implements needed for animal herding. In such clans, the family group is organized around and related to an older male. This man is usually, but not always, the dominant personality in the extended family. Yet even where the man is dominant, there is not the demeaning subordination of women found in later class-divided and exploitive societies. So although no Neolithic community shows matriarchy, or all-out female dominance, neither does any Neolithic community show all-out male domination. Each sex continues to do its own important jobs in its own area; there is no oppression.

In a Neolithic community combining some agriculture and animal herding, the men probably cleared the land, built most of the homes, herded the animals, hunted, and manufactured weapons and some tools. The women did all the other agricultural work on the land, made the clothing, made all the pottery, ground the grains, and cooked the food.[21] In these communities men and women had a rough equality of status.

THE ADVENT OF SLAVERY

The Neolithic life was a hard life for all, but the relationship between men and women tended to be characterized by "dignity, freedom and mutual respect."[22] The clan had a collective economy and no slaves. How did all this change in a few thousand years?

Men provided milk and meat from cows, while women hoed the fields. Then great progress was made in lifting the burden of hoe-

[19]Leavitt, op. cit., p. 398.
[20]Ibid.
[21]Childe, op. cit., p. 67.
[22]Kathleen Gough, "The Origin of the Family," in Rayna R. Reither, ed., *Toward An Anthropology of Women* (New York: Monthly Review Press, 1975), p. 75.

ing from women when it was discovered that animals could be domesticated to do the work instead. "The first step, perhaps, was to make a pair of oxen to drag over a field a variant on the hoe that women had hitherto wielded—a plough."[23] Since men had tamed and herded the cattle and oxen, it was men who followed the plough and thus took over the main agricultural duties. Agriculture was totally changed from a female to a male occupation by the use of the plough. This ended some of the hardest labor for women, but it also ended their control of the food supply and reduced their socioeconomic status.[24]

Women, whose shoulders were the oldest means of transport, were replaced by animals pulling wheeled vehicles. Along with the animals came male drivers. Besides the wheel for vehicles, men also invented the potter's wheel; henceforth pottery was done by men. These male inventions helped women live better, but reduced their status. When women no longer carried the heaviest burdens, did most of the agriculture, and made the pottery, the economic bases of women's equal status were removed as well. After men took over agriculture, transport, and pottery, as well as cattle raising, most societies became patriarchal. The male dominated the family or household, which included married sons and their families.

Yet even male economic dominance did not automatically mean the total subordination of women—any more than it did in predominantly herding societies. What sealed the doom of women was the coming of slavery and/or serfdom, which put an end to both collective ownership and the matrilineal clan system. The clan system slowly gave way to a society of individual families with their own private property, beginning with the cattle owned by the male.[25] The process by which the patriarchal family replaced the matrilineal clan as the basic economic unit was always long and usually painful.

The new inventions utilizing animal power greatly increased human productivity. When, in addition, bronze was substituted for wood and stone, a worker could for the first time produce more than enough to guarantee his or her own subsistence. This meant that a surplus of food and other wealth could be accumulated. It meant that specialists could concentrate on one task, such as metalworking, while others could produce food. It meant, above all, that it would be profitable to keep slaves or serfs. Before a worker could produce

[23]Ibid., p. 88.
[24]Ibid., p. 89.
[25]Leacock, op. cit., pp. 40–41.

a surplus, war prisoners were adopted or killed or eaten. When they could produce a surplus, however, they were made into slaves or serfs to be exploited for their master's benefit.

As certain men accumulated wealth in goods or cattle or slaves, they gained the power to oppose the democratic and collective clan structure. The ancient commune was poisoned by class division, private property became the rule, and internal government and armed forces were formed to support the rule of the wealthy owners over the slaves and serfs. The formerly temporary elected war chief could consolidate his position as ruler with this new wealth. Moreover, the male chief found ways to give his sons not only his private wealth but also his authority, and this ruling line of wealth and power became hereditary.[26]

In such societies, even ruling-class women came to be treated as property, the same as slaves and serfs, sometimes more valuable, sometimes less so. Woman's value declined because slaves could do the productive work and because slave women could be used for sexual pleasure. The double standard was instituted whereby a husband could have sex with any woman but the wife was to be strictly monogamous. The reason for the strict control and seclusion of wives was to ensure that only legitimate sons inherited the private wealth.

In ancient Greece, slave women sometimes worked in the fields, but most did household work. They were completely the property of the patriarchs, who could enjoy them sexually at will. Some of the women were allowed slave husbands, but they were still at the master's pleasure—and their children could be taken and sold at any time. Yet it was a crime for any women of the household to have sex with a stranger. In Homer's *Odyssey,* when Odysseus returns home, he first kills his wife's suitors. Then he discovers that 12 of his servant women have had sex (he was gone 10 years), so he orders his son Telemachus: "Take the women out of the hall . . . and use your long swords on them, till none are left alive to remember their lover and the hours they stole in these young gallants' arms."[27] Thus he punishes his property.

Later, in Athenian Greece, 80 percent of all women were slave women; that is, property. The slave owner's wife was to be seen, not heard. She was well-off materially, but even in so-called demo-

---

[26]Childe, op. cit., p. 95.
[27]Quoted in Julia O'Faolain and Lauro Martines, eds., *Not in God's Image* (New York: Harper & Row, 1973), p. 4.

cratic fifth-century Athens, she was not to leave the house. Women were completely secluded—as in some Islamic countries today—and were prohibited from playing any role in the active political life of the city.[28] They were secluded not because of romantic love (a modern concept), but to ensure legitimate heirs. In ancient Greece, even in the ruling-class woman's own home, she could not be present at her own dinner parties unless everyone present was a family member. Moreover, she was required to spend most of her day in the *gynaeceum,* an isolated area of the house that was off limits to any stranger.[29]

Woman's place was in the home with children. Demosthenes said: "Mistresses we keep for our pleasure, concubines for daily attendance upon our person, wives to bear us legitimate children and be our faithful housekeepers."[30] While women were secluded to bear "legitimate children," men were out on the town having sex where they pleased. Euripides has Medea say: "If a man grows tired of the company at home, he can go out, and find a cure for tediousness. We wives are forced to look to one man only."[31] This was the double standard with a vengeance. For lower-class and slave women, life was very different. Many, often against their will or from dire necessity, were forced to become prostitutes, mistresses, or concubines.

The ruling-class man did not stay at home with his wife. Concern with household matters was considered demeaning. He spent his time in the market or the forum or the public baths, talking about economics and politics with other men. Women had no political rights in "democratic" Greece. They could not make contracts for more than a bushel of barley. They were required to have at all times a legal guardian—father or husband or someone appointed. The guardian could give a woman in marriage and could even will her to someone else at his death. Moreover, a man could easily divorce a wife, provided only that he returned her dowry to her father or other guardian. A woman could get a divorce only on rare occasions and under extreme provocation. The husband owned all the property and slaves, and his sons inherited most of it. Ruling-class women usually learned to read and write, but higher education was reserved for boys. Slaves were never educated, except when their job necessitated it.

[28]Childe, op. cit., p. 216.
[29]Cornelius Nepos, quoted in O'Faolain and Martines, op. cit., p. 16.
[30]Quoted in ibid., p. 9.
[31]Quoted in ibid., p. 15.

FEUDALISM

In Western Europe, slavery was followed by feudalism. Under feudalism, human beings were no longer owned by other human beings; rather, serfdom prevailed. Serfs were slightly better off than slaves in that they were not owned, but were merely bound to the landlord's land. Men and women serfs had to labor a certain number of days a year for the landlord; in return, he was supposed to "protect" them. In the earliest period, serfs did need protection from wandering barbarian tribes, but later they needed protection only from the economic and sexual exploitation of the landlords. The landlords, in turn, held their land at the pleasure of the feudal nobility, to whom they owed military support. The same hierarchy of obligations continued through the lesser nobility, to the greater nobility, and thence to the king, who owed allegiance only to God.

The nobility was divided into secular and religious nobles. The Church was the largest single landowner, the holder of most accumulated knowledge, and the greatest power in Europe during this period. The Church had a very low opinion of women. In the first century, St. Paul said: "The head of the woman is the man. . . . For a man . . . is the image and glory of God. . . . I suffer not a woman to teach, nor to usurp authority over the man, but to be in silence."[32] A few hundred years later, St. Augustine repeated the notion: "The woman herself is not the image of God; whereas the man alone is the image of God. . . ."[33] Finally, in the thirteenth century, St. Thomas Aquinas could still write: "As regards the individual nature, woman is defective and misbegotten, for the active force in the male seed tends to the production of a perfect likeness in the masculine sex; while the production of woman comes from a defect in the active force. . . ."[34]

Although the Church stated clearly that women were the weaker and inferior sex, that did not stop either secular or religious landlords from working their women serfs in the fields the same as the men. Women did every kind of agricultural labor except heavy plowing. In England, in 1265, a serf's widow had the following obligations to the lord of the manor: ". . . From Michaelmas to the Feast of St. Peter in Chains she must plow half an acre every week. . . . And from the Feast of St. John the Baptist until August she must perform manual service 3 days every week. . . ."[35] She was also re-

---

[32] Quoted in ibid., p. 128.
[33] Quoted in ibid., p. xi.
[34] Quoted in ibid., p. 131.
[35] An old manual, quoted in ibid., pp. 160–161.

quired one day a week to transport goods on her back anywhere the bailiff told her to go. In addition, she had to find 4 days in the spring to mow the landlord's meadow, 4 more days to gather hay for him, and 2 more days for weeding his land. In some places, female serfs were exempted from work on the lord's land, but that only meant they did most of the work on the serf's own plot.

Female serfs were also used in the lords' homes. Their lot was described by an English Franciscan monk in the thirteenth century. He stated that the domestic serf or chambermaid had to do the heaviest and foulest jobs, was given the poorest food and clothing, had to marry whomever the lord told her to marry, and had to give her children to the lord as serfs. The monk stated matter-of-factly: "Chambermaids are frequently beaten, . . . they rebel against their masters and mistresses and get out of hand if they are not kept down. . . . Serfs and that sort are kept in place only through fear."[36]

During the early feudal era even free women and the wives and daughters of lords had little freedom. One important outlet for women was the nunnery. There, serf women still did all the hardest work but were protected from male exploitation. Upper-class women had the opportunity to get an education, which they were otherwise denied. Furthermore, they could live their own lives, practice management and business, and assume leadership roles respected by the whole community. From the sixth to the twelfth centuries, nuns were treated on an equal basis with monks. In fact, the women who headed the larger nunneries often were the representatives of the king or the pope in that area. They had judicial powers to try and to sentence people, and they sometimes even raised armies. Education and scholarship were highly regarded in nuns, so there were some famous women scholars at a time when most people lived in total ignorance.

Later, the Protestant Reformation closed many nunneries, but by that time increased urbanization and the spread of commerce and industry had opened up new opportunities for upper-class women. The wives of some of the powerful lords themselves grasped power when their husbands were away fighting wars. Some of the crafts in the cities were opened to women. However, in most of the guilds, which were a sort of combined monopoly and trade union organization of small craftsmen, women were not admitted to full status—and everywhere women were paid lower wages. Yet in Paris, by 1300, five different crafts were completely dominated by women, some

[36]Quoted in ibid., p. 163.

of whom accumulated considerable fortunes. Women monopolized weaving and spinning in most of Europe—hence the name "spinster" for older unmarried women. Women in England were also barbers, apothecaries, armorers, shipwrights, and tailors.[37] By the late medieval period, a few bourgeois women were in business for themselves as wholesale and retail merchants.

As early as the thirteenth century, the beginning of capitalist relations caused some improvements in the lives of well-to-do bourgeois women, due to their greater economic strength. They were still treated as inferiors, however. There were legal changes that allowed a married woman who was engaged in trade to be considered legally as a *femme sole* or single woman.[38] In other words, feudal law gave married women no rights, so when women began to go into business they were treated as if they were single. As women went into commerce on a wider scale, their legal and social position began to rise, although very slowly. Even the nonbusinesswoman who was married to a bourgeois husband had a wide range of duties, including acting as a doctor for her family and taking over the family business when necessary. Under these conditions, increased respect was fostered between husband and wife.

Although women played a greater economic role in the feudal period than stereotypes would indicate, they continued to be fettered legally and prohibited from participating in public life, as they had been under slavery. Married women had no power over property and no power to make contracts. Men managed and had complete power over all the family property. A late sixteenth-century English lawyer wrote:

> Every Feme Covert (married woman) is a sort of infant. . . . It is seldom, almost never that a married woman can have any action to use her wit only in her own name: her husband is her stern, her prime mover, without whom she cannot do much at home, and less abroad. . . . It is a miracle that a wife should commit any suit without her husband.[39]

The only exception, even in the late feudal period, was the right of

---

[37]See A. Abram, "Women Traders in Medieval London," in Susan Bell, ed., *Women: From the Greeks to the French Revolution* (Belmont, Calif.: Wadsworth, 1973), p. 153.

[38]Eileen Power, "The Position of Women," in ibid., p. 163. Ms. Power has written a great deal on medieval women in other books and articles.

[39]Quoted in O'Faolain and Martines, op. cit., p. 145.

a married woman engaged in trade to make certain binding contracts. Acts making this possible were not passed till the fifteenth century. Only in the seventeenth century did the equity courts of England devise ways for rich women to hold separate property while married. In most areas, in the feudal period, even widows usually did not own family property but could use it only in their lifetimes as trustees for their male children. The only woman who regained full rights to property and contractual rights was the childless widow. Among the feudal lords, all marriages were arranged by the parents, often while the children were still in their cradles. The important criteria for a good marriage were the joining of another family's land and military power. Love had nothing to do with it. In the late feudal period, when bourgeois families first emerged into riches and power, the same custom prevailed. Marriages were arranged on the basis of the relative fortunes of different families. Again, love had nothing to do with it.

The feudal lords also generally had the right to decide whom their underlords and ladies should marry. They even had the right to decide whom a widow should marry—though she was to be given a year to herself. The lesser lords, in turn, might decide whom their serfs should marry. On the whole, though, no one cared whom a serf married because no land or power was involved. The father of a serf sometimes decided whom the son or daughter would marry, but sometimes he didn't pay any attention. In fact, many serfs lived together without marriage. Thus at least a few serfs may have married or lived together for love (though there is no evidence one way or the other).

Since marriage was not founded on "love," even in theory, divorces were never granted for incompatibility, nor in fact were divorces granted for any reason under Church law. A marriage might be annulled for very specific reasons: fraud in the marriage contract, nonconsummation of marriage, or the parties' being too closely related. A legal separation might be granted for adultery or leprosy, but not much else. Only in very rare cases in which the woman's family was very powerful would a legal separation be granted for extreme brutality and cruelty. A "normal" amount of violence against the wife was expected. A writer in late thirteenth-century France said: "In a number of cases men may be excused for the injuries they inflict on their wives, nor should the law intervene. Provided he neither kills or maims her, it is legal for a man to beat his wife when she wrongs him—for instance, when she is about to surrender her body to another man, when she contradicts or abuses him, or when she refuses, like a decent woman, to obey his reasonable commands."[40] A woman's husband was her lord, so if she attacked him she was a traitor. She could be burned at the stake if she killed him for any reason; he could kill her for adultery.

Since almost all marriages were marriages of convenience, arranged by the couple's parents, it was assumed that they involved no romantic love. Thus the concept of romantic love in literature first arises in reference to the extramarital liaisons of wandering knights or troubadours with the love- and sex-starved wives of lords. It is this image of medieval love that comes down to us: of knights chivalrously saving ladies from ogres, eternal but unsatisfied devotion, and serenades.

As we have seen, this image bore no relation to the usual marriage under feudalism. It might be added that the religious lords were supposed to be celibate, so their sexual activity was an even greater transgression of God's law. The songs of chivalrous love seem to reflect only the frustrations of the ruling-class women and the illegal desires (and activities) of some of the men. Of course such extramarital sex was mostly condoned for men but not for women.

The idea of mixing romantic love with marriage began to have a little more substance only when a middle class grew larger in the cities of the late feudal period:

> The aristocracy and the upper classes of the towns tended to regard sex with the greedy cynicism and tolerant amusement we find in Boccaccio's stories. . . . On the other hand, the artisan class in the towns followed a life-pattern that gave new meaning to marriage. The growth of craft production established a mutuality of interest within the family. The master of a trade performed his tasks at home, assisted by his wife and children.[41]

In these circumstances, the woman assumed a more important role in the family, ensuring its survival if the man died. The woman was treated somewhat more equally, and marriage for love, or at least the development of love within marriage, became a little more common. Nevertheless, the double standard carried over from feudalism to modern capitalism, so much so that the following description of sexist views of women might characterize the early twentieth century as well as it characterized the thirteenth century in Western European society: "The degradation of women is based on class dis-

---

[40]Quoted in ibid., p. 175.
[41]John Howard Lawson, *The Hidden Heritage* (New York: Citadel, 1968), p. 57.

tinctions, and is exhibited in the treatment of the upper-class woman as a prized sexual object as well as the assumption that women of the less privileged classes are available to the conquering male for casual gratification."[42] The only difference was that this outlook was partly institutionalized in the feudal period. For example, the feudal lord had the right of the first night—the right to have the first sexual intercourse with the new bride of a serf—though in the later feudal period it was often bought off by a monetary tribute.

Partly because of their double oppression, serf women generally played a major role in the peasant rebellions and protest movements. In some areas where heretics tried to found more egalitarian communities, there were more equal relationships between men and women. As a consequence, the first charge against the founders of these communities was always "free love." Similarly, when the peasants organized nocturnal assemblies pledged to rebellion against lay and clerical lords, their enemies often described them as "witches' sabbaths" because of the leading role women played in them. Women were the main doctors and healers for several centuries, and this also gave those in power a chance to persecute them as witches. Because ignorance was so pervasive in those times, all medical cures were ascribed to magic. "The idea of the woman as a witch—which led to such brutal persecutions over the centuries—is in part a superstitious acknowledgement of her special medical skill. But the more profound reason for accusations of sorcery lay in the fear of the woman's social influence, her role in organizing protest against oppression, and the necessity of *keeping her in her place.*"[43]

THE TRANSITION TO CAPITALISM

In the fourteenth and fifteenth centuries, some forms of commercial capitalism began to appear in Northern Italy and Flanders (Holland and Belgium). In the towns of these areas, the new socioeconomic conditions gave rise to the whirlwind of changing ideas known as the Renaissance. One major strain of the Renaissance was the humanist philosophy expressed by scholars like Erasmus. The humanists emphasized that the widest possible education leads to the greatest virtue. For the first time a large number of writers argued in favor of educating women as well as men, both for their own sakes and for the further education of their children. In 1516 Thomas More

[42]Ibid., p. 60.
[43]Ibid., p. 61.

wrote in his *Utopia* that women must be educated equally with men, though some books were more appropriate to one sex and some to the other.[44]

Humanist prescriptions were actually put into effect for most upper-class Western European women. This education and new appreciation for women's minds resulted in a large number of famous women scholars and doers in this period. In Italy, Beatrice d'Este (1475–1497) showed considerable political skill. Her sister Isabella (1474–1539) brought order and affluence to her husband's impoverished estate and used the new wealth to become the patron of many great poets and artists. In Spain, Queen Isabella (1451–1504) successfully unified Spain, founded new universities, subsidized scholars, and funded Columbus' expedition. Princess Marguerite of Angoulème in France (1492–1549) encouraged and protected many humanist scholars as well as some persecuted Protestant reformers. She was a writer of note, including in her works both lofty poems of mystical religious beauty and a book of lewd stories, the *Heptameron,* which has been compared with Boccaccio's *Decameron.* Yet she also found time to deal carefully with statesmen and ambassadors on behalf of her brother, the king of France.

Another woman who played a very important political role was Catherine de Medici (1519–1589), the niece of a powerful pope and herself regent of France. Still another Renaissance woman worthy of mention was Elizabeth I of England (1533–1603), whose education was of the highest caliber. Her tutor gave her the sexist compliment that "the constitution of her mind is exempt from female weakness, and she is endowed with a masculine power of application. No apprehension can be quicker than hers, no memory more retentive."[45] There was much more to this than flattery. Elizabeth I kept peace between the warring English factions, actively led England to a successful defense against the Spanish Armada, and encouraged the great artists and writers of what we call the Elizabethan period.

Unfortunately, this early rise in the status of women was cut short by increasing religious bigotry during the wars accompanying the Protestant Reformation. The Protestant preachers gave thunderous sermons against sinful wives. Their very practical advice told husbands how to keep their wives meek and subservient.[46] Thus

[44]See excerpts of humanist writers in Susan Bell, op. cit., Part 5.
[45]Quoted in ibid., p. 215.
[46]Ibid., p. 200.

much of the feminine advance, but not all of it, was set back in the sixteenth and seventeenth centuries. The Protestant sects particularly saw the husband as the secular ruler and religious head of his household, charged with making sure that the whole household was obedient to the desires of king and church. Women still could own no property, were expected to be silent, and were required to obey their husbands and God.

Yet at the same time the Reformation led to greater political participation by some women—those who participated in the most radical religious sects. At this time the political spectrum was represented in the spectrum of religious sects. The more radical sects—the Brownists, the Baptists, and the Quakers, for example—did strive for socioeconomic as well as religious change. All agreed that women should have spiritual equality, though none argued for social equality. As a result, many women joined these sects and played a prominent role in their struggles. In them, women could express themselves publicly; they learned more about the world, and many emancipated themselves from the restrictions of the family—though those who were married still had to render obedience to their husbands.

St. Paul had prohibited women from preaching. Yet by the 1630s and 1640s, women were preachers in the radical sects in Holland, England, and Massachusetts. There were so many women among the Quakers that some thought the sect was limited to women.[47] Women were important among the Quakers even in the universities, and in the 1670s they started to hold their own women's meetings and to send delegates to take part in the church's governing bodies.

Women also played a major role in the Revolution of 1640–1666 that ended feudalism in England. Upper-class women took over estates when their husbands were exiled and directly helped them escape. Many working-class women joined the radical Levellers. In 1649 their leader, Lilbourne, and three other leaders were arrested: "When the men durst not any more petition in behalf of Lilbourne and his associates, the women took it up."[48]

During the sixteenth and seventeenth centuries, capitalism was spreading throughout Western Europe. Many bourgeois women became involved in business in town and country. Willy-nilly, education—at least the learning of arithmetic—spread to these women. In

[47]Ibid., p. 226.
[48]Quoted in O'Faolain and Martines, op. cit., p. 268.

Holland, women learned accounting and kept the books in most businesses.

Still, there was plenty of resistance to the education of women; many men insisted they should be kept in their place in the home. Molière satirized these sentiments when he had a man in his play *Les Femmes Savantes* (1672) say:

> I'm speaking to you, sister. . . . I don't like all these useless books of yours. Apart from that big Plutarch that keeps my neckbands pressed, you should burn them all. . . . It's not decent . . . for a woman to study and know so much. Teaching her children good principles, running her household, keeping an eye on her servants, and managing her budget thriftily are all the study and philosophy she needs.[49]

Meanwhile, working-class women of town and country were kept too busy to even entertain the possibility of acquiring an education. In 1555, Sir Anthony Fitzherbert explained carefully the chores of a good country wife:

> First set all things in good order within thy house, milk the kine, suckle thy calves, strain up thy milk . . . get corn and malt ready for the mill to make and brew. . . . Thou must make butter and cheese when thou may, serve thy swine both morning and evening . . . take heed how thy hens, ducks, and geese do lay. . . . In the beginning of March is time for a wife to make her garden and to get as many good seeds and herbs as she can. . . . March is time to sow flax and hemp . . . to help her husband to fill the muck wain or dung cart, drive the plow, to load hay, corn and such other.[50]

THE ENLIGHTENMENT AND THE FRENCH REVOLUTION

The English Revolution of 1648 ended feudalism in one country, helped raise the status of women, and produced several philosophers, like John Locke, who were dedicated to equality and freedom. The American Revolution of 1776 ended colonial control in another country, spread revolutionary ideas of liberty and the pursuit of happiness for all, and encouraged some people to raise the question of women's rights (see Chapter 9). But the French Revolution—which was influenced directly and indirectly by the English and American revolutions—had a much wider and more profound impact on all of Europe and the United States. It ended feudalism and encouraged

[49]Quoted in ibid., pp. 244–245.
[50]Quoted in ibid., p. 253.

capitalism and parliamentarianism over a large part of Europe. More important, perhaps, its philosophers, like Voltaire and Rousseau, put on everyone's tongue the ideas of liberty, equality, and *fraternité,* or brotherhood.

These philosophers of enlightenment spoke only of brotherhood, not sisterhood. Some of them, like Condorcet, did speak in favor of women's rights, but they were in the minority. Many spoke of liberty and equality for all *men* but continued to hold an utterly reactionary position on women. This position was stated baldly by Jean-Jacques Rousseau in *Emile,* his manual on education:

> Men and women are made for each other, but their mutual dependence is not equal. . . . We could survive without them better than they could without us. . . . Thus women's entire education should be planned in relation to men. To please men, to be useful to them, to win their love and respect, to raise them as children, care for them as adults, counsel and console them, make their lives sweet and pleasant; these are women's duties in all ages and these are what they should be taught from childhood.[51]

In spite of such male attitudes, women did play a role in the French Revolution. Upper-class women held *salons,* meeting places for the elite and the intelligentsia, in which a vast amount of criticism was voiced and digested. Much of the critical discussion of the seventeenth century was literary and artistic, but by the eigthteenth century many of the salons turned to religious, philosophical, and finally political criticism. Many of the ideas of the Enlightenment and the Revolution were first discussed in these salons, which played the role the news media play today. Many of the initial contacts necessary for the Revolution were made in these salon gatherings. The salon of Madame Roland, for example, became the intellectual center of the Girondist party.

During the Revolution itself, working-class women played a very important part. Since feeding the family was seen as a feminine role, women were the leaders in the bread riots that formed the background of the Revolution. And many women took part in storming the Bastille and liberating its prisoners.

Moreover, women finally found voice to speak for themselves. In 1789, the French Assembly proclaimed the Rights of Man. In 1791, Olympe de Gouges replied with a *Declaration of the Rights of Woman:*

---

[51]Quoted in ibid., pp. 246–247.

Woman is born free and her rights are the same as those of man.
. . . The law must be an expression of the general will; all citizens,
men and women alike, must participate in making it. . . . Women have
the right to go to the scaffold; they must also have the right to go to
parliament. . . .[52]

One of the most remarkable people of her time was Mary Wollstonecraft, an English writer and activist. At a time when most
women stayed in the home and were uneducated, she made a living
by writing novels, critical essays, and book reviews. She lived an independent life, despite the economic and social constraints on
women. She lived with a man without marriage for some time, participated in an artistic and liberal discussion circle on an equal basis,
married a leading anarchist philosopher (William Godwin), and was
the mother of Mary Shelley (author of *Frankenstein* and wife of the
poet Percy Bysshe Shelley). When married, she continued to live in
a separate residence and to act and write independently.

When the French Revolution broke out, its liberal philosophy
and actions were attacked by the conservative Edmund Burke. Wollstonecraft wrote *A Vindication of the Rights of Men* which was the
first reply to Burke. She even went to France in order to live in a freer
country. Most important of all, in 1792, Wollstonecraft wrote *A Vindication of the Rights of Woman*. This book reflected the liberal
ideas of Locke and Voltaire and Rousseau, but argued that they must
now be applied equally to women. It was the first full-scale book
favoring women's liberation, and nineteenth-century leaders of the
women's movement in Europe and the United States read it and were
much affected by it. Wollstonecraft argued that human limitations
are given not by nature but by social environment, that men *and*
women can learn anything if they are given the opportunity. She described the average woman as totally subordinate and dehumanized
by social constraints and lack of education. She spoke of the constraints and limitations on women's education and opportunities in
very personal terms, as she herself suffered most of them in her early
years. Women, she claimed, had been reduced to sex objects: A
woman is "the toy of man, his rattle, and it must jingle in his ears
whenever, dismissing reason, he chooses to be amused."[53]

Although Wollstonecraft accepted Rousseau's liberal philoso-

[52]Quoted in ibid., p. 307.
[53]Quoted from Wollstonecraft, "Vindication," in Eleanor Flexner, *Mary Wollstonecraft* (Baltimore: Penguin, 1973). Flexner's is an excellent, moving biography, a delightful experience to read.

phy, she wrote a detailed critique of his views on women's education, tearing them to shreds as a piece of sexist nonsense. As a substitute, she expressed some of the earliest ideas on progressive education for both male and female, rich and poor. Her earlier works argued for the fullest education possible for middle-class and upper-class women. She later became aware of and exposed the crimes against working-class women, their miseries, and their need for liberation. In her *Rights of Women* she wrote: "It is time to effect a revolution in female manners—time to restore to them their lost dignity—and make them, as part of the human species, labour by reforming themselves, to reform the world."[54]

WOMEN UNDER FRENCH CAPITALISM

In 1787, on the eve of the French Revolution, an economic study in France showed that working women in manufacturing made only 15 sous a day. The cost of a day's food was at least 14 or 15 sous, so these women had no money for anything but food. The average wage for men was twice as much, or 30 sous, so women were dependent on men for survival. A petition to the king in 1789 by women described their lot: "If nature has not granted them good looks, they get married . . . to unfortunate artisans and drag out a grueling existence in the depths of the provinces, producing children whom they are unable to bring up. If . . . they are pretty, . . . they fall prey to the first seducer, make one slip, come to Paris to conceal it, . . . and end up dying as victims of debauchery."[55]

After the Revolution, there were three interrelated changes. First, the feudal nobility were destroyed and the political balance swung to the bourgeoisie. Second, feudal economic relations were replaced by capitalist ones; that is, serf labor was replaced by "free" labor. Capitalists hired, if it looked profitable, free men and women; the workers were free to work for what the capitalists offered, or starve. Third, the Industrial Revolution meant a vast increase in all of Western Europe of jobs in industry and commerce and resulted in a great population movement from rural to urban areas (though France changed more slowly than England).

These changes did eventually affect women, but for a long time the effects were hardly noticeable. A study in 1840 found that women still worked 15 hours a day, they were still paid about the same 15 sous a day, and men still earned about twice as much.

[54]Ibid., p. 151.
[55]Quoted in O'Faolain and Martines, op. cit., p. 305.

"Generally speaking, a man can earn enough to save, but a woman scarcely makes enough to subsist on and a child of less than twelve years hardly earns the price of his food."[56] Since machinery required less physical strength, employers hired more women and children, who could be paid very little for very long hours. Yet since the whole family could survive if all its members worked, capitalists were able to reduce the wages of men accordingly.

In 1793, many women were still active in political clubs (the main driving force of the Revolution), such as the club of Revolutionary Republican Women, but in that year all the women's clubs were suppressed. Women's participation in politics was violently opposed during the whole nineteenth century. In government employment, women were only allowed to be schoolmasters and postmasters. The Napoleonic Code gave all management of family funds to the husband, punished female but not male adultery, and did not allow a married woman to bring suit without her husband's permission. The Revolutionary Assembly legalized divorce in 1792, but reaction resulted in a reversal in 1814, when divorce was again forbidden. Legalizing legislation was not finally passed till 1884.

The awful conditions and wages of working women inspired the first socialist women's liberationist. In 1843, Flora Tristan wrote a pamphlet called the *Workers Union*. In it she advocated both socialism and equal rights for women in politics, education, and work. She admitted that the bourgeoisie resisted her socialism, while the workers resisted her ideas on women's liberation.

In 1849, two women socialists formed a workers' union dedicated to women's liberation and socialism. They and the men who joined it were arrested for forming a political association, which was a crime, and sent to prison. The two women, Jeanne Deroin and Pauline Roland, had also launched the first feminist socialist newspaper, *L'Opinion des Femmes*. The newspaper and union were formed in the aftermath of the Revolution of 1848. But the return of reaction in 1851, when they had just gotten out of prison, forced them into exile. No more political activity was undertaken by women until the Paris Commune of 1871, when many women participated and were killed along with the men.

Only very slowly did middle-class women in France win any rights. During the 1870s, they were finally admitted to French universities. Women were allowed to practice medicine by 1875 but not to practice law until 1900. Married women could not dispose of their

[56]Contemporary statistician, quoted in ibid., p. 309.

own earnings until 1907, and they had no independent legal capacity until 1938. Women were not allowed to vote in France until after the liberation from German fascism in 1944!

French women had struggled for the vote ever since 1870, when universal suffrage was granted to men. In 1885, Madame Barbarousse claimed that the law said "all French" *(tout français)* were enfranchised, so women could also vote; but the court held that *tout français* did not include French women.

In spite of the barriers, some French women did distinguish themselves. The most outstanding was Marie Curie, one of only two people ever to receive *two* Nobel prizes. She received the prize for physics jointly with her husband in 1903 and won the chemistry prize by herself in 1911.

WOMEN UNDER BRITISH CAPITALISM
The Industrial Revolution was most rapid in England. It reduced physical work requirements and brought women and children into the factories and the mines—where they could crawl into smaller tunnels than men. Employers generally tried to hire a whole family for the same wage they had previously paid for the man alone. The Victorian ethic proclaimed that the family should instill discipline and hard work and that women should produce many children. Protestant sects, such as the Wesleyan, preached against any freedom for women of the working classes.

Working conditions were so bad and wages so low that thousands of women were forced into prostitution. Men have always had a double standard toward this institution. On the one hand, they condemn the poor women forced into prostitution, and applaud every time the police round them up. On the other hand, society seldom arrests the men who patronize prostitutes or the pimps and organized criminals who make most of the profits from prostitution. Men often defend it on the "sewer theory," first enunciated by St. Augustine: "Rid society of prostitutes, and licentiousness will run riot throughout. . . . Prostitutes in a city are like a sewer in a palace. If you get rid of the sewer, the whole palace becomes filthy and foul."[57] Throughout the Industrial Revolution, women remained at the bottom of society, both as prostitutes and as workers in the dirtiest jobs.

In England during the early nineteenth century, women still had few legal rights. In 1840 a judge ruled:

[57]Quoted in O'Faolain and Martines, op. cit., p. 290.

The question raised in this case is, simply, whether by common law the husband, in order to prevent his wife from eloping, has a right to confine her in his own dwelling-house, and restrain her from liberty, for an indefinite time, using no cruelty. . . . There can be no doubt . . . "the husband hath by law power and dominion over his wife, and may keep her by force . . . and may beat her, but not in a violent or cruel manner."[58]

Moreover, a husband could get a divorce on the ground that his wife committed adultery, but a woman could get a divorce only on the grounds that her husband committed adultery *and* was extremely cruel. Only Parliament could grant divorces and almost all divorces were granted to men. Only four women got divorces in 200 years; all four were cases of incest and/or bigamy plus adultery plus cruelty. In the first case, the woman's husband had committed adultery with her sister. Yet divorce was *rejected* for a Ms. Dawson, where it was admitted that her husband committed adultery and beat her with a horsewhip and hairbrush.

Only very slowly and under pressure from organized women's protests were any changes made. In 1856, 26,000 women petitioned Parliament to allow married women to keep their own earnings and inherited property.[59] In 1857, divorced women were finally granted the same rights as single women; married women obtained these rights only slowly in acts of 1870, 1882, and 1893. These acts concentrated mainly on property ownership and benefited primarily the middle-class women who constituted most of the women's movement up to that point.

The feature of the British scene that most affected the women's movement was the very strong hold of elitism and upper-class control of the political process. Thus in much of the nineteenth century, radicals were concerned primarily with extending the vote to working-class men (who were barred by property qualifications) and only secondarily concerned with suffrage for women. On the other hand, many conservatives wanted to extend suffrage to aristocratic or propertied women to increase the vote of the Conservative party. Since the Liberals feared this increase, they opposed all measures that would have enfranchised single women who were property owners. The Liberal politician, Lord Acton, wrote: "Girls and widows are Tories, and channels of clerical influence."[60]

[58]Quoted in ibid., p. 318.
[59]Ibid., p. 331.
[60]Quoted in Andrew Sinclair, *The Emancipation of the American Woman* (New York: Harper & Row, 1965), pp. 277–278.

The first British women's political groups formed in the 1830s to combat slavery around the world. In the 1840s, middle-class women organized the first women's rights groups in the industrial towns of Sheffield and Manchester—where many middle-class men were radicals because they felt left out of British political life. These groups were local and temporary. The first permanent group was the Manchester Women's Suffrage Committee, founded in 1867 by Lydia Becker. By 1868, more than 5000 Manchester women were organized for suffrage. And in 1869, unmarried women householders were given the right to vote in local elections. Ms. Becker fought for women's rights for the rest of her life and edited the *Woman Suffrage Journal* for 20 years.

At this time, middle-class women were beginning to enter the economy. Florence Nightingale helped found nursing as a proper profession for middle-class women. Thousands of women became school teachers and hundreds of thousands became office workers, bookkeepers, and typists.

On the basis of this economic activity, middle-class women exerted more and more pressure for suffrage. Harriet Taylor, whose husband was the philosopher John Stuart Mill, was one of the first writers in England to press for women's rights. In 1867, she persuaded her husband to move an amendment to an election reform bill in Parliament to give women the right to vote. It was defeated by 194 votes to 73, but the strength shown for it was a surprise to everyone. For the rest of the century, similar bills were introduced every year, but all were unsuccessful. In 1868 Mill, with help from his wife, wrote *On the Subjection of Women,* in which he advocated equal political rights for women. Many conservative members of Parliament moved bills to enfranchise only propertied women, and these won majorities three times, but they never reached the necessary second reading because the government always took a neutral position on them.

In the 1880s and 1890s, the women's movement grew as Lydia Becker gathered all the local groups into a National Union of Women's Suffrage Societies. This group worked mainly for a limited suffrage restricted to educated middle-class women. There was still, however, unremitting opposition from much of Victorian society. Victoria herself, when she heard that a Lady Amberley had publicly demanded the vote, said: "The Queen is most anxious to enlist everyone who can speak or write to join in checking this mad, wicked folly of 'Woman's Rights' with all its attendant horrors, on which her poor feeble sex is bent, forgetting every sense of womanly feeling and propriety. Lady Amberley ought to get a good whipping."[61]

The women's movement picked up real steam when the militant Emmeline Pankhurst, widow of a radical Manchester Labourite, joined the fight for suffrage. She and her two daughters, Christabel and Sylvia, were at first socialists who worked through the Labour party. They were important enough to be widely slandered. Even a modern British historian, writing in 1971, describes them in an utterly sexist fashion and worries primarily over whether they were ladies. He writes:

> Mrs. Pankhurst was a lady, and a lady of immense determination, considerable skill in speaking and . . . [had] no regard for her health . . . or her life itself if they had to be sacrificed for the cause. Christabel was . . . very obviously good-looking, she had immense vitality, she had her mother's skill as a speaker; it was not quite so clear that she was a lady. Sylvia was fairly certainly not a lady.[62]

(Such cutesiness characterizes the writings of most male historians of the women's movement, except when they very seriously worry about how many of the leaders were lesbians.)

The British Labour party refused to support the Pankhurst demand of suffrage for a limited number of middle-class women, most of whom would probably vote Conservative. Pankhurst and her daughters then formed the militant Women's Social and Political Union in 1903. It immediately derived considerable support from the women in the factories due to the efforts of Annie Kenney, herself a mill worker.

The Pankhursts decided that the previously respectable tactics of the suffrage movement would never get anywhere, that publicity was needed, and that spectacular actions would get publicity. In 1905 Christabel and Annie Kenney were arrested for causing a disturbance at a political meeting. In the following decade, hundreds of British women were arrested for stone-throwing, hitting policemen (who hit them brutally in return), and chaining themselves to the railings in front of Number 10 Downing Street, the prime minister's residence. The police were usually very, very careful about upper-class women, but in 1905 they brutally clubbed *any* women demonstrat-

[61]Ibid., p. 283.
[62]Trevor Lloyd, *Suffragettes International* (New York: American Heritage Press, 1971), p. 60.

ing for their rights. The press reacted with sympathy, as did the general public.

The women protesters particularly heckled Herbert Asquith, prime minister from 1908 to 1916, who bitterly opposed votes for women as a Conservative device. Many were imprisoned as a nuisance for ringing his bell. In 1907 there was a large, peaceful parade by moderate supporters of suffrage. Three days later a parade by the militants was attacked by mounted police who rode down many women. A Ms. Drummond was arrested for breaking into a cabinet meeting and yelling, "Votes for women." A Ms. Matters dropped leaflets from a balloon high over London. In 1908 Pankhurst's WSPU held a meeting in Hyde Park, which, according to the *London Times,* was attended by 500,000 people.

Also in 1908, Pankhurst and two others were arrested and convicted of trying to provoke a breach of peace at a meeting. In 1909, they and every other suffragist in prison went on a hunger strike. At first the government released each woman when she grew weak. But that was too easy and made the government look silly. So they started force-feeding the women, which aroused immense public opposition.

In 1910, the Conservatives introduced a bill to allow voting by women who owned property. It got a majority on first reading but was finally killed by the Liberals. The next year, Asquith's government announced that it would introduce a bill to give the vote to all men and would allow amendments to give the vote to women. But the government stalled until 1913, when it killed its own bill by parliamentary maneuvering. Women in this period showed their anger by breaking all the windows in Piccadilly Circus one day, for which 200 were arrested. They also wrote "Votes for women" in acid on some golf courses. In 1912 the Labour party conference voted that it would support no further extension of suffrage without suffrage for women—a remarkable stance, since it went contrary to their own immediate objective of expanding the working-class male vote.

Against this rising tide of support for women's rights there was a reactionary backlash. A "distinguished" doctor, Sir Almroth Wright, wrote to the *London Times* that half the women in England go somewhat mad during menopause and all the militant women were mentally ill.[63] A "distinguished" criminologist named Lambroso said that "even the normal woman is a half-criminaloid being."[64]

[63]Quoted in ibid., p. 86.
[64]Quoted in ibid., p. 87.

The government passed a so-called Cat and Mouse Act, by which it could release from prison a militant woman who became weak from a hunger strike, and then rearrest her as soon as she regained her health.

In 1914, the outbreak of the war suddenly ended almost all suffrage activity. Both moderate women and militants suddenly became superpatriots. Only a small socialist women's organization led by Sylvia Pankhurst (who had split with her mother and sister as they became more friendly to the Conservatives) remained true to women's suffrage. She went to jail for opposing the war on the grounds that it was both inhuman and a mask for British and German imperialism.

The war, however, did have a major effect on the position of women. Hundreds of thousands went into munitions factories, where they ran the risk of being blown up. Many others kept the rest of the economy and government agencies running during the war. Still others became nurses at the front, drove army trucks, and ran the army communications system. Much of this involvement was amply reported in the British press.

In 1918, partly as a reward for helping win the war and partly under the continued pressure of socialist militants, the government at last gave universal suffrage to men and women. Men were eligible to vote at 21, while women could not vote until they were 30. This age difference was justified on the basis that women constituted a majority of the population. For most women leaders the granting of suffrage largely ended the fight. They continued to argue only for legal rights to property and political equality, all of which were granted in the 1920s. In 1928, women were given the right to vote at 21, and that completely ended the suffrage movement.

WOMEN
IN THE
CONTEMPORARY WORLD

9

A thorough analysis of the status of women around the world would require many books. A brief survey of different kinds of societies can provide an overview of the progress women have made and of changes that are still necessary. In this chapter, we will examine women's place in the capitalist democracies of Western Europe, in several socialist societies, and in selected Third World countries.

WESTERN EUROPE
Although the Western European countries differ among themselves, they are more similar to each other and to the United States than the other countries we will examine. Most of the Western European countries are more generous in their social welfare policies than the United States, but their economies are quite similar to our own. As we will see, the status of women in Western Europe is also not radically different from that in the United States.

Legal rights
The English common law, with its doctrine of coverture, granted very few rights to married women. Women who lived in countries with legal systems derived from Roman Law were even worse off. There, even unmarried women remained under the guardianship of a male relative all their lives.[1] The Code Napoleon, a codification and standardization of Roman Law that spread across Western Europe, classified women with children along with "persons of unsound mind"

[1] Kathleen Newland, *The Sisterhood of Man* (New York: Norton, 1979), pp. 12–13.

as incapable of entering into contracts. Obedience to her husband was made a woman's legal obligation and she had to seek his permission for almost anything she wanted to do.

Some Western European countries began to make reforms during the mid-nineteenth century and all have done so during the twentieth. During the 1850s, for example, the Scandinavian countries passed legislation ensuring women's right to engage in trade and commerce and between 1845 and 1857, equal inheritance rights for men and women were established.[2] In 1880 Denmark changed the law that committed women to the guardianship of their husbands; Norway followed suit in 1888, but Sweden did not until 1920. Other countries were a great deal slower. In France, the law stating that a wife owed complete obedience to her husband was not repealed until 1938.[3] Legislation passed in 1970 changed the French law requiring a husband's signature for a wife to buy on credit, start a new business, take a job, or open a bank account. In Italy, divorce was not legalized until 1970.

Political rights and political power

Today women have the right to vote in every Western European country except tiny Liechtenstein.[4] Women obtained suffrage earliest in the Scandinavian countries. In 1901, women gained the right to vote in municipal elections in Norway and, in 1913, gained full voting equality. Finland began female suffrage in 1907 and Sweden in 1918. In contrast, French women did not obtain the right to vote until 1944, and Italian women did not until 1947.

Suffrage has not, however, been translated into political power. As Table 9.1 shows, women are severely underrepresented in Western European parliaments. Women do best in the Scandinavian countries. Norway, for example, had a woman prime minister for a short time.

Women and employment

Western Europe, like the United States, has seen an increase in the number of women entering its labor force. In the last several dec-

---

[2]Ingunn Norderval Means, "Scandinavian Women," in Lynne Iglitzin and Ruth Ross, eds., *Women in the World* (Santa Barbara: Clio Books, 1976), p. 377.

[3]Catherine Bodard Silver, "France: Contrasts in Familial and Societal Roles" in Janet Giele and Audrey Smock, eds., *Women: Roles and Status in Eight Countries* (New York: Wiley, 1977), pp. 266–267.

[4]Newland, op. cit., p. 98.

TABLE 9.1
Women in Western European Parliaments

Country	Legislative body	Year	Percent women
Finland	Euduskunta	1978	22
Sweden	Parliament	1979	26
Norway	Parliament	1978	24
United Kingdom	House of Commons	1975	4
West Germany	Bundestag	1975	7
France	Parliament	1978	2

Source: Kathleen Newland, *The Sisterhood of Man* (New York: Norton, 1979), pp. 126–127; and *Political Life in Sweden,* no. 4 (June 1980), 1.

ades, the proportion of women working outside the home has risen substantially in most, though not all, Western European countries. As Table 9.2 shows, female labor force participation tends to be highest in the Scandinavian countries and lowest in southern Europe.

In Europe, as in the United States, the composition of the female labor force has changed. No longer are working women primarily young and unmarried. In Sweden, for example, 67.7 percent of married women were in the paid labor force in 1976.[5] In the common market countries, except for the Netherlands where more traditional patterns prevail, slightly more than half of all working women

[5]Ronnie Steinberg Ratner, *Equal Employment Policy for Women* (Philadelphia: Temple University Press, 1980), p. 4.

TABLE 9.2
**Female Labor Force Participation
  Rates in Western Europe**

Country	1950	1977
Denmark	49.6	67.3
Finland	59.9	64.7
France	49.5	50.1
West Germany	44.3	48.4
Italy	32.0	37.1
Norway	36.6	58.5
Portugal	26.3	50.4
Sweden	35.1	70.0
United Kingdom	40.7	57.3

Source: Organization for Economic Co-operation and Development, *Women and Employment,* 1980, p. 22.

are married. Labor force participation by women with children has also been increasing. In Sweden, 68.5 percent of the mothers of preschool children work outside the home; in Germany more than one-third do and, in France, more than 40 percent.[6] Women with school-age children are even more likely to be employed; in 1976 their labor force participation rate was 78 percent in Sweden, 48 percent in France, and 41 percent in Germany.[7]

Although working for pay is increasingly the norm for Western European women, they, like their American sisters, are segregated in the labor force. Women are concentrated in clerical, sales, and service occupations and in the "female" professions of teaching and nursing.[8] The percentage of women who are clerical, sales, and service workers is 54 percent in Germany, 49 percent in France, 56 percent in Sweden and 63 percent in the United Kingdom.[9] This segregation results in a wage gap between men and women just as it does in the United States. Women's jobs are undervalued and, thus, women earn less than men. Table 9.3 does show that some European countries have made significant progress in narrowing the wage gap.

During the 1960s and early 1970s many of the Western European countries passed equal pay legislation. More recently, a number have adopted broader equal opportunity policies.[10] The approaches used vary from country to country. In France, for example, the legal strategy places heavy emphasis on litigation whereas in Britain, it involves administrative enforcement mechanisms.[11] Austria, West Germany, and the Scandinavian countries rely upon trade unions to implement equal opportunity policy through collective bargaining.[12] Ronnie Steinberg Ratner, in her careful review of various strategies, concludes that "litigation of individual cases is probably the most inefficient and ineffective."[13] The collective bargaining strategy has produced quite impressive results in Sweden but has been less effective in West Germany. Ratner believes that multiple strategies hold the greatest promise of success. One important component of such

[6]Organization For Economic Co-operation and Development (OECD), *Women and Employment,* 1980, p. 23.

[7]Sheila Kamerman, "Child Care and Family Benefits: Policies and Six Industrialized Countries," *Monthly Labor Review* 103 (November 1980), 24.

[8]OECD, op. cit., p. 24.

[9]Ratner, op. cit., p. 16.

[10]For a summary of the policies, see OECD, op. cit., pp. 110–117.

[11]Ratner, op. cit., p. 420.

[12]OECD, op. cit., p. 68.

[13]Ratner, op. cit., p. 421.

TABLE 9.3
The Wage Gap in Western Europe— Average Female Earnings as a Percent of Average Male Earnings*

Country	1968	1977
Denmark	.74	.85
France	.86 (1972)	.86
West Germany	.69	.73
Norway	.75	.80
Portugal	.64 (1974)	.73
Sweden	.78	.87
United Kingdom	.60	.72

*Ratios are not strictly comparable across countries.
Source: Organization for Economic Co-operation and Development, *Women and Employment,* 1980, p. 32.

an approach is expanding women's opportunities to train for more lucrative male jobs. A number of European countries, including France, West Germany, and Norway, now have specific programs to assist women to train for traditional male occupations.[14] In Sweden, one goal of the government's Labor Market Board, which conducts much of the vocational training, is the promotion of equality between the sexes.

Social policy

Effective equal employment opportunities for women depend not only on antidiscrimination laws but on reasonable maternity leave and child-care policies. In these areas, the European countries are well ahead of the United States. Most of the European countries provide paid maternity leave.[15] In France, for example, a woman can receive full pay for 16 weeks after she gives birth. In West Germany, a woman can take up to 7½ months of leave, part at full pay and part at a lower rate. Sweden is unique in that there, the 9-month leave is available to either parent. In all these countries, the woman's job, seniority rights, and pension entitlements are protected during the period of childbirth or maternity leave. If she takes additional unpaid leave, her job continues to be protected.

Most of the Western European countries have free public pre-

---

[14]OECD, op. cit., p. 62.
[15]Kamerman, op. cit., p. 25.

school programs for children age 3 to 6.[16] In France and Belgium, 95 percent of children in this age group are enrolled in such programs; in Germany, 75 percent are. Italy has room for about 70 percent of its 3- to 6-year-olds in public preschools. Although a number of these programs are gradually being extended to 2-year-olds, mothers must generally make their own arrangements for younger children. Afterschool care is also a problem for many mothers. France and Sweden are beginning to provide supervised care for children after school hours, but much still needs to be done. Nevertheless, Europeans are ahead of Americans by far in recognizing that society has an interest in and a responsibility for the provision of quality child care.

Western European countries have made progress in another area of importance to women—the right to a safe, legal abortion. Iceland, Sweden, and Denmark pioneered liberal abortion laws in the 1930s, but the non-Scandinavian countries had highly restrictive laws until very recently. Britain liberalized its laws in 1967, France in 1974, Austria in 1975, Germany in 1976, and Italy in 1978. In Spain and Portugal, abortion, except to save the life of the woman, is still illegal.[17]

In heavily Catholic areas, even where it is legal, abortion can be very difficult to obtain. In Italy, for example, most doctors refuse to perform abortions and waiting lists are long. Furthermore, anti-abortion movements have developed in most Western European countries and are trying to roll back the progress that has been made.[18] Like their American sisters, European feminists are faced with a formidable task in protecting their gains.

Feminist movements in Western Europe

A feminist movement exists in every Western European country. In most countries both autonomous groups and women's caucuses within various leftist parties are active. In Sweden, for example, the powerful Social Democratic party's strong endorsement of equality has led the majority of feminists to work through that party. The Democratic French Labor Confederation (CFDT) has made working women's problems a top priority and, in the early 1970s, the union's national secretary, Jeannette Laot, was a leader of the movement to legalize abortion. An independent group of French feminists is engaged in the development of highly sophisticated and controversial

[16]Ibid., p. 26.
[17]Los Angeles Times, June 12, 1981.
[18]Newsweek, January 7, 1980, p. 37.

feminist theory.[19] In Britain and Germany, there are a multitude of small autonomous groups. A vigorous feminist movement has developed in Italy. Italian feminists were instrumental in defeating attempts to repeal the divorce law and the liberalized abortion law. Despite strong backing by the Pope, Italian voters overwhelmingly rejected both changes. The Union of Italian Women, a multipartisan organization, can claim major credit for these victories. It informed and organized women, and its pressure led the powerful Communist party to throw its full weight behind the feminist cause.[20]

These feminist movements have plenty of work ahead of them. The European countries have made progress in raising the status of women but, as in the United States, true equality is still only a dream.

SOCIALIST COUNTRIES

The Soviet Union and the People's Republic of China emerged out of revolutions aimed at sweeping away traditional oppressive laws, customs, and social and economic relations. Their official ideology, Marxism, explicitly advocates women's liberation. How well have these countries actually done in improving conditions for women?

Women and Marxism

A concern for women's liberation has always been evident in Marxist ideology. Karl Marx and Frederick Engels founded the modern socialist movement in the 1840s when women and children worked under the most terrible conditions in factories. In the *Communist Manifesto* (1848) they wrote of the impact of early capitalism on the family:

> On what foundation is the present family, the bourgeois family, based? On capital, or private gain. . . . But this state of things finds its complement in the practical absence of the family among the proletarians, and in public prostitution. . . . The bourgeois clap-trap about the family and education, about the hallowed relation of parent and child, become all the more disgusting, the more, by the action of Modern Industry, all family ties among the proletarians are torn asunder and their children transformed into simple articles of commerce and instruments of labor.[21]

[19]For a discussion of some of the French theorists, see *Feminist Studies* 7 (summer 1981). On the CFDT, see *In These Times,* July 30–August 12, 1980.

[20]Carl Marzani, *The Promise of Eurocommunism* (Westport, Conn.: Lawrence Hill, 1980), pp. 119–137.

[21]Quoted and discussed in Peggy Morton, "A Woman's Work is Never Done," in Edith Altbach, ed., *From Feminism to Liberation* (Cambridge, Mass.: Schenkman, 1971), pp. 216–217.

All of their later writings emphasized that there are many forms of the family, each corresponding to different socioeconomic conditions. Marx, in *Capital* (1869), made the new point that although factory work exploited women, their entry into the economy outside the home would eventually lead to a whole new social atmosphere:

> However terrible and disgusting the dissolution, under the capitalist system, of the old family ties may appear, nevertheless modern industry, by assigning as it does an important part in the process of production, outside the domestic sphere, to women, . . . creates a new economic foundation for a higher form of the family and of the relations between the sexes. It is, of course, just as absurd to hold the Teutonic-Christian form of the family to be absolute and final as it would be to apply that character to the ancient Roman, the ancient Greek, or the Eastern forms . . .[22]

The first full-scale Marxist work on women's liberation was written by Engels: *The Origin of the Family, Private Property, and the State* (1884). Engels traced various forms of the family and various changes in the status of women to the underlying economic division of labor and the power relations in each society. Although his anthropological data were wrong in detail, he correctly stressed that women have higher status in many primitive societies, where they are responsible for a large part of the economic production. He shows that the dominance of men is established when they come to dominate agriculture through the use of cattle to pull plows, and then start to utilize their war prisoners as slaves to further enhance heavy agriculture and construction.

Only then, he shows, are women also treated as slaves. Only then is there "monogamous" marriage, in which women must remain faithful though men may indulge in extramarital sex as they will. Only with slavery and private property do "monogamy" . . . and the double standard become institutionalized. These, Engels says, are "based on the supremacy of the man; [their] express aim is the begetting of children of undisputed paternity, this paternity being required in order that these children may in due time inherit their father's wealth as his natural heirs."[23] Engels showed how male supremacy and this form of the family persisted in all class-divided societies up to and including capitalism. He indicted capitalism for the social infe-

---

[22]Quoted and discussed extensively in the very useful essay by Hal Draper, "Marx and Engels on Woman's Liberation," in Roberta Salper, ed., *Female Liberation* (New York: Knopf, 1972), p. 92.

[23]Quoted in ibid., p. 94.

riority of women and for legal and economic discrimination against them.

Engels believed that all this could change only under socialism. Then relations between women and men would not be dominated by economic considerations but would be built on love and companionship. Moreover, the form of the family would probably change; at least, marriage and divorce would become much simpler.

Marx and Engels strongly encouraged women's liberation within the European socialist movement at a very early period. In 1868, Marx wrote that "of course" women could join the International Workers Association on the same basis as men. He proposed a resolution to the General Council of the International to encourage the formation of women's branches of the International, without interfering "with the existence or formation of branches composed of both sexes."[24] Moreover, under Marx's leadership a woman— Harriet Law—was elected a member of the General Council.

Another important book in the socialist movement advocating women's liberation was August Bebel's *Women and Socialism,* written in 1879. Under the influence of Engels and Bebel, the German Marxists strongly endorsed women's liberation. Clara Zetkin published a socialist woman's newspaper, *Equality (Gleichheit),* that had a circulation of 100,000. Not all socialists agreed with Zetkin. In 1875, when the Marxist Bebel presented a resolution for equal rights for women at the Social Democrats' congress, it was defeated. Finally, at the 1891 congress, when the Marxists were in the majority, a resolution was passed favoring the full legal and economic equality of women. However, right-wing socialists continued to oppose that program.

Engels and all the Marxist leaders, including the women's leadership—Rosa Luxemburg, Zetkin, and Marx's daughter Eleanor— strongly supported all the working women's organizations that fought for socialism and women's liberation. At the same time, they criticized the bourgeois feminist movements, which advocated equal legal and property rights but which ignored the need for revolutionary socioeconomic change. Engels commented that for these groups "the separate women's rights business" was a "purely bourgeois pastime."[25] Marxists believe in fighting for equality for women under capitalism, but argue that only socialism can lay the foundation for complete women's liberation.

[24]Quoted in ibid., p. 102.
[25]Quoted in ibid., p. 106.

The Marxist emphasis on equality for women was later to have an important effect on countries that became socialist. Both Russia and China, as we shall see, were very backward at the time of their socialist revolutions. In neither country were the social conditions conducive to women's liberation. Yet in both countries, under the influence of Marxism and of economic necessity, tremendous progress has since been made.

Women in the Soviet Union

Women in tsarist Russia were oppressed badly. They had few if any rights, either political or economic. According to law, they were required to obey their husbands in all matters. They could be jailed for running away and could not get a divorce. The male supremacist ideology was very strong; women were considered inferior to men in most ways. Although literature depicted some strong-minded heroines among educated women, most upper-class women were idle and suffered from boredom. Peasant and industrial working women often worked all day in factory or field, then took sole responsibility for the housework in the evening.

Women reacted to these bleak conditions with a women's liberation movement of considerable scope. The Women's Political Club, a left-wing bourgeois feminist group, attacked the political and psychological aspects of women's oppression and called for equal rights. A socialist women's movement—the Society for Mutual Help Among Working Women—also existed. The socialist women were critical of the feminists, urging the need for a deeper class analysis of society; they argued that socialism was a prerequisite to complete women's liberation because women could never be free under capitalism. The socialist women had a remarkable leader in Alexandra Kollantai. She was a revolutionary, later a novelist, and still later a diplomat for Bolshevik Russia.[26]

Women fought in the Revolution, and the women's liberation movement expanded afterward. In November 1918, a Soviet women's conference was held in Moscow with 1147 delegates, including many peasant women. In the same year, the Central Committee of the Party established a women's section, called *Zhenotdel*, to push women's liberation. Yet even the creation of Zhenotdel—

[26]The historical background is discussed in Erica Dunn and Judy Klein, "Women in the Russian Revolution," *Women: A Journal of Liberation* 1, no. 4 (summer 1970), 22–26. Also see Marilyn Goldberg, "Women in the Soviet Economy," *Review of Radical Political Economics* 4 (July 1972), 60–65.

which replaced the earlier Society for Mutual Help as the main socialist women's organization—was opposed by some Communist men. They argued that it was too "feminist" to have a separate organization of women, and was totally unnecessary in a socialist state. These arguments reflected both the extreme backwardness of Russian attitudes toward women and the incompleteness of Marxist theory on women's liberation up to that time.

Long before the Revolution, Lenin had endorsed Engels's analysis of the oppression of women and the need for women's liberation. Indeed, he himself did considerable writing in favor of women's liberation. He wrote: "Women grow worn out in the petty, monstrous household work, their strength and time dissipated and wasted, their minds growing narrow and stale, their hearts beating slowly, their will weakened."[27] And he attacked male attitudes: "Very few men . . . think how much labour and weariness they could lighten for women . . . if they would lend a hand in 'women's work.' . . . Our communist labours among the masses . . . involves a considerable effort to educate the men. We must root out the ancient outlook of the lord and master to the last fiber."[28] Moreover, Lenin lived in a free and open relationship with the revolutionary woman Krupskaya, who was herself an independent leader in the women's movement. Yet Lenin seems to have underestimated the need for consciousness raising among women, since he thought it "feminist" to waste time discussing love and marital problems. He also underestimated, like all socialists of his day, the effort necessary to root out sexism in a socialist society.

Nevertheless, in the 1920s, with Lenin as its leader, the Soviet government propagandized for equal rights, allowed freedom of divorce, legalized abortion, and pushed for women's liberation in many ways (even helping women remove the veil in Central Asia). Marriages and divorces could be registered by a simple postcard, but many intellectuals did not register at all, feeling that registration of marriage was "too bourgeois." Even where marriages were registered, women often kept their previous name—while some couples combined the two names. The formal equality of men and women has remained unchanged ever since the Revolution. Article 122 of the Soviet constitution (1936) says that "women in the USSR are accorded equal rights with men in all spheres of economic, cultural, political, and other public activities."

[27]Quoted in Dunn and Klein, op. cit., p. 24. Lenin has a pamphlet called "The Emancipation of Women" (New York: International Publishers, n.d.).
[28]Quoted in ibid.

Among the equal rights granted were completely equal property rights within the marriage and the right of either spouse to a divorce by submitting a postcard to the government. At the same time, the women's organization, Zhenotdel, was greatly encouraged and spread to all areas, although it was always stronger in the cities than in the countryside. It published magazines, helped Eastern women remove the veil, and propagandized against arranged marriages and wife beating. It helped organize cooperatives through which women could both produce and sell products and buy more cheaply as consumers. Since women had little or no education before the Revolution and more than 90 percent were illiterate, an educational drive was launched. Kollantai wrote a widely read novel, *Red Love,* which described the life and problems of a liberated woman.

But male attitudes were slow to change, especially in the rural areas. In the 1920s, most of the Soviet Union remained agricultural, and in most peasant communities, the traditional subservient role of women did not change. As late as 1933, an American woman in the Soviet Union wrote: "On a motor trip I visited many cottages in outlying villages; the women stood while the men sat down and ate; kept their heads bent and their hands folded, not speaking until they were spoken to."[29]

Moreover, the highly democratic processes of government just after the Revolution were replaced by a harsh dictatorship under Stalin by about 1928. The dictatorship resulted from the civil war and foreign intervention of 1918–1921, the lack of literacy and of any democratic tradition in Russia, and—most important—from a need to industrialize backward Russia almost overnight if the Soviet Union was to survive. The terrible economic conditions plus the dictatorship were catastrophic for the women's movement.

In 1929, Stalin abolished the Zhenotdel and all other women's organizations, many of whose leaders had opposed him. In order to encourage industrialization, Stalin and other leaders believed a more regimented society was necessary. This included a more stable family and more stringent divorce laws. Divorce was made more complicated in 1926, and in 1944 it was made quite difficult to obtain and expensive by Soviet standards. The People's Court had to hear the plaintiff's reasons for divorce—always ultimately granted if the woman persisted, but hard for a man to get if children were involved—and a fee of 100 rubles had to be paid. The court attitude became quite rigid: ". . . the USSR Supreme Court has pointed out that courts trying divorce cases must begin with the task of strength-

---

[29]Ella Winter, *Red Virtue* (New York: Harcourt Brace Jovanovich, 1933), p. 101.

ening the family, and that temporary discord in the family and conflicts between spouses due to random and transient factors must not
be regarded as sufficient grounds for divorce."[30]

At the same time, to stabilize the family as Stalin had ordered,
the government put out a great deal of puritanical propaganda: "So-
called free love is a bourgeois invention and has nothing in common
with the principles of conduct of a Soviet citizen. Moreover, marriage receives its full value for the State only if there is progeny."[31]
This was a reversal of the early casual attitude toward marriage.

Stalin's 1944 law ended the father's obligations to children
born outside marriage. Before that time, the father's obligations to
all children, born in or out of marriage, were the same. In 1968, a
new law gave the single mother the right to receive a state allowance
and the right to place the child in an institution to be brought up at
the state's expense if the identity of the father was not established.
(The mother is once again entitled to child support if the father's identity is established.)

Immediately after the Revolution, birth control information and
devices were made free and available. In 1936, Stalin radically
changed the policy. Birth control by contraception was still legal, but
discouraged (especially by the very, very low production of contraceptives for at least two decades). All abortions that were not medi-
cally necessary were banned. Under Stalin a doctor performing an
abortion was imprisoned for 2 years, and the woman was subject
to public censure for the first offense and fined 300 rubles for a second offense.

To increase the population and provide more labor for industrial expansion, a policy of family subsidies was begun. Payment increased with the number of children. Women who had a great number of children were also given special awards. Women with five
children received a Motherhood Medal, Second Class; those with
six children, the Motherhood Medal, First Class; those with seven
children, the Order of Glory of Motherhood. The Presidium of the
Supreme Soviet presented the woman with ten children with a scroll
and the title Mother Heroine.[32]

After Stalin's death, the frantic rush to industrialize slackened
as the initial goals had been achieved, and some loosening of political

[30]A. Gorkin, "Concern for the Soviet Family," *Soviet Review* 10 (fall 1969), 49.
[31]Commissariat of Justice, *Sotsialisticheskaya Zakonnost,* no. 2 (1939).
[32]Dunn and Klein, op. cit., p. 26.

control took place. Dissenters are still often arrested and sent to jail or to an insane asylum, though they are no longer executed. In this somewhat better atmosphere, the older Marxist attitude toward the family has begun to reassert itself. In 1955, abortion was again legalized. Abortions were made free for all urban working women but cost 5 rubles for housewives and students and 2 rubles for farm women. The abortion rate has been quite high, especially because of a persistent shortage of contraceptives. Only in the late 1960s was some priority given to the increased production of contraceptives, mostly owing to alarm over the high abortion rate.[33] Therefore, in spite of continuing official propaganda favoring big families, the number of children per woman in the USSR had dropped to 1.9 in rural areas and 1.5 in urban areas by 1969. This foreshadows a declining population for the Soviet Union.

In 1955 and again in 1965, the divorce laws were much further liberalized. It still takes 3 months to get a divorce, but if there are no children, no fee is involved. When there are children, there are fees and hearings to determine what should be done. The husband or the wife—whoever has a job and does not have the children—must pay child support, but no alimony. The number of divorces has risen sharply but is still far below the U.S. rate. Finally, a 1968 law gives unmarried women the same state subsidies for children as it gives to married women, and equal rights to all state facilities.

In spite of all these ups and downs on family policy, the status of women has greatly improved since the oppression of tsarist Russia. The all-out drive for industrialization required the largest possible labor force, and women went to work in unprecedented numbers. They also flooded into the schools and colleges. In 1967, the number of employed women with higher education was 54 times as high as in 1928. Women have made up over 50 percent of the whole labor force ever since 1945. In fact, according to 1975 data, 64.3 percent of women between the ages of 15 and 70 are in the labor force; and 83.1 percent of women between the ages of 16 and 54 are in the labor force.[34]

Just before the Revolution, women made up only 25 percent of all students enrolled in universities. Since the Revolution, the num-

[33]See David Heer, "Abortion, Contraception, and Population Policy in the Soviet Union," *Soviet Studies* 17 (July 1965), 76–83.

[34]Alastair McAuley, *Women's Work and Wages in the Soviet Union* (London: Allen and Unwin, 1981), p. 37.

ber of girls and boys in grades 1 through 10 has been equal, except in the more backward republics where girls leave school at an earlier age than boys. Beyond the tenth grade, the percentage of women tends to decline. Nevertheless, in urban areas, the proportion of women with secondary education is higher than that of men.[35] In 1933, the percentage of women with the degree of *kandidat* (similar to our Ph.D.) was close to zero. In 1968, women received 31 percent of all kandidat degrees.

Women are well represented in the professions. About 40 percent of engineers, 74 percent of physicians, 36 percent of lawyers, and 40 percent of university professors are female.[36]

Although women have made great strides, there are still some major problem areas. Equal pay for equal work is a firmly established principle; there are no mechanisms by which a man and a woman doing the same job could be paid differently. In the blue-collar sector, however, there is very considerable segregation, with women more often found in the lower-paying jobs.[37] Furthermore, women's progress into better-paid positions has been very slow. In management and the professions, women are well represented, but the top jobs still go mostly to men. Thus, although women are three-fourths of all physicians—a profession that does not have the same prestige in the USSR as in the United States—they are only 53 percent of chief physicians. Seventy-two percent of primary and secondary school teachers are women, but only 32 percent of school principles are.[38] In the non–blue-collar area, however, women have made considerable gains. Women enterprise directors increased from 7 percent in 1939 to 13 percent in 1970; in middle management and above, women increased from 22 percent in 1939 to 44 percent in 1970.[39] In industrial management, women account for 49 percent of the engineers, including chief engineers, 53 percent of the chief and senior accountants, and 26 percent of the department heads and their deputies.[40]

Women have made less progress in the political sphere. One-

[35]Ibid., p. 148.

[36]Ibid., pp. 72–73, 87. See also Norton Dodge, "Women in the Soviet Economy," in Athena Theodore, ed., *The Professional Woman* (Cambridge, Mass.: Schenkman, 1971), pp. 207–226.

[37]McAuley, op. cit., pp. 67–97.

[38]Ibid., p. 87.

[39]Ibid.

[40]Ibid., p. 88.

third of the members of the Supreme Soviet are female, but this parliament has little power. Of the 319 voting members of the more powerful Central Committee of the Communist party, only 8 are women.[41]

Like their counterparts in the West, employed women in the Soviet Union carry a double burden. Women are expected to assume primary responsibility for children and housework. Industry in the Soviet Union, however, does have an adequate system of maternity leaves. Women are allowed 8 weeks prenatal and 8 weeks postnatal leave at full pay. They may also choose to take their annual paid vacation (2 to 3 weeks) after that and an additional 3 months unpaid leave if they desire.[42] An extensive system of child-care centers also exists. In 1969, Soviet child care facilities had provisions for 9 million children. Nevertheless, Soviet women complain of the shortage of facilities, since there are places for only 70 percent of urban children and less than that for children in rural areas. They also complain about the poor quality of the facilities. The Soviet Union is far behind the United States in the availability of household appliances and convenience items such as frozen foods. Services that make an employed woman's life easier are also underdeveloped.

Given the problems Soviet women still face, one might expect the development of a feminist movement. Recently, in fact, several Leningrad women organized a feminist group and circulated a collection of critical essays called *Women and Russia*. The authorities promptly suppressed the group and deported one of its organizers.[43] The Soviet government is, however, attempting to increase production of consumer items, hoping thereby to prevent further such developments.

Considering the status of women in Russia before the revolution, remarkable progress has been made. Nevertheless, the USSR's low level of development combined with a one-party dictatorship means that men at the top have their own political and material reasons for perpetuating an authoritarian family, with women doing most of the housework as well as holding down a job. Since 1929, the top leadership has always—rightly—feared and prevented the emergence of a militant women's liberation movement because it might jeopardize their own power.

[41]*Los Angeles Times,* March 9, 1982.
[42]William Mandel, *Russia Re-Examined* (New York: Hill and Wang, 1967), pp. 174–175.
[43]*Los Angeles Times,* March 9, 1982.

Women in Communist China

For thousands of years, most Chinese were peasants who lived on the brink of starvation. From 108 B.C. to A.D. 1911, 1828 famines are recorded. The landlord gentry, the ruling class that ruthlessly exploited the peasants, amounted to less than 20 percent of the population. In both classes, the family was rigidly authoritarian, with females dominated by males and young people by old. The Confucian text, *Li Chi,* set the tone: "The woman always follows the man."

In old China women were clearly subordinate. They were not recognized as independent entities under the law; they could not own property or inherit land. Women were taught only one virtue—obedience. A young girl was sold to a strange husband in a strange family. From then on, she was a member of that family and was under the control of her husband or, if he died, her mother-in-law and father-in-law. No matter at what age she might become a widow, she was forbidden to remarry. "She was terrified and often terrorized, frequently beaten by both her husband and her mother-in-law."[44]

Women of the upper classes were kept physically secluded, preparing the meals for men but eating separately. In addition to the first wife, the gentry also had "secondary wives," concubines, prostitutes, or simply female slaves. To show that the man was wealthy and the woman a useless ornament, women of the gentry had their feet bound to prevent them from growing to be more than 2 or 3 inches long! The binding of feet was still common as late as the 1940s.

Peasant women were often used as slaves and prostitutes. Daughters were considered such a curse that they were often killed at birth. When a peasant woman was married, however, her position with regard to her husband might be a little better and the family a little less rigid than among the gentry. Peasant women had to work in the fields in the south and in heavy domestic labor in the north. Therefore their feet could not be bound. Neither could the peasant man afford more than one woman; therefore the peasant woman usually had more decision-making power than gentry women, and her position was a little closer to equality.

When revolt against the old regime became endemic in the nineteenth century, women immediately joined. Many urban women became bourgeois feminists as early as the 1850s. In the

---

[44]The quotes and the material in the preceding paragraph are from Charlotte Cohen, "Experiment in Freedom: Women of China," in Robin Morgan, ed., *Sisterhood is Powerful* (New York: Vintage, 1970), p. 388.

peasant revolt called the Taiping Rebellion, which lasted from 1850 to 1864, women fought in the peasant army. Their program included communal ownership of property, complete equality of men and women, no foot binding or prostitution, and a monogamous family built on love. The emperor, with foreign support, defeated them in a bloody civil war.

In the early 1900s some gentry began to send their daughters to schools, and the bourgeois feminist movement grew. An early leader, Chi'iu Chin, established the first women's newspaper, *Chinese Women's Journal,* and wrote poems like this one:

> May Heaven bestow equal power on men, women.
> Is it sweet to live lower than cattle?
> We would rise in fight yes! drag ourselves up.[45]

Women fought in Sun Yat-sen's liberation wars, but were given only a few new rights in the republican constitution of 1912. Women also joined in the massive student demonstrations of the May Fourth Movement from 1917 to 1921, in which they fought against the restraints of Confucianism, against foreign imperialism, and against the native warlords, but also raised the banner of women's liberation. Many young students, including Mao Tse-tung, refused to marry because all marriages were still arranged and were thus a prison for men as well as for women. When the Communist party was organized in 1921, many women broke with the bourgeois feminist movement, saying it was necessary to go further. The militant Hsiang Chin-yu said: "The emancipation of women can only come with a change in the social structure which frees men and women alike."[46]

From 1921 to 1927, the Communists and the bourgeois republican Kuomintang formed a coalition. During this period both bourgeois and socialist women's movements flourished in the cities. The Women's Department of the coalition organized 1,500,000 women. But in 1927, the Kuomintang broke the coalition and killed every Communist available, as well as every "Communist sympathizer," including every women's leader. Many women organizers were tortured and imprisoned; some had their noses and breasts cut off. Any women's emancipation was suspect, so a girl whose only crime was that she had freely chosen her fiancé was tortured and shot. The Kuomintang soldiers shouted: "You have had your free love now."[47] Although in 1931 the Kuomintang, under Chiang Kai-shek, promul-

[45]Quoted in ibid., p. 390.
[46]Quoted in ibid., p. 392.
[47]Quoted in ibid., p. 393.

gated a code of equal rights for women, it was never enforced, and the authoritarian family was strongly encouraged.

In contrast, the Communists actively organized a women's movement through groups called Women's Associations. They favored equality both for ideological reasons and because they felt that the strength of women was required in order to make the revolution successful. They had often witnessed "divide and rule" tactics by the conservatives. For example, in a 1924 strike the male union failed to support the women's strike for equal pay, and both unions were weakened. The Communist party admitted that its organizers viewed work among women workers as less important than among men and set out to correct this tendency. A very strong women's movement was launched in the liberated areas of the countryside. The party announced that all marriages must be free and equal and by mutual consent, gave equal property rights, and prohibited concubines, female infanticide, and foot binding. Attracted by this program, women played a vital role in the Revolution.

In 1949, after the Revolution, militant women organized the All China Democratic Women's Federation, which spearheaded the movement for women's rights. In 1950, a new marriage law was promulgated in the People's Republic.

Article 1 of the Marriage Law:

> The arbitrary and compulsory feudal marriage system, which is based on the superiority of man over woman . . . is hereby abolished. The new Democratic marriage system, which is based on free choice of partners, on monogamy, on equal rights for both sexes, and on the protection of the lawful interests of women and children, shall be put into effect.

Article 7:

> Husband and wife are companions living together and shall enjoy equal status in the home.

The law prohibited polygamy, concubinage, child betrothal, infanticide, marriage by purchase, and interference with the remarriage of widows. It gave equal rights to women and men to pursue any career, to manage the family property, to use their own family names, and to inherit property. Children born out of marriage were given the same rights as legitimate children. Free divorce by mutual consent was allowed: "Divorce shall be granted when husband and wife both desire it." If there was disagreement, a wife could still always get a divorce. A man could get a divorce also, except when the wife was pregnant or had a child under 1 year old.

China was very poor, and propaganda emphasized the need for women to work hard if they would be equal participants in society. Women reacted as to a renaissance. One confessed:

> . . . the gongs and drums of "liberation" woke me up like thunder in the spring and I began to crawl out of the dirt. . . . I want to shout with millions of sisters. . . . We want to be masters of the new society. We have to break the chains on our hands and create the garden of happiness for humanity.[48]

The women had to enforce the new ideas and the new marriage law against intense resistance. One important technique was the "speak bitterness" meeting. If a man were found to be oppressing his wife, all the active women in the village would go to him and reason with him. If that failed, as it often did because the women weren't taken seriously, they would put him in jail for 2 or 3 days to think it over. Then, the Women's Association would haul him out of jail to a public meeting attended by all the women of the town. The man was allowed to tell his story. Then, whether he spoke or not, the woman was encouraged to speak publicly, usually for the first time in her life. After that, the accused man was given a chance to confess and promise to act reasonably toward his wife in the future. If he refused, he was beaten, and he was not released until he gave a public promise to behave with equality toward his wife.[49]

The male resistance, however, also resorted to such tactics, especially where the local Communist party cadres were themselves sexist. "In Kwangsi province . . . ten women were ordered to be tortured and made the object of 'struggle' meetings for their audacity in desiring to marry for love."[50] The central government, however, always backed the women, so the struggle was largely successful. Moreover, many women were brought into the lower government levels; party decree proclaimed women must constitute at least 10 percent of every village council.

Another major fight was to eradicate venereal disease and prostitution. George Hatem, an American doctor who spent many years in China, says that in prerevolutionary Shanghai 10 percent of the people had syphilis, and many parents were forced to sell their daughters to brothels in order to stay alive.[51] He adds that in the

[48]Quoted in ibid., p. 401.

[49]Diane Feeley, "Speak Bitterness," *Women: A Journal of Liberation* 1 (summer 1970), 5.

[50]Cohen, op. cit., p. 403.

[51]George Hatem, in *Parade,* August 12, 1973, p. 4.

old China enormous numbers of people had venereal diseases, and prostitution was almost as widespread as poverty. "Shanghai was really a hell-on-earth except for the very rich."[52]

Hatem explains that in communist China VD was conquered by voluminous propaganda and through educational campaigns involving thousands of volunteers. Prostitution was wiped out in a similar manner. Prostitutes who had been in the business only a short time were given other jobs. Those who were longtime prostitutes were given a rehabilitation course in which they were told that the old society had forced them into such jobs for survival but that the new society would teach them trades and guarantee jobs. The women were encouraged to speak their own bitterness about their past lives at long, friendly sessions, a catharsis that helped many. "Once they were cured and rehabilitated, they were sent out as nurses, teachers, clerks, with the assurance that never again would the government permit poverty to drive them or their children into prostitution."[53]

From 1954 to 1958, much greater emphasis was put on women's participation in the economy. But the movement of women into the economy, plus the high divorce rates as women broke up unwanted marriages, led to a very unstable and disoriented family situation. In response, party policy swung back to an emphasis on family virtues, though the family emphasized was one of equality. People were encouraged to marry late, have fewer children—a major birth control campaign was launched—and avoid divorce, which was considered bourgeois.

There were, however, contradictions within this policy, since women were encouraged to take outside jobs but also told to build stable families—which meant investing a lot of time in child care. This situation was partly resolved in the Great Leap Forward of 1958, when communes were set up in both rural and urban areas. The communes were supposed to take over all housework and child rearing for working mothers. But the communes tried to go too far too fast, and the services provided were often inadequate. The resources needed for communal kitchens and child care often were not available. Nevertheless, there was no retreat from the basic principle of providing communal facilities to lighten the women's burden—though many of the initial extremes were quickly abandoned.

One result of the commune system was perhaps the world's most extensive free and collective child-care system. Two U.S.

[52]Ibid.
[53]Ibid., p. 5.

women journalists reported in 1973 that 90 percent of all Chinese women now work outside the home.[54] Their children, even very small ones, are cared for in nurseries, often right next door to the office or factory where the women work. Still, about 50 percent of children under 3 are cared for by grandparents. From 3 to 7, only 20 percent are cared for by grandparents; the rest are cared for by nurseries.

Since women as well as men worked outside the home, equality within the home was emphasized even more. In addition, women were further encouraged to raise their consciousnesses, to get out of purely private life and into public life; and many did take on executive responsibilities. The percentage of women on the party's Central Committee rose from 4.5 percent in 1956 to 8 percent in 1969, and the number of women in higher education also began to rise. In 1960, women accounted for 18 percent of the engineering students, 42 percent of the medical students, 28 percent of the agronomy students, and 24 percent of the education students.

What has China achieved? On the one hand, turning millions of women from foot-bound slaves into revolutionary activists in industry and government is a major miracle. In terms of sheer numbers, this is the greatest single emancipation of women in history. The provision of education and communal facilities for meals and child care has put real teeth into the Chinese drive for women's equality.

On the other hand, real problems still exist. Women in China seem to have some of the same problems as Soviet women. They have made great strides in the economy, in education, and in politics—but they still constitute only a very small portion of those at the top of economic and political pyramids. They are equal in family rights before the law, but many, many marriages still follow the traditional path—with the male dominant and the woman doing all the household chores. In 1965, a Chinese woman complained that "women work much more than men. We have two jobs; we work in the fields and in our homes."[55] Thus women bear a double burden. Chinese women have come a remarkably long way, but they still have a long way to go.

WOMEN IN THE THIRD WORLD
While the countries of the Third World vary tremendously in culture and social structure and thus in the position that women hold, they

---

[54]Janice Perlman and Lois Goldfrank, "How China Schools Its Children," *Parade,* November 25, 1973, p. 11.

[55]Quoted in Cohen, op. cit., p. 413.

resemble one another in that they all are less developed economically than the countries discussed earlier. They remain very poor,
rural, agricultural, with high rates of disease and illiteracy—in other
words, they resemble countries in Western Europe in 1750. Many
of them, such as India, had very advanced cultures before they were
conquered by British, European, or U.S. imperialism. In most cases,
imperialism reversed cultural development, plundered and ruined
economic development, and reduced the position of women.

In Africa, for example, women used the hoe to conduct almost
all of the agricultural production, while men limited themselves
mostly to hunting and warfare. But European colonialism ended the
intertribal war activities of the men. Since the African men then appeared idle to the Europeans, the Europeans used every means to
force them into farming. They believed that agriculture was by nature
a male job. Therefore, they never perceived that almost all African
agriculture was done by women. They assumed that "men could become far better farmers than women, if only they would abandon
their customary 'laziness.' "[56] Hence, they taught modern farming
techniques to the men only.

Modern methods meant introduction of the heavy plow instead of the hoe, which usually meant substitution of men for women
in farming. This change resulted in the same drastic lowering of the
status of African women as had occurred in ancient Neolithic communities when the same substitution was made. The smooth functioning of African society was totally destroyed as men were forced
into farming, for which they were unprepared, while women lost
their main economic role and were relegated to comparative useless-
ness.

In addition to giving men control of the land, the Europeans
attracted or coerced many men to the cities to do the lowest-paying
work there. Yet the administrators and missionaries often completely
blocked the women, who had previously been the main traders,
from even entering the towns. Only married women were allowed
in because it was assumed that any single woman in the towns would
become a prostitute. Because no normal social life was allowed to
Africans in the towns, this was a self-fulfilling prophecy.

Since they have won formal independence, the African countries have gotten rid of most of the legal restrictions on women and
have granted them the right to vote (of little use in one-party states)

[56]Ester Boserup, *Women's Role in Economic Development* (New York: St. Martin's,
1970), p. 54.

and the right to hold public office. Nevertheless, "few women are in high public office or in the upper echelons of industry and the professions."[57]

In most of the Third World countries, European imperialism relied on the support of the most reactionary groups, so it tended to encourage and support all the most conservative customs regarding women. For example, in India under the British, the custom of arranging marriages and virtually selling a young woman for her dowry continued unabated. Even today, "a majority of unmarried young women in India say the men look at their fathers' bankbook even before they look at them as prospective brides."[58] The dowry system persisted under British rule along with laws that gave only men the right to hold or inherit property. Only men could be educated, and in all except the lowest castes, only men could work outside the home. To provide the dowry, many poor families went into debt. Others looked ahead and simply murdered all girl children at birth.

Many Indian women in the cities have rejected the arranged marriage-dowry system and have fought a long battle against it. Angered women forced the government to ban dowries by law in 1961. Yet these measures have not penetrated at all into the rural areas, where most people live. Even in Delhi, in 1973, "a groom's father threatened to call off the wedding at the last moment unless the girl's father produced a transistor radio worth $200 as part of the dowry."[59] The father of the bride didn't have $200 because he had already spent a great deal of money on the wedding—and his salary was only $150 a month. To save his daughter's marriage, he was forced to borrow at exorbitant interest rates from a money lender.

The status of women is probably lowest in the Muslim countries. Islamic law endorses both patriarchy and polygyny.[60] A woman owes her husband obedience; it is his legal right to beat her for disobedience. Husbands can force their unwilling wives to live with them, even to the point of physically imprisoning them in the house. An Islamic man can divorce his wife simply through divorce-by-renunciation, which requires no legal proceedings or even a state-

[57]Ruby Leavitt, "Women in Other Cultures," in Vivian Gornick and Barbara Moran, eds., *Women in Sexist Society* (New York: Basic Books, 1971), p. 418.

[58]M. G. Srinath, "Indian Marriages Are Made in Counting House, Not Heaven," Riverside, California, *Press Enterprise,* November 22, 1973.

[59]Ibid.

[60]Newland, op. cit., pp. 14–15.

ment of cause. It is almost impossible for her to divorce him. A number of Muslim countries have recently begun to reform their laws but many highly unequal provisions remain.[61]

Women in the Arab states are more likely than those anywhere else to be illiterate. In 1970, 85 percent of the women as compared with 60 percent of the men could not read or write.[62] The cultural norm that restricts women from having contact with men who are not relatives, as well as the low education level, results in a very low employment level among women. The average female work participation rate in nonagricultural occupations is only 4 percent.[63]

Recently, women's access to education has been increasing. The more education a woman has the more likely she is to be employed. In Turkey, Syria, and Egypt, for example, a mere 4 percent of women with only some primary schooling are employed, while 21 percent of those with secondary school diplomas are working. Two-thirds of female university graduates are employed in professional occupations.[64] As women get more education and move into the labor force, their status will rise. Currently, however, the impact of reforms for women is mostly confined to those in the upper class. In most Muslim countries, women of the lower classes have made very little progress.

Third World women have made their greatest gains by joining men in national liberation struggles. In North Vietnam, women's equality was proclaimed a goal of the Vietnamese Communist party. Vietnamese women belong to the party as well as to the separate Women's Union, created specifically to fight for women's liberation. They are campaigning for equality in the party, in the army, in labor, and in the family. In the economy, the number of women has risen from 500 unskilled workers in 1954 to 50 percent of the industrial workers and 70 percent of the agricultural workers in 1973.[65] In 1960 new marriage laws outlawed polygamy and gave women equal rights to obtain divorces, equality in the family, and equality in property ownership. Before that, men had sole control of the family and property and the sole right to divorce. A woman could not even re-

---

[61]Nadia H. Youssef, "Women in the Muslim World," in Inglitzin and Ross, op. cit., pp. 204–206.

[62]Newland, op. cit., p. 30.

[63]Youssef, op. cit., p. 204.

[64]Ibid., pp. 208–209.

[65]Charlotte Bunch-Weeks, "Asian Women in Revolution," *Women: A Journal of Liberation* 1, no. 4 (summer 1970), 6.

marry if her husband died! Women now get equal pay for equal work, paid maternity leaves, and some child care.

Although this progress is spectacular, Vietnamese men's attitudes are still sexist, and few women have obtained top management or political positions. An American woman visitor was told that there are still three problem areas for women in North Vietnam. First, their self-image is still one of inferiority, so they shy away from responsible jobs. Second, even though the number of women in politics has greatly increased, there are still too few, and there is resistance to putting women into positions of leadership. Third, women are still expected to fulfill traditional roles in the family. The Women's Union is fighting on all three fronts, but expects to win only after housework is socialized and adequate child care becomes available.[66]

Women participated actively in the national liberation wars of both Mozambique and Angola and, in both countries, women's liberation has been a top national priority. Before the revolution, women's place was very low. Women provided most of the agricultural labor yet had little power in the family. Because most women were illiterate, education has been emphasized. The Organization of Mozambiquan Women runs intensive literacy courses in the countryside. Women study 5 days a week for 4 months, only going home on weekends.[67] Although some husbands have objected—sometimes violently—the women, supported by the government, are determined to learn so they can participate more fully in public life. New laws have banned many traditional oppressive customs. But changing centuries-old practices is very difficult. A Canadian visitor to Mozambique was once told, "Compared to our fight to wipe out polygamy and *lobolo* [bride-price], getting rid of the Portugese was easy."[68] That the person who made the statement was an old Muslim male indicates that real progress has been made.

This quick survey of women's status in a number of countries shows that the position of women has varied tremendously over time and from place to place. Women's inferior status is not immutable. Modernization seems to bring some improvements in women's position automatically. Women have, however, moved furthest and fastest when they have organized themselves and demanded change. Certainly, women have made tremendous progress in some societies, yet everywhere there is much still to be done.

[66]Ibid., p. 8.
[67]Rick Salutin, "Notes on A Week in Cabo Delgado," *Monthly Review* 32 (July–August 1980), 62–64.
[68]Ibid., p. 68.

A CENTURY OF STRUGGLE: AMERICAN WOMEN, 1820-1920

10

Recently, a few historians have noted the omission of the women's movement from all conventional histories.[1] For example, the suffrage movement gets only two sentences, but prohibition gets three pages, in Morison's *Oxford History of the American People*.[2] In his *New Viewpoints in American History,* Arthur Schlesinger said: "If the silence of the historians is to mean anything, it would appear that one-half of our population have been negligible factors in our country's history."[3] This neglect is still the case in all general U.S. histories.

The typical history text mentions that women were *given* the vote in 1920. Susan B. Anthony may be mentioned in a condescending sentence or two. That women struggled for almost a century, that many endured ridicule as well as physical hardships, that the early women's leaders were fighting not just for the vote but for full social, political, and economic equality—these facts are never mentioned.

WOMEN'S STATUS IN PREREVOLUTIONARY AMERICA
Many women came to the United States as indentured servants, sold from London prisons or kidnaped from London streets. They were treated as slaves for 7 years, then freed, but given no money. Most black women were kidnaped in Africa, then shipped as cargo to

[1]See Eleanor Flexner, *A Century of Struggle* (New York: Atheneum, 1971), Preface. This is the best single work on the women's movement from 1820 to 1920. The most complete documentation is in Elizabeth Stanton et al., *History of Woman Suffrage* (New York: Fowler & Wells, 1881–1922), 6 vols.

[2]Samuel Morison, *Oxford History of the American People* (New York: Oxford University Press, 1965).

[3]Quoted in Flexner, op. cit., Preface.

America, where they were enslaved for their entire lives. (The situation under slavery in the American South is discussed later in this chapter.)

Even "free" women had very few rights in early America, where the laws were based on British common law. A married woman's property, even property from a dowry or inheritance, belonged completely to her husband. Married women did not exist as legal entities apart from their husbands. They couldn't testify in court, they couldn't sue or sign contracts, their earnings belonged to their husbands, and they did not have the right to their own children even if they were legally separated. Few women were allowed to remain single, but the harsh frontier conditions created many widows. The widow usually carried on with her husband's farm or other craft. A widow's life was, in fact, freer than a wife's. The laws concerning married women's property were not changed anywhere until the mid-nineteenth century, and many states retained them until much later.

The subordinate status of women was supported by the dominant ideology of the period, the strongest medium of which was religion. In this very religious atmosphere, all of the sects preached "that woman's place was determined by limitations of mind and body, a punishment for the original sin of Eve. However, . . . to fit her for . . . motherhood, the Almighty had . . . endowed her with such virtues as modesty, meekness, . . . piety."[4]

All women on the frontiers—except a few very upper-class women—led a hard life, working from dawn until dusk. Among the pioneers, the men had to hunt and fight wars, build houses, and clear the fields. The women had to plant, tend, and harvest the crops, and turn animal skins into clothing and meat into edible food.[5] This lifestyle continued on the frontiers in much the same manner from the sixteenth to the end of the nineteenth century.

It is important to understand that a woman's status in such a society was fairly low and her work was very hard, yet her status was far higher than in European societies of the same period. In frontier society, ideology gave way to the necessities of survival, and woman's work was indispensable. Furthermore, women were always scarce on the frontier, as will be shown in some detail in later sections. Since women were both absolutely necessary and very scarce, their status rose. As husband and wife worked side by side, a companionate, though still unequal, relationship often developed.

[4]Ibid., p. 8.
[5]Ibid., p. 5.

The laws and the ideology had a much firmer grasp in the older communities than in the newer frontier communities.[6] In later sections, we shall see that the frontier perspective was important in making the western states the first in the United States to grant women suffrage.

Many women gained political experience when they organized the Daughters of Liberty to support the Revolutionary War. The Daughters of Liberty educated women to boycott British goods, keep the farms going during the war, and supply clothing to the army.

Tom Paine spoke for women's rights and described women in the 1770s as "robbed of freedom and will by the laws, the slaves of opinion, which rules them with absolute sway and construes the slightest appearances into guilt; surrounded on all sides by judges, who are at once tyrants and their seducers. . . ."[7] In 1777, during the Revolutionary War, Abigail Adams wrote to her husband, the future president: "In the new code of laws . . . I desire you would remember the ladies. . . . Do not put such unlimited power into the hands of the husbands. Remember, all men would be tyrants if they could. If particular care and attention is not paid to the ladies, we are determined to foment a rebellion, and will not hold ourselves bound by any laws in which we have no voice or representation."[8] These isolated arguments made by a few individuals here and there were the sole reflections of women's protest up to the war—and beyond it until the 1830s.

CONDITIONS FROM THE REVOLUTION TO THE CIVIL WAR

Before the Revolutionary War and up to 1820, there was no education for most women. A few rich women were tutored in French, embroidery, painting, singing, and harpsichord playing in institutions called female seminaries.[9]

In 1819, Emma Willard, who had studied and taught mathematics, presented a petition to the New York legislature for a women's seminary. She would not speak publicly because it was considered unladylike, but she lobbied in private. The legislature

[6]Ibid., p. 9. The fullest discussion of the frontier conditions and effects on the women's movement is in Alan Grimes, *The Puritan Ethic and Woman Suffrage* (New York: Oxford University Press, 1967).

[7]Quoted in Flexner, op. cit., p. 14.

[8]Quoted in ibid., p. 15.

[9]The definitive work on women's education is Mabel Newcomer, *A Century of Higher Education* (New York: Harper & Row, 1959).

gave her a charter but no money. She founded her school in Middle-bury, Vermont, in 1814. When she finally got money from the city of Troy, New York, she moved the school there and called it the Troy Female Seminary (now called Emma Willard School). She taught not only history and geography and a little math but also the indelicate subject of physiology: "Mothers visiting a class at the Seminary in the early thirties were so shocked at the sight of a pupil drawing a heart, arteries and veins on a blackboard . . . that they left the room in shame and dismay."[10] All of the women's seminaries at this time were on the high school level—there was no higher education for women.

Public education was slow in coming for both males and fe-males in the nineteenth century. By 1840, a free public education was given to 50 percent of the children in New England, 25 percent in the Middle Atlantic states, 16 percent in the West, and only 8 per-cent in the South. New England took the lead because the area needed skilled workers in industry. Women were admitted immedi-ately to the earliest elementary schools but were resisted at the high school level. There were no free high schools for women until after the Civil War.

The first coeducational college, and the first to admit blacks, was Oberlin, founded in 1833. At first women were given a special course intended to prepare them for homemaking or teaching. More-over, women students had special duties: "Washing the men's clothes, caring for their rooms, serving them at table, listening to their orations, but themselves remaining respectfully silent in public as-semblages, the Oberlin 'co-eds' were being prepared for intelligent motherhood and a properly subservient wifehood."[11] Most women were still trained to be helpmates, not independent scholars. Not until 1841 did the first women graduate from the regular (men's) pro-gram at Oberlin.

In 1834, the first college for women, Wheaton College, was founded by Mary Lyon at Norton, Massachusetts. In 1837, Lyon helped found Mt. Holyoke. It was little more than a seminary for a number of years and was called one until 1893. Mary Lyon proposed the idea of such a college herself, but stayed in the background until men failed to raise enough money, when she went out and did it herself.

In the South it was illegal to teach any slave to read. In the North, black men were barred from almost all public schools, even

[10]Alma Lutz, *Emma Willard* (Boston: Houghton Mifflin, 1929), p. 181.
[11]Quoted in Flexner, op. cit., p. 30.

though they paid taxes for them. Black women received even poorer treatment. In 1833, a private school for black girls was opened by Prudence Crandall in Canterbury, Connecticut. The "respectable" community attacked it with threats, then jailed Crandall for vagrancy, then tried to legislate against the school in the state legislature, then broke windows, then stoned the teachers and students when they went walking, dropped manure in their well, got shopkeepers to refuse to sell them food, forced doctors to refuse to treat them, and finally destroyed the schoolhouse physically.

While the majority of Americans still lived on farms, women were moving into industry during the first half of the nineteenth century. Women did over 100 different industrial jobs before the Civil War, mostly in the textile industry. By 1850, there were 225,000 women in industrial jobs. At first they worked for the textile industry by sewing at home, where it was "respectable"; then they moved into the factories. They worked 13 to 14 hours a day at very low pay. Women were excluded from many other jobs; and, with few skills besides sewing, thousands were forced to compete against each other in the garment industry. This competition brought their wages down. Women were paid from one-seventh to one-fourth of what men were paid in the same industries. Many short-lived unions were formed to protest these conditions. In the "good" cotton mills, women worked from 13 to 16 hours a day. In 1835 there was a strike in Paterson, New Jersey, for a 12-hour day!

In 1845, at the Lowell, Massachusetts, textile mills, a union called the Lowell Female Labor Reform Association was formed. It proved that women workers could develop a stable organization, give it dynamic leadership, and carry on a systematic and partly successful campaign. The union spread to all the mill towns, and delegates went to statewide labor conventions. The association took part in a drive for a 10-hour day and presented petitions to the Massachusetts legislature. Sarah Bagley, leader of the union, spoke bluntly to a legislative committee on working conditions, telling how "she worked in a room with more than 150 people, where 293 small lamps and 61 large lamps burned mornings and evenings all winter, making the air foul; sometimes as many as 30 women were sick in one day from the fumes."[12] The 1830s and 1840s thus saw the first women's efforts for equal pay and better conditions. Women in working-class struggles were an important part of the women's movement in several periods; in fact, the three movements—

[12]Quoted in ibid., p. 59.

workers', blacks', and women's—have often intertwined in U.S. history.

Married women in the 1840s still couldn't manage their own property, sign legal papers, or control their own wages. Husbands controlled everything and could drink or gamble away all of a family's money, even if nothing was left for the wife or children. A woman had no legal rights at all in marriage: She could not make a will, sue or be sued, or help choose where to live. Her husband still had control of her earnings and property, control of her person, and exclusive control and guardianship of their children, even after a divorce.

Between 1839 and 1860, most states passed legislation that enabled married women to own property. This was an upper-class reform led by wealthy fathers and even by wealthy husbands who sought protection against creditors. When the law permits a married woman to hold property in her own name, her husband's creditors cannot take her property if her husband goes bankrupt. The law left all other inequalities untouched.

One such inequality was the denial of women's right to vote. In the democratic atmosphere that existed immediately after the Revolutionary War, many states allowed free blacks to vote, but not women. Only one state, New Jersey, allowed all men and women to vote if they were over 21 and if they owned property worth 50 pounds. But, by 1800, conservatives in almost all states had limited the vote to free, white males who held property. As a result, only 10 to 13 percent of the population could vote. In 1806, New Jersey also fell into line, limiting the vote to "free, white, male citizens with property."

American slavery

American slavery before the Civil War was quite similar to slavery in ancient Athens in regard to the position of both slaves and women. Millions of Africans were kidnaped and sent to the United States as slaves. Their first ordeal after being kidnaped was the Atlantic voyage, on which the slaves were treated as "cargo." During a 5- or 6-week voyage in small, often storm-tossed ships, the slaves were "chained in pairs to platforms . . . sometimes with as little as eighteen inches between the 'floor' and the 'ceiling' . . . occasionally they would have to double up their legs, with no room to move them."[13] Over one-third of the slaves were women, and there are many re-

[13]Ibid., p. 18.

corded cases in which slave women gave birth to children under these inhuman conditions.

When the slaves who survived the voyage reached the United States, the women were sold at auctions, where they were undressed and carefully inspected. A majority of the women were sold for the same job as men, field hand in the cotton-growing states. A few "lucky" ones were made "house servants," in which job they took care of the house and served the sexual needs of the white master. He often got them pregnant, then sold his own children for a profit. Another large number of slave women were sold to the breeding states, Virginia, North Carolina, Maryland, Delaware, Kentucky, Tennessee, and Missouri. In these states the most important cash crop were slaves that could be sold to the cotton states of the Deep South. A typical advertisement for a slave woman read: "Negroes for sale: A girl about twenty years of age . . . and her two female children. . . . She is very prolific in her generating qualities and affords a rare opportunity to any person who wishes to raise a family of strong and healthy servants for their own use."[14]

What kind of life did the wives of slaveowners lead? They lived in material luxury, but slavery was a disaster for them in every other way. According to the southern literary image, the white slave-owning woman was a perfect lady, delicate in looks and manner and submissive to her husband; she brought up the children, managed the house, and was very religious. A southern male wrote: "Her life was one long act of devotion—devotion to God, devotion to her husband, devotion to her children, devotion to her servants, to the poor, to humanity."[15] She was certainly devoted to God and husband, but we may be more skeptical about her devotion to the slaves, whom she too exploited.

The slave-owning woman's religion told her she was inferior to men (though superior to slaves, just as Aristotle had argued in ancient Greece). Religion told her to be meek, obey her husband, and suffer. The same message of "ladylike" obedience and lack of independence or creativity was impressed on her by schools, parents, books, and magazines. It was said to be her only road to respect and love.

As in every other slave society, the power of the man over the slaves made him the authoritarian patriarch of the family. The South

[14]Quoted in ibid., p. 21.
[15]Quoted in Anne Scott, *The Southern Lady* (Chicago: University of Chicago Press, 1970), p. 5.

remained strongly patriarchal long after the rest of the country had begun to change.

Contrary to the image of romantic love, most marriages among the slave holders were arranged for economic reasons, just as they were under slavery in Greece. A southern newspaper wrote in 1808 that ". . . when a young man is about to get him a wife, the first inquiry he makes is, Has such a young lady much property . . . ?"[16] Essentially, the young white woman was also sold, but more politely than her black sister. She was often shocked to find that she didn't live romantically but had to supervise a hectic operation. One southern white woman wrote: "Her large family, the immense retinue of slaves who all had to be fed, clothed, nursed, not to mention the incessant demands of hospitality, made her the real burden-bearer of the community."[17] No doubt the white woman found this life a burden, but think what the burden was on the black woman who slaved for her. We might add that much harder work than the slave-owner's wife did was done by the small, free farmer's wife in the South, who not only minded house and children but also hoed the cornfields, often cut firewood, and did her own spinning and weaving.

The myth glorified motherhood, but even for the white woman reality included endless pregnancies, real danger of death in childbirth, and numerous children to care for. Because of the lack of contraceptives, white women were often unenthusiastic about sex. The slave-owning men increasingly exploited their female slaves sexually as relations with their wives deteriorated. The wives were then jealous of the slaves and felt demeaned by their husbands' sexual relations with slave women. As one southern white woman wrote: "Under slavery we live surrounded by prostitutes; like patriarchs of old, our men live in one house with their wives and concubines."[18]

The slave-owning woman usually hated black slave women for the sex that they were forced to supply to male slaveowners. Yet some black and white women formed alliances and friendships across the slave-master boundary for mutual support against the white male patriarch. For these and other reasons, most white southern women who wrote about it opposed slavery. A few even went north and joined the abolitionist movement.

As in ancient Greece, education for women was very limited,

[16]Quoted in ibid., p. 22.
[17]Quoted in ibid., p. 29.
[18]Quoted in ibid., p. 52.

since it was believed that women had inferior minds. Sarah Grimke, a Southern white woman who became an abolitionist, wrote: ". . . The powers of my mind have never been allowed expansion; in childhood they were repressed by the false idea that a girl need not have the education I coveted."[19] Just before the Civil War there was some increase in finishing schools for southern slave-owning women. This occurred because it was felt that educated women might be more pleasant companions; the education consisted mostly of learning to read and practicing the fine arts. And what of education for slave women? To teach a slave to read and write was a crime punishable by prison or even death.

THE MOVEMENT FROM THE REVOLUTION TO THE CIVIL WAR

The rise of industry and the creation of a bourgeois class from the eighteenth-century owners of industry and commerce led to several revolutions against feudalism. The most important of these was the French Revolution, which spread the idea of equality across the world. The American Revolution was fought for independence, but it also initiated the slogan of equality that was assumed and amplified by the French Revolution. These two revolutions shook American society and changed the ideological outlook of many people. At first, the idea of equality was applied only to white males, but it was inevitable that every oppressed group would make this slogan its own.

The Jacksonian movement in the late 1820s and 1830s continued the democratic ferment for equality. At the same time, conflict between the southern slaveowners and the capitalist owners of industry in the North became evident over who was to be the dominant political-economic power. Using the rhetoric of equality, some northern businessmen supported a movement to abolish slavery. Many women joined the abolitionist movement and gained their first political experience in it. This movement was the most important direct cause of the upsurge of women's liberation activity that occurred in the 1830s and 1840s.

One other immediate source of the women's movement was the militant unionism in which working women participated during the 1840s. This early unionism was semipolitical in character and was closely tied to the first working people's political parties of the 1840s. Unionism was, of course, another natural result of the spread of industry throughout the northern United States.

19Quoted in ibid., p. 64.

Finally, we must recognize that people need time and money in order to participate in political movements. The rise of U.S. industry and commerce created a class of upper- and middle-class women who had some leisure and a little money. About this time, these women began to have access to some education, which brought them into contact with the theories of equality then popular. Working women, on the contrary, had no leisure time or money and no education. The underrepresentation of working women in the nineteenth-century movement can also be attributed to discrimination against them by some of the leaders of the movement. When working women did find any extra energy for organization, most spent it in the fight for higher wages and better working conditions. Some, however, did become involved in the suffrage movement.

The 1830s witnessed an upsurge of the antislavery movement. The American Anti-Slavery Society was formed in 1833. Twenty women attended, but they were not allowed to sign the Declaration of Purposes. So the women formed their own Female Anti-Slavery Society, though they asked a man to preside at their meeting. The society spread, and the women became more confident. By 1837, when a man volunteered to be the presiding officer, they wrote to him that "when the women got together, they found they had *minds* of their own, and could transact their business *without* his directions."[20]

All abolitionists—but especially the militant women in the movement, who were thought to be "unnatural"—suffered persecution and mob violence over and over again. Many women did particularly dangerous work helping slaves escape through the Underground Railroad.

The most successful railroad "conductor" was Harriet Tubman, herself an escaped slave. This black woman actually made many trips into the South and brought out slaves, whom she then delivered to the next station on the railroad to freedom. Her code name in the underground was Moses. "The white slaveholders put a price on her head. They wanted her captured, dead or alive. But the slaveholders couldn't believe that 'Moses' was a woman. One slaveholder even offered a reward of $40,000 for the capture of 'the escaped male slave known as Moses.' "[21] Ms. Tubman fought in the

---

[20]Quoted in Flexner, op. cit., p. 42.

[21]Susan Brownmiller, *Shirley Chisholm* (New York: Pocket Books, 1972), p. 25. For Tubman's biography, see Earl Conrad, *Harriet Tubman* (New York: International Publishers, 1942).

Union Army during the Civil War, and led a successful raid by 300 black soldiers against the Confederates. She was denied a soldier's pension for many years because she was a woman.

The earliest women to speak publicly for the abolition of slavery were Sarah and Angelina Grimke. They were born into a South Carolina slave-owning family, so their hatred of slavery was based on personal knowledge. In the 1830s, they spoke to small groups of women, then to larger groups, and finally to large public meetings of women and men. For this the Council of Congregationalist Ministers of Massachusetts violently denounced them. Speaking publicly was going beyond women's "God-given place." In answering the attack, they began to speak not only for the slaves but for women. Sarah said: "I ask no favors for my sex. . . . All I ask of our brethren is that they will take their feet off our necks and permit us to stand upright. . . ."[22]

The male abolitionists, even the radicals, cautioned the Grimkes to be quiet because pushing for women's rights might hurt the cause of abolitionism. This tactical argument divided the black and women's movements time and time again. Angelina replied: "Why, my dear brothers, can you not see the deep laid scheme of the clergy against us lecturers? . . . If we surrender the right to *speak* in public this year, we must surrender the right to petition next year, and the right to write the year after, and so on. What *then* can *woman* do for the slave . . . ?"[23] Here we have a clear instance of sexist ideology used to split and weaken a progressive moment.

In 1840, women delegates to the World Anti-Slavery Convention in London were denied seats and forced to sit in the gallery. This treatment made the women even more aware of their inferior status. Discussion by these women finally led to the first Women's Rights Convention at Seneca Falls, New York, in 1848. (Here *convention* meant a meeting of interested people, not delegates.) They declared: "We hold these truths to be self-evident: that all men and women are created equal."[24] The forms of social, economic, and legal discrimination against women were listed and the women pledged to use every means to end discrimination. The only disagreement was on whether to demand the vote—some said it was too radical and ridiculous—but a suffrage resolution was finally passed by a small majority. Until 1860, there were frequent meetings, primarily just talk aimed at trying to agree on a program; there was no national

[22]Quoted in Flexner, op. cit., p. 47.
[23]Quoted in ibid., p. 48.
[24]Quoted in ibid., p. 75.

organization. In fact, the women's movement was run mostly by married women in their few spare moments after doing all the housework and child care.

Many newspapers attacked the women's suffrage movement. For example, the *New York Herald* attacked the suffragist Lucy Stone, who spoke well and might have been a lawyer, saying, "How funny it would sound in the newspapers that Lucy Stone, pleading a case, took suddenly ill . . . and perhaps gave birth to a bouncing boy in court."[25] The same nonsense was repeated for decades.

To answer these attacks and state their own views, women started their own newspapers: *The Lily, The Una, Pittsburgh Visiter, Women's Advocate*. No national organization was formed because women thought it would be cumbersome, might stifle individual initiative, and was not necessary. They concentrated on issues of equality—social, economic, and legal—but very few of the women emphasized the vote. Some didn't see the vote as being really important; others just thought that it was impossible to achieve.

The three most important personalities in the movement were Lucy Stone,[26] its most gifted orator, Elizabeth Stanton,[27] its best philosopher and program writer, and Susan B. Anthony,[28] its best organizer.

It was probably Lucy Stone's upbringing on a poor Massachusetts farm that turned her into a feminist. She saw that her mother worked as hard as her father, yet her father was indisputably the master in the house. She taught school for 7 years to earn enough money to attend Oberlin College, where she was one of the first women to graduate from the full course. She became a lecturer for the Anti-Slavery Society, but often included the subject of women's rights in her talks. Abolitionists, afraid she was hurting the cause, asked her to drop the incendiary topic. Finally a compromise was made; she would speak on abolition on Saturdays and Sundays; on women's rights the rest of the week. The breadth of issues with which the early women's movement was concerned is shown by Stone's three stock lectures on women. One was on women's social and industrial dis-

---

[25]Quoted in ibid., pp. 81–82.

[26]See Alice Blackwell, *Lucy Stone* (Boston: Little, Brown, 1930).

[27]See Alma Lutz, *Created Equal: A Biography of Elizabeth Stanton* (New York: Day, 1940). Also see Mary Oakley, *Elizabeth Cady Stanton* (New York: Feminist Press, 1972).

[28]See Ida Harper, *The Life and Work of Susan B. Anthony* (Indianapolis: Hollenbeck Press, 1898, 1908), 3 vols.

abilities, another on legal and political handicaps, and the third on moral and religious discrimination.

The marriage of Lucy Stone and Henry Blackwell in 1855 received wide public attention because of the statement they incorporated into the ceremony. In this statement Blackwell repudiated the superior status the law granted him as husband, and the couple declared themselves equal partners in the marriage. Lucy Stone retained her maiden name throughout her life. Marriage did not hamper her. She continued her lecturing and was active in the suffrage movement throughout the second half of the nineteenth century.

Elizabeth Cady Stanton attended the 1840 World Anti-Slavery Convention in London and was denied a seat because of her sex. Eight years later, she was to be the moving force in calling the first women's rights convention in Seneca Falls, where she introduced a resolution calling for women's suffrage. Despite being married and having seven children, she was to be active in the women's movement for the rest of her life. A good speaker, her greatest contribution was as the movement's philosopher. Her attention was never restricted to suffrage. She called for equality in all spheres, advocating marriage and divorce law reform at a time when this was considered a topic that should not even be mentioned. She strongly criticized the Bible for its statements on women.

Susan B. Anthony, Stanton's lifelong friend and co-worker, came to the women's movement via the temperance movement and soon became its greatest organizer. In 1854, Anthony led a petition campaign in New York for women to control their own wages, to have guardianship of their children after a divorce, and to be allowed to vote. Her 60 women "captains," one in each county, collected 6000 signatures in 10 weeks in spite of harassment. When she presented the signatures and spoke to a Joint Judiciary Committee of the State Legislature, the committee turned down the petition with "humorous" arguments, saying that the ladies ". . . always have the best seat. . . . They have their choice on which side of the bed they will lie . . . if there is any inequity or oppression . . . , the gentlemen are the sufferers."[29] But continuous struggle brought some success. In 1860, Stanton addressed a joint session, and the state legislature passed a law giving women control over their own wages, allowing them to sue in court, and giving them inheritance rights similar to their husbands'.

Unmarried, Anthony bore the brunt of the traveling and lecturing when her married friends could not get away from home. She

[29]Quoted in Flexner, op. cit., p. 85.

spent much of her life on the lecture circuit, enduring hostility, ridicule, extreme cold and heat, bedbugs, and miserable food. Although agreeing with Stanton that real equality would require many social and legal reforms, Anthony concentrated on suffrage. The vote, she believed, was the prerequisite to other reforms. She also felt strongly that women would not be free until they could support themselves, until marriage became a luxury and not a necessity for women as well as for men. Education she saw as one key, and because she believed sex-segregated education would always be unequal, she advocated coeducation.

A woman who fought equally well for both abolition and women's rights was Sojourner Truth, a freed slave. At a women's meeting in Akron, Ohio, in 1851, a clergyman argued that women were weak and helpless and ridiculed their desire to vote. The women all hesitated to answer until Sojourner Truth rose and said:

> The man over there says women need to be helped into carriages and lifted over ditches, and to have the best place everywhere. Nobody ever helps me into carriages or over puddles, or gives me the best place—and ain't I a woman? [She raised her bare black arm and said:] Look at my arm! I have ploughed and planted and gathered into barns, and no man could head me—and ain't I a woman? I could work as much and eat as much as a man—when I could get it—and bear the lash as well! And ain't I a woman? I have borne 13 children, and seen most of 'em sold into slavery, and when I cried out with my mother's grief, none but Jesus heard me—and ain't I a woman?[30]

The women's movement was confined to the North and the West. No women spoke for women's rights in the South before the Civil War. The white women slaveowners were supposed to be on a pedestal, but they were (metaphorically) chained to it and made to keep silent. Black women were more literally chained.

CONDITIONS FROM THE CIVIL WAR TO 1900

On the farm, where most people still lived, full-time work by both sexes was absolutely necessary. Furthermore, in the frontier states women were very scarce. The ratio of men to women was 3 to 1 in California, 4 to 1 in Washington, 8 to 1 in Nevada, and 20 to 1 in Colorado.[31] On the frontier, women worked just as hard as men. A frontier woman wrote about a typical day in her diary: "churned and made a cheese . . . painted . . . front door. Washed and cleaned

[30]Quoted in ibid., p. 90.
[31]Ibid., p. 157.

furniture for painting. . . . Dipped 24 dozen candles. . . . Our house [windows] is wholly glassed though to complete it I had to set 47 squares of glass."[32] The obvious indispensability of women's work, combined with the scarcity of women, led to greater egalitarianism in the West and thus to greater receptivity to women's suffrage.

Free high schools for women were first opened in Boston and Philadelphia just after the Civil War. Still, there was great opposition to any higher education for women. It was argued that too much study would fatigue women (because they were thought to have smaller brains) and ruin their reproductive organs. In the 1850s and early 1860s, women were permitted to enter some midwestern universities, such as Iowa and Wisconsin. They were turned down until 1870 at Michigan, Ohio, and Illinois. For the most part, these universities admitted women only when they lacked students, particularly when the men went off to fight in the war.

In the East, women were mostly restricted to single-sex colleges, which had to give much remedial work because women lacked the needed preparation. Vassar paid women faculty lower salaries and didn't allow them on faculty committees. A number of women's colleges were established during the second half of the nineteenth century—Vassar in 1865, Smith and Wellesley in 1875, the "Harvard Annex" (later Radcliffe) in 1879, and Bryn Mawr in 1885.

A scarcity of male teachers resulted in many women going into teaching during the Civil War. After the war, teaching became a mostly female profession, though it had been considered a male job previously. The change occurred, at least in part, because women could be paid lower salaries—in New York in 1853, women teachers were paid 10 percent of the male salary! In most states, women teachers were fired if they married. The reason for this rule was that unmarried women would be more submissive because they had no alternative source of support, and so they could be paid less.

In the western pioneer states, women gained the right to control their own property and earnings during the years between 1860 and 1900. In the East, there was less progress. In 1900, a married woman in Pennsylvania still couldn't sign a contract without her husband's approval. In the South, almost no progress was made in the laws, and almost no women were educated beyond elementary school. Even in the West, as late as 1900 in Minnesota, if a woman was divorced for adultery, she had to forfeit all property, including

[32]Quoted in ibid., p. 158.

her own; but there was no similar penalty for men. The same was true in many other states. This was the double standard with a vengeance.

Pioneer and working women dressed roughly, but the mid–nineteenth-century middle- and upper-class "lady" was forced to follow Queen Victoria. Corsets made of steel ribs or whalebone and tight laces were the style, and some young girls had to sleep in them to "narrow the waist." Petticoats and skirts added another 15 pounds to the baggage they had to carry around. Women could hardly move or breathe, their muscles atrophied, and they fainted with the slightest exertion (no wonder!). A number of early women's leaders attempted to institute a change in style or at least give women an option by adopting the bloomer costume—a short skirt worn over long, full pants. They were subjected to so much ridicule that they came to believe they were hurting the chances of more important reforms and gave up the costume. Women continued to wear long skirts until the feminist upsurge of the 1920s.

During the Civil War women worked in factories, in addition to doing their traditional work at home. Women kept the farms going. Women became nurses in the Union Army, even though the Army Medical Corps was mostly hostile to them. Women became teachers in order to keep the schools open.

Although in the mid-nineteenth century women were allowed into industry, they were resisted in the professions. A perceptive woman wrote in 1853 that "millions of women . . . are condemned to the most menial drudgery . . . for one fourth the wages [of men]. . . . They plough, reap, dig . . . chop wood . . . do anything that is hard work, physical labor, and who says anything against it. But let one presume to use her mental powers . . . take up any profession . . . which is deemed honorable and requires talent, and O! . . . unloose his corsets! . . . What, a fainting fit Mr. Propriety has taken! Just to think that 'one of the deah creathures' . . . should foresake the sphere—woman's sphere—to mix with the wicked strife of this wicked world.[33]

Elizabeth Blackwell wanted to be a doctor but was turned down by 29 medical schools. She was then admitted to one as a joke, but persisted and, in 1849, became the first woman M.D. In New York, however, she couldn't find a house or office to rent, had no private patients, and was given no access to hospitals. Finally, in 1857, she started her own hospital, which was run completely by

[33]Quoted in ibid., p. 113.

women. After the war there was still no reputable medical school that would admit women, so in 1868 she opened the Woman's Infirmary Medical School.

In 1872 a woman was prohibited from getting a license to practice law in Illinois. But women were entering law practice in some other states, and Belva Lockwood was admitted to the bar of the United States Supreme Court in 1879.

After the Civil War, vast industrial expansion commenced. Permanent, national unions came into being in the 1870s. Women factory workers increased. There were 226,000 in 1850, 271,000 in 1860, and 323,000 in 1870. Most were still in the sewing trades, which were overcrowded and paid very low wages. Women were admitted to the printers' union and to the cigar makers' union in 1869. They were important members in the militant federation called the National Labor Union in the 1860s and 1870s—but this union lasted only a short while.

Women not only got low wages but often were not paid at all. Many suits for unpaid wages were brought by the Legal Aid Society. At a meeting to discuss legal aid in 1864 several women said: "Oh, if we could always get paid for our work, we could get along."[34]

In 1868, Susan B. Anthony helped form a Working Women's Association. Some of the members wanted to teach work skills—Ms. Anthony herself wanted to campaign for suffrage—but most members wanted to fight economic discrimination. In 1869, they organized the Women's Typographical Union, Local #1, which was strongly encouraged by some of the men's locals. Because of the male expression of solidarity, the women steadfastly supported the union. The national president of the typographers said: "Though most liberal inducements were offered to women compositors to take the places of men on strike, not a single member of the women's union could be induced to do so."[35] Yet most other union locals did not support the women. A woman organizer reported to the printers' union convention in 1871, "We refuse to take the men's situations when they are on strike, and when there is no strike if we ask for work in union offices we are told by union foremen that 'there are no [jobs] for us.'[36] So the tactic of divide and rule by sexism won again; the women's locals died out. Other short-lived unions run by women in the 1870s were those of the laundry workers, who worked

[34]Quoted in ibid., p. 132.
[35]Quoted in ibid., p. 135.
[36]Quoted in ibid., p. 136.

in rooms where temperatures reached 100°; and the shoemakers, who called themselves Daughters of St. Crispin. In all cases, the women's anger at awful conditions and unequal pay led to organization and some success, but sexism by male unions led to eventual defeat.

In 1880, there were 2,600,000 women workers making up 15 percent of the labor force. In 1890, there were 4,000,000 women workers making up 17 percent of the labor force. Of these women, 1,000,000 were domestic servants, 523,000 were clothing and textile workers, and 109,000 were laundry workers.

In 1881, the Knights of Labor became a national labor federation. It set up craft locals but also established regional "assemblies," covering all the workers in a geographical area. In 1886 there were 113 women's assemblies including all kinds of women workers, from teachers to laundry workers. The Knights had women national delegates—16 women out of 660 delegates in 1886. They also had a woman organizer. Some of their women investigators found that the average woman worker worked 10 hours a day for $5 a *week*. The women organizers complained that ". . . many women are deterred from joining labor organizations by foolish pride, prudish modesty . . . religious scruples . . . and expectancy that in the near future marriage will lift them out of the industrial life. . . ."[37] Thus women's sexist social conditioning as well as male sexism presented obstacles to women's unionization.

In the 1890s, the Knights of Labor died and the American Federation of Labor became the most important labor organization. The AFL mostly organized skilled craft workers. It included few women, gave women no encouragement, and had only one woman organizer (Mary Kenney, for 5 months in 1892), then none for a long time.

The 1890s saw much social tension. The frontier no longer existed as a safety valve. Millions of workers were in sweatshops and slums; but there were 4047 millionaires! "Muckraking" journalistic attacks on big business were frequent, as were radical proposals for better societies (e.g., Edward Bellamy's utopian novel, *Looking Backward*). In the 1870s and 1880s, many utopian colonies formed. The rise of the Populist party occurred in the 1880s and 1890s. The period was characterized by strikes, much hysteria about communism, anarchism, bomb-throwing, and considerable class polarization.

Nevertheless, many middle-class women joined reform organi-

[37]Quoted in ibid., p. 200.

zations. In 1899 the New York Consumers League exposed the terrible working conditions of women; it had branches in 20 states by 1896 and at its height was led by Florence Kelley. Middle-class women also formed "settlement houses," which gave charity and advice but also helped organize the poor and working women. The main settlement house in Chicago was founded by Jane Addams, who worked closely with organized labor. For the most part, however, middle-class reform movements had little to do with working-class radicals and labor organizations.

THE MOVEMENT FROM THE CIVIL WAR TO 1890

No women's rights activity took place during the Civil War; in the North, women concentrated on propagandizing and petitioning for the abolition of slavery. These women expected equality for blacks *and* women after the war. Thus they felt betrayed when the Fourteenth and Fifteenth amendments were introduced in Congress in 1866 and restricted the protection of the right to vote to male citizens. This was the first time the word *male* was used in the Constitution. The women knew it would take many more decades to get another amendment for women.

Tragically, the abolitionist movement and the women's movement split. Why? The white male abolitionists consisted of northern businessmen and intellectuals. The businessmen wanted an end to slavery so that northern business could expand. As soon as slavery was abolished, they quit the fight for equality, feeling that their purpose had been accomplished. Social and economic equality for the freed slaves was not a part of their program. The businessmen were against equality and better wages for all workers; many were still for limiting the male vote by property qualifications. They opposed women's suffrage because it might disturb the status quo. Northern politicians wanted the black vote because they believed it would ensure Republican victories in the South and enable them to dominate national politics. They could see no gain from women's votes. The intellectuals were middle class; they felt that formal equality for the ex-slaves was sufficient, and they still had biases against women. Black males wanted the vote urgently because blacks were still being lynched and physically and legally attacked. Black leaders didn't want to jeopardize the right of blacks to vote by adding women's right to vote to the amendment.

The militant women's leaders, who were white and middle class, reacted with violence that bordered on racism against putting "Sambo" Africans, Chinese, and "ignorant" foreigners ahead of women. Ms. Stanton said that male suffrage "creates an antagonism between black men and all women that will culminate in fearful outrages on womanhood, especially in the southern states."[38]

The joint movement had formed an American Equal Rights Association for pushing both blacks' and women's rights, but it split in May 1869. Stanton and Anthony were for an immediate women's suffrage amendment. When many others opposed it, they formed the National Woman Suffrage Association (hereafter called the National), which did not admit men and worked militantly for suffrage. The National published a paper called *Revolution,* and campaigned not only for suffrage but against the exploitation and terrible conditions of women (and men) workers and the unequal social situation of women. It ran campaigns against the double standard, even publishing some writers who advocated "free love," which shocked the Victorian world. The *Revolution* even criticized the churches for their sexist ideas and support of discrimination.

In November 1869, the moderates organized the American Woman Suffrage Association (hereafter called the American), which included men and whose first president was a man. The organization's main spokesperson was Lucy Stone, who brought in many middle- and upper-class club women and professionals. The American's newspaper, the *Woman's Journal,* was well financed, unlike the more outspoken *Revolution,* which went bankrupt in just 2½ years. The *Journal* was quite conservative in style and soft-pedaled suffrage. It said nothing about exploitation at work or domination in marriage and did not attack the churches.

The more radical National also utilized much more militant tactics. For example, in 1876, at a centennial celebration of U.S. independence in Philadelphia, Ms. Anthony suddenly got up on the stage and read a Declaration of Rights for Women, which her supporters then distributed as a leaflet. The National also protested by having 150 women try to vote in 1872. Ms. Anthony was prosecuted for voting illegally. The judge would not even allow her to testify, since, he said, women were "incompetent" to do so. She was found guilty and fined $100, but refused to pay. The government never tried to collect because it didn't want the case to be appealed.

In 1872, the National supported a case by Virginia Minor, who tried to vote on the ground that voting was a privilege granted all citizens by the first section of the Fourteenth Amendment. But in 1874, the United States Supreme Court ruled against Ms. Minor on the grounds that states have the right to set property qualifications or deny the vote to criminals, insane people, or women.

[38]Quoted in ibid., p. 144.

The National campaigned for a federal suffrage amendment. Known as the Anthony Amendment, it was introduced every year from 1868 on. Actually, the first test in Congress was a bill in 1866 to give women the vote in the District of Columbia. During the debate Senator Williams claimed that if women could hold political views apart from their husbands it would "make every home a hell on earth." Senator Frelinghuysen said that "the God of our race" has stamped on American women a "higher and holier mission" than politics. "Their mission is at home, by their blandishments . . . to assuage the passions of men as they come in from the battle of life. . . ."[39] These two arguments—that women belong in the home and that giving women the vote would ruin the home—were used against suffrage by congressmen *ad nauseam.* The bill lost by 37 to 9.

The American worked for suffrage state by state, with success first in the West, where most women in fact worked equally with men. When Wyoming first became a territory, a woman named Esther Morris lobbied most of the territorial legislators. Her lobbying took the form of serving them both a dinner and a speech patterned on one of Ms. Anthony's. In 1869, Wyoming gave women suffrage, mainly on the argument that women were very scarce there and the vote would attract them. Wyoming also gave women control of their own wages and property and admitted them to jury duty. Ms. Morris was appointed the first woman justice of the peace, and served her full term despite verbal attacks by the newspapers and physical attacks by hooligans.

When Wyoming tried to become a state in 1889, some congressmen argued that it should not be admitted with women's suffrage because the Fourteenth Amendment makes it unconstitutional for women to vote! Southern congressmen argued that *states* have no right to grant suffrage, quite contrary to their usual talk about states' rights. The Wyoming territorial delegate thought that Wyoming would not be admitted with women's suffrage, so he telegraphed his legislature to ask if they would drop women's suffrage to get statehood. The state legislature, elected partly by women's votes, telegraphed back: "We will remain out of the Union a hundred years rather than come in without the women."[40] Finally, in 1890, Wyoming was admitted by a slim margin in Congress, and became the first state with women's suffrage.

The territory of Utah, run by the Mormons, was locked in a

[39]Quoted in ibid., p. 148.
[40]Quoted in ibid., p. 178.

battle with the federal Congress over the issue of plural marriages. The issue of women's suffrage became involved as a political tactic on both sides.[41] In 1870, in order to gain political support for plural marriages among women in Utah and elsewhere (and to prove that Mormon women would also vote for plural marriage), the government of Utah, composed mainly of Mormon men, suddenly gave women the right to vote. Then, in 1887, when Congress outlawed plural marriages, it added another clause in the same bill revoking women's suffrage in Utah. Finally, in 1896, when Utah became a state, having renounced plural marriage, the state constitution again gave women the right to vote.

Before women's suffrage was won in 1920, the women's organizations conducted 56 referendum campaigns, 480 campaigns to get state legislatures to allow suffrage referenda, 47 campaigns at state constitutional conventions for suffrage, 277 campaigns to include women's suffrage in state party programs, 30 campaigns to get women's suffrage in national party programs, and 19 campaigns to get the Nineteenth Amendment—the women's suffrage amendment—through Congress.

In Congress, the Nineteenth Amendment did not get out of committee for many years. After much lobbying, it finally got to the floor of Congress in 1886. The southerners spoke against it because they felt that black women shouldn't get the vote. Senator West said it would ruin the home and make women into dangerous agitators, as they had become during the French Revolution: "Who led those bloodthirsty mobs? Who shrieked loudest in that hurricane of passions? Women!"[42] The amendment was defeated 34 to 16, with 22 of the negative votes from the South. It was proposed and defeated every year after that until 1896—after which it wasn't brought up again until 1913, as we shall see.

Both the National and the American suffrage organizations remained rather small, elite, and ineffectual in this early period. But other women's organizations were formed. The housework of middle-class women in the cities was getting easier with better technology and use of immigrant women as maids. So these middle-class women had more time, and they formed women's clubs. Also, there were more women working as semiprofessionals—in 1870 there were 90,000 women teachers; by 1890, the number had increased to 250,000—and they also formed organizations. There were huge numbers of women's clubs for literary study, "self-improvement,"

[41]Discussed in ibid., pp. 162–163.
[42]Quoted in ibid., p. 175.

and discussion of reforms. In 1890, the most stable ones formed the General Federation of Women's Clubs. At least 20 black women's clubs also existed, but these were rejected for membership in the General Federation, so they formed the National Association of Colored Women. Once again, racism divided black and white women in a way that made it easier for all women to be controlled.

Alcoholism was widespread as the last refuge of downtrodden male workers. Its burden fell on wives, whose entire family shopping money might be spent on their husbands' drink. For this reason, among others, most women reformers favored prohibition. The Women's Christian Temperance Union (WCTU) was formed in 1874 and in 1879, Frances Willard became its president. She was very able and experienced, having been a dean at Northwestern University until she found it impossible to work with the all-male board of trustees. Willard organized WCTU chapters in every state and increased its membership to over 200,000. This remarkable woman not only worked for prohibition but openly and strongly pushed for women's suffrage. Before her death in 1898, the WCTU put more money and organizers into the suffrage campaigns than the official suffrage associations. The organization's activity also sparked intensified opposition to suffrage by the liquor interests.

THE MOVEMENT IN THE 1890s

In 1890, the National and the American merged into the National American Woman Suffrage Association (NAWSA). The National had grown less radical in its tactics and much less interested in working-class causes, limiting itself to suffrage. The American had become even more strongly in favor of suffrage, and more willing to use political tactics. The combined organization slowly became more conservative and respectable, attracting many former WCTU leaders. It devoted itself to the single issue of suffrage and even gave up on the federal amendment, concentrating most of its small numbers and limited efforts on state referenda.

Why this change in tone and direction? By 1890 the women in NAWSA were the Boston and New York elite of leisured club women, plus a few professional women. They were fighting for a cause that had become almost respectable among the middle class and in Congress. A highly educated woman speaker was no longer a rarity. The women in NAWSA were totally isolated from working women, whom they often looked down on with contempt. As we have seen, this was an era of growing labor-versus-capital disputes and increasing class polarization.

As the movement became more respectable, the typical member was no longer a nonconformist and iconoclast. Women who agreed with their middle-class male contemporaries on every issue but suffrage entered NAWSA. Antiimmigrant and antiblack feeling and rhetoric were very strong at the time, and both were reflected in the new, prosuffrage rhetoric. Partly from belief—and partly as a tactic to win equally prejudiced male legislators, voters, and the business interests of the East and South—the NAWSA leaders often advocated *limited* suffrage for women during this period. They argued that the vote could be limited to all men and women who were educated and propertied, thus excluding most workers, immigrants, and blacks.

In 1902, the suffrage leader, Ms. Stanton, said in answer to the objection that women's suffrage would double the "ignorant vote" of immigrants: "The patent answer to this is to abolish the ignorant vote. . . . There have been various restrictions in the past for men. We are willing to abide by the same for women."[43] In 1903, NAWSA President Anna Shaw said: "Never before in the history of the world have men made former slaves the political masters of their former mistresses. . . . There is not a nation from pole to pole that does not send its contingent to govern American women."[44] Southern suffragists especially pandered to racism, one exclaiming: "How can I, with the blood of heroes in my heart . . . quietly submit to representation by the alien and the negro?"[45]

The women's movement grew out of the abolitionist movement and had its closest ties with the black liberation movement until the Civil War. Conflict began when the Fourteenth and Fifteenth amendments gave the vote to blacks but not to women. The two movements remained friendly until the 1890s, when the women's movement completely dissociated itself from blacks in order to become "respectable." In the early 1900s, the women's movement became antiblack in order to win the South. Woman suffrage associations affiliated with NAWSA appeared in every southern state by 1900, and two southerners, Laura Clay and Kate Gordon, held seats on the national board until 1910. These southern women argued on every occasion that white supremacy would benefit from women's suffrage because white women would outnumber blacks.

[43]Quoted in Andrew Sinclair, *The Emancipation of the American Woman* (New York: Harper & Row, 1965), p. 299.

[44]Quoted in ibid., p. 296.

[45]Quoted in ibid.

Ironically, southern white males did not buy the argument. White men opposed all change in the status quo; they were afraid women might seek social equality and were most afraid, in the words of an Alabama pamphlet, "that *Woman Suffrage* means a reopening of the entire *Negro Suffrage* question. . . ."[46]

Part of the change in tactics was an end to the old argument, originating in the American and French revolutions, that justice requires that women as well as men be allowed to rule themselves, that they not be taxed without representation. The suffragists switched to an argument from expediency; they told reformers that women were purer than men and would vote for reforms. Therefore progressive or reform-oriented men need not *share* votes and power with women but could *double* their votes and power.[47]

Similarly, they argued that because women are better and purer than men, politics would improve when good, motherly women were allowed to participate. Thus they accepted Victorian sexist stereotypes as a basis for their arguments. They extended this argument to claim that women should work for various reforms. For example, women should support the pure food and drug acts because they are good for the family, and women should fight for minimum wage and hour acts for women because delicate women need protection—but the vote was the necessary prerequisite for all such struggles.

Why did they concentrate on the sole issue of the vote? Middle-class women had already won the right to a higher education, provided that the family could pay for it. They had also won new property laws that protected a woman's right to control her own property, if she had any. So their immediate needs had been won, and they now mainly wanted formal equality with men in the Constitution—and some believed that the vote would give them such equality. Many believed in sexist stereotypes themselves, and so they felt that it was not "natural" for women to work or to be equal in the family. Hence they largely ignored the two areas of labor and family relations.

From 1870 to 1910, the suffragists were remarkably unsuccessful. This was partly due to their own conservative tactics and racist, elitist positions, which alienated their potential allies. Partly, too, it was due to continued opposition from those who feared women's

---

[46]Quoted in ibid., p. 298.
[47]See the excellent and comprehensive discussion in Aileen Kraditor, *The Ideas of the Woman Suffrage Movement, 1890–1920* (New York: Columbia University Press, 1965), pp. 200 ff.

votes for even more conservative and elitist reasons; this opposition included southern politicians, the liquor industry, city bosses, and big business, as we shall see later. Since NAWSA devoted little attention to it, the federal amendment never even reached the floor of Congress from 1893 to 1913. In the states, a huge number of campaigns resulted in only 17 actual referendum votes, almost all in the West. Only two of these were won, those in Colorado and Idaho, where the radical Populist movement was powerful. Since Wyoming and Utah were admitted as states with women's suffrage, the result of all the suffragists' work up to 1910 was four and only four states, all in the West, won for suffrage.

CONDITIONS, 1900–1920

Since the AFL didn't organize women, in 1903 a National Women's Trade Union League was formed by some middle-class, some professional, and some union women. It lobbied Congress to provide money for an investigation of the terrible working conditions of women and children. The report resulting from this investigation, which was issued in 19 volumes from 1908 to 1911, helped pass protective labor laws for women. By 1907, some 20 states had laws limiting women's hours of work. The United States Supreme Court had declared such laws unconstitutional for all workers on the basis that they were an unreasonable, unnecessary, and arbitrary interference with the right and liberty of the individual to contract in relation to his or her labor. But in *Muller* v. *Oregon* (1908) the Supreme Court held that women were especially delicate creatures who needed special protection, and on that basis it upheld protective labor laws for women only.

The number of women workers continued to climb: 4,000,000 in 1890, 5,300,000 in 1900, 7,400,000 in 1910. In 1900, 1,800,000 women were in domestic or other service; 700,000 were farm laborers; 325,000 were teachers; 878,000 were clothing and textile workers; 174,000 were clerical workers; and 217,000 were sales clerks.

In 1900, women started organizing the International Ladies Garment Workers Union. The garment industry employed many immigrant women and paid very low wages. Because the immigrant women had no power to collect their wages, sometimes they were not paid at all. For the most part the industry used small wooden buildings, with little or no sanitation and little protection from fire; as a result, several tragic fires occurred. The women worked very long hours in ill-lit rooms amid very noisy machinery. ILGWU officers were, for the most part, white males and still are, though most of the members are now Puerto Rican and black women. In 1909, a strike was considered, and a mass meeting was held in New York, at which Samuel Gompers of the AFL, Socialist party leaders, and other union leaders all gave very long speeches. The meeting almost died from too much rhetoric until one young worker got up and said: "I am a working girl, and one of those who are on strike against intolerable conditions. . . . I offer a resolution that a general strike be declared—now!"[48] The strike grew to between 20,000 and 30,000 women. It was helped by the AFL and by the Women's Trade Union League, which called a massive support rally in the New York Hippodrome addressed by the president of NAWSA. Still, the strikers almost starved during a very cold winter. The women picketed every day; the police often assaulted them and arrested many. The courts supported the bosses and approved the police attacks, with one judge telling a striker: "You are on strike against God and Nature, whose prime law it is that man shall earn his bread in the sweat of his brow." To this profound observation, George Bernard Shaw retorted: "Delightful. Medieval America always in intimate personal confidence of the Almighty."[49]

In spite of all the obstacles, women workers continued to organize in this period. During a militant strike in 1912 in the textile industry at Lawrence, Massachusetts, the women said they fought for beautiful lives as well as for money, they fought for both "bread and roses."

> As we come marching, marching,
> Un-numbered women dead
> Go crying through our singing
> Their ancient song of bread;
> Small art and love and beauty
> Their drudging spirits knew—
> Yes, it is bread we fight for,
> But we fight for roses, too.
>
> As we come marching, marching,
> We bring the greater days;
> The rising of the women
> Means the rising of us all.
> No more the drudge and idler,
> Ten that toil where one reposes,
> But a sharing of life's glories,
> Bread and Roses, Bread and Roses.

[48]Quoted in Flexner, op. cit., p. 241.
[49]Quoted in ibid., p. 243.

Another part of the song, which was inspired by the strike, said: "Hearts can starve as well as bodies, Give us Bread and give us Roses."[50]

Led by middle-class presidents until 1921, the Women's Trade Union League organized women, worked for protective laws, and propagandized in support of working women. The AFL was cordial, gave much praise, but offered little concrete help. Only 5 percent of women workers in manufacturing were unionized by 1910, and almost none were organized in the service occupations.

Women workers wanted equal pay, a shorter workday, safer conditions, and less harassment—including sexual harassment—from foremen. They were too busy getting a job with decent pay and conditions to worry about the vote. Some early women unionists were suspicious of the suffragists and reformers. Mother Jones, an organizer for the mine workers, said the plutocrats want women to concentrate on "suffrage, prohibition, and charity" rather than the real issues of class struggle, and added: "you don't need a vote to raise hell!"[51] Only in the period from 1908 to 1920 did some socialist women and militant union women join the fight for the vote, but then they were very important in swinging large numbers of working-class men toward women's suffrage. The suffrage movement itself remained white, Anglo-Saxon, and middle class, and never had many working-class members.[52]

The Socialist party and women
The Socialist party helped greatly to make workers conscious of and sympathetic to woman's suffrage. At its first convention, in 1901, its program demanded "equal civil and political rights for men and women."[53] It was the only political party to allow participation by women. On the other hand, in its early years the party ignored most of the special demands of women, even suffrage, and made no special effort to recruit women.

Until 1908, women made up only a small portion of party members although there were a number of auxiliary or women's locals composed mostly of the wives of members. In 1904, a Woman's

[50]The full text of the song, "Bread and Roses," may be found in Irwin Silber, ed., *Lift Every Voice* (New York: People's Artists, 1953), pp. 32–33.

[51]Quoted in William O'Neill, *Everyone Was Brave* (New York: Quadrangle, 1969), p. 54.

[52]See Kraditor, op. cit., pp. 105–128.

[53]Quoted in the excellent article by Mari Jo Buhle, "Women and the Socialist Party, 1901–1914," in Edith Altback, ed., *From Feminism to Liberation* (Cambridge, Mass.: Schenkman, 1971), p. 67.

National Socialist Union was organized. It was the first radical U.S. women's organization—but it got nowhere except in California, where both socialism and suffrage were already strong among women. At the same time, the party began to eye the growing suffragist numbers as a source of recruits. They proudly pointed to their stand for equal rights, but their own sexism prevented them from doing anything about it. One socialist man admitted that "when we come to practice, we are not always in accord with this highly respectable principle of ours."[54] One woman complained that her husband had been going to socialist meetings for 6 years, but "he has never yet asked me to attend any of them with him."[55] Most socialists' wives were still expected to conform to the Victorian image by doing nothing but stand at their husbands' sides and "cheer their efforts."

In 1907, however, Josephine Kaneko founded a newspaper called the *Socialist Woman,* which thundered for both socialism and women's rights for the next 7 years—during which time its circulation rose to 500,000. The *Socialist Woman* immediately complained that the party ignored women's rights and that most locals discussed only men's issues and even met in places where women were not likely to go.

At its 1908 convention the party debated its neglect of women and the need for special organizational forms. A woman delegate said: "It makes very little difference whether we approve of a separate organization for Socialist women or not. We have one—a real, live revolutionary movement, writing its own literature, managing its own newspapers, planning its own campaign."[56] Some delegates at the convention argued that women, like blacks, needed no special demands or special organization but should just join the party; the victory of socialism would solve all problems. Nevertheless, the 1908 convention approved woman suffrage and other women's rights, elected a National Woman's Committee, headed by May Simons, and provided it with money for one organizer.

The committee helped form a Federation of Socialist Women's Clubs, but this organization only aided coordination of the women's auxiliaries. The local Socialist Women's Clubs often met hostility from the party locals and seldom got any support or funds. Some women belonged to both the Socialist party and the Socialist

---

[54]Quoted in ibid., p. 69.
[55]Quoted in ibid., p. 70.
[56]Quoted in ibid., p. 73.

Women's Clubs, but most belonged only to the Women's Clubs. One woman activist said bitterly that in one instance, the women were using a little local party money for their Women's Club and getting very good results when "the local woke up to the fact that the women were really handling some money, a part of their own dues, and spending it as they thought best! This would never do of course, since in this respect even a Socialist man still has a capitalist mind, and still thinks the purse strings belong to the male sex."[57]

Yet in some areas a little cooperation was given, with ads for meetings saying "Women Especially Invited." In these areas, such as Kansas and Illinois, it was estimated that the number of women in the party rose tenfold in 1908 and 1909.

Just as they did 60 years later, the socialist women debated whether to recruit primarily working-class or middle-class women. As it turned out, their best efforts could attract few women who worked in the factories because they were too tired and lacked the leisure to attend meetings. Socialist propaganda for suffrage, however, attracted and held thousands of professional women and middle-class housewives from 1908 to 1912. In that period many women worked in both movements, women accounted for 15 percent of the party, and several held leadership positions. By 1913–1914, however, the suffrage movement had become so large and respectable that it could ally itself with the far larger and more influential Progressive party, and even some elements of the Republican and Democratic parties.[58] The socialists then stopped getting many recruits from this source, though many socialist women continued to play a role in the suffrage movement.

THE SUFFRAGE MOVEMENT
NAWSA had two new leaders in this period. One was Carrie Chapman Catt[59] and the other was Anna Howard Shaw.[60] Catt was born in 1859 on a farm in Wisconsin. She graduated from Iowa State College and practiced teaching and school administration, then journal-

[57]Quoted in ibid., p. 77.

[58]A full-scale discussion of suffrage in relation to the party politics of 1913–1920 is in David Morgan, *Suffragists and Democrats* (Ann Arbor: Michigan State University Press, 1972).

[59]Catt gives her view of the movement, including each campaign in detail, in Carrie Catt and Nettie Shuler, *Woman Suffrage and Politics: The Inner Story of the Suffrage Movement* (New York: Scribner's, 1926).

[60]See her autobiography, Anna Howard Shaw, *The Story of a Pioneer* (New York: Harper & Row, 1915).

ism. She married a successful engineer, who supported her while she worked for suffrage. She was an outstanding organizer of new locals and instituted better procedures at headquarters for keeping track of membership and fund raising. After Susan Anthony retired in 1900, Catt became president of NAWSA.

Shaw was born in a western pioneer family. She studied divinity and became a minister. She then studied medicine, received her M.D. in 1886, and practiced medicine in the Boston slums. She was a great orator, first for the WCTU and then for NAWSA. She became president of NAWSA in 1904.

From about 1896 to 1910, NAWSA did little and accomplished almost nothing. It had no national headquarters, and its leaders communicated by mail. Its first significant accomplishment was a petition with 400,000 names collected in 1908–1910. Elizabeth Cady Stanton's daughter, Harriot Blatch, wrote: "The suffrage movement was completely in a rut . . . at the opening of the twentieth century. It bored its adherents and repelled its opponents. . . . Supporters in private drawing rooms and in public halls . . . listlessly heard the same old arguments."[61]

Blatch was exhilarated by the far more militant tactics she had witnessed in England; so in 1907 in New York she organized a new group, the Women's Political Union. The Union set out to be more dramatic and to make contact with business and professional women, whereas NAWSA still consisted mostly of "women of leisure." The Union also contacted and interested labor unions, and introduced working women to state legislators. The women told the truth about their awful working conditions, thereby shocking the legislators. It initiated the first open-air meetings for suffrage in 30 years. Finally, it launched a set of mass parades, which met with opposition by "respectable ladies" but soon became the most successful tactic of the suffrage movement.

A number of other new organizations were launched independently among college women, scientists, and union women. Even NAWSA started to revitalize itself, and by 1908 it had 2000 precinct captains in New York City to put pressure on Tammany Hall.

Then, in 1910, a referendum for women's suffrage was won in the state of Washington, mostly by sending speakers to local granges, labor unions, and churches.[62] In California a very important

---

[61]Quoted in Flexner, op. cit., p. 250.

[62]For a first-hand discussion of the struggles in Washington and Oregon, see Abigail Duniway, *Path Breaking, An Autobiographical History of the Equal Suffrage Movement in Pacific Coast States* (New York: Source Book Press, 1914, 1970 reprint).

suffrage referendum was won by a narrow margin through imaginative use of speakers and meetings, big billboard ads, plays, pageants, essay contests, and a touring limousine with speakers and a small theater group performing "How the Vote Was Won." The new, splashy, militant tactics were successful in California. There was powerful opposition from business and liquor interests, and thousands of votes were stolen, but enough were protected by militant women poll watchers to win.

In 1910, NAWSA received a gift of $1 million from a millionaire's wife to set up a national headquarters. Moreover, working women became more outspoken as a result of their own militant union struggles. One unionist, Rose Schneiderman, answered a New York State senator who claimed that women would lose their feminine qualities if they voted: "We have women in the foundries, stripped to the waist . . . because of the heat. Yet the Senator says nothing about these women losing their charm. . . . Women in the laundries . . . stand for 13 or 14 hours in the terrible steam and heat with their hands in hot starch. Surely these women won't lose any more of their beauty and charm by putting a ballot in a ballot box once a year. . . ."[63]

In 1912, suffragists, with the aid of radical farmers, won referenda in Arizona, Kansas, and Oregon. They also won in Michigan, but the election was stolen by means of false returns from some precincts. Even the governor accused the liquor interest of election fraud. In the same year, Teddy Roosevelt's Progressive party made women's suffrage part of its program. In 1913 the Progressive party, composed of radical farmers and city reformers, held the balance of power in Illinois, and forced the state legislature to approve women's suffrage.

The Progressive movement

The Progressive movement was not merely a political movement; it was a pervasive ideology for reform in the 1900–1920 period. With roots in the earlier Populist movement, it advocated reforms intended to restore America to an earlier, better age. In the cities, it represented small businessmen and artisans who wanted antitrust laws to end industrial concentration, break up the big corporations, and return to a mythical state of pure competition. In the country, it was supported by the small farmers who wanted laws to prevent takeovers by big corporate farmers, laws to break the power of rail-

63Quoted in Flexner, op. cit., p. 259.

roads, and laws to break the power of monopolies supplying machinery and fertilizer to the farmer and monopolies buying wholesale from the farmer. To achieve these laws, they also wanted more democratization, such as the popular election of senators and the initiative and referendum, all of which they thought would break the power of the bosses and of the big businessmen who controlled them and return power to the "people" (by which they meant the native-born middle class).

The suffragists promised the Progressives that the vote for women would double the number of reform-minded middle-class voters who could be counted on to vote against corruption and against monopoly. Teddy Roosevelt said in 1910 that "the prime duty of the average woman is to be a good wife and mother," but he agreed that good women might add the duty to vote for middle-class reform "to help the unfortunate."[64] The various women's and Progressive groups were closely linked. As early as 1908, the General Federation of Women's Clubs was a prime mover and lobbyist in the successful Progressive drive for the Pure Food and Drug Act. By 1914, the General Federation officially supported suffrage.

By 1914, 9 of the 11 states with women's suffrage also had strong Progressive movements and had adopted the initiative and referendum. In fact, many of the same people were in the leadership of the Progressives, NAWSA, the General Federation of Women's Clubs, the Women's Trade Union League, and the settlement house movement. Jane Addams, for example, was a founder of the first settlement house and a leader in all the other organizations.

Militant tactics, 1914–1920

In spite of Progressive and Socialist help and widespread middle-class support, the constitutional amendment for woman suffrage was still getting nowhere in 1914. Then Alice Paul came back from England, where she had been impressed by the militant tactics used there. Paul was made head of NAWSA's Congressional Committee, which had a yearly budget of $10 because NAWSA thought federal action was very unlikely and so gave it a low priority. She gathered new funds, plus a small group of militant women, including the historian Mary Beard. Paul was a charismatic speaker and leader, and she and her small group managed to organize a parade of 5000 women in Washington, D.C., the day before Woodrow Wilson's inauguration.

---

[64]Quoted in Sinclair, op. cit., p. 325. Sinclair gives quite a bit of information on this period.

The women . . . had to fight their way from the start and took more than one hour in making the first ten blocks. . . . It was where Sixth Street crosses the avenue that police protection gave way entirely and the two solid masses of spectators on either side came so close together that three women could not march abreast. It was here that the Maryland boys [supporters of the women, from Maryland Agricultural College] formed in single file on each side of the "Pilgrims" and became a protective wall. . . . The parade itself . . . was a great success . . . the marchers, for the most part, kept their tempers . . . few faltered.[65]

The public was so outraged by the attack on the women and the lack of police protection that the chief of police lost his job.

The committee also organized car caravans to Washington and presented 200,000 signatures for a federal amendment. But its tactics were too militant for NAWSA, so it was expelled. It changed its name to the Congressional Union, then merged with the Women's Political Union to form the Women's party, which still exists. In 1914 and 1916, the Women's party campaigned against *all* Democrats because, when in power, they had not endorsed women's suffrage.

In 1914, only Montana and Nevada, with strong Progressive and Socialist movements, voted for women's suffrage; suffrage lost in five other states. While NAWSA kept changing officers, but doing little more, the militant Women's party held meetings and parades, presented petitions, and lobbied—and finally got the Nineteenth Amendment to the floor of Congress. It was defeated in 1914 by 35 to 34 in the Senate and 207 to 174 in the House.

In 1915, NAWSA pushed referenda in New York, New Jersey, Pennsylvania, and Massachusetts, but after hard campaigns— opposed by the saloons in Philadelphia and by the Catholic Church in Massachusetts—it lost all four. Finally, in 1915, NAWSA tossed out Shaw and put in its best organizer, Catt. Catt, helped by a $2 million bequest from a rich sympathizer, organized in detail both a series of state campaigns and a federal campaign. Also in 1915, the first important antisuffrage organization was formed in the South; its slogan was "Home Rule, States Rights, and White Supremacy."[66]

In 1916, both major parties came out for women's suffrage, but didn't say how or when. Because of southern influence, the Democrats said the issue should be left to the states. Catt and NAWSA worked closely and politely with President Wilson, even

[65]A newspaper account, quoted by Flexner, op. cit., p. 264.
[66]Quoted in ibid., p. 275.

though he still equivocated in public, and Catt designed a secret "winning plan" outlining what each state organization was to do year by year, a plan that proved to be successful.

In 1917, the Women's party turned to all-out militant tactics, picketing Wilson and the White House for doing nothing to advance women's suffrage. In that year the first woman representative, Jeannette Rankin of Montana, took her seat in the House. Then came war. NAWSA supported the war and worked with the Wilson administration, advocating both patriotism and women's suffrage.

The Women's party, which included many Quaker pacifists, did not support the war or engage in any part of the war effort. Jeannette Rankin, the only woman in the House, voted against the declaration of war. The Women's party picketed the White House with signs saying "Democracy Should Begin at Home."[67] When they were attacked by hysterical mobs of hoodlums and soldiers, they, not the mobs, were illegally arrested for exercising their right of free speech: 218 women were arrested and 97 jailed. "When the women protested against the illegality of their arrests, the bad conditions, and the brutality of their treatment by going on hunger strikes, the authorities . . . resorted to forced feeding, and made martyrs wholesale."[68] NAWSA strongly attacked the pickets in several public statements in order to show its own patriotism and respectability.

In addition to the militants' protest, other events helped women's suffrage during the war. Because men were in the army, thousands of women were given jobs in occupations that had previously excluded them, and thousands more moved from the home into industry for the first time. Women, led by NAWSA, also sold Liberty bonds, raised food in gardens, and did nursing at home and in front-line hospitals in France. NAWSA emphasized women's patriotism and participated in a government committee to mobilize women, a committee that led, in 1920, to the formation of the Women's Bureau in the Department of Labor. Only the Women's party and some women socialists actively opposed the war, arguing that it was an imperialist war.

Because of women's war role, the White House pickets, and some usual suffrage activity by NAWSA, in 1917 women were granted the right to vote by state legislatures in North Dakota, Ohio,

[67]Quoted in ibid., p. 284.
[68]Ibid., p. 285.

Rhode Island, Nebraska, Michigan, and Arkansas—still mostly western states. A referendum was defeated in Maine, but in New York a suffrage referendum fared better. After a hard campaign, Tammany Hall was persuaded to remain neutral because it feared revenge by women voters if they did get the vote. Women's suffrage won by 100,000 votes in New York City, and this crucial state was finally won.[69]

In January 1918, Wilson spoke publicly for women's suffrage, and the amendment came to a vote in the House. Last-minute efforts were frantic, and the women brought several representatives from hospital beds. The amendment passed by exactly the two-thirds necessary for a constitutional amendment. The deep South still voted almost solidly against it, as did a few industrial states—Massachusetts, Pennsylvania, New Jersey, and Ohio.

In this period the militancy of women and the spread of suffrage sentiment was reflected in the explosive growth of NAWSA (see Table 10.1). The Women's party remained quite small, perhaps never comprising more than 40,000 to 50,000 members. NAWSA was happy to recruit anyone, including many who were not active participants. Since the women's party demanded and got concentrated participation from all its members, it probably accomplished as much as NAWSA.

[69]The story of the New York campaign is told in detail in Mildred Adams, *The Right to Be People* (Philadelphia: Lippincott, 1967).

TABLE 10.1
Membership of National American Woman Suffrage Association

Year	Number of members
1893	13,150
1905	17,000
1907	45,501
1910	75,000
1915	100,000
1917	2,000,000

Source: Aileen Kraditor, *The Ideas of the Woman Suffrage Movement, 1890–1920* (New York: Columbia University Press, 1965), p. 5. These are very rough estimates.

To get the amendment through the Senate took another year and a half, until late 1919, since its opponents went all-out to delay it. Suddenly, in mid-1918, these opponents thought they could defeat the amendment, so they called it to the floor. In an extraordinary gesture designed to get votes in the next election, Wilson spoke in its favor on the Senate floor. He argued patriotism: ". . . the early adoption of this measure is necessary to the successful prosecution of the war. . . ." He said that the country needed enthusiastic war workers and warriors willing to fight for "democracy" and that most ordinary people "think in their logical simplicity, that democracy means that women shall play their part in affairs alongside men and upon an equal footing with them."[70] The opposition argued "states' rights" and fear of black women voters. The vote was 62 in favor to 34 opposed, 2 short of the needed two-thirds. The 34 negative votes almost all came from conservative Republicans in New England and conservative southern Democrats. The southerners spoke against votes for black women; but one newspaper noted that they really represented the cotton industry, which employed thousands of women and children at miserable wages and opposed any strengthening of women's position.

Also in 1918, three more states, South Dakota, Michigan, and Oklahoma, gave women the vote by referenda, in spite of attempts to steal the election in Oklahoma by fraud. Six states (Iowa, Minnesota, Missouri, Ohio, Wisconsin, and Maine) gave women the vote by legislative action. Still, in February 1919 the Senate again defeated the amendment by one vote. In May and June 1919, both houses of Congress finally passed it, though the southerners still voted against it.

Opponents then used every dirty trick to defeat ratification by the states. NAWSA launched a campaign in every state for ratification. Finally it won in 35 states (none in the South), but needed one more that proved very hard to get. By August 1920, the only apparent possibility in the near future was the border state of Tennessee. If the amendment lost there, opponents might delay until postwar conservatism buried it for good. All the forces both for and against poured into Tennessee. The liquor interests handed out so much liquor that on the night before the vote "legislators . . . were reeling through the halls in a state of advanced intoxication."[71] The deep South sent hundreds of men and women to spread racist and sexist propaganda. Catt wrote: "Women, including Kate Gordon and Laura

[70]Quoted in Flexner, op. cit., p. 308.
[71]Quoted in ibid., p. 322.

Clay [former members of NAWSA's own board!], are here, appealing to Negrophobia and every other cave man's prejudice."[72]

On the other side, the mother of one legislator wrote to him: "Hurrah! And vote for suffrage. . . . I notice some of the speeches against [suffrage] . . . were very bitter. . . . Don't forget to be a good boy and help Mrs. Catt. . . ."[73] He changed his position and voted for the amendment, which passed by two votes. The opponents desperately tried to enjoin and overthrow Tennessee's vote in the courts, but they failed. And the Nineteenth Amendment became a part of the Constitution!

Who opposed women's suffrage?

Interests opposed to the amendment were: (1) liquor businesses; (2) big-city bosses; (3) the Catholic church; (4) southern whites; and (5) big business. The opposition organized antisuffrage organizations, led by wealthy women, as fronts for their own activity. Oppositionists spent huge amounts of money on all kinds of advertising and propaganda. They bought votes wholesale and paid bribes to steal elections. Besides sexist prejudice, they had economic and political interests to protect against possible votes by women.

The liquor industry, fearing women's votes for prohibition, spent millions against suffrage. One brewer wrote to another in 1914 that "a new anti-suffrage association . . . in Illinois . . . is a retail liquor dealer's affair."[74] But he said that the connection should be kept secret.

The big-city machines and bosses were afraid women voters would want reforms, such as the abolition of child labor, and—horrors—would want to "clean up" politics.

The Catholic church felt that women might get out of hand if they voted and might oppose its sexist teachings on "woman's place." In 1916, a cardinal sent a message of support to an antisuffrage convention; and in many state referenda religion-oriented antisuffrage leaflets were sent to Catholic voters.

Southern white politicians denied the vote to blacks in practice. They were afraid to extend suffrage again, or to have any discussion of suffrage, because then the Fourteenth Amendment might be enforced, giving blacks the vote. In 1919, Senator Smith of South Carolina still warned his fellow southerners that votes for women would cause a new "clamor for Negro rights" and argued that this

---

[72]Quoted in ibid.
[73]Quoted in ibid., p. 323.
[74]Quoted in ibid., p. 297.

could be avoided by adherence to states' rights rather than a federal amendment: "By thus adding the word 'sex' to the 15th Amendment you have just amended it to liberate them all [black women as well as white women], when it was perfectly competent for the legislatures of the several states to so frame their laws as to preserve our civilization without . . . involving women of the black race."[75]

Although southern opposition was rooted in social conservatism and fear of blacks, the issue of child labor was also heavily involved. In the years after 1890, textile manufacturing had become of major importance in the South, and this industry depended on cheap labor from women and children. Because the suffragists had become associated with child labor reform and because it was assumed that women generally would oppose child labor, cotton textile manufacturers in the South were bitterly opposed to women's suffrage. Some of the racist statements made in opposition to the amendment may even have been a cover for opposition on the basis of protecting the textile interests. In the October 1, 1918 Senate vote, one senator from Mississippi and one from Louisiana, both states with heavy black populations, voted for suffrage. The only southern states from which both senators voted against suffrage were North and South Carolina, Georgia, and Alabama—the four leading textile states.[76]

Big business was worried that any change might disturb its power, and so it opposed women's suffrage as it had opposed popular election of U.S. senators (the Seventeenth Amendment) and the "communistic" income tax established by the Sixteenth Amendment. In every referendum battle women reported huge antisuffrage expenditures by the railroads, oil industries, and manufacturers. There were large numbers of antisuffrage lobbyists financed by the same interests in every legislative battle. A congressional investigation found that Swift and Company, the meat packers, made secret antisuffrage contributions. An antisuffrage appeal in Nebraska in 1914 was signed by nine railroad executives, seven bankers, and two Episcopal ministers. Other antiwomen interests included the Texas Business Association, Santa Fe Railroad, American Express, Portland Cement, and the Union Pacific, Illinois Central, and Southern Pacific railroads. The "Man Suffrage Association" included wives of bankers, wives of railroad and corporate executives, and the son-in-law

[75]Quoted in ibid., p. 303.
[76]Morgan, op. cit., p. 175.

of J. P. Morgan. The head of NAWSA's Congressional Committee wrote that some senators, who had been put in office by big-business money, "were not really in favor of our form of government. They believed in an oligarchy of the well-to-do, and they were fearful that tariff schedules might be reduced or railroad regulation extended if women had a chance to vote."[77]

Why success in 1920?

In spite of the powerful opposition, women's suffrage was won in 1920. Why? One reason was the support of the Progressives. The Progressives, in turn, were strong at that time because of the last-ditch effort of small business and small farmers to avoid total elimination by big business and big farming interests. Suffrage came to be seen as a middle-class reform expected to expand that group's voting power. A second reason was the support of the Socialists and trade unions, which helped mobilize workers. Perhaps most important were the growing numbers of women in industry and the professions, women with knowledge and some political interest, who could no longer be ignored. Finally, World War I served as a catalyst in that it brought still more women into industry, government, and nursing—and made it useful for Wilson and others to argue for women's suffrage as part of the war for democracy.

[77]Quoted in Flexner, op. cit., p. 302.

FORTY YEARS IN THE DESERT: AMERICAN WOMEN, 1920-1960

11

Suffragist leaders entered the 1920s with bright hopes, but legal changes cannot alter attitudes overnight. For many years after the passage of the Nineteenth Amendment, women voted in smaller numbers than men. It has been estimated that in the 1920 election only 43 percent of the eligible women voted. As late as 1940, only 49 percent of women as compared to 68 percent of men voted.[1] Many women and men still believed that politics was a male preserve.

Throughout the period, the difference between the percentages of men and women voting has been greatest in groups where sex role differences are most marked. Among the poor and the poorly educated, in rural areas, and in the South, women have tended to vote in considerably smaller numbers than men.

A women's bloc vote, which the suffragists had hoped for and male politicians had feared, never really materialized. Women tended to vote very much like men. Party affiliation and class, not sex, influenced voting choice.

Few issues have clearly split the sexes. Women have tended to be more in favor of the welfare state—of government intervention and government ownership—and have tended to be more pacifist than men.[2] The latter tendency has worried male politicians and military men. In 1925, Rear Admiral Fiske said:

[1]Martin Gruberg, *Women in American Politics* (Oshkosh, Wis.: Academia Press, 1968), p. 9.
[2]Ibid., pp. 12–13.

No man respects and admires women more than I do, but some women have faults, and the fault most commonly found is a seemingly insatiable desire to interfere in matters they do not understand. War they understand least and from it they instinctively recoil. There is danger in this situation. Women now have the vote and they outnumber the men. There must be some action by the men which will bring women to realize that it is for their comfort and protection that all wars are fought. It is to the interest of women that they permit men to obtain the necessary armament. Only in this way can they be assured of the comfort and protection they need. In spite of themselves, we must protect the ladies![3]

THE WOMEN'S MOVEMENT, 1920–1940

Early data showed some evidence of political independence by women, enough to scare male politicians. In Chicago in 1915, men gave a plurality to the machine candidate for mayor, but women gave as big a vote to the reform candidate. In 1918, women organized a nonpartisan coalition that defeated the antisuffrage Senator John Weeks. In 1918 in Columbus, Ohio, 500 women volunteers registered 21,000 new voters, and a reformer won by 19,000 votes over an incumbent corrupt mayor. In 1921, the National Women's party threatened to run as a third party.[4]

The male politicians caved in before this danger. The Democratic and Republican parties included most demands of organized women in their 1920 platforms. Both parties put women on their national committees and gave them some patronage jobs. In 1920–1921, most state legislatures gave women the right to jury duty; some passed minimum wage and hour laws for women; two passed equal pay laws; and Wisconsin passed a general equal rights bill. Even some southern states passed reforms pushed by women lobbyists. Women lobbyists in Washington got Congress to pass (reluctantly, but under the goad of fear of defeat) the following: (1) in 1921, money for teaching mothers how better to care for babies; (2) in 1921, a bill for meat inspection; (3) a 1922 bill to equalize citizenship requirements for men and women; (4) a 1923 bill to extend the merit system in the civil service; and (5) the Child Labor Amendment to the Constitution in 1924. Even the American Medical Association, which should have

[3]Quoted in ibid., p. 13.
[4]William Chafe, *The American Woman* (New York: Oxford University Press, 1972), p. 26. The fullest description of the successes of the women's movement from 1920 to 1924 is in J. Stanley Lemons, *The Woman Citizen: Social Feminism in the 1920s* (Champaign: University of Illinois Press, 1973).

known, said that women's organizations were "one of the strongest lobbies that has ever been seen in Washington."[5]

The women's movement was divided over priorities after suffrage was attained, but seemed very much alive. The more militant National Women's party said suffrage had achieved little, that women were still "subordinate to men before the law, in the professions, in the church, in industry, and in the home."[6] The Women's party pledged to work for full equality, and succeeded in getting the Equal Rights Amendment introduced in Congress in 1923 (and every succeeding year until 1972, when it was passed). The Equal Rights Amendment states that "equality of rights under the law shall not be denied or abridged by the United States or by any state on account of sex." The Women's party was the only organization that consistently fought for women's rights from 1920 to 1960.

The Women's party, however, was limited to a relatively small group, having only 8000 members by 1923 (down from 50,000 in 1920). It focused on legal equality and—to a much lesser degree—eventual equality in the home. It never really challenged the Victorian image of women and was horrified by advocates of sexual freedom. It also had nothing to do with battles on behalf of blacks, the poor, or workers. Partly because of its narrowness but mainly because of the hostile sociopolitical climate, it slowly declined after the mid-1920s. Its leaders and members grew older and more isolated, and its influence decreased.

On the right wing of the women's movement was the League of Women Voters, which in 1919 evolved directly from the National American Woman Suffrage Association (NAWSA). Its white, middle-class membership declared that the fight for women's rights had been won with suffrage; in 1931 the league's president claimed that "nearly all discriminations have been removed."[7] The league did very little for women's rights and focused mainly on child labor laws, minimum wages and hour laws, pacifism, and many general reforms. It advocated gradualism and attacked all sudden "radical changes." Because it never fought for women's liberation, used conservative tactics, and was generally dull, and because of the hostile political climate, it never gained the allegiance of most American women. Whereas NAWSA had about 2 million members in 1920, the League of Women Voters was down to about 100,000 by 1923.

[5]*Journal of the American Medical Association,* quoted in Chafe, op. cit., p. 28.
[6]Quoted in ibid., p. 114.
[7]Quoted in ibid., p. 115.

The league violently attacked the Women's party over the Equal Rights Amendment (ERA). League members argued that the ERA would be used to overturn all the protective labor laws for women (minimum safety, wages, and hours) for which the League had worked. The Supreme Court had voided all protective laws for male workers on the basis that freedom of contract was guaranteed to corporations as "persons" entitled to the due process and privileges given in the Fourteenth Amendment. But in 1908 the Supreme Court had allowed protective laws for women on the basis that women are delicate creatures needing protection. The league favored that decision, philosophy and all. In 1922, the league said, "investigations have shown a lower resistance on the part of women to the strain and the hazards incident to industry."[8] The Women's party favored the Equal Rights Amendment and equal protective laws for men and women. But its position was difficult until 1938, when the New Deal passed and, in 1941, forced a reluctant Supreme Court to accept several protective labor laws for both men and women.

Reaction, mid-1920s

In the mid-1920s, conservative reaction resulted in an attack on all progressive legislation and helped wipe out the women's liberation movement. Congress cut down funds for the Women's Bureau and the Children's Bureau, and refused to pass more reforms. Besides the conservative swing throughout the nation, politicians noted that women cast only about 35 percent of the vote in 1923 and 1924, and voted about the same as men on most issues.[9] Many women did not vote because they still felt that voting was for men. Only slowly did this attitude change, and the percentage of women voting crept up very slowly. It now equals the percentage of men voting.

The Child Labor Amendment (to prevent children from being forced to work) was defeated in the states in the mid-1920s by conservatives, big business, and the church. The National Association of Manufacturers, aided by the agribusiness-oriented National Farm Bureau, led the fight against it. Amid the red-baiting hysteria of the period, it was charged that the amendment was a Bolshevik plot paid for by Moscow. The Catholic church's official magazine said: "There never was a more radical or revolutionary measure proposed for the

[8]Quoted in William O'Neill, *Everyone Was Brave* (New York: Quadrangle, 1969), p. 278.
[9]Chafe, op. cit., p. 31.

consideration of the American people than this so-called Child Labor Amendment, that . . . would set aside the fundamental principles of states' rights, . . . would destroy parental control over children, and would commit this country forever to the communistic system of the nationalization of her children."[10]

In addition, there was a general red-baiting smear against all women's groups. In 1924, an employee of the Office of Chemical Warfare of the War Department, run by ex-Senator Weeks (who had been defeated by women's votes and wanted revenge), produced a chart showing that all liberal women's groups were part of a "spider web" directed from Moscow![11] In 1927, a conservative veterans' leader, head of the Military Order, said in a speech to the DAR that the WCTU, the YWCA, and the American Association of University Women were all part of the "radical, pink, or intelligentsia group."[12]

The conservative swing reflected the economic upswing in the 1920s, the continuing decline in the number of small farmers (who had supported radical Populists and Progressives), and the fact that a large, native-born industrial labor movement was still nascent and weak. The women's confused response to the all-out attack on them was also conditioned by the narrow, legalistic ideology of the suffragists that propagandized suffrage as the single goal—neglecting basic social and economic equality. As a result, the women's liberation movement disappeared almost completely after 1923 and, for other reasons as well, remained dormant for 40 years (from about 1923 to 1963).

Only the tiny and narrowly legalist Women's party continued the struggle for equal rights—and its members grew fewer and older year by year. The League of Women Voters swiftly declined to one-tenth or less the size of its parent, NAWSA. It became very conservative on women's issues, devoting almost all its time to general reform issues. The Women's Trade Union League stopped organizing, did purely educational work, and died away in the late 1920s. Similarly, the liberal National Consumers' League became more conservative, electing as president a man who was head of the Cleveland Chamber of Commerce, and likewise swiftly died. The Women's Bureau in the Department of Labor was always very conservative, favoring only some protective labor laws while opposing the Equal Rights Amendment. The bureau continued to argue that woman's place was not

[10]Quoted in O'Neill, op. cit., p. 235.
[11]See ibid., p. 229; also Chafe, op. cit., p. 262.
[12]Quoted in O'Neill, op. cit., p. 229.

at work but in the home. In 1923, the head of the bureau said that equality between the sexes was an impossible myth.[13]

Only a few specialized, middle-class women's organizations survived. Many women did work in pacifist organizations of a reformist, nonrevolutionary nature. In 1919, the National Federation of Business and Professional Women's Clubs was formed. A very narrow and "respectable" organization, it did support the Equal Rights Amendment. In 1921, college women formed the American Association of University Women. The General Federation of Women's Clubs continued, but became mainly social and apolitical. In 1919 its president attacked revolutionaries "of many grades, from certain intellectuals to 'down and outers.' "[14] In 1927, the federation's president advocated a superpatriotic line and told her members to look out for communists in schools and churches, "for I have information from the most authoritative sources that it is among our young people . . . that the communists are working."[15]

The Equal Rights Amendment fight

In 1926, at a meeting sponsored by the Women's Bureau (which was against the amendment), there was a violent fight, with only the Women's party supporting the ERA. The Women's party won time for a debate on the ERA only by disrupting one of the meeting's other sessions. Using militant liberation tactics, its floor leader said: "Get up and yell—you've got good lungs."

Senate hearings on the ERA in 1931 revealed the different ideologies involved. The Women's party argued that the ERA was necessary because of discrimination against women in wages, employment, education, and numerous laws. It listed at least 1000 discriminatory state laws, including laws in 11 states giving control over a wife's wages to her husband, laws in 16 states forbidding a wife to make a contract, laws in 20 states barring women from jury service, and a law in Minnesota allowing a husband—but not a wife—to collect damages from a lover for adultery!

The ERA was opposed by women connected with the AFL, the Women's Bureau, and the League of Women Voters. They all argued that the ERA might destroy the protective labor laws for women (against long hours, heavy weight lifting, etc.). The League argued that it was getting rid of discriminatory laws state by state, slowly

[13]See Chafe, op. cit., p. 124.
[14]Quoted in O'Neill, op. cit., p. 257.
[15]Quoted in ibid., pp. 261–262.

and gradually; "that it is undesirable to interfere with the State-right principle . . ." ; and that the League is for protective laws, which are needed for "true" equality, in view of the "actual biological . . . differences between men and women."[16]

The Women's party answered that discriminatory laws had oppressed women for centuries. Getting rid of them on a state-by-state basis would take decades, and it was not willing to wait. Furthermore, it argued in favor of certain protective legislation for both men and women workers. They pointed out that many so-called protective laws actually discriminate against women—for example, laws limiting women to 8 hours' work a day in banks or insurance companies—and that many of these were being pushed by male union leaders to force women out of such work.

After the Fair Labor Standards Act was passed in 1938 and was approved by the courts in 1941, protective laws for both men and women became feasible. That basis for opposing the ERA became less tenable. The Women's party got a favorable committee report on the ERA to the Senate floor in 1939, and got the Republican party to endorse it in 1940.

Women as party workers

Some of the suffragists had hoped that once women obtained the vote they would shun the major parties that had treated them so shabbily and act as an independent force or even form their own party. No independent mass women's movement emerged, but many women entered mainstream party politics.

A number of women had been active in the Progressive party before passage of the Nineteenth Amendment. In 1912, Jane Addams seconded Theodore Roosevelt's nomination and campaigned across the country for him. Both major political parties set up women's divisions—the Democrats in 1916, the Republicans two years later. Eager to capture the women's vote, both parties instituted the 50–50 rule on their national committees. Under the rule each state is represented by one man and one woman. "Fifty-fifty looks better on paper than it has worked out in practice," Eleanor Roosevelt said. "Too often the vice chairmen and the committeewomen are selected by the men, who naturally pick women who will go along with them and not give any trouble. Thus they are apt to be mere stooges. . . . Too often the selection of a national committee

---

[16]Quoted in Aileen Kraditor, ed., *Up from the Pedestal* (New York: Quadrangle, 1968), pp. 300–301.

woman is based on her bank account, social prestige or party service rendered by a deceased husband."[17]

Too often, then, women in party leadership positions were mere tokens. A few women did manage to become powerful in their own right, but the barriers to such achievement were very great.

While women were seldom welcomed into the inner councils of the major parties, they were increasingly making up the rank-and-file work force. Civil service reform radically decreased the number of patronage jobs available, with the result that men willing to do the unexciting everyday party work became hard to attract. Middle-class women with some leisure became the mainstays of the parties, doing everything from envelope stuffing to canvassing.

Work within the party was seldom rewarded with nomination to elective office. According to India Edwards, who was for many years vice-chairman of the Democratic National Committee, "if the Party backs a woman you can be pretty sure they do it because they think it is a lost cause but they know they have to have *some* candidate."[18]

The first woman to serve in the U.S. Congress was elected in 1916, four years before the passage of the Nineteenth Amendment. She was Jeannette Rankin of Montana, a state that had granted women suffrage in 1914. A leader in the suffrage campaign, she kept the statewide organization she had built for that purpose intact and won the primary and general election handily.

During her tenure she worked for the suffrage amendment in the House of Representatives. She served as ranking minority member on the Woman Suffrage Committee, which she had been instrumental in forming. She led the floor debate on the amendment, which passed the House by the two-thirds vote needed. The measure was, however, killed by the Senate.

Ms. Rankin is best remembered for her vote against the declaration of war. Defeated in 1918 in a try for the Senate, she became a lobbyist for the National Consumers' League and for the Women's International League for Peace and Freedom.

Running for Congress again in 1940, she won on a "keep our men out of Europe" platform. She cast the only dissenting vote against the declaration of war. Realizing that she had little chance of reelection, she retired from elective office but remained active.

17Quoted in Gruberg, op. cit., p. 62.
18Quoted in Kirsten Amundsen, *The Silenced Majority* (Englewood Cliffs, N.J.: Prentice-Hall, 1971), p. 83.

A strong critic of the Vietnam War, in 1968 she led a women's protest parade to the U.S. Capitol. The antiwar women fittingly called themselves the Jeannette Rankin Brigade.[19]

WOMEN IN POLITICS, 1920–1940

No great flood of women entered the U.S. House of Representatives during the 1920s and 1930s. Between 1920 and 1924, three women each served one term in the House; none was reelected. The three elected in 1924 were to be the first professional congresswomen. Florence Kahn of California succeeded her husband but managed to make a reputation on her own. She served 12 years in the House and was the first woman appointed to the powerful Appropriations Committee. After a long political career on the state level, Mary Norton was elected to Congress from New Jersey. She served for 26 years and rose to chair the Labor Committee. Edith Nourse Rogers, also a congressman's widow, served in the House for 35 years. She became chairwoman of the Veterans' Affairs Committee in 1947, and much veterans' legislation bears her name.

Most of the women elected during the remainder of the 1920s and during the 1930s had much less distinguished careers. Seven of the 16 were widows of congressmen; 10 served one term or less.

The first woman senator was appointed in 1922 and served for only 2 days, at which time her term ended.[20] The second managed to last considerably longer. Hattie Caraway of Arkansas was appointed in 1931 to fill her late husband's seat. She was elected to the Senate on her own and won reelection in 1938. In 1944, she was defeated by J. William Fulbright. As the first woman elected to the U.S. Senate, she broke an important barrier, but she accomplished little else.

During this period only two women were elected governor, and neither won the office in her own right. Nellie Taylor Ross succeeded her husband as governor of Wyoming when he died in 1925. Lacking political experience and being in mourning, she left campaigning and probably governing to her campaign manager. Miriam ("Ma") Ferguson succeeded her husband as governor of Texas. He had been impeached and therefore could not run. Their campaign slogan, "Two governors for the price of one," indicated that the Fergusons were simply trying to circumvent the Texas constitution. She served from 1924 to 1926 and again from 1932 to 1936.

---

[19]Hope Chamberlin, *A Minority of Members, Women in the U.S. Congress* (New York: Praeger, 1973), pp. 5–18.

[20]Gruberg, op. cit., p. 123.

Women were a little more successful in attaining lower state offices. In a few states, some relatively powerless offices have become women's preserves. In Kentucky, New Mexico, and South Dakota, for example, women were elected secretary of state during the 1920s, and that position has been held almost exclusively by women ever since.

In the 1930s, the Great Depression politically awakened and radicalized millions of women. But because their central concern was full employment, not women's rights, they joined existing movements from the New Deal Democrats and the CIO to the Socialist and Communist parties. Eleanor Roosevelt played a major political role in behalf of liberal causes as did Ms. Roosevelt's close friend, Mary Dewson. Dewson thought women were different from men, purer and concerned mostly with the "security of the home"; on this basis, she felt, they would naturally support many New Deal reforms, such as social security. She directed all women's work for the Democratic party in the 1930s. By 1936, she had over 60,000 women out explaining and advocating Roosevelt's policies, door to door.

As a result of women's work for the Democrats, the party convention of 1936 had women (as alternates) equal in number to men on the Platform Committee. The committee passed seven of the eight planks advocated by Dewson. Moreover, these successful activists were paid with patronage jobs: Women got 26 percent of all postmasterships by 1938, Frances Perkins became the first woman cabinet member, Ruth Rhode and Florence Harriman were made ambassadors, and Florence Allen became a judge on the U.S. Circuit Court of Appeals.

It should be noted that the Democrats were not greatly enlightened on women's rights. In 1928, Al Smith ridiculed the notion, saying, "I believe in equality, but I cannot nurse a baby."[21] This strange "logic" forced the Women's party to support Hoover. Even under Roosevelt, the National Recovery Administration codes specifically allowed lower wages for women.

WOMEN AT WORK, 1920-1940

In the very early 1920s, it was fashionable for young middle-class women to go to work, and many looked for liberation by way of a career. "Even the girls who knew that they were going to be married pretended to be considering important business positions."[22]

---

[21]Quoted in O'Neill, op. cit., p. 292.
[22]Sinclair Lewis, *Main Street* (1920), quoted in Chafe, op. cit., p. 49.

The euphoria and the emphasis on women's emancipation in the mass media was, however, very, very brief.

World War I lasted such a short time that only a few new women workers actually entered the economy. As early as 1919, with the number of jobs declining, the usual attempt was made to push women out. In that year, the New York Central Federated Union stated: "The same patriotism which induced women to enter industry during the war should induce them to vacate their positions after the war."[23] Women were forced to give up jobs as streetcar conductors by the unions; 20 women were forced to resign as judges by New York City; and the U.S. government still excluded women from 60 percent of all civil service jobs. The warm myth about women's economic emancipation in the 1920s is deflated by the cold facts (see Table 11.1).

There is a long-run increase in the number of working women as a percentage of all workers and as a percentage of all women. The first major jump in women's labor force participation occurred in 1900–1910 (a 3-percentage-point jump). Why? Because women were becoming emancipated and wanted to work to be liberated or to have fun? Unfortunately not. Women increasingly *had* to work. The urban population rose rapidly (doubling between 1890 and 1920), and 40 percent of big-city populations were foreign-born by 1900. On top of that, another tremendous wave of immigrants (19 million from 1900 to 1930) filled the new factories. Because the men were paid terrible wages, women (and children) had to work if the family was to survive.

From 1910 to 1920, there was actually a decline in women's

[23]Quoted in Chafe, op. cit., p. 53.

TABLE 11.1
Women at Work, 1890–1940

Year	Working women as percentage of all workers	Working women as percentage of all women
1890	17%	18%
1900	18	20
1910	21	25
1920	20	23
1930	22	24
1940	25	29

Source: U.S. Department of Labor, Women's Bureau, *1969 Handbook on Women Workers* (1969), p. 10.

role in the labor force (in spite of the war). Moreover, in the next period, from 1920 to 1930, women's participation rose only slightly. The greatest wave of immigration was over by 1910, and the increase in native-born women working was much less than it was in native-born men. So the "normal" pattern of men dominant in the economy and women relegated to the kitchen continued, with only slight improvement, to 1930.

The next jump in the percentage of women workers came in the 1930s (another 3-percentage-point increase). Perhaps this was due to greater liberation? Unfortunately, no. During the Depression, more than half of all U.S. families had incomes of less than $1200 a year. Wives went to work so their families wouldn't starve. They did not go into glamorous occupations; 36 percent of working wives were in domestic and personal services, and 20 percent were in apparel and canning factories—with the highest percentages working in the deep South, which was least liberated but most depressed.[24]

All during the 1930s, employers, unions, and government made the sexist plea that women should go back to the great reserve army of unemployed to solve men's employment problem. By the end of the 1930s, women's unemployment rate was twice that of men, and it has remained higher ever since. Mrs. Samuel Gompers said that it was "unnatural" for women to work and that working women took jobs from men who really needed them. "A home, no matter how small, is large enough to occupy [a wife's] mind and time."[25] Even the Women's Bureau declared: "The welfare of the home and family is a woman-sized job in itself," and that wives who worked were destroying their families—this despite the fact that the same bureau found that 90 percent of all women who worked in the 1930s absolutely had to do so for economic reasons.[26]

The jobs performed by women were changing in type but not in status. In 1900, most women workers were domestic servants, farm laborers, unskilled factory workers, and teachers. By the 1920s, women had entered white-collar work; in 1930, some 30 percent of all women held clerical and sales jobs. In factory work, 40 percent of the women were in the textile mills. Ever since, most women have remained segregated mainly in the categories of clerical work, retail sales, domestic service, elementary school teaching, nursing, and other services, such as waitressing.

[24]See ibid., p. 57.
[25]Quoted in ibid., p. 64.
[26]See ibid., pp. 63–64.

WOMEN AND UNIONS

We saw that there was a long and heroic strike by women garment workers in 1909. By 1920, the International Ladies Garment Workers Union had 65,000 members and the Amalgamated Clothing Workers had 66,000. Both unions had a female majority in membership but an all-male leadership. Outside of the garment trades, women were mostly unorganized. One out of every 9 male workers was organized compared to only 1 out of every 34 women workers. This was a major reason for the lower wages of women.

Why were so few women organized? First, for the most part the AFL organized skilled craft workers, while women were primarily unskilled factory workers. Second, many women and most unions assumed that women were transient, not permanent, workers. Third and most important, sexist attitudes prevented unions from organizing women workers, even when the women themselves were enthusiastic. The AFL unions and leaders were openly hostile. Women printers, candy workers, hairdressers, and streetcar workers were all turned down for union membership on the grounds that women weren't serious, wouldn't stick together, wouldn't fit. Samuel Gompers said that the AFL wasn't prejudiced, it just wouldn't accept "any nonassimilable race." When, in the late 1930s, the CIO (Congress of Industrial Organizations) organized unskilled workers and welcomed women, thousands of women joined and were among the CIO's steadiest and most militant supporters.

THE SEXUAL REVOLUTION OF THE 1920s

Where did most historians get the false idea that women were emancipated in the 1920s? Partly because they focused on suffrage, but mostly because they were struck by the revolution in life-styles. Women's skirts got shorter (these were the "flappers"). Women bobbed their hair and smoked and drank in public. Men and women danced wildly to jazz bands.

Sex did indeed become freer. The results of a study of white middle-class women are shown in Table 11.2. Many other studies have confirmed the same trend. The greatest increase in premarital intercourse occurred in the 1920s, with comparatively little change since then.

But greater sexual freedom for women did not mean freedom to get an equal higher education, or to choose a career, or to be paid equal wages, or to be equal in the family. Girls stressed their individual "freedom" (of sex), but showed no interest in women's rights or equal social position with men. The "revolution" in sexual mores

TABLE 11.2
Sexual Activity of Women

Year of birth	Percentage virgins at marriage
Before 1890	87%
1890–1899	74
1900–1909	51
Since 1910	32

Source: William O'Neill, *Everyone Was Brave* (New York: Quadrangle, 1969), p. 298.

was real, but superficial. The same books and magazines that celebrated the "flapper's freedom" attacked working women. In 1922, a popular novel, *This Freedom,* said that career women were traitors and claimed that "the peace of the home . . . rests ultimately on the kitchen."[27]

Although in the early 1920s some articles defended the right of women to work, the conservative reaction of the late 1920s produced many articles such as the one that said "the office woman, no matter how successful, is a transplanted posey."[28] Others played up the joys of homemaking and said the important thing for women was "no longer smartness, but charm." As we have seen, the scarcity of jobs during the Great Depression greatly intensified the "back to the home" clamor.

EDUCATION

Although large numbers of women were going to college, a change occurred in the women's colleges in the mid-1920s and after. The high-quality comprehensive training of the early years was replaced by an emphasis on preparation for "woman's place" in the home. In 1924, Vassar started offering courses called "Husband and Wife," "Motherhood," and "The Family as an Economic Unit." Even coed colleges, such as Cornell and the University of Chicago, started undergraduate and graduate programs in home economics for women.

The long-run trends are shown in Table 11.3. In the portion of B.A. degrees going to women, there is an incredible jump of 11 percentage points from 1910 to 1920. This reflects to some extent the height of the suffrage movement and its liberating effect on women's thinking. In part, it also reflects the greater willingness of

[27]Quoted in ibid., p. 99.
[28]From *McCall's,* quoted in Chafe, op. cit., p. 105.

TABLE 11.3
Women's Education, 1890–1940

Year	Percentage of all degrees awarded to women B.A.	M.A.	Ph.D.
1890	17%	19%	1%
1900	19	19	6
1910	23	26	10
1920	34	30	15
1930	40	40	15
1940	41	38	13

Source: U.S. Department of Labor, Women's Bureau, *1969 Handbook on Women Workers* (1969).

universities to take women when men were drafted for the war. Then, in the 1920s, there is a further jump, but of only 6 percentage points, perhaps reflecting the continuing liberation of middle-class women. In the 1930s, there is a gain of only 1 percentage point, reflecting the very negative impact of the Depression on women's position.

The trend in the women's portion of M.A. degrees is similar, except that the greatest jump is a 10-percentage-point leap in the 1920s. Since one needs a B.A. degree to get an M.A., this is partly a normal lagged response to the earlier jump in B.A.'s, and partly reflects the continued increase in freedom in the 1920s. But in the portion of M.A. degrees awarded to women, the negative impact of the Depression shows up in a 2 percent decrease.

Finally, it was clearly much, much more difficult for women to break into the highest educational sphere, the Ph.D., which is the gateway to many of the higher professions. Only in 1900 did women finally win a significant portion (a mere 6 percent) of these degrees. And there are only two further increases in the portion of Ph.D.'s going to women—a 4-percentage-point increase in the 1900s and another 5 percentage points in the 1910s. In the supposedly liberating 1920s, there was no increase. And among the losses of the Great Depression was a 2-percentage-point decrease in the still-small portion of Ph.D.'s awarded to women.

PROFESSIONAL WOMEN

The portion of women workers who were "professionals" increased from 12 percent in 1920 to 14 percent in 1930. But 75 percent of these were in the "women's professions" of nursing or teaching, with low status and very low pay. Women remained only 3 percent of architects and lawyers, and the absolute number of women doctors actually declined.[29] From 1925 to 1945, there was a 5 percent quota on women in almost all medical schools—and only 40 out of 482 general hospitals accepted women interns.

Finally, a 1929 survey of women in university teaching found most women faculty discontented but resigned to the fact that "no matter how much a woman studied or taught, she was likely to remain an instructor, burdened with the greatest teaching load and recompensed with the smallest salary."[30] As an example of discrimination at that time, a woman dean was fired from a midwestern college because she got married; the college president told her this was not discrimination because "marriage itself is for a woman an adequate career."[31]

Things got much, much worse for professional women during the 1930s. As we saw, the portions of M.A.'s and Ph.D.'s going to women actually dropped. Even in lower-level professions, such as elementary and high school teaching, men in search of jobs entered and displaced women. In addition, these new men teachers received higher pay. In 1939, male teachers were paid a median salary of $1,953 a year, while women teachers were paid only $1,394.[32] Finally, the percentage of working women who were "professionals" (including teachers and nurses) fell during the Depression from 14 percent back to 12 percent.

WAR, 1940–1945

It is one of the great historical ironies that only war could lift the U.S. economy and all its oppressed sectors from the depths of the Great Depression. Because of the all-out demand for war production, workers achieved full employment and rapid unionization; blacks came out of the South to industrial jobs and began the long march toward equal civil rights; and women moved in vast numbers into the economy, broke the sexist image, and started their own long march toward liberation. The changes are astonishing: (1) a 50 percent rise in women at work, (2) a large rise in wages, (3) twice as many wives at work, (4) four times as many women in unions, and (5) a vast change in the public's attitude toward women.

Even the aggregate data are exciting (see Table 11.4). During the war the portion of women at work jumped 9 percentage points, while their portion of the labor force jumped 11 percentage points.

[29]See ibid., p. 58.
[30]Quoted in ibid., p. 91.
[31]Quoted in ibid., p. 101.
[32]Ibid., p. 61.

TABLE 11.4
Women at Work, 1940–1950

Year	Women workers as percentage of all workers	Women workers as percentage of all women
1940	25%	29%
1945	36	38
1947	28	32
1950	29	34

Source: U.S. Department of Labor, Women's Bureau, *1969 Handbook on Women Workers* (1969), p. 10; and U.S. Department of Labor, *Manpower Report of the President* (1973), p. 129.

There was a tremendous slip backward immediately after the war, during reconversion and the return of veterans. Then the numbers of women in the economy resumed their upward march; both in absolute numbers and percentages there were many more women working in 1950 than in 1940 (though considerably fewer than at the war's peak).

The great increase in women workers did not come without resistance. Of 1,750,000 workers trained for war industries by December 1941, only 1 percent were women. War industry employers claimed women had the ability to fill only 29 percent of the jobs available. Six months later, with millions of men going into the army and a drastic labor shortage, the tune changed. Already, 13 percent of the trainees were women, employers declared that women were able to fill 55 percent of open jobs, and the government said they could do 80 percent of the jobs.[33]

And women did. They shattered the sexist image by becoming—with little training—railroad switchmen, precision toolmakers, crane operators, lumberjacks, acetylene torch operators, and so on *ad infinitum.* Even the giant corporations hired women as chemists and engineers; Wall Street hired women stock analysts; and the U.S. government hired women lawyers and doctors.

Moreover, the war industries, which at first declared it impossible, suddenly were able to provide women with decent rest rooms and toilets. Since these corporations were making astonishing profits from the war and needed workers badly, they were also suddenly able to put in better lighting, chairs, cafeterias, and 40 percent higher wages than the consumer industries.

[33]Joan Trey, "Women in the War Economy—World War II," *Review of Radical Political Economics* 4 (July 1972), 44.

Furthermore, the unions, which had neglected women, suddenly needed their power. The number of women unionists jumped from 800,000 in 1939 to over 3 million in 1945. Women were concentrated in the CIO unions in the electrical, auto, and steel industries.

Particularly crucial to the changing image of women was the fact that, since it was now encouraged, wives went to work. In 1940, most women workers were young and single. By 1945, over half were married, and their average age was over 35.

Most astounding of all was the change in propaganda. In the 1930s, women were told to stay in the home, that going to work was unnatural. Overnight, with the heavy demand for labor, all of the media, advertising, and government posters declared that it was both natural and patriotic for women to work. Some radio stations had a "Working Women Win Wars Week."[34] Rosie the Riveter, the woman with an acetylene torch, became a national heroine—and *Life* magazine showed women pilots on its cover. The War Department issued a pamphlet telling industry in its title: "You're Going to Employ Women." Moreover, it was emphasized everywhere that Hitler's Germany tried to keep women in the home for nothing but sexual reproduction, that fascism tried to push these sexist attitudes on the world, and that American women must fight fascism and sexism by working in the war economy.

And lo and behold! Public attitudes changed—both because of the change in the media and because of the obvious change in reality. In 1935, when over one in four workers was unemployed, a poll showed that 80 percent of Americans thought it was wrong for women to work, particularly if they were married. By 1942, 71 percent thought that more married women could and should be employed.[35]

Yet even during the war there was resistance to women working on the part of some reactionaries. Clare Booth Luce could still tell women to go back to the home to care for their children. The Children's Bureau called working mothers "a hazard to the security of the child in his family."[36] The army refused to commission women doctors until 1943, when Congress commanded it to do so. Private industry kept women as segregated as possible. Industry also gave women the dullest jobs because, as one capitalist put it, they can

[34]See Chafe, op. cit., p. 146.
[35]Ibid., p. 148.
[36]Quoted in ibid., p. 150.

"do the monotonous, repetitive work . . . that drives a man nuts."[37]
In government, the Women's Advisory Commission on War Manpower was kept as an ornament, given no power, and hardly ever consulted, even on decisions about working women.

The government did urge equal wages for women—and some progress was made—but firms could pay women less if they were in a job that was "historically" a woman's, or if they were in a different plant, or if their job was called something different (e.g., General Motors called male jobs "heavy" and women's "light," even though they were exactly the same). The loopholes were thus as big as the rules. Consequently, women were paid much lower wages (about 65 percent of men's), and this was sanctioned in some union contracts by reference to the legal loopholes. Unions and management mostly agreed that women should get seniority on a different list or only "for the duration."

Even worse was the child-care situation. With millions of mothers working, it would seem obvious that child-care facilities were urgently needed. But many sexists, like Clare Booth Luce and her husband, believed this would destroy children and the sanctity of the home. As if leaving children unattended wouldn't destroy them— when mothers *had* to work and the war effort needed them. Only when industry found itself inconvenienced because women workers were exhausted or absent trying to care for children and do their jobs as well did the government take some action—much too little and too late. Under pressure from industry and many women's organizations, Roosevelt allotted some emergency funds for child care. Congress then allowed a very small portion of the funds from the Lanham Act for wartime facilities to be used for child care. Congressman Lanham from Georgia, who didn't want any of "his" funds going to communistic child care, did his best to obstruct. Eventually, only about one-tenth of all children of working mothers received some kind of government-financed child care.

THE END OF THE WAR, 1945–1949

What would happen when the war ended? The Women's Advisory Committee demanded retention of women workers, and in 1944 Senator Harry Truman said, "they are entitled to the chance to earn a good living at jobs they have shown they can do."[38] Many, however, feared that there would not be enough jobs to go around. Power-

[37]Quoted in ibid., p. 152.
[38]Quoted in ibid., p. 176.

ful forces pushed for the "natural" solution of sending women back to the reserve army of unemployed, to wait in the kitchen until they were needed again. By 1945, the head of the National Association of Manufacturers stated the grim message very politely: "From a humanitarian point of view, too many women should not stay in the labor force. The home is the basic American institution."[39] A soldier wrote the Women's Bureau: "Wishing you success in your work, and hoping for the day when women relax and stay in her beloved kitchen."[40] More bluntly, a southern senator, Charles Andrews of Florida, told Congress it should force wives and mothers back to the kitchen "to give jobs to veterans."

Naturally, after the war, industry followed the sexist urgings. Veterans were given priority and, in the layoffs accompanying reconversion, women were fired at a rate 75 percent higher than men. From 1945 to 1947, the number of women at work declined by 4 million! The percentage of women at work declined from 38 percent back to 32 percent, and the percentage of women in the total labor force declined from 36 percent to 28 percent—almost, but not quite, back to prewar levels. All this occurred in spite of the fact that two-thirds of all women workers said they wanted to keep their jobs.[41]

Fortunately for women, the long expansion of the U.S. economy in the postwar period began very soon. By 1950, the number of women working started creeping up again—and this long-run tendency has continued ever since. In 1950, almost half of all women workers were married, and the median age of all women at work had risen to 36.5—quite a difference from the typically young and single woman worker of the prewar period.

Of course the fact that the economy needed and got more women workers did not mean it needed high or equal wages for women. Discrimination continued. Women's median wage continued to be about 35 percent lower than men's. Women continued to be denied admission to many professional schools, and the percentage of women in well-paying business and professional positions continued to decline.

A few women tried to outlaw such discrimination by political action. Representative Helen Gahagan Douglas fought for an equal pay act in Congress in 1945; the act was defeated then, and was introduced and defeated every year thereafter until it was passed in 1963. Opponents included the Chamber of Commerce, which said

[39]Quoted in Trey, op. cit., p. 51.
[40]Quoted in ibid.
[41]Ibid., p. 47.

capitalists would correct unequal pay voluntarily, and the AFL, whose President Meany said it should be left to collective bargaining.

A second issue pushed anew was the Equal Rights Amendment. Recognizing the "magnificent wartime performance" of women, Harry Truman, Henry Wallace, and both major parties supported it. The Women's Bureau, fearing the amendment might nullify protective legislation, still opposed it. In 1946, the Senate voted approval by 38 to 35, but this was below the two-thirds needed. The Senate passed it in 1950 and 1953, but with the rider that sex-specific protective legislation was not affected, which made it meaningless. The ERA never came to a vote in the House.

The third issue of concern to women was continuation of federal help for child-care centers. Congress finally extended funding for 6 months, then refused to do any more. In New York, permanent state funds were refused, but the state agreed to temporary funds for children whose mothers could prove poverty. The state youth commissioner even said it would be better for mothers to go on relief so they could stay home! In 1947, the New York *World Telegram* declared that the child-care campaign was masterminded by communists in "social work cells."[42] All New York State child care ended in 1948.

William Chafe says the late 1940s presented "a strange paradox" because "unprecedented numbers of females joined the labor force," but "only minimal progress was made in . . . women's rights" to equal pay, equal promotion, and child care.[43] On the basis of their on-the-job education in the war and the wartime propaganda against fascism (and against the vicious fascist brand of sexism), women briefly renewed the fight for equal rights. Similarly, with their work experience and the volume of propaganda against fascist racism, blacks pressured for more rights. For a time they were supported by millions of veterans whom the war had made more cosmopolitan and liberal—they, too, had been filled with antifascist propaganda. Women were also encouraged by many greatly strengthened radical CIO unions. All these forces coalesced briefly in the Progressive party campaign of 1948.

The counterattack by the conservative advocates of "return to normalcy"—supported by the press, big business, the church, and both old parties—was, however, much too strong at the time. The causes of women's rights, black rights, civil liberties, and better labor laws were all buried under the avalanche of the cold war, the red

---

[42]See Chafe, op. cit., p. 187.
[43]Ibid., p. 188.

scare, and the anticommunist crusade. These red herrings justified enormous military spending, which provided enough jobs to allay the workers' discontent. For women, the conservative reaction took the form of the "feminine mystique"—a glorification of the traditional female role. Nevertheless, a few determined women refused to stay in their place. In the political sphere, some progress was made.

WOMEN IN POLITICS, 1940-1960

In the 1940s and 1950s, 34 women were elected to the House of Representatives. There were still a large number of congressmen's widows elected—13 of the 34—but more qualified women made it on their own, and a number were to make the House their career.

Frances P. Bolton, elected in 1940 to succeed her late husband, remained in Congress until 1968 and rose to become ranking minority leader on the House Foreign Affairs Committee. Another widow elected the same year was to have an even more distinguished career. Margaret Chase Smith spent 8 years in the House. In 1948, she ran for the Senate without party endorsement. A big vote-getter in Maine, she won and was reelected until 1972. She was the first senator to speak out against McCarthyism and the first woman to hold a party leadership post in the Senate.

Helen Gahagan Douglas, an opera singer and actress, was elected to the House in 1944. A liberal Democrat, she had been active in California politics for a number of years. Her liberal activist record was used against her when she ran for the Senate in 1950. Her opponent, Richard Nixon, based his campaign on the red smear—calling her the "pink lady." His vicious campaign during a period of national hysteria about domestic communists was successful, and Helen Douglas, one of the most capable of women politicians, was retired from public life.

Despite the sway of the feminine mystique, the 1950s saw a number of capable women enter the House for lengthy careers. Lenor Sullivan, elected in 1952, became a leading exponent of consumer protection legislation. The 1954 election raised the number of women in the House to 16—a record to that date. The election brought in two women who were to have long and distinguished careers in the House. Edith Green, Democrat from Oregon, made education her specialty and rose to become second-ranking member on the Education and Labor Committee. Martha Griffiths, the first woman appointed to the powerful Ways and Means Committee, was one of the most outspoken feminists in Congress. She worked for laws barring sex discrimination throughout her tenure.

Despite the increase in women in the House, progress for women in politics was slow. No woman was elected governor or mayor of a major city during the 1940s and 1950s. Only two women served in cabinet posts. Frances Perkins, first appointed secretary of labor by Franklin Roosevelt in 1933, served in that post until 1945. Oveta Culp Hobby was named to head the new Department of Health, Education and Welfare in 1953 and served until 1955. Two women served as lieutenant governor and one as attorney general during this period.

Stereotyped notions about woman's place have retarded progress for women in the political arena. For many women the thought of going into politics is simply inconceivable. For those who try, the barriers to success are great. Party pros generally believe a woman's place is stuffing envelopes. Women are not encouraged and are seldom supported as candidates. Being a congressman's widow is more useful in getting a congressional nomination than intelligence and willingness to work hard. A widow has name recognition and presumably sympathy from the electorate. Sometimes, also, a widow is nominated in order to prevent a divisive intraparty fight for the nomination.

Women's inferior role in politics is often attributed to their family duties. "Edith Green disagrees. . . . Women, she feels, are the victims of a form of psychological warfare, systematically waged by men who consider the political world their exclusive domain. 'When I entered politics,' she says, 'a thousand and one times in a condescending tone, I heard: How did it ever happen that you [meaning a woman] are running for office?' "[44]

Helen Gahagan Douglas was asked during her campaigns, "Hey, Helen, why aren't you home with the kids?"[45] Coya Knutson's congressional career was destroyed by her opponents' use of such sentiments. They extracted from her alcoholic husband a letter saying "Coya come home,"[46] and she was defeated for reelection. According to columnist Doris Fleeson,

> Many in Washington, not all of them women . . . feel that she was marked down as "fair game" simply because she was a woman and roughly treated in a manner that the men in her business are not. . . . There are many better stories here than *l'affaire* Knutson and they are about much more prominent people, but it is not considered

[44]Quoted in Chamberlin, op. cit., p. 258.
[45]Quoted in ibid., p. 183.
[46]Quoted in ibid., p. 264.

cricket to use them as a political weapon.

The lesson is that, as a practical matter, women are held to a far higher standard of accountability in politics than men are. Women clearly cannot count on the club spirit for protection.[47]

THE COUNTERREVOLUTION OF THE 1950s

With the U.S. army playing world policeman, with a high level of employment and prosperity at home, and with liberal or radical voices stilled by the witch-hunting of Senator McCarthy and others, the Great American Celebration was on. *Conformity* was the catchword, and the best description of students and youth in general was "the silent generation." The cause of women's liberation could not flourish in this atmosphere; it always reflects the general climate and the state of protest movements in particular. We have seen that the women's movement arose with the abolitionist movement, scored a victory on suffrage in alliance with the Socialist and Progressive movements, and raised its head again, though not in an organized way, in the atmosphere of the all-out antifascist war.

We saw, on the other hand, that the movement died out in the extremely anti-red reactionary period of economic expansion in the mid-1920s. Now we find, as no surprise, that in the prosperity and renewed anti-red hysteria of the 1950s, the possibilities for a revival of the women's liberation movement were cut off. As in the 1920s, the ideological drive of the 1950s, reflected in the media, was toward privatism. It was an apolitical period during which idealism or concern with social problems was considered rather weird. Men learned that the highest virtue was money-making; women were told that the highest virtue was to be a child-producing machine surrounded by lots of glittering gadgets in a little box in the suburbs; and sex was glorified, since there was nothing else exciting left to glorify.

Particularly for women, this ideological picture diverged further and further from reality. The ideology declared that men made enormous salaries so women could have "leisure" to care for a huge number of children and mind a beautiful, time-consuming house. In reality, more and more women had to go to work if the family was to earn the minimal socially acceptable income.

Despite the rising tide of back-to-the-kitchen ideology, more and more women went to work outside the home (see Table 11.5). Thus both the percentage of women working and the ratio of women to all workers increased steadily each decade. In fact, the trend ac-

[47]Quoted in ibid., p. 265.

TABLE 11.5
Women at Work 1940–1970

Year	Women workers as percentage of all workers	Women workers as percentage of all women
1940	25%	29%
1950	29	34
1960	33	38
1970	40	43

Sources: U.S. Department of Labor, Women's Bureau, *1969 Handbook on Women Workers* (1969), p. 10; and U.S. Department of Labor, *Manpower Report of the President* (1973), p. 129.

celerated. From 1890 to 1940, the portion of women working rose by only 1½ percentage points per decade; from 1940 to 1970, it rose by 5 percentage points per decade!

Sexist ideology portrayed all married women and mothers of small children as being at home—otherwise, child-care centers might be a reasonable idea. In 1940, married women constituted only 30 percent of all women workers, but that number had risen to 48 percent by 1950, to 54 percent by 1960, and to 60 percent by 1970. The increase of women workers did not come from single women; the percentage of single women at work rose only from 48 percent in 1940 to 51 percent in 1970. But the percentage of married women at work rose from 17 percent in 1940 to 40 percent in 1970.

Particularly contrary to sexist ideology's picture was the rise in the number of working mothers. The percentage of women at work who had children below age 6 increased from 13 percent in 1948 to 29 percent by 1967. These greater numbers at work reflected socioeconomic necessities and changing attitudes, and helped change attitudes further.

BRAINWASHING IN THE 1950s
We were all brainwashed in the 1950s to believe that the Red Menace was about to eat us, so we must spend billions of dollars and thousands of lives to prevent revolution in Korea and Vietnam and Guatamala and everywhere else. But women were especially brainwashed to reverse the effects of the liberating World War II experience.

The old antiwomen interest groups continued to push the sexist view of women's subservience and "place." Big business did not mind the increase in jobs for women; it needed millions of women workers. Knowing their "place," however, meant that these women should be submissive and should not organize for higher wages. Moreover, if women workers think of themselves as transient and "returning" to full-time housework "eventually," then they will more easily accept a low wage in times of prosperity and unemployment in times of depression. Middle-class woman's place was said to be in the home and/or in a "woman's job" on the lowest levels of teaching or nursing or as a humble secretary—but not in positions of power in business or politics. Southern white males continued to oppose any degree of equality for blacks or women. Organized religion, particularly the Catholic church, continued to urge women's subservience to men and to the church.

The 1950s, however, saw several new twists. Freudian psychology, stated in a sophisticated fashion in university classrooms and in crude ways in the popular media, was used as a major weapon to keep women in their traditional place. The big-selling magazines, such as *McCalls, Life,* and *Ladies Home Journal,* popularized what Betty Friedan called "the feminine mystique." In Friedan's survey of these magazines, she found "the image of woman that emerges . . . is young and frivolous, almost childlike; fluffy and feminine; passive; gaily content in a world of bedroom and kitchen, sex, babies, and home."[48] The women's magazines mentioned no national and world issues—because these were beyond women—but stuck to recipes and clothing styles. They emphasized as a new, "modern" view the concept of family "togetherness," a sticky mixture of man barbecuing, woman playing with baby, and all praying together ("the family that prays together stays together").

Another "modern" twist was to warn of the dangers of being a "dried-up career woman" (à la Freudian psychology), while emphasizing that a woman could be "highly creative" in the home by doing fancy cooking, baking her own bread, sewing, interior decorating, and redecorating. The feminine mystique was extolled in magazine articles like "Femininity Begins at Home," "Have Babies While You're Young," "How to Snare a Male," and "Cooking to Me Is Poetry."[49]

In 1949, only one-third of the fictional heroines in magazines had careers, and they were always psychologically sick and unhappy until they gave it up for the home. By 1959, there were *no* heroines with careers (or a real interest in art or politics), only happy housewives. One typical housewife heroine exclaimed: "I'm so grateful for my blessings! Wonderful husband, handsome sons with disposi-

[48]Betty Friedan, *The Feminine Mystique* (New York: Dell, 1963), p. 30.
[49]Ibid., p. 38.

tions to match, big comfortable house. . . . I'm thankful for my good health and faith in God and such material possessions as two cars, two TV's and two fireplaces."[50]

The politicians echoed the same sexist line. Even the liberal Adlai Stevenson said that a woman's political job was to

> . . . inspire in her home a vision of the meaning of life and freedom. . . . This assignment for you, as wives and mothers, you can do in the living room with a baby in your lap or in the kitchen with a can opener in your hand. . . . I think there is much you can do about our crisis in the humble role of housewife. I could wish you no better vocation than that.[51]

The 1950s were the period in which psychoanalysis reached full bloom; many middle-class men—and women—yearned to be analyzed out of all their problems. The most widely quoted Freudian book was *Modern Woman: The Lost Sex,* by Marynia Farnham and Ferdinand Lundberg, published in 1947. The authors began by repeating all the old slanders against the early women's liberation leaders—that they were sex-starved and frustrated, that they envied men's penises and wanted only to castrate all males, that "feminism . . . was at its core a deep illness."[52] Since women were created to be biologically and psychologically dependent on men, they could not be happy in independent careers. Women's independence and education caused all their neuroses. ". . . The more educated the woman is, the greater chance there is of sexual disorder. . . ."[53] This is contrary, of course, to all known studies, which consistently show women's sexual satisfaction rising with education. On the basis of their faulty analysis, they argued that the government should favor childbearing and larger families by propaganda and subsidies; bar married women from many occupations, even teaching; and pay for psychoanalysis for all neurotics infected by women's liberation.

Similar arguments were made by sociologists like Talcott Parsons, who found our present sexist ideology and family structure to be "functional" or useful for preservation of the status quo (true, but that assumes we want the status quo). Even the anthropologists, like Margaret Mead, whose work had shown the great variety of men's and women's roles in primitive cultures, went back to look again

[50]Quoted in ibid., p. 57.
[51]Quoted in ibid., p. 54.
[52]Marynia Farnham and Ferdinand Lundberg, *Modern Woman: The Lost Sex* (New York: Harper & Row, 1947), p. 142.
[53]Ibid.

armed with Freudian categories. And lo and behold! They found what they looked for: that primitive women were very happy because they did nothing but have babies, fulfilling their "true" sexual roles.

All of this was transmitted not only in the popular media but also in the universities. Counselors told women not to prepare for architecture or law or medicine but to take home economics so as to prepare for "the happiest career." Those who were interested in science or any creative subject were discouraged because too much of the wrong education would make a girl unhappy sexually and in general. One women's college boasted, "We are not educating women to be scholars; we are educating them to be wives and mothers."[54] A good education for women, according to Lynn White, former president of Mills College, would not include courses in which men are "naturally" better—like the sciences. It would not only begin with a "firm nuclear course in the Family, but from it would radiate curricular series dealing with food and nutrition, textiles and clothing, health and nursing, house planning and interior decoration, garden design and applied botany, and child development."[55] He urged fellow educators to make a course on the "theory and preparation of a Basque paella" as difficult and exciting (for women) as a course in post-Kantian philosophy.

Others made use of the same sexist nonsense in more directly "functional" ways. The advertising industry, a multibillion-dollar business devoted to encouraging waste, discovered that women do 75 percent of consumer household buying. When she researched the sexual selling game of the 1950s, Betty Friedan was told by one advertising executive that "properly manipulated, . . . American housewives can be given the sense of identity, purpose, creativity, the self-realization, even the sexual joy they lack—by the buying of things."[56]

DISCRIMINATION IN THE 1950s
Although reality had little to do with the picture painted by sexist ideology, we should not assume that the brainwashing was unsuccessful. True, more and more women, many of whom were wives and mothers, worked outside the home. Sexist ideology and overt discrimination, however, were successful in preventing any women's liberation movement in the 1950s; keeping women segregated in

[54]Friedan, op. cit., p. 150.
[55]Quoted in ibid., p. 152.
[56]Quoted in ibid., p. 199.

"women's jobs"; keeping women's wages low; preventing many women from attaining higher education, prestigious professional positions, or positions of power in business or politics; and keeping women as a flexible reserve, easily employable and easily fired.

Since 1950, in every recession the rate of unemployment of women workers has been about twice that of men workers. In the period from 1950 to the present, the wages and salaries of women have shown a *declining* trend relative to those of men (see Table 11.6).

Why did women's wages suffer this relative decline? The answer to this is increased discrimination, but with a change in the forms of discrimination. There was no change in the differential wage that was paid for the same job, but there has been an increase in the percentages of women holding the lower-paying jobs in each occupation. More important, most of the large increase of women in the labor force went into the traditional "women's jobs," so the de-

TABLE   11.6
Women's Median Wage as
   Percentage of Men's

Year	Percentage
1950	65%
1955	64
1956	63
1957	64
1958	63
1959	61
1960	61
1961	59
1962	60
1963	60
1964	60
1965	60
1966	58
1967	58
1968	58
1969	61
1970	59

Source: U.S. Department of Labor, Women's Bureau, *Fact Sheet on the Earnings Gap* (1970), p. 1.

gree of segregation into the lower-paying occupations increased considerably. Let us examine the evidence for these trends.

There is plentiful evidence that within each occupation the higher-paying jobs are going to men in ever-increasing proportions. For example, women have remained over 80 percent of all elementary school teachers, but men have increasingly monopolized the better-paying and higher-status administrative jobs (see Table 11.7).

The same trend toward male dominance is observable in the higher-paying administrative jobs in several other "women's occupations," such as social workers, librarians, high school teachers, bank clerks, and telephone operators. The increased predominance of men in the top business and professional positions may also be reflected in the fact that 6 percent of those listed in *Who's Who* in 1930 were women, but only 4 percent of the entries were women in 1970.

The most important type of economic discrimination to increase in this period is the segregation of women into "women's jobs." The increasing numbers of women at work have gone largely into sex-typed jobs, thus intensifying the overcrowding of these areas and further lowering, or at least keeping low, the wages paid in those occupations. Specifically, from 1950 to 1960, sexist ideology and overt discrimination forced 48 percent of the total increase in women in the labor force into occupations that are 70 percent or more female. Moreover, in the same period a startling 59 percent of the growth in number of women at work occurred in occupations in which over half the workers are women.

When we examine detailed classifications, such as telephone operators or stenographers, the pattern is very clear. Yet even in the very broadest classifications encompassing all workers, the long-run trend toward increased segregation is very striking (see Table 11.8).

These data tell a grim story. During the years 1940 to 1970,

TABLE 11.7
Elementary School Principals,
1928–1968

Year	Percentage of women
1928	55%
1948	41
1958	38
1968	22

Source: Kirsten Amundsen, *The Silenced Majority* (Englewood Cliffs, N.J.: Prentice-Hall, 1971), p. 38.

TABLE   11.8
Economic Segregation by Sex, 1940–1970

Occupation	Women as percentage of total in occupation	
	1940	1970
Mainly male occupations		
Foreman	2%	3%
Laborer (nonfarm)	3	3
Farmer and farm worker	8	15
Manager and proprietor	12	16
Mixed occupations		
Factory worker	26	31
Professional and technical	45	39
Salesperson	28	42
Mainly female occupations		
Service (nondomestic)	40	61
Clerical	53	75
Domestic service	94	98
Total	25	40

Source: U.S. Department of Labor, Women's Bureau, *1969 Handbook on Women Workers* (1969), plus current Labor Department publications.

the percentage of all workers who were women increased from 25 percent to 40 percent, but most of this increase came in the segregated "women's occupations." Thus the big jumps are in nondomestic service jobs, such as waitresses, and in clerical jobs. By 1970, three out of every four clerical workers were women, and one in every three women workers was a clerical worker. Both areas are low paying and low status. In domestic service, the lowest paying of all, the percentage of women rose still further, from 94 percent to 98 percent.

In the mixed areas, the relatively low-paying categories of factory worker and salesperson showed large increases in percentages of women. In the mainly male areas, the only large increase in the percentage of women came in the categories of farmers and farm workers—but more detailed data show that the increase was all in low-paid farm work, while the percentage of female farm owners actually declined.

Foremen remained 97 percent male. The only faint ray of hope was the slight increase in female managers and proprietors, from 12 percent to 16 percent, an increase of 4 percentage points in 30 years.

On the other side of the coin—in this period when the proportion of women to all workers increased greatly—the only major decline in the portion of women in an occupation was in the higher-paying and more prestigious professional area, a decline that has continued since about 1930. We shall see that women in all the professional areas suffered greatly from the sexist offensives of the 1930s and the 1950s.

The Labor Department's "professional" category is very broad, and we are concerned not only with the declining percentage of women in the whole area but also with their increased segregation within it. Over 75 percent of the women classified as professionals are in the low-paying and low-status occupations of teaching and nursing. The picture in these semiprofessional mainly female, areas of the "professional and technical" category is shown in Table 11.9.

Women held their own in the 1950s (and still do) in elementary school teaching and nursing. The percentage declined somewhat among social workers and librarians, and by 1970 the percentage of female librarians had decreased further, to 80 percent. All of these remained mainly female occupations, but men were moving into them, particularly into the top jobs, taking over most head librarian jobs, social work directorships, and even most jobs as elementary school principals. Most striking was the male invasion of high school teaching; the percentage of women in this area declined from 60 percent in 1940 to only 46 percent in 1970. Moreover, by 1970, over 95 percent of all high school principals were men.

The greatest losses suffered by women, however, were in the highest-paying and most prestigious professions. For example, the percentage of female college faculty (including instructors, professors, and presidents) continued its decline from the 1930 high point (see Table 11.10).

The percentage of women scientists also declined in the 1950s,

TABLE 11.9
Low-paid Professional Occupations, 1950–1960

Occupation	Percentage of women	
	1950	1960
Elementary school teacher	87%	86%
High school teacher	60	49
Nurse	98	97
Librarian	89	85
Medical-dental technician	57	62
Social worker	66	57

Source: U.S. Department of Labor, Women's Bureau, *1969 Handbook on Women Workers* (1969), plus current Labor Department publications.

TABLE 11.10
Female College Faculty, 1910–1970

Year	1910	1920	1930	1940	1950	1960	1970
Percent female	19%	30%	32%	27%	23%	19%	18%

Source: U.S. Department of Labor, Women's Bureau, *1969 Handbook on Women Workers* (1969), plus current Labor Department publications.

TABLE 11.11
Female Scientists, 1950–1960

Specialty	Percentage of women	
	1950	1960
Biologist	29%	27%
Chemist	10	9
Mathematician	38	26
Physicist	7	4
Geologist	6	2
All natural scientists	11	10

Source: U.S. Department of Labor, Women's Bureau, *1969 Handbook on Women Workers* (1969), plus current Labor Department publications.

though it was low to begin with (see Table 11.11). Women were barely accepted in the physical sciences in 1950, but the percentage dropped still further in the 1950s and 1960s. The percentage of female natural scientists dropped again in the 1960s; women were only 8 percent of the total by 1970. The percentage of women mathematicians also dropped again, to only 10 percent in 1970. In most of the social sciences the percentages remained low, the highest being in psychology, with 23 percent women in 1970. Several of the lower-paying areas in the humanities have much higher percentages of women.

Another indication of the changing status of women is their educational attainment (see Table 11.12). From their high point in 1930, the percentage of women earning academic degrees drops precipitously to a low point in 1950. The decline is due in some large part to the renewed climate of sexism in the 1930s and late 1940s. It is also due partly to the large influx of veterans from World War II. Yet the low figure for 1950 is not an accident, because the decline begins in the 1930s and because the recovery takes so long. In the face of the sexism of the 1950s, the percentage of women B.A.'s slowly recovers until it is slightly higher in 1970 than in 1930, but

TABLE 11.12
Recipients of Academic Degrees,
1930–1970

Year	Percentage of women		
	B.A.	M.A.	Ph.D.
1930	40%	40%	15%
1940	42	38	13
1950	24	29	10
1960	35	35	11
1970	42	40	13

Sources: U.S. Department of Labor, Women's Bureau, *1969 Handbook on Women Workers* (1969); and Rudolf Blitz, "Women in the Professions," *Monthly Labor Review* 97 (May 1974), 38.

the portion of Ph.D.'s going to women has not yet recovered to the 1930 level.

THE WOMEN'S LIBERATION MOVEMENT: 1940–1960

With two slight qualifications, there was *no* organized women's liberation movement from 1940 to 1960. First, most of the older women's organizations survived. The League of Women Voters continued, though declining; it had inherited a mailing list of 2 million names from NAWSA, but had only about 200,000 members in the mid-1920s, and only 106,000 in 1960. Also continuing were the YWCA, the Business and Professional Women's Clubs, the General Federation of Women's Clubs, and the American Association of University Women. But all had primary interests—social, professional, or reform—not related to women's liberation, or else they saw no relationship. Another continuing conservative influence was the Women's Bureau.

Second, women's liberation was advocated by the National Women's Party and by the old left-wing parties, particularly Communist and Socialist Workers—but all these were small, sectarian, and without influence. The left-wing parties suffered severe government persecution in the 1950s; they also saw women's liberation as only a secondary priority.

In short, there was no significant women's liberation movement in the 40 years from the mid-1920s to the mid-1960s. One reason was the limited ideology and elite class base of the suffragists. So strongly had they emphasized the vote, and only the vote, that their successors—like the League of Women Voters—could declare in the 1920s that there was no more discrimination against women and that liberal women should use their energies for general reforms for all people. The sole successor to the most militant suffragists—the Women's party—was narrow in other ways. It continued to fight for equal legal rights but paid little or no attention to women's inferior position in the family, to the exploitation of women workers, or to the special problems of black women. This lack of interest in the major social, economic, and racial issues alienated radical women, while the hostile social atmosphere prevented them from winning over the moderate women.

By the mid-1920s, the relative stability of capitalism, the disappearance of the small radical farmer, the red-baiting, and the internal splits destroyed the Socialist and Progressive parties and brought a period of conservatism hostile to the women's movement. The radicalism of the 1930s concentrated on unemployment and, in the late 1930s, on the threat of war with fascism to the practical exclusion of all other issues. Again, during the war other issues could not be raised. The postwar 1946–1960 period was a time of U.S. economic expansion and world dominance, of the cold war and superpatriotism ensured by the witch-hunting of McCarthyism. All radical and liberal groups suffered repression; and possible women's liberation causes—such as child care—were smothered with the rest.

THE NEW STRUGGLE FOR LIBERATION: AMERICAN WOMEN, 1960 TO THE PRESENT

12

As the 1960s began, the myth of the American woman as the "happy housewife heroine" increasingly came into conflict with reality. Twenty-three million women—36 percent of all women 16 and older—worked for pay. These working women were not just single girls spending a few years in the labor force; more than half (54 percent) were married, and many had children. Of all women with school-age children, 43 percent worked for pay. By the end of the 1960s, a *majority* of women between 18 and 64 worked at paid jobs.

While the women's magazines' picture of the full-time housewife and mother was valid for fewer and fewer women, an alternate picture—that of the career woman successfully competing in what had been a man's world—was equally false. Women worked in factories, as domestics and secretaries, as teachers and nurses. The prestigious and remunerative positions in the professions and business were overwhelmingly held by men. Educationally, women were not doing as well relative to men as they had in 1930. In 1960, 35 percent of all B.A.'s went to women; in 1930, women had received 40 percent. Whatever a woman's education, when she entered the labor force she encountered discrimination. She made less money than a man with the same education, and her chances of promotion were much slimmer.

Women's position in the public sphere was, if anything, even worse. Forty years after winning the vote, women were voting at almost the same levels as men. Millions worked in political campaigns, stuffing envelopes, typing, canvassing. But despite their numbers as voters and their efforts as party workers, women were barely represented in government decision-making positions. The 1960 elections brought the highest number of women ever into Congress; 15 out of 435 in the House of Representatives and 2 out of 100 in the Senate.[1] There had, of course, never been a woman president or a woman Supreme Court justice. In neither case had a woman ever been seriously considered. Only two women had served in the cabinet, and few had been appointed to other high administrative posts. Federal judges, all appointed by the president, were also overwhelmingly male. On the state level the situation was hardly better. Even by 1967, only about 4 percent of state legislative seats were held by women.[2] No women served as governors in 1960. The only woman to be elected to that office during the 1960s—Lurleen Wallace—was governor in name only, like the two women governors elected previously.

Women's representation was better on the local level, but only when relatively unprestigious and badly paid positions such as library board members and treasury clerks were counted.[3] In 1966, there were 100 women mayors, but none of these served as mayor of a major city.[4] Even on school boards, an area that, according to the stereotype, should be of special interest to them, women were underrepresented—only 9.7 percent of board members were women.[5]

Thus, despite doing the major part of the unglamorous but essential political work, women were neither rewarded with high appointive office nor given encouragement and help in running for elective office. John Bailey, one-time Democratic national chairman, expressed the common view of male professionals toward women in politics: "The only time to run a woman is when things look so bad that your only chance is to do something dramatic."[6]

In the other centers of power in the United States, women were again conspicuous only by their absence. The corporate elite was a male preserve. As late as 1967, the boards of directors of the top 20 industrials, the top 15 banks, and the top 15 insurance companies included no women.[7] By 1970, women were represented on the

---

[1]Judith Hole and Ellen Levine, *Rebirth of Feminism* (New York: Quadrangle, 1971), p. 401.

[2]Kirsten Amundsen, *The Silenced Majority* (Englewood Cliffs, N.J.: Prentice-Hall, 1971), p. 78.

[3]Ibid., p. 70.

[4]Ibid., p. 79.

[5]Ibid., p. 80.

[6]Ibid., p. 83.

[7]Ibid., p. 91.

boards of 2 of the 3 major broadcasting networks. At NBC, 1 out of 18 directors was female; at CBS, 1 out of 16. No woman served on ABC's board of directors. In 37 states, no woman held a top position—president, vice-president, or general manager—in any local tv station. In the other states there were a few; for example, in California, of 34 such positions, 4 were held by women. Women did a little better on the boards of major newspapers. There was a woman on the governing board of the *Washington Post,* the *Chattanooga Times,* the *Houston Post,* and the *New York Post.* But in several of these cases, the woman's unquestioned talent was backed up by ownership of the newspaper.[8]

The professedly egalitarian unions provided little more opportunity for women to rise to major decision-making positions. In the late 1960s there was no woman on the 28-member executive council of the AFL-CIO. Of the council's 16 standing committees, none had a woman chairperson. The Amalgamated Clothing Workers of America and the International Ladies' Garment Workers' Union—both with a predominantly female membership—had no woman officer at the national level.[9]

As the 1960s began, then, women were a silent and powerless majority—but not, as the myth of the 1950s had it, a contented one. Even the women's magazines, the prime propagandizers of the feminine mystique, came to recognize the "trapped housewife" syndrome. A Gallup poll taken in 1962 found that 90 percent of the housewives surveyed did not want their daughters to lead the same type of life they had led. They hoped their daughters would get more education and marry later.[10]

The widening of the gap between ideology and reality had reached a critical point. Extreme disparities between social ideology and social reality are conducive to the formation of social movements. This was the situation for women in the early 1960s. According to the ideology, the typical American woman was an affluent housewife, happy and completely fulfilled in that role. In reality, more and more women worked because their financial contribution was needed for family support. Yet the ideology was used to deny them good jobs, promotions, and equal pay. The affluent housewife, on the other hand, was finding that living up to the feminine mystique exacted heavy costs. Generally college educated, she was relegated to housework, which offered little intrinsic satisfaction and no pres-

[8]Ibid., p. 100.
[9]Ibid., p. 97.
[10]Ibid., p. 122.

tige. Thus many women had been educated too much to find satisfaction in the housewife role; yet when from choice or need, women went to work, they found themselves discriminated against because of their sex. The preconditions for a social movement were present.

During the early 1960s, however, it was the discontent of blacks, not of women, that became articulated and held center stage. Blacks were saying: "We're tired of waiting; we want in *now,* and we're backing rhetoric with action." Sit-ins and freedom rides led to nationwide organizations, and many white students of both sexes became deeply involved in the civil rights movement. Here many young women learned both the rhetoric and the organization of protest. Not surprisingly, as they became more sensitive to the blacks' second-class status, they became aware of their own.

The mid-1960s saw an increased politicization of American college students. Many who started in the civil rights movement became involved in the free speech movement and in Students for a Democratic Society. The antiwar movement attracted additional tens of thousands. Organizing and protesting became a way of life for many on campus. The movement's lack of success in ending the war despite its spectacular growth led to radicalization—to the emergence of the New Left. The early antiwar movement had seen the war as a ghastly mistake; later, the war was increasingly perceived as a natural outgrowth of U.S. imperialism. With this change in view came an increasingly radical critique and analysis of American society. The women in the movement were to learn the New Left lesson well; they were to carry the critique to a more fundamental level than the men expected.

EARLY SYMPTOMS

In December 1961, John Kennedy established a Presidential Commission on the Status of Women. The idea originated with Esther Peterson, a member of Kennedy's campaign staff and his appointee as head of the Woman's Bureau. Kennedy seemed to have accepted the proposal at least in part because it was a cheap way of repaying the hundreds of women who worked in his campaign, none of whom, with the exception of Esther Peterson, had been appointed to a high-level government job. There has also been speculation that Kennedy saw the commission as a way of finessing the Equal Rights Amendment issue. The amendment had been included in the platforms of both major parties in nearly every election from 1940 to 1960. But the major labor unions, which were important Kennedy supporters, were opposed to it. Such a commission would, at minimum, postpone any need to consider the amendment and, if it were to find no need for the ERA, would give Kennedy an excuse for never bringing it up.[11]

The commission's report did not come out until late 1963, but meanwhile there were other stirrings. In early 1963, Betty Friedan's *The Feminine Mystique* was published.[12] A powerful indictment of the ideology that forced women into the role of full-time housewife and a description of the psychological costs of such a limited life, it became an instant best-seller.

In the summer of the same year, the Equal Pay Act was passed by Congress. This act required that, in the jobs covered by it, women be paid equally with men doing the same job. The act had been introduced in 1945 by Representative Helen Gahagan Douglas and was reintroduced in every session until it was finally successful in 1963.[13]

The report of the President's Commission on the Status of Women was made public in October 1963. The report of the Commission itself was moderate, although the reports of some of its committees, released at the same time, were somewhat stronger. Its recommendations included greater availability of child-care services, removal of the remaining property law restrictions, greater opportunities for women in politics, and equal opportunity in employment. The commission's total lack of militancy is shown by its position on the last point. While it recommended that the president issue an executive order embodying the principle of equal opportunity in employment, it recommended no enforcement procedures. Voluntary compliance was to be relied upon.[14] The report favored the removal of all barriers to women's full participation in American society; at the same time, it accepted the assumption that it is the woman who is fundamentally responsible for homemaking and child rearing, even if she also works outside the home. To make this dual role easier, it recommended greater opportunities for part-time workers. The report favored the retention of protective laws for women, at least until such laws could be extended to cover all workers.[15] It also concluded that the Fifth and Fourteenth Amendments provided sufficient basis for the equality of women under the law and that the ERA was not needed.

The importance of the commission lies more in its being an ex-

[11]Hole and Levine, op. cit., p. 18.

[12]Betty Friedan, *The Feminine Mystique* (New York: Dell, 1963).

[13]Lucy Komisar, *The New Feminism* (New York: Warner Paperback Library, 1972), p. 118.

[14]Hole and Levine, op. cit., p. 21.

[15]Ibid., p. 435.

ample and a publicizer than in its recommendations. It was the first official body to make a thorough study of the status of women in the United States.[16] By 1963, a number of states had followed the federal example by setting up state commissions on the status of women, and by 1967 every state had such a commission.

Two of the commission's recommendations were of immediate importance. In November 1963, Kennedy, as the commission had urged, set up the Interdepartmental Committee on the Status of Women and the Citizens' Advisory Council on the Status of Women. The first was composed of governmental officials; the latter, composed of private citizens, was to play an important role in pressuring the government to live up to its official nondiscriminatory position.

A major weapon in the fight for equality came into being in 1964. Its inadvertent forger was Congressman Howard Smith, a southern gentleman of the old school—he approved of both women and blacks as long as they stayed in their place. A comprehensive civil rights bill was up for debate, and it looked as if there were sufficient votes to pass it. Smith, the powerful chairman of the Rules Committee and wily leader of the die-hard southern contingent in the House, realized that drastic steps were needed. He could not win on the floor, and he dared not bottle up the bill in committee, as he had done in the past. During his appearance on "Meet the Press," May Craig, a member of the White House Press Corps and a feminist, suggested a strategy by asking him to include women under Title VII, the equal employment section of the bill.[17] Perhaps the bill could be laughed to death.

Congresswoman Martha Griffiths had intended to make that motion, but knowing Smith would bring more votes, she waited to see if he would actually do so. Smith did in fact move to include women in Title VII. Many of the liberal supporters of the civil rights bill, convinced, like Smith, that this might kill the bill, opposed his amendment. Even Edith Green, sponsor of the 1963 Equal Pay Bill and long-time advocate of equal rights for women, worked and voted against Smith's amendment. The other congresswomen supported it, and on February 8, this strange coalition of feminists and southerners passed it by 168 to 133.

Smith must have been surprised, as were others, when the whole bill, amendment included, passed in the House. The Senate might well have dropped the provision had not a lobbying campaign gotten under way. Pauli Murray, a black woman lawyer, wrote a

---

[16]Ibid., p. 18.

[17]Caroline Bird, *Born Female* (New York: Pocket Books, 1971), p. 3.

"Memorandum in Support of Retaining the Sex Amendment," which was used by women representing the Business and Professional Women's Clubs in their effort to persuade senators. Caroline Bird reports that Lady Bird Johnson very discreetly let it be known that the administration supported the amendment.[18] Under these circumstances, there were enough senators who decided that voting against the rights of half their constituents was not politically smart. The bill passed, amendment and all.

When the law went into effect in July 1965, it became illegal to discriminate against women in hiring and promotions. But laws are of little use unless vigorously enforced. The Equal Employment Opportunity Commission (EEOC), set up to enforce Title VII, considered the sex provision, in the words of its director, "a fluke . . . conceived out of wedlock."[19] Most of the commissioners seemed to consider the provision at best a joke, at worst a distraction from their real work in behalf of black men. Perhaps the Playboy Clubs would have to hire male "bunnies," someone said at a White House Conference on Equal Opportunity in August 1965. The press, finding equal opportunity for women at least as funny as did the EEOC commissioners, labeled the amendment the Bunny Law and asked, "Can she pitch for the Mets?"[20]

It became clear to interested women that, given this attitude, little could be expected of the EEOC unless pressure was applied. A particular danger lay in the provision that made it legal to discriminate if sex were a bona fide occupational qualification (bfoq) for the job in question. Interpreted loosely, this could nullify the act. In November 1965, under pressure from the Citizens Advisory Council, the EEOC came out with guidelines that interpreted the bfoq provision narrowly. The council argued and the EEOC accepted the position that exceptions should not be allowed ". . . based on stereotypes of characteristics of the sexes; the preferences of the employer, co-workers, clients, or customers; or assumptions of the comparative characteristics of women (or men) in general."[21] The EEOC, however, rejected the council's recommendation that sex-segregated want ads be outlawed.

[18]Ibid., p. 11.
[19]Ibid., p. 13.
[20]Ibid.
[21]"Report on Progress in 1965 on the Status of Women," *Second Annual Report of Interdepartmental Committee and Citizens' Advisory Council on the Status of Women,* December 31, 1965, p. 25.

NOW IS ORGANIZED

The situation, then, seemed ripe for the formation of a women's organization. In 1965–1966, Betty Friedan was often in Washington conferring with interested women on what could be done to combat discrimination. In the spring of 1966, the controversy over sex-segregated want ads was in full swing, and in June, Congresswoman Martha Griffiths strongly attacked the EEOC for its lack of enforcement. The two EEOC commissioners who were interested in enforcing the sex provision of Title VII had decided that an organization to pressure the government into enforcement was needed and were discreetly letting their views become known.

The third annual meeting of the National Conference of State Commissions, which opened in Washington on June 28, provided an opportunity. This meeting, held under the sponsorship of the Citizens Advisory Council and the Interdepartmental Committee on the Status of Women, brought together a large number of concerned women. An informal meeting of some of them to discuss the possibility of an independent women's group produced no results. Some of the state commissioners present felt that such an organization was not necessary, that it would be better to work through the official bodies already established. But when Kathryn Clarenbach, head of the Wisconsin Commission, found that the conference was not allowed to pass resolutions or take action and, thus, that she could not introduce a resolution against the EEOC's position on want ads, it became clear to her and to many others that working through the state commissions would not be sufficient. At the final luncheon, the National Organization for Women (NOW) was formed. NOW's first action, decided upon during the luncheon, was to send telegrams to the EEOC commissioners asking them to change their position on want ads.

NOW announced its existence, with a charter membership of 300, at a press conference on October 29, 1966. Betty Friedan became its first president. Its purpose was stated thus: "To take action to bring women into full participation in the mainstream of American society *now,* exercising all the privileges and responsibilities thereof in truly equal partnership with men."[22]

NOW went into full swing right from the beginning. It immediately got involved in several sex discrimination cases under Title VII. The EEOC was petitioned to hold hearings on the want-ad guidelines. After considerable pressure, they were held in May of the following

[22]NOW Statement of Purpose, adopted at organizational conference, October 29, 1966.

year. Task forces were set up to study and make recommendations about discrimination against women in education, employment, and religion. Others worked on the media image of women, the problems of poor women, and the family.[23] Government officials from the EEOC commissioners to the president were petitioned in person and by mail.

During its early years, NOW's tactics included the mainstays of "establishment" protest—setting up task forces, bringing suit, lobbying government officials. The organization did not, however, restrict itself to such ultrarespectable activities. In 1967, NOW members picketed *The New York Times* to protest its sex-segregated want-ad policy; NOW organized a national day of demonstration against the EEOC and set up picket lines in cities with EEOC offices. Later, NOW members were to disrupt a Senate committee hearing, demanding that hearings on the Equal Rights Amendment be held.

At NOW's second national conference in November 1967, the growing pains that often afflict a young movement became apparent. As the first national women's group, NOW's membership was extremely heterogeneous, and ideological conflicts were inevitable. At the conference, a major order of business was the drawing up of a women's Bill of Rights. Eight demands were eventually included:

    I.   Equal rights constitutional amendment
    II. Enforcement of laws banning sex discrimination in employment
    III. Maternity leave rights in employment and in social security bene-
         fits
    IV. Tax deduction for home and child care expenses for working
         parents
    V.   Child care centers
    VI. Equal and unsegregated education
    VII. Equal job training opportunities and allowances for women in
         poverty
    VIII. The right of women to control their reproductive lives[24]

Two of the planks engendered major controversies and were adopted only after bitter fights. Women from the United Auto Workers objected to the inclusion of the Equal Rights Amendment plank because their union's official position was still one of opposition. They did not carry out their threat to walk out when the plank was adopted, but they withdrew the secretarial services they had been

---

[23]Hole and Levine, op. cit., p. 86.
[24]Reprinted in ibid., p. 88.

providing, throwing NOW "into administrative chaos for months."[25] The passage of the abortion plank did lead to a walkout. The opponents argued that abortion was not a women's rights issue and that taking such a controversial position would destroy the effectiveness of the organization.

At the next annual meeting a split-off on the left took place. Ti-Grace Atkinson, president of the New York chapter, and some of her radical followers walked out after losing their fight to dismantle NOW's hierarchical structure.

These splits did not retard NOW's growth. By 1971, NOW had over 150 chapters and from 5,000 to 10,000 members. By late 1973, it had grown to about 30,000. During the late 1960s women were becoming aware of their second-class position at a rate sufficient to keep both the moderate and the radical wings of the movement growing at an accelerating pace.

A number of other moderate women's groups were founded in quick succession. The Women's Equity Action League (WEAL), incorporated on December 1, 1968, has been particularly active in cases of sex discrimination in higher education and in the ERA campaign. The group has a fairly conservative style—"League of Women Voter types," according to a member—and its Washington, D.C., chapter includes congresswomen and high government officials as members.[26] Federally Employed Women (FEW) was founded in 1968 for the purpose of pressuring the Civil Service Commission to enforce the executive order banning sex discrimination in federal employment. Human Rights for Women, Inc., also founded in 1968, is a nonprofit, tax-exempt organization dedicated to providing legal aid in sex discrimination cases.

RADICAL WOMEN ORGANIZE

The radical wing of the women's movement had somewhat different origins than the moderate wing and developed concurrently. During the middle 1960s, women in the civil rights movement and its offshoots were becoming aware that, even in groups dedicated to human liberation, they were second-class members—useful at the typewriter, in the kitchen, and in bed, but expected to leave policy making to the men. The first stirrings of organization seem to have occurred in 1964, when a small group of women in the Student Non-Violent Coordinating Committee (SNCC) began to meet and talk about their role in that organization. Ruby Doris Smith Robin-

[25]Ibid.
[26]Ibid., p. 96.

son presented a paper stemming from these talks at a SNCC staff meeting. The men's reaction is well expressed by the response of Stokely Carmichael: "The only position for women in SNCC is prone."[27] The women in these groups found again and again that men considered their complaints trivial. Bringing up the women's issue is "bourgeois," the women were told; it diverts attention from the real problems. A paper written by two SNCC women in 1965 produced such a reaction from male radicals. "Catcalls, storms of ridicule and verbal abuse"—"she just needs a good screw"—greeted attempts to bring up the women's issue at a 1965 SDS conference. Women demanding attention for women's liberation at an SDS convention in 1966 "were pelted with tomatoes and thrown out of the convention."[28]

Despite such treatment, women did not leave the New Left *en masse.* Some did begin to meet together to discuss their position in the movement. These women's caucuses were small and informal. The first effort to organize radical women as women did not occur until 1967.

During the spring of that year, two Chicago women—Heather Booth and Naomi Weisstein—held a seminar on women's issues under the auspices of a free university program. At the same time, a national meeting of New Left groups was being planned for Chicago in the fall. The seminar spurred a group of women to consider presenting a list of women's demands to the National Conference for a New Politics. These women finally decided not to participate as a group. The members who attended as individuals joined with other women to form an ad hoc women's caucus at the convention. The strong women's rights resolution that the caucus prepared was shunted aside by the convention leadership on the basis that there was not sufficient time. When it became clear that the convention did have time to take up additional resolutions as long as they were on other subjects, two of the caucus women, Jo Freeman and Shulamith Firestone, protested. "They were told in no uncertain terms that their 'trivial' business was not going to stop the conference from dealing with the important issues of the world."[29]

"Rage at what happened at the convention kept us going for at least three months," reported one of the participants, and spurred regular women's meetings in Chicago.[30] From these beginnings two

[27]Ibid., p. 110.
[28]Marlene Dixon and Robin Morgan, quoted in ibid., p. 112.
[29]Ibid., pp. 113–114.
[30]Quoted in ibid., p. 114.

groups emerged—the Woman's Radical Action Project and the Westside group. Jo Freeman, a founder of the latter, started the first newsletter of the movement in early 1968, thus providing some link with interested women across the country.

In the fall of 1967, Shulamith Firestone and Pam Allen organized Radical Women in New York. The group's first public action took place during an antiwar demonstration by a coalition of women's peace groups in January 1968. The Radical Women, joined by 300 to 500 women from the Jeannette Rankin Brigade, as the coalition was called, staged "The Burial of Traditional Womanhood" in a torchlight parade at Arlington Cemetery. Many New Left women opposed this action as being nonpolitical and basically irrelevant. The Radical Women responded that before women could hope to influence public policy, they must overcome their own subjugation, that the problem of women in America was social, not personal. Thus dealing with the women's issue was seen as both political and basic. ". . . We cannot hope to move toward a better world or even a truly democratic society at home until we begin to solve our own problems."[31]

The responses to the demonstration highlighted a conflict that had been developing in the new movement. The male-dominated New Left organizations had defined the women's problems as trivial. To the extent that a problem was recognized at all, it was assumed that it would automatically be righted by socialism, increasingly the goal of the New Left. Some New Left women agreed with this position, but those who formed the women's caucuses and then the independent women's groups did not. Nevertheless, even the women who saw the oppression of women as important disagreed in their analysis of its origins and thus in their tactics and proposed solutions. Is woman's inferior place due to "the system"—to private property and capitalism? Or is it due to men—to the male's psychological need to dominate? Is women's liberation part of the larger struggle for a socialist restructuring of society? Or is it *the* issue—the most basic and first form of exploitation of one human by another? Should women's groups, even if not a part of larger organizations, work closely with the New Left? Or must they be independent and work alone? This conflict between socialists and feminists was to be a recurring issue in many groups as the movement grew. The two approaches eventually came to be called *socialist feminism* and *radical feminism.*

---

[31] Kathie Amatniek, "Funeral Oration for the Burial of Traditional Womanhood," *Notes from the First Year,* June 1968.

THE MOVEMENT GROWS

Many people first became aware of the women's liberation movement in September 1968. The Radical Women's protest of the Miss America Contest was the first feminist activity to get front-page coverage. The purpose was to "protest the image of Miss America, an image that oppresses women in every area in which it purports to represent us." A Freedom Trash Can into which to throw "bras, girdles, curlers, false eyelashes, wigs" and other such "woman's garbage" was provided and a sheep was crowned Miss America.[32]

By 1969, women's liberation was getting considerable, if often condescending and inaccurate, publicity. But even before the media discovered the movement, it had begun to spread. During 1968, groups were forming throughout the country. Sometimes they were the result of a specific event; sometimes a woman active in one area moved to another and organized a group; sometimes they just seemed to spring up out of nowhere, amongst women who were unaware of activities elsewhere. The catalyst in the formation of a group in Seattle was a sexist SDS speaker at the University of Washington. "Balling a chick together" is an excellent way of enhancing the political consciousness of poor white youth, he said.[33] Many of the women were active in or dropouts from the New Left. A member of an early San Francisco group explained its origins:

> Some of us had been friends before the group began. We had discussed the problems we had as women. . . . At this time we had heard about women's groups being formed in other parts of the country, but our experience in the "movement" had burned us so badly that anything that hinted of organizing, meetings or objectivity was synonymous with manipulation, rhetoric and ego-trips, so for a long time we didn't seriously consider meeting in any kind of formal way. But finally we did decide to meet.[34]

In August 1968, a meeting of radical women's groups took place in Maryland. Although attendance was small (about 30) and representation was not really national (most of those present were from the East Coast and the Midwest), this was the first attempt at forming a national movement.[35] At Thanksgiving of the same year, a much larger conference was held in Chicago. Over 200 women

[32]Robin Morgan, ed., *Sisterhood Is Powerful* (New York: Vintage, 1970), p. 521.
[33]Hole and Levine, op. cit., p. 120.
[34]Pamela Allen, *Free Space* (Washington, N.J.: Times Change Press, 1970), p. 9.
[35]Hole and Levine, op. cit., p. 122. See also Jo Freeman, *The Politics of Women's Liberation* (New York: McKay, 1975), pp. 106–107.

from across the country and from Canada attended. The conflict between the socialists and the feminists took the form of a debate over the value of consciousness raising. A paper was presented that attempted to formalize and politically justify the technique developed by the New York Radical Women.

While the socialist women had a ready-made ideology that provided an analytic and tactical guide, the feminists had rejected Marxism as inadequate. Most were, in fact, socialists in that they accepted the Marxist critique of capitalism, but they felt that Marxism overemphasized economic determinants and did not provide an adequate analysis of women's subjugation. The feminists had not yet developed an alternate ideology. During the next several years, groups arose that attempted to develop distinctly feminist analyses and tactics.

ORGANIZATION AND IDEOLOGY

In early 1969, several members of the New York Radical Women formed a new group, which they called the Redstockings. Intended by its founders to be specifically feminist and militantly activist, the group immediately became involved in the fight for abortion. In February, the group disrupted state legislative hearings on reform of the laws prohibiting abortion, demanding repeal instead, and the next month it held its own counterhearings.

The thrust of the group, however, changed rather rapidly. A growing commitment to consciousness raising replaced its activism. Redstockings fully developed the theory of consciousness raising, providing an analysis of its uses and purposes. Consciousness raising was likened to the Chinese "speak bitterness" technique—a way of getting one's "personal" problems into the open not in order to adjust but to discover that the problems are, in fact, social and require a collective solution. The Redstocking Manifesto spoke of female *class* consciousness in order to emphasize the political nature of the technique.[36] The value of consciousness raising is now generally accepted by feminists but is seen as a first step to be followed by collective action. The Redstockings, however, turned more and more inward, concentrating on the technique to the exclusion of all else. This eventually led to the group's demise.

The history of the Feminists, another group formed at about the same time as the Redstockings, illustrates some of the other problems the young movement had to confront. At the second annual NOW convention, Ti-Grace Atkinson, president of the New York

[36]Hole and Levine, op. cit., p. 138.

chapter, and some other New York members left the organization after an argument over the decision-making structure of NOW. Atkinson, several NOW members, and some former members of the New York Radical Women formed the October 17th Movement, which was later called the Feminists. The Feminists' objective was to develop a theoretically sound feminist analysis, to work out in practice a new, nonoppressive organizational form, and to take public actions. Their analysis led them to see the source of women's oppression in the male-female role division and to define their goal as the annihilation of sex roles.[37]

Like the Redstockings, the Feminists' first public action was on the abortion issue. In January 1969, they demonstrated at the trial of an abortionist and demanded the repeal of all laws on abortion. To dramatize their position that the family is central to the oppression of women, the Feminists picketed the New York Marriage License Bureau. In a leaflet they distributed, they labeled marriage a "slavery-like practice" and summarized a number of the laws on marriage.[38] They concluded: "We can't destroy the inequalities between men and women until we destroy marriage. *We must free ourselves. And marriage is the place to begin.*"[39]

The group's most original contribution lay in its experiment with internal organization. Atkinson had left NOW over the issue of organizational hierarchy. All hierarchy is oppressive, she contended. "You cannot destroy oppression by filling the position of the oppressor."[40] Participatory democracy and nonhierarchy had been important ideological tenets of the New Left movement, whatever the situation in actual practice. Women's liberation groups, because of the members' often unhappy experiences in the New Left, were even more strongly committed to nonhierarchy. But often an informal leadership would emerge because of the women's differences in experience and skill—or, structureless, the group would flounder, incapable of any action.[41] The Feminists, too, learned that good intentions are not sufficient.

To overcome this problem, the Feminists devised the Lot System and the Disc System. Tasks were divided into creative and word tasks, and two sets of lots were used. Thus no one could draw the same type of job twice in a row. Not only would this sharing of both

[37]Ibid., p. 143.
[38]Morgan, op. cit., p. 536.
[39]Ibid., p. 537.
[40]Quoted in Hole and Levine, op. cit., p. 145.
[41]Morgan, op. cit., p. xxvii.

the fun and the "shit" work foster a better spirit in the group, but everyone would develop skills and expertise.

The Disc System was used to prevent a few members from monopolizing group discussions. Each woman began with a certain number of discs and every time she spoke she used a disc. At the beginning, the results were more humorous than effective. According to the perhaps apocryphal story, everyone used up all her discs within a quarter hour when the system was first used. The second time, the women were overly careful with their discs, and the meeting dragged on in virtual silence. "Gradually, the device worked its way into everyone's consciousness as a symbol for the need to listen to each other, and not interrupt or monopolize the conversation."[42]

The Feminists' commitment to egalitarianism degenerated into "an anti-individualist mania," in the words of a former member.[43] In the summer of 1969, while part of the membership was on vacation, the remainder passed a new set of rules demanding total commitment to the group. Performing one's assignments and attendance at meetings were made compulsory. To further ensure the dedication of the group, it was decided that at any given time no more than one-third of the membership could be living with a man. Both the new rules and the way they were passed led a number of members to quit, leaving the group in the hands of the ultras. In the summer of 1970, Atkinson left the group. She had been criticized for becoming a "star," and rules to prevent such "star making" were passed. Any contact with the media had to be approved by the group and the spokesperson chosen by lot.

In December 1969, the Stanton-Anthony Brigade, the founding unit of the New York Radical Feminists, was formed. Most of its early members were from the Redstockings or Feminists and were determined to avoid these groups' ideological and structural mistakes while incorporating what was useful. The group's manifesto— "Politics of the Ego"—sets forth a clearly feminist position:

> Radical Feminism recognizes the oppression of women as a fundamental political oppression wherein women are categorized as an inferior class based upon their sex. It is the aim of radical feminism to organize politically to destroy this sex class system. We believe that the purpose of male chauvinism is primarily to obtain psychological ego satisfaction, and that only secondarily does this manifest itself in economic relationships. For this reason we do not believe that capitalism, or any other economic system, is the cause of female oppression,

[42]Ibid., p. xxviii.
[43]Reprinted in ibid., p. 440.

nor do we believe that female oppression will disappear as a result of a purely economic revolution.[44]

The early years of the radical movement were very fertile in the development of ideology. Elements of the ideology and the new issues to which the ideology directed women's attention—rape, for example—were to spread to the moderate women's movement. The radical wing was less successful in developing new structures that were both nonhierarchical and effective. Most of the early groups eventually dissolved due to structural problems. Their experimentation did, however, sensitize moderate as well as radical women to the need for conscious struggle with the question.

SOCIALIST FEMINISTS

The problems faced by socialist feminists were somewhat different from those of the radical feminists. They did not need to develop an ideology from scratch; they found Marxism adequate and only needed to apply it to the special problems of women. In Engels' *Origin of the Family, Private Property and the State,* a persuasive explanation of the subordination of women as a result of class society already existed. Marxist theory on the need for a reserve army of labor under capitalism could easily be used to explain the discrimination against women in the labor market.

Where the radical feminists emphasized personal and family oppression of women, the socialist feminists emphasized the economic oppression of women (though they also discussed the social oppression). Where the radical feminists, like Shulamith Firestone, explained the origins of women's oppression in terms of sex differences in strength and in reproductive roles, the socialist feminists pointed to the coming of male predominance in agriculture and the introduction of private property and slavery as the original causes of female subordination. Radical feminists argued the need for revolution to give the female "class" equality with the male, after which socialism might emerge. Socialist feminists claimed that a socialist revolution was the necessary prerequisite to full liberation for women. However, they opposed the dogma of some male socialists that socialism would automatically lead to immediate women's liberation. Therefore they saw the need for a continuing, independent women's movement under both capitalism and socialism. As this brief outline indicates, the socialist feminists believed they had a consistent theory of the origins, present uses, and solution to sexist op-

---

[44]Reprinted in ibid., p. 440.

pression—though they were the first to admit a need for much more elaboration.

Relationships with men in the New Left and with radical feminists were a problem for socialist feminists. Because their ideological stance was close to that of the male-dominated Left, they found it hard to break away. Even after they had formed independent women-only groups, many members still felt psychologically tied to the male Left. The male Left's opinion that feminist activities were bourgeois hung heavy over many groups. Working on feminist issues had to be justified in terms of the greater goal of socialism. For a long time Bread and Roses, an early socialist feminist group, accepted Weathermen positions even when they did not "stem from their own understanding or experience."[45] Radical feminists, because of their bad experiences in the New Left, tended to be suspicious of and disdainful toward socialist feminists. They were afraid that socialist feminists saw the movement only as a recruiting ground for new socialists. Because socialist feminists maintained close ties with the male Left, radical feminists did not consider them feminists at all.

With the decline in the New Left and the growth of the women's movement, socialist feminists gained self-confidence and independence. They no longer felt guilty about working on women's issues. Alliances with other groups could be made when the women thought them useful for their own purposes. They no longer felt they must help leftist groups to prove their socialist credentials. With the change came a new flexibility and creativity. This was expressed by the Hyde Park Chapter of the Chicago Women's Liberation Union in "Socialist Feminism: A Strategy for the Women's Movement," one of the best statements of the nonsectarian, flexible position.

During the early 1970s, autonomous socialist-feminist groups—frequently called women's unions—formed in dozens of cities. These groups were independent not only of mixed Left groups but of one another. No national organization existed, and frequently little communication among the groups took place. A coalition of socialist feminists from the New American Movement, a nonsectarian socialist group with a heavy feminist emphasis, and from some of the autonomous groups in the East and Midwest decided to organize a national socialist feminist conference in 1975.[46] Six to eight hundred women were expected to attend. Even though the lack of a

---

[45]Cellestine Ware, *Woman Power: The Movement for Women's Liberation* (New York: Tower Publications, 1970), p. 67.

[46]Barbara Dudley, for the Berkeley-Oakland Women's Union, "Report on the Conference," *Socialist Revolution* (October–December 1975): 107–116.

communications network among the autonomous women's groups meant that publicity was spotty, over 2000 women came. There were physical facilities for only 1600, so many had to be turned away.

RELATIONS BETWEEN MODERATES AND RADICALS

Despite their differences in analysis and style, the moderate wing and the two radical wings of the movement managed to work together occasionally. The Congress to Unite Women, held in November 1969, brought together over 500 women, both moderate and radical. The groups represented ranged from NOW to the Stanton-Anthony Brigade, from the Women Lawyers—Boston to the Daughters of Bilitis. This disparate group managed to agree on a 10-point set of demands, including nationwide, free 24-hour child-care centers staffed equally by men and women; abortion prohibition repeal; the ERA; and women's studies courses in colleges. It also called for an end to sex role socialization of children, and for equality in education and employment.[47]

Another case of cooperation, as well as an indicator of the movement's strength and appeal, was the massive Women's Strike for Equality. The strike, set for August 26, 1970, the fiftieth anniversary of women's suffrage, was coordinated by NOW, but the participants ranged across the ideological spectrum and included many women who had not been active in the movement before. Three major demands were agreed upon—24-hour child care centers, abortion on demand, and equal opportunity in education and employment. Thousands of women across the country marched and picketed, held rallies and teach-ins. In New York, women set up a child-care center in City Hall Park; in Chicago, sit-ins at restaurants barring women were held. On the West Coast, women were given radio time to discuss women's liberation, and some mayors dedicated the day to equality for women.

Respectable housewives and "hippie" students, secretaries and women lawyers marched together carrying signs that read "Don't Cook Dinner—Starve a Rat Today!" "Eve Was Framed," "End Human Sacrifice! Don't Get Married!!" and "Washing Diapers Is Not Fulfilling."[48]

Despite the strike's undeniable success, the differences within the movement were too great to make joint action possible on a regular basis. The moderate groups were afraid of being identified with

[47]Bird, op. cit., p. 222.
[48]Komisar, op. cit., pp. 125–126.

the "wild, man-hating" rhetoric and tactics of the radical groups. Many radical feminists saw groups like NOW as hopelessly compromised by their establishment membership and ties, as demanding "let us in" rather than "set us free."

On both sides there was considerable ambivalence. Betty Friedan warned NOW that the basic support for the women's movement would come from young women, however alien their style might be. Some radical women felt that both types of organizations were necessary and valuable. "The more we talk about test-tube babies, the more NOW can demand child-care centers and abortion repeal."[49] Others were ambivalent. They knew that organizations like NOW appealed to women who would never join the more radical groups and they believed that much of the work the moderate groups did was valuable. Yet, they feared that, under the influence of these groups, the women's movement might make the same mistake as the suffragists—that of "creating a bourgeois feminist movement that never quite dared enough, never questioned enough, never really reached beyond its own class and race."[50]

Despite the movement's only occasional success at united action and the splits within each wing, it continued to grow and had an effect on the attitudes of many women who were not members of any group.

FURTHER GROWTH AND RESPONSES
The early media treatment of the movement led a few radical women's groups to refuse all contact with media personnel and many to attempt to regulate such contact. The media had created the myth of the bra-burning feminist out of an incident that never occurred. The movement was treated with condescension, usually just for laughs. A member of NOW, a group usually less hostile to the media, explained her reaction to tv coverage of the April 26 strike in which she had participated. "I was shocked how warped it was. . . . My reaction was the media was showing the women's movement as silly."[51]

Women's liberation was news. By the spring of 1970, nearly every major magazine had run a cover story on the movement and the networks had given it prominent attention. By fall of that year, after the strike, 80 percent of a sample of adults knew of the move-

---

[49]Quoted in Hole and Levine, op. cit., p. 92.
[50]Morgan, op. cit., p. xxii.
[51]Honolulu *Advertiser,* July 18, 1973.

ment.[52] The quality of the coverage began gradually to improve—perhaps because of the radical groups' policy of talking only to women reporters, perhaps because, with the growth of the movement, the media grew afraid of offending a significant portion of its audience.

Despite the often biased coverage, the movement was having an effect on women's attitudes. A 1972 poll showed that 48 percent of women favored efforts to strengthen or change women's status in society, while 36 percent opposed such efforts.[53] A poll taken the previous year had found only 40 percent in favor and 42 percent opposed. Support varied, being highest among single women (67 percent) and black women (62 percent); lowest among the widowed (40 percent), the rural (40 percent), and those 50 and older (41 percent). Asked about the effectiveness of organizations trying to change women's status, 43 percent felt that most or some were helping—up from 34 percent the previous year; 44 percent felt that only a few or none were effective, down from 51 percent. Sympathy for women's liberation groups per se still was not high among women generally—39 percent were sympathetic, 49 percent unsympathetic. But among certain groups sympathy was high—62 percent among single women and 67 percent among black women favored it. While a majority of women (60 percent) agreed that picketing and participating in protests was "undignified and unwomanly," an even larger majority (71 percent) felt that "if women don't speak up for themselves and confront men on their real problems, nothing will be done." Thus women generally were awakening, although many were not yet sure about what could and should be done.

Women who had never before been politically active began to discuss women's issues and sometimes to form groups. OWL (Older Women's Liberation) had formed by 1970 and took part in the Second Congress to Unite Women held in that year. Kaffee klatsches in the suburbs turned into consciousness-raising sessions and sometimes into formal groups such as the Croton (New York) Women's Liberation Organization.

Although even today membership in the movement is predominantly young and middle class, it is beginning to penetrate into the working class. Susan Jacoby has described a group in a working-class community of the East Flatbush section of Brooklyn. The women

[52]Hole and Levine, op. cit., p. 269.
[53]All data in the paragraph from Lou Harris and Associates, Inc., *The 1972 Virginia Slims American Women's Opinion Poll.*

were in their forties; most graduated from high school, married soon thereafter, and quickly had children. A woman who did have contacts outside the neighborhood through her volunteer work and who was hearing more and more about the movement suggested setting up a formal consciousness-raising group. She and her three closest friends quickly recruited others from the neighborhood until they had a dozen members.[54]

Following the advice they got from a copy of *Ms.,* the women decided on regular weekly meetings, agreeing that only a true emergency would be allowed to interfere. Despite the objections of many husbands, the women managed to stick to their meetings.

Many of the women had joined because, with their children grown, they saw 20 or 30 empty years ahead of them and had little idea how to fill them. The groups gave some the confidence to try something new. Ruth Levine, who had never held a job, became the first to begin working. Lacking training, she became a file clerk in an advertising agency; but for her this opened the door to a whole new world. When her young co-workers asked why she was working, she told them "because it's better than sitting home and being a vegetable and that they should get themselves some more training or they'll be file clerks 20 years from now, whether they get married or not."[55] The money she brought home was also important. "It makes me feel both that I'm independent and that I'm contributing something to the household." Initially opposed, her husband, a taxi-driver, gradually began to cut down on his 14-hour workday. They spent more time together and their sex life improved. "That little bit of extra money makes a big difference to us. We go to bed together more than we did for the last 10 years," Levine said.

Many of the women reported an improvement in their sex lives. As in so many consciousness-raising groups, sexual problems were a major topic of discussion during the group's early period. Many of the women who had never discussed sex with their husbands found the courage to broach the subject and then found that simply discussing sex could lead to improvement. Masters and Johnson's finding that healthy men and women can and do enjoy sex into their sixties and seventies came as a revelation to many husbands. One woman reported that her husband said, "You know, Rose, we were brought up in ignorance even if we did manage to have four kids. This Masters-Johnson thing you're telling me

---

[54]Riverside, California, *Press Enterprise,* June 17, 1973.
[55]Ibid.

about—I thought a wife would think her husband a dirty old man if he kept trying to take her to bed when they were 50 years old."

These women followed the ideal path for a consciousness-raising group—analysis and then action. Although they could not identify with many of the leaders of the movement ("Gloria Steinem with her streaked hair and slinky figure"), they were concerned about the same issues: child-care centers, equal pay for equal work, the right to abortion and contraceptive information, the need to educate young girls to view themselves as independent human beings and not just as wives and mothers. They attempted to introduce these ideas into the community. One of their specific projects was to provide a health information service for girls and women in their area. A year after its founding, the group took in five new members to replace those who had dropped out because they were too busy with jobs and college courses. "All of the women call that progress," Susan Jacoby reported.[56]

The movement filtered down into the high schools and below. Groups sprung up for consciousness raising and action. Individual girls challenged school policies denying them the right to take shop courses or forcing them to take home economics. A New York girl forced the board of education to desegregate Stuyvesant High School, a highly regarded all-male science school. Girls also protested their exclusion from tennis teams and from participation in other sports. New York State changed its policy in 1971 and began allowing high school girls and boys to compete in noncontact sports. A 16-month experiment revealed that coed participation had no bad effects. Under intense pressure from feminists, even the Little League agreed to admit girls.

Activities on college campuses varied from consciousness-raising groups to abortion referral services, from the establishment of women's centers to ad hoc actions such as the "nude-in" at Grinnell College to protest *Playboy's* portrayal of women. When a *Playboy* representative began to speak on campus, a group of students stripped.[57] He left in embarrassment. Pressure from women students and faculty at many colleges and universities led to the establishment of women's studies courses. By mid-1971, almost 100 colleges offered at least one course for credit on women. Some colleges had set up full-fledged programs; the first was started at San Diego State College in the fall of 1970.

---

[56]Ibid.
[57]Hole and Levine, op. cit., p. 232.

The change in spirit was to be seen everywhere. Women tennis players organized, protesting the much larger amounts of prize money received by men players. Kathy Kusner, an Olympic rider, won her place as the first woman jockey after taking her case to court. Women artists picketed the Whitney Museum, alleging sex discrimination in the selection of works for a show of contemporary American sculptors. Women members of the Washington press corps picketed the Gridiron Club because of its exclusion of women. Colonel Jeanne Holm, director of women in the Air Force and Hester Turner, chair of the Defense Advisory Committee on Women in the Services, spoke out publicly about the treatment of women in the armed services.

LESBIANS

The new feminist movement attracted many lesbians. Oppressed both for their sex and for their sexual preference, such women saw the need for organization and action. They, after all, could not rely on men to support them and thus felt particularly the brunt of job discrimination. Many had rejected the feminine role and had long ago recognized its oppressiveness and absurdity.

At first, lesbians in the movement hid their sexual orientation. They were afraid of being rejected by their straight sisters, who constituted the vast majority, and they were afraid of hurting the movement. In the early years, the taunt of lesbian had often been used against women's liberationists. At that time, everyone seems to have believed that if the women's movement became tainted with lesbianism, it would be destroyed. With increasing gay consciousness and the growth of the gay liberation movement, lesbians active in women's groups became less willing to stay in the closet. "Why, in a movement dedicated to the liberation of all women, must we hide our sexual orientation?" they asked. Equal rights for lesbians should be a demand of the women's movement. With this change in attitudes and this new militancy, the issue could no longer be swept under the rug. How the lesbians' demands were to be received was to be a test of the movement. Was it to remain dedicated to the liberation of all women, or would it abandon some of its sisters whenever politically expedient?

In some groups and areas, a gradual change in attitude took place, and lesbian demands were incorporated without bitter battles. In others, the issue proved extremely divisive. New York NOW was almost destroyed by internal struggles over lesbian demands. Betty Friedan had always opposed any recognition of the lesbian issue, calling it the "lavender herring." NOW had, however, never barred lesbians from membership and had allowed at least one lesbian couple to join at the reduced "couple rate."

In 1969, Rita Mae Brown joined New York NOW and became very active. She refused to hide her lesbianism and spoke out on homosexual oppression. Considerable pressure was applied, and in January 1970 she resigned, saying "Lesbianism is the one word which gives the New York N.O.W. Executive Committee a collective heart attack."[58] At the national level, the issue was also heating up. The national director who had supported the lesbians' demands was forced out of office. A gay feminist group was formed in response to these events. Rita Mae Brown called a meeting to discuss sexism within the movement. From this group, which was later to call itself the Radicalesbians, came the position paper, "The Woman-Identified Woman."

In 1970, the lesbians decided to force the movement to confront the issue at the second Congress to Unite Women. On Friday night, when congress participants were all assembled in a large hall, the lights suddenly went out. When they were turned on again, 20 lesbians wearing "Lavender Menace" T-shirts were at the front of the hall. They spoke of their oppression both within and outside the movement and invited sympathetic members of the audience to join them. One of the women who spoke was a member of the scheduled panel. It was the first time Kate Millett talked about her bisexuality. Reactions among straight women were varied. Some felt that an important issue had finally been brought out into the open; others were dismayed and felt that the congress had been destroyed.

A few feminists did begin speaking to lesbian groups. Ti-Grace Atkinson made a rather ambivalent speech to the Daughters of Bilitis (DOB), an older lesbian organization. Caroline Bird, after at first refusing, spoke very positively. Many NOW members still hoped they would be able to contain the issue. A candidate for the presidency of NOW spoke to DOB members, telling them they were welcome so long as they were not openly homosexual. When the mass media got into the act, however, containment proved impossible.

At a Columbia University Forum on Sexual Liberation, a lesbian challenged Kate Millett to openly declare her bisexuality. Ms. Millett did so. A *Time* reporter with a tape recorder was in the audience. On December 8, 1970, *Time* printed a vicious attack on Ms. Millett and on the movement. Under the title, "Women's Lib: A Second

---

[58]Quoted in Sidney Abbott and Barbara Love, *Sappho Was a Right-On Woman* (New York: Stein and Day, 1973), p. 112. The following account is based on the excellent discussion in Abbott and Love.

Look," the article said that Millett's admission of bisexuality had ". . . contributed to the growing skepticism about the movement." It also claimed, "The disclosure is bound to discredit her as a spokeswoman for her cause, cast further doubt on her theories, and reinforce the views of those skeptics who routinely dismiss all liberationists as Lesbians."[59]

Such an attack could not go unanswered. A lesbian woman persuaded the Women's Strike Coalition to make support for Millett part of a march already planned in New York. On December 12, 1970, both gay and straight women marched wearing lavender arm bands handed out by the president of New York NOW. The leaflet handed out to members and to the press explained the crux of the issue as well as it has ever been explained:

> It is not one woman's sexual preference that is under attack—it is the freedom of *all women* to openly state values that fundamentally challenge the basic structure of patriarchy. If they succeed in scaring us with words like "dyke" or "Lesbian" or "bisexual," they'll have won AGAIN. They'll have divided us, AGAIN. . . . *Time* Magazine wants us to run scared, disown Kate and all our gay sisters. . . . That's why we're all wearing lavender Lesbian armbands today—to show we all stand together as women. . . . They can call us all Lesbians until such time as there is no stigma attached to women loving women.[60]

Gay and straight women found they could work together openly. Yet the media completely ignored the event. Something further had to be done. On December 17, 1971, a press conference was held. Its purpose was to show movement support for Millett. Movement luminaries like Ti-Grace Atkinson, Gloria Steinem, and Florynce Kennedy participated. Bella Abzug and NOW National President Aileen Hernandez sent supporting statements. This cast was too much for the media to ignore. Press coverage was extensive and fair, and media lesbian-baiting decreased.

Within NOW the controversy still raged. At the national level, the executive committee attempted to come to a decision. An angry closed session disclosed that the committee was split almost evenly, and no decision was reached. The New York NOW elections of 1971 turned into a dirty political brawl with accusations of lesbianism used as weapons. A woman who had shown sympathy toward lesbians was, in effect, purged.[61]

[59]"Women's Lib: A Second Look," *Time,* December 8, 1970, p. 121.
[60]Quoted in Abbott and Love, op. cit., p. 122.
[61]Ibid., p. 127.

In other parts of the country, change came much more smoothly. In April 1971, the West Coast regional membership passed a resolution demanding acceptance of lesbians and lesbianism. They voted to present their resolution to the full NOW membership in the fall. Other chapters also had come to terms with the problem and were prepared to bring it up at the convention.

The fifth annual conference of NOW, held in Los Angeles in September 1971, passed a strongly worded prolesbian resolution. There was no bitter floor fight, and the vote was nearly unanimous. The resolution recognized and admitted NOW's culpability:

> Afraid of alienating public support, we have often treated lesbians as the step-sisters of the movement, allowed to work with us, but then expected to hide in the upstairs closet when company comes. Lesbians are now telling us that this attitude is no longer acceptable. Asking women to disguise their identities so they will not "embarrass" the group is an intolerable form of oppression, like asking black women to join us in white face.

It then resolved:

> That NOW recognizes the double oppression of women who are lesbians,
> That a woman's right to her own person includes the right to define and express her own sexuality and to choose her own lifestyle,
> That NOW acknowledges the oppression of lesbians as a legitimate concern of feminism.[62]

THIRD WORLD WOMEN

Although a few Third World women participated in the women's liberation movement from the beginning, the movement was predominantly white and middle class. How to get more Third World women involved was a constant topic of conversation in women's groups. Socialist feminists concerned about building a class movement were especially worried about their white, middle-class membership.

Many black and Chicana women were repelled by the racial and class composition of the women's movement. Especially during the early years, they felt that they had little in common with movement women and that the movement did not attack problems of central concern to them. In class and color, movement women looked too much like "Miss Ann," the employer and oppressor of the black

---

[62]Fifth Annual Conference of the National Organization for Women, Los Angeles, September 3–6, 1971, *Revolution: From the Doll's House to the White House* (a report from NOW to its membership), pp. 15–16.

woman domestic. Even when militant Third World women became aware that they were playing the traditional subservient feminine role in black or Chicano liberation groups, racial or ethnic loyalty often kept them from public revolt.

The first feminist protest by radical minority women occurred in the Student Non-Violent Coordinating Committee. In 1964, Ruby Doris Robinson, a black woman, presented a paper protesting women's role in the organization. The men's violent reaction, however, made it clear that women would have to choose between feminism, which was labeled bourgeois, and black liberation. At that time the men were not willing to incorporate feminist demands into their basic program. Many Third World women still feel that they must choose—they can either become feminists or support their brothers. They must decide whether their basic identity is racial or sexual. Most have chosen to work within the black or Chicano movements.

But ideological tendencies within parts of the black movement eventually led many black women to decide that a black feminist movement was necessary. Black women found that too many black men were blaming them for their situation. Black matriarchy and the "castration" of the black male by the black female became accepted tenets of "revolutionary" rhetoric. Black men were telling their women to take a subordinate position so as to build up the damaged black male ego. In effect, women were being told that the black liberation movement could succeed only at their expense.

Some black men had swallowed basic tenets of white establishment ideology, which they believed they had rejected *in toto.* The black woman who was economically and socially oppressed for both her sex and her race, who made less money and was more frequently unemployed than the black man, yet who frequently had to rear her children alone, was seen as a problem, not a sister. She was called an ugly black bitch for not looking and acting white, a castrating bitch for having the strength that made her and her children's survival possible. According to Cellestine Ware, a black woman and a founder of New York Radical Feminists, "it is the fear and anxiety of the black male that led to the construction of the 'evil' black female. By now, the superstructure of the 'black bitch' bears as little relation to the real black woman as any myth to the reality."[63]

The black movement's position on birth control and abortion disturbed many women. Male radicals charged that white America planned genocide. Forced sterilization and the availability of birth control and abortions were all part of the plan. Black women should

[63]Cellestine Ware, "Black Feminism," *Notes From the Third Year,* 1973, p. 25.

refuse to use the pill; they should breed and rear warriors for the revolution. Many black women agreed with the analysis, but not with the recommendation. The "no pill/have-kids/mess-up-the-man's-plan notion" is oversimplified, they charged.[64] "Seems to me the Brother does us all a great disservice by telling her to fight the man with the womb. Better to fight with the gun and the mind."[65]

Many black women felt that neither the white women's movement nor the male-dominated black movement addressed some of their basic concerns. A black woman's organization was the obvious solution, but because women feared that such a group would be considered divisive, it was not until 1973 that a national group was formed. In August 1973, 30 black women, all of whom had been active in the women's movement, formed the National Black Feminist Organization. Margaret Sloan, NBFO chairwoman, explained, "We decided we needed a group of black women to come out and say 'We're here, we understand feminism—it's okay.' "[66]

The group's membership grew to over 1000 by the end of 1973. Four hundred women attended its first convention in December of that year. The organization then decided to admit only black women, but to work with both the women's and the black movements. Keynote speaker Shirley Chisholm brought up one issue—that of stereotypes. "One of the cruelest labels has been that the black woman is a matriarch. First society forces her into that condition, then it criticizes her for it. Black women had to have strength and power to survive, but their strength is no sign of liberation, nor do they have power in terms of society."[67]

Black feminists' priorities differ somewhat from those of the white movement. A minimum wage for domestics and safeguarding the rights and improving the position of welfare mothers are high on the list. According to Eleanor Homes Norton, formerly New York City Commissioner on Human Rights, "what the women's movement as a whole badly needs is a black nuance and nuances from Spanish-speaking women. The movement will only be truly sensitive to them when they join up." Black and white feminists do agree on most basic issues. Child care is, for example, considered a priority by both.

The increasing cooperation between civil rights and women's

[64]Toni Cade, "The Pill: Genocide or Liberation?" in Cade, ed., *The Black Woman* (New York: Signet, 1970), p. 168.

[65]Ibid., p. 167.

[66]*Newsweek,* December 17, 1973.

[67]Shirley Chisolm, quoted in ibid.

groups at the national level and in a number of states has eased the position of black feminists. Sensitized to discrimination by their own experiences, black men have often been more receptive to feminist concerns than white men. But friction does arise. Women were outraged when some black Illinois legislators voted against ratification of the ERA for rather convoluted political reasons. Generally, however, black legislators have been supportive of women's issues. Because many problems affect both women and minorities, feminist and civil rights groups often work together in lobbying. As a result, black feminists are less likely to feel torn between their racial and sexual loyalties.

Like black women, Chicanas have experienced inner conflicts trying to contend with both ethnic and sexual discrimination. They must worry that if they fight for their rights as women, they may be abandoning the struggle of their people as a whole. Chicanas have responded in diverse ways. Some work in mixed community service organizations; others, in all-Chicana groups; still others in Chicana caucuses within Anglo women's groups.

Southern California, with its large Mexican-American population, is in the forefront of the Chicana movement. Comision Femenil Mexicana Nacional, one of the earliest Chicana organizations, now has 16 chapters in California and a handful in other states.[68] The Chicana Service Action Center, one of the organization's projects, provides job training for about 500 women a year and operates a child-care center and a shelter for battered women. Las Mujeres for Political Action is an informal group of politically active Chicanas which lobbies for legislation and pressures government for the appointment of Chicanas. Two Chicana chapters of the National Women's Political Caucus have been formed in the Los Angeles area. At the national level, the Mexican-American Women's National Association tries to provide some overall coordination, though this has not been easy. Women have become more prominent in some of the older and traditionally male-dominated organizations. Vilma Martinez heads the Mexican-American Legal Defense and Education Fund. That influential organization now has a Chicana Rights Project, which is directed by a woman.

UNION WOMEN

The class composition of the women's movement is slowly beginning to change. Working-class women's lack of interest in the movement seems to have been due to several distinct factors—their greater ac-

---

[68]*Los Angeles Times,* September 23, 1981.

ceptance of sexist ideology, lack of time, and the perception that the movement did not address their special problems. In working-class families, sex role socialization tends to be even more intense than in middle-class ones. The effect on attitudes can be seen in a 1973 survey.[69] Noncollege women were less likely than college women to believe that women are discriminated against (42 and 63 percent, respectively, felt they were); noncollege women were less likely than college women to agree that the statement "women's place is in the home" was nonsense (47 percent to 64 percent). Because most working-class women are employed and are also solely responsible for the housework, time is always a problem. Furthermore, the women's movement has been perceived as alien and radical. "Women's libbers" have been seen as "women who want to be men" or as persons advocating sexual promiscuity.

Nevertheless, the women's movement does seem to have had an effect on working-class women. Union women especially are becoming aware of job discrimination and are determined to do something about it. In March 1974, over 3000 women members of 58 labor unions met in Chicago and formed the Coalition of Labor Union Women (CLUE).[70] Olga Madar, vice-president of the United Automobile Workers and an active feminist, was elected president. The organization's objectives include fighting sexism within unions as well as in society at large. It encourages unions to place a greater emphasis on organizing unorganized women, to give women a greater policy-making role within the union, and to be more aggressive in fighting job discrimination. The women have also worked for child-care legislation, an increased minimum wage law, ratification of the ERA, and the extension of protective laws to men.

By 1982, CLUE's membership had grown to 16,000 and its efforts had born some fruit.[71] The organization has chosen a nonconfrontationist stance with respect to the AFL-CIO. Although some feminists considered this strategy a recipe for ineffectualness, it has had some payoffs. CLUE persuaded the AFL-CIO to reverse its stance on the ERA. Due, in part, to CLUE prodding, the AFL-CIO has thrown its very considerable sophistication and resources into lobbying for women's issues such as the pregnancy disability bill. Unions with large female memberships have been promoting women and hiring

---

[69]Study by Daniel Yankelovich, reported in Riverside, California, *Daily Enterprise,* June 3, 1974.
[70]Riverside, California, *Daily Enterprise,* April 3, 1974.
[71]*Los Angeles Times,* January 5, 1982.

more women organizers.[72] In 1980, the AFL-CIO paid for and cosponsored with CLUE a conference on organizing women. Also in 1980, the AFL-CIO Executive Council voted to expand representation of women and minorities by waiving the tradition requiring that council members be general officers of affiliated unions. That year Joyce Miller, president of CLUE, was elected to the Executive Council.[73] In the last few years, the labor movement has become significantly more sensitive to feminists' concerns. CLUE can claim at least a little of the credit for that.

Only about 12 percent of employed women are members of labor unions. Since women who are union members make about a third more than those who are not and receive better fringe benefits as well, unionization is a potentially fruitful strategy for increasing women's pay.[74] CLUE and the AFL-CIO are involved in attempting to organize women. The most exciting development, however, is the agreement recently reached by Working Women, a feminist group which is the largest organization of women office workers, and the Service Employees International Union (SEIU), the seventh largest labor union in the United States. The two groups created a new nationwide union, District 925, to organize office workers. Karen Nussbaum, founder and executive director of Working Women, said the agreement represents "a new chapter in labor history, a partnership between the women's movement and the trade union movement."[75] SEIU will provide the money, while both organizations will supply the needed expertise. Nussbaum will remain executive director of Working Women as well as become acting president of District 925 and chair of the District 925 Organizing Committee.[76] If this effort is even partially successful, it will represent one of the most significant accomplishments of the women's movement.

WOMEN AND THE CHURCH

The world's major religions have played a role in preserving women's subordinate status. Founded at a time when women's social position was vastly inferior, they have continued to reflect an earlier social reality. Women were excluded from the priesthood by the Catholic and Episcopalian churches and by some Protestant sects. Among Orthodox Jews, women are still segregated physically

[72]*Nation,* November 17, 1979, p. 492.
[73]*AFL-CIO Federationist,* April 1980, p. 8.
[74]Ibid, p. 3.
[75]*Los Angeles Times,* March 6, 1981.
[76]*Spokeswoman,* April 1981, p. 4.

in the synagogue and are not counted in the *minyan,* the quorum of 10 needed for a service.

The development of feminist consciousness led women to question church practices and to attempt to change them. "Church authorities, usually entirely male, have misused the Bible to reinforce their prejudices against women," charged Virginia Mills, a member of the United Presbyterian Task Force on Women.[77] Nuns formed a liberation group and demanded freedom from domination by priests. The publication of a new Roman Catholic missal supposedly extending women's rights within the church received a sharp reaction from NOW's Ecumenical Task Force on Women and Religion. The missal stated that women could read the Bible and act as lectors during mass, but only when there were no men available—and women could not stand within the altar rail, as men did. The Task Force burned the missal and sent its ashes, tied with a pink ribbon, to the president of the American bishops.

On August 27, 1973, a group of Hawaiian women calling themselves the Ad Hoc Committee for Equal Rites for Women protested in front of Our Lady of Peace Cathedral in Honolulu. On the day proclaimed Women's Rights Day by the governor, the biblical passage used for the prescribed second reading was Ephesians 5:21–32, which reads in part: "Wives be subject to your husbands, as to the Lord. For the husband is the head of the wife as Christ is head of the Church. . . . As the Church is subject to Christ, so let wives also be subject in everything to their husbands. . . ." Reactions to the protest were mixed. "It's a good example of liberation in action," one female parishioner said. "I wouldn't want one of my grandchildren out there," another responded. The church hierarchy attempted to defend itself, claiming that the women were misinterpreting the passage. Bishop Scanlan's defense that the Catholic church had exalted women "more than any organization that ever existed" showed, however, that there was no real understanding of the women's point. Ms. Leopold, the organizer of the protest, had the last word. According to newspaper reports, a priest attempting to end a discussion with her said, "God bless you." "Thank you," Ms. Leopold replied, "She will."[78]

Women have demanded the right to become priests, rabbis, and ministers. In most Protestant denominations there are no formal barriers, but finding a church willing to accept a woman minister is still difficult. As late as 1975, only 2 percent of all ministers were

[77]Komisar, op. cit., p. 139.
[78]Honolulu *Advertiser,* August 26 and September 1, 1973.

women.[79] The first woman reform rabbi was ordained in 1972, and over 30 others have been ordained since.[80] Jewish feminists have also gotten some changes in ritual.[81] More congregations now allow women to receive *aliyahs* (the honor of blessing the Torah) and count women in the *minyan.* The *bar mitzvah,* the celebration of a boy's coming of age, is increasingly being extended to girls.

The most intense and well-publicized conflict over women's right to serve as priests took place in the Episcopal church. Under pressure from feminists, the church's general convention voted to allow women to be ordained as deacons in 1970. In 1973, a proposal to ordain women priests was voted down. Feminists and sympathetic priests decided some dramatic move was needed. In July 1974, 4 bishops ordained 11 women as priests. Because the ordination was unauthorized, the House of Bishops voted to censure the bishops who had taken part. The publicity attendant upon these proceedings resulted in a great deal of support both for the unofficially ordained women and for the prowomen bishops. In 1976, the church reversed its 1973 position and voted for the ordination of women. Since then, more than 40 women have become Episcopal priests.[82]

Roman Catholic feminists have had considerably less success in changing their church's centuries-old practices. Feminist agitation for women priests seems to have precipitated Pope Paul's declaration reaffirming the traditionalist view. The declaration said:

> The same natural resemblance is required for persons as for things; when Christ's role in the Eucharist is to be expressed sacramentally, there would not be this natural resemblance which must exist between Christ and his minister if the role of Christ were not taken by a man; in such a case it would be difficult to see in the minister the image of Christ. For Christ himself was and remains a man.[83]

The Vatican statement was intended to cut off the debate, but it has not done so. The arguments used were not persuasive to groups such as the National Coalition of American Nuns and the National Assembly of Women Religious, which continued to push for the ordination of women.

Recently, Pope John Paul II has reiterated the Catholic church's traditional notions about women. The Pope's vocal opposition to

[79]*Newsweek,* October 13, 1975.
[80]*Washington Post,* September 25, 1981.
[81]*Newsweek,* May 31, 1976.
[82]Riverside, California, *Daily Enterprise,* September 16 and 17, 1976.
[83]Quoted in *Los Angeles Times,* January 28, 1977.

abortion, divorce, homosexuality, and the ordination of women during his visit to the United States in 1979 led the NOW workshop on Women and Religion to suggest a resolution stating, "Sexism is a Sin" and urging the Pope and the U.S. Catholic hierarchy to repent.[84] This Pope's statements, like those of his predecessor, are less likely to still the debate than they are to convince some women to leave the church.

Not only are women fighting for equality within the church structure, but a feminist theology is beginning to emerge. "Patriarchal religion emphasizes guilt, judgment, and death rather than love, joy, and life-giving attributes of God,"[85] which are at the heart of feminist theology. Mary Daly, a leading feminist theologian, has called on women to leave the patriarchal church, which she believes is beyond reform, and to form an antichurch of their own based on sisterhood.[86]

WOMEN'S STUDIES

The rising feminist consciousness quite naturally created a demand for women's studies programs in universities. Movement women realized that they knew very little about woman—about female sexuality and psychology, about women's history and literature. The college curriculum, designed by men and largely taught by men, sets up male culture as the standard and frequently ignores the female completely.

Using the black experience as an example, feminists pushed for women's studies courses and programs. Perhaps because administrators did not want to repeat the often bitter battles that had preceded the acceptance of black studies, success came relatively quickly. San Diego State College set up the first women's studies program in 1970. By the beginning of 1974, women's studies programs were functioning at 78 institutions, and about 2000 courses were being offered on another 500 campuses.[87] The number continued to increase throughout the 1970s. There are now about 350 women's studies programs on college campuses and another 600 institutions offer at least 25 women's studies courses. All together, about 20,000 women's studies courses exist nation-

---

[84]Riverside, California, *Daily Enterprise,* October 10, 1979.

[85]Gayle Kimball, "Feminist Theology," in Kimball, ed., *Women's Culture* (Metuchen, N.J.: Scarecrow Press, 1981), p. 232.

[86]Ibid., p. 233.

[87]*Newsweek,* December 10, 1973.

wide.[88] Although the progress has been slow, some of what is taught in these courses is beginning to penetrate precollege education.

In 1972, the *Women's Studies Newsletter* was begun to serve as a communications channel among feminist educators. The National Women's Studies Association was formed in 1977.

The last decade has seen a flowering of feminist scholarship. The early teachers of women's studies had difficulty finding sufficient published materials to use in their courses, now the problem is keeping up with and, in survey courses, choosing among the wide variety available. In all the disciplines of the social sciences and the humanities, feminists are at work asking new questions and providing new answers to old ones. This work is being published in book form, in the increasing number of feminist scholarly journals such as *Signs* and *Feminist Studies,* and, to some extent, in traditional scholarly journals. Feminist scholars still face difficulties. Some of their male colleagues may not take their work seriously or give it as much weight in tenure and promotion decisions as they would more traditional work. Still, progress has been considerable. The Schlesinger Library at Radcliffe, which is devoted to the history of women in America, has become one of the busiest research centers on campus, and throughout the country the number of university professors who specialize in women's history has grown to several thousand.[89] The psychology of women has become one of the most active research subfields in psychology. Recently, a journal devoted to women and politics began publication.

Most feminists agree that the purpose of women's studies is not just to teach about women but to prepare women to change society. This activist thrust dictates a close relationship between the women's studies programs and the movement. Ideally, the program should serve all university women—secretaries, cafeteria workers, and faculty wives, as well as students and community women. The program should serve as a mobilizing device. Given the broad constituency to which the programs try to address themselves and the movement's emphasis on nonhierarchy, the question of administrative structure has frequently caused problems. University administrators are less than friendly to nonstructured programs in which no one is in charge. Thus most women's studies programs have set up a coordinating board or committee with representation from faculty, students, and sometimes staff. Involvement of community women has been spotty.

[88] Florence Howe, quoted in Riverside, California, *Daily Enterprise,* January 4, 1981.
[89] *Los Angeles Times,* January 4, 1982.

Feminists criticized traditional education not just because of its course content, but also for its structure. The usual relationship between student and instructor is characterized by sharp differentiation of roles and of power. In such a situation students are, in effect, passive objects to be acted upon by the instructor. Emphasis on objectivity, on learning the material that is given to one, guarantees that the student will keep academic knowledge and her own life experiences separated. To break out of this sterile, power-dominated form of education, feminists have deemphasized lectures and have used small-group discussions as much as possible. Team teaching—in which both students and faculty are involved as instructors—is used, especially in beginning classes. Students are encouraged to work together on projects to break down the competitive feelings the educational system fosters. Students in advanced classes often do original research in the library and in the field, and thus add to knowledge of the female experience. There are still many experiments to be tried. But in providing participatory, noncoercive education, women's studies has been more successful than traditional programs.

The relationship of women's studies to the university has raised problems to which no ideal solution has yet been found. In some colleges, the women's studies "program" consists of courses on women given within the traditional departments. Under this arrangement, feminists have no control over staffing or course content. Women's studies programs set up as separate units do have greater autonomy. Control over hiring is usually far from complete, but the program board at least has considerable say and finds it easier to hire women who are not "qualified" according to traditional criteria. Community women without the necessary degrees but with valuable experience are sometimes used as part-time instructors. The independent program makes experimentation much more feasible. Unfortunately, autonomy may result in isolation and vulnerability. The existence of an independent women's studies program may take pressure off the traditional departments to hire feminists. Such a program can be easily dismissed as academically unsound, composed of a bunch of kooky females, and, when financial adversity hits the college, easily cut. The innovative and highly successful program at SUNY/Buffalo found itself in this position in 1972. Because it had established close working relationships with other units on campus, however, it came out of the struggle in good shape.[90] At present,

[90]Christine Grahl et al., "Women's Studies: A Case in Point," *Feminist Studies* 1, no. 2 (fall 1972).

women's studies programs need allies if they are to survive and grow.

Some women have decided that the compromises necessary to stay on campus are not worth the results and have started independent feminist liberation schools. Breakaway in Berkeley, for example, has declined to affiliate even with a free or people's school: "The only way we can learn without intimidation, inhibition, and frustration is from and with each other. Women must have their own school where they can meet together in a warm, supportive atmosphere to share experiences and knowledge."[91] Breakaway has offered courses on everything from "Women Over Thirty" and "Women Who Are Coming Out" to karate, carpentry, and auto mechanics. The student body is fairly heterogeneous—composed of students, housewives, and other women.

Whether independent or within the university, women's studies courses usually reach students who already have some feminist awareness. Those who need the exposure most are least likely to get it. Integrating feminist material into traditional courses is the only way of ensuring that all students get some exposure. It is for this reason that the growing respectability of feminist scholarship is important. Wheaton College has recently made the first effort to remove sexism from all aspects of its coursework and curriculum and integrate the new feminist scholarship. The process will not be easy and has already met with resistance from some faculty. President Alice Emerson and provost Ruth Schmidt, however, are committed to a basic reorientation—"not adding courses but transforming courses."[92] This is an effort worth watching; it may provide a model for the future.

FEMINISTS IN PRINT

In March 1968, Jo Freeman and other Chicago feminists began putting out *Voices of the Women's Liberation Movement.* The little newsletter—only six mimeographed pages—was the first modern feminist publication.[93] As the women's movement grew and more and more small groups formed across the country, so did the need for a means of communication. Many of the women who were active in the movement used their experience with New Left underground publications to begin newsletters and journals across the country. By 1971, over 100 were being published; by 1977, both

[91]Quoted in Kirsten Grimstad and Susan Rennie, eds., *The New Women's Survival Catalog* (New York: Coward-McCann, 1973), p. 123.

[92]*Los Angeles Times,* November 13, 1981.

[93]Hole and Levine, op. cit., p. 270.

the number of publications and their circulation had increased many times over.

Feminist publications range from local newsletters in mimeo form to slick magazines with national distributions. The focus of these publications vary too, including coverage of the movement locally and nationally, legal developments, personal testimonials, theoretical articles, and, frequently, feminist fiction and poetry. Some of these publications are one-woman enterprises; a few are run along traditional lines. Most are put out by groups of women who share all the tasks, menial as well as creative, as equally as possible.

In recent years, the number of special-interest feminist journals has increased greatly. *Signs: A Journal of Women in Culture and Society* and *Feminist Studies* are scholarly journals. *Calyx* is devoted to art and literature by women. *Quest* focuses on feminist political analysis and ideological development. *Spokeswoman* provides current information on developments in law and politics that especially concern women. *Working Woman* is oriented toward employed women. *Feminist Periodicals,* published bimonthly by the University of Wisconsin at Madison, is a review of current feminist periodicals.

The financial success story among feminist publications is *Ms.* magazine. In 1972 a group of women with publishing experience decided a feminist magazine that would reach nonmovement women was needed. Substantial financial backing was required if the magazine was to have a national circulation and look respectable. Such backing was not easy to find; people who controlled sufficient funds were convinced there was no market for such a publication. Finally *New York* magazine was persuaded to put out a sample issue. The 300,000 copies of the sample were sold out in 8 days. The women editors were left without enough copies to honor their promises for free ones.[94] Regular publication was begun in July 1972. By October 1973, *Ms.* had a monthly circulation of 350,000 and a 70 percent renewal rate.[95] With the magazine doing so well, the women have branched out into television, books, and records. Marlo Thomas's record for children, "Free To Be . . . You and Me," was produced by *Ms.* and was an instant hit, selling 95,000 copies.[96]

Within the more radical segment of the movement, sentiments toward *Ms.* have been mixed. The sexist advertising run in the sample issue appalled most feminists. The women who put out the sam-

[94]See "A Personal Report," *Ms.* 1 (July 1972).
[95]*Newsweek,* October 15, 1973.
[96]Ibid.

ple, however, had no control over advertising in that issue. Since becoming an independent publication, they have refused the worst sort of advertising. Virginia Slims ("You've Come a Long Way Baby") has repeatedly attempted and failed to get its ads accepted, even though Billie Jean King has spoken for them. Nevertheless, sexism is so ingrained in our society that a totally pure policy is not possible. Ads offensive to feminists still appear in *Ms.* To their credit, the editors print letters criticizing their choices and attempt to take such criticism into account. There has been criticism, both amongst *Ms.*'s staff and from the feminist community, on content as well. Not enough space is devoted to the problems of blue-collar women, Third World women, and lesbians, it has been charged. The magazine is not radical enough; it reflects a middle-class bias.

Despite such criticism, most feminists would agree that, on balance, *Ms.* has been a good influence. *Ms.* is reaching women who wouldn't be caught dead reading *Ain't I A Woman?* or *No More Fun and Games.* According to Onka Dekker, writing in *Off Our Backs,*

> *Ms.* is making feminist converts of middle class heathens from academia to condominium-ville. A slick, reputable-looking magazine breaks down defenses and lets the word worm its way into the brain. *Ms.* is almost in violation of Truth in Packaging laws. There is a female mind-set on those glossy pages slipping into American homes concealed in bags of groceries like tarantulas on banana boats. . . . Curious girl children will accidentally discover feminism in *Ms.* the way we stumbled onto sex in our mother's *Ladies Home Journal.*[97]

From newsletters and magazines, feminists expanded into books—not just writing them but publishing them as well. A number of feminist presses are in operation, turning out beautifully printed and inexpensive feminist works. Diana Press, Inc., is owned and operated by three women. It grew out of an ideologically heterogeneous women's collective. One of the owners explains: "The name, Diana Press, for example, was agreed upon as a compromise between those who wanted to commemorate weatherwoman Diana Oughton and others who viewed Diana as a symbol of ancient woman's culture."[98] Diana Press operates both as a publisher and as a commercial printshop, in which capacity it has done much work for women's groups.

---

[97]Quoted in Grimstad and Rennie, op. cit., p. 35.
[98]Quoted in ibid., p. 9.

The Feminist Press of Old Westbury, New York, was a pioneer in the publication of nonsexist children's books. In addition to its substantial list of adult and children's books, it publishes a women's studies newsletter. Since no nationally organized women's studies association existed until recently, the newsletter provided a much-needed communication channel among feminists involved with women's studies around the country.

Among women's presses, KNOW, Inc. is unique and has become an institution of the movement. Members of Pittsburgh NOW founded the press in the fall of 1969 to reprint movement articles for use at local NOW meetings. When word got around, KNOW discovered there was a great need for such reprints and decided that the press could support itself by selling them at slightly over cost.[99] The demand proved so great that KNOW found it could actually pay a staff member. By late 1973, the press was run by six full-time and four part-time staffers, who work as a collective. KNOW's vice-president was formerly a typical housewife whose husband never wanted her to work. "He still looks at me in amazement some days," she says. "I just say to him—'You're not Vice-President of your company.'"[100] KNOW's list includes some 200 articles and pamphlets, some full-length books, and a Female Studies series that consists of course syllabi and essays on women's studies.

This outpouring of feminist literature made it possible for women's bookstores to spring up across the country. The typical feminist bookstore is a place to meet other women, discuss literature, and find out what's going on around town. Browsing is encouraged; comfortable chairs and hot coffee are often provided. The women who work there are not "hired help" but committed feminists ready to help the beginner find what to start with, or discuss feminist theory with the experienced.

Most women's bookstores carry a wide selection of feminist literature—nonfiction from both standard and feminist presses, novels by women past and present, a full range of feminist periodicals, and a section of nonsexist children's books. Most also have a bulletin board where news of movement events is posted.

In addition, feminist literature is becoming easier to find in traditional bookstores. Such stores have always carried the big best-sellers such as Kate Millet's *Sexual Politics* and Susan Brownmiller's *Against Our Will.* But now more and more traditional bookstores have entire sections devoted to women's books. The selection is

[99]Ibid., p. 10.
[100]Quoted in ibid.

much more restricted here than in women's bookstores—some of the books included in these sections would make a feminist blanch. Still, these developments do indicate that feminist works are more available to the general public than ever before.

THE MEN'S MOVEMENT

Very slowly and sporadically, a feminist men's movement has begun to develop. The lives of many men have been affected by the women's movement. Men living with committed feminists have been most affected. Many relationships have broken up because men could not adjust to the changes the women were going through, but in other instances, men have altered their attitudes and behavior in response. Because the movement has influenced the attitudes and expectations even of women who do not consider themselves feminists, their men have also been affected.

Because of their ideological stances, some men have become intellectually as well as personally committed to feminism. Although in the 1960s and early 1970s the Left had been resistant to feminism, by the mid-1970s under pressure from their women members, most left groups had changed their stance. Some men, when exposed to feminist analysis, began to see the costs of adoptioning the male role in a patriarchical society. Warren Farrell's *The Liberated Male* and Herb Goldberg's *The Hazards of Being Male,* which examined those costs, carried the message beyond the small circle of men familiar with early feminist works. Some men, who were emotionally committed to feminists, realized that their relationships were doomed if they did not change.

Men learned, just as women had earlier, that real personal change was not easy. Habits of thought and behavior ingrained since childhood could not be altered simply by one day making an intellectual decision to do so. For those men who were truly committed to changing, the solution has been the same as for movement women— the consciousness-raising group. The first known men's consciousness-raising group was set up in 1972 by Jane Wagner for the male partners of NOW members.[101] Since then and especially in the late 1970s many more have formed. The men's movement is certainly not a mass movement. Still it does seem to be growing. In 1981, 200 men attended the Fourth Annual California Men's Gathering for feminist men.[102] The Seattle YMCA has even put out a book called the *Facilitator's Manual for Men's Consciousness Raising.*

[101]*Los Angeles Times,* March 1, 1981.
[102]*Los Angeles Times,* September 23, 1981.

Because of male socialization, consciousness raising is more difficult for them than it is for women. Everyone familiar with men's groups agrees that one major problem that must be overcome is men's desire to talk rather than listen. Another is that men too easily perceive themselves as victims: Group discussion can degenerate into a series of complaints about how the male role oppresses men with no examination of how the men themselves acquiesce in the oppression of women. Jane Wagner, now an expert on men's consciousness-raising groups, reported that groups led by women were more effective than all-male groups. "Groups led by men bond together," she reported. "It's harder for them to get to the issues."[103] But she also reported that real attitude change does occur. "When men come in they see themselves as oppressed, more so than women. By the end they do not. They understand they sit in a power position. It's hard for a man to understand what women do. But he is able to do so which wasn't there ten years ago."[104]

WOMEN IN POLITICS
The change in the climate of opinion and the growth of the women's movement resulted in an increasing role for women in politics. A major increase in the number of women running for and winning election to public office did not occur until the early 1970s. But in the 1960s, women politicians sympathetic to feminist demands found that they finally had an active constituency, and this allowed them to push for prowomen policies with a greater chance of success.

Congresswoman Edith Green was instrumental in getting the Equal Pay Act of 1963 passed. "To get it passed took eight years," she said, "eight years to persuade Congress that a woman doing identical work with a man ought to be paid the same salary."[105] In 1972, with backing from the women's movement, Green got Congress to pass a provision prohibiting educational institutions receiving federal funds from discriminating on the basis of sex.

The inclusion of sex in Title VII of the 1964 Civil Rights Act was a major victory for women, for which Martha Griffiths deserves much of the credit. Less well known is her work on the Ways and Means Committee to make the social security system more equitable. She pushed through a provision allowing divorced women who

[103]*Los Angeles Times,* March 1, 1981.
[104]Ibid.
[105]Hope Chamberlin, *A Minority of Members: Women in the U.S. Congress* (New York: Praeger, 1973), p. 257.

had been married 20 years or more to collect on their former husbands' social security.[106] As the original sponsor of the ERA, she steered it through the House twice and helped lobby it to success in the Senate.

The 1964 election of Patsy Mink to the House of Representatives signaled the advent of a new breed of women politicians. Young (only 36 when first elected) and a lawyer, she made it on her own. Ms. Mink was personally aware of discrimination against women. When, after graduation from law school, she attempted to find a job with a law firm, she was told, "Stay home and take care of your children."[107] Whenever possible, Congresswoman Mink used the powers of her office to change discriminatory practices. The abolition of a Post Office regulation barring women from becoming postal inspectors was one such victory.

Shirley Chisholm had two strikes against her—she is female and she is black. Through hard work, brains, and self-confidence, she made it to the House in 1968. An activist on a wide variety of liberal issues, she has been criticized in her constituency for involvement in the women's movement. Assemblyman Thomas Fortune accused her of spending "so much time with women's lib and gay lib that she has forgotten all about black lib in Bedford-Stuyvesant."[108] James Farmer ran a blatantly sexist campaign against her. He brought in the issue of "matriarchal dominance" and emphasized the need for "a strong male image" and "a man's voice in Washington."[109] Given such criticism, it is not surprising Ms. Chisholm believes that, in politics, she has faced more discrimination on account of her sex than on account of her race. In 1972, Shirley Chisholm ran for the presidency. Attempting to forge a coalition of youth, blacks, women, and the poor, she amassed 151.95 delegate votes at the Democratic convention.

Bella Abzug, a committed feminist, was elected to Congress in 1970. A lawyer and a founder of Women Strike for Peace, she, like Chisholm, is an activist. As a new member of Congress, she became known nationally. She introduced and worked for a large variety of feminist legislation—comprehensive child care, the right to abortion, and prohibitions against the use of the discriminatory titles "Miss" and "Mrs." by the federal government.

Chisholm and Abzug were among the founders of the National

[106]Ibid., p. 261.
[107]Ibid., p. 309.
[108]Ibid., p. 329.
[109]Ibid., p. 328.

Women's Political Caucus in July 1971. According to Chisholm, "the function of the NWPC is not to be the cutting edge of the women's liberation movement, but the big umbrella organization which provides the weight and muscle for those issues which the majority of women in this country see as concerns."[110] Women in the moderate wing of the movement felt that, although gains had been made, a specifically political organization was needed. Women, they felt, should not only influence decision makers, but become decision makers themselves.

The caucus is a multipartisan organization whose basic goal is "to awaken, organize, and assert the vast political power represented by women—53 percent of the population—by: organizing state and local caucuses around the country; raising women's issues at every level of the political process; electing to office women committed to women's concerns; educating women through political action."[111] The swift growth of the caucus showed the need for such an organization. By 1973, every state, the District of Columbia, and Puerto Rico had active caucuses. Caucus members tend to be middle class and politically experienced. Almost 9 out of 10 members have worked in political campaigns, and 37 percent have held party leadership posts.[112] There seems to be a good deal of overlap between caucus and NOW membership. Although the present chairperson is a Republican, the membership seems to consist predominantly of liberal Democrats.

The caucus played an active part in the 1972 Democratic convention. The new delegate selection rules resulted in women's constituting 40 percent of the delegates. The NWPC had pressured for enforcement of the new rules and held delegate training sessions all over the country. It wrote and successfully passed a women's plank in the Democratic platform. Bella Abzug, a member of the platform committee, had fought for the plank. Federal funding for comprehensive child-care programs as well as support for the ERA were included. In order to help women delegates become successful participants, the caucus sponsored a meeting to inform women of key votes and of the Rules, Credentials, and Platform committees' procedures. A "nerve center" where women could get questions answered was set up. NOW was also present in force. To the extent possible amid the usual confusion of a convention, the two groups worked together.

[110]Shirley Chisholm, speech delivered to the national convention of the National Women's Political Caucus (NWPC), 1973.

[111]NWPC pamphlet, 1973.

[112]NWPC press release, August 26, 1973.

The right to abortion was not included in the platform as passed by the platform committee. At a June meeting between caucus members and George McGovern, McGovern had shown signs of vacillation on the issue. By convention time, the McGovern forces had decided that abortion was too dangerous an issue. Tremendous pressure to drop the issue was applied, but the women decided to fight. At a caucus meeting for women delegates, a vote on the minority plank won by 9 to 1. The women introduced the minority plank, although they feared a humiliating defeat. The fight raged late into the night. When a vote was taken, the women were defeated, but by a narrow margin.

Exhilarated by the near win, the women activists decided to run a woman for vice-president. Frances "Sissy" Farenthold, who had run for governor in Texas and won 46 percent of the vote in the runoff, was chosen as the candidate. There was little time to line up support, yet Farenthold came in second to McGovern, the chosen nominee. According to Gloria Steinem, "in one final, glorious push, our jerry-built system of floor-contacts actually worked. Most of the women had never heard of Sissy Farenthold before Miami, yet they trusted their floor leaders' information enough to vote for another woman."[113]

The Republican convention was much less exciting, and progress was slower. Pressure from Congresswoman Margaret Heckler and from the caucus resulted in a child-care plank, but it was much weaker than the one adopted by the Democrats. A bright spot was the increase in women delegates, from 17 percent in 1968 to 30 percent in 1972.

The 1972 presidential election was a disappointment to committed feminists. Nixon, although occasionally paying lip service to feminist aspirations, was a major stumbling block to legislative progress. His statements on abortion, his veto of the child-care bill, and his generally conservative stance made most feminists regard him as an enemy. On other levels, the election year had less dismal results. Encouraged by support from women's groups, more women than ever ran for office, and 28 percent more women were elected to state legislatures.[114] Results of the House elections were also encouraging. Five new women were elected: all were lawyers, four were under 40 when elected, and two were black. The four Democrats, all of whom are liberal activists, soon had an impact on the House. While none of these women ran for office as feminists, all

[113]Gloria Steinem, "Coming of Age with McGovern," Ms., October 1972, p. 105.
[114]NWPC pamphlet, 1973.

were sympathetic. A number received support from women's groups.

The NWPC's clout and credibility continued to increase. The caucus was active at the 1974 Democratic miniconvention in Kansas City.[115] For women, the most important issue was the revision of delegate selection rules. Old-line elements in the party wanted to gut the reformed selection rules, which in 1972 had for the first time given women and minority men an equal chance to become delegates. The coalition of women and minorities was not strong enough to prevent all change, but it did manage to preserve some elements of the reforms. Women had developed enough clout that they had to be included in the private negotiating sessions.

The results of the 1974 elections were generally encouraging. All incumbent women members of Congress were reelected, most by a very wide margin. Although 4 congresswomen retired, 6 new women were elected, bringing the total number of women in the U.S. House of Representatives to a record high of 18. The 6 new women were notably representative of states across the nation; they included two from New Jersey, one from Kansas, one from Tennessee, one from Maryland, and one from Nebraska.

At the state level, the most important victory was won by Ella Grasso in her bid for the governorship of Connecticut—the first governorship won by a woman in her own right. Mary Krupsak was elected lieutenant governor of New York; March Fong, secretary of state of California; and Susie Sharp, chief justice of the North Carolina Supreme Court. Janet Hayes was elected mayor of San Jose, California, a city of more than half a million people. All of these were new political records for women. Extremely important for the future was the fact that 27 percent more women were elected to state legislatures. Five of the seven new state senators in Arizona were women, and in Massachusetts, an avowed lesbian was elected to the lower house.

Many of the women who ran were supported by the caucus and by other women's organizations. The caucus has provided technical assistance of various sorts to women candidates. It and the Women's Campaign Committee, an independent group dedicated to supporting progressive women candidates, have provided financial help also.

Preparations for the 1976 campaigns began early. The NWPC's Campaign Support Committee geared up to provide assistance to women candidates. Presidential candidates were polled to

[115]*NWPC Newsletter* 4 (January–February 1975), 2.

ascertain their positions on 16 women's issues ranging from health care to the ERA. Candidates' campaign staffs were scrutinized to determine whether women held decision-making positions in them. The delegate-selection process was monitored, with many women running for delegate slots. The Democratic Task Force, which consists of caucus members who are active Democrats, worked to ensure that women's interests were included in the Democratic platform.

When the Democratic convention opened, women were organized and ready to take part as a major force. The Democratic Women's Agenda, a coalition of the NWPC's Democratic Women's Task Force and the Women's Caucus of the Democratic National Committee, held daily morning caucuses for hundreds of delegates.[116] The NWPC established a network of contacts in each state delegation for lobbying, polling, and meeting notification. Abortion and delegate-selection procedures were the two major issues. Women successfully pressured the Carter forces to include in the platform a statement saying that a constitutional amendment prohibiting abortion would be "undesirable." Although feminists would have liked a stronger plank, the compromise was an advance over 1972, when no mention of abortion was included.

Under the strong, affirmative-action–oriented delegate-selection procedures in force during 1972, women were elected to 40 percent of the delegate slots at the Democratic convention. The rules were subsequently weakened, and as a result, only 34 percent of the 1976 delegates were women. Because of this decrease, feminists were especially concerned that rules for future conventions include strong affirmative action provisions. Women proposed a 50-50 rule whereby all state delegations would have to have equal numbers of men and women. When the proposal lost in committee, the women threatened a floor fight. Eager to avoid such a fight, which would be broadcast on prime-time tv, Carter was willing to negotiate. A negotiating group from the caucus struck a bargain with Carter that dropped the 50-50 requirement. Instead, the rules would read: "Future conventions shall promote equal division between delegate men and delegate women. . . . The national party shall encourage and

[116]The following discussion of the Democratic and Republican conventions is based upon Lucy Komisar, "Women Come into Their Own," *The Nation,* September 18, 1976; Jo Freeman, "Something Did Happen at the Democratic National Convention," *Ms.,* October 1976; Jo Freeman, "Republican Politics—Let's Make a Deal," *Ms.,* November 1976; and National Women's Political Caucus, *Women's Political Times* (July 1976, August 1976).

assist state parties to adopt provisions to achieve this goal. . . ."[117] In return for this concession, Carter promised to strengthen and make more independent the party's Women's Division and to appoint women to high positions in his administration.

When the negotiation group brought this compromise back to the rest of the women, a spirited debate over whether to accept it took place. Bella Abzug and various caucus leaders spoke in favor. They knew, from a poll that had been taken, that the 50-50 rule would lose on the floor. Karen DeCrow, president of NOW, spoke in favor of a floor fight anyway. The compromise was accepted. Women did not get everything they wanted at the convention, but they showed they were a force to be reckoned with. Some symbolic "firsts" also occurred: Barbara Jordan was the first woman to give the keynote address, Lindy Boggs chaired the convention.

Even though female representation at the 1976 Republican convention was up slightly over 1972—31.5 percent in contrast to 29.8 percent—women were much less successful there than at the Democratic convention. The NWPC's Republican Women's Task Force was active, but its only victory was preventing conservatives from removing support for the ERA from the platform. A plank supporting a constitutional amendment to prohibit abortion was included in the platform.

Despite the dismal Republican convention, there were other signs that women were being taken seriously as a political force. President Ford had appointed a woman—Carla Hills—to the cabinet. Women played a more prominent role in the campaign than ever before. Two of Carter's deputy campaign managers were feminists. Four of his 10 regional coordinators and 10 of the 48 state coordinators during the primary campaign were women.[118] On October 2, 1976, Carter spoke to the National Women's Agenda Conference and thus became the first presidential candidate ever to give a major speech on women's issues.

From a feminist viewpoint, the results of the election were mixed. Carter's victory was generally applauded, as a Democratic administration was thought likely to be more sympathetic to women's concerns than previous Republican ones. All incumbent congresswomen who ran were reelected, even though some faced strong challengers. An issue in Martha Keys' reelection campaign in a Kansas district was her marriage to a congressman from Indiana.

[117]Quoted in Freeman, *Ms.,* October 1976, op. cit., pp. 114–115.

[118]Komisar, *The New Feminism*, op. cit., p. 232.

Would her loyalties now be divided between Kansas and Indiana, some asked. Needless to say, her husband's constituents did not raise such questions about his loyalties. Two new congresswomen were elected. One, Barbara Mikulski of Maryland, had been a long-time NWPC activist. Despite these victories, the total number of women in the House of Representatives actually declined from 19 to 18 because several women retired. The United States Senate remained all male. Congresswomen Patsy Mink and Bella Abzug gave up safe seats to run for the Senate, but both were defeated in the primaries. The only woman to win a senatorial primary lost in the general election. Dixie Lee Ray became governor of Washington. A woman for the first time won statewide elective office in Oregon. Women again increased their numbers in state legislatures, but still made up only 9.1 percent of the total membership.[119]

The 1978 elections brought an even greater increase in the number of women elected officials. Women climbed to 10.2 percent of all state legislators.[120] The number of women lieutenant governors increased from three to six; six women won elections for state treasurer; six won election or confirmation to major state judicial offices. Ella Grasso was overwhelmingly reelected as governor of Connecticut and Nancy Kassebaum became the first woman elected to the U.S. Senate in 12 years. But not all the news was good. The number of women in the House of Representatives dropped from 18 to 16, and several good women, including Martha Keys, were defeated in reelection bids.

The results of the 1980 elections, which will be discussed at greater length later, have been bemoaned by feminists as a disaster. The negative outcome of the elections are all too obvious, yet under the surface, there were some hopeful developments. Women state legislators increased to 11.9 percent of the total.[121] In the 12 years from 1968 to 1980, the number of women's state legislators nearly tripled so that now, no state lower chambers and only five state senates are all male. The number of women in the U.S. Congress reached an all time high of 21—19 in the House and 2 in the Senate. Unfortunately, Paula Hawkins, the new woman senator, strongly opposed the ERA and reproductive freedom, and several of the new women House members are quite conservative as well.

[119]*Los Angeles Times,* November 14, 1976.
[120]All data in the paragraph are from the *Washington Post,* November 10, 1978.
[121]All data in the paragraph are from the *Houston Post,* December 27, 1980; and *Congressional Quarterly Weekly Report,* November 8, 1980, p. 3303.

Two women now serve as mayors of cities whose population is more than 1 million—Jane Byrne of Chicago and Kathy Whitmire of Houston. The 1980 election saw women gain a majority of the San Francisco Board of Supervisors, which governs both the city and the county. A woman, Dianne Feinstein, also became mayor of San Francisco in 1980. Both the San Jose City Council and the Board of Supervisors of the county in which San Jose is located now have female majorities. According to the National Women's Political Caucus, these are the first instances in which women dominate the city and county governments in major metropolitan areas.[122]

Although women have been making progress, they are still very much underrepresented in elective offices. What are the barriers a woman candidate faces? A group of articles recently in *Ms.* on women running for office was entitled, "Too Fat, Too Chic, Too Shrill, Too Weak: The Plight of the Woman Candidate."[123] That title tells part of the story. Down deep, maleness is an essential ingredient of many voters' image of an acceptable candidate. This puts women in a no-win situation. No matter how they look or act, it is not right. Barbara Mikulski, a short, plump woman, said of her campaign for the U.S. Senate, "One of my problems is that I don't fit the image of a U.S. Senator. You know, an Ivy-League–looking male, over fifty and over six feet tall."[124]

Most women candidates believe that prejudice among party leaders and others of the politically active elite is a much greater problem than voter attitudes. According to Gary Hoggard, a pollster who has worked for a number of women candidates, "No one thinks the woman can win, and they won't give her the bucks unless they think she can win, and she can't win unless she gets the bucks."[125] Consequently, women have to rely much more heavily on volunteers and grassroots organizing. Such campaigns have some real advantages for the candidate and for the political system in general, because they get more people deeply involved. However, in large constituencies, sole reliance on grassroots strategies will result in defeat; to reach large numbers of voters, heavy television advertising is essential and that is very costly.

Unfortunately, men's unwillingness to take women in politics seriously extends beyond the campaign. In 1977, the Center for the

[122]*Los Angeles Times,* November 8, 1980.
[123]*Ms.,* May 1981.
[124]Ruth Mandel, "The Trouble with Women Candidates," in ibid., p. 76.
[125]Quoted in Riverside, California, *Daily Enterprise,* October 10, 1980.

American Woman and Politics of the Eagleton Institute of Politics at Rutgers surveyed women officeholders. When they were asked, "What special difficulties, if any, have you experienced as a result of being a woman holding public office?" these women reported that they were not taken seriously, they were stereotyped and regarded as sex objects, they were excluded from "old boys' networks," and they were discriminated against in committee assignments.[126] Some reported that their ideas and programs had been met with opposition simply because a woman had initiated them.

Despite these barriers, many women have become effective public officials. In Congress, for example, virtually all of the legislation on behalf of women passed in the last 2 decades was sponsored by and shepherded through the legislature by women.[127] The number of female elected officials has grown enough to make the formation of women's caucuses possible within a number of associations, such as the National League of Cities and the National Conference of State Legislatures.[128] In early 1977, the women then serving in the House of Representatives institutionalized their informal cooperative arrangement by forming the Congressional Women's Caucus. Similar organizations exist in a few state legislatures. These caucuses have allowed women to share information and expertise and have thereby contributed to their effectiveness in office.

Are women elected officials different from their male colleagues? Although the data are limited, the studies that do exist find that women are generally more liberal and more feminist than men.[129] After pointing out the speculative nature of her conclusion, Marilyn Johnson, former director of research at the Center for the American Woman and Politics, said,

> Nonetheless, the evidence to date invites the conclusion that if women today were to hold half the public offices in the nation, the ERA would now be ratified, federal abortion policy would differ from its present form, income-maintenance among older women would be more secure, government generally would be more active in assuring equal rights for women.[130]

[126]Marilyn Johnson, "Women and Elective Office," in *Society,* May–June 1980, p. 66.
[127]Riverside, California, *Press-Enterprise,* November 2, 1980.
[128]Johnson, op. cit., p. 68.
[129]Ibid.,pp.66–67.
[130]Ibid., p. 67.

INTERNATIONAL WOMEN'S YEAR AND THE WOMEN'S AGENDA

The United Nations declared 1975 International Women's Year. Each member country was expected to draw up a plan to equalize the status of women. When it became clear that the U.S. government did not intend to take the UN mandate seriously, women's groups decided to act. With the Women's Action Alliance acting as coordinator, over 100 women's groups were contacted and asked to submit a list of goals. Sufficient areas of mutual concern were found to draw up the U.S. National Women's Agenda. The 90 groups representing 30 million women supporting the agenda ranged from the YWCA and the Future Homemakers of America, the National Women's Political Caucus and the National Black Feminist Organization, to the National Gay Task Force.[131] Despite the diversity of the support, the document was strongly feminist. Specific goals were listed under 11 headings: fair representation and participation in the political process, equal education and training, meaningful work and adequate compensation, equal access to economic power, quality child care for all children, quality health care and services, adequate housing, just and humane treatment in the criminal justice system, fair treatment by and equal access to media and the arts, physical safety, and respect for the individual (including extension of civil rights legislation to prohibit discrimination based on sexual preference).[132]

In the media, the June announcement of the agenda was overshadowed by the International Women's Year Conference. Held in Mexico City, it really consisted of two conferences—the official UN conference, the delegates to which were appointed by and represented UN member governments, and the unofficial Tribune sponsored by nongovernmental organizations. The official conference was a disappointment to feminists. According to Elizabeth Reid of Australia, one of the few feminists among the official delegates, "government 'politicos' were permitted to carry on their old-hat squabbles without even feeling embarrassed by the fact that these squabbles, as they presented them, in no way related to women."[133] The official delegates' behavior showed that, by and large, the governments they represented did not care about

---

[131]Nancy Seifer, "Best-Kept Secret of Women's Year," Riverside, California, *Press-Enterprise,* October 5, 1975.

[132]The full Agenda is reprinted in *Ms.,* December 1975, pp. 110–111.

[133]Elizabeth Reid, "Between the Official Lines," *Ms.,* November 1975, pp. 88–89.

women. Governments used the conference to continue the ongoing rhetorical conflict over Zionism, imperialism, racism, and the redistribution of the world's wealth. Some of these issues are of major concern to women, yet the way in which they were presented indicated that few delegates understood this. The level of feminist consciousness of the conference was indicated by the fact that a man was chosen as chair.

Despite the diversion of the conference from its stated aim, the World Plan of Action adopted did contain elements important to women. Political participation, education, employment, health and nutrition, and population were areas in which governments were urged to better the position of women.[134] That these women-related matters remained in the draft plan is largely due to the fact that the conference ran out of time before the draft could be extensively amended.

The unofficial Tribune attended by approximately 7000 women was, in the words of most participants, "where the action was." Here too bitter conflicts erupted; attempts to disrupt meetings occurred. Yet real communication also occurred. In the words of a participant, "There, the primary concern was the lives of women—how women work, eat, learn, participate, reproduce, survive. Without doubt, political issues also disturbed the peace at the Tribune but it was, in most cases, a fruitful disturbance, exploring the relationship of female oppression to other forms of oppression."[135]

NOW women organized several large sessions called *Global Speak-Outs,* which were chaired by a panel of representatives from all over the world. Innumerable smaller workshops and informal get-togethers were held. Out of the Tribune came a plan for strengthening and implementing the World Plan of Action. Unfortunately, the official conference refused to consider it because it did not come from an official body.

In December of 1975, the UN General Assembly endorsed the World Plan of Action and proclaimed 1976–1985 UN Decade for Women. A world conference to evaluate progress on the plan was scheduled for 1980.

Meanwhile, in the United States feminists continued to push

[134]Ibid., p. 90.

[135]Ellen Boneparth, "International Women's Year: The Ecstasy and the Agony." Paper presented at the 1976 Annual Meeting of the Western Political Science Association, April 1–3. See also Mary Jo McConahay, "Trials at the Tribune," *Ms.,* November 1975; *Do It Now,* July/August 1975.

the Women's Agenda. December 2, 1975, was declared Agenda Day and women around the country sought endorsements of the agenda from political figures at all levels of government. In 1976 women attempted to get as much of the agenda as possible included in the party platforms.

BACKLASH

Social change is painful for many, and thus a backlash is inevitably provoked. When social roles and expectations are changing rapidly, many people will feel insecure and anxious. The values and behavior patterns they were taught as children are challenged. The world becomes a confusing and threatening place. The reaction to the changing role of women has taken a number of forms. Some academics have revived pseudoscientific theories that purport to show that traditional sex roles are biologically based. Attempts to "fool mother nature" will result in disaster, they claim.

The success of books like *Total Woman* and *Fascinating Womanhood* is another reaction. Both tell women that if they return to traditional patterns, total happiness will be theirs. "It is only when a woman surrenders her life to her husband, reveres and worships him, and is willing to serve him, that she becomes really beautiful to him,"[136] writes Marabel Morgan, the author of *Total Woman*. Outward submissiveness, manipulation of the feminine-wiles sort, and plenty of slightly exotic sex (greet him at the door wearing only net stockings and a frilly apron) is the recipe for holding onto one's husband and meal ticket.

Courses propounding these views have been set up by the authors and have attracted sizable numbers of women. Those who attend—mostly not very affluent wives with children—seem to feel that something is missing from their lives and their marriages, that somehow the American dream has eluded them. That these women turn to solutions like *Fascinating Womanhood* indicates that feminists have not been successful in conveying their message to all segments of society. In part, this is the fault of women's groups themselves; the media treatment of the movement also must bear much of the blame. The media generally and television in particular report primarily the picturesque, the exotic, and the outrageous. Thus mass marches, sit-ins, and demands for test-tube babies get covered; the hard and less glamorous work such as attempting to secure laws providing financial security for housewives does not. In the process, the

[136]Quoted in Joyce Maynard, "Different Kind of Liberation," Riverside, California, *Daily Enterprise,* October 5, 1975.

real effects of the changes advocated by the women's movement are distorted.

Such misinformation accounts for the defeats in 1975 of state equal rights amendments in New York and New Jersey. Because both are liberal states that easily ratified the national ERA, proponents were overconfident. Many ERA supporters neither gave money nor worked for ratification. In contrast, opponents went all out. In New York, Conservative party members, fundamentalist churches, Right-to-Lifers, the John Birch Society, and some conservative Catholics were the backbone of the organized opposition.[137] This coalition was similar to that which worked against the national ERA in the unratified states, and the same falsehoods were used. The ERA would result in unisex toilets, homosexual marriages, and husbands no longer supporting their wives, they claimed. That such a campaign succeeded shows again that the women's movement must do a better job of communicating. Some of the opposition to the changes the movement advocates is based on deep-seated ideological differences. Much, however, is due to a diffuse fear of social change and can at least be alleviated by an understanding of the true roots and effects of such change.

The growth of the New Right and the emergence of conservative Christian groups as a political force confront feminists with a serious challenge. These groups have used people's fears about social change to amass political power. Opposition to the gains women have made is basic to their program and, unless they are effectively countered, feminists are likely to be dealt some very serious setbacks.

THE MOVEMENT IN THE MID-1970s

The strong reactions the women's movement has provoked are a sign that it has had an impact on society. Although the backlash has not stopped the movement's growth, internal conflicts have created problems. As NOW's membership expanded, the organization became more heterogeneous. Feeling the need for some national organization, many radical women joined NOW while still maintaining their roles in local autonomous groups. The logic of feminist analysis radicalized some NOW members. They began to see that major structural changes were required to make true equality possible. At the 1975 NOW convention, the brewing conflict between such

---

[137] Lisa Cronin Wohl, "The ERA: What the Hell Happened in New York," *Ms.,* March 1976, p. 66.

women and more conservative members came to a head.[138] One group, which called itself the Majority Caucus, advocated a greater emphasis on improving the quality of life for masses of women through worksite organizing of women in stereotypic jobs, recognizing the bond between oppression based on sex, race, sexual preference, poverty, and ethnic background, and struggling against all these types of oppression simultaneously. It called for greater recruitment of minority women and more militant tactics. The opposition consisted of women who considered this program ideologically uncongenial and of others who believed that, because of the backlash, NOW should adopt a more moderate program even though they themselves agreed with the Majority Caucus position. The caucus, led by Karen DeCrow, won a close but decisive victory. But considerable bitterness resulted from the conflict and at first a lasting split within NOW seemed imminent. That this did not occur indicates that much of the opposition was based upon tactical rather than ideological considerations. At its 1977 national convention NOW was clearly united again. Ratification of the ERA was adopted as the top priority. Other resolutions passed called for working to pass legislation to assist displaced homemakers, legislation to establish a homemakers' "bill of rights," full employment, a comprehensive childcare act, and a guaranteed minimum income.[139]

With a membership of almost 60,000 and internal conflicts under control, NOW entered its second decade in good shape.

A multitude of specialized women's groups formed during the 1970s. The National Congress of Neighborhood Women, a Brooklyn-based, multiethnic organization, is devoted to issues affecting working-class women. California Women in Higher Education includes faculty, administrators, and staff women from colleges and universities working to end discrimination in higher education. The Appalachian Women's Rights Organization attempts to deal with the special problems of poor mountain women. Women's caucuses within professional organizations are still going strong. A number of groups dedicated to organizing women working in clerical occupations have formed. Even in smaller cities, a number of women's groups with no official ties to one another often exist. The number

---

[138]For descriptions of the convention, see Judy MacLean, "N.O.W.," *Socialist Revolution,* July–September 1976, pp. 39–50; and Pam Proctor, "Has the Feminist Movement Reached a Turning Point?" *Parade,* February 15, 1976, pp. 13–16.

[139]Judy MacLean, "United NOW Enters its Second Decade," *In These Times,* May 3–9, 1977, pp. 12–13.

usually runs into the dozens in metropolitan areas. Women's centers, which have been established on many campuses and in many cities, frequently provide some coordination. Some centers serve as umbrella organizations and are run by representatives of a number of groups. Almost all function as information clearinghouses. Joint activities are often planned through the centers.

The demise of some of the autonomous radical feminist groups and the conflict within NOW led some commentators to declare the death of the movement. The women's movement changed, but this is a sign of life, not death. The easy victories have been won; the struggle for changes that are more difficult to achieve but more significant continues.

HOUSTON: THE IWY CONFERENCE AND ITS AFTERMATH

The Houston Women's Conference in November 1977 demonstrated that the movement had truly come of age. The meeting showed that women of all ages, races, and economic conditions were concerned with feminist issues and that, despite their diversity, they could work together.[140]

The Conference was the result of federal legislation authorizing the International Women's Year Commission to "convene a national women's conference, preceded by state conferences, to evaluate the status of women and issues of concern to them." Five million dollars was appropriated for this purpose.

Many of the state meetings at which delegates to the Houston Conference were to be chosen saw feminists challenged by right-wingers opposed to the most basic feminist positions. Some meetings were disrupted, and there were numerous charges that, in the western states, the Mormon church had instructed its members to attend. In Utah, a resolution to deny women the right to vote was proposed but failed. In several states, men with walkie-talkies seemed to be directing strategy. Altogether 130,000 women attended the state and territorial meetings, and although a few meetings were dominated by conservatives, feminists prevailed in most. Most of the resolutions approved by the state meetings were strongly feminist. The 1442 delegates chosen to go to Houston were a diverse group—17.4 percent

---

[140]The following account is based upon Karen Wellisch, "Winning Big in Houston," *In These Times,* December 6–12, 1977; Lucy Komisar, "Feminism as National Politics," *The Nation,* December 10, 1977; and Lindsy Van Gelder, "Four Days That Changed the World," *Ms.,* March 1978.

were black, 8.3 percent were Hispanic, and almost 10 percent were members of other minority groups. The conservatives had won fewer than 20 percent of the delegate slots.

Nevertheless many women worried that Houston would become a confrontation between feminists and the right wing. The media had played up the dissension in the state meetings and seemed to be anticipating, rather gleefully many women thought, a battle of major proportions.

The meeting started on a high note. A torch that had been carried by relays of women runners from Seneca Falls, site of the first women's rights convention in 1848, was handed to Susan B. Anthony, great-niece of the nineteenth-century women's leader. Bella Abzug, presiding officer of the International Women's Year Commission and sponsor of the legislation mandating the conference, and Billie Jean King, the feminist tennis star, joined the runners for the final yards. The opening session was addressed by Rosalynn Carter, Betty Ford, Lady Bird Johnson, Coretta Scott King, and Congresswoman Barbara Jordan.

The large number of delegates and the existence of the right-wing minority made organization mandatory. The Pro-Plan Caucus formed by leaders of various feminist state delegations and supported by NOW, the NWPC, the labor caucus, and many other groups, provided the coordination. The agenda for the Houston meeting was the 26-point national agenda put together by the IWY Commission from resolutions passed in the state meetings. The Pro-Plan Caucus was formed to support this agenda. The Pro-Plan conveners held meetings with state delegations, special-interest caucuses, and national organizations to urge acceptance of the plan without change. The conveners believed this the safest strategy because they feared that once the convention began to amend the plan, the process might get out of control. Eventually the strategy was agreed upon with exceptions being made for the minority, disabled, and welfare caucuses. The substitute minority women's resolution, which the Pro-Plan Caucus agreed to support, was developed by the American Indian-Alaskan Natives caucus, the Asian-Pacific caucus, the Hispanic caucus, and the black caucus working together.

The long consultations and careful planning paid off when the time to consider resolutions came. The debate was often passionate, and many demonstrations briefly interrupted the proceedings. But all sides including the right wing (dubbed the "antis") were given an opportunity to speak, and the agenda was considered in a timely and orderly fashion. The plan was passed almost in its entirety. Although the resolution on abortion, the ERA, and lesbian rights received the most press attention, the plan covered the full spectrum of women's concerns from better treatment for homemakers to welfare reform, from equal opportunity in employment and in politics to help for older, disabled, and rural women. Only a resolution calling for the establishment of a cabinet-level women's department failed, and on this measure, even the feminists were split.

The "antis," finding they were massively outnumbered, did not make a serious attempt to disrupt the meeting as some had feared. A counter rally of some 10,000 held in the Astro-Arena was addressed by Phyllis Schlafly, a leader in the anti-ERA movement, and did receive considerable press coverage. Ironically the influence of the "antis" was the opposite of what they had intended. The prospect of a catfight among women resulted in much more media coverage of the Houston meeting than probably would have occurred otherwise. For the overwhelming majority of feminist delegates, the threat from the "antis" made it clear that unity was essential. After the tone of press coverage of the Mexico City IWY meeting, feminists knew that dissension at Houston was a luxury the women's movement could not afford. Even so, the press did give disproportionate coverage to the minority of "antis"; but what was accomplished by women at Houston was so impressive that the media did present a largely favorable image.

The National Plan of Action approved at the Houston conference was submitted to the president and Congress. President Carter named Bella Abzug cochair of the National Advisory Committee for Women which, among other things, was to assist in advising him on the implementation of the plan. Feminists knew that getting the plan adopted would require a lot of hard work and they geared up to perform. High inflation during the late 1970s, however, eroded public support for new social programs and made the task harder. At anniversary meetings 1 and 2 years after the Houston Conference, participants agreed that the most important result of the conference had been the establishment of a sophisticated and extensive feminist political network. "The communication that resulted among women was the most important single benefit of the conference. The good ole girl network is firmly in place," one participant said.[141] There were some legislative victories as well—extension of the ERA ratification deadline, pregnancy disability legislation, some funding for displaced homemaker programs, and passage of the Women's Education Equity Act authorizing funds to aid in obtaining sexual equality in school programs. Those proposals that would require large

[141]*Los Angeles Times,* November 21, 1978.

amounts of money, such as a comprehensive child-care program or welfare reform, made no progress. "We got a lot of things," one feminist leader said, "but we didn't get the things that cost money."[142]

However, after the conference, feminists became increasingly disillusioned with President Carter. Although he usually paid lip service to feminist goals, he seemed to lack a real understanding and commitment to them. Carter's firing of Bella Abzug as cochair of the Women's Advisory Committee confirmed feminists' suspicions. Abzug had put out a press release pronouncing Carter's budget cuts harmful to women, and in response Carter fired Abzug and, in effect, told the committee to stick to women's issues and not to meddle in economic and budget policy. More than half of the committee's members resigned in protest.

Although Carter may have lacked a real appreciation of feminism, he did understand that women had become a political force to be reckoned with. He far surpassed his predecessors—or his successor—in appointing women to positions of influence. After the 1976 election, an ad hoc coalition of Women's Groups, including representatives of over 40 national women's and public interest organizations, was formed to pressure the administration to appoint women to high-level positions.[143] The coalition compiled a list of qualified women, which it made available to the administration. After considerable pressure had been used on him, Carter met with leaders of the coalition and with other officials. The pressure produced results. Two women were appointed to cabinet posts—Juanita Kreps as secretary of commerce and Patricia Roberts Harris, first as secretary of housing and urban development and later as secretary of health and human services. A National Women's Political Caucus study found that the number of women in noncareer Schedule C jobs (Government Service grades 13–18), which are policy-making and subject to presidential appointment, increased from 14 percent in 1976 to 31 percent in 1979. In cabinet and subcabinet jobs—the top positions—the number of women increased from 4 to 8 percent of the total—not good but still a major improvement.[144] Most important for the future were the women appointed to the federal judiciary. Carter appointed 40 women—15.8 percent of his appointments—to judgeships. This was more than all of his predecessors combined.[145] Eleven women were appointed to the U.S. Court of

[142]*Washington Post,* November 19, 1978.
[143]National Women's Political Caucus, *Women's Political Times,* winter 1977.
[144]*Women's Political Times,* December 1980, p. 13.
[145]Ibid., p. 10.

Appeals and 29 to the U.S. District Courts.[146] Although this represents tremendous progress, women still make up only about 6.6 percent of the federal bench.[147]

THE UN MID-DECADE CONFERENCE FOR WOMEN

When the United Nations proclaimed 1976–1985 UN Decade for Women, a mid-decade conference to evaluate progress was scheduled. Convening in Copenhagen on July 14, 1980, the conference opened on a sober note. Although there had been some progress made in selected areas, women by and large were worse off than they had been 5 years before, the UN data indicated. Women, who represent half of the world's adult population, account for nearly two-thirds of the world's working hours but receive only one-tenth of the world's income and own less than one percent of the world's property.[148]

Feminists saw Copenhagen as a test of the progress that governments had made in recognizing the problems of women. At the Mexico City conference in 1975 many governments had shown an almost complete lack of understanding. If little progress had been made in actually bettering women's position, had there at least been some increase in comprehension and sensitivity?

The conference indicated that yes, there had been some increase but not a lot. There were more women delegates at Copenhagen than there had been at Mexico City, and most of the top conference officials were women. The U.S. delegation was a diverse one that included Sarah Weddington, assistant to the president and a feminist, as cochair and feminist Congresswomen Barbara Mikulski and Mary Rose Oaker as delegates. The Programme of Action and the 48 resolutions adopted at the conference contain much of value. The Programme recognized that measures for women isolated from major priorities and strategies for development and conceived of simply as welfare programs could not produce substantial improvements. It stated that positive and concerted action to change attitudes and prejudices and special supportive measures aimed at women must accompany legislative change.[149]

On the negative side, many governments used the conference as simply another forum for rehashing current political questions

---

[146]*Congressional Quarterly Weekly Report,* February 14, 1981, p. 300.
[147]Ibid.
[148]*U.N. Chronical,* September–October 1980, pp. 54–55.
[149]Ibid., pp. 54–62; and *Department of State Bulletin,* November 1980, pp. 85–86.

such as the Israeli-Arab problem. The United States, although it expressed support for most of the Programme, refused to sign because of references to Zionism and the PLO. According to Caren Grown, a consultant to the Secretariat of the World Conference for the United Nations Decade for Women, "The problem of Copenhagen for [feminists] was not that political issues were discussed; rather delegates reiterated the same old battle weary statements and positions without developing a new understanding of how these issues relate to and affect women."[150] Committed feminists within the official delegations often found their efforts "stifled by formal bureaucratic procedure."[151] Another negative was the press coverage. The media sensationalized and blew out of proportion walkouts by some delegates during the Israeli and Egyptian statements and other conflicts, and largely ignored productive exchanges and results.[152]

As in Mexico City, a nongovernmental conference was held to parallel the World Conference. This Mid-Decade Forum was attended by 8000 participants from 128 countries. According to Carolee Heileman,

> The major subjects on which the organizers of the Forum had arranged panel discussions and workshops were: equality, development, peace, health, education, employment, racism, sexism, refugees, migrants and the family. These were supplemented by workshops and discussion groups on almost every imaginable subject of interest to women, organized by the participants themselves. They covered such diverse areas as credit unions for women, feminist spirituality, female circumcision, how to get a job in mass media, women in the struggle for national liberation, children's views of sex roles, barefoot doctors in rural China, uses of appropriate technology, aging, how to silk screen banners, and many more. Women, and some men, from all walks of life and all regions of the world, shared experiences, information and resources, challenged one another in an exchange of ideas, and joined together for collective action. Activity was not confined to discussions alone—films, displays, audio visual presentations, cultural events, demonstrations, and informal gatherings seemed to mushroom everywhere, and the University buildings were festooned with banners, notices, posters and all manner of paraphernalia."[153]

---

[150]Caren Grown, "Conference on the U.N. Decade for Women," *URPE Newsletter,* September 1980, p. 18.

[151]Ibid.

[152]Robin Morgan, "Sisters at a Summit," *Los Angeles Times,* August 3, 1980.

[153]*Women's Caucus for Political Science Quarterly,* November 1980, p. 17.

The emphasis at the Forum was on practical suggestions: how to run a health clinic, set up a day care center, and attack problems of rural development. Women from Senagal shared information with women from Peru, India, and Montana. Out of these exchanges came new networks for information, ideas, and support. The Tribune Center, which was established after the Mexico City Conference, continues to serve as an information center keeping individuals and groups in touch with what is going on. Copenhagen, while not all that feminists would have wished, did produce some useful results. Women can use the Programme of Action to pressure their governments and agitate for change. The excitement of the Forum regenerated many participants' feminist energies and led to the forging of fruitful relationships. But all this and more is necessary if the worldwide status of women is to be substantially bettered.

EXPERTISE AND ALLIES

The least well-known but perhaps the most important developments of the last few years have been in the growth of feminist expertise and the movement's forging of alliances with other progressive forces in society. During the 1970s, women with expertise in a wide variety of areas—from medical care delivery to education to politics to advertising—became feminists, and feminists working on projects from health clinics to publishing developed expertise. As a result there are now feminist experts on almost any subject imaginable able to use their in-depth knowledge of institutions and processes to effectuate real change.

In a number of cases, the expertise has been institutionalized in specialized organizations. Some are primarily oriented to research; others combine research and action. Recently, the Women's Research and Education Institute of the Congresswomen's Caucus—itself an example of the institutionalization of expertise—compiled a list of women-oriented research centers. The list includes 20 centers that study a wide range of issues affecting women.[154] One of the many groups involved in both research and action is the National Center on Women and Family Law, which collects and disseminates information in that area.[155] It has, for example, conducted a study of the marital rape exemption in states' criminal laws and has pre-

[154]For the names and addresses of the centers, see Spokeswoman, September 1981, p. 6.

[155]For the address of this and the following two organizations discussed, see Women's Rights Law Reporter (spring 1980), 159.

pared a comprehensive training module for advocates for battered women. The Inter-Agency Minority and Female Recruiters Association maintains a register of women and minorities for personnel offices of government agencies to use in hiring and provides assistance to women and minorities dealing with the complexities of federal job-seeking. The National Sexual Harassment Legal Back-Up Center of the Working Woman's Institute offers a variety of services to lawyers handling sex discrimination claims, including help in the preparation and development of cases and amicus briefs and the provision of expert witnesses and legal memoranda on the admissibility of such testimony. The Working Women's Institute has developed a national network of over 200 attorneys available for work in sexual harassment cases. The Women's Legal Defense Fund provides *pro bono* representation for persons complaining of sex discrimination in employment. It attempts to bring cases that will establish important legal precedents on behalf of women.[156] The NOW Legal Defense and Education Fund is involved in both legal work and educational campaigns. The names of some of its projects—the Family Law Project, the Family Education Project, the Media Reform Project, the Project for Equal Education Rights—indicate the broad range of issues in which LDEF is involved.

That feminists have been able to establish and maintain these and many other specialized organizations is the more amazing when one considers the meager foundation funding that exists for such projects. A study supported by the Ford Foundation found that, in 1976, women's programs received about $12 million—less than 1 percent of the $2 billion given away each year by foundations. The reason, according to the study, was that women's projects "touch economic, political and social issues that challenge many accepted public policies and traditional life styles."[157]

The development of feminist expertise has increased the movement's ability to mount an effective challenge to those traditional policies and life-styles. Because the easy victories have been won, further progress will require a greater mobilization of skill and clout. Feminists' increased expertise has become evident in lobbying efforts in Washington, D.C. For instance, without expert research by the Center for Women's Policy Studies, the Equal Credit Opportunity Act probably would not have passed or, if it had, would not have gotten such tough requirements for lending institutions from the Federal Re-

[156]See ibid., p. 158.
[157]*Los Angeles Times,* November 14, 1979.

serve Board.[158] In order for feminist lobbyists to hold their own on such a highly technical subject, access to sympathetic experts was essential.

For feminist groups, the decision to get involved in lobbying on a regular basis has not been an easy one. To many feminists, traditional lobbying smacks of joining rather than fighting the system, and the organizational requirements for effective lobbying seem to conflict with the feminist commitment to nonhierarchial organization. Within both NOW and the National Women's Political Caucus, the decision to open legislative offices in Washington in 1973 were associated with considerable internal conflict.[159] In both organizations it took several years before the conflicts were resolved and the lobbying operation began to function effectively. Some other feminist groups had fewer problems. The Women's Equity Action League, with its smaller membership and its commitment to establishment tactics, moved its office to Washington in 1972 without incident. The Women's Lobby, Inc., was formed in late 1972 to lobby for the ERA. According to Carol Burris, its president, the motto of the Women's Lobby is, "If you don't do something to Congress, Congress will do something to you."[160]

To be effective in influencing Congress, a group needs allies. Allies are especially important to new groups without extensive congressional contacts. For feminist groups, traditional women's groups like the League of Women Voters, the National Federation of Business and Professional Women, the American Association of University Women, and the National Council of Jewish Women were the first allies.[161] A number of these groups had feminist origins, which the women's movement reawakened after a long period of dormancy. These traditional groups had a great deal of experience in Washington lobbying and a respectability that the newer feminist groups still lacked. Working with women members of Congress, this coalition of women's groups scored a number of victories—the establishment of a minimum wage for domestic workers, equal credit legislation, the Women's Education Equity Act, the admission of women

[158]Joyce Gelb and Marian Lief Palley, "Women and Interest Group Politics: A Comparative Analysis of Federal Decision-Making," *The Journal of Politics* 41 (May 1979), 370–371.

[159]Anne N. Costain, "Representing Women: The Transition from Social Movement to Interest Group," *Western Political Quarterly* 34 (March 1981), 102–105.

[160]Quoted in Riverside, California, *Daily Enterprise,* June 28, 1973.

[161]Ibid., pp. 108–109.

to military academies, and the establishment of a national commission on the observance of International Women's Year.[162]

In the late 1970s, the feminist lobby developed an increasing number of allies. As the lobby gained in expertise and clout, more groups saw the advantage to working with feminist groups. Women's groups have worked with the American Civil Liberties Union, Common Cause, civil rights groups, and with a number of education groups on various issues. For example, the National Coalition for Women and Girls in Education, which is dedicated to the preservation and enforcement of Title IX, includes NOW, WEAL, the NWPC, many of the older women's groups, and a number of education groups.[163]

A new and perhaps shaky but extremely important ally of the feminist lobby is labor. The labor movement's financial resources and political sophistication make it a formidable lobbying force in Washington. In the early and middle 1970s feminists found that, although the unions would sometimes endorse a woman's issue, they seldom were willing to use their political clout on its behalf.[164] The first important joint effort of feminists and unions was the campaign to reverse through legislation the *Gilbert* decision. A broad-based coalition called the Campaign to End Discrimination Against Pregnant Workers was formed.[165] Both feminists and the unions were very active, and the effort proved to be completely successful. In the past few years, feminists and labor have found themselves increasingly on the same side of big issues. Both are highly concerned with protecting social programs from spending cuts and they are working together regularly in this effort. The feminist lobby has become a full-fledged member of the loose progressive coalition in Washington.

The growing coalition between feminists and labor has progressed beyond Washington lobbying. Women's groups took part in the massive Solidarity Day rally on September 19, 1981. Initiated and organized by the AFL-CIO, a half-million people converged on Washington to protest Reagan's policies. Not only was there a feminist delegation but many union members, male as well as female, carried ERA banners that had been handed out by feminists. Eleanor Smeal, president of NOW, was one of the featured speakers. Smeal

[162]Ibid., pp. 109–110.
[163]Gelb and Palley, op. cit., p. 380.
[164]Costain, op. cit., p. 110.
[165]Gelb and Palley, op. cit., p. 386.

was also invited to address the AFL-CIO's national convention in late 1981. These developments attest to the women's movement's increasing clout, to real attitude changes on the part of labor leaders, and to recognition by both feminists and labor of the extent of their common interests.

Feminists have also become a force within the Democratic party. In 1978, they won a rule requiring that half of all national convention delegates be women. The 1980 convention showed the clout that feminists now wield within the party. Feminists passed two minority reports opposed by Carter.

The preparations that made these victories possible started early. During 1979, the National Women's Political Caucus held 22 workshops in 18 states to prepare its members to win delegate positions.[166] The NWPC also held a series of meetings with other women's groups to prepare for the convention. The caucus and NOW organized feminists into the Coalition for Women's Rights. The coalition's purpose was to fight for two minority planks—one stating that "the Democratic party shall offer no financial support and technical campaign assistance to candidates who do not support the ERA," the second advocating federal funding for abortions for poor women. The Carter forces worked hard against the ERA plank and at the last moment, when the situation looked bad for them, tried to work out compromise language. "We just made up our minds not to compromise because we held all the cards," Iris Mitgang of the NWPC said.[167] And, indeed, the feminists did hold the cards. When the National Education Association delegates decided to support the feminists, the Carter people knew they had lost and agreed to concede defeat on a voice vote. The Carter forces did not work actively against the abortion plank, and it passed on a 2005 to 956 roll-call vote. Although many feminists were less than enthusiastic about Jimmy Carter and NOW officially opposed his renomination, the Democratic convention showed the strength feminists had attained in the party. In the words of Eleanor Smeal, "We have arrived in the Democratic party."[168]

Some feminists worry that the compromises required for effectiveness in conventional politics will result in a women's movement that is narrowly reformist and that looses sight of its truly radical aims. That is a danger, but one lessened by the existence of a multitude

---

[166]The following is based primarily on the excellent account by Jo Freeman, *In These Times,* August 27–September 2, 1980, p. 2.
[167]*Newsweek,* August 25, 1980, p. 27.
[168]Ibid.

of autonomous feminist groups. So long as such groups continue to produce and disseminate feminist theory and to place new issues on the agenda, the groups involved in establishment politics are not likely to stagnate. Furthermore, given the current threat to past feminist gains, the women's movement cannot afford to stay out of conventional politics.

FEMINISM, THE NEW RIGHT, AND THE REAGAN ADMINISTRATION

All the expertise and allies that feminists have developed are going to be needed during the 1980s. The aim of those in the New Right is to roll back the gains women have made, and the results of the 1980 election give them some chance of success.

During the second half of the 1970s the New Right became a vocal presence on the American political scene. Evangelical conservative groups such as the Moral Majority, the National Conservative Political Action Committee (NCPAC), ultraconservative direct-mail expert Richard Viguerie, and secular New Right groups such as the Committee for the Survival of a Free Congress not only received a great deal of media attention but, because of the large amounts of money they raised, became a potent political force. Playing upon people's fears of social change, these groups made antifeminism a core part of their program. They opposed abortion, affirmative action, "sex-intermingling" in school sports, sex education, the provision of birth control information to minors, and any government "interference" in the family—including programs against child abuse, funding for battered women's shelters, and child-care programs.[169]

Ultraconservatives came very close to denying President Gerald Ford renomination in 1976. In 1978, they defeated some liberal incumbents in House and Senate races. Candidates backed by the New Right won Senate seats from liberals Dick Clark in Iowa and Thomas McIntyre in New Hampshire. In 1980, the conservatives' favorite, Ronald Reagan, won the Republican nomination for president.

For feminists, the 1980 Republican convention was a disaster. The Republican Women's Task Force of the National Women's Political Caucus was in operation but, because of the conservativism of most of the delegates, accomplished little.[170] For the first time since 1940, the Republican platform did not include endorsement of the ERA. (Feminists' efforts may have prevented an outright repudiation

---

[169]*Congressional Quarterly Weekly Report* 38 (September 6, 1980), 2630.
[170]The following is based on the account by Jo Freeman, *In These Times,* July 30–August 12, 1980, p. 5.

of the ERA.) The Task Force did not make an effort on the abortion issue, and the Republicans endorsed a constitutional amendment to outlaw abortion.

Although he claimed to favor equal rights for women, Ronald Reagan continued to oppose the ERA and reproductive freedom during his campaign. These stands as well as his image as a warmonger resulted in women showing much less enthusiasm for Reagan than men did. Polls showing Reagan lagging among women reportedly led to his promise to appoint a woman to the Supreme Court.[171] But despite this gesture, Americans voted along sex lines in 1980, an extremely unusual occurrence. The New York Times/CBS election-day exit poll found that, while 54 percent of men voted for Reagan, only 46 percent of women did.[172] Among the majority of women who favored the ERA, only 32 percent voted for Reagan. Since the election, women have consistently rated Reagan's performance less favorably than have men.

Nevertheless, Reagan won the presidency. Other republicans made significant gains in the House of Representatives and won control of the Senate for the first time in 28 years. Many senior Senate liberals were replaced by New Right conservatives. Thus the Senate elected in 1980 has a conservative majority and contains a large contingent of committed Republicans from the New Right.

President Reagan's record on appointments of women to influential positions has been dismal. He did fulfill his campaign promise when he appointed Sandra Day O'Connor to the Supreme Court, but as of early 1982, she was the only woman Reagan had appointed to the federal bench.[173] None of the heads of the major departments are women and only one woman—Jeane Kirkpatrick, U.S. ambassador to the United Nations—holds cabinet rank. Reagan has appointed only about half as many women to subcabinet positions as Carter did, and those women he has appointed are not feminists but, often, virulently antifeminist. For example, Anne Gorsuch, head of the Environmental Protection Agency, attempted to dismantle the state Commission on Women when she served in the Colorado legislature.[174]

Just as worrisome are the men Reagan has appointed to positions of special interest to women. Most of those in the health area

[171]*Congressional Quarterly Weekly Report* 38 (October 25, 1980), 3223.

[172]The poll results in this paragraph are reported in *National NOW Times,* October 1981, p. 8.

[173]Data in this paragraph are from *Los Angeles Times,* January 29, 1982.

[174]Rep. Patricia Schroeder in *Los Angeles Times,* November 3, 1981.

are strong opponents of abortion. Those charged with enforcement of antidiscrimination laws are, by and large, hostile to affirmative action and generally insensitive to the problems women and minorities face. Perhaps the most outrageous choice was that of William Bell to head the Equal Employment Opportunity Commission. Lacking any record of civil rights activity or of the managerial experience necessary to administer the 3000-employee EEOC, Bell's only "qualification" was that he was black.[175] Vigorous protests by women's, black, and other minority groups eventually forced Reagan to withdraw the nomination.

The policies pursued by the Reagan administration are exactly what one would expect of an administration that appoints such people. By changing administrative regulations and altering enforcement strategies, the administration is attempting to stop enforcing antidiscrimination laws (see Chapter 13). The Reagan budget cuts also have a disproportionately devastating impact upon women. The elimination of the minimum social security benefit, which Reagan won but which Congress reversed after a storm of protest, primarily would have affected women, many in their seventies and eighties. Not only have benefits been reduced under the Aid to Families with Dependent Children program, but the rules governing benefits have been rewritten so as to eliminate work incentives. Because the expenses related to holding a job—child care, for example—are now treated differently, many poor women can no longer afford to work and must rely completely on welfare.[176] Consequently, poor women's chances of working their way up to a decent standard of living are much reduced. One could go on and on. Increasingly in this country, the poor are women and their children, and the social service cuts hit them hardest.

Proposals under consideration in Congress are potentially even more devastating for women. A multitude of constitutional amendments to outlaw abortion have been introduced. Legislation sponsored by Senator Jesse Helms would not even allow abortion in cases where it would save the life of the mother. A constitutional amendment introduced by Orrin Hatch would outlaw affirmative action.[177] The Family Protection Act, sponsored by Senators Roger Jepsen and Paul Laxalt, has been characterized as "a tidy wish list for the New Right."[178] This act would, among other things, weaken Title IX and

[175]Los Angeles Times, November 5, 1981.
[176]Los Angeles Times, November 3, 1981.
[177]Congressional Quarterly Weekly Report 39 (September 12, 1981), 1749.
[178]Congressional Quarterly Weekly Report 39 (October 3, 1980), 1916.

prohibit the use of federal funds for educational materials that "do not reflect a balance between the status role of men and women, do not reflect different ways in which women and men live and do not contribute to the American way of life as it has been historically understood."[179] Even family planning programs are under attack.[180]

All the opinion polls show that the 1980 elections were not a mandate for turning back the clock on women's issues or on civil rights and social progress generally. Nevertheless, if progressives had not mobilized, the consequences could have been dire. The New Right rhetoric roused many women who previously had not belonged to feminist organizations to take action. During the first year of the Reagan presidency, the membership of the National Women's Political Caucus increased by 8,000.[181] In July 1981 alone, 14,000 new members joined NOW, whose current membership is close to 150,000.[182] The membership of the National Abortion Rights Action League jumped from 90,000 to 130,000, and many other progressive groups have reported very sizable increases.[183]

Feminists declared February 4, 1981, Women's Rights Day in Congress, and 3000 women representing 80 different organizations converged on Washington to lobby. Feminist, civil rights, church, and labor groups were involved.[184] Since then, women's groups, in coalition with other progressive organizations and on their own, have continued the work. The progressive coalition was not able to prevent deep cuts in the budgets of social programs but, to this point, none of the retrogressive legislation or constitutional amendments advocated by the New Right has emerged from Congress. The feminist battle certainly has not been won. The Reagan administration is attempting to cripple antidiscrimination programs. An antiabortion constitutional amendment and other antifeminist measures may yet emerge from Congress. Simply to prevent major damage to the status of women, feminists will have to be willing to contribute both money and time to the opposition effort. The next few years will be difficult ones; luckily the women's movement has developed the political sophistication to meet the challenge.

[179]Ibid.
[180]*Women's Political Times,* August 1981, p. 5.
[181]*Los Angeles Times,* January 29, 1982.
[182]*Los Angeles Times,* October 4, 1981.
[183]*Los Angeles Times,* January 29, 1982.
[184]*In These Times,* February 18–24, 1981.

CURRENT ISSUES OF
THE WOMEN'S MOVEMENT

13

In the decades before 1920 the women's movement focused almost all its attention on a single issue—the vote for women. The contemporary women's movement concerns itself with the full range of women's oppression. Struggles concerning a wide variety of issues are in full swing.

This chapter records the arguments used and the campaigns launched on the main issues of the women's movement today. These are (1) changing the way women are portrayed in the media, (2) equal opportunity in employment and education, (3) child care, (4) upgrading the position of the homemaker, (5) woman's right to control her own body, (6) violence against women, and (7) the Equal Rights Amendment. These issues all grow out of the fundamental principle of the movement: that all internal and external barriers to women attaining full personhood must be destroyed. Increasingly, women are realizing that society itself must be fundamentally changed before this goal can be reached.

CHANGING THE IMAGE

Movement women agree that the image of women in the print and broadcast media is both a symptom of and a contributor to sexism in our society. Without a change in this degrading and not really human picture of women, changes in other spheres will be much more difficult.

The treatment of women in the adult media is bad enough, but in children's books and tv programs it is really dangerous. What children read and see during their preschool and early school years will strongly influence their view of what the world is like and what sorts of behavior are expected of them. Knowing this, women who became involved in the movement began to look at their children's schoolbooks in a new light. What they saw led several groups to make detailed studies. A group studying elementary school texts in New Jersey found that girls were portrayed as passive, fearful creatures who cried a lot and provided an adoring audience for their assertive, curious, and brave brothers. Women were housewives/mothers and were often as fearful and incompetent as their daughters. The group, an offshoot of NOW, published its findings under the title *Dick and Jane as Victims.* [1] When other studies found that the same situation prevailed across the country, pressure was brought on both publishers and school boards. Task forces have been organized in many cities, including Berkeley, Dallas, and Minneapolis, that attempt to introduce nonsexist materials into the public school curriculum and run workshops for teachers on the subject. But progress has been slow. The authors of *Dick and Jane as Victims* reported that their examination of texts copyrighted in 1973 showed no real progress. Both publishers and educators frequently refused to see a problem. "It might confuse young children a little bit to be shown women out working," said Daniel E. O'Connel, director of curriculum development for the Boston schools. [2] "Concern about sexism is a bunch of baloney—it is just something else to clutter up thought processes," one teacher said.

Nevertheless, the pressure did have some effect. In Detroit, Evanston, and Seattle, official policy now calls for the rejecting of blatantly sexist material. In Wellesley, Massachusetts, a committee has been set up to screen textbooks for sexism. The New York City Board of Education has warned more than 150 textbook publishers to pay "special attention to the relative neglect . . . of the role of women," and said that "books and materials should concern themselves, among other things, with the new roles of women in the economy and the changing patterns of family life." Some publishers have also reacted favorably. Both the American Book Company and Scott, Foresman, among the largest textbook publishers, said there would be changes in their new editions.

In 1976, the Association of American Publishers issued a "Statement on Bias-Free Materials" that recognized the importance of textbooks in children's lives and acknowledged that racial and sex-

---

[1] *Dick and Jane as Victims,* Women on Words and Images, 1972 (P.O. Box 2163, Princeton, N.J., 68540).

[2] Quoted in Riverside, California, *Daily Enterprise,* June 14, 1973.

ual stereotypes had been pervasive in many school materials. Noting that many publishers had issued guidelines to eliminate stereotyping, it listed a number of suggestions for overcoming previous negative biases including "placing women and minority group members in positions of prominence, leadership and centrality."[3]

Around the country feminists involved in precollege education have been developing nonsexist materials for use in the classroom. Informal networks allowed for some sharing of such materials but this form of dissemination has tended to be haphazard. In 1981, *TABS: Aids for Ending Sexism in School* received funding from the Women's Education Equity Act Program to establish Project Share.[4] The goal has been to establish a network in school districts around the country for sharing bias-free lessons and activities and other teaching techniques.

Children's books other than textbooks have also been scrutinized. A women's group studying 1000 such books found that only 200 could be labeled nonsexist. The list of "good" books has been widely distributed, and many women's bookstores stock nonsexist children's books. Some women have even decided to write children's books to fill the void.

Kathi Gibeault, a California woman, found that by age 6 her daughter was already affected by the negative image of women in children's books. She decided to do something about it. *Susan in the Driver's Seat* is a "blow-by-blow account of several weeks of running around with her daughter to actually meet women with exciting careers." Her second book, *Mommies Are People Too,* is the "story of the adjustment a young girl goes through when she realizes her mother is determined to go back to work and no longer spend all her time in the home."[5]

Children's tv programs have not escaped criticism. Jo-Ann Gardner, a movement activist and psychologist, raked "Sesame Street" over the coals. "Virtually all [the programs] emphasized that there is men's work and then there is women's work—that men's work is outside the home and women's work is in the home."[6] She accused the show of "promoting 'femininity,' motherhood and

[3]U.S. Commission on Civil Rights, *Window Dressing on the Set: An Update,* January 1979, p. 17.

[4]*Spokeswoman,* November 1981, p. 6.

[5]Riverside, California, *Daily Enterprise,* May 31, 1973.

[6]Quoted in Judith Hole and Ellen Levine, *Rebirth of Feminism* (New York: Quadrangle, 1971), p. 215.

homemaking as the most desirable and only appropriate roles for females."[7] Joan Cooney, the executive producer, agreed to make some changes, but the staff felt, according to one member, that "our target audience—ghetto and culturally deprived children—needs strong male figures with which to identify."[8] Despite this seeming reluctance, "Sesame Street" has changed immensely since the early 1970s. It now offers strong women role models and is one of the few bright spots in children's tv.

Criticism of the adult media for their portrayal of women predates the movement. In *The Feminine Mystique,* Betty Friedan bitterly attacked the women's magazines and advertisers as accessories in the creation and prime transmitters of the mystique. The women's magazines portrayed women only as full-time housewives and mothers interested in a beautiful house, a happy husband, and lots of children. Being feminine, which meant being not only pretty and submissive but also childlike and basically incompetent at anything other than housework, was the most important thing in life. True fulfillment for a woman meant giving birth—the more often the better. All news of the world outside was resolutely kept out of the magazines. An editor explained to Friedan, "Our readers are housewives, full time. They're not interested in the broad public issues of the day. They're not interested in national or international affairs. They are only interested in the family and the home. They aren't interested in politics, unless it's related to an immediate need in the home, like the price of coffee."[9] Women's lack of interest in the "broad public issues" was the result, not the cause, of these magazines' policies, Friedan claimed. "Ideas," she pointed out, "are not like instincts of the blood that spring into the mind intact. They are communicated by education, by the printed word."[10]

Friedan's discussion of advertising was concerned mostly with its manipulative aspects—with advertisers' exploitation of the void in most housewives' lives to get them to buy more and more, with their claims that a woman could express herself by using 10 different types of cleaners rather than 1 all-purpose one or that fulfillment lay in having the cleanest laundry on the block.

The movement launched an all-out attack on the portrayal of women by advertisers. In the world of tv commercials, there were two types of women. One was the housewife-mother—usually

[7]Quoted in ibid.
[8]Quoted in ibid.
[9]Quoted in Betty Friedan, *The Feminine Mystique* (New York: Dell, 1963), p. 31.
[10]Ibid., p. 45.

blandly pretty; always interested exclusively in trivia, the whitest laundry, and the shiniest floors; and often stupid. Some man had to tell her what products to use even in her supposed area of expertise, and she would listen to any man no matter how strange his form— tornado, knight, or disembodied voice from the ceiling. The other variety of woman was the sex kitten. She also was not very bright, but then clearly she was good for only one thing, and that presumably didn't require brains. Very infrequently a deviant like Josephine the Plumber was thrown in for comic relief. She, of course, was neither young nor pretty.

The campaign against sexist advertising has taken several forms. Women have been encouraged to write to offending companies to criticize and threaten a boycott of their products. NOW has presented "Barefoot and Pregnant in the Kitchen" awards to advertising agencies that produce particularly blatant ads. Stickers have appeared on billboards and subway and bus ads—particularly those depicting women as sex objects—reading, "This ad exploits women."

The campaign seems to have had at least some marginal effect. The Geritol commercial in which a man says of his wife, "I think I'll keep her," is no longer being run. Employed women seem to appear in commercials more frequently now than in the past, but their depiction tends to be highly unrealistic. A recent report by the Women's Action Alliance indicated that commercials are still fostering sexist stereotypes. The monitoring project, which involved 465 women and surveyed over 40,000 commercials, found that men outnumbered women two to one in television commercials and five to one in radio commercials. Furthermore, only 27 percent of the women who appeared could be characterized as "confident."[11]

NOW has decided that advertising can be a tool as well as a target. One of its members, a woman who had been active for many years in advertising, set up and coordinated its ad campaign. After prolonged negotiations, the Advertising Council, which handles public service campaigns, endorsed the project in February 1973. Both magazine ads and tv and radio commercials were prepared and run in cities all across the country. One showed a toddler. The copy reads, "This healthy, normal baby has a handicap. She was born female. As she grows up, her job opportunities will be limited, her pay low. She may earn half of what a man does. Isn't it time to change all that? Job discrimination based on sex is against the law. And it's a waste. Think about your own daughter—she's handicapped too."

[11]*Spokeswoman*, July 1981, p. 8.

Another, showing a fancy college diploma, says, "Congratulations, you just spent twelve thousand dollars so she could join the typing pool."[12]

Although advertising has been a special target, other aspects of the media have not escaped attention. The portrayal of women on tv has received a great deal of feminist criticism. Studies done under the auspices of the U.S. Commission on Civil Rights show that, unfortunately, there is still a lot to complain about. The first study of prime-time television drama during the years 1969 through 1974 found that women were severely underrepresented and those women who did appear were disproportionately in their twenties and held stereotyped occupational roles.[13] To see if any change had occurred, a follow-up study of the years 1975 to 1977 was carried out. Not much had changed. Of the total number of characters in prime-time television, 62.7 percent were white males, 24.1 percent were white females, and 3.6 percent were minority females.[14] White male characters continued to be seen in a much wider variety of occupations than other characters. In short, in the world of prime-time tv there are few women, and those there are are less than 30 years old and either have no identifiable occupation or are secretaries, nurses, homemakers, household workers, or students.

The studies also examined the representation of minorities and women in network television news. Few of the news stories sampled dealt with women or minorities; most of the newsmakers were white males. Female newsmakers were shown primarily in two roles—as victims or as wives and mothers.[15] The only bright spot was in the area of news correspondents. Although only 10 percent of the correspondents were women and 7.8 percent were minority males, these correspondents more often reported stories of national and international importance in 1977 than they had in previous years. In 1974–1975, women and black correspondents largely had been relegated to stories related directly to minorities and women.[16]

Spokespersons for the women's movement have also criticized newspapers for their condescending attitude toward women and toward the movement. The women's page, with its assumption that women's interests are restricted to recipes, fashion, and bridal announcements, particularly has been considered an affront. The con-

[12]Honolulu *Advertiser,* July 18, 1973.
[13]*Window Dressing,* op. cit., p. 7.
[14]Ibid., p. 9.
[15]Ibid., p. 23–25.
[16]Ibid., p. 26–27.

stant references in news stories to women as divorcees or grand-mothers, blondes or brunettes—facts that have absolutely nothing to do with the story and would never be used to identify a man—are considered even worse. Edith Green reports that when she was first elected to Congress all the newspapers wanted pictures of her in the kitchen. A classic in the "putting down women" category was achieved by a highly respectable newspaper when it headlined a story about a physicist receiving the Nobel Prize "Grandmother Wins Nobel Prize."

Pressure has resulted in at least one newspaper officially changing its policy and in some others being a little more careful. Reportedly, rumors that women reporters at the *Washington Post* were planning a women's liberation group led the editor of the paper to issue a memorandum directing reporters to stop using degrading descriptive words such as brunette, cute, and the like and to stop being condescending in their stories about successful women.[17]

The most dramatic action against the women's magazines was the sit-in at the *Ladies Home Journal.* The Media Women, a feminist group, occupied the offices of the magazine's editor-in-chief and publisher for 11 hours on March 18, 1970. In a press release the women charged that the *Journal* "deals superficially, unrealistically or not at all with the real problems of today's women; . . . the *Journal* depicts no life style alternative for the American woman, aside from marriage and family."[18] Of the demands made—a woman as editor-in-chief, a child-care center, a $125-per-week minimum wage, a less hierarchical structure, a "liberation" issue put out by the protesters—only the last was, in part, agreed to. The women were paid for producing a short supplement to the August 1970 issue. They used the supplement to explain feminism and various women's issues to the *Journal*'s readership.

Although some of the women who participated in the action felt that it was a failure because no permanent changes resulted, the women's magazines have begun to change. Probably due more to the growth of the movement than to any specific pressures, women's magazines have started to run articles on abortion, child care, and even jobs. After the defeat of the state ERAs in New York and New Jersey, editors of several magazines decided the defeats had resulted from a lack of reliable information and that the traditional women's magazines could provide such information to women unlikely to get it elsewhere. The joint effort eventually grew to 36 magazines, in-

---

[17]Hole and Levine, op. cit., p. 263.
[18]Media Women, press release, March 18, 1970.

cluding *Ladies' Home Journal, Family Circle, Good Housekeeping, Playgirl,* and a number of the confession magazines, all of which published stories about the Equal Rights Amendment in July 1976.[19]

There are other signs of change as well. Most major publishers now send their authors instructions on how to avoid sexist language. Dr. Spock, in the latest revision of his bestselling *Baby and Child Care,* has significantly changed his earlier sexist outlook. The new version emphasizes the role of the father and includes a chapter on working mothers.[20] Instead of their usual man of the year, *Time* Magazine honored 12 outstanding women as women of the year in 1975. Very gradually, advertising seems to be improving. A study by the National Advertising Review Board may result in further change. The study found that not just feminists but also very conservative women were offended by the portrayal of women in advertising.[21]

Ms. runs a regular feature called "No Comment" of particularly blatant sexist advertisements sent in by readers. The magazine has not had any trouble filling that space, but enough positive advertisements have been sent in to justify a new feature called "One Step Forward." Most major newspapers have renamed their women's sections "Living" or "Style" or "Consumer Affairs" and have expanded their content respectively. Stories about women's accomplishments in untraditional fields, about issues of concern to feminists, and about the women's movement appear fairly frequently in these sections, at least in the big city papers. Some films with clear feminist themes, most notably *Norma Rae* and *9 to 5,* have been box office successes.

Attitudes generally are changing. Every 2 years since 1972, the Center for Political Studies has been polling a cross-section of the American public: "Some people feel that women should have an equal role with men in running business, industry, and government. Others feel that women's place is in the home. What do you think?" In 1972, 47 percent agreed that women should have an equal role; 29 percent said that women's place was in the home; and 19 percent had mixed feelings. By 1980, those who chose the equal role option had increased to 58 percent, and those who said women's place was in the home had decreased to 20 percent.[22] Attitude change has

---

[19]Riverside, California, *Daily Enterprise,* July 4, 1976.

[20]*Newsweek,* May 3, 1976, p. 86.

[21]*Los Angeles Times,* January 24, 1977.

[22]Center for Political Studies, University of Michigan, American National Election Studies.

been especially dramatic among women. In 1970, women were more likely to say they opposed most of the efforts to strengthen and change women's status in society than they were to favor them. But between 1970 and 1980, the percentage who said they favored efforts to strengthen women's status increased from 40 to 64 while the percentage opposed decreased from 42 to 24.[23] Black women, young women, single and divorced women, and women with college educations were most heavily in favor of changes in women's status.[24] But by 1980, majorities of all categories of women except widows were in favor. A majority of women (58 percent) and of men (54 percent) now believe that most sexually differentiating characteristics involving "masculine" and "feminine" behavior are "a result of the way people are raised and how they are taught to act." Only 22 percent of women and 25 percent of men attribute them to "basic physical differences" between the sexes.[25] When one considers that attitudes about sex roles are learned in earliest childhood, the speed and magnitude of these attitude changes are truly remarkable.

Nevertheless, a great deal still needs to be done. Parents attempting to raise their children in nonsexist ways often feel that the whole world is conspiring against them. Schools, peers, and tv still convey sexist attitudes. The sexist messages may be less blatant than they were a few years ago, but they certainly haven't disappeared. Thus feminists must keep up the pressure on those who determine the content of all forms of the media. Everything from textbooks to tv commercials must continue to be monitored, and protests such as those by NOW's National Media Reform Committee must be made whenever necessary. Positive strategies must also be pursued. Feminists have produced several television programs that have been shown on the networks. A number of women's groups now produce radio shows, and numerous feminist films are being made. These examples must be followed; and new ones set.

EMPLOYMENT AND EDUCATION

When stated abstractly, equal pay for equal work and equal opportunity in the labor market are the least controversial tenets of the women's movement. These demands are so directly derived from mainstream American ideology that few people are willing to take issue with them publicly. Furthermore, the Equal Pay Act of 1963

[23]Roper Organization, *The 1980 Virginia Slims American Women's Opinion Poll*, p. 15.
[24]Ibid., p. 17.
[25]Ibid., p. 27.

and Title VII of the 1964 Civil Rights Act have made these views the law of the land. The women's groups found, however, that given the pervasive sexist assumptions in our society and the vested interest of many groups in keeping women "in their place," these laws were not solutions, only weapons that could be used in the fight for equality. With the passage of these bills the battle had just begun. Much hard and sustained work was still required if the laws were to have any impact.

Keeping a watchful and threatening eye on the Equal Employment Opportunity Commission became one of NOW's first activities. How effective Title VII would be depended on how strict the EEOC guidelines on sex discrimination were and on how vigorously they were enforced. Most of the EEOC commissioners were clearly not interested in enforcing the sex provision in Title VII. After considerable pressure from the Citizens Advisory Council, the EEOC had issued guidelines giving a narrow interpretation to the provision for "bona fide occupational qualifications" (bfoq), restricting its applicability to situations such as male actors for male roles. Nevertheless, the EEOC had allowed sex-segregated want ads to continue, claiming that the headings simply "indicate that some occupations are considered more attractive to persons of one sex than the other."[26] Congresswoman Martha Griffiths attacked the EEOC while on the floor of Congress, labeling its attitude toward the sex provision "specious, negative and arrogant. I would remind them that they took an oath to uphold the law, not just the part of it that they are interested in."[27]

NOW pressure resulted in EEOC hearings in May 1967 on the sex discrimination guidelines. Both the want-ad policy and the problem of so-called protective laws were discussed. In December, keeping the pressure on, NOW picketed EEOC offices across the country, and in February 1968 it filed a suit against the EEOC to "force it to comply with its own governmental rules."[28] In August, the EEOC reversed its position, declaring sex-segregated want ads illegal. The American Newspaper Publishers Association sued the EEOC but lost, and the order finally went into effect in January 1969.

Suits have also been brought against individual newspapers under Title VII and under various state and local laws. In December 1968, when charges were filed against New York City newspapers with the New York Fair Employment Practices Commission, they gave up sex-segregated want ads. Although a number of papers com-

[26]*Congressional Record,* June 20, 1966, p. 13055.
[27]Ibid., p. 13054.
[28]Quoted in Hole and Levine, op. cit., p. 406.

plied either voluntarily or under court order, there were many hold-outs. In June 1973, a suit brought by NOW was decided by the Supreme Court. Rejecting the argument that freedom of the press was endangered, the Court ruled that a city ordinance outlawing sex-segregated advertising was constitutional.[29]

The relationship between Title VII and state protective labor laws for women presented an especially difficult problem, and the EEOC's policy vacillated. Most women's groups argued that such "protective" laws really protect jobs for men, that their effect most often has been to prevent women from getting higher-paying jobs. An incident that took place during a drive to revise the New York State protective laws seems to bear out their contention. Assembly-woman Mary Ann Krupsak reported that a memo distributed by organized labor to legislators "simply said in essence, 'We must protect jobs for men.' "[30] Furthermore, by 1970 about 75 percent of all women workers were covered by the federal, non–sex-specific Fair Labor Standards Act; and most of the rest were in occupations such as private household work that were not covered by the state laws. Women's groups were especially concerned that state protective laws not be interpreted as making sex a bfoq for jobs covered, since this would, to a large extent, have nullified the sex provision of Title VII. Pressure from women's groups finally had the desired effect; in August 1969, the EEOC decided that state protective laws were superseded by Title VII.

While bringing pressure on the EEOC, women's groups were also bringing suits under Title VII in the federal courts. A number of the suits specifically concerned the protective law issue, resulting from women having been denied promotion on the basis of state or company regulations on weightlifting or hours. The court decisions tended to invalidate state laws. (For a discussion of these cases, see Chapter 7.)

Complaints to the EEOC have snowballed—some resulting in accommodation, some in court suits. Airline stewardesses have challenged company rules whereby they would be fired upon getting married or on attaining the age of 32 or 35. In 1970, a group of stewardesses filed suit against TWA, charging the airline with sex discrimination because it paid pursers, who are male, $2500 to $3500 more per year than hostesses who do the same work.

Also in 1970, editorial staff women at *Newsweek* and *Time*

[29]Riverside, California, *Daily Enterprise,* June 22, 1973.
[30]New York City Commission on Human Rights, *Women's Role in Contemporary Society* (New York: Avon, 1972), p. 334.

charged their companies with sex discrimination. In both cases a settlement giving women greater opportunities for promotion was reached without court action.

The Department of Justice filed its first sex discrimination suit under Title VII in 1970. Brought against Libbey-Owens and the United Glass and Ceramic Workers of North America, the suit charged that women were hired in only one of the five plants in Toledo, Ohio, and were assigned to the less desirable and lower-paying jobs. The consent agreement that settled the case included an agreement by Libbey-Owens to change its policy and to publicize the change to its women employees. The settlement did not include back pay.

The years 1972 and 1973 saw some significant progress in the area of equal employment opportunities. Vigorous lobbying by feminist groups resulted in an extension of the EEOC's powers. The commission may now directly sue an employer in federal court for violation of the civil rights laws. Title VII was extended to apply to educational institutions and to government employment. Also in 1972, the Equal Pay Act was extended to cover executive, professional, and administrative jobs. In 1973, AT&T was forced to give $50 million in back pay to women and minority workers. The EEOC, NOW, and the NAACP had challenged AT&T's rate increase request on the basis that 1800 individual discrimination complaints had been filed against the company. The agreement worked out with the EEOC was much below what women and minorities were really owed—that was figured at $3.5 billion for the period 1965 to 1973. Still, it was the largest back-pay settlement reached up until that time.

In contrast, the settlement with the steel industry that was announced in April 1974 was severely criticized by both NOW and the NAACP. The settlement included $30.9 million in back pay to about 40,000 minority males and about 4,000 women and it committed the steel companies to opening up more jobs to minorities and women. In return, however, the companies would not be subject to any equal employment opportunity suits for 5 years.[31]

With its new powers and an expanded legal staff—up from 30 to 220 during 1973—the EEOC seemed to become more vigorous. In September 1973, discrimination charges were filed against a number of large corporations and unions, including General Motors, Ford, General Electric, Sears, the United Automobile Workers, and the United Electrical Workers. Continued understaffing, poor man-

[31]Riverside, California, *Daily Enterprise,* April 16, 1974.

agement, and lack of support from Republican administrations, however, hindered the effectiveness of the EEOC. By early 1977, the backlog of cases had grown to 126,000.[32]

Because of these problems, women have frequently been forced to hire private attorneys. Helen O'Bannon, for example, filed a class-action sex discrimination suit against Merrill Lynch.[33] She had applied for a job as account executive and had passed the early screenings. On the final test, which included such questions as "When you meet a woman for the first time, what impresses you most?" ("correct" answers—beauty and affectionateness), she did not do well. She filed a complaint with the EEOC, but when nothing had happened after 15 months, she filed a suit on her own. Later, the EEOC did join her suit. Merrill Lynch agreed to a $3.5 million settlement that committed the firm to pay compensation to women and minorities against whom it had discriminated and to recruit and hire women and minorities.

From 1972 through 1976, enforcement of existing antidiscrimination laws seemed to be the major problem in the employment area. The EEOC's administrative rulings interpreting Title VII were strongly prowomen and most precedent-setting court cases were favorable. The Supreme Court decision on pregnancy handed down in late 1976, however, indicated that women would have to go to Congress for more legislation. The EEOC's rulings state that pregnancy must be treated like any other temporary disability, but the Court ruled that General Electric could exclude pregnancy from its temporary disability plan even though almost any other imaginable disability would be covered. Immediately after the Court ruling, representatives of women's groups got together to form the Coalition to End Discrimination Against Pregnant Workers.[34] The effort was successful and, in 1978, Congress passed a law overturning this decision.

Another weapon that has been used in the fight for equal employment opportunities is Executive Order 11375. In October 1967, after intense lobbying by women's groups and by the head of the Women's Bureau, President Johnson signed this executive order. Banning discrimination on the basis of sex in federal employment and by federal contractors and subcontractors, it was a revised version of an order signed 2 years previously that banned discri-

[32]*Los Angeles Times,* April 21, 1977.
[33]*Ms.,* January 1977, p. 19.
[34]*New York Times,* December 15, 1976.

mination on the basis of race, color, religion, or national origin.

With the signing, the campaign to get the order enforced began. The Department of Labor, which is charged with enforcement in most cases, was pressured to hold hearings and issue tough guidelines. But when new guidelines were finally published in February 1970, they did not refer to women at all. Contractors were required to come up with affirmative action programs with specific goals and timetables for minorities, but presumably, given the omission, not for women. After more pressure, guidelines on sex discrimination were issued, but they were much weaker than those that applied to minorities, as they lacked any specific goals or timetables. Secretary of Labor James D. Hodgson expressed the department's attitude when he said he had "no intention of applying literally exactly the same approach for women" as for minorities.[35] He backed down to a certain extent when the outraged reactions began coming in, saying that new guidelines incorporating "some kinds of goals and timetables applying to some kinds of federal contractors" would be issued. New guidelines were finally issued on December 4, 1971.

Even without strict guidelines, women's groups began to make use of the executive order. Because a federal contract may be denied a contractor found in violation of it—a very costly result—the order is potentially a powerful weapon. The Women's Equity Action League was the first to make use of the order against an educational institution. In January 1970, the group filed charges of sex discrimination against the University of Maryland. By the end of 1971, suits had been brought against over 300 colleges and universities by various women's groups. NOW brought a suit against Harvard, and federal contracts were held up for 2 weeks. WEAL filed suits against the entire public university system in Florida, New York, and California. Until these suits were filed, the government had made no attempt to enforce the sex provision of the executive order.[36]

Suits have also been filed against all U.S. medical and law schools charging them with discrimination in admissions policies. NOW has charged 1300 major U.S. corporations with sex discrimination under the order.

Attempts to combat sex discrimination also took place within the professions. In September 1969, women's caucuses were formed at the annual meetings of the American Political Science Association, the American Sociological Association, and the American Psycho-

---

[35]Quoted in Hole and Levine, op. cit., p. 46.
[36]Irene L. Murphy, *Public Policy on the Status of Women* (Lexington, Mass.: Heath, 1973), p. 37.

logical Association. By the end of 1971, a women's caucus existed in nearly every professional association.

In some cases the caucus was established by moderate women. Thus Alice Rossi, an established scholar and a founder of NOW, was instrumental in the formation of the caucus in sociology. More frequently, younger women who had come to feminism via the New Left took the lead and, in some cases, continued to cooperate with the radical mixed caucus in the association.

These groups demanded that commissions be established to study the place of women in their particular profession. Often the caucuses hold panels to present and discuss research on women. Child-care facilities at the convention are often demanded and frequently obtained. Some caucuses have run their members for association offices and have won a few positions.

Enforcing legislation that runs counter to the vested interests of powerful groups in the society is always difficult. When the administration is hostile, it becomes almost impossible. According to Irene Murphy, who has made a careful study of public policy on the status of women, Nixon made no effort "to give strong and continuous support to antidiscrimination programs"[37] and opposed most bills designed to strengthen such programs.

During the last year of the Ford administration, a battle to prevent weakening of the executive order took place.[38] During the summer of 1976 rumors that the Office of Federal Contract Compliance Programs intended to weaken affirmative action regulations began to spread. A leaked copy of the proposed regulations allowed women's groups to prepare for the battle ahead. Published in mid-September, the proposed regulations would have exempted approximately 20 percent of the companies that were doing business with the government from preparing an affirmative action plan. In addition, the review of a potential contractor's affirmative action plan before a contract was awarded would have been practically eliminated.

Leading the fight against these changes were several working women's groups, including "9 to 5" and Women Employed. Their strategy was to delay issuance of the regulations as long as possible. If Carter won the election, the regulations probably would be scrapped. A public hearing on the changes was demanded; sympathetic congresspeople were asked to contact the secretary of labor; and a letter-writing campaign was started. When OFCCP capitulated

---

[37]Murphy, op. cit., p. 42.

[38]For an excellent account, see Judy MacLean, "Coalition Winds Ford Benign Neglect In Its Own Red Tape," *In These Times,* April 6–12, 1977, p. 6.

and held public hearings, so many people asked to testify that the hearings lasted twice as long as originally planned. By this time the election was over, but preventing the regulations from being issued before the inauguration was still necessary. A telegram blitz and threats of a lawsuit won the day. "The strategy of winding up the bureaucracy in its own red tape worked," said Day Creamer of Women Employed. "We learned that a coalition of women's and civil rights groups can be incredibly powerful. If we work together, we can win, even against incredible odds."[39]

During the Carter administration significant progress was made in the enforcement of antidiscrimination laws. Eleanor Holmes Norton, a black feminist, was appointed to head the EEOC. She undertook a thorough reorganization of the agency, reduced the backlog of cases, and increased the impact of the agency. Norton reported to Congress that total monetary benefits obtained during the first 8 months of the field reorganization amounted to $11.43 million, which accrued to 3643 individuals, while another 1952 individuals received nonmonetary benefits such as training opportunities. Monetary benefits averaged $3300 per person for newly filed charges and $3000 per person for backlog charges. The average remedy rate through negotiation and conciliation for new charges was nearly 50 percent, as compared with 14 percent under the old system.[40]

The guidelines issued by the EEOC such as those on sexual harassment continued to be strong and the agency began to show interest in the concept of equal pay for comparable work. In 1978, President Carter assigned to the EEOC the responsibility for coordinating the federal government's anti-employment discrimination efforts.[41] The aim was to eliminate duplication and increase the efficiency of enforcement.

In 1979 in the Weber case, the Supreme Court ruled positively on the validity of voluntary affirmative action programs.[42] Earlier the courts had confirmed the right of the federal government to require affirmative action from federal contractors pursuant to its power to establish the terms of the contract. However, private employers who are not federal contractors are not required by Title VII to take affirmative action. Only after the EEOC has found reasonable cause to be-

---

[39]Quoted in ibid.

[40]U.S. Department of Labor, Women's Bureau, *Employment Goals of the World Plan of Action: Developments and Issues in the United States* (Washington, D.C.: Government Printing Office, 1980), p. 20.

[41]Ibid.

[42]This discussion is taken from ibid., pp. 20–21.

lieve that an employer is discriminating does it seek a conciliation agreement, or if that fails, a court order requiring remedial affirmative steps. The EEOC has, however, increased its emphasis on systematic discrimination and has encouraged employers to examine their practices and voluntarily undertake affirmative action to remedy inequities.

When white males began to charge that affirmative action was discriminating against them, the EEOC issued guidelines describing circumstances that would warrant affirmative steps and carefully specifying what those steps should be. In the case which brought the issue to the Supreme Court, the United Steelworkers of America and the Kaiser Aluminum and Chemical Corporation had voluntarily entered into a collective bargaining agreement that included a training plan to eliminate conspicuous racial imbalances in Kaiser's then almost all-white craft work forces. Rather than continuing its plan of hiring skilled outsiders, Kaiser agreed to train production workers to fill craft openings and to reserve 50 percent of the openings for blacks. A white worker who had not been selected for the training program filed suit, claiming that he had been discriminated against in favor of blacks with lower seniority.

The Supreme Court ruled that the nondiscrimination provisions of Title VII did not condemn all private, voluntary, race-conscious affirmative action plans. The Court found that the purposes of the Kaiser plan mirrored the purposes of the act, which was designed to break down old patterns of segregation and open new employment opportunities to blacks. The plan had offered half of the new training opportunities to white workers. Further, the plan was a temporary measure; it had not been intended to maintain a racial balance, but simply to eliminate a racial imbalance. Commentators on the Court's decision assumed that the same principles would apply to an affirmative action plan designed under similar circumstances for women.

During this period a number of important cases were settled. In June of 1978, the General Electric Company entered into a conciliation agreement estimated to cost $32 million. This included training programs, an open promotion system, and bonuses of $500 to $800 for women and minorities who succeeded in higher-level jobs. The Chase Manhattan Bank also settled a class-action suit brought against it by its female managerial employees by developing a $2 million program to identify and train women and minority employees who had management potential.[43] In 1980, Ford Motor Company settled the

---

[43]Ibid., p. 19.

bias suit against it for $23 million. The company agreed to pay cash damages of $13 million dollars and to spend $10 million on training and other affirmative action programs to help employees develop skills needed for higher-paying jobs.[44] Also in 1980, Western Electric agreed to pay $7 million in damages to 2000 women and to set up an affirmative action plan to increase the number of women in management positions.[45] In 1981, Nabisco agreed to pay $5 million in damages as well as to provide training programs for female employees, expand publicity of promotion possibilities, increase recruitment of women, and take necessary steps to discourage the sexual harassment of female employees.[46] A number of big city police departments have recently settled suits against them by agreeing to hire more women and minorities. In 1980, Philadelphia agreed to hire women for 30 percent of its next several thousand vacancies and the Los Angeles Police Department agreed to increase the number of women employees until 20 percent of its sworn work force is female. More than 30 other major cities are now under court order to increase the numbers of women and minorities in their police departments.[47]

Equal opportunity in education is a prerequisite to equal job opportunity. Title IX has its defects (see Chapter 7) but it is strong enough to offer women another lever for increasing opportunities. Again enforcement is the key.

After the act was passed in 1972, the Department of Health, Education and Welfare undertook to write specific guidelines interpreting the legislation. Lobbying by interested groups was intense. Women's groups wanted strong, explicit rules. The most vocal opposition came from spokepeople for men's sports.[48] Groups representing high school and college coaches attempted to have sports exempted from the guidelines. Almost all schools have flagrantly discriminated against women in sports. There are fewer choices available to women, funding levels are much below those for men's sports, and women have access to many facilities, such as basketball courts, only when the men have finished. Coaches in big-time men's sports such as football and basketball lobbied hard against any rules that would lessen their privileged position.

[44]*Los Angeles Times,* November 28, 1980.

[45]Riverside, California, *Daily Enterprise,* July 25, 1980.

[46]*Spokeswoman,* October 1981, p. 2.

[47]*Los Angeles Times,* October 2, 1980 and November 21, 1980.

[48]Riverside, California, *Daily Enterprise,* June 19, 1974.

The guideline-writing process dragged on and on, and final regulations did not go into effect until July 1975. In athletics, the guidelines require equal opportunity for women to participate, but not equal expenditures on women's sports.[49] In 1979, then secretary of HEW Patricia Harris issued further guidelines on intercollegiate sports programs that were considerably stronger (see Chapter 7).

Although the Title IX guidelines are far from perfect, they are strong enough to make a difference if they are enforced effectively. Having learned that enforcement occurs only when sufficient pressure is applied, women's groups set out to monitor progress. The most ambitious effort has been run by the Project on Equal Education Rights (PEER) of the NOW Legal Defense and Education Fund. PEER women are reviewing every sex bias complaint from women employed or students enrolled in primary and secondary schools in 4 regional offices, or 17 states.[50] From this monitoring, PEER will be able to assess how effectively the law is being enforced. No doubt the knowledge that they are being watched affects the behavior of officials responsible for enforcement. PEER also publishes a newsletter to keep people informed about enforcement proceedings.

The National Advisory Council on Women's Educational Programs reported that Title IX has in fact contributed to major improvements for females at every level of American education. In its report entitled *Title IX: The Half Full, Half Empty Glass* released in October 1981, the council cited an increase in the proportion of women enrolled in traditionally male vocational courses, from 5 percent in 1972 to 11 percent in 1978. It also reported increases in the proportion of master's and Ph.D. degrees earned by women and in the number of women enrolled in professional schools.[51] Despite the intense opposition, gains have been most dramatic in the area of athletics. The council found that the proportion of girls in high school interscholastic sports increased from 7 percent in 1971 to 35 percent in 1981. By 1980, females were 30 percent of all participants in intercollegiate athletic programs compared to only 15 percent before Title IX. Seven years ago, only 60 colleges offered athletic scholarships to women, now 500 do. In 1974, females received approximately 1 percent of all athletic scholarships awarded by institutions

[49]Riverside, California, *Daily Enterprise*, June 4, 1975.

[50]*New York Times*, August 31, 1976.

[51]This discussion of the report is based on *Peer Perspective* 7 (November 1981), 4–5.

belonging to the two major athletic associations; today they receive 22 percent. But as the report's title implies, not all the findings were so cheering. The least progress has been made by women employed in education. For example, the council found that women were 13 percent of principals in 1974 and only 14 percent in 1978. In 1981, it found, women were still less than 1 percent of the approximately 16,000 district superintendents. The percentage of women faculty at the level of full professor showed *no* increase from 1975 to 1981, although women managed gradual improvements in lower academic ranks. The council's report also found that increases in faculty women's salaries lagged behind men's and their earnings relative to men's declined in recent years.

If women are to succeed in education or employment, their environment must be reasonably conducive to study or work. The extent of sexual harassment and its impact on that environment have only recently come to public attention. Like rape and wife-beating, sexual harassment was considered rare, something women brought upon themselves, and certainly not something to be discussed openly. Yet studies show it is far from rare. Barbara Hayler, reporting on an Illinois study, said:

> Fifty-nine percent of the women reported experiencing one or more incidents of sexual harassment in their present place of employment, ranging from suggestive looks and sexual remarks to propositions and coercive sex. Respondents were asked to report only those incidents of unwanted sexual attention that made them feel humiliated or threatened. 52% had been subjected to sexual remarks or teasing, 41% had been the target of suggestive looks or leers, 26% had experienced subtle sexual hints and pressure, 25% had been physically touched or grabbed, 20% had been sexually propositioned, 14% had been repeatedly pressured to engage in personal relationships, 9% reported other miscellaneous forms of unwanted sexual attention, and 2% had experienced some form of coercive sex. These figures total more than 100% because most women reported several kinds of harassing experiences. The less serious forms of harassment were usually reported as part of a larger pattern of abuse. For example, 93% of those who reported receiving suggestive looks also reported other, more serious forms of sexual harassment. . . .
>
> Retaliation for refusal to tolerate or cooperate with sexual harassment is a more explicit form of sexual harassment, where both the threats and the consequences are readily apparent. When asked about the consequences of sexual harassment, 6% of the respondents reported they had been denied promotions at some time, and 14% said this had happened to a woman they knew; 3% had been involun-

tarily transferred, and 10% knew of other such cases; 3% had been fired, and 13% knew of other women who had been fired. In addition 7% had quit a job because of sexual harassment.[52]

The findings of a Los Angeles study were quite similar; 53 percent of the women surveyed reported they had been harassed at work, one-third said they had experienced some kind of negative job consequence because of harassment, and 10 percent reported quitting jobs because of such harassment.[53] Harassment of female students by male professors has been reported at a number of colleges and universities.[54]

Professors or job superiors who engage in sexual harassment are exploiting their power over women, to whom the negative consequences are obvious whether or not explicit threats are employed. Harassment by co-workers, customers, and clients can also make it impossible for a woman to do her job. Victims report a variety of psychological and physical symptoms—feelings of powerlessness, fear, anger, decreased job satisfaction, diminished ambition, headaches, and nausea.[55]

In the 1970s, a few courageous women took their harassers to court on charges of sex discrimination. The courts, in the early cases, refused to interpret sexual harassment as sex discrimination, but, in 1976, in *Williams* v. *Saxbe,* such harassment was recognized as a form of sex discrimination falling under Title VII.[56] As we saw in Chapter 7, the EEOC in 1980 issued strong guidelines.

Since the guidelines make the employer responsible for such occurrences, they provide a strong incentive for employers to take preventative measures. A number of large companies are publicizing the guidelines and setting up grievance procedures.[57] Increasingly, universities are doing the same. Even before the guidelines were is-

---

[52]State of Illinois, House Judiciary II Committee, Testimony of Barbara Hayler on Research Conducted by Sangamon State University and the Illinois Task Force on Sexual Harassment in the Workplace, March 4, 1980.

[53]*Los Angeles Times,* September 13, 1981.

[54]*Time,* February 4, 1980, p. 84.

[55]Joan Vermuelen, "Comments on the Equal Employment Opportunity Commission's Proposed Amendment Adding Section 1604.11, Sexual Harassment, to Its Guidelines on Sexual Discrimination," *Woman's Rights Law Reporter* 6 (summer 1980), 287–288.

[56]Catharine A. MacKinnon, *Sexual Harassment of Working Women* (New Haven: Yale University Press, 1979), pp. 59–60.

[57]Riverside, California, *Press-Enterprise,* November 16, 1981.

sued, pressure from women students forced the firing of one California professor and the reprimanding of another.[58]

The guidelines are a major step forward in dealing with this problem. Various resources are available to women caught in this situation. Working Women United Institute is a national research and action center established to focus specifically on sexual harassment on the job. It offers workshops, speakers, and organizational resources for women concerned about the issue.[59] Many other women's groups offer various forms of help. Bringing a complaint can be exceedingly unpleasant, but all of these tools will have little effect unless women are willing to make use of them.

Although women are increasingly entering better-paying, nontraditional fields, the vast majority still work at jobs that are overwhelmingly sex-segregated. Economic equality for women requires not just women's having an opportunity to enter previously male jobs, but also the upgrading of traditionally female jobs. At least 10 independent working women's organizations dedicated to this task have formed in cities around the country. Groups such as "9 to 5" in Boston, Women Employed in Chicago, and Women Organized for Enforcement consist of women employed in clerical jobs.[60] One focus of these groups has been to assist individual employees with job problems—sex discrimination, harassment, unfair firings. Thus when Iris Rivera, a secretary at the Public Defenders Office in Chicago, was fired for refusing to make coffee, members of Women Employed demonstrated on her behalf.[61] The publicity that ensued resulted in Ms. Rivera's reinstatement. These organizations also engage in political action such as lobbying for legislation and pressuring for the enforcement of affirmative action laws. The groups took a leadership role in the fight against the Ford administration's attempt to weaken affirmative action rules.

Boston's "9 to 5" has gone one step further and formed a union.[62] Since one-third of all women are clerical workers and most clerical workers are not unionized, this may be the most promising strategy for upgrading women's jobs. Unions run by women could give clerical workers the clout to obtain better wages as well as respect and dignity on the job.

[58]*Los Angeles Times,* January 9, 1980.

[59]*In These Times,* March 14–20, 1979.

[60]*Moving On,* March 1977, pp. 6–10; *New American Movement,* January 1976; *Do It Now,* March 1977.

[61]*In These Times,* February 23–March 1, 1977.

[62]*Do It Now,* op. cit.

NOW has also decided that the upgrading of traditional women's jobs must be a top-priority goal. As Eleanor Smeal, NOW president, said: "The jobs that women do are often complicated and highly skilled. A secretary needs training on business machines, a command of the English language, discretion, the ability to make decisions. We have to ask why she is paid on a lower end of the scale than men in less skilled jobs."[63] The thrust among feminists is to demand "equal pay for work of equivalent value—work that is not identical to that of men, but is equal in terms of training, skill and importance."[64]

The concept of equal pay for comparable work has gained the attention not only of women's groups but of unions and of the EEOC. In the late 1970s the EEOC laid the groundwork for using the concept to attack the male-female wage gap.[65] In response to pressure from women's groups, the state of Washington hired a private consultant to carry out a comparable worth study. The study evaluated 121 positions in which at least 70 percent of the employees were members of one sex and found that average pay rates for predominately female positions were about 20 percent lower than rates for male-dominated jobs requiring comparable skill and responsibility.[66] The state refused to accept the study's results and a suit is being brought.

Although the Washington study did not result in steps being taken to rectify the disparity, a study done in San Jose, California, led to a real breakthrough.[67] In 1978, the American Federation of State, County, and Municipal Employees (AFSCME) pressured the San Jose city council to commission a comparable worth study of the city's work force. AFSCME, a progressive union with many women members, had been developing the concept of comparable worth for a number of years. San Jose mayor Janet Hayes, a feminist, was basically sympathetic. The study, delivered to the city in December 1981, concluded that the salaries of women working in female-dominated jobs were on the average 15 percent lower than those of men in comparable jobs in male-dominated areas. In contract talks with the union, the city offered to begin to rectify the disparity, but AFSCME considered the offer inadequate. Mayor Hayes and the city

[63]*Los Angeles Times,* May 26, 1977.

[64]Ibid.

[65]*Business Week,* December 17, 1979, pp. 66–69.

[66]Jane von Frank, "Equal Pay for Comparable Work," *Harvard Civil Rights and Civil Liberties Law Review* 15 (fall 1980), 479–480.

[67]This account is based on *In These Times,* July 29–August 11, 1981; and *Los Angeles Times,* June 30; July 6, 13, 15, 1981.

council—which now had a female majority—claimed the city could not afford more. The union went on strike. After a 9-day strike, which received national media attention, a precedent-setting agreement was reached. The city agreed to spend $1.5 million over a 2-year period toward equalizing women's pay. The settlement meant that workers in 67 different job classifications would receive pay increases of from 5 to 15 percent in addition to cost-of-living increases. The first strike over the issue of comparable worth had been won.

A Supreme Court decision handed down in the midst of this controversy has offered further hope that the comparable worth concept will become a major tool for rectifying pay discrimination. In the case of *Washington County, Ore.* v. *Gunther,* the Court ruled that women could file suit under Title VII even if they were not doing the same jobs as men.[68] The case was brought by a group of jail matrons who were paid $200 per month less for guarding female prisoners than deputy sheriffs were paid for guarding males. The matrons guarded fewer prisoners and had more clerical duties.[69] They did not claim the jobs were identical and did not sue under the Equal Pay Act but under Title VII.

The Court's decision by no means established comparable worth as the law of the land. The Court, in fact, specifically declined to address that issue. Still, the decision was important because in it, the Court allowed comparable worth arguments to be made under Title VII. A contrary decision would have foreclosed the whole issue and thus would have been a disaster.

The comparable worth concept is still in its infancy. Feminists' efforts to apply it will face intense resistance from employers, whom it will cost a lot of money. A variety of strategies can and must be pursued. Cases can be brought; legislation concerning employment in public agencies can be sought. A 1981 California law authorized, but did not mandate, state government to take comparable worth into consideration in setting salaries.[70] As weak as this law is, it is a first step. Making comparable worth a union demand in collective bargaining discussions may also be a promising strategy, as the San Jose case shows. Pressuring various governmental employers to undertake comparable worth studies is a useful first step, as the results are likely to build pressure for further action.

Unfortunately, the time and energy needed to make further progress in employment and education may have to be used to pro-

[68]*Congressional Quarterly Weekly Report,* June 13, 1981, p. 1049.

[69]Riverside, California, *Press-Enterprise,* March 22, 1981.

[70]*ACLU Open Forum,* November 1981.

tect past gains instead. The Reagan administration has mounted an across-the-boards attack on the strategies women and minorities have been using to combat discrimination. William Bradford Reynolds, assistant attorney general of the Civil Rights Division of the Justice Department, has announced that in suits brought to enforce Title VII and similar statutes, "We no longer will insist upon or in any respect support the use of quotas or any other numerical or statistical formulae designed to provide to non-victims of discrimination preferential treatment based on race, sex, national origin or religion. To pursue any other course is, in our view, unsound as a matter of law and unwise as a matter of policy."[71] Rep. Augustus F. Hawkins, Chair of the Subcommittee on Employment Opportunities, called the administration's position "patently idiotic." The policy, he said, "irresponsibly abandons the only effective tool with which to attack and eliminate the effects of past discrimination."[72] Reynolds had also announced that the Justice Department would restrict itself to dealing with discrimination on a case-by-case basis, a procedure NOW President Eleanor Smeal likened to "using a plastic spoon to move a mountain."[73] The Office of Federal Contract Compliance Programs has proposed new guidelines that would slash by 75 percent the number of federal contractors required to have written affirmative action programs. Present rules require such a program of any contractor with 50 or more employees and a contract with the federal government worth $50,000 or more. The Reagan administration would raise the number of employees to 250 and the worth of the contract to $1 million.[74] Furthermore, contractors would be required to comply only if a single contract was worth $1 million; with several contracts that in combination totaled $1 million, the contractor would be under no obligation. The Women's Equity Action League has found that at least 219 of the 272 colleges and universities that, in 1980, were required to have written affirmative action plans would be exempt under the new rules.[75]

The Reagan administration has also attacked Title IX. Vice-president Bush has announced that the guidelines barring sex discrimination in intercollegiate athletics would be reviewed. The Department of Education has taken the position that Title IX does not cover employment and is advocating that federal student loan

[71]Quoted in *Spokeswoman* 6 (October 1981), 1.
[72]Quoted in ibid.
[73]Quoted in ibid.
[74]*New York Times,* August 31, 1981.
[75]*Spokeswoman* 6 (August 1981), 4.

monies not be regarded as aid to educational institutions. The department also seems to be moving toward a program-specific—rather than a broad-based—interpretation of the applicability of Title IX, which Senator Orrin Hatch is attempting to write into law.[76] These are all attempts to limit severely the applicability of Title IX.

Women's groups, civil rights groups, and other progressives have mounted a campaign against the drastically retrogressive policies of the Reagan administration. The Labor Department has received about 1200 comments from the public on the proposed guidelines concerning federal contractors. Comments are reported to be running four to one against the changes.[77] Women's and civil rights groups do not have much leverage in this administration. Consequently, pressure will have to be brought to bear from the outside, by working with friendly members of Congress and by publicizing the effects of proposed administration policy. Only pressure from large numbers of women will prevent the administration from carrying out its plans.

CHILD CARE

By 1969, child care had become a major issue not only in the movement but among women generally. The inclusion of child care in NOW's bill of rights occasioned no controversy. "We demand," the statement read, "that child care facilities be established by law on the same basis as parks, libraries, and public schools, adequate to the needs of children from the preschool years through adolescence, as a community resource to be used by all citizens from all income levels."[78] The disparate groups that participated in the Women's Strike for Equality in 1971 made 24-hour child-care centers one of their three central demands.

Not only feminists but nonfeminist education experts, liberals, and people interested in getting welfare mothers to work are active on the issue. The feminists' analysis and justification for child care is, however, very different from the traditional arguments:

> A basic cause of the second-class status of women in America and the world for thousands of years has been the notion that . . . because women bear children, it is primarily their responsibility to care for them and even that this ought to be the chief function of a mother's existence. Women will never have full opportunities to participate in

[76]*Peer Perspective* 7 (November 1981), 3–5.
[77]*Spokeswoman* 6 (December 1981), 2.
[78]Reproduced in Hole and Levine, op. cit., p. 439.

our economic, political, cultural life as long as they bear this responsibility almost entirely alone and isolated from the larger world. . . . [We believe] that care and welfare of children is incumbent on society and parents. We reject the idea that mothers have a special child care role that is not to be shared equally by fathers.[79]

Feminists do not see child care simply as a way of making women's dual role—both mother and worker—easier, but as a first step toward breaking down society's view that the sole responsibility for child care necessarily rests with the woman. All agree that men should participate in the running of such centers on the same basis and in the same numbers as women.

Cooperative child-care centers have sprung up all over the country. Because of state licensing requirements and high costs, many have folded, but some have survived and new ones continually start up. Perhaps the most unusual is the Artemis Child Experience Center, which was set up and is staffed by antisexist men.[80] The increasingly vocal demand for child care has led some companies to set up centers. It has even attracted private entrepreneurs. Several franchised chains of child-care centers have been started.

Radical women are especially concerned with these trends. Realizing the desperate need for child care, they still feel that commercial and some types of governmental centers would be worse than none at all. Commercial centers run for the sake of profit, not for children, would only train children even earlier and thus more thoroughly to be compliant workers and unthinking order-followers. The centers must be community- and parent-controlled, they contend, if they are to help break down sex role socialization.

Some of the moderate women's groups have also participated in setting up child-care centers. NOW and Princeton University joined in sponsoring a nursery school in Princeton, New Jersey. Being less mistrustful of governmental activity, however, they have spent the greater part of their effort in lobbying for federal assistance. At the White House Conference on Children in December 1970, NOW organized a strong feminist lobby, with the result that the conference recommended to the president a federally financed national child-care network.

In December 1971, Congress passed the Office of Economic Opportunity Bill, which included a comprehensive child develop-

[79]NOW, quoted in ibid.
[80]Kirsten Grimstad and Susan Rennie, *The New Women's Survival Sourcebook* (New York: Alfred A. Knopf, 1975), p. 73.

ment program. The bill authorized $2 billion for the program in 1973 and stipulated that care was to be available to all children regardless of their parents' economic status. Debate was vigorous, with opponents using the same arguments employed during World War II. James Buckley said that no need for such a program had been established, that costs would be prohibitive, and that "the proposal threatens the very foundations of limited government and personal liberty."[81] Walter Mondale, then a senator and author of the proposal, responded, "The whole purpose behind the child development provisions in the bill is to improve and strengthen the family relationship. The program is entirely voluntary. It builds upon parentally controlled committees. The whole purpose is to strengthen the family and to run it at the local level."[82]

The bill, while far from perfect, was a good one. It met two of the major feminist criteria for child care. Considerable control was to be vested in parent- and community-staffed committees. The centers were to be open to all children. Poor families would not have to pay; a sliding scale of payments based on income was to be established for other families. On December 9, 1971, President Nixon vetoed the OEO bill because he objected to the comprehensive child development program. Echoing the most conservative congressmen, he claimed that the bill had "family-weakening implications." A veto override attempt failed in the Senate.

Various comprehensive child-care bills have been introduced in each house of Congress since then. Even though such bills had no real chance of passing so long as Nixon or Ford was president, a right-wing scare campaign against federally funded child care began.[83] Flyers claiming such a bill would take control over children away from parents, that it was a communist scheme, spread across the country and led to masses of hysterical mail being sent to Congress. With a Democrat in the White House and the Senate sponsor of the child-care bill as vice-president, the prospect for passage looked somewhat brighter. The high inflation of the late 1970s, however, made passing new social welfare legislation increasingly difficult, and no comprehensive child-care bill came close to enactment. The chances of any progress whatsoever during the Reagan administration are dim.

Yet the need for affordable, reliable, high-quality child care

[81]Quoted in *Congressional Quarterly Report* 20 (January 29, 1972), 216.
[82]Quoted in ibid.
[83]*Newsweek,* April 5, 1976.

grows ever more intense. In 1980, 45 percent of women with children under 6 were in the labor force. More than half of all children under 18 have working mothers. Survey after survey has found that child care is one of the most severe problems these women face.[84] According to Senator Alan Cranston, "At least 2 million school age children between the ages of 7 and 13 are simply left alone without any supervision."[85] A government study found that "in 1978 almost 52 percent of the country's 24.4 million families with children under 13 have a work-related need for some form of day care."[86] Yet it has been estimated that in 1978, licensed day care centers served only about 900,000 children.[87]

The lack of adequate child care is directly related to the low economic status of women in the United States. A U.S. Commission on Civil Rights study has concluded that "lack of child care, or inadequate child care, prevents women from participating in the labor force, prevents them from participating in federally supported education and training programs, reduces the amount of time they can devote to employment or education, makes them unable to take advantage of job promotions or training necessary for advancement and conflicts with their ability to perform their work."[88]

An actual case illustrates the problem better than a host of statistics. In 1978, Cheryl Petska became the first woman state trooper in Virginia. During a coal miners' strike in late 1978, she was ordered on 48 hours notice to report for a 2-week tour of duty in the coalfields 400 miles from her home. Because she could not arrange for overnight baby-sitting for her children on such short notice, she refused the assignment and was fired for "insubordination."[89]

Federal child-care programs and policies are grossly inadequate. The Tax Reform Act of 1976 provided a nonrefundable credit for child care expenses. The allowable credit is 20 percent of expenses up to $2000 for one child and 20 percent of expenses up to $4000 (e.g., a maximum of $800) for the care of two or more children. This is of some help to middle- and upper-income families, but of little to no help to lower-income families for whom the prob-

[84]United States Commission on Civil Rights, *Child Care and Equal Opportunity for Women,* June 1981, p. 9.
[85]Ibid.
[86]Ibid., p. 13.
[87]Ibid., p. 14.
[88]Ibid., p. 9.
[89]Ibid., p. 7.

lem is most acute.[90] Title XX of the Social Service Amendments of 1974 pays directly for child care for some low-income women.[91] Approximately 800,000 children receive day care services with Title XX assistance each year.[92] Unfortunately, as the U.S. Civil Rights Commission has concluded, "Title XX eligibility criteria tend to restrict women to low-income jobs."[93] The problem is that when a woman's income rises above a certain point, the day care subsidy is completely withdrawn but the cutoff is set so low that the woman is unable to afford the full cost of child care. "Title XX thus helps women move towards self-sufficiency but makes them ineligible for child care subsidies before they have achieved it," the Civil Rights Commission concluded.[94]

Again, an individual's experience shows the impact of such rules. A single mother, Hannah Robinson got off welfare when she found a job at a VA hospital. Her salary was so low that she was eligible for child-care assistance. When she received a raise, however, her income exceeded the eligibility level, but the extra money was not nearly sufficient to allow her to pay the full cost of child care. She had to accept a demotion in order to keep her salary below the cutoff point and thus remain eligible for child-care assistance.[95] Her only alternative would have been to go back on welfare.

Some companies have found that providing subsidized child-care centers for their employees is good business. Intermedics, a Texas company that makes heart pacemakers, found that turnover dropped by 23 percent during the first year of its on-site child care center and by another 40 percent during the second year. Absenteeism fell by 15,000 hours in the manufacturing section alone.[96] On-site centers have real advantages. Parents can have lunch with their children, they are close in case of an emergency, and they can better monitor the quality of care. In 1978, there were 105 employer-sponsored centers nationwide; by mid-1981, at least 100 more companies had started programs and about 200 others were investigating the possibility.[97] Because of a shortage of nurses, hospitals have been

---

[90] Ibid., pp. 25–26.
[91] For details of the program, see ibid., pp. 17–21.
[92] Ibid., p. 17.
[93] Ibid., p. 18.
[94] Ibid., p. 18.
[95] Ibid., p. 7.
[96] *Los Angeles Times,* January 6, 1982.
[97] Ibid.

in the forefront of this development. So long as parents monitor the quality of care, these child-care centers in the workplace are a positive development. They represent a recognition that women are now a core part of the labor force.

Still, only government action can make significant improvements in the area of child care. Many claim that an adequate federal program would be too expensive. To that argument, one can respond that the costs of doing nothing are much higher. Too many children receive inadequate supervision, and many miss out on the enriching early childhood education that good child care provides. Bearing the full responsibility for arranging child-care in a society that provides little help, too many women are kept in low-paying, dead-end jobs. To those unconcerned by the costs to women and children, one can point out the costs to the economy. Problems of child care contribute heavily to keeping women in poverty and on welfare.

Most European countries have developed much more adequate programs without bankrupting themselves. A five-country study covering Sweden, France, Hungary, and the two Germanys found that these countries provided a paid childbirth leave of from 3 months to 3 years, with 6 months being the average.[98] In Sweden a 9-month leave is available to either parent. In all the countries studied, most children age 3 to 6 attend a free public preschool program that is open to all children whether or not their mothers are employed. In France, for example, 95 percent of 3- to 6-year-olds are enrolled. In a number of countries, the programs are being extended to 2-year-olds. These programs are provided not simply to allow mothers to work, but because most Europeans believe that group participation is good for children and that the state has partial responsibility for its next generation of citizens. The European countries have not solved all their child-care problems. Afterschool care is still a need in many areas. Only Sweden provides post-childbirth leave for both parents, thus encouraging fathers to assume a greater share of the responsibility. Nevertheless, the United States, which prides itself on being in the forefront in so many areas, can learn a great deal from Europe.

UPGRADING THE POSITION OF THE HOMEMAKER

The work the full-time homemaker does has been estimated as being

[98]Sheila B. Kamerman, "Child Care and Family Benefits: Policies of Six Industrialized Countries," *Monthly Labor Review,* November 1980, pp. 23–28.

[99]*Ms.,* January 1977.

worth from $20,000 to $40,000 per year. Yet the homemaker lacks the most elementary protection afforded most employed people.[99]If she is hurt, she is not eligible for disability pay. If she is divorced or widowed, she does not get unemployment compensation. She is not eligible to receive social security payments on her husband's account until she reaches age 60. And if at the time of divorce she had been married less than 20 years, she has no claim to any part of her husband's social security. She cannot build up social security or pension rights on her own. If her children are over 18, she is not even eligible for welfare.

The women's movement has begun an attack on the laws and customs that place the full-time homemaker in such a vulnerable position. Attempts are being made to change social security laws so as to provide homemakers with accounts in their own name. A recent law makes it possible for housewives to establish individual retirement accounts. There is considerable discussion of changing state family laws to give the housewife some present interest in her husband's income, and the possibility of a salary for housework has even been brought up.

But progress has been slow. In the mid-1970s, Representatives Bella Abzug and Barbara Jordan introduced legislation that would have given women social security credits for the time they were at home rearing their children.[100] This proposal, based on the system in effect in Britain, got nowhere. Rep. Mary Rose Oaker is currently sponsoring a bill based upon the philosophy that marriage really is a partnership and that the homemaker's contribution should be valued equally with that of the wage-earner. Social security benefits for a married person would be based upon one-half of the combined earnings of the partners.[101] Despite the support of feminists and of senior citizens groups, the bill seems to be making little progress.

In the area of helping displaced homemakers cope with the myriad of problems they face, somewhat more progress has been made. A woman divorced or widowed after many years as a full-time housewife confronts immense emotional and financial problems. Lacking employment experience, confronted with discrimination on the basis of both her sex and her age, she frequently can get only the most menial of jobs. California was the first state officially to recognize these problems and do something about them. In 1975, the first Displaced Homemaker Center was set up in Oakland with state

[100]*In These Times,* July 1–14, 1981.
[101]Ibid.

funding.[102]In the next few years, at least 22 other states provided funds to establish centers. The centers offer individual and group counseling, skills training, and financial and legal guidance. They run workshops on resume writing, skills assessment, assertiveness training, and money management. A "learning contract" distributed to the participants at the Oklahoma Center for Displaced Homemakers says:

> What we cannot do: guarantee you a job; put you through school; solve all your problems; make you rich; make you happy; make your career decisions for you. What we can do: we can show you new ways of thinking about yourself to increase your confidence in yourself; teach you about some of the choices you have open to you and help you locate more information about them; help you identify your interests, aptitudes, and skills; teach you ways of setting goals, making plans for the future, solving day-to-day problems; help you learn how to help each other; teach you skills for finding jobs and succeeding on the job once you're there; provide you with information about the "world of work."[103]

The coalitions fighting for passage of displaced homemaker legislation at the state and national levels include feminist groups and traditional homemakers who have never previously been involved with and sometimes have even opposed feminist concerns. The coordinators of the NOW Task Force on Older Women, which is very active in the Alliance for Displaced Homemakers at the national level, believe that the experience of traditional women and feminists working together will broaden and deepen the movement.[104] In 1978, the battle to obtain federal legislation resulted in the allocation by Congress of $5 million for centers. This federal funding allowed for the establishment of centers in areas previously without such services. The funding came through the CETA program, and with most CETA programs discontinued by the Reagan administration, it is now seriously endangered. As in so many areas of concern to feminists, women will have to redouble their efforts if past gains are to be protected.

A WOMAN'S RIGHT TO CONTROL HER OWN BODY

In the years before 1970, about 1 million abortions were performed

---

[102]Jeanne Crabtree, "The Displaced Homemaker: Middle-Aged, Alone, and Broke," *Aging* (January–February 1980), p. 18.

[103]Ibid., p. 19.

[104]*Do It Now,* December 1976.

every year in the United States; of these only 10,000 were legal.[105] One expert estimated that as of 1970, over 350,000 patients were admitted to hospitals every year with complications resulting from abortions.[106] Although the number of deaths yearly was disputed— estimates range from over 10,000 to a low of 500—it is well known that it was the poor, the black, and the brown who died. Unable to pay for safe illegal abortions, they turned in desperation to "back-alley butchers."

While most Americans resolutely ignored these grisly statistics, there were individuals and groups working without much success to change the laws before the women's movement emerged. Occasionally a particular incident would bring the abortion problem into public view. In 1962, Sherri Finkbine's attempt to obtain a legal abortion received front-page coverage. She had been taking thalidomide, which results in severely deformed babies, yet she was denied an abortion in the United States. The birth of over 20,000 deformed babies after a German measles epidemic also stirred up discussion for a while.

The early groups, for ideological or tactical reasons, worked for abortion law reform. They often pushed for laws modeled on suggestions by the prestigious American Law Institute. This group recommended that abortion be legal not only if the woman's life was at stake but also if pregnancy would gravely impair her physical or mental health, if the baby was likely to be deformed, or if pregnancy was the result of rape or incest.

The women's movement, which became involved in the abortion fight soon after its inception, demanded repeal, not reform. Instead of basing its argument on the need for population control or on the fact that an abortion properly performed would be safer than having a baby, it argued that a woman's right to control her reproduction was a matter of simple justice:

> Repeal is based on the quaint idea of *justice;* that abortion is a woman's right and that no one can veto her decision and compel her to bear a child against her will. . . . [Other justifications] are only embroidery on the basic fabric: *women's right to limit her own reproduction.* [107]

---

[105]Lucinda Cisler, "Unfinished Business: Birth Control," in Robin Morgan, ed., *Sisterhood is Powerful* (New York: Vintage Books, 1970), p. 258.

[106]Robert Hall, "The Abortion Revolution," in Arlene and Jerome Skolnick, eds., *Family in Transition* (Boston: Little, Brown, 1971), p. 260.

[107]Cisler, op. cit., p. 276.

The Association to Repeal Abortion Laws in California, founded in July 1966 by Patricia Maginnis, seems to have been the first total-repeal group. The group compiled and distributed lists of abortionists, intending to provoke arrest in order to test the laws in court.[108] In January 1969, the New York chapter of NOW founded New Yorkers for Abortion Law Repeal. This was the first repeal group to justify abortion in strictly feminist terms. Its activities included publicizing the issue, lobbying, and some referral work.

The radical women's liberation groups often preferred more dramatic action. Redstockings disrupted New York State legislative hearings to protest the list of witnesses—14 men and a nun! When they were not allowed to testify as they demanded, Redstockings held counterhearings in which, before a large audience, women told about their own abortions.

In Detroit, women staged a funeral march mourning women murdered by back-alley abortionists. In Minneapolis, they presented a guerrilla theater skit on the issue. In Washington, D.C., women's liberation groups, joined by welfare women and the Medical Committee for Human Rights, picketed a hospital that had approved a legal abortion for a woman and then at the last moment withdrew the approval.

Abortion referral groups, some set up by radical feminists, some chapters of NOW, some independent, sprang up across the country in neighborhoods and especially on college campuses.

During the period 1968–1970, court actions against abortion laws were under way in more than 20 states. Some favorable rulings had resulted at the lower court levels. But the first real breakthrough occurred in 1970 at the state legislative level. Between 1967 and 1970, 12 states had reformed their abortion laws along American Law Institute lines, but this was not considered much of a step forward. In 1970, Hawaii, Alaska, and New York passed much more liberal laws that came close to allowing abortion on request.[109]

Public opinion supported the change. A Lou Harris nationwide poll in the spring of 1969 found that 64 percent of all those polled believed that the decision on abortion should be a private one; 60 percent of the Catholics questioned agreed.[110] Nevertheless, in New York, where the Catholic church is strong, the battle was a vicious one. Women's groups lobbied for total repeal, the Catholic hierarchy for no change. During the fight, New York's eight Catholic bishops

[108]Hole and Levine, op. cit., p. 295.
[109]Hall, op. cit., pp. 268–269.
[110]Cisler, op. cit., p. 277.

several times issued joint pastoral letters that were read from 1700 pulpits, reaching an audience of 6½ million.[111] The deciding pro vote was cast by a Catholic assemblyman, despite the knowledge that he was jeopardizing his career. He was denied reendorsement by the local Democratic party and defeated by his heavily Catholic constituency. The liberalized laws, though a step forward, still did not meet the criterion of total repeal. Most required the permission of the woman's husband or, if she was a minor, of her parents. Frequently the operation had to be performed in a licensed hospital and by a licensed physician and could not be done after the pregnancy had advanced to a certain point.

Feminists argued against all such restrictions. The decision, they said, should be the woman's alone; no one should be able to force her to have a baby she does not want. An abortion done early is a simple and safe procedure that can be done in a doctor's office and by well-trained paramedics under a doctor's supervision. If both hospital and doctor are required, the cost of abortions would be prohibitive for the poor and difficult for everyone to get because of the shortage of hospital beds and of physicians. Finally, a woman's right to an abortion should not be limited to a certain number of months after conception. If a woman decides to terminate a late pregnancy, she undoubtedly has a very good reason and should have the right to make that decision.

By 1972, a large number of cases challenging various state laws had been brought, and lower courts had declared some state abortion laws unconstitutional. Then, in early 1973, the Supreme Court handed down decisions on *Roe* v. *Wade* and *Doe* v. *Bolton*. Although not establishing a woman's right to abortion on demand, the decisions were major victories. The state may still prohibit abortion during the last 3 months of pregnancy and may regulate abortion to ensure the woman's health during the second 3 months; during the first 3 months, the decision must be left to the woman and her doctor.

The opponents of abortion greeted the decision with dismay, and an organized movement to overturn it was soon formed. Right-to-life groups, backed by the Catholic church, launched an extensive and well-financed campaign. The National Right-to-Life Committee has opened an office in Washington, D.C. Right-to-Lifers have organized mail campaigns directed at officeholders; as a result, mail to Congress ran 100 to 1 in opposition to freedom of choice. Pressure at the local level resulted in the Supreme Court's decision being ignored in many areas. Antiabortion groups seem willing to use almost

[111]Hall, op. cit., p. 277.

any tactics. The children of abortion advocates have been harassed; a Minneapolis hospital that was performing abortions had its phone lines jammed.[112]

The Catholic church has poured a great deal of money into the antiabortion fight.[113] Pressure is being brought on both legislators and parishioners. The executive secretary of the Maryland Catholic Conference in effect threatened Catholic legislators with excommunication if they voted for legalized abortion.[114] The bishop of the San Diego diocese ordered priests in his diocese to refuse communion to Catholics who publicly admitted membership in NOW or any group that supported the right to abortion.[115] The move led NOW to call a Day of Outrage against the Catholic church on Mother's Day, 1975. In Washington, D.C., NOW members picketed the Vatican embassy; in cities across the country, protests were staged.[116] Late in 1975, Catholic bishops unveiled a plan to create "tightly knit and well-organized" antiabortion groups in all congressional districts to pressure members of Congress.[117] A year later, the National Conference of Bishops launched a political pledge drive for support of a constitutional amendment barring abortion.[118] During the 1980 elections, Cardinal Humberto Medeiros issued a pastoral letter to Massachusetts Catholics calling it a "deadly sin" to vote for proabortion legislators.[119] The statement was generally interpreted as encouraging a vote against congressional candidates Barney Frank and James Shannon. Nevertheless, both were elected.

Conservative evangelical groups have become increasingly active politically in recent years, and opposition to freedom of choice has been one of their major emphases. Because they have money and an effective communications system, they are potentially an extremely formidable force. Jerry Falwell of the Moral Majority has grossed over $50 million a year in donations from viewers of *Gospel Hour,* his television program.[120] The religious shows, many of which have acquired an overtly political tone in recent years, are estimated

[112]*Ms.,* October 1973, p. 92.

[113]Ibid., p. 92.

[114]Ibid., p. 94.

[115]Riverside, California, *Daily Enterprise,* April 9, 1975.

[116]Riverside, California, *Daily Enterprise,* May 12, 1975.

[117]Quoted in *New York Times,* November 21, 1975.

[118]*Do It Now,* April 1977.

[119]*The Washington Post,* September 27, 1980.

[120]*Congressional Quarterly Weekly Report,* September 6, 1980, p. 2634.

to have 10 to 15 million regular viewers, and as many as 100 million may tune in once a week.[121] These groups also have impressive mailing lists. The Moral Majority claims a list of over 400,000, of whom 72,000 are pastors or preachers.[122] The function of the organization, according to one of its officers, is "to create a moral climate in which it is easier for politicians to vote right than wrong."[123] These conservative evangelical groups have close links with the Right-to-Lifers and with secular New Right groups such as the Committee for the Survival of a Free Congress, the Conservative Caucus, and the National Conservative Political Action Committee.[124]

The antiabortion campaign has influenced elected officials. Every year from 1976 to the present, Congress has passed the Hyde Amendment restricting medicaid funding for abortions for poor women. Feminist groups have attempted to counter the antiabortionists with letter-writing campaigns, counterdemonstrations, and lobbying. The National Abortion Rights Action League's lobbyist on Capitol Hill has worked full time on this issue, and many other organizations have been involved in lobbying members of Congress. Despite these efforts, the Hyde Amendment became progressively more restrictive. The Supreme Court's holding the Hyde Amendment to be constitutional was a serious blow to feminists. The fight to insure poor women access to federally funded abortions has been lost. A major change in the political climate may make it possible to reopen the issue, but for now, feminists have been defeated and poor women are paying the price.

The 1980 elections were a serious blow to advocates of freedom of choice concerning reproductive rights. While the Democratic platform clearly and strongly supported freedom of choice, the platform of the victorious Republican party advocated a constitutional amendment to ban abortion and supported the Hyde Amendment.[125] In a provision that even some antiabortionists considered overwrought, the platform pledged Republicans to "work for the appointment of judges at all levels of the judiciary who respect traditional family values and the sanctity of innocent human life."[126]

[121]Ibid.
[122]Ibid., p. 2628.
[123]Ibid.
[124]Ibid., p. 2629.
[125]Zillah Eisenstein, "Antifeminism in the Politics and Elections of 1980," *Feminist Studies* 7 (summer 1981), 194.
[126]*Congressional Quarterly Weekly Report,* July 19, 1980, p. 2008.

President Reagan's appointments have reflected this antiabortion thrust. Richard Schweiker, secretary of the Department of Health and Human Services, is a long-time abortion foe. Dr. C. Everett Koop, the surgeon general who heads the Public Health Service, has no background in public health but is a leading antiabortion spokesman and an opponent of Planned Parenthood.[127]

The 1980 elections also increased the strength of the New Right in Congress, very much encouraging abortion opponents. Although preoccupation with the economy prevented much attention to social issues during 1981, a number of antichoice measures were introduced. Constitutional amendments banning abortion have been reintroduced as in previous congresses. There are two types of such amendments: One would allow no exceptions whatsoever to the prohibition, the second would allow abortions only when it is necessary to prevent the death of the mother.[128] In addition to these straightforward measures, antiabortionists are trying other tactics. Senator Jesse Helms and Congressman Henry Hyde introduced bills to declare that life—and U.S. citizenship—begins at conception.[129] In essence, this legislation would make abortion, as well as the use of some means of birth control such as the IUD, murder. Since it is simply legislation, not a constitutional amendment, passage of the bill requires only a majority vote in each chamber. The bill is, however, of doubtful constitutionality. Also, the hearings that Senator John East held concerning the legislation did not help the antiabortionists' cause. East, an extremely conservative Republican, handpicked the witnesses to support his own antiabortion stance and refused to let anyone who disagreed testify.[130] This patent unfairness caused a great deal of negative publicity and forced East to hold more hearings at which opponents of the legislation did testify.[131]

Probably the most dangerous measure under consideration is the constitutional amendment introduced by Orrin Hatch. It states, "A right to abortion is not secured by this Constitution. The Congress and the several states shall have the concurrent power to restrict and prohibit abortion: Provided, that a law of a state which is more restrictive than a law of Congress shall govern."[132] The amendment,

---

[127]National Now Times, November 1981, pp. 3, 11.
[128]Congressional Quarterly Weekly Report, February 28, 1981, pp. 386–387.
[129]Ibid., p. 383.
[130]In These Times, May 6–12, 1981.
[131]Washington Post, June 19, 1981.
[132]Los Angeles Times, January 16, 1982.

thus, would allow either the national or the state government to outlaw abortion. This amendment is a greater threat than proposed amendments that would straightforwardly ban abortion because it can be sold on a states-rights basis. Many members of Congress who are not committed antiabortionists would very much like to get abortion off the congressional agenda and thereby relieve themselves of the lobbying pressure to which they have been subjected. Consequently, the Hatch Amendment may be appealing. Such members can claim they were neither voting for nor against abortion but simply for the right of the states to decide for themselves.

Although the National Right-to-Life Committee narrowly endorsed the Hatch Amendment, antiabortionists are split on strategy.[133] They really want an amendment banning abortion, but many are becoming convinced that the votes needed for passage are not obtainable. Advocates of freedom of choice are gaining allies. Organizations ranging from Tom Hayden's Campaign for Economic Democracy[134] to unions have become actively involved.[135] Public opinion favors freedom of choice. A 1981 Yankelovich poll asked 1015 American women, "On the whole, do you agree or disagree with those who feel that any woman who wants an abortion should be permitted to obtain it legally?" Sixty-seven percent agreed and 29 percent disagreed.[136] The difficulty of enacting a constitutional amendment, the split within antiabortionist ranks, and the public and organizational support for freedom of choice are factors favoring the feminists' prochoice position in the battle for reproductive freedom. They do not, however, ensure victory. The gains so painfully won may soon be wiped out unless large numbers of women take an active part in the struggle.

The costs of losing the fight would be very high. A study by the National Centers for Disease Control, suppressed by the Reagan administration but leaked to the press, reported that legalized abortion has produced a dramatic decline in abortion-related disease and death and significantly reduced the incidence of teenage marriages and out-of-wedlock births.[137] The availability of both amniocentesis and abortion has led to an increase in successful births in families with genetic risks. Women in such families can now conceive without fear that they will bring badly deformed babies into this world.

[133]Ibid.

[134]*Economic Democrat* 2 (July 1981), 3.

[135]*Democratic Left* 9 (November 1981), 9–10.

[136]Ibid., p. 11.

[137]*Los Angeles Times,* July 12, 1981.

The report concludes that outlawing abortions would result in "a predictable increase in illness and disease of American women."[138]

The right to choose must, of course, include the right to choose to have children. When cases of forced sterilization of women on welfare came to light, pressure was brought on HEW to write guidelines protecting women from this indignity. The final regulations for federally funded sterilization procedures, published in 1979, were good ones. According to them, the medical personnel must certify that the patient has received an explanation of the procedure, advice about alternative forms of birth control, and assurance that no federal benefits will be lost if sterilization is refused. Federal funding for sterilization of those institutionalized in prisons or mental hospitals is prohibited.[139] These much stricter rules are a major advance but enforcement will have to be monitored.

As their self-awareness grew, women increasingly began to realize that control over one's own body required *knowledge* about one's body. Many found they actually knew very little about their bodies. Little girls are taught not to touch or look at their genital area—"It's not nice," "It's dirty." "Sex" education in the schools, when it existed at all, tended to be restricted to the film on menstruation put out by Kotex. Gynecologists often treat women as if they were children; they seldom explain what they are doing to women, much less provide the background information they need.

The self-examination movement grew out of the felt need for knowledge as a prerequisite of control. With the help of some trained person—a paramedic, a nurse, or a doctor—women have learned how to do pelvic examinations on themselves and how to teach others to do so. Self-examination makes women more comfortable with their own bodies; it demystifies the gynecological examination given by doctors. The attitude of male doctors during such examinations had only increased women's feelings of helplessness and incompetence. By becoming familiar with their own bodies, women were serving notice that they would no longer let doctors play God; they would know enough so that they could ask intelligent questions and demand answers.

The Feminist Women's Health Center in Los Angeles grew out of a consciousness-raising group that became a self-help group.[140] The center, which offers courses on self-examination, free pregnancy

[138]Ibid.
[139]*Women's Rights Law Reporter* 5 (winter/spring 1979), 75.
[140]Kirsten Grimstad and Susan Rennie, eds., *The New Woman's Survival Catalog* (New York: Coward-McCann, 1973), p. 71.

screening, and counseling, opened a gynecological clinic in August 1973. There a patient may choose a private examination by a woman gynecologist. Women paramedics demonstrate self-examination as well as provide traditional treatment. Alternately, the patient may be treated along with a group of women with similar problems, in which case she can observe the treatment given other women. The center has opened a licensed abortion clinic where cheap and nontraumatic abortions are available. Each woman is accompanied during the procedure by a woman counselor, and women paramedics handle everything but the abortion itself. The Los Angeles group has helped organize self-help groups, as well as two other Feminist Women's Health Centers in Santa Ana and Oakland.

A number of other women's clinics have sprung up around the country. Women's unwillingness any longer to put up with gynecologists who degrade them has been one spur. The high cost of abortions and the often unsympathetic treatment given by the medical establishment to women requesting abortions are others. The women's health movement is growing so quickly that it is difficult to estimate the number of clinics and centers in operation. By 1975, there were at least 42 in the United States, and a number were known to be operating in Canada, Australia, and England.[141] Groups often start by offering counseling and training in self-examination, then include lab work and treatment for VD and vaginitis, and then, where funds and facilities are available, offer abortion services. A newsletter, the *Monthly Extract,* keeps workers in the area informed of what others are doing.[142] The Feminist Women's Health Centers run 7-week summer sessions to train women to staff these health facilities. In 1979, the National Women's Health Network was formed.[143]

As the number of women's clinics increases, gynecologists will have to change their behavior or lose their patients. Thus the self-help movement may have an impact beyond the women it actually treats. By educating women who have never been near a feminist clinic, the movement has already had a significant impact. *Our Bodies, Ourselves,* written by the Boston Women's Health Collective, has sold over 2 million copies in 13 languages. The book, according to Belita Cowan of the National Women's Health Network, "has touched the life of every woman in the country, whether she realizes it or not. . . .

[141]Grimstad and Rennie, *Sourcebook,* op. cit., pp. 35–36.
[142]Grimstad and Rennie, *Catalog,* op. cit., p. 73.
[143]*Los Angeles Times,* November 11, 1979.

The knowledge in the book is very powerful. It gives women that sense of entitlement—that they have the right to know."[144]

VIOLENCE AGAINST WOMEN

In the early 1970s, rape became a major feminist issue. The increase in rape and growing feminist consciousness led to a questioning of society's views on rape and a new, specifically feminist analysis.

The common view holds that rape is committed by a few sick men driven by insatiable sexual urges. Not infrequently, it is assumed that the crime is usually committed by black men on white women. But society's view toward the victim is at best ambivalent. It is frequently assumed that she asked for it, that nice women don't get raped. Even if the victim can show that the attack was completely unprovoked, she is stigmatized. Somehow, it is felt, she is to blame for having been raped. These attitudes are lodged deep in the consciousness of most men and women. All consciousness-raising groups include sex and female sexuality as a major topic of discussion. Such discussions frequently begin with the participants' sexual hangups and progress to an analysis of the socialization process that produced them. Early consciousness-raising groups often did not carry the analysis much further, but as the movement's awareness increased, women came to see the relationship between sex and dominance in our society. Men often see sex as something men do *to* women, an act that certifies the male's superordinate position. The connection between sex and violence is not restricted to hard-core pornography; words like *fuck* and *screw* signify both sexual intercourse and doing someone in. Women came to see that frequently their sexual relationships had had masochistic-sadistic overtones, at least on the psychological level. They learned to acknowledge that, whatever their rhetoric, many men still regarded sexual relationships as conquests.

When the topic of rape came up, most women would say: Yes it's a problem, but it's never happened to me. As the discussion progressed, however, women would frequently realize that their denial was not completely accurate. Almost all had been sexually harassed by men. Being shouted at and followed on the street, being pressured into bed through the use of psychological warfare (the threat of being labeled a "cock teaser, frigid bitch") were common experiences. Even the use of threats and physical force by "dates" was not unusual. Such experiences left women feeling not just sexually used but

[144]Ibid.

psychically put down. The essence of such situations was not sex but domination. Sexual harassment was men's way of asserting their supremacy, of warning women to stay in their place.

From an understanding of the sex-dominance relationship, a new analysis of rape emerged. Rape, women discovered, is a political act, not a sexual one. It is a political act of terror against an oppressed group. According to one of the first feminist analyses of rape, by Pamela Kearon and Barbara Mehrhof, "rape teaches . . . the objective, innate and unchanging subordination of women relative to men."[145]

Kearon and Mehrhof's 1971 analysis has become a feminist classic. They say:

> [In our sexist society the] sexual act [is] a renewal of the feeling of power and prestige for the male, of impotence and submission for the female. Rape adds the quality of terror. . . .[146]

Society's real attitude toward rape is shown by its treatment of the victim. Frequently the accused rapist is treated better than the victim. Police often refuse to believe rape took place unless the victim can show severe injuries. They ask demeaning questions, such as "Did you enjoy it? Did you come?" The victim is repeatedly forced to describe the rape in excruciating detail to various male police officers. Her past sex life is scrutinized. A woman who once says yes to a man who is not her husband is assumed to have lost her right to say no to any male. Eva Norman, a founder of the Los Angeles Commission on Rape, says: "The crime of rape has no parallel. It is the *only* crime in which the victim is treated like a criminal by the police, the hospitals, the courts."[147]

Not infrequently, the police will make only a nominal effort to catch the rapist. "If he is white, and middle class, forget it. They figure that the chances of getting a conviction in court wouldn't be that good."[148] If a woman has let a man into her apartment and he has raped her, she might as well forget it too. Both the police and juries take that as consent. If the accused rapist is black or lower class and the woman is white, the police are more likely to pursue the matter.

In 1972, 46,497 forcible rapes were reported. Criminologists

---

[145]Pamela Kearon and Barbara Mehrhof, "Rape: An Act of Terror," *Notes from the Third Year,* 1972, p. 80.

[146]Ibid.

[147]Quoted in Grimstad and Rennie, *Catalog,* op. cit., p. 155.

[148]Quoted in ibid., p. 145.

estimate that only 1 out of 10 rapes are reported.[149] Given the police harassment of the victim, the low reporting rate is hardly surprising. But even if a woman is willing to endure the experience of going to the police, the chances of conviction are very slim. In 1972, 3,562 rapes were reported in Chicago; 833 arrests were made, 23 defendants pleaded guilty; and 8 were found guilty and sentenced after a trial. Thus fewer than 1 percent of the rapes resulted in jail sentences.

The situation is not new, nor was it a well-guarded secret. But it required a strong feminist movement and a new analysis of rape to make women see that collective action was necessary. The first political action was a Rape Speak Out organized by the New York Radical Feminists in 1970.

The first rape crisis center seems to have been the one in Washington, D.C. Formed in the summer of 1972, it at first concentrated on counseling and giving emotional support to rape victims. Since then it has gone more heavily into helping women deal with hospitals and the police. Members accompany the woman to the hospital and to the police. They make sure the medical examination form is filled out properly. This is necessary for conviction, but according to one of the members, "the intern, either out of ignorance or not wanting to testify, fudges the report" unless watched.[150]

The presence of rape crisis center members not only provides emotional support to the victim but results in better treatment by the police and the hospital. The police take the case more seriously and moderate their behavior. The Washington center's existence has even had an effect on the treatment of victims who come in independently. A member explained: "When we first started, we wouldn't say that we were members of the Rape Crisis Center—we would simply say that we were friends of the victim. So, now, whenever a woman comes in with a friend, they assume that she is from the Crisis Center, even if she's really not, and they behave very nicely."[151] Members accompany the women to court and can refer her to a free lawyer. They are also involved in the D.C. Task Force on Rape, which is working for changes in police, hospital, and court procedures.

Such services, while essential, will not directly prevent rape. Thus the center has also set up self-defense classes to aid women in protecting themselves. Karate, judo, and street-fighting techniques

[149]Ibid., p. 150.
[150]Quoted in ibid., p. 145.
[151]Ibid.

are taught. Asked how effective the classes were, a member replied:

> No matter how much karate or self defense you know, it's not worth shit if you don't have the mind set to use it. What we try to do is politicize the women. Middle-class women, especially, are very afraid of being aggressive. We try to break that down and make women realize that if someone is fucking her over, she has the right to hit him back—just enough so that she can get out of the situation and run.[152]

Rape crisis centers have sprung up by the dozens. As Mary Ann Langen of NOW said in 1977, "In 1972 there were three rape crisis centers in this country. Today there are over 150."[153] Frequently centers are started by former rape victims. Many are modeled on the D.C. center; its booklet, "How to Start a Rape Crisis Center," is often used as a guide. Every center has a crisis line that women who need help can call. Most try to staff the line 24 hours a day, but because this is often difficult, compromises are frequently made. Center members check out hospitals to determine which offer the best and most sympathetic care. They compile lists of gynecologists, VD clinics, and Planned Parenthood chapters where further medical help can be obtained. A list of sympathetic, nonsexist psychiatrists and psychologists is also necessary.

Some women may need professional help, but many find that talking to previous victims working at the center is even more useful. Because society tends to blame the victim for the rape, women often need to be reassured that they are still worthwhile people, that in fact they are not responsible. The Washington, D.C., center sets up meetings at which rape victims and their families can discuss their reactions and learn from each other to overcome their shame and fear. Rape crisis centers frequently get calls from women who were raped years before. Often it is the first time the woman has told anyone about the experience. Center members will accompany a victim to the police if she decides to report the crime. But the decision is left up to the woman. Most women agree in principle that all rapes should be reported and prosecuted, but the emotional ordeal involved is such that few women feel they should persuade someone who is reluctant to go to the police.

Some centers have managed to establish reasonable relationships with police and prosecutors' offices. In a number of areas, rape crisis personnel are even involved with police training. Janet Taggart

[152]Quoted in ibid., p. 146.
[153]Quoted in *In These Times*, March 9–15, 1977.

of Seattle's Rape Reduction Project says, "We do a part of each new patrol person's training. It is very extensive and it's generally been successful."[154] Even if these officials cannot be made more sympathetic by reasoned discussion, the presence of an active center often has a salutary effect. If they know that any misbehavior will be publicized, they tend to be more careful.

A center organized on different lines began operation in May 1973 in Philadelphia. Women Organized Against Rape (WOAR) has its headquarters in Philadelphia General Hospital, where rape victims are examined. When a rape victim enters the hospital, the WOAR room is notified and a member on duty is immediately available for help. Because of its location, WOAR sees all rape victims who report the crime. A member explained why they worked so hard to get their location inside the hospital: "It was obvious to us that hotlines and crisis centers which work outside the system would reach mostly middle-class and movement women. We felt we had to be available to poor and Third World women who are particularly vulnerable to rape, and who are the most abused by medical and legal agents of the patriarchy."[155]

Getting into the establishment took a 3-year campaign. In August 1970, women began to collect the names of people interested in starting a rape crisis center. In November, WOAR was formed by 150 women. WOAR talked to various prominent Philadelphia women—a district attorney, a judge, members of the city council, and several black leaders. WOAR's documentation of the abusive treatment of rape victims persuaded these women to serve on the WOAR board of directors and to use their influence to get the group into the hospital. Opposition collapsed under this kind of pressure, and during its first 3 months, WOAR counseled over 300 rape victims. Of these, 90 percent were black and 60 percent were girls under 16.[156] This approach has begun to spread; in several other cities, centers are now located in hospitals.

Action against rape has taken a variety of other forms. Most centers do some community education such as giving talks at schools and to local organizations. Self-defense for women has become more prevalent. Classes, how-to booklets, and even schools are proliferating.

Efforts to educate those who deal with rape victims is continu-

[154]Quoted in ibid.
[155]Quoted in Grimstad and Rennie, *Catalog,* op. cit., p. 147.
[156]Ibid.

ing. In 1981, the Los Angeles Commission on Assaults Against Women undertook a survey of the needs and problems of rape victims in Los Angeles County. The worst problems, the survey found, were medical.[157] According to the survey, the county's emergency rooms were frequently unhelpful and insensitive. "We found out minors were being turned away if they didn't have parental consent. This is illegal. Women who did not report the rape to the police were being turned away from treatment. By and large, rape victims were seen as low priority," the commission's executive director reported.[158] Evidence was often improperly collected and preserved, making prosecution difficult or impossible. Rape victims were forced to wait in public waiting rooms, and police officers were often present during the medical examination. To change this deplorable situation, the commission, along with the National Council of Jewish Women and the Los Angeles Police Department, has launched an educational program for hospital emergency room personnel. By late 1981, almost half of the hospitals in the county have signed up for the program. Similar educational efforts undoubtedly are needed across the country.

But, the progress that has been made is now threatened. In the late 1970s and early 1980s, cuts in government spending for social services severely affected rape crisis centers. Although most were established by volunteers on shoestring budgets, the costs of maintaining a center are high. Many eventually obtained some government funding and, when such money became scarce, were forced to cease operation. In mid-1981, before the full effects of the Reagan budget cuts were felt, about a quarter of the approximately 600 centers that had been established during the 1970s had closed.[159] Some centers have managed to tap private funding sources effectively. For example, the Santa Monica Rape Treatment Center, a model hospital-based, comprehensive-treatment center, has developed a reliable support base among the affluent Los Angeles liberal community.[160] For most centers, however, relying upon purely private funding will mean at best a hand-to-mouth existence. Furthermore, if more cuts in government social spending are made, the competition for private funds will become even more fierce.

Not all the news is bad. The campaigns to change rape laws

[157]*Los Angeles Times,* December 13, 1981.
[158]Ibid.
[159]*New York Times,* August 31, 1981.
[160]*Los Angeles Times,* October 18, 1981.

and judicial proceedings launched in the 1970s have shown important results. Most states have made some reforms in their rape laws, with the most frequent change being a restriction on the admission of evidence about the victim's previous sexual history. But although progress has been made, recent rape cases show that the old misogynist assumptions are far from dead. In Madison, Wisconsin, a teenage boy convicted of raping a 16-year-old girl was "sentenced" to a year of supervision by his parents. In explaining his leniency, the judge called the rape "a normal reaction . . . to sexual permissiveness and provocative clothing."[161] Feminist groups and other outraged citizens organized a recall petition drive in which they obtained almost twice the required number of signatures. The judge was removed from the bench in September 1977 in the first judicial recall election in Wisconsin history. He lost to a feminist candidate. Another Wisconsin judge, hearing a case in which a 24-year-old man sexually assaulted a 5-year-old girl, blamed the attack on the girl. Incredibly, he called the 5-year-old "an unusually sexually permissive young lady" and "the aggressor" in the assault.[162] A recall campaign is now underway.

More important than these judges' attitudes is the response they have provoked. Attitudes about rape do seem to be changing. The feminist position has received considerable favorable coverage in the press. Because of its large audience, the "All in the Family" episode in which Edith Bunker is raped may have contributed significantly to a change in public perceptions of rape. People who work with rape victims also report a change. "The women I get today feel better about themselves as women," said Pamela Klein of the National Coalition Against Sexual Assault. "They are less willing to hold themselves responsible for what happened."[163]

A major change in attitudes was a prerequisite to raising the problem of marital rape. Even now it is difficult to get many legislators to treat it as a serious issue. "If you can't rape your wife, who can you rape?" a California state senator said to a group of feminist lobbyists.[164] The campaign on marital rape is still in its infancy. Marital rape is considered a crime in only a few states (see Chapter 7). The National Center on Women and Family Law has conducted a study of the marital rape exemption in the states' criminal laws and

[161]*Los Angeles Times,* June 3, 1977.
[162]*National NOW Times,* January/February 1982, p. 6.
[163]*New York Times,* August 31, 1981.
[164]*Express,* May 16, 1980.

provides information to feminists who want to launch reform campaigns.[165] This is an area in which a great deal of public education is needed. A campaign to change the law, even if it is not initially successful, is an excellent way of focusing public attention on the problem.

The feminist movement has also forced people to look at other aspects of reality that many would rather pretend did not exist. One of these seldom-discussed subjects is wife-beating. Contrary to myth, this is not a rare occurrence, nor is it restricted to the "lower classes." During 1973, approximately 14,000 wife-abuse complaints reached the New York State Family Courts.[166] And cases that make it to court are only the tip of the iceberg. Virtually all police personnel agree that wife-beating is the most underreported of all crimes; it has been estimated that a million women a year are subjected to domestic violence.[167]

Guilt and fear frequently prevent battered women from reporting the crime. As with rape, prevalent attitudes in our society are such that women who have been beaten often believe that somehow it's their fault. Many feel a public admission would expose them as failures at the role of wife. Economically dependent upon their husbands, lacking any place to go, battered wives fear that calling the police will only increase their husbands' wrath.

If a battered wife does call the police, her complaint is often not taken seriously. The husband will be arrested only at last resort and only if he has inflicted considerable injury. Police do not like getting involved in domestic conflicts, and unfortunately, too many seem to believe that there's nothing wrong about a husband slapping his wife around a little. Yet according to a Kansas City study, 96 percent of that city's family homicides had been preceded by at least one "domestic disturbance" call.[168]

The magnitude of the problem first became apparent in London. A Women's Aid center, opened in 1971 to provide advice and support to women, found battered women coming in seeking shelter. The refuge that was established provided shelter to almost 5000 women and children in its first 3 years.[169] There are now about 50 such shelters in England. The first center in the United States had a

---

[165]*Women's Rights Law Reporter* 6 (spring 1980), 159.

[166]Judith Gingold, "One of These Days—Pow Right in the Kisser," *Ms.*, August 1976, p. 52.

[167]*In These Times,* May 18–24, 1977.

[168]Gingold, op. cit., p. 54.

[169]Grimstad and Rennie, *Sourcebook,* op. cit., p. 214.

similar history. Women Advocates of St. Paul, Minnesota, started in 1972 as a phone service for answering women's legal questions.[170] Staffers were soon deluged by women seeking emergency housing, which was not available. A fund-raising campaign resulted in enough money to open a shelter in 1974. Rape hot-lines also frequently received calls from battered women desperate for someplace to go.

Although a number of privately funded shelters for battered women have been opened around the country, the need much exceeds the supply. Lengthy waiting lists are intolerable when delay may mean serious injury or death. Because of the high cost of operating shelters, government funding has often been sought. A group in Orange County, California, obtained federal grant money to open a shelter. The NOW Wife Assault Task Force in Ann Arbor, Michigan, which provides emergency housing as well as other services, paid one full-time staff member out of Federal Government Comprehensive Employment and Training Act (CETA) funds.[171] A Brooklyn program operated jointly by the YWCA and the National Congress of Neighborhood Women received a $200,000 grant from New York State as start-up money.[172] The California legislature provided money for a pilot program to establish a limited number of shelters there.

By 1978, there were about 300 shelters, and the National Coalition Against Domestic Violence had been formed. Trying to develop reliable funding sources has been a top priority. Several states have been induced to increase their marriage license fees and earmark the money raised for spouse-abuse prevention programs. Florida took the lead in 1978. Since then Montana, California, Michigan, Kansas, North Dakota, and Ohio have followed. Indiana has imposed an antiabuse fee on divorce filings. This source of funds has been of immense help to those shelters that receive it because it is not dependent upon the vagaries of politics or the whims of private donors. The fees are not sufficient, however, to support the total budget of most shelters. Mercy House, one of four shelters in Montana, is probably typical. About $18,000 of its $60,000 budget comes from fees; the rest must be raised from foundations, churches, the United Way, and individual donations.

The National Coalition Against Domestic Violence, supported by other feminist groups, mounted a campaign to establish a federal program. In 1979 the House and in 1980 the Senate passed a domes-

---

[170]*Do It Now*, June 1976.

[171]Ibid.

[172]*In These Times*, May 18–24, 1977.

tic violence bill authorizing $65 million over 3 years, mostly for emergency shelters. The House passed the bill easily, but in the Senate, the vote was 46–41. Incredibly, conservative Christian groups targeted the bill for defeat and, led by the Moral Majority, subjected Senators to intense pressure. These groups opposed the bill because, in the words of Senator Gordon Humphrey, the federal government had "no business" intruding in family disputes. In the end, the Moral Majority defeated the broad coalition of women's, civil rights, and social service organizations who supported the bill. Although the conference report was easily approved in the House, opponents of the legislation threatened a filibuster in the Senate and, because it was so late in the session, killed the bill.

The defeat of the bill proved to be a tragedy because the little federal money shelters had been getting from other government programs fell victim to Reagan's 1981 budget cuts. Shelters may still get some money from federal block grants to the states, but competition for these funds will be fierce. Unfortunately, retrogression is a real possibility in many areas. Many women will be forced to endure abuse because they have nowhere to go.

While essential, sufficient emergency housing is by no means a solution to the problem. Social service agencies and the police must be made more sensitive to domestic violence. A good deal of feminist effort is going into getting the police to enforce the law. In New York, a class-action suit on behalf of battered wives was filed in 1976. The suit charged that the police "deny the existence, prevalence, and seriousness of violence against married women or treat it as a private privilege of marital discipline."[173] The police frequently refused to respond to requests for assistance from battered wives and were extremely reluctant to arrest the husband.[174] In June 1978, the New York City Police Department entered into a consent judgment with the plaintiffs. In the agreement, the police bound themselves to guaranteeing battered women the same police protection and assistance afforded other crime victims. What this obligation entails is spelled out in considerable detail.[175] That this settlement represents an important victory indicates how little protection battered women formerly received from the police. A massive monitoring campaign to make sure the police live up to the agreement is underway. Encouragingly, the settlement appears to be having an impact beyond

---

[173]*Ms.,* April 1977, p. 19.
[174]Laurie Woods, "Litigation on Behalf of Battered Women," *Women's Rights Law Reporter* 5 (fall 1978), 7–34.
[175]Ibid., 28–31.

New York. Feminists, using it as a model, have pressured police departments in a number of cities to change their procedures.[176] The National Center on Women and Family Law has prepared a comprehensive training module to aid advocates for battered women.[177]

The roots of the physical abuse of women lie in our society's beliefs about appropriate sex roles and the institutional arrangements that result from these beliefs. Men are expected to be aggressive and physically assertive, to be head of the household. Women are expected to be dependent and passive. Within the traditional family structure, women are economically dependent upon their husbands and thus basically powerless. Under these circumstances, it is not altogether surprising that men take out their frustrations by beating their wives—often the only person over whom they have power. A real solution thus requires basic changes in attitudes and power relationships.

Some of the uglier symptoms of the underlying attitude toward women in our society are the prevalence of violence against women in films and the bizarre record jackets put out by a number of reputable firms and popular rock groups. On the record jackets, women have been shown badly beaten and seemingly enjoying it. Women Against Violence Against Women was formed to combat such outrages. The group forced a billboard advertising one such record to be removed and organized a boycott of the companies involved. After a 2½-year struggle, Warner Communications, Inc., one of the worst offenders, agreed to renounce such promotional tactics. "The WCI record group opposes the depiction of violence, against men or women, on album covers and in related promotional material," the company's president said in a joint statement issued by WCI and WAVAW in Los Angeles and New York.[178] Although this was a major breakthrough, it was only one battle in a much bigger war.

Recently, some feminists have extended the attack to include pornography. The image of women in pornography is extremely negative and demeaning. In it, women are depicted as objects, not as feeling individuals. Violence against women is a major theme in pornography, and women are frequently shown as enjoying it. Although all feminists oppose pornography's depiction of women, there is some argument about what should be done. Some advocate censorship; others are concerned that this would violate the right to freedom of speech. Large reputable record and film companies can be

[176]Ibid., p. 31 n. 156.

[177]*Women's Rights Law Reporter* 6 (spring 1980), 159.

[178]*Los Angeles Times,* November 9, 1979.

subjected to the pressure of public opinion as was done with WCI. This tactic is, unfortunately, much less likely to be successful with the small and more marginal companies that produce pornography and that do not have reputations to lose. The best answer in the long run is to destroy the market for pornography through education. In the short run, there may not be an answer short of breaching the First Amendment.

THE EQUAL RIGHTS AMENDMENT

The Equal Rights Amendment had been introduced in every session of Congress since 1923, but in 1963 the possibility of favorable action seemed more remote than ever. In that year, the President's Commission on the Status of Women opposed the ERA, declaring that it was unnecessary and in fact undesirable, since it would void state protective laws for women. The AFL-CIO, the United Auto Workers, the Women's Bureau, and the League of Women Voters all opposed the amendment. Only the tiny National Women's party and the National Federation of Business and Professional Women's Clubs supported it—and the latter was not actively working in its behalf. With the resurgence of feminism, interest in the amendment revived. Passage of the ERA was included in NOW's bill of rights, although only after a struggle. In late 1967, President Johnson said he personally favored the amendment, and Nixon came out in support during the 1968 campaign. Nixon's Task Force on the Status of Women supported passage in its report, and the Citizens Advisory Committee strongly urged passage.

The voiding of some state protective laws on the basis of their being in conflict with Title VII of the 1964 Civil Rights Act made it easier for some groups to change their position. At their national convention in 1970, the United Auto Workers reversed themselves and came out for the ERA. While the national board of the AFL-CIO remained opposed, a statewide AFL-CIO women's conference in Wisconsin endorsed the amendment and stated its opposition to state protective laws. Elizabeth Koontz, head of the Women's Bureau, persuaded the Department of Labor to change its position by June 1970.

In May 1970, hearings on the amendment began in a subcommittee of the Senate Judiciary Committee. The result of pressure by NOW—members had disrupted Senate hearings on the 18-year-old vote, demanding hearings on the ERA—the hearings were devoted predominantly to friendly witnesses and reported the amendment to the full committee with a favorable recommendation on June 28, 1970.

The House Judiciary Committee, under the chairmanship of Emanuel Celler, a long-time opponent of the ERA, refused to hold hearings or issue a report. To get the amendment out of committee, Martha Griffiths, the primary sponsor, resorted to the use of the discharge petition. This tactic is considered an insult to the chairman and to the committee and thus is seldom successful. Since 1910, only 24 bills had been brought to the floor in this way.[179]

Griffiths filed the petition on June 11; by July 20, she had gathered the necessary 218 signatures. "I didn't let anyone forget this one," she said.

> I chased fellow congressmen ruthlessly. I'd even listen to roll calls for the names of any who hadn't signed. Having spotted the face, I'd promptly corner him for his autograph. Louisiana's Hale Boggs, Democrat whip, was opposed to the amendment. But he promised to sign as Number 200, convinced that I would never make it. You may be sure that when I had Number 199 signed up, I rushed to his office, and Hale Boggs became Number 200.[180]

Pressure from women's groups had made opposition politically dangerous. On August 10, the House passed the ERA by an overwhelming 352–15 vote.

The ERA fared less well on the Senate floor. An amendment by Senator Sam Ervin exempting women from the draft was added. A totally unrelated amendment guaranteeing the right of nondenominational prayer in the public schools also passed. These crippling amendments sealed the ERA's fate for that session. No further action was taken.

Pressure by women's groups continued. On June 22, 1971, the House Judiciary Committee reported out the ERA by a 32–2 vote. Chairman Celler was still opposed, but other committee members, fearing another successful discharge petition and the wrath of their women constituents, voted overwhelmingly against him. The victory was only a partial one. The committee had added the Wiggins Amendment, which allowed Congress to exempt women from the draft and permitted either Congress or the states to enact laws allowing different labor standards for men and women. As Don Edwards, an ERA supporter, pointed out on the floor, the Wiggins Amendment was added to kill the ERA. It would, he said, in effect repeal the por-

---

[179]*Congressional Quarterly Almanac* (Washington, D.C.: Congressional Quarterly, 1970), p. 707.
[180]Quoted in Hope Chamberlin, *A Minority of Members* (New York: Praeger, 1973), pp. 259–260.

tion of Title VII that prohibits sex discrimination in employment. Bella Abzug said that the clause intended to retain protective labor laws would "protect women from only one thing—from participating effectively in society, despite the fact that many are compelled by economic conditions to work and participate. Believe it or not, my friend, some of us even choose to work and participate."[181] Martha Griffiths, the original sponsor of the ERA, said that if the Wiggins Amendment were approved, she would vote against the ERA as amended and would ask others to do so. Celler, a die-hard opponent to the end, supported the Wiggins Amendment on the floor, but it was defeated 87 to 265. On October 12, the House passed the ERA by a 354–23 vote. Nine of the 11 congresswomen voted for it; one, Edith Green, did not vote; Lenore Sullivan, who was dependent on labor backing for reelection, voted against it.

The Senate Judiciary Committee reported out the ERA on March 14, 1972, without amendments. In committee, only Sam Ervin voted against it. The committee's report said that "the basic principle on which the amendment rests may be stated shortly: sex should not be a factor in determining the legal rights of men or of women. The amendment thus recognizes the fundamental dignity and individuality of each human being."[182]

On the floor of the Senate, Sam Ervin was the major opponent. "During the debate he quoted the Bible, recited poetry, spun North Carolina tales, and discoursed at length on constitutional law."[183] If the amendment were ratified, women would be drafted and "sent into battle to have their fair forms blasted into fragments by the bombs and shells of the enemy."[184] Amending the Constitution to get rid of discriminatory state laws, he said, "would be about as wise as using an atomic bomb to exterminate a few mice."[185]

Ervin offered amendment after amendment: to exempt women from the draft and from combat service, to retain protective laws, to secure sexual privacy, and so forth. Supporters countered all his arguments and voted down all his amendments. If any one of them had passed, the ERA would have been severely compromised. If a conference to resolve House-Senate differences had been necessary, Celler, the archfoe, would have represented the House.

Finally, on March 22, the Senate passed the ERA without

[181]*Congressional Quarterly Almanac,* op. cit., p. 657.
[182]*Congressional Quarterly Weekly Report* 20 (March 25, 1972), 693.
[183]Ibid., p. 692.
[184]Quoted in ibid., p. 694.
[185]Quoted in ibid.

change by an 84–8 vote. Two southern Democrats and six Republicans voted against it. Martha Griffiths, aided by Congresswoman Margaret Heckler, had lobbied hard in the Senate and won.

The *Congressional Record* noted that there were demonstrations in the galleries when the vote was announced. Women's groups had worked hard for passage. They had lobbied, organized letter-writing campaigns, and put out publicity to inform women across the country. One group of middle-aged women lobbied every Wednesday afternoon for months on Capitol Hill. They called themselves Crater's Raiders, after Flora Crater, organizer of the Virginia Women's Political Caucus and later the feminist candidate for lieutenant governor. Without such pressure the amendment would have failed. Other groups, such as Common Cause, participated in the effort.

There was little time to celebrate passage. For ratification, approval by 38 states would be needed. The first states came easily. Hawaii ratified the ERA only minutes after congressional passage. By the end of 1972, 22 states had ratified. NOW, the National Women's Political Caucus, the League of Women Voters, and other women's groups lobbied vigorously in many states. Personal visits with state legislators and letter-writing campaigns were organized. In many places, statewide coalitions of women's groups were formed. Pro-ERA speakers were present to testify at legislative hearings; close watch was kept on the position of each legislator. In those states where the ERA had not been ratified, women challenged anti-ERA legislators in the 1974 elections and defeated many of them.

Early in the ratification fight, major opposition came from the AFL-CIO, which still based its argument on the protective laws. Most of the major groups on the far right joined in fairly quickly. The John Birch Society, the National States' Rights party, the White Citizens Council, Young Americans for Freedom, the Ku Klux Klan, and the Christian Crusade were prominent among opposition groups.[186] Phyllis Schlafly surfaced as the most prominent opposition spokesperson. A self-proclaimed ordinary housewife and author (she has written a number of right-wing tracts including *A Choice Not an Echo*), she headed STOP ERA, a nationwide organization of indeterminate size.[187] Her arguments are the usual ones and are stated in the most inflammatory way possible: Under the ERA

---

[186]See Lisa Cronin Wohl, "The Sweetheart of the Silent Majority," *Ms.,* March 1974; and *Do It Now: Monthly Newsletter of the National Organization for Women* 7, no. 4 (April 1974), 10.

[187]Wohl, op. cit., p. 55.

rest rooms and prisons would be desegregated; unwilling mothers would be forced to go to work; women would be sent into combat. Misstatements and half-truths seemed to be a basic part of her strategy. Expounding the virtues of the present support laws on William Buckley's "Firing Line," she told of a case in which the court had forced a husband to buy his wife a mink coat.[188] She implied that this was his obligation under the support laws; she did not explain that the woman had charged the coat, and under a law protecting creditors, the husband was liable for the woman's debts. Nor did she add that if the man had charged the coat, the woman would have been liable.

Schlafly traveled around the country speaking against the ERA. Anti-ERA legislators were very generous with their time, and Schlafly returned the favors by testifying at many legislative hearings. Whenever an ERA proponent appeared on tv or radio, Schlafly requested and usually got equal time. Thus she received a great deal of media exposure.

Business involvement in the anti-ERA campaign, when it occurred, was very discreet. NOW charged that in Nebraska the opposition was heavily funded by the insurance industry, and similar rumors surfaced elsewhere.[189]

Eight more states ratified the ERA during 1973. In late 1974, the AFL-CIO reversed itself and endorsed the amendment. Reportedly, pressure by union women and the organization's increasing discomfort with the legislative company it was keeping caused the reversal. But even with this new support, victories became more and more difficult. In 1974, three additional states ratified; in 1975, one; 1976 saw no new states added to the list; 1977, only one.

Although only three additional states were needed, time was running out; March 22, 1979 was the deadline for the ratification campaign. Although the ERA had the support of the Carter administration, this did not translate into victories in any of the unratified states. When it became clear that meeting the deadline would not be possible, feminists went to Congress to request an extension. After an intense lobbying campaign, Congress extended the deadline until June 30, 1982.

ERA supporters pursued a variety of strategies. In the electoral arena they attempted to replace opponents with supporters. Legislators who were declared supporters and won with movement support but then voted against the ERA came under attack, and a number

[188]Ibid., p. 56.
[189]Ibid., p. 88.

were defeated. NOW and other women's groups urged organizations not to hold conventions in unratified states. By late 1977, more than 45 organizations—ranging from the American Association of Law Librarians to the American Home Economics Association—had joined the boycott, and cities such as Chicago, Atlanta, and St. Louis were losing millions as a result. The state of Missouri sued NOW, but in 1979 the convention boycott was ruled a legitimate political tool.[190] By mid-1980, almost 200 organizations had joined the boycott, including even the American Psychiatric Association.[191] In late 1981, the Directors Guild of America promised to boycott film and tv production in the unratified states.[192] A host of celebrities were enlisted in the effort. Former First Ladies Betty Ford and Lady Bird Johnson were prominent in the ratification effort, as were actors Alan Alda, Ester Rolle, and Jean Stapleton. NOW made ERA ratification its foremost goal, and large numbers of women left their families, their jobs, or their schools to work as "equality riders" in the unratified states.

But despite all this effort, pro-ERA forces lost the battle for ratification. A 1981 Gallup poll showed that 63 percent of the American people supported ERA, so clearly a lack of popular support was not the problem.[193] Most of the traditional women's groups like the League of Women Voters and the National Federation of Business and Professional Women supported the ERA and worked actively for its ratification. Almost every progressive organization in the country endorsed the amendment. Thus feminists did not lack allies or organized support. But, because 38 states are required, amending the Constitution is very difficult. ERA opponents were strong in the remaining unratified states—most of which are in the South or are states in which the Mormon church is powerful. The Mormon church has been a strong opponent of the ERA. In late 1979, it excommunicated Sonia Johnson for supporting the ERA; it sent money and organizers into unratified states to work against feminist ratification drives.[194] It was a Mormon judge who ruled that Congress's extension of the ERA deadline was unconstitutional but that the recision voted by five states was valid. Laurence Tribe, a Harvard Law School professor of constitutional law, called the decision "a naked exercise of unjustified judicial power," and it was stayed by the Supreme

190*Washington Post,* February 22, 1979.
191*Los Angeles Times,* May 9, 1980.
192*Los Angeles Times,* October 23, 1981.
193*Women's Political Times,* August 1981, p. 19.
194*In These Times,* February 20–26, 1980.

Court.[195] The growing organizational strength of far-right groups and the boost that the 1980 election results gave them made the ratification drive immensely more difficult. Feminists can take pride in the growth in public support for the ERA, despite the virulent and temporarily successful right-wing campaign against it. Furthermore some of the constitutional amendments proposed by the right wing and its congressional supporters make the wisdom of the framers more apparent. The fact that it is extremely difficult to amend the Constitution can work for us as well as against us.

The failure of the ratification drive means the women's movement has lost an important battle, but not the war. Furthermore, the 10-year struggle did have some payoffs. Large numbers of movement women learned important political organizing skills. The movement discovered it could raise large amounts of money; millions were raised during the first 6 months of 1982. The ERA will be reintroduced in Congress, but NOW intends to concentrate on electing more women to legislatures before mounting another major ERA drive. The NWPC also plans to intensify its electoral activities. The women's movement has emerged from the ratification effort with impressive political skills; if supporters' energies can be successfully redirected, impressive progress in electing good women is possible. "In the final analysis we were begging men for our rights," NOW president Eleanor Smeal said of the failed ratification drive.[196] The task now is to make sure that next time, that will not be necessary.

CONCLUSION

Although the women's movement is under attack, there is no real cause for discouragement. The attack is the direct result of the movement's impact on society. Indeed, for a young movement, its achievements are impressive. The next few years may have to be devoted primarily to protecting past gains, even though there are so many more changes that still need to be made. We must remember that bringing about fundamental social change is an enormous enterprise, one that usually requires not years but decades.

Can the necessary changes be accomplished within the present system? In order to create a humane and nonsexist society, will a revolution be necessary? Different feminists have widely different answers to these questions.

[195]*Houston Post,* December 29, 1981.
[196]Riverside, California, *Daily Enterprise,* June 25, 1982.

THEORIES
OF WOMEN'S LIBERATION

14

All feminists agree that women at present have lower status than men; that women are discriminated against socially, economically, and politically; and that this state of affairs is unjustified and must be changed. They differ in their analysis of the origins of women's inferior status, of why the lower status has persisted, and of what changes are necessary to end sexism.

Within the women's movement, the three major ideological positions are those of the moderate or women's rights feminists, the radical feminists, and the socialist feminists. Not all women active in the movement can be neatly placed into one of these categories, nor do all adherents of any one position agree among themselves on all matters. The ideologies are still flexible and in the process of development. The discussion that follows will sketch the ideas prevalent within each of the three groups at present.

SOCIALIST FEMINISM

Having the rich tradition of Western socialism to draw upon, socialist feminist ideology is the most elaborate and extensive of the three. Following Engels, socialist feminists see the oppression of women as stemming from the class system. They believe that women did not always occupy an inferior place. "Throughout primitive society, which was the epoch of tribal collectivism, women were the equals of men and recognized by man as such."[1] Women were, in fact, the social and cultural leaders in an egalitarian society because dur-

---

[1] Evelyn Reed, *Problems of Women's Liberation* (New York: Pathfinder Press, 1969), p. 65. This discussion of the socialist theory of origins closely follows Reed's.

ing the hunting and gathering stage their labor was the more important. Hunting, which was done by the men, was an unreliable source of food; the vegetable foods the women found and prepared were the staples of primitive peoples' diet. Women discovered agriculture, domesticated small animals, and developed the arts of pottery and weaving. Thus, in primitive society there was a sexual division of labor and women worked very hard. But in the socialist view, the assumption of some anthropologists that women were therefore oppressed is completely wrong. "The primitive woman is independent because, not in spite of, her labor."[2]

How, then, did women lose their position of equality? "The downfall of women coincided with the breakup of the matriarchal clan commune and its replacement by class-divided society with its institutions of the patriarchal family, private property and state power."[3] Hunting and gathering were gradually replaced with agriculture and stock raising. A more complex division of labor developed. Increasingly, a surplus product above subsistence needs was produced. Society, which had been homogeneous, began to be differentiated into groups that differed in the labor in which they engaged. These divisions eventually led to classes, in which some produced and others received the surplus.

> By virtue of the directing roles played by men in large-scale agriculture, irrigation and construction projects, as well as in stock raising, this surplus wealth was gradually appropriated by a hierarchy of men as their private property. This, in turn, required the institution of marriage and the family to fix the legal ownership and inheritance of a man's property. Through monogamous marriage the wife was brought under the complete control of her husband who was thereby assured of legitimate sons to inherit his wealth.[4]

Thus according to the socialist view, women's inferior status is due to the institution of private property and class-divided society and to their corollary, the family. The family did not develop to fulfill human needs for companionship, emotional support, and children— needs amply fulfilled by the communal clan. Its function at origin was the preservation of wealth within the paternal line. Woman's function within the family was preeminently that of breeder; she became in effect a possession of her husband.

Women have been oppressed as a sex in all succeeding class

---

[2]Robert Briffault, quoted in ibid., p. 43.
[3]Ibid., p. 65.
[4]Ibid.

societies. In modern capitalism, women are oppressed by their sub-ordinate role in the family and are doubly exploited as workers. Women are still defined in terms of the traditional female role as pri-marily housewives, and this is a role with little status. As Margaret Benston points out, "In a society in which money determines value, women are a group which works outside the money economy. Their work is not worth money, is therefore valueless, is therefore not real work."[5] Even when women do work at paid jobs, their position in the labor force is not taken seriously—it is not really where they be-long. Therefore, say the socialists, women serve as a reserve army of labor—to be employed when needed and fired, without political repercussions, when not.

Sexism, like racism, is seen as functional for the capitalist sys-tem.

> . . . It is not just male supremacist ideas, or individual men, who keep women doing unpaid labor in the home and low paid labor outside. It is capitalism's need for a reserve labor force, to keep wages down and profits up. The system cannot afford to free women. It cannot afford the social services necessary to allow women to be out of the home. . . . Nor can capitalism afford to give women control in areas like child-raising and reproduction, because they would then be free to demand jobs that do not exist.[6]

The nuclear family, in which the husband is the major bread-winner, also serves important functions in a capitalist society. As an economic unit, the nuclear family is a valuable stabilizing force.[7] Be-cause the husband is solely responsible for supporting his wife and children, his ability to strike or to change jobs is limited. Because the wife is economically dependent, she is also likely to become emo-tionally dependent and passive. Her economic vulnerability is apt to make her fearful and interested only in security. Therefore, she will exert a conservative influence on her husband and children. Thus the family, as currently organized, keeps both men and women from making trouble.

Capitalists thus gain from sexism. The low wages paid "work-ing" women result in higher corporate profits, while the unpaid work

[5]Margaret Benston, "The Political Economy of Women's Liberation," in Edith Hoshino Altbach, ed., From Feminism to Liberation (Cambridge, Mass.: Schenkman, 1971), p. 202.

[6]"Working Draft—Socialist Feminist Paper," in Women's Studies Program: Three Years of Struggle (Publication of Inside the Beast, California State University at San Diego, May 1973), p. 12.

[7]Benston, op. cit., p. 205.

women do in the home is essential for the reproduction and maintenance of the work force. If women did not cook, clean, and do laundry for their husbands and children, society would have to provide these services. Sexist conditioning makes women docile workers who can be easily fired when not needed. The present family structure supports the economic and political status quo. The inculcation of the sexist ideology through education and the media makes sexism, like racism, a basis for dividing the working class. When workers are split along sexual and racial lines, unions are weakened and the workers' economic bargaining power is decreased. Furthermore, such divisions make workers easier to rule politically and thus contribute to the capitalists' hold on power.

The socialist feminist explanation of women's oppression, then, places major emphasis on economic factors. The oppression of women is traced to the institution of private property and the first division of society into classes. Sexist ideology and structures such as the family, which maintain women's inferior status, persist because they are an integral part of and perform important functions for the capitalist system.

Juliet Mitchell, an English socialist feminist, enriches this analysis by emphasizing that, in analyzing the position of women at a given point in time, reproduction, sex, and the socialization of children as well as production must be considered. Women's position at any given point in history is determined by the particular combination of these elements in force at that time.[8] The extent to which reproduction is voluntary, the extent to which the socialization of children is considered primarily the women's task, and the extent of sexual freedom all affect the position of women. These factors are ultimately related to but not directly derivable from the economic factor—the mode of production:

> The contemporary bourgeois family can be seen as a triptych of sexual, reproductive and socializatory functions (the woman's world) embraced by production (the man's world)—precisely a structure which in the final instance is determined by the economy.[9]

Since, from the socialist perspective, private property and class divisions are at the root of women's oppression and since that oppression is useful for the capitalist system, a socialist revolution is needed to free women. "As long as a system works better with sex-

[8]Juliet Mitchell, "Women: The Longest Revolution," in Altbach, op. cit., p. 99.
[9]Ibid., p. 121.

ism and racism, it will not be able to 'reform' them out."[10] The women's struggle is a part of the larger struggle based on class.

Unlike earlier socialists, socialist feminists do not believe that socialism will automatically free women. The position of women in the Soviet Union and China, while much improved from that of pre-revolutionary days, is still not equal to that of men. Women must make sure, through their struggle, that the revolution is a socialist feminist one:

> Socialism that is really feminist will only come about with sharp and conscious struggle led by women. The ideas and concepts of sexism . . . will persist for a long time. In addition to changing these ideas, men's concrete power and privilege will have to be done away with. Some Socialist groups argue that men are sexist only out of false consciousness, since sexism divides the working class and keeps it from uniting against its real oppressors. But men also benefit from sexism: they gain material advantages (skills, jobs, positions), status, power and service. . . . Men, too, will benefit from ending sexism—by ending their own oppressive roles (tough, hard, competitive, etc.) and by having more human relationships—but they will also have to give up that power and privilege.[11]

To free women, the objective conditions and structures that now keep women in their place must be changed. Margaret Benston emphasizes that fighting for free and equal entry into the productive sector is not sufficient. Housework must be socialized. Otherwise the "working" woman simply ends up with two jobs. Child care, cooking, cleaning, and the other work that is done in the home must not remain the woman's private responsibility. Mitchell makes the same point in a more general way when she calls for changes in all four factors that determine women's position. While economic demands are most basic, the other elements must not be neglected. Furthermore, strategy will sometimes dictate emphasizing one or another of the noneconomic elements over the economic.[12]

Working for present reforms so long as the ultimate objective is not forgotten is imperative. Marxist women should struggle with their sisters for equal pay for equal work; equal opportunity in education and employment; free abortion on demand; and free community-controlled child-care centers. "Mobilizing women behind these

[10]"Working Draft—Socialist Feminist Paper," op. cit., p. 12.
[11]Ibid., pp. 12–13.
[12]Mitchell, op. cit., p. 121.

issues not only gives us the possibility of securing some improvements but also exposes, curbs and modifies the worst aspects of our subordination in this society."[13]

Women must maintain their independent struggle for liberation but must not fall into the trap of believing that men per se are the enemy. "No segment of society which has been subjected to oppression . . . can delegate the leadership and promotion of their fight for freedom to other forces—even though other forces can act as their allies."[14] During the course of the struggle men can and must be re-educated. Male workers must learn that "their chauvinism and dominance is another weapon in the hands of the master class for maintaining its rule."[15]

What, then, is the socialist feminist vision of the good society after the revolution? No one has drawn up blueprints, but the general outlines are clear. The society would be democratic both politically and economically. The means of production would be publicly owned and the fruits of production equably distributed. Factors like sex and race would no longer predetermine one's status or life-style. Most of the functions the family now performs—child care, for example—would be socially performed, and as a result, the oppressiveness of the present bourgeois family would cease. According to Mitchell, the result would be not the destruction of the family, but "a plural range of institutions—where the family is only one. . . ."[16]

RADICAL FEMINISM

Because it is a newer ideology, radical feminism is less fully developed than socialist feminism, and there is less agreement among its adherents. All radical feminists agree, however, that the oppression of women is the first and most basic case of domination by one group over another. "Male supremacy is the oldest, most basic form of domination. All other forms of exploitation and oppression (racism, capitalism, imperialism, etc.) are extensions of male supremacy: Men dominate women, a few men dominate the rest."[17]

The problem, then, is the sex class system through which women have been relegated to being breeders and have been excluded from the creation of and any real participation in culture.

[13]Reed, op. cit., p. 75.
[14]Ibid.
[15]Ibid., pp. 75–76.
[16]Mitchell, op. cit., p. 123.
[17]"Redstockings' Manifesto," in Betty and Theodore Roszak, eds., *Masculine/Feminine* (New York: Harper & Row, 1969), p. 273.

"Radical feminism recognizes the oppression of women as a fundamental political oppression wherein women are categorized as an inferior class based upon their sex."[18] The function of sexism is primarily psychological, not economic. According to the New York Radical Feminists,

> . . . The purpose of male chauvinism is primarily to obtain psychological ego satisfaction, and . . . only secondarily does this manifest itself in economic relationships. For this reason we do not believe that capitalism, or any other economic system, is the cause of female oppression, nor do we believe that female oppression will disappear as a result of a purely economic revolution. The political oppression of women has its own class dynamic; and the dynamic must be understood in terms previously called "non-political"—namely the politics of the ego. . . . Man establishes his "manhood" in direct proportion to his ability to have his ego override woman's, and derives his strength and self-esteem through this process.[19]

Among radical feminists, only Shulamith Firestone has developed a comprehensive theory of the origins of women's oppression. The origins of the sex class system, she says, lie in the biologically determined reproductive roles of men and women; in short, in the fact that women bear and nurse children. "Unlike economic class, sex class sprang directly from a biological reality: men and women were created different and not equally privileged."[20] Until reliable birth control methods became available, women were "at the continual mercy of their biology."[21] Biology made women dependent on males for their physical survival. Thus "the biological family is an inherently unequal power distribution."[22] The result is power psychology and the economic class system. "Natural reproductive differences between the sexes led directly to the first division of labor at the origins of class."[23]

The exploitation of woman by man and of man by man has its origins in biology, not economics, say the radical feminists. The male's biological advantage in not being the bearer of children made

---

[18]"Politics of the Ego: A Manifesto for N.Y. Radical Feminists," in Anne Koedt, Ellen Levine, and Anita Rapone, eds., *Radical Feminism* (New York: Quadrangle, 1973), p. 379.

[19]Ibid., pp. 379–380.

[20]Shulamith Firestone, *The Dialectic of Sex* (New York: Bantam, 1970), p. 8.

[21]Ibid.

[22]Ibid.

[23]Ibid., p. 9.

the female dependent on him. This dependency of female on male is the prototype of all power relationships and the origin of the power psychology—the desire to dominate others. The first division of labor—that between man and woman—contained a power component. From this developed the exploitative economic class system. According to Firestone, "current leftist analysis [is] outdated and superficial because this analysis does not relate the structure of the economic class system to its origins in the sexual class system, the model for all other exploitative systems and thus the tapeworm that must be eliminated first by any true revolution."[24]

Although women's oppression has its origins in biology, it is not therefore immutable. Technological developments—reliable birth control and, in the future, artificial reproduction (i.e., test-tube babies)—have the potential for freeing women. However, oppression will not cease just because its biological determinants are overcome. The supporting structures for maintaining that oppression are still functioning. A feminist revolution is needed, and its first stirrings are already occurring.[25]

While not all radical feminists would subscribe to Firestone's exclusively biological explanation, all would agree that all past and present societies are patriarchies. Men institutionalized their domination over women via social structures such as the family and religion. "The oppression of women is manifested in particular institutions, constructed and maintained to keep women in their place. Among these are the institutions of marriage, motherhood, love, and sexual intercourse (the family unit is incorporated by [these])."[26] To free women, these institutions and the sexist ideology they foster must be destroyed. Revolution, not reform, is needed.

According to Firestone, revolution is possible because of the control over reproduction technology has made possible; it is necessary simply for survival. The population explosion must be controlled, and soon, if disaster is to be averted. But the family structure and the psychology it fosters make such control impossible. People have too many babies and for the wrong reasons—to satisfy ego needs by possessing and living through a child. The reduction of population growth and the rearing of psychologically healthy children will be possible only when the family is destroyed.

The revolution envisioned by the radical feminists, then, aims at a total restructuring of society. The abolition of capitalism and the

24Ibid., p. 37.
25Ibid., p. 31.
26"Politics of the Ego: A Manifesto for N.Y. Radical Feminists," op. cit., p. 381.

institution of a socialist economy, while necessary, are not sufficient. Nor is it reforms in the status of women that are sought. "The end goal of feminist revolution must be . . . not just the elimination of male *privilege* but of sex *distinction* itself: genital difference between human beings would no longer matter culturally."[27] Thus all sex role typing must be abolished. Still, integrating women into the male world is not the answer.

> We believe that the male world as it now exists is based on the corrupt notion of "maleness vs. femaleness," that the oppression of women is based on this very notion and its attendant institutions. . . . We must eradicate the sexual division on which our society is based.[28]

Women must make the revolution; they can expect little help from men. The first step is to free themselves from the self-destructive, sexist notions they have internalized:

> We must begin to destroy the notion that we are indeed only servants of the male ego, and must begin to reverse the systematic crushing of women's egos by constructing alternative selves that are healthy, independent and self-assertive. We must, in short, help each other to transfer the ultimate power of judgment about the value of our lives from men to ourselves.[29]

Radical feminists believe that the destruction of the sex class system will ultimately benefit men by freeing them from the masculine role, which is also oppressive, and thus make possible genuinely human relations. Men cannot, however, be expected to realize this. They have been warped by the power psychology, and they derive real benefits from the present system. "*All men* receive economic, sexual, and psychological benefits from male supremacy. *All men* have oppressed women."[30] Thus only women working together can bring about a nonsexist, nonoppressive society.

What, then, will the new society be like? Firestone sets out four conditions that it must fulfill.

1. Women must be freed from the "tyranny of their reproductive biology."[31] Child rearing and even childbearing will become the responsibility of society as a whole. Men, as well as women, will be involved. Further advances in the biologi-

---

[27]Firestone, op. cit., p. 11.
[28]Bonnie Kreps, "Radical Feminism 1," in Koedt et al., op. cit., p. 239.
[29]"Politics of the Ego: A Manifesto for N.Y. Radical Feminists," op. cit., pp. 382–383.
[30]"Redstockings' Manifesto," op. cit., p. 273.
[31]Firestone, op. cit., p. 206.

cal sciences should make artificial reproduction possible for those who wish to make use of it. Changes in child rearing require radical social reorganization.

2. "The full self-determination, including economic, of both women and children"[32] will be necessary. Feminist socialism in a land of plenty will provide economic independence for everyone whether they "work" or not. With increasing automation, work as we know it would disappear. Dull, repetitive, uncreative tasks would be done by machines. Human beings would be free to occupy themselves at whatever they found interesting, whether socially useful or not.

3. "The total integration of women and children into all aspects of the larger society"[33] would be required.

4. Full sexual freedom must be guaranteed to both women and children.[34]

The fulfillment of the first two conditions would strip the family of its reproductive and economic functions and thus destroy it. The latter two would ensure an end to any form of social oppression.

While disclaiming any intention or desire to provide a detailed blueprint of the future society, Firestone does present sketches meant to stimulate further thought. "The most important characteristic to be maintained in any revolution is flexibility," she says.[35] There should, she says, be a multitude of options. People should be able to choose the life-style that suits them best and change it at will. This would be possible in an affluent, highly automated, socialist society in which no one had to work.

She suggests two nonreproductive styles—single professions and "living together." The first she describes as "a single life organized around the demands of a chosen profession, satisfying the individual's social and emotional needs through its own particular occupational structure."[36] More satisfactory for some people would be "living together"—the "loose social form in which two or more partners, of whatever sex, enter a nonlegal sex/companionate arrangement the duration of which varies with the internal dynamics of the relationship."[37]

[32]Ibid., p. 207.
[33]Ibid., p. 208.
[34]Ibid., p. 209.
[35]Ibid., p. 227.
[36]Ibid.
[37]Ibid., p. 228.

These two forms provide for various combinations of privacy and companionship, and one or both would probably be the choice of most people for at least part of their lives. They are not, however, suitable for children. For children and adults who like and want to be around children for part or all of their lives, there would be households—a group of adults and children living together. To provide the stability needed for the children, the adults would contract to live together for a specified time—7 to 10 years, Firestone suggests. After that period each individual and the group as a whole could decide whether to remain together. Both child care and other chores would be equally shared by all the adults and thus would not be burdensome. Children born into a household would have the right to transfer out if they so wished. This setup would make it possible for children to form close relationships with adults and other children without being anyone's "property," as is the case in the nuclear family.

Radical feminists and socialist feminists thus differ over the origins and the present function of women's oppression. Socialist feminists see the origins in the institution of private property and the division of society into classes; radical feminists emphasize female biology—particularly the woman's reproductive role. Sexism, according to the radical feminists, primarily serves a psychological function for men. Socialist feminists, in contrast, see sexism as primarily serving an economic function for the capitalist.

Radical feminists, then, see patriarchy (male supremacy) as the defining characteristic of our society; for socialist feminists, the defining characteristic is capitalism. They agree that to free women a revolution that is both socialist and feminist is necessary; but, differing in their prior analysis, they place differing emphases on the two elements. Socialist feminists see a socialist revolution as a necessary but not sufficient condition for a nonsexist society. Participation by active, committed socialist feminists in the revolutionary struggle and in the new society will ensure the demise of sexism. Radical feminists believe that a feminist revolution against the patriarchy will destroy sexism and also institute socialism. The two groups' ideals of the good society, then, do not differ greatly.

Socialist feminists and most radical feminists believe androgyny to be a major defining characteristic of the good society. With the destruction of sex roles, both male and female would be free to develop and express the full range of valued human traits. Creativity, independence, nurturance, and sensitivity would be considered desirable characteristics in all human beings. Liberation consists not in women "becoming" men but in both male and female being free to become truly human. In a good society both men and women would be different from what they are in our society. Personality differences among people would still exist, but they would not be related to sex. Furthermore, society would be structured so as to encourage the development of traits such as cooperativeness and sensitivity toward others.

A few women have rejected androgyny and substituted the notion of matriarchy. These women have tended to glorify all traits presently labeled feminine—even those that most feminists see as self-destructive. One version of this position is based on the biological differences between the sexes. Women are, by nature, mothers, it is claimed; but rather than justifying women's inferior place, the capacity for motherhood makes women superior. "Female biology is the basis of women's powers."[38]

Although this position is rare in the movement, the publication in the August 1973 *Ms.* of an open letter by Jane Alpert gave it considerable publicity. Alpert, formerly closely associated with the Weathermen, presented a theory of "mother right." The feminist revolution, she said, "must be an affirmation of the power of female consciousness, of the Mother."[39] The good society will be one in which women are revered and powerful because of their capacity to bear children. ". . . [T]he point of Mother Right is to reshape the family according to the perceptions of women, and to reshape society in the image of this new matriarchal family."[40]

This extreme position is unlikely to gain many adherents because of the theoretical and practical problems it presents. To base the argument for women's liberation on the female's capacity to bear children at a time when motherhood will occupy decreasing amounts of women's time seems foolhardy. A reversal in the status of present sex roles will not end oppression. The sex roles themselves must be destroyed.

WOMEN'S RIGHTS FEMINISM

Moderate feminists have been less inclined toward abstract analysis and theorizing than their more radical sisters. Their ideology is the least integrated and least clear-cut of the three major positions. Most start from liberal principles—that all people are created equal and that there should be equal opportunity for all. They see that these

[38]Jane Alpert in *Ms.,* August 1973, p. 91.
[39]Ibid., p. 94.
[40]Ibid., p. 93.

principles have not been applied to women and demand that henceforth they should be.

No moderate has written on the origin of women's lower status. Most would probably subscribe to a biological explanation similar in content to Firestone's but very different in tone. Before reliable contraceptives and baby bottles were available, a woman had no choice but to spend the greater part of her life bearing and rearing children. By the time the technology to free women from this biologically determined role became available, the male-female division of labor had been so completely accepted as natural and right that little changed. Thus tradition maintains a form of social organization that is no longer necessary.

In *The Feminine Mystique,* Betty Friedan analyzes the costs of maintaining the traditional male-female division of labor. She concentrates on the sterile life of the middle-class housewife. Under mid–twentieth-century circumstances, housework and child rearing are not sufficiently challenging for any adult. Yet women have been taught that true self-fulfillment lies in being wife and mother exclusively. When women do not realize the promised self-fulfillment and, in fact, become miserably unhappy, they blame themselves, not their situation. Friedan's solution is for women to educate and find professions for themselves.

Since 1963, when her book was published, Friedan's analysis has broadened considerably. She and other moderates no longer concern themselves only with the plight of middle-class women. Friedan's early analysis implied that only the brainwashing of women by the schools and the media kept them from achieving professionally. Moderates now realize that legal inequalities, employment discrimination, and the lack of facilities such as child-care centers are also real barriers. They realize that women's secondary status has been institutionalized and that women cannot free themselves individually merely through a change in consciousness. A mass movement of women is needed.

Moderates do not carry their critique of motherhood and the family to the same basic level as the radical feminists do, but they agree that as now constituted, the institution of the family is oppressive to women. Betty Friedan says that as long as women are relegated to being mothers and mothers only, "motherhood is a bane and a curse."[41] When women are free to be full, equal human be-

---

[41]Betty Friedan, "Our Revolution is Unique," in Mary Lou Thompson, ed., *Voices of the New Feminism* (Boston: Beacon, 1970), p. 36.

ings, the family will no longer be oppressive. Moreover, other life-styles will also be available for those who prefer them.[42]

Although moderates have picked up some of the vocabulary of the other wings of the movement—they speak of the "oppression of women"—and see many of the same problems, their analysis of the functions sexism serves is quite different. In *The Feminine Mystique,* Friedan points out that keeping women in the home is profitable for business because it fosters overconsumption. Middle-class women with nothing interesting to occupy their time will go out and buy products they do not need. More generally, however, moderates see sexism as dysfunctional for society—it deprives society of the talents of half its members. Furthermore, moderates do not see sexism as performing a vital function for an appreciable segment of society. It doesn't really help anyone. Opposition to feminists' demands is interpreted most frequently as stemming not from self-interest but from false consciousness due to sexist socialization.

Given this analysis, moderates place great emphasis on the benefits men will derive by ending sexism. According to Friedan, "Man . . . is . . . the fellow victim of the present half-equality."[43] Radical feminists point out that men will also have to give up advantages they now enjoy. The moderates, because they do not see men as truly benefiting from sexism, do not consider men the enemy.[44]

Moderate feminists have been relatively optimistic about working with men. Organizations like NOW admit male members. Nevertheless, moderates believe that women must depend primarily on themselves. ". . . it would be as much of a mistake to expect men to hand this to women as to consider all men as the enemy, all men as oppressors," Friedan has said.[45] Like "any other oppressed group," women must lead the fight for their own liberation.

While moderates are increasingly using the term *"revolution,"* they do not mean it literally. A nonsexist society can be attained by working through the present system, they feel. Many may hope that an accumulation of reforms will transform society, but feel that radical restructuring, such as that envisioned by the socialist or radical feminists, is not necessary.

Two beliefs explain the moderates' optimism that the needed changes can be accomplished within the system. As no significant

[42]Ibid., p. 38.
[43]Ibid., p. 32.
[44]Ibid., p. 36.
[45]Ibid., p. 39.

segment really benefits from sexism, opposition to feminist demands should eventually wither away under the impact of education. Furthermore, the moderates, working from a liberal ideology, see the distribution of power in the United States as pluralist. Competition among many groups determines government policy, they feel; no single group dominates. Organized women can get into the game and, like other groups, can expect to have their demands met if they put on enough pressure.

The moderates have not sketched out their ideal society very clearly. They are often accused by their more radical sisters of demanding "let us in," not "set us free"—of simply wanting a slice of the pie. Although this may have been a fair criticism in the early days of the movement, it is considerably less so now. Moderate groups have increasingly concerned themselves with the problems of poor women—welfare mothers, for example—and of social outcasts— lesbians and prison women in particular. The notion of androgyny has also taken hold. Moderates do not advocate that women adopt the more unattractive male traits, such as aggressiveness and super-competitiveness, in order to be successful. Like socialist feminists and radical feminists, moderates believe that each person should be free to develop his or her full humanity independent of what is now labeled masculine or feminine. In a good society, valued human traits such as independence (now labeled masculine) and tenderness (now labeled feminine) would be characteristic of both men and women.

FROM IDEOLOGY TO ACTION
The three major groupings in the movement are more clearly distinct in ideology than in tactics and strategy. Much cross-fertilization has taken place. Forms of action that originated in one segment of the movement have spread to others.

Consciousness raising
Consciousness raising was developed as a feminist technique primarily by radical feminists. Rejecting the male New Left's emphasis on antiseptic, abstract theorizing, the early feminists insisted that theory must grow out of their feelings and experiences.

They quickly discovered that becoming aware of women's secondary status was only a first step. Through the socialization process women have internalized many of the assumptions of patriarchal society. Recognizing that society's notions of masculinity and femininity are assumptions, not facts, tracing out the ramifications of these assumptions, and truly freeing oneself of them is not an easy process.

A sudden revelation brought on by some blatantly sexist incident may provide the impetus for further examination; it does not make one a free woman or a true feminist.

Becoming a feminist requires both an emotional and an intellectual understanding of the patriarchal nature of society. A woman must discover how she herself has been molded by that society and how its structures affect her. To do so, she needs the warm, supportive environment provided by other women going through the same process.

From these realizations grew the theory of consciousness raising (CR). Of course the first CR groups, frequently called *rap groups* at the time, developed without the aid of theory. Dissatisfied and increasingly angered by their treatment within the New Left, women got together to discuss their problems. They soon realized that their problems were not personal and idiosyncratic but systemic and thus political. Such discussions led to increased awareness of the sexist nature of society and thus to more basic analysis and criticism.

The male Left ridiculed women's problems as trivial and CR groups as bourgeois therapy. Feminists countered that CR was highly political because it aimed for fundamental change, not adjustment. Theory and analysis, if it is to be valuable as a guide to action, must stem from personal feelings and experiences. In a CR group, women discuss their own feelings and experiences. In discovering how similar these are from one woman to another, women discover the political nature of their problems. The individual woman learns that she is not a misfit, a kook, or sick but rather that society is sick. From such discussion comes an analysis that is truly meaningful because it has been developed by the women themselves and because it is based not on abstractions but on the women's own life experiences. Such an analysis becomes an integral part of the way a woman looks at the world; it shapes the way she thinks and behaves. From this analysis strategies for action are developed. The ideal course for a CR group is from discussion of feelings and experiences, to analysis, and then to action. Each succeeding stage should grow organically from the preceding stages.

Although the consciousness-raising technique was developed by radical feminists, it has spread to all sections of the movement. Most NOW chapters have set up CR groups; all women's centers serve as a way of bringing together women who want to form groups; and many suburban homemakers otherwise unaffiliated with the movement have participated in independent CR groups.

Most groups consist of 5 to 15 women who meet weekly for

a period ranging from 6 to 18 months. A general rule is that attendance should take precedence over anything but a true emergency. How structured the discussion is varies from group to group. In some cases a woman who has previously been through CR acts as facilitator—she guides the discussion, attempts to keep participants on the topic, and helps them move from personal experiences to societal analysis. In others, all the women are new to the process and either rotate the position of facilitator or do not use it. Most groups will set a particular topic for each session—early childhood experiences and learning what being a girl means, relations with parents and siblings, first menstruation and adolescence, sex, marriage, motherhood, growing old. To what extent discussion is kept on the topic varies from group to group. Ideally, all members should participate equally and should be absolutely honest. Because of the very intimate nature of the matters discussed, reaching the ideal is not easy. Many women find it difficult at first to open up and then painful to be honest with themselves. Again ideally, the atmosphere should be so warm and supportive as to make complete honesty possible. Because the discussion brings out such basic beliefs and values, conflicts do occur and feelings sometimes run high.

Despite the problems, women who have participated in CR groups almost universally consider the experience not just worthwhile but one of the most important of their lives. Reexamining the notions one has held since childhood and being truly honest with oneself is painful, yet it is necessary if one is to start on the long journey toward becoming a free woman.

A critique of the CR technique frequently voiced a few years ago was that, whatever the theory, in practice CR often has not led to action. The problems encountered in translating analysis into action are, however, due not to the CR technique but to feminists' notions of structure.

The problem of structure

Radical feminists again took the lead in making a critique of traditional organizational structures a central tenet of feminism. A disliking of hierarchy was evident in the New Left. Despite this, feminists were offended by the power-tripping they had seen in New Left organizations. In their new movement they were determined to prevent the same structures and behavior patterns from arising.

Starting from the premise that all hierarchy and leadership is oppressive, many radical feminists concluded that the only good structure was no structure at all. All tasks should be shared, they felt; no one should be in the position of telling anyone else what to do.

Decisions should be made by consensus. *Elitist* or *star* became the worst epithet one could hurl at a sister. Women who assumed responsibility and got something done frequently were not praised but accused of ego-tripping or self-aggrandizement.

The notion that no structure at all was necessary made action very difficult, if not impossible. With no agreed-upon mechanism for making decisions, decisions frequently were not made; with no one responsible for a task, the task frequently was not done.

After a time frustrations built up and a reaction set in. Joreen's article, "The Tyranny of Structurelessness,"[46] was well received when it appeared in 1972. She points out that while structurelessness inhibits action, it does not prevent the development of an elite. If a group lacks a formal structure, a friendship clique within it will become an informal elite, and because it was not chosen by the members, it cannot be held responsible by the members. "If the movement continues to deliberately not select who shall exercise power, it does not thereby abolish power. All it does is abdicate the right to demand that those who do exercise power and influence be responsible for it."[47]

Radical feminists have increasingly come to realize that the structureless, leaderless group appropriate to consciousness raising is not appropriate to action. They have not, however, given up their commitment to nonoppressive organization. Most groups do attempt to come to decision by consensus whenever possible. Tasks are shared; no one is left with all the grubby work while others do the more creative tasks. Increasingly, an apprenticeship system is being used. Instead of expecting a woman to undertake a task with which she has had no experience—frequently the result of rotating tasks without attention to participants' skills—a younger woman and a more experienced one will work together. Leaders are more frequently officially designated, but their titles—*facilitator* or *coordinator*—indicate a real difference in function. They are expected to facilitate, not direct or dominate. The group as a whole makes policy.

These less extreme ideas about organization are now prevalent throughout the movement. NOW chapters are, in reality, autonomous. They are no longer required to get their bylaws approved by national NOW, and each chapter decides on its own what activities to undertake. Many have abandoned traditional officers' titles such as *president* for those favored in the rest of the movement. As in

[46]Joreen, "The Tyranny of Structurelessness," in Koedt et al., op. cit., pp. 285–299.
[47]Ibid., p. 297.

the more radical groups, great stress is placed on consensus decision making.

The problem of structure has not been solved. Developing organizational forms that make effectiveness possible without hierarchy or coercion is no simple task. Groups still flounder for lack of structure or disintegrate because of conflicts over structure. When groups have organized for a task, the pressures of operating in this society often create new and unforeseen quandaries and conflicts. What should be the relationship between full- and part-time workers at a self-help clinic? Should the full-timers, who do know more about the task, have greater say in its operation? Should women working at a feminist bookstore, at a self-help clinic, or on a feminist periodical pay themselves a salary? Are they taking advantage of their sisters, or are they simply making it possible to spend full time on feminist causes? If some women are paid, will a professional feminist elite emerge?

Despite the problems and the further need for experimentation with organizational forms, many groups are engaged in actions. The types of activities undertaken can be broadly divided into two categories: the setting up and running of counterinstitutions and attempts to bring about changes in governmental policy through political action.

Counterinstitutions

Feminist analysis bears heavily on the many legitimate needs of women that the institutions in our society do not adequately fulfill. One feminist response has been to set up counterinstitutions such as women's clinics, independent feminist schools, rape crisis centers, and child-care centers. Women's centers, bookstores, periodicals, and publishing houses also can be placed in this category.

Radical and socialist feminists took the lead in the development of such counterinstitutions, and most are staffed by women from these groups. Moderate feminists have, to a lesser extent, also become involved in this form of action. KNOW, Inc., discussed in the last chapter, was begun by NOW members, and moderate women have been active in rape crisis work in some areas.

Women engaged in such work see it as serving several purposes. A needed service is provided—support for rape victims, nonoppressive and inexpensive gynecological care, feminist psychological counseling, nonsexist child care. These counterinstitutions are also intended to raise women's consciousness. A rape victim helped by feminists will not only have an easier time surviving the trauma but will be more likely to interpret the experience in feminist terms.

A woman who has learned self-examination will never again let herself be cowed into silence by the coldly superior manner of a gynecologist. Made aware that there are better alternatives, women will question the way establishment institutions treat women. Thus consciousness raising takes place through experience. Its effects are not limited to women who use the services or hear about them through friends or the media. For the women who provide the services, the work is a continuation of the consciousness-raising process. Other women's experiences enrich their understanding of sexist society and increase their dedication to change.

For radical and socialist feminists, these counterinstitutions are also intended to serve as models for structures in the future good society. Some women may hope that, through an evolutionary process, their counterinstitutions will replace establishment institutions. Most believe that this is impossible without major structural change. However great the need for the services provided, our present society will limit the growth of feminist institutions and will not allow them to become a threat to the system. Constrained by lack of money, harassed by establishment groups who see them as a threat to their monopoly position, feminist counterinstitutions will be able to fill only a fraction of the need for their services.

They are, nevertheless, of real importance as experiments and as models. Nonoppressive forms of organization must be developed, and these institutions serve as laboratories. If postrevolutionary society is to be better than what exists at present, there must be models. That is a function feminist organizations can serve.

Change through the polity

All segments of the movement have been involved in traditional forms of political action aimed at changing government policy. The emphasis placed on such action and the rationale for engaging in it differ.

Moderate groups have devoted the greater portion of their effort to getting legal changes and to seeing that feminist-supported laws are actually enforced. Because most moderates believe significant change can be accomplished within the system, their emphasis on influencing government follows logically. Their form of organization—national in scope and more structured than in the rest of the movement—is well suited to such action.

Moderates use the full gamut of political tactics. They lobby, testify at legislative hearings, and organize letter-writing campaigns. They have also picketed and disrupted legislative hearings. Moderate groups have brought thousands of suits charging sex discrimination.

Lacking the money and frequently the organization for the more establishment type of political activity, socialist and radical feminists have tended to use demonstrations and the like to bring political pressure. Still, in terms of types of action, no sharp distinction between segments of the movement can be made. Groups like the New York Radical Feminists have testified at legislative hearings on rape laws; petitions opposing antiabortion amendments to the Constitution are circulating throughout the movement.

The rationale given by radical and socialist feminists for such action does differ from that of the moderates. They do not believe reform is sufficient. Certain kinds of reforms—those that pacify people through tokens—are, in fact, pernicious. Still, some reforms will ameliorate conditions. Bringing up demands around which a mass movement can be built and keeping pressure on the system will bring the revolution nearer. Thus for socialist and radical feminists, reforms are not an end in themselves but a means toward a more distant goal.

The diversity of viewpoints and the number of independent groups involved in the women's movement is a strength—not a weakness. There is a great need for experimentation, both in organizational forms and in tactics. As long as there are many groups, if one or another gets sidetracked into nonproductive activities or even disintegrates, the movement will not be endangered.

Building a movement that is viable for an extended period of time is crucial. We cannot expect a quick and easy victory. But if we can avoid the mistakes of the suffragists, who limited their goals too much and were too easily satisfied, our chances of building a humane, nonsexist society are good. After all, women do constitute more than half of the world's population.

Women, even movement women, are not yet all sisters. Class and race divide us. Old fears, prejudices, and suspicions are hard to overcome. Yet we do have many basic interests in common. Even those women who benefit materially from the status quo do so, by and large, only as adjuncts to men. They pay for their comforts through dependency. As more and more women begin to realize that the present system does not serve their interests—that it serves only the interests of a few upper-class white males—a mass movement aimed at basic socioeconomic change may emerge.

FURTHER READINGS

Those who wish to explore in greater depth any of the topics covered in this book will find the materials cited in the footnotes useful. Many of the books cited include bibliographies and most are heavily footnoted.

Because extensive bibliographies already exist, this listing is not intended to be exhaustive. I have included only those works that I consider to be especially useful.

CHAPTER 1

Figes, Eva. *Patriarchal Attitudes.* Greenwich, Conn.: Fawcett Publications, Inc., 1970. A beautifully written historical study of sexist ideology—guaranteed to both anger and amuse.

Morgan, Robin, ed. *Sisterhood is Powerful.* New York: Vintage Books, 1970. Gornick, Vivian, and Moran, Barbara, eds. *Women in Sexist Society.* New York: Signet, 1971. These are two of the earliest and still among the best collections. Both contain articles on sexist ideology and its effect on the lives of women. They provide a good introduction to the range of concerns that have activated the women's movement.

CHAPTER 2

Weisstein, Naomi. "Psychology Constructs the Female, or the Fantasy Life of the Male Psychologist." In *Roles Women Play,* edited by Michele Hoffnung Garskof. Belmont, Calif.: Brooks/Cole, 1971. This particular article is also available in many other collections. A devastating critique of psychologists' views on women, its author is a psychologist and movement activist. The article is a movement classic.

Maccoby, Eleanor E., and Jacklin, Carol N. *The Psychology of Sex Differences.* Stanford, Calif.: Stanford University Press, 1974. This is a thorough and scholarly survey of the psychological literature on sex differences.

Chesler, Phyllis. *Women and Madness.* New York: Avon Books, 1972. A powerful book about the damage that psychiatry has done to women.

Hyde, Janet Shibley, and Rosenberg, B. G. *Half the Human Experience.* Lexington, Mass.: D. C. Heath, 1976. See also Deaux, Kay. *The Behavior of Women and Men.* Monterey, Calif.: Brooks/Cole, 1976. These two brief texts are highly readable for the beginner, and both are written from a feminist point of view.

Unger, Rhoda K. *Female and Male: Psychological Perspectives.* New York: Harper & Row, 1979. A comprehensive and relatively advanced presentation of the current state of knowledge in the psychology of gender, it is very useful to the student with some background in psychology.

CHAPTER 3

Bem, Sandra L. and Daryl J. "Training the Woman to Know Her Place: The Power of a Nonconscious Ideology." Freeman, Jo. "The Social Construction of the Second Sex." Both in *Roles Women Play,* edited by Michele Hoffnung Garskof. Belmont, Calif.: Brooks/Cole, 1971. Both articles survey the socialization process from a feminist theoretical perspective.

Rivers, Caryl; Barnett, Rosalind; and Baruch, Grace. *Beyond Sugar and Spice.* New York: Putnam, 1979. This discussion of socialization is aimed at helping parents rear their children in a nonsexist way.

Sex Roles. A scholarly journal, it presents recent research, much of which relates to socialization.

The books by Shibley and Rosenberg, Deaux, and Unger cited under Chapter 2 also discuss the socialization process.

CHAPTER 4

Friedan, Betty. *The Feminine Mystique.* New York: Dell, 1964. An important book in the history of the contemporary feminist movement, it is an excellent study of the problems faced by middle-class housewives and a good analysis of the institutions that perpetuate the feminine mystique.

Bernard, Jessie. *The Future of Marriage.* New York: Bantam, 1973. A survey and analysis of the sociological literature on marriage, the book confirms Friedan's contention that marriage, as presently constituted, is not good for women.

Rubin, Lillian Brestow. *Worlds of Pain.* New York: Basic Books, 1976. This is an excellent study of the working-class family.

Pepitone-Rockwell, Fran, ed. *Dual-Career Couples.* Beverly Hills, Calif.: Sage, 1980. This collection examines the problems and rewards of dual-career couples.

CHAPTERS 5 AND 6

The Women's Bureau, U.S. Department of Labor is the best source of data on women in industry and the professions. Its *Handbook on Women Workers,* 1975, contains a mass of relevant data. The Bureau periodically issues new bulletins, a list of which can be obtained by writing the Bureau.

The Department of Labor puts out a monthly report entitled *Employment and Earnings* that contains up-to-date data broken down by sex. The Department of Labor also publishes many special reports. Information can be obtained in the government publications sections of most university libraries.

Amsden, Alice H., ed. *The Economics of Women and Work.* New York: St. Martin's Press, 1980. This interesting collection is appropriate for students with some background in economics.

Edwards, Richard; Reich, Michael; and Gordon, David. *Labor Market Segmentation.* Lexington, Mass.: D. C. Heath, 1975. This book presents a new theory of the labor market that explains why women are relegated to the worst jobs. Some of the articles are technical, but the introduction and Chapters 8 through 11 can be read by the noneconomist.

Blaxall, Martha, and Reagan, Barbara B., eds. *Women and the Workplace: The Implications of Occupational Segregation.* Published as Spring 1976 Supplement of *Signs: Journal of Women in Culture and Society* 1, no. 3. This is a good collection of articles on sex segregation in employment.

CHAPTER 7

Babcock, Barbara Allen; Freedman, Ann E; Norton, Eleanor Holmes; and Ross, Susan C. *Sex Discrimination and the Law: Causes and Remedies.* Boston: Little, Brown, 1975. This 1000-page volume is the most comprehensive single source on women and the law.

Raffel, Norma K. ''Federal Laws and Regulations Prohibiting Sex Discrimination." Marguerite Rawalt, "Constitutional Rights for Women—The Equal Rights Amendment." In *The Study of Women: Enlarging Perspectives of Social Reality,* edited by Eloise C. Snyder. New York: Harper & Row, 1979. These two articles with self-explanatory titles are useful analyses.

Women's Rights Law Reporter. Published twice a year, this journal is exclusively devoted to reporting on the legal status of women. Each edition includes analytic articles and a summary of recent cases. It is the single best source on the fast-changing legal scene.

Peer Perspective. This newsletter, published by the Project on Equal Education Rights of the NOW Legal Defense and Education Fund, is the best source for information on Title IX.

CHAPTER 8

Leacock, Eleanor. Introduction to Frederick Engels' *The Origin of the Family, Private Property, and the State.* New York: New World Paperbacks, 1972. This is an excellent contemporary discussion by an anthropologist of the issues raised by Engels.

Reiter, Rayna R., ed. *Toward an Anthropology of Women.* New York: Monthly Review Press, 1975. In this excellent collection, women anthropologists present a feminist analysis of women's status in various "primitive" societies.

Mead, Margaret. *Sex and Temperament in Three Primitive Societies.* New York: Dell, 1935, 1971. Mead's very readable study shows how sex roles vary across societies.

O'Faolain, Julia, and Martines, Lauro, eds. *Not in God's Image.* New York: Harper & Row, 1973. This collection contains selections on women written by people in each of the periods from ancient times to the nineteenth century.

Bell, Susan, ed. *Women: From the Greeks to the French Revolution.* Belmont, Calif.: Wadsworth, 1973. This is a collection of historical documents and writings.

Flexner, Eleanor. *Mary Wollstonecraft.* Baltimore: Penguin, 1973. This excellent biography of a great woman is a pleasure to read.

CHAPTER 9

Boserup, Ester. *Women's Role in Economic Development.* New York: St. Martin's Press, 1970. A study of the changes in women's role that occur during the process of economic development, it documents the importance of women in the economy of many "primitive" societies.

Iglitzin, Lynne B., and Ross, Ruth, eds. *Women in the World.* Santa Barbara, Calif.: Clio Books, 1976. This is a comprehensive collection of articles on women in both developed and developing societies.

Giele, Janet Zollinger, and Smock, Audrey Chapman, eds. *Women: Roles and Status in Eight Countries.* New York: Wiley, 1977. Another good collection, this book covers fewer countries in greater depth. The introductory chapter in which Giele attempts to explain the variation in women's status is particularly interesting.

Newland, Kathleen. *The Sisterhood of Man.* New York: Norton, 1979. A survey of the status of women around the world.

Lapidus, Gail W. *Women in Soviet Society.* Berkeley, Calif.: University of California Press, 1978. A thorough and scholarly analysis, it traces the position of women from the revolution to the present.

CHAPTER 10

Flexner, Eleanor. *A Century of Struggle.* New York: Atheneum, 1971. This is the best single work on the women's movement in the United States from 1820 to 1920. It is a social as well as a political history and is very well written.

Kraditor, Aileen. *The Ideas of the Women Suffrage Movement, 1890–1920.* New York: Columbia University Press, 1965. This is an excellent history of the ideological issues raised and arguments used by the suffrage movement.

Newcomer, Mabel. *A Century of Higher Education for American Women.* New York: Harper & Row, 1959. The definitive historical work on the education of women in the United States.

Martin, Wendy, ed. *The American Sisterhood.* New York: Harper & Row, 1972. A collection of feminist writings from colonial times to the early 1970s.

Stage, Sara. *Female Complaints: Lydia Pinkham and the Business of Women's Medicine.* New York: Norton, 1979. This delightful book combines a history of the well-known patent medicine company with an analysis of women's changing status in the nineteenth and early twentieth centuries.

Friedman, Jean E., and Shade, William G., eds. *Our American Sisters: Women in American Life and Thought.* Boston: Allyn and Bacon, 1973. This collection of articles by contemporary historians covers the colonial period to the present.

Lutz, Alma. *Emma Willard.* Boston: Beacon, 1970. *Created Equal:*

A Biography of Elizabeth Cady Stanton. New York: John Day, 1940. *Susan B. Anthony.* Boston: Beacon, 1959. All of Lutz's biographies are informative and truly enjoyable to read.

Wertheimer, Barbara Mayer. *We Were There: The Story of Working Women in America.* New York: Pantheon Books, 1977. This is a readable history of American working women.

Gordon, Linda. *Woman's Body, Woman's Right: A Social History of Birth Control in America.* New York: Grossman, 1976. This fascinating book is written by a feminist historian.

CHAPTER 11

Chafe, William. *The American Woman, 1920–1970.* New York: Oxford, 1972. This political and social history contains much useful information.

The Friedman and Shade reader cited under Chapter 10 includes some useful articles on this period.

Trey, Joan. "Women in the War Economy—World War II." In *Review of Radical Political Economics* 4 (July 1972). This article gives a good detailed description of the enormous increase in participation by women during World War II.

Gruberg, Martin. *Women in American Politics.* Oshkosh: Academia Press, 1968. This book provides a great deal of data on women in politics during this period.

Women's history is now a very active field of scholarship. Whatever period or topic one is interested in, chances are good there exists some recent work. Check your library's card catalogue for books, and scholarly feminist journals such as *Signs* and standard history journals such as the *Journal of American History* and *American Quarterly* for articles and book reviews.

CHAPTERS 12 AND 13

Hole, Judith, and Levine, Ellen. *Rebirth of Feminism.* New York: Quadrangle Books, 1971. An excellent history and analysis of the early period of the contemporary women's movement, it is must reading for anyone interested in the movement.

Ware, Cellestine. *Woman Power: The Movement for Women's Liberation.* New York: Tower Publications, 1970. The development of the movement is discussed in this interesting book by an early participant.

Freeman, Jo. *The Politics of Women's Liberation.* New York: David McKay, 1975. Freeman, another early participant, presents an excellent description and analysis of the development of the movement.

Brownmiller, Susan. *Against Our Will: Men, Women and Rape.* New York: Bantam, 1976. An extremely provocative book, it has caused a great deal of discussion within the movement.

Lederer, Laura, ed. *Take Back the Night: Women on Pornography.* New York: Morrow, 1980. This collection analyzes pornography from a feminist perspective.

Githens, Marianne, and Prestage, Jewel L. *A Portrait of Marginality: The Political Behavior of the American Woman.* New York: McKay, 1977. This is a good collection of articles on women as voters and as public officials.

Women's Political Times, published by the National Women's Political Caucus, *National NOW Times, Spokeswoman,* and *Ms.* are good sources for current information. The August 1980 issue of *Ms.* contains a list of general and specialized women's organizations, along with their addresses and phone numbers.

CHAPTER 14

Reed, Evelyn. *Problems of Women's Liberation.* New York: Pathfinder Press, 1969. Reed presents the orthodox Marxist position. Her discussion of the origins of women's oppression is especially interesting.

Mitchell, Juliet. "Women: The Longest Revolution." Reprinted in *From Feminism to Liberation,* edited by Edith Altbach. Cambridge, Mass.: Schenkman, 1971. This seminal article, which first appeared in the *New Left Review,* has had an important impact on the thinking of socialist feminists.

Firestone, Shulamith. *The Dialectic of Sex.* New York: Bantam, 1970. The most complete statement of radical feminist theory, it is extremely thought-provoking.

Koedt, Anne; Levine, Ellen; and Rapone, Anita; eds. *Radical Feminism.* New York: Quadrangle, 1973. A number of articles from the very influential *Notes* are reprinted in this collection. Also of interest is an article by Joreen called "The Tyranny of Structurelessness," which is an excellent analysis of the problems that the movement has had with questions of organization and structure.

Friedan, Betty. "Our Revolution Is Unique." In *Voices of the New Feminism,* edited by Mary Lou Thompson. Boston: Beacon, 1970. A founder of the moderate wing of the movement briefly presents her position in this article.

Kimball, Gayle, ed. *Women's Culture: The Women's Renaissance of the Seventies.* Metuchen, N.J.: Scarecrow Press, 1981. This interesting collection presents a feminist theory based upon women's culture. Kimball's introductory essay, "Women's Culture: Themes and Images," provides an excellent introduction to this new and provocative theoretical development.

Jaggar, Alison M., and Struhl, Paula Rothenberg. *Feminist Frameworks: Alternative Theoretical Accounts of the Relations Between Women and Men.* New York: McGraw-Hill, 1978. As its title implies, this collection presents alternative theoretical approaches to the position of women. The frameworks included are conservativism, liberalism, traditional Marxism, radical feminism, and socialist feminism.

INDEX

occupational discrimination against, 173
oppressiveness of, 461–462
overmothering, 67–68
reality of, 61–66
Soviet medals for, 228
stereotypes of, 34, 35, 61
working, and children, 82–83, 85
working, as role models, 46
Mt. Holyoke, 245
Moynihan, Daniel, 115
Mozambique, 241
Ms., 338, 355–356, 367, 396, 460
Muller v. *Oregon,* 167–168, 267
Muncy Act, 152
Murdock, George P., 75, 98
Murphy, Irene, 403
Murray, Pauli, 322–323
Myrdal, A., 63

N

NAACP, 400
Nabisco, 406
Name in marriage, 159–160
Napoleon Bonaparte, 5
Napoleonic Code, 209, 216
National, The. *See* National Woman Suffrage Association
National Abortion Rights Action League, 388, 426
National Academy of Sciences, 130
National Advertising Review Board, 396
National Advisory Committee for Women, 376–377
National Advisory Council on Women's Educational Programs, 407
National American Woman Suffrage Association (NAWSA), 264–268, 271–280, 284, 286, 315. *See also* League of Women Voters
National Assembly of Women Religious, 350
National Association of Colored Women, 263
National Association of Manufacturers, 285, 301
National Black Feminist Organization (NBFO), 345, 369

National Center on Women and Family Law, 380, 437, 440
National Centers of Disease Control, 428
National Coalition Against Domestic Violence, 439
National Coalition Against Sexual Assault, 437
National Coalition for Women and Girls in Education, 382–383
National Coalition of American Nuns, 350
National Commission on Uniform State Laws, 160
National Conference for a New Politics, 327
National Conference of State Commissions, 324
National Conference of State Legislatures, 368
National Congress of Neighborhood Women, 373, 439
National Conservative Political Action Committee (NCPAC), 385, 426
National Consumer's League, 286, 289
National Council of Jewish Women, 382, 436
National Education Association, 384
National Federation of Business and Professional Women's Clubs, 287, 382, 442, 447
National Gay Task Force, 369
National Labor Relations Board, 87
National Labor Union, 258
National League of Cities, 368
National Office Managers Association, 93
National Organization for Women (NOW), 330, 331, 335, 336, 351, 358, 361, 365, 375, 382–384, 388, 390, 397, 402, 403, 411, 413, 422, 434, 462, 464
abortion and, 326, 423, 425
advertising as target of, 393–394
autonomy of chapters of, 466–467
child-care issue and, 414–415
early years of, 325–326
Ecumenical Task Force on Women and Religion, 349
Equal Employment Opportunity Commission and, 398–400

88 89 90   10 9 8 7